T0190294

Communications
in Computer and Information Science   **2159**

Rationale

The CCIS series is devoted to the publication of proceedings of computer science conferences. Its aim is to efficiently disseminate original research results in informatics in printed and electronic form. While the focus is on publication of peer-reviewed full papers presenting mature work, inclusion of reviewed short papers reporting on work in progress is welcome, too. Besides globally relevant meetings with internationally representative program committees guaranteeing a strict peer-reviewing and paper selection process, conferences run by societies or of high regional or national relevance are also considered for publication.

Topics

The topical scope of CCIS spans the entire spectrum of informatics ranging from foundational topics in the theory of computing to information and communications science and technology and a broad variety of interdisciplinary application fields.

Information for Volume Editors and Authors

Publication in CCIS is free of charge. No royalties are paid, however, we offer registered conference participants temporary free access to the online version of the conference proceedings on SpringerLink (http://link.springer.com) by means of an http referrer from the conference website and/or a number of complimentary printed copies, as specified in the official acceptance email of the event.

CCIS proceedings can be published in time for distribution at conferences or as post-proceedings, and delivered in the form of printed books and/or electronically as USBs and/or e-content licenses for accessing proceedings at SpringerLink. Furthermore, CCIS proceedings are included in the CCIS electronic book series hosted in the SpringerLink digital library at http://link.springer.com/bookseries/7899. Conferences publishing in CCIS are allowed to use Online Conference Service (OCS) for managing the whole proceedings lifecycle (from submission and reviewing to preparing for publication) free of charge.

Publication process

The language of publication is exclusively English. Authors publishing in CCIS have to sign the Springer CCIS copyright transfer form, however, they are free to use their material published in CCIS for substantially changed, more elaborate subsequent publications elsewhere. For the preparation of the camera-ready papers/files, authors have to strictly adhere to the Springer CCIS Authors' Instructions and are strongly encouraged to use the CCIS LaTeX style files or templates.

Abstracting/Indexing

CCIS is abstracted/indexed in DBLP, Google Scholar, EI-Compendex, Mathematical Reviews, SCImago, Scopus. CCIS volumes are also submitted for the inclusion in ISI Proceedings.

How to start

To start the evaluation of your proposal for inclusion in the CCIS series, please send an e-mail to ccis@springer.com.

Aurona Gerber
Editor

South African Computer Science and Information Systems Research Trends

45th Annual Conference, SAICSIT 2024
Gqeberha, South Africa, July 15–17, 2024
Proceedings

 Springer

Editor
Aurona Gerber ⓘD
Department of Computer Science
University of the Western Cape
Bellville, South Africa

ISSN 1865-0929 ISSN 1865-0937 (electronic)
Communications in Computer and Information Science
ISBN 978-3-031-64880-9 ISBN 978-3-031-64881-6 (eBook)
https://doi.org/10.1007/978-3-031-64881-6

This Springer imprint is published by the registered company Springer Nature Switzerland AG
The registered company address is: Gewerbestrasse 11, 6330 Cham, Switzerland

If disposing of this product, please recycle the paper.

Preface

This volume of Springer CCIS (CCIS 2159) contains the revised accepted research papers of SAICSIT 2024, the 45th *Conference of the South African Institute of Computer Scientists and Information Technologists*. SAICSIT 2024 was held from 15–17 July 2024 in the Boardwalk Hotel, Gqeberha, South Africa. The theme of the conference, *Human-Machine-Digital-Convergence* aimed to stimulate robust engagement to generate new insights into the transforming relationship between humans and machines.

The role of the 45th SAICSIT conference was to support and connect the Southern African computing community so that innovation and creativity can flourish. The SAICSIT conference aims to provide a space to meet and exchange ideas on addressing the challenges of the fast-evolving digital future.

The review process was double-blind and rigorous, with every paper sent to at least three and receiving at least two substantive reviews from our program committee. The program committee comprised more than 125 members with over 50 national and international affiliations. The technical committee, consisting of the technical chairs and track chairs, managed the review process and supported the authors in revising their papers to the quality results that are published in these proceedings.

This SAICSIT 2024 proceedings book contains 26 full research papers organised in their respective Computer Science and Information Systems research tracks. These submissions were included for presentation in the SAICSIT 2024 programme. With more than 90 papers submitted (from national and international authors) and more than 80 submissions in total sent out for review, the acceptance rate for full research papers for this CCIS volume is 32.5%. In the Information Systems track, 38 submissions were sent out for review and 12 were accepted for this volume of Springer CCIS, amounting to an acceptance rate of 31.5%. In the Computer Science track, 48 submissions were sent out for review, and 14 were accepted for this volume, amounting to an acceptance rate of 29%.

We want to express our gratitude to the track chairs and program committee reviewers for their hard work and dedication. Thank you to the authors of all the submitted papers for sharing their research results. We hope the opportunity to participate in SAICSIT 2024 will have a lasting impact on the quality and productivity of future research in our scholarly community.

We also acknowledge the enthusiasm and outstanding contributions of the local organisers of SAICSIT 2024, the Computer Sciences Department and the School of Information Technology at Nelson Mandela University. Thank you to everyone who contributed to the success of SAICSIT 2024.

June 2024

Aurona Gerber
Bukelwa Ngoqo

Organisation

General Chair

Mathys C. du Plessis   Nelson Mandela University, South Africa

Technical Co-chairs

Aurona Gerber   University of the Western Cape and CAIR, South Africa

Bukelwa Ngoqo   Nelson Mandela University, South Africa

Computer Science Co-chairs

Hein Venter   University of Pretoria, South Africa

Lester Cowley   Nelson Mandela University, South Africa

Information Systems Co-chairs

Marié Hattingh   University of Pretoria, South Africa

Melissa Makalima   Nelson Mandela University, South Africa

Publication Chair

Aurona Gerber   University of the Western Cape and CAIR, South Africa

Programme Committee

Computer Science Track

Adedayo, Oluwasola Mary   University of Winnipeg, Canada

Adigun, Matthew   University of Zululand, South Africa

Bagula, Antoine	University of the Western Cape, South Africa
Bradshaw, Karen	Rhodes University, South Africa
Casini, Giovanni	ISTI - CNR, Italy
Chavula, Josiah	University of Cape Town, South Africa
Chindipha, Stones	Rhodes University, South Africa
Dlamini, Moses T.	CSIR, Pretoria, South Africa
du Plessis, M.C.	Nelson Mandela University, South Africa
Dunaiski, Marcel	Stellenbosch University, South Africa
Furnell, Steven	University of Nottingham, UK
Greyling, Jean	Nelson Mandela University, South Africa
Grobler, Trienko	Stellenbosch University, South Africa
Gruner, Stefan	University of Pretoria, South Africa
Hazelhurst, Scott	University of the Witwatersrand, South Africa
Henney, Andre	University of the Western Cape, South Africa
Hutchison, Andrew	Google Switzerland, Switzerland
Isafiade, Omowunmi Elizabeth	University of the Western Cape, South Africa
James, Steven	University of the Witwatersrand, South Africa
Jembere, Edgar	University of KwaZulu-Natal, South Africa
Klein, Richard	University of the Witwatersrand, South Africa
Kotzé, Eduan	University of the Free State, South Africa
Kuttel, Michelle	University of Cape Town, South Africa
Leenen, Louise	University of the Western Cape, South Africa
Makura, Sheunesu	University of Pretoria, South Africa
Marais, Patrick	University of Cape Town, South Africa
Medupe, Abiodun	University of Pretoria, South Africa
Meyer, Thomas	University of Cape Town and CAIR, South Africa
Modipa, Thipe	University of Limpopo, South Africa
Mokwena, Sello	University of Limpopo, South Africa
Motara, Yusuf	Rhodes University, South Africa
Nel, Stephan	Stellenbosch University, South Africa
Ngoqo, Bukelwa	Nelson Mandela University, South Africa
Norman, Michael	University of the Western Cape, South Africa
Nyathi, Thambo	University of Pretoria, South Africa
Nyirenda, Clement	University of the Western Cape, South Africa
Olivier, Martin	University of Pretoria, South Africa
Rananga, Seani	University of Pretoria, South Africa
Sanders, Ian	University of South Africa (UNISA), South Africa
Serfontein, Rudi	North-West University, South Africa
Shibeshi, Zelalem	Rhodes University, South Africa
Singh, Avinash	University of Pretoria, South Africa
Suleman, Hussein	University of Cape Town, South Africa
Timm, Nils	University of Pretoria, South Africa

Vadapalli, Hima Bindu   University of Johannesburg, South Africa
van Alten, Clint   University of the Witwatersrand, South Africa
van der Merwe, Brink   Stellenbosch University, South Africa
Van Zijl, Lynette   Stellenbosch University, South Africa
Van Heerden, Willem   University of Pretoria, South Africa
Velempini, Mthulisi   University of Limpopo, South Africa
Venter, H. S.   University of Pretoria, South Africa
Venter, Isabella   University of the Western Cape, South Africa
Wa Nkongolo, Nkongolo   University of Pretoria, South Africa
Watson, Bruce   Stellenbosch University, South Africa
Zugenmaier, Alf   Hochschule München, Germany

Information Systems Track

Adebesin, Funmi   University of Pretoria, South Africa
Adeliyi, Timothy   University of Pretoria, South Africa
Baduza, Gugulethu   Rhodes University, South Africa
Beelders, Tanya   University of the Free State, South Africa
Bottomley, Edward-John   Stellenbosch University, South Africa
Campher, Susanna E. S.   North-West University, South Africa
Chindenga, Edmore   University of Fort Hare, South Africa
Davids, Zane   University of Cape Town, South Africa
De Wet, Lizette   University of the Free State, South Africa
du Plessis, M. C.   Nelson Mandela University, South Africa
du Preez, Madely   University of Pretoria, South Africa
Eybers, Sunet   University of South Africa (UNISA), South Africa
Harmse, Rudi   Nelson Mandela University, South Africa
Hattingh, Marié   University of Pretoria, South Africa
James, Steven   University of the Witwatersrand, South Africa
Jere, Nobert   Walter Sisulu University, South Africa
Le Roux, Daniel   Stellenbosch University, South Africa
Maasdorp, Christiaan   Stellenbosch University, South Africa
Makalima, Melissa   Nelson Mandela University, South Africa
Masinde, Muthoni   Central University of Technology, South Africa
Matthee, Machdel   University of Pretoria, South Africa
Mawela, Tendani   University of Pretoria, South Africa
Mennega, Nita   University of Pretoria, South Africa
Mohammed, Nouralden   University of the Witwatersrand, South Africa
Mujinga, Mathias   University of South Africa (UNISA), South Africa
Mwansa, Gardner   Walter Sisulu University, South Africa
Ncube, Zenzo Polite   University of Mpumalanga, South Africa
Nel, Wynand   University of the Free State, South Africa

Ngoqo, Bukelwa	Nelson Mandela University, South Africa
Oki, Olukayode	Walter Sisulu University, South Africa
Olaitan, Oo	Walter Sisulu University, South Africa
Oluwadele, Deborah	University of Pretoria, South Africa
Parry, Douglas	Stellenbosch University, South Africa
Pillay, Komla	University of Johannesburg, South Africa
Pretorius, Henk	University of Pretoria, South Africa
Serfontein, Rudi	North-West University, South Africa
Seymour, Lisa	University of Cape Town, South Africa
Sigama, Khuliso	Tshwane University of Technology, South Africa
Smit, Imelda	North-West University, South Africa
Smit, Danie	University of Pretoria, South Africa
Smuts, Hanlie	University of Pretoria, South Africa
Snyman, Dirk	University of Cape Town, South Africa
Steyn, Riana	University of Pretoria, South Africa
Taylor, Estelle	North-West University, South Africa
Tuyikeze, Tite	Sol Plaatje University, South Africa
van der Merwe, Thomas	University of South Africa (UNISA), South Africa
van der Vyver, Charles	North-West University, South Africa
van Eck, Rene	Vaal University of Technology, South Africa
Van Staden, Corné	University of South Africa (UNISA), South Africa
Wa Nkongolo, Nkongolo	University of Pretoria, South Africa
Weilbach, Lizette	University of Pretoria, South Africa

Postgraduate Symposium

Wesson, Janet	Nelson Mandela University, South Africa

SAICSIT 2024 Sponsors

The sponsors of SAICSIT 2024 are herewith gratefully acknowledged.

Contents

Information Systems Track

Computer Science Track

Deep Learning Classification for Encrypted Botnet Traffic: Optimising Model Performance and Resource Utilisation

Lucas Carr$^{(\boxtimes)}$ and Josiah Chavula

Computer Science Department, University of Cape Town, Cape Town, South Africa
crrluc003@myuct.ac.za, jchavula@cs.uct.ac.za

Abstract. Detection of malicious traffic on a network is critical to ensuring the safety and security of internet systems. Classical approaches to this task increasingly struggle with modern networking procedures, like encryption. Deep learning (DL) offers an alternative approach to traffic classification problems. We address two major problem classes: (1) botnet detection and (2) botnet family classification. For each problem, we explore five implementations of DL architectures: a multi-layer perceptron (MLP), shallow and deep convolutional neural network (CNN v1 and CNN v2), an autoencoder (AE) and an autoencoder + convolutional neural network (AE+CNN). Our evaluation of models for each respective problem class is based on the classification performance and computational requirements of each model. We further investigate the effect of training the models on an input with a reduced feature space, where we evaluate the impact this has in terms of a trade-off between computational and classification performance. For botnet detection, we find that all models attain good (≥ 0.979 accuracy) classification performance on a normal testing set; however, this performance drops fairly substantially when evaluated on a set of unknown botnet families. Furthermore, we observed a clear trend between increased feature space and memory utilisation, while finding no evidence of a trend between inference time and feature space. For botnet classification, we found that models which implement CNN architectures outperform others by a substantial margin (≈ 6 percentage points). We observe the same trend between feature space and memory utilisation, and absence of apparent relationship between feature space and inference time.

Keywords: Deep Learning · Machine Learning · Malware Classification · Malware Detection · Botnets

1 Introduction

The proliferation of computers and networks as tools essential to modern life has resulted in innumerable benefits. However, adoption of the associated technologies has created new security dynamics to consider; specifically in the form of

A. Gerber (Ed.): SAICSIT 2024, CCIS 2159, pp. 3–29, 2024.
https://doi.org/10.1007/978-3-031-64881-6_1

malicious software, or malware. Malware is an umbrella term that encompasses various types of software designed to infiltrate systems without permission, aiming to cause harm or exploit vulnerabilities, often with a financial motive [15].

While there are numerous sub-categories of malware, we focus attention on botnets, out of recognition that the increasing number of security-vulnerable Internet of Things (IoT) devices offer an ideal landscape for botnets [3]. A botnet defines a distributed network of computers, or *bots*, infected with software that enables the bots to be controlled by a malicious operator, or *botmaster* [1,17]. A botnet typically leverages one of many additional types of malware - such as a worm - to propagate itself across multiple computers, and can incorporate a centralised or decentralised operating procedure [17]. Moreover, botnets attempt to hide themselves by transmitting normal traffic amongst their botnet traffic [17]. However, a defining characteristic of botnets is the presence of command and control channels, through which the malicious operator is able to transmit instructions or receive information. A common instruction would be a distributed denial-of-service (DDOS) attack, where the bots flood a target to disrupt its service [1,3]. It is this characteristic of botnets - that the bot must at some point connect to its botmaster - that may be leveraged to build detection models. When a bot connects to the botmaster, a sequence of network flows, defined as a grouping of related traffic, can be extracted from the generated traffic, from which a deep learning (DL) model will be able to learn distinguishing patterns [17]. DL is a field within machine learning which is defined by the use of multi-layered architectures, enabling models to learn complex, hierarchical patterns from data without requiring feature engineering [12,20].

Preventative measures against malware and botnets, are not a novel concern; there are existing approaches to detect and block malicious traffic on networks. These approaches typically deploy a Network Intrusion Detection System, or NIDS [18]. NIDS operate by implementing a broad range of techniques to detect and identify malicious traffic: notably, port analysis, blacklisted IP addresses, and inspecting packet payloads [16,29]. Recently adopted practices around networking have dampened the effectiveness of these techniques, making NIDS which use them less reliable. Port numbers have become less reliable indicators of application type; additionally, the existence of port-obfuscation enables creators of malware to avoid detection [29]. Similarly, dynamic IP addresses and IP spoofing make systems which filter traffic based on blacklisted IPs unreliable. Finally, approaches which aim to detect malware by inspecting the payload contents of packets flowing through the network face increasing difficulty as more network traffic adopts encryption protocols - a Cisco report from 2017 noted that $\approx 75\%$ of analysed malicious traffic made use of encryption [26].

In recognition of the shortcomings of existing malware detection practices, we define an objective to evaluate the effectiveness of different DL algorithms when tasked with detection and classification of botnet traffic using network flows. More specifically, we implement a series of binary classification models to detect malicious traffic, and a secondary series of multiclass classification models to classify botnet traffic into respective families. While this approach is not itself novel, much of the existing literature evaluates the effectiveness of DL models in terms of the accuracy, F1-score, False Positive Rate (FPR), and False Negative Rate (FNR) [17, 19, 28].[1] These metrics provide insight into classification performance; however, we argue that insight into the computational requirements of a model are important. A model which attains good accuracy scores might be impractical due to its computational requirements, especially on smaller, lower-resourced networks. Moreover, models are trained on a datasets made up of only a subset of existing botnets, while newer botnets are continuously developed. Evaluating models on an unseen testing set comprised of botnet families present in their training set ignores this concept. As a result, there is greater uncertainty into a model's ability to generalise to newer botnets.

This paper evaluates the effect of feature space size has computational performance, in terms of a model's inference time and memory utilisation. Furthermore, a supplementary set of unknown botnet families is used to evaluate a model's ability to generalise to zero-day attacks. More specifically, this paper makes the following contributions:

1. Evaluate the performance of five binary classification models, an MLP, shallow CNN (v1), deep CNN (v2), AE, and AE+CNN, on the standard and proto zero-day test set.
2. Implement and evaluate performance of five multiclass classification models, an MLP, shallow CNN, deep CNN, AE, and AE+CNN, which aim to identify respective families of botnets.
3. Evaluate how reducing the feature space, into 50% and 30% samples, effects the memory requirements and inference time, in relation to the overall accuracy of a model.

2   Related Work

2.1   Classification Approaches: Payload vs. Flow Based

Network traffic is made up of discrete blocks of data, called packets, which travel through a network. Approaches to classify network traffic typically make use of training data comprising of either the individual packets' payload, or network flows. Informally, network flows represent a sequence of packets between a source and destination [29]. Statistical features can be extracted from network flows, which explain metrics such as the rate at which packets flow back and forth, and the mean packet size of the flow [7].

Another approach is to use the core contents of a packet (the payload) as training data. The notion is that the payload of malicious traffic contains at least part of the malware binary, from which a model would be able to recognise patterns belonging to this binary [11]. Payload based approaches face the difficulty of classifying encrypted traffic - a problem that flow-based analysis avoids, since only the packet headers are required, which are not encrypted [12]. There

---

[1] Definitions for these are found in Sect. 5.1.

have been implementations of payload-based classifiers which are able to handle encrypted traffic [4,10,11]. These approaches typically require thorough processing steps to prepare the data for classification, which makes payload-based approaches ill-suited to real world application. Conversely, aggregated network flows are comparatively easy to extract [18].

2.2 Machine Learning Approaches

Hadidi et al. [7] evaluate the effectiveness of different machine learning approaches to botnet detection. Their approaches include Support-Vector Machines (SVM), K-Nearest Neighbour (KNN), and Bayesian Networks (BN) to classifying botnet traffic based of either payloads or network flows, using Detection Rate (DR) and False-Positive Rate (FPR) as evaluation metrics.[2][3] Simulated network traffic was captured in a sandbox environment. Non-encrypted traffic was used, so as to make their payload-classifier able to handle the traffic captures. Notably, in the network flow preprocessing phases, identifying features such as IP addresses and port numbers were removed from the datasets [7]. In the majority of evaluations, payload-based classifiers have been shown to be superior to flow-based methods. Specifically, the payload-based models such as KNN, SVM, and BN have recorded detection rates (DRs) of 1, 0.995, and 0.938 respectively. In contrast, the flow-based models have posted comparatively lower scores, with DRs of 0.968, 0.910, and 0.838. This trend of better performance by payload-based classifiers is also evident in terms of false positive rates (FPRs).

Yeo et al. [28] evaluate four different ML architectures (Random Forest, CNN, MLP, and SVM) to be used as binary classifiers for botnet detection. The models were trained on bi-directional network flows extracted from PCAPs in the CTU-13 dataset - a dataset containing botnet traffic from 7 different families. Typical measurements of accuracy, precision and recall were used as evaluation metrics, while the performance of a classifier was evaluated w.r.t an individual botnet family.

2.3 Autoencoders

Autoencoders (AE) are a type of unsupervised learning algorithm that aim to compress input data into a lower-dimensional "latent" vector. As output, an approximation of the input is reconstructed from the latent vector, through a decoding process [6]. When applying AEs to classification tasks, the decoding process can be replaced with a classification layer (like a softmax or sigmoid layer). The encoding portion of the AE focuses on detecting crucial features in the input data and encoding them into a condensed representation. This process of dimensionality reduction ideally encodes the most significant features which aid the subsequent classification layer.

---

[2] Detection Rate is identical to Recall.

[3] DR and FPR defined as $\frac{TP}{TP+FN}$, $\frac{FP}{FP+TN}$, respectively.

Deep Packet, an approach proposed by Lotfollahi et al. [11], is a system which incorporates both feature extraction and classification stages. This approach is not directly related to malware detection or classification, and instead aims to identify major traffic classes or application. While this is a significant divergence from the aims of our paper, the approach to solving their problem using DL has strong parallels to ours. They propose a five-layered Stacked Auto Encoder (SAE) connected to a softmax layer, and 1D-CNN as classifiers made up of two convolutional layers and a softmax layer [11]. Following convention, Precision, Recall and F1-score were the chosen evaluation metrics.

2.4   Convolutional Neural Networks

Convolutional neural networks (CNNs) have become increasingly popular algorithms for classification [14]. Typically CNNs work with grid-like inputs, such as an image, where a convolutional operation will sweep over the grid, producing a feature map which represents significant areas of the input. These feature maps enable the model to learn identifying spatial patterns in data. Most applications of CNNs use two-dimensional image data, or image-representations of streams of one-dimensional data. However, the fundamental principle of a sequence of convolutional layers that identify increasingly complex patterns in the data holds for inputs which are not grid-like in nature - for instance, a network flow, which is a one-dimensional vector [2].

Marín et al. [12] used flow-based and packet-based approaches to detect (a binary classification) and further classify (a multiclass classification) botnet traffic. These approaches implement a 1D CNN which is connected to an LSTM. For the binary classification task, the flow-based approach is the best model by a significant margin, with an accuracy of 0.986, compared to the packet-based model's 0.776. They note the flow-based model is able to achieve this accuracy with a FPR of ≈0.025. For the multiclass classification, they were unable to use a flow-based approach due to limitations relating to their dataset. Bearing this in mind, their packet-based model, which aimed to classify traffic into classes of Benign, Neris, Rbot, and Virut, attained accuracies of $0.878, 0.635, 0.999$, and 0.547 for each respective class, with an overall accuracy of 0.765.

Pektas & Acarman [17] proposed using a deep neural network (DNN) as a binary classifier for botnet detection. They employed the CTU-13 dataset for botnet captures, which was also used in Yeo et al. [28]. To process the data, they constructed a graph representation of the network captures where nodes represent connected hosts. This approach allowed them to extract statistical information about network flows. Alongside source and destination IP addresses and port numbers, they computed five statistical metrics for each flow: mean, median, maximum, minimum, standard deviation. These metrics were applied to the duration, byte size, number of packets and periodicity of each flow. For evaluation, they focused on accuracy, precision, recall, and the F1-score.

3   Datasets and Preprocessing

Detection and classification of botnet traffic using DL algorithms is a task that lends itself towards supervised learning. Supervised learning requires the use of high quality, labelled datasets with sufficient samples for the training and evaluation process - the existence of such datasets is rare [26].

Network traffic is typically captured through programs like WireShark, where the information is stored in PCAP files. For the task at hand, network flows, and ideally bidirectional network flows, are extracted from these PCAP files, and preprocessed into suitable training data. We developed a preprocessing pipeline which received traffic captures in the form of PCAP files as input, and after a series of steps, outputted datasets in the form of .csv files. Information concerning the original source of the dataset is discussed in Sect. 3.1, after which Sect. 3.2 describes the preprocessing steps taken in the pipeline.

3.1   Dataset

The Stratosphere Research Laboratory host an online repository[4] of malicious and normal network captures. Specifically, they have created the CTU-13 dataset, which contains network captures of real traffic from seven distinct botnet families [5]. The dataset is made up of thirteen captures; each capture containing the malware binary, extracted network flows, and a PCAP file containing only botnet traffic from that scenario's capture (these PCAP files have had their normal and background traffic removed due to privacy considerations) [21].

The bidirectional network flows provided by the CTU-13 dataset, which were extracted using the open source tool, openArgus, offer comparatively limited information, relative to what could be extracted when using CICFlowMeter [8].[5] Consequently, only the PCAP files containing botnet traffic were used from this dataset. These were then supplemented with the Stratosphere Research Laboratory's repository of normal captures, which are captures of network activity which imitate a typical user's activity on a network, and are restricted to contain only benign network activity. The inclusion of benign traffic was necessary in order to facilitate the measurement of True Negatives and False Positives; as well as encourage models to be able to generalise to a real-world environment [22].

Captures 10 and 11 were omitted from the CTU-13 collection, as they were instances of a malware family which had sufficient representation from the remaining scenarios. The resultant eleven scenarios were supplemented with five 'normal' captures.

For the binary classification process, the botnet families Murlo and NSIS-ay were excluded from the training and testing sets. This was to enable the creation of an additional testing set, hereafter referred to as the 'proto zero-day'

---

[4] The repositories can be found at: www.stratosphereips.org/datasets-overview.

[5] openArgus can be found at: https://openargus.org.

set, which contained botnet families to which the model had not been exposed. Unlike traditional test sets, which present models with unseen instances of known botnet families, our set introduces entirely new categories. This additional measure is analogous to concept of zero-day attacks, which are malware attacks that have never appeared before [30]. While measuring a model's exact ability to detect zero-day attacks would be impossible, we argue that this approach reasonable indication of the model's performance when encountering previously unseen attacks.

3.2   The Pipeline

Illustrated in Fig. 1, the preprocessing pipeline begins with a collection of PCAP files representing traffic captures. These were the eleven botnet captures and five normal captures. Individually, each PCAP represents a capture of either entirely normal traffic, or a single botnet family [5]. The bi-directional network flows were extracted using CICFlowMeter [8]. The extracted flows from each PCAP file would be stored in a corresponding .csv file.

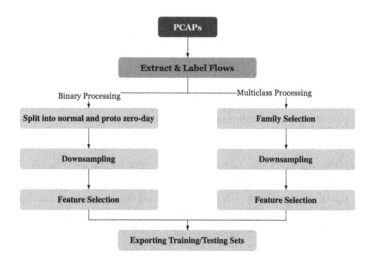

Fig. 1. Illustration of the preprocessing pipeline, showing the divergence in processing steps for the binary and multiclass classification datasets

Flow Extraction and Labelling. An essential part of the preprocessing was to assign accurate labels to the data. The CTU-13 dataset includes labelled bi-directional network flows for each scenario, extracted with the openArgus. However, these flows are not as detailed as flows extracted using an alternative tool: CICFlowMeter [8]. A consequence is that flows extracted using CICFlowMeter needed to be labelled manually. The nature of the sourced PCAP files was that they contained either entirely malicious or entirely benign traffic [21]. As such, the labelling process was straightforward to implement: the labels corresponding to the flows generated from the previous stage could be identified by knowing which PCAP file the flows originated from - which was simple to do, given that each PCAP file would produce a single .csv of its extracted flows. The labelling process was automated through a python script, *FlowLabeller.py*.

For the binary classification dataset, the data was either labelled as 0 indicating benign, or 1 meaning malicious. For the multi-class classification, benign traffic was labelled 0, and the malware classes were labelled from 1-7.

Feature Selection. The bidirectional flows are one-dimensional vectors, made up of 82 features. Each feature is a specific measurement of how the data behaves in the flow, from which patterns can be learned during the training process. For example, there is a feature (Total Fwd Pkt) which provides the total number of forward flowing packets in the bi-directional flow. However, we recognised that allowing certain features to persist in the dataset could potentially be detrimental to the models' classification performance.

Features relating to IP addresses and port numbers were removed. Dynamic IP address, port-obfuscation and IP spoofing are techniques which make relying on these features for classification a poor idea [7,18]. Additionally, the models should be able to generalise to unseen data as best as possible, and inclusion of these features in the training set is antithetical to this goal, since they are not intrinsic to the identity of the malicious traffic [18].

In the end, each bi-directional flow is represented as a one-dimensional vector with 75 features. We then create two additional datasets containing a random sample of 50% and 30% of the features (37 and 22 features, respectively). This would facilitate investigation into how reducing the feature space might lower memory requirements and inference time, and what effect it would have on classification performance.[6]

Balancing. The datasets for the binary classification task were balanced to have an even distribution of benign and malicious samples. The malicious samples were made up of Neris, Rbot, Virut, Menti, and Sogou botnet families. Murlo and NSIS.ay families were excluded as they were used for the creation of the proto zero-day dataset. The approximately 110,000 malicious flows were downsampled to 59,000, which was the number of benign samples in the dataset; the datasets were split into training, validation, and testing sets in a 72%, 8%, and 20% ratio.

To balance the classes in the datasets for multiclass classification, we ensured that classes would have a sufficient number of respective samples, so as to allow the model to train well on that class. Empirically, we determined that a class required a minimum of 30,000 samples in order for the classifiers to perform effectively. A consequence of this being that botnet families Sogou, Menti, NSIS.ay, and Murlo were removed from the training set. As indicated in Table 1, these families did not have enough samples for practical up-sampling. The resultant

---

[6] The specific features present in these datasets are described in Table 2 in the Appendix.

Table 1. Botnet Families and Network Flows from the CTU-13 Dataset with additional Benign Traffic

Family	#Flows	Family	#Flows
Neris	190,028	Sogou	72
Rbot	46,796	dMurlo	11,537
Virut	85,779	NSIS.ay	7,645
Menti	4,810	Benign	56,665

dataset included traffic labelled as benign, Rbot, Virut, or Neris. These classes were then down-sampled to consist of 45000 samples each; the datasets were split into training, validation, and testing sets in a 72%, 8%, and 20% ratio.

4 Implementation

4.1 Hyperparameter Tuning

The performance of a DL model is heavily influenced by hyperparameters. Discovering optimal hyperparameters typically involves references to existing literature, and exploring iterations of training slightly different models and evaluating which parameters yield better results (for example, Grid-Search). This process is both computationally expensive and time consuming. We adopt an alternate approach using an extension of Keras Tuner called Hyperband [9,13]. Starting with a predefined set of options, including ranges of layer sizes, activation functions, learning rates, and dropout rate, Hyperband adopts an early-stopping strategy to identify promising combinations of hyperparameters. These are trained for a small number epochs to assess their performance. The top-performing configurations are kept for further training, while the rest are discarded. This process is iterated until the algorithm converges on a network topology and set of hyperparameters that yield near-optimal performance [9].

4.2 Architectures

To achieve our aims of both detecting and classifying botnet traffic, we decided that for each model, we train a binary classifier (for botnet detection) and a multiclass classifier (for botnet classification). This section describes the topology and hyperparameters of each model - arrived at through implementation of the Hyperband process discussed in Sect. 4.1.

Multilayer Perceptron. The MLP is, by design, our simplest model. The MLP binary classifier has an input layer, connected to a single densely connected layer with 33 neurons using the Tanh activation function. The output of this layer is fed into another densely connected layer with a Sigmoid activation function for classification. The architecture for the multiclass classification model is markedly similar, the difference being an increase in the size of the hidden layer, with 128 neurons, and a classification layer which uses a Softmax function.

Convolutional Neural Networks. For both classification tasks we introduced two CNN architectures inspired by the implementations of 1D-CNNs as per [25,29]. Each task has a respective shallow CNN (CNN v1), and deeper CNN (CNN v2). Across all models, we adopted the Adam optimiser during the training phase, which has had widespread success in related literature [11,26,29]. Furthermore, all networks shared a common filter size of 3×1, with a stride of 1. Following these convolutional layers, MaxPooling was employed as a down-sampling technique to reduce spatial dimensions and retain critical features of the input.

With respect to the binary classifiers, CNN v1 had two 1D convolutional layers made up of 128 and 416 filters, respectively. The output from the final MaxPooling layer was flattened, and fed into a densely connected layer with 352 neurons. A final Sigmoid layer was used for classification. CNN v2 implemented three 1D convolutional layers, with 40, 136, and 232 filters. After the final Max-Pooling layer, a dropout of 0.5 was introduced to combat overfitting. The result was flattened, and channelled into a dense layer of 104 neurons, followed by another dense layer of 40 neurons before a final Sigmoid layer for classification. Aside from the classification layer, all applicable layers made use of the Rectified Linear Unit (ReLU) activation function, which introduced non-linearity to the model - a decision determined through the hyperparameter tuning process.

For multiclass classifiers, CNN v1 had two 1D convolutional layers made up of 232 filters each; after the second MaxPooling layer, the output was flattened and inputted to densely connected layer of 72 neurons, before a final Softmax classification layer. CNN v2 implemented three 1D convolutional layers, made up of 232, 104, and 40 filters, respectively. After the third MaxPooling layer, we introduced a 0.5 dropout to the model for overfitting. The output was then flattened and inputted to a densely connected layer of 296 neurons, after which another dropout layer of 0.25 was introduced. Two more densely connected layers sized 456, and 168 were implemented before the Softmax classification layer. The dense and convolutional layers used the Tanh activation function - the decision to implement Tanh was made through empirical findings, through the hyperparameter tuning process.

Autoencoders. The architecture of the AEs we implemented for the binary classification and multiclass classification problems were very similar, with differences appearing in the size of the layers. Drawing inspiration from [11], each AE had five fully connected hidden layers, and a classification layer (Sigmoid or Softmax). The sizes of these layers for the binary classifier were $[232, 72, 40, 104, 232]$, whereas the multiclass classifier has layers sized $[168, 104, 104, 40, 104]$. Both the binary and multiclass classifiers implement a Tanh activation function in each layer.

AE+CNN. The AE + CNN is an ensemble of the previously implemented AE and CNN v1. For the binary classification task, five densely connected layers were used for the encoding process, which had $136, 136, 72, 104, 136$ neurons, respectively. The output from the fifth layer was reshaped in order to be suitable input for the CNN. Subsequently, two one-dimensional convolutional layers were implemented with 64 and 32 filters, respectively. Each convolutional layer was followed by a MaxPooling layer, where the final MaxPooling layer was flattened and channelled into a densely connected layer with 8 neurons, connected to the final classification layer which used the Sigmoid activation function. All of the applicable layers used a ReLU activation function, and the Adam optimiser - for the same reasons as before.

The multiclass AE+CNN implemented a similar architecture, with five densely connected encoding layers with $136, 104, 72, 40, 104$ neurons, respectively. The same reshaping and subsequent convolutional and MaxPooling layers were included, with 32 and 96 neurons in each respective convolutional layer. These layers, where applicable, implemented a Tanh activation function, as opposed to the binary classification model's ReLU. A final softmax layer was used for classification.

5   Experiment Design

5.1   Evaluation Metrics

To evaluate the performance of a model, we use accuracy, FPR, FNR, mean inference time (MIT), and mean memory usage (MMU). While accuracy is a standard metric w.r.t. determining the effectiveness of a classifier, much of the related work prefers F1-score [10,11,18]. The advantage F1-score offers is that it provides a fairer representation of a model's performance in the case of unbalanced datasets [27]. In our case, measures were undertaken to ensure a balanced training and testing set; consequently, accuracy was preferred to F1-score.

FPR quantifies the fraction of benign results incorrectly identified as malicious by the model [7]. Conversely, FNR measures the proportion of actual threats misclassified as benign. In the context of intrusion detection systems, both metrics are important. High FNRs undermine the essential purpose of an IDS - to detect threats. On the other hand, an elevated FPR can erode trust in the system. If users are frequently alerted to false threats, they may begin to ignore genuine threats [7]. These metrics are defined as:

$$\text{Accuracy} = \frac{TP + TN}{TP + FP + FN + TN}$$

$$\text{FPR} = \frac{FP}{FP + TN}$$

$$\text{FNR} = \frac{FN}{FP + FN}$$

where TP refers to true positives, TN to true negatives, FP to false positives, and FN to false negatives.

MIT and MMU provide the mean time for a model to make an inference, and memory required to make 100 inferences, respectively. These measurements require multiple iterations of measurements for each model, in order to extract the mean. An alternate approach of taking the worst-case performance of these measurements was considered. The advantage of a worst-case measurement is that it enables us to infer the hardware specifications needed to implement the model without fear of failure, providing an upper bound on the memory usage or inference time. However, we recognise that there are significant difficulties in ascertaining accurate measurements of memory usage or CPU time, (see Sect. 5.2 for further discussion of these challenges).

5.2   Binary Classification Task

Classification Performance on Normal vs Proto Zero-Day Test Sets. This experiment establishes a baseline evaluation of how MLP, CNN v1, CNN v2, AE, and AE+CNN perform, in terms of classification accuracy, FPR, and FNR on the conventional testing set. Subsequently, these models are evaluated on the additional testing set, as discussed in Sects. 3.1 and 3.2 to ascertain their ability to generalise to unseen botnet families. Accuracy is determined through the use of the Keras framework's 'evaluate' function. For calculation of FPR and FNR, a model makes predictions on a testing set which are compared with the set of ground truths to determine the FP, FN, TP, TN values used in the formulas outlined in Sect. 5.1.

Effect of a Reduced Input Feature Space on Computational and Classification Performance. While DL has largely alleviated the necessity for feature engineering, as is present in machine learning, larger feature spaces typically incur a greater computational cost [11,20]. We aim to explore the relationship between computational and classification performance of the five DL models when trained on inputs of 100%, 50%, and 30% of the feature space.

We define computational performance as the memory usage (MMU) and inference time (MIT) of a model. Determining accurate values for these metrics presents significant difficulties: during the execution of a program, there are invariably other processes running concurrently. Furthermore, memory management of an operating system is largely beyond our control. Empirically, we found that a when a program iterated over each model, measuring memory use and inference time, there was a consistent increase in memory consumption with each subsequent iteration, irrespective of model complexity. To minimise the potential impact these factors may introduce, we elected to measure the inference time and memory utilisation across batches ($b = 10$) of the test dataset, each batch composed with fixed number of samples ($n = 100$). In this approach, the system was rebooted after each subsequent evaluation of a batch. Memory use was measured using the 'Memory Profiler'[7] python package, which provides a list of memory usage taken at snapshots during the program's execution. We record the model and memory usage for each batch, extracting the mean usage from these results. Inference time was determined using the 'timeit' package from Python's Standard Template Library [23]. We measure and record the time taken for a model to make predictions over a batch, extracting the mean from these records. We implement this procedure three times for each model, using training and testing sets containing $100\%, 50\%$, and 30% of the available features.

5.3   Multiclass Classification Task

Multiclass Classification Accuracy for Each Botnet Family. This experiment evaluates the MLP, CNN v1, CNN v2, AE, and AE+CNN models to determine their overall accuracy scores, as well as their accuracy scores for each specific botnet family. Metrics like FPRs and FNRs are not applicable to multiclass classification problems, as they require a binary relation. It is still useful, however, to determine how each model performs relative to each class in the multiclass classification. We evaluate each model on the normal testing set only, and from this evaluation we are able to determine a general accuracy for each model, as well as the accuracy of each model respective to the available classes. Reiterating the discussion from Sect. 5.1, we use accuracy because we have ensured that each class has an equal representation of samples, at 8000. For each model, we make classifications using the Keras Library's 'predict()' method, and store the results in a confusion matrix.

Evaluating the Effect of a Reduced Input Feature Space. We evaluate how datasets with reduced feature spaces influence the computational and classification performance of models. More specifically, five models are trained on three datasets containing a random sample of 100%, 50%, and 30% of the total features - this translates to datasets with $74, 37$, and 22 features, respectively. We then observe the effect that a reduced feature space might have on a single, or group of models' computational and classification performance. We regard the computational performance to be the MIT and MMU of a model, while classification performance is largely defined as a model's accuracy across all classes, with a secondary focus on the portion incorrectly classified traffic. This latter focus enables us to determine which models might struggle to classify specific families, or if certain families are poorly classified by all models.

We determine the MIT and MMU by taking measurements over a series batches ($b = 10$) containing a fixed number of samples ($n = 100$).

---

[7] Memory Profiler can be accessed at https://github.com/pythonprofilers/memory_pro filer.

6   Results and Discussion

In the following, we present and discuss the findings from the experiments outlined in 5. We begin with the discussion of binary classifiers, followed by multiclass classification results.

6.1   Binary Classifiers for Botnet Detection

Performance on Normal and Proto Zero-Day Test Sets. Figure 2 displays the accuracy, FPR, and FNR of the MLP, CNN v1, CNN v2, AE, and AE+CNN when evaluated on the normal and proto zero-day testing sets. Performance on the normal testing set provides an indication of a model's ability to generalise to unseen traffic that belongs to botnet families which were present in the training set. On the other hand, results relating to the proto zero-day testing set relates to a model's ability to classify traffic from botnet families which were entirely excluded from the training set.

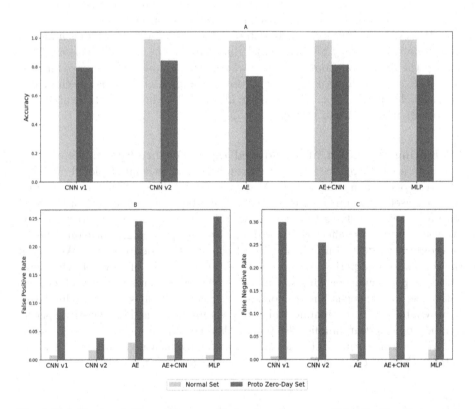

Fig. 2. Sub-Figures A, B, and C, respectively, show Accuracy, False-Positive Rates, and False-Negative Rates of each model when evaluated on the normal and proto zero-day testing sets.

All models achieved relatively high ($\geq$0.979) accuracy scores when evaluated on the normal testing set. The MLP, our least complex model, attained a score of 0.986, indicating that the task of botnet detection from known families is fairly simple. The CNN v2 attained the highest classification accuracy of 0.993, while the AE was the lowest with a score of 0.979. A possible explanation for the poor performance of the autoencoder models is that latent vectors created by the encoding phase fail to capture some distinguishing features of the input data. When comparing best and worst models - CNN v2 and AE - there is an absolute improvement by the CNN v2 of 0.014. While this improvement is small, we calculate that the error rate of the CNN v2, at 0.007, represents a 0.667 reduction in errors relative to the error rate of the AE, at 0.021.[8]

To recognise the significance of this reduction, we need to contextualise the problem. Networks are often required to handle a large volume of traffic; for example, a network on a college campus with $10,000$ users may see a typical transfer of 7TB of data every 24 hour period [24]. For an intrusion detection system monitoring this network, a relative reduction in error rate of 0.667 could entail thousands of fewer errors.

These errors can be broken down into two categories: false negatives and false positives. From this, we determine the FPR and FNR for each model. When FPR was evaluated on the normal testing set, the CNN v2, AE+CNN, and MLP were the best performers with FPRs of 0.008. The CNN v2 attained an FPR of 0.016. The poorer performance of the CNN v2 in comparison to the CNN v1 might be explained by the increased complexity of CNN v2, with the additional convolutional layer and fully connected layers causing overfitting. The worst performer w.r.t FPR was once again the AE, with a measure of 0.030. It is difficult to suggest an acceptable tolerance for FPR and FNR: factors around the type of information being secured, the size of the organisation, and general security posture may all influence what might be deemed acceptable. However, the FPRs achieved by the CNN v2, AE+CNN, and MLP, with respective accuracies of $0.993, 0.983$, and 0.986, present an improvement on existing work [12,28].

Evaluation on the proto zero-day testing set showed a decline in performance in terms of accuracy, FPR, and FNR across all models. The best performing model w.r.t. this classification performance was the CNN v2, which achieved an accuracy of 0.842, FPR of 0.038, and FNR of 0.255. The same model evaluated on the normal testing set achieved scores of $0.990, 0.016$, and 0.004 for each respective metric. The decline in classification performance aligns with our understanding that distinct botnet families are likely to exhibit, at least partially, different behaviour. It is this difference which causes the models to struggle when classifying traffic belonging to families entirely excluded from the training set. However, the model's performance on the proto zero-day testing set remains a significant improvement on guessing. We suggest that an explanation for this improvement rests on the notion that while there are certainly some differences, distinct botnet families must express certain shared behaviour that is not present in benign traffic. This would be behaviour intrinsic to all sampled

---

[8] Formulas and calculations provided in Appendix.

botnet families, as opposed to behaviour distinct to individual families. This shared behaviour among botnet families is what a model would recognise in the proto zero-day testing set.

There was also a more pronounced degree of variability in classification performance of the five models when evaluated on the proto zero-day testing set, relative to the evaluation based on the normal testing set. For instance, the mean accuracy, over all five models, when evaluated on the proto zero-day testing set was 0.783 with a standard deviation of 0.047. In contrast, when evaluated on the normal testing set, we determined a standard deviation of 0.005 around a mean of 0.986. This variability indicates that there is a fairly substantial difference between each models' ability to learn the more complex, intrinsic botnet behaviour which enable better detection of unknown botnet families.

From these two ideas - that good performance on the proto zero-day testing set requires learning more complex behaviour patterns intrinsic to all botnets, and that there is greater variability in model's classification performance when evaluated on the proto zero-day testing set - we make the claim that certain models, specifically models which implement convolutional layers, are significantly more capable of learning these more complex patterns. We ground this claim in the observation that the CNN v1, CNN v2, and AE+CNN achieved accuracies on the proto zero-day set of $0.842, 0.793$, and 0.810, respectively, whereas, the AE and MLP achieved accuracies of 0.732 and 0.740. A potential explanation for the efficacy of convolutional layers towards learning these behaviour patterns is that they are particularly good at learning patterns which emerge from the relationship between closely related features - which may represent the more intrinsic behaviour general to all botnets. The AE and MLP are able to achieve high (>0.979) accuracies on the known botnet families because they can learn the defining features of each individual family, as opposed to learning some underlying pattern seen in all families. This is sufficient for binary classification on known families, but generalises poorly to classification of unknown families, because these 'defining' features may not be present.

Effect of a Reduced Input Feature Space on Computational and Classification Performance. Sub-Fig. 3C and 3D show the MIT and MMU for each model when using $30\%, 50\%$, and 100% of the available input feature space. From Fig. 3D, we observe a small but clear trend whereby increasing the feature space of a model's input has an associated increase in the memory usage of that model. This result aligns with the position outlined by Sarker [20], that the absence of feature engineering in DL may increase computational requirements of DL models. While the trend is consistent across all models, the proportional increase in memory is small; going from feature spaces of 30% to 100% (that is, 22 to 74 features), we observe a mean increase in MMU of $\approx 10\%$. In the most extreme case, CNN v1, the jump from 30% to 100% of features saw an increase in MMU of ≈ 90 MB, or 20.726%. For CNNs, an explanation for the relatively small increase to MMU when given larger feature spaces is likely found in their use of sparsely connected layers and parameter sharing, which reduce the number of trainable parameters in a model.

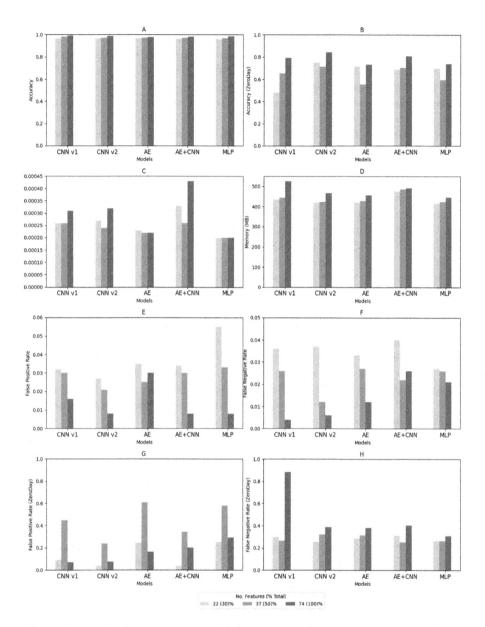

Fig. 3. Figures illustrating model performance on testing sets comprised of 30% (22 features), 50% (37 features), 100% (74 features) of total features. The figures show Normal Accuracy (A), Proto Zero-Day Accuracy (B), Mean Inference Time (C), Mean Memory Usage (D), False Positive Rate (E), False Negative Rate (F), False Positive Rate on Zero-Day set (G), and False Negative Rate on Zero-Day set (H).

From sub-Fig. 3D, we observe that the CNN v1 sees the largest increase in memory utilisation when evaluated on larger feature spaces. However, larger feature spaces in this model also result an improvement to classification performance. From sub-Fig. 3A, the normal accuracy improves from 0.968 to 0.993, sub-Fig. 3E shows that the FPR improves from a rate of 0.027 to 0.008, and FNR (sub-Fig. 3F) improves from a rate of 0.037 to 0.006. These improvements to classification performance when using larger feature spaces are significant. Moreover, they are, to lesser extents, observable in the four other models. Consequently, we make the claim that the increase in memory utilisation associated with larger feature spaces is justified by the improvements made to classification performance, given the informal notion that it is easier to buy more memory than it is to attain higher classification accuracy.

This argument is made clearer when we evaluate the impact of a reduced feature space on the proto zero-day testing set. To this end, sub-Fig. 3B shows that the best performing model using 100% of features, in terms of accuracy, was the CNN v2 with a score of 0.842. When this model was trained and tested on the set of 30% of features, the accuracy declined to 0.751. Furthermore, sub-Fig. 3G shows that the FPR increased from 0.038 to 0.076, and similarly that the FNR declined from 0.255 to 0.389, evident in sub-Fig. 3H. An explanation for the more significant decline in classification performance when evaluated on the proto zero-day set compared to the normal testing set is that detection of botnet traffic from a range of known botnet families is a fairly simple task, enabling (relatively) high accuracies to be obtained with fewer features. On the other hand, echoing the discussion in Sect. 6.1, detection of botnet traffic from a range of unknown botnet families requires models to learn complex patterns shared by all botnets, which the datasets with reduced feature spaces are not rich enough to support.

6.2   Multiclass Classifiers for Botnet Classification

Classification Accuracies of Each Model Overall, and for Each Botnet Family. The classification performance of each of the five multiclass classifiers is shown in Fig. 4; each model has a corresponding confusion matrix which displays its predictions, and enables evaluation of how the model performs w.r.t. each botnet family. Sub-Figure 4F offers a holistic representation of all the models' performance on each respective family. Evident in Fig. 4F, the overall accuracies of the models when classifying traffic into respective families of Benign, Neris, Rbot, and Virut were expectedly lower than the binary classification task model accuracies, with a mean accuracy score across all classes of 0.850, compared to 0.986. The best performance was observed in the CNN v1, which achieved an average accuracy across all families of 0.907. We observed that there was again a marked improvement, in terms of overall classification accuracy, seen in the models which used convolutional layers, with the exception of the AE+CNN model. CNNs are known for their efficacy when learning hierarchical relationships between features, which is a useful way of reasoning about the necessary and sufficient conditions when making a classification [6]. In the context of this classification task, this ability may be an explanation for their performance, as they are better able to combine the surface level and more complex features of network flows in order to learn more detailed patterns from the data.

As with the binary classification task, the shallow CNN (v1) outperforms the deep CNN (v2) by a small margin, with accuracies of 0.907 and 0.898, respectively. This is a percentage point increase of 0.009, which is fairly negligible. These findings allow us to make the claim that whichever patterns are learned by the CNNs are able to be learned with a shallow network, and that additional complexity (and associated dropout layers to combat overfitting) is unnecessary.

In the discussion from Sect. 6.1, concerning binary classification accuracy on the proto zero-day set, we suggested that the models that implemented convolutional layers (CNN v1, CNN v2, and AE+CNN) performed better due to the ability of CNNs to learn complex underlying behaviour patterns present in all botnet families. With respect to multiclass classification accuracy, CNN v1 and v2 are the best performers with overall accuracies of 0.907 and 0.898, respectively; while the AE+CNN has substantially worse classification performance, with an accuracy of 0.837. We have just proposed that a CNNs' ability to capture hierarchical relationships in data may be an explanation for their effectiveness for this problem; consequently, we suggest that an explanation for the relatively poor performance of the AE+CNN, which should benefit from this property of the convolutional layers, is that the encoding phase of the network reduces the complexity of the data to a point where the subsequent CNN is unable to learn the necessary hierarchical relationships, because they no longer 'exist' in the encoded representation. We further suggest that the reason for this is that the typical purpose of an autoencoder is to encode the input into a lower-dimensionality representation, from which an approximation of the original input can be reconstructed. This process may encourage the encoder to prioritise the more 'visible', surface-level patterns as they would be the best way to approximate the input. The consequence being that the encoder begins to act as a bottleneck - the features which aid more complex pattern learning are not present in the encoding, preventing a subsequent CNN from exploiting them. When we compare the results of the AE+CNN to the AE, similar accuracy rates are observed across the board, with overall accuracies of 0.837 and 0.836, respectively. This appears to reaffirm the notion of the encoder acting as a bottleneck for further classification.

Marín et al. [12] implemented a multiclass classifier of a deep CNN fed into an LSTM, trained on a dataset of Benign, Neris, Rbot, and Virut classes. Our best performing model, the CNN v1, showed an improvement on their CNN+LSTM, with an overall accuracy of 0.907 to their 0.765. Apart from the model architecture, a significant difference between our model and theirs is that our CNN v1 uses network flows as data, while they use bytes from the packet payloads, which are encrypted. We suggest that the difference in classification performance is caused by their model struggling to learn meaningful representations from the encrypted data. In support of this notion we refer to their binary classification experiments, where their payload-based classifier obtained an accuracy of 0.650, a result significantly lower than their flow-based classifier at 0.900, and our best performing binary classifier at 0.979 [12].

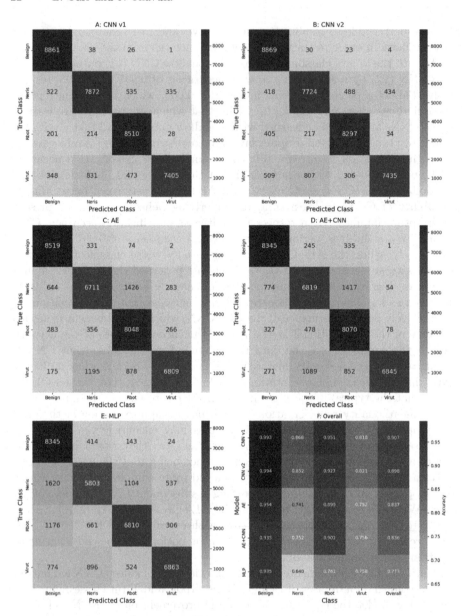

Fig. 4. Sub-Figures A to E show the respective confusion matrices for CNN v1, CNN v2, AE, AE+CNN, and MLP models, showing performance of each model w.r.t. individual classes. Sub-Figure F shows the overall accuracy, false-positive rate, and false negative rate of each model w.r.t. each class.

Notably, the CNN+LSTM struggled the most when classifying instances of Neris and Virut families. Figures 4B and F quite clearly show that this trend is observable across all models. Marín et al. suggest that an explanation of this is a result of the similarity between the Neris and Virut botnet families, causing models to misclassify one as the other. The results in Fig. 4 show that Virut samples are most frequently misclassified as Neris, supporting this notion. However, Neris samples are most frequently misclassified as Rbot, which may indicate that there is some other cause for the models' confusion.

Impact of Reduced Feature Space on Computational and Multiclass Classification Performance. Figure 5A shows the accuracy of each model given the size of the feature space. As the number of features is reduced we observe an associated decline in classification accuracy. This aligns with the intuition that more features enable a model to use the relationships between features to learn more complex patterns, facilitating better classification performance. The two CNN models show a more substantial decline in accuracy when the features are reduced from 50% to 30%, when compared to 100% reduced to 50%. In some sense, this is an unintuitive result; the larger reduction in feature space is accompanied by a smaller reduction in accuracy. An explanation for this lies in the notion that the CNN's success is a consequence of their ability to learn useful patterns from relations between features. When the feature space is reduced from 100% to 50%, there remains a sufficient number of features to enable the models to learn these patterns. In the reduction from 50% to 30%, while fewer features are removed, the resultant dataset is not detailed enough for CNN's to learn useful information. However, an alternate explanation of why the decline in accuracy is more pronounced when going from 50% to 30% of feature space, as opposed to 100% to 50%, is that the process of reducing the feature space uses random sampling to select features. This may have resulted in important features being absent from the 30% dataset. To this end, the cause of the decline might be a result of quality, rather than quantity of features.

We observe that the three models that employ a CNN appeared to use more memory than the AE and MLP. We expect the MLP to use the least memory, as it is the least complex model. However, the CNN v1 has fewer trainable parameters than the AE, while using more memory. We suggest that the cause of this, and a general explanation for why CNNs seem to have the largest MMU, is that the CNN has to store filters and their respective activation maps in memory, which can become fairly expensive [6].

We find that in every model, there is an increase to MMU as the feature space increases. This was an expected result, reaffirming the position outlined in Sect. 6.1 that larger input feature spaces are associated with an increase to a model's MMU. However, we maintain that this increase to MMU represents a relatively small improvement to computational performance, and is often coupled with a fairly substantial improvement in classification performance. For instance, when going from 30% to 100% of features the MLP's MMU performance declines, with an increased utilisation of only ≈28 MB; however, there is an accompanied improvement to accuracy of 0.089.

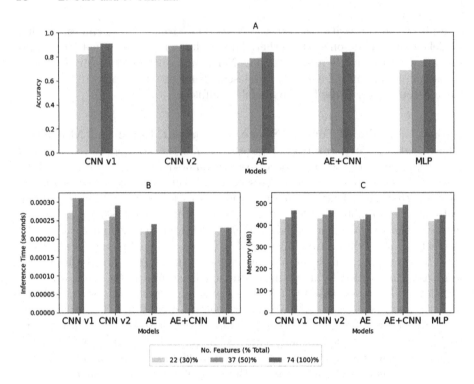

Fig. 5. Sub-Figures A, B, and C show the respective accuracy, Mean Inference Time, and Mean Memory Usage when evaluated on datasets of varying feature size.

The CNN v1, v2 and AE+CNN models have the three slowest inference times when evaluated on 100% of the feature space. This result matches our expectations, as CNNs operate by executing a convolution operation for each filter across all output elements of the preceding layer [6]. This convolutional process is computationally intensive and is not a requirement in the Autoencoder (AE) and Multilayer Perceptron (MLP) architectures. While these trends seemingly continued as the feature space was reduced, we found no discernible relation between the MIT and the size of the feature space.

7   Conclusions and Future Work

In this paper we evaluated the classification and computational performance of DL models for botnet detection, and classification. We further explored the effects of reducing feature spaces on performance. For our first research objective, we found that all models achieved accuracy ≥ 0.979, FPRs ≤ 0.033, and FNRs ≤ 0.026, suggesting that the classification problem was fairly simple. Classification performance on the proto zero-day set saw models which implemented convolutional layers have substantially better classification performance. Additionally, there was considerably more variation between models' performance, indicating that architecture choice plays a more significant role when detecting unknown botnet families. We suggest this was a result of the ability of convolutional layers to learn the more complex behaviour, general to botnets, as opposed to surface-level features. Learning the behaviour patterns of botnets in general enables the models to perform well on testing sets made up of entirely unknown botnet families. We further observed a clear trend that larger feature spaces where associated with a larger memory utilisation (MMU), affirming our expectation that feature selection might improve computational performance. However, in reducing feature space we also observe a substantial decline in classification performance. We found no evidence of a trend between feature space size and MIT; however, we acknowledge that there were serious limitations to the accuracy of measuring MIT. The consequence of this is that an 'optimal' size for a feature space should be determined on a per case basis, it is dependent on relevant constraints.

While we found little evidence of a reduced feature space improving the inference time of models, we did observe that CNNs in general seemed to have longer inference times, which we attributed to the expense of the convolution operation. Furthermore, we found that CNNs appeared to have a greater associated MMU, which we suggest is a result of the filters and respective activation maps, and not solely their complexity. With respect to MMU across varying feature space, we observed in all models that a reduction in feature space was clearly associated with a lower MMU. However, as was argued with respect to the binary classification problem, the fairly minor improvements to the computational cost of models are accompanied by an arguably more significant degradation to classification performance.

With respect to the second research objective, we found a fairly large differential between the classification performance of models which used convolutional layers and those that did not. We suggest that the efficacy of CNNs at learning hierarchical relations between features is an explanation for this. As with the binary classifiers, we observed a trend where larger feature spaces were associated with slightly greater MMU. However, the larger feature spaces resulted in substantially better classification performance.

The most significant observation from this work is in the classification performance of binary classifiers on the proto zero-day set. In this area, we observed accuracies high enough to act as a proof of concept: that models are able to generalise what they learn from training data to entirely unseen botnets. However, these results leave considerable room for improvement.

Future work might take one of two directions; while we explored the theoretical capabilities of DL models to detect and classify encrypted botnet traffic, an interesting extension would be a practical implementation of some of this work. We suggest that a good starting point would be to implement a binary classifier for detection - as detection, when contrasted with family classification, seems to have more immediate utility. On the theoretical side, we suggest ablation studies to investigate both feature and hyperparameter importance. The notion being that model size could be reduced if we knew more about the importance of certain features, or parts of the model. This may further yield insight into behaviours common between botnets, and consequently enable tuning models specifically for handling new botnet families.

A   Appendix

For comprehensive information, see Project Website or Github.

A.1   Feature Sets

Table 2. All the features present in flow extraction from CICFlowMeter. Bold and/or underlined indicate inclusion in 30% and 50% feature-spaces, respectively. All features present in 100% feature space.

No.	Feature Name	No.	Feature Name	No.	Feature Name
1	Flow ID	30	**Fwd IAT Max**	59	**Average Pkt Size**
2	Src IP	31	Fwd IAT Min	60	Fwd Segment Size Avg
3	Src Port	32	<u>Bwd IAT Total</u>	61	Bwd Segment Size Avg
4	Dst IP	33	<u>Bwd IAT Mean</u>	62	**Fwd Bytes/Bulk Avg**
5	Dst Port	34	**Bwd IAT Std**	63	**Fwd Pkt/Bulk Avg**
6	Protocol	35	<u>Bwd IAT Max</u>	64	Fwd Bulk Rate Avg
7	Timestamp	36	Bwd IAT Min	65	Bwd Bytes/Bulk Avg
8	<u>Flow Duration</u>	37	Fwd PSH Flags	66	Bwd Pkt/Bulk Avg
9	<u>Total Fwd Pkt</u>	38	Bwd PSH Flags	67	Bwd Bulk Rate Avg
10	<u>Total Bwd Pkts</u>	39	Fwd URG Flags	68	<u>Subflow Fwd Pkts</u>
11	**Total Length of Fwd Pkt**	40	Bwd URG Flags	69	**Subflow Fwd Bytes**
12	**Total Length of Bwd Pkt**	41	**Fwd Header Length**	70	Subflow Bwd Pkts
13	**Fwd Pkt Length Max**	42	Bwd Header Length	71	**Subflow Bwd Bytes**
14	Fwd Pkt Length Min	43	**Fwd Pkts/s**	72	FWD Init Win Bytes
15	Fwd Pkt Length Mean	44	Bwd Pkts/s	73	Bwd Init Win Bytes
16	Fwd Pkt Length Std	45	**Pkt Length Min**	74	<u>Fwd Act Data Pkts</u>
17	Bwd Pkt Length Max	46	Pkt Length Max	75	**Fwd Seg Size Min**
18	Bwd Pkt Length Min	47	Pkt Length Mean	76	<u>Active Mean</u>
19	Bwd Pkt Length Mean	48	Pkt Length Std	77	**Active Std**
20	**Bwd Pkt Length Std**	49	Pkt Length Variance	78	Active Max
21	Flow Bytes/s	50	FIN Flag Count	79	**Active Min**
22	Flow Pkts/s	51	SYN Flag Count	80	Idle Mean
23	Flow IAT Mean	52	RST Flag Count	81	**<u>Idle Std</u>**
24	<u>Flow IAT Std</u>	53	PSH Flag Count	82	<u>Idle Max</u>
25	<u>Flow IAT Max</u>	54	ACK Flag Count	83	**Idle Min**
26	Flow IAT Min	55	**URG Flag Count**	84	**<u>Label</u>**
27	Fwd IAT Total	56	CWR Flag Count		
28	<u>Fwd IAT Mean</u>	57	**ECE Flag Count**		
29	<u>Fwd IAT Std</u>	58	Down/Up Ratio		

A.2   Classification Results

(See Tables 3, 4, 5 and 6)

Table 3. Results of Binary Classifiers on Default Test Set

Model	Accuracy			Precision			Recall			FPR			FNR		
	100	50	30	100	50	30	100	50	30	100	50	30	100	50	30
CNN v1	.990	.972	.966	.990	.972	.966	.990	.972	.966	.016	.030	.032	.004	.026	.036
CNN v2	.993	.983	.968	.993	.983	.968	.993	.983	.968	.008	.021	.027	.006	.012	.037
AE	.979	.974	.966	.979	.974	.966	.979	.974	.966	.030	.026	.035	.012	.027	.033
AE CNN	.983	.974	.963	.983	.974	.963	.983	.974	.963	.008	.030	.034	.026	0.022	.040
MLP	.986	.971	.959	.986	.971	.959	.986	.971	.959	.008	.033	.055	.021	0.026	.027

Table 4. Results of Binary Classifiers on Proto Zero-Day Test Set

Model	Accuracy			Precision			Recall			FPR			FNR		
	100	50	30	100	50	30	100	50	30	100	50	30	100	50	30
CNN v1	.793	.653	.480	.904	.777	.671	.700	.736	.116	.092	.448	.071	.300	.264	.884
CNN v2	.842	.714	.751	.960	.777	.909	.745	.677	.611	.038	.240	.076	.255	.323	.389
AE	.732	.552	.716	.783	.581	.824	.713	.683	.619	.245	.609	.163	.287	.317	.381
AE CNN	.810	.705	.687	.957	.727	.785	.688	.746	.597	.038	.346	.202	.312	.254	.403
MLP	.740	.594	.698	.782	.610	.744	.734	.736	.691	.253	.580	.294	.266	.264	.309

Table 5. Computational Performance of Binary Classifiers

Model	Memory (MB)			Inference Time (S)		
	100	50	30	100	50	30
CNN v1	465.89	422.91	422.39	0.00032	0.00024	0.00027
CNN v2	526.16	443.78	435.83	0.00031	0.00026	0.00026
AE	457.02	428.02	420.16	0.00022	0.00022	0.00023
AE CNN	490.94	485.50	475.42	0.00026	0.00023	0.00033
MLP	446.05	422.70	416.67	0.00020	0.00020	0.00020

Table 6. Classification and Computational Performance of Multiclass Classifiers

Model	Accuracy (%)			Memory (MB)			Inference Time (S)		
	100	50	30	100	50	30	100	50	30
CNN v1	.907	.881	.819	465.96	434.63	425.77	.00030	.00031	.00027
CNN v2	.898	.889	.809	465.85	446.88	431.28	.00029	.00026	.00025
AE	.836	.786	.745	447.98	427.21	419.70	.00024	.00022	.00022
AE CNN	.836	.807	.755	492.95	478.88	458.87	.00028	.00030	.00030
MLP	.773	.764	.684	445.69	425.44	418.13	.00023	.00023	.00022

References

1. Abu Rajab, M., Zarfoss, J., Monrose, F., Terzis, A.: A multifaceted approach to understanding the botnet phenomenon. In: Proceedings of the 6th ACM SIG-COMM Conference on Internet Measurement, IMC 2006, pp. 41–52. Association for Computing Machinery, New York (2006). https://doi.org/10.1145/1177080.1177086
2. Aceto, G., Ciuonzo, D., Montieri, A., Pescapé, A.: Mobile encrypted traffic classification using deep learning. In: 2018 Network Traffic Measurement and Analysis Conference (TMA), pp. 1–8. IEEE (2018)
3. Bertino, E., Islam, N.: Botnets and internet of things security. Computer **50**(2), 76–79 (2017)
4. Cheng, R.: D 2 pi : identifying malware through deep packet inspection with deep learning (2017). https://api.semanticscholar.org/CorpusID:53062187
5. García, S., Grill, M., Stiborek, J., Zunino, A.: An empirical comparison of botnet detection methods. Comput. Secur. **45**, 100–123 (2014). https://doi.org/10.1016/j.cose.2014.05.011, https://www.sciencedirect.com/science/article/pii/S0167404814000923
6. Goodfellow, I., Bengio, Y., Courville, A.: Deep Learning. MIT Press (2016). http://www.deeplearningbook.org
7. Haddadi, F., Le Cong, D., Porter, L., Zincir-Heywood, A.N.: On the effectiveness of different botnet detection approaches. In: Lopez, J., Wu, Y. (eds.) ISPEC 2015. LNCS, vol. 9065, pp. 121–135. Springer, Cham (2015). https://doi.org/10.1007/978-3-319-17533-1_9
8. Lashkari, A.H., Gil, G.D., Mamun, M.S.I., Ghorbani, A.A.: Characterization of tor traffic using time based features. In: Proceedings of the 3rd International Conference on Information Systems Security and Privacy - Volume 1: ICISSP, pp. 253–262. INSTICC, SciTePress (2017). https://doi.org/10.5220/0006105602530262
9. Li, L., Jamieson, K., DeSalvo, G., Rostamizadeh, A., Talwalkar, A.: Hyperband: a novel bandit-based approach to hyperparameter optimization. J. Mach. Learn. Res. **18**(1), 6765–6816 (2017)
10. Lim, H.K., Kim, J.B., Kim, K., Hong, Y.G., Han, Y.H.: Payload-based traffic classification using multi-layer LSTM in software defined networks. Appl. Sci. **9**(12), 2550 (2019)
11. Lotfollahi, M., Jafari Siavoshani, M., Shirali Hossein Zade, R., Saberian, M.: Deep packet: a novel approach for encrypted traffic classification using deep learning. Soft Comput. **24**(3), 1999–2012 (2020)
12. Marín, G., Caasas, P., Capdehourat, G.: DeepMAL - deep learning models for malware traffic detection and classification. In: Data Science – Analytics and Applications, pp. 105–112. Springer, Wiesbaden (2021). https://doi.org/10.1007/978-3-658-32182-6_16
13. O'Malley, T., et al.: Kerastuner (2019). https://github.com/keras-team/keras-tuner
14. O'Shea, K., Nash, R.: An introduction to convolutional neural networks. arXiv preprint arXiv:1511.08458 (2015)
15. Pachhala, N., Jothilakshmi, S., Battula, B.P.: A comprehensive survey on identification of malware types and malware classification using machine learning techniques. In: 2021 2nd International Conference on Smart Electronics and Communication (ICOSEC), pp. 1207–1214 (2021). https://doi.org/10.1109/ICOSEC51865.2021.9591763

16. Papadogiannaki, E., Tsirantonakis, G., Ioannidis, S.: Network intrusion detection in encrypted traffic. In: 2022 IEEE Conference on Dependable and Secure Computing (DSC), pp. 1–8 (2022). https://doi.org/10.1109/DSC54232.2022.9888942

17. Acarman, T.: Botnet detection based on network flow summary and deep learning. Int. J. Netw. Manage. **28**(6), e2039 (2018). https://doi.org/10.1002/nem.2039, https://onlinelibrary.wiley.com/doi/abs/10.1002/nem.2039

18. Piskozub, M., Gaspari, F.D., Barr-Smith, F., Mancini, L., Martinovic, I.: MalPhase: fine-grained malware detection using network flow data. In: Proceedings of the 2021 ACM Asia Conference on Computer and Communications Security. ACM (2021). https://doi.org/10.1145/3433210.3453101

19. van Roosmalen, J., Vranken, H., van Eekelen, M.: Applying deep learning on packet flows for botnet detection. In: Proceedings of the 33rd Annual ACM Symposium on Applied Computing, pp. 1629–1636 (2018)

20. Sarker, I.H.: Cyberlearning: Effectiveness analysis of machine learning security modeling to detect cyber-anomalies and multi-attacks. Internet Things **14**, 100393 (2021)

21. Stratosphere: Stratosphere laboratory datasets (2015). https://www.stratosphereips.org/datasets-overview. Accessed 13 Mar 2020

22. Torres, P., Catania, C., Garcia, S., Garino, C.G.: An analysis of recurrent neural networks for botnet detection behavior. In: 2016 IEEE Biennial Congress of Argentina (ARGENCON), pp. 1–6. IEEE (2016)

23. Van Rossum, G., Drake, F.L.: Python 3 Reference Manual. CreateSpace, Scotts Valley (2009)

24. Villa, A., Varki, E.: Characterization of a campus internet workload. In: Proceedings of CATA, pp. 140–148 (2012)

25. Wang, W., et al.: HAST-IDS: learning hierarchical spatial-temporal features using deep neural networks to improve intrusion detection. IEEE Access **6**, 1792–1806 (2017)

26. Wang, Z., Fok, K.W., Thing, V.L.: Machine learning for encrypted malicious traffic detection: approaches, datasets and comparative study. Comput. Secur. **113**, 102542 (2022). https://doi.org/10.1016/j.cose.2021.102542

27. Weisz, S., Chavula, J.: Community network traffic classification using two-dimensional convolutional neural networks. In: Sheikh, Y.H., Rai, I.A., Bakar, A.D. (eds.) AFRICOMM 2021. LNICST, pp. 128–148. Springer, Cham (2022). https://doi.org/10.1007/978-3-031-06374-9_9

28. Yeo, M., et al.: Flow-based malware detection using convolutional neural network. In: 2018 International Conference on Information Networking (ICOIN), pp. 910–913 (2018). https://doi.org/10.1109/ICOIN.2018.8343255

29. Zeng, Y., Gu, H., Wei, W., Guo, Y.: $deep - full - range$: a deep learning based network encrypted traffic classification and intrusion detection framework. IEEE Access **7**, 45182–45190 (2019). https://doi.org/10.1109/ACCESS.2019.2908225

30. Zhou, H., Hu, Y., Yang, X., Pan, H., Guo, W., Zou, C.C.: A worm detection system based on deep learning. IEEE Access **8**, 205444–205454 (2020)

Quantitative Analysis of Zambian Wikipedia Contributions: Assessing Awareness, Willingness, Motivation, and the Impact of Gamified Leaderboards and Badges

Christabel Chalwe⦿, Chisanga Chanda⦿, Lweendo Muzyamba⦿,
Joe Mwape⦿, and Lighton Phiri$^{(\boxtimes)}$⦿

Department of Library and Information Science, University of Zambia,
P.O Box 32379, Lusaka, Zambia
{2019092387,2019036843,2019009650,2019090295}@student.unza.zm,
lighton.phiri@unza.zm

Abstract. Wikipedia is a widely recognized and valuable source of information, However, it encounters persistent challenges in attracting and retaining active contributors. It is recorded that only 10 people from Zambia contribute and create content on wikipedia in the month of may 2023. While a large number consumes Wikipedia content, there is a noticeably low number of Wikipedians that contribute content on and about Zambia. This paper presents a Facebook plugin, WikiMotivate, aimed at motivating Zambian Wikipedians to update pre-existing content, add new entries, and share their natural expertise. WikiMotivate was implemented as a Facebook plugin that utilizes leaderboard and badge gamification features to encourage and incentivize active Wikipedia content contribution. Using a mixed-methods approach, historical Wikipedia edit histories were used to quantify content contributed by Zambian Wikipedians. In addition, user surveys were conducted to determine relative levels of awareness about Wikipedia, willingness to contribute to contribute content on Wikipedia and perceived motivating factors that affect content contribution on Wikipedia. Furthermore, a Facebook plugin, WikiMotivate, was implemented in order to be used an a service for motivating potential Zambian Wikipedians. Finally, in order to determine the most effective approach, a comparative analysis of leader-boards and badges was conducted with nine (9) expert evaluaters. The results clearly indicate that a significant proportion of Wikipedia content on and about Zambia is authored by Wikipedians from outside Zambia, with only 11% of the contributors, out of the 224, originating from Zambia. In addition, study participants were largely unaware of the various editing practices on Wikipedia; interestingly enough, most participants expressed their willingness to contribute content if trained. In terms of motivating factors, "Information Seeking and Educational Fullfilment" was as the key motivating factor. The Facebook plugin implemented suggests that incorporating leaderboards and badges is a more

A. Gerber (Ed.): SAICSIT 2024, CCIS 2159, pp. 30–44, 2024.
https://doi.org/10.1007/978-3-031-64881-6_2

effective approach to motivating contributions to Wikipedia. This study provides useful insight into the landscape of Wikipedia content contribution in the Global South.

Keywords: Wikipedia · Crowdsourcing · Facebook · Gamification

1 Introduction

Digital content contribution from contributors originating from countries located in the so-called Global South is noticeably low, with a recent study by Graham et al. reporting that Sub-Saharan Africa stands out with the lowest levels of participation on GitHub-1% of GitHub users hail from the region-and shocking low levels of Wikipedia contributions, with contributions originating from the whole of Africa being lower than those from Hong Kong [7]. Interestingly enough, of the Wikipedia articles on and about Africa, only 5% of the contributions were reported to have been generated locally [7]. Recent statistics on Wikipedia contributions suggest that Wikipedia content contribution participation from the so-called Global South is still low.

While there are a considerable number of Global South Internet users that consume content from Wikipedia, there is a corresponding disproportionate number of users that contribute content to the same platform. The Republic of Zambia provides a classic case example for this problem; for instance, there were a total of 2,347,000 Wikipedia page views against a mere 20 editors from The Republic of Zambia in the month of April 2024[1].

The motivation for conducting this is three-fold; first, there is a reported disproportionate content on Wikipedia on about the Global South; second, statistics compiled by Wikipedia indicate that there is a vast difference between Wikipedia content consumption and creation in the Global South [8]; finally, with the rapid adoption of Large Language Models (LLMs), such as ChatGPT [17], it becomes crucial to ensure that data sources used to train the LLMs are updated with content from underrepresented regions of the world. Incidentally, Wikipedia is reported as one of the well-know pre-training and fine-tunning dataset for most LLMs [11,15].

This paper presents work conducted to explore how gamification could be utilised in order to increase the number of Zambian Wikipedians with the potential to increase content creation and contribution. Specifically, the study was guided by the following specific objectives:

– To quantify Wikipedia content creation and contribution about Zambia by Zambians
– To determine the levels of awareness and willingness to create and contribute content on Wikipedia
– To identify the perceived motivation factors that affect content contribution on Wikipedia.

---

[1] https://stats.wikimedia.org/#/metrics/en.wikipedia.org.

– To design and implement a software that will use gamification to motivate and increase content creation and contribution on Wikipedia.

The remainder of this paper is organised as follows: Sect. 2 is a review of existing literature related to the study conducted; Sect. 3 describes the methodological approach followed when executing the studies linked to this research; Sect. 4 presents study findings and their discussions and; finally, Sect. 5 provides concluding remarks.

2   Related Work

2.1   Wikipedia Content Contribution Awareness, Willingness and Motivation

Several studies have been conducted to understand the willingness and motivations linked to contributing content on Wikipedia. The motivations linked to content contribution can, in part, be best understood using existing theories on motivation; there are a series of theories that explain the factors that drive and direct human motivations. Popular theories include Maslow's Theory of Hierarchical Needs [25], Hertzberg's Two-Factor Theory [2], McClelland's Theory of Needs [23], Vroom's Theory of Expectancy [24] and McGregor's Theory X and Theory Y [12]. In addition, the Uses and Gratification Theory [3,10] has been applied extensively in understanding content contribution.

Xu and Li's empirical study revealed that Wikipedia content contribution is largely driven by extrinsically oriented motivations, including reciprocity and the need for self-development [26]. Yang and Lai set out to determine how conventional and self concept-based motivation on individual willingness affect the sharing of knowledge in Wikipedia, with internal self-concept motivation identified as the key motivation for knowledge sharing on Wikipedia [27]. Crowston and Fagnot argue that motives for contributing content differ at various stages [5].

The study presented in this work extensively used the Uses and Gratification in order to understand how digital content contribution gratifies users due to its successful application in prior studies [4,20]. For instance.

2.2   Quantifying Digital Content Contributions

There have been a number of studies conducted to empirically analyse various aspects of Wikipedia. Reagle [21] and Ortega [18] both conducted studies focusing on quantitative analysis of Wikipedia, aimed at measuring various aspects of the Wikipedia platform in order to gain insights into its collaborative nature. These studies utilised large datasets of user-contributed data from Wikipedia, including article edits and revisions. The quantitative studies measured engagement and impact within the Wikipedia community, analysing factors such as the number of edits, revisions per page, and user distribution to uncover patterns of contribution and participation. Ortega's work, in particular focused on identifying the fraction of authors responsible for most changes in Wikipedia articles and how their behavior evolved over time.

Some existing works have explored the measurement of user participation on digital platforms, with Riquelme and Gonzalez [22] investigating the factors influencing participation levels on Twitter using user activities and contribution patterns.

2.3 Gamification for Enhanced User Engagement

Gamification has been reported to increase motivation and participation during crowdsourcing, with different implementations using a combination of simpler implementations such as point system and other richer mechanisms [14].

Studies specific to Wikipedia include work by Eisenschlos et al. [6] in which a gamification framework used badges and reputation systems to motivate users to create and contribute high-quality content. Oceja and Sierra explore how the presence of tangible rewards vs. badges impacts the user's behaviours, with tangible rewards proving to be more effective [16].

The work presented in this paper focuses on the use of leaderboards and badges and is aligned with work by Katz and Suleman as the Facebook platform is used as the primary platform for users to engage [9].

3 Methodology

This research study employed a mixed method approach, blending both qualitative and quantitative research methods to provide a more comprehensive understanding of the study. A total of three (3) sub-studies were conducted. First, an empirical study involving the analysis of Wikipedia edit histories for pages on and about Zambia was conducted as outlined in Sect. 3.1. In addition, a survey, outlined in Sect. 3.2 was conducted to determine the levels of awareness of Wikipedia content contribution; perceived willingness to contribute content to Wikipedia; and perceived motivation factors linked to Wikipedia content contribution.

3.1 Quantifying Wikipedia Content Contributions

In order to determine the relative quantity of Wikipedia content contributed by Zambians, Wikipedia edit history records were extracted and analysed from Wikipedia. Wikipedia page with content on and about Zambia were purposively sampled. The total number of contribution was used as an inclusion criteria.

The history view page of the candidate pages served as the measurement instrument. In essence, data of both user account editors as well non-user editors (anonymous editors) was collected from the history view page of the pages quantified. Registered user contributions have a corresponding hyperlinked username for the contributors, with the hyperlink leading to the profile page of the

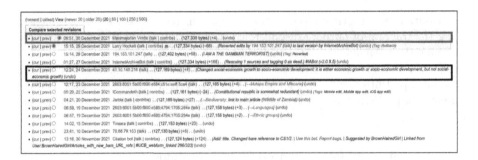

Fig. 1. Revision History for Zambia Wikipedia Page

contributor. Anonymous contributions on the other hand, have the IP address associated with the contributor. Figure 1 shows an example history view page for the Zambia Wikipedia page. The history entry highlighted in the red bounding box shows a sample contribution from a registered user "Maximajorian Viridio", while the history entry highlighted in black bounding box shows a sample contribution from an anonymous contributor.

The data collection process involved retrieving IP addresses from editors without Wikipedia user accounts, identified as IP accounts, through the Wikipedia view history of pages relevant to Zambia. The IP addresses were then used to determine the origin of the editors in order to assess the level of engagement. For editors with user accounts, the procedure involved a manual retrieval of their origin information by checking their biography on Wikipedia.

As shown in Fig. 1, Wikipedia contributions are of varying types, including additions and deletions of content; the magnitude of the contributions represented in terms of bytes. The definition of a contribution in the study presented in this paper was agnostic of the type—addition or deletion—and size.

3.2   Levels of Awareness, Willingness and Motivation Factors

The goal of assessing the level of awareness and willingness was to measure the level of awareness and willingness among individuals from Zambia to participate in content creation and contribution on and about Zambia-related articles on Wikipedia. Furthermore, the aspect of the study linked to motivating factors was focused on determining factors with the potential to motivate content contribution on Wikipedia.

Study participants were randomly sampled from The University of Zambia (UNZA) students and informed Zambian employees were the target population for assessing the level of awareness and willingness to create and contribute content on Wikipedia about Zambia.

Online Google Forms[2] questionnaires were used to collect data on their perceived awareness and willingness to contribute content to Wikipedia. The questionnaires included items for assessing awareness, willingness and, additionally,

---

[2] https://www.google.com/forms/about.

Table 1. Awareness, Willingness and Motivation Questionnaire Items

Aspect	Items	Scale
Demographics	Age	Interval
	(Student/Employee) Gender	Categorical
	Level of Study	Categorical
	Year of Study	Categorical
	(Employee) Highest Qualification	Categorical
	(Employee) Profession	Categorical
	(Employee) Geographic Location	Categorical
	(Student/Employee) Experience Editing	5-Point Likert Scale
Awareness	Editing content on Wikipedia	5-Point Likert Scale
	Anonymously editing on Wikipedia	5-Point Likert Scale
	Contributing minimal edits on Wikipedia	5-Point Likert Scale
	Creating a new article on Wikipedia	5-Point Likert Scale
	Adding multimedia on Wikipedia	5-Point Likert Scale
	Processes and guidelines for Wikipedia	5-Point Likert Scale
Willingness	Willing to contribute content on Wikipedia	5-Point Likert Scale
Motivation	Information Seeking & Educational Fullfilment	5-Point Likert Scale
	Self-Expression & Identity	5-Point Likert Scale
	Social Interaction	5-Point Likert Scale
	Achievement and Recognition	5-Point Likert Scale

subjective views on motivating factors aligned with the Uses and Gratification Theory [20]. The questionnaire was designed to include the items summarised in Table 1

3.3   Design, Implementation and Evaluation of WikiMotivate

The WikiMotivate platform is a multifaceted Web application developed primarily using the Python programming language and the Flask Web framework [19]. Specifically, the XTools API [1] to retrieve data about top editors, dynamically creating visually appealing leaderboard images, and seamlessly sharing these images on the dedicated WikiMotivate Facebook page. The integration between the WikiMotivate Web application and Facebook was facilitated using the Facebook Graph API [13].

WikiMotivate sends HTTP GET requests to the XTools API endpoint specific to each Wikipedia page, resulting in a response with data about top editors, edit counts and other relevant metrics. An additional feature facilitates the automatic generation of data and information for the leaderboard and badges. The badge and leaderboard specific information is then posted on a WikiMotivate public Facebook page[3]. Facebook was identifed as an appropriate host environment as it is one of the most widely used social medial platforms in Zambia.

---

[3] https://www.facebook.com/profile.php?id=100094560138473.

4   Results and Discussion

As outlined in Sect. 3, a total of three (3) sub-studies—outlined in Sects. 4.1 to 4.3—were conducted as part of the research presented in this paper.

4.1   Quantifying Wikipedia Content Contributions

As of October 24 2023, there were 6,733,541 articles in the English Wikipedia, out of which a total of 244 were identified as being related to Zambia. A total of four (4)—Zambia[4], History of Zambia[5], Victoria Fall[6] and Economy of Zambia[7]—Wikipedia articles were analysed during the empirical evaluation.

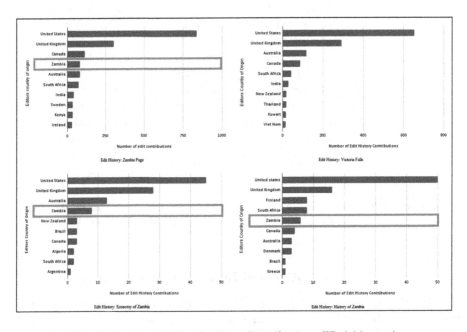

Fig. 2. Zambian Wikipedia Page Contributions (IP Addresses)

Analysis 1. Anonymous Contributions. Figure 2 shows the top 10 Wikipedia edit history countries by anonymous editors, with results for the Zambia, History of Zambia, Victoria Falls and Economy of Zambia Wikipedia pages. The results indicate that the United States is the source country with the highest number of edits for all the four (4) Wikipedia pages.

---

[4] https://en.wikipedia.org/wiki/Zambia.
[5] https://en.wikipedia.org/wiki/History_of_Zambia.
[6] https://en.wikipedia.org/wiki/Victoria_Falls.
[7] https://en.wikipedia.org/wiki/Economy_of_Zambia.

Surprisingly enough, Zambia is not on the top 10 list for the Zambia Wikipedia page, a Wikipedia page on and about Zambia with the largest number of edit histories. These results provide a compelling case for why the problem with the lack of active Zambia Wikipedians. Interestingly enough, Zambia is on the top 5 list of couries for the History of Zambia and Economy of Zambia Wikipedia pages. A potential explanation for this is arguably that the two pages fall within the category of pages that attract little interest from non-Zambian Wikipedians. This is in fact further supported by the results for the Victoria Fall Wikipedia page in which Zambia is the country with the least Wikipedians in the top 10 list.

Analysis 2. Registered Users' Contributions. The contributions from registered users are summarised in Fig. 3 and Table 2. The contributions from Zambia are not on the top 10 list of contributions for the "Economy of Zambia" and "History of Zambia" Wikipedia Pages. Interestingly enough, the total contributions from Zambia are the highest for the "Zambia" Wikipedia page, however, upon further analysis, it was discovered that there were a number of contributors who had contributed significantly more. This is in fact illustrated in Table 2 were the total number of contributors from Zambia were a mere 14, accounting for 11%.

An analysis of overall contributors from Zambia presents a compelling case for how serious the problem of few Global South contributors. Out of the 224 contributors of the four (4) Wikipedia pages analysed, a mere 18—representing 8%—were identified as originating from Zambia. A further breakdown of this distribution highlights the severity of the problem; the proportion of contributors from Zambia for the "Zambia", "History of Zambia", "Economy of Zambia" and "Victoria Falls" pages was 11% (14 out of 124 contributors), 3% (1 out of 39 contributors), 3% (1 out of 34) and 7% (2 out of 27 contributors), respectively.

4.2   Levels of Awareness, Willingnesss and Motivation

As outlined in Sect. 3.2, the second objective was aimed at determining the levels of awareness of content contribution on Wikipedia, perceived willingness to contribute content on Wikipedia and, additionally, identifying motivating factors that could encourage content contribution on Wikipedia. Online surveys were used in order to elicit responses.

Demographic Factors. A total of 60 participants responded to the Employee questionnaire, with varying values for gender, education qualifications, ages, professions and geographic locations. 82 students participants responded to the Student questionnaire with varying gender, age, level of education, year of student and experience with Wikipedia.

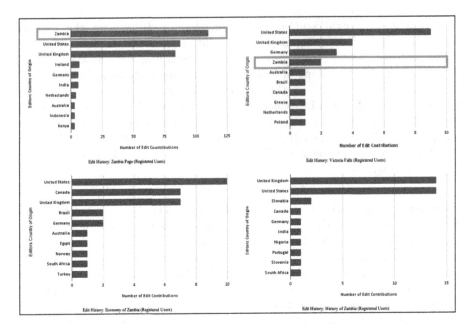

Fig. 3. Zambian Wikipedia Page Contributions (Registered Users)

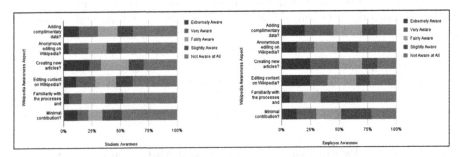

Fig. 4. Survey Participants' Perceived Levels of Awareness

Analysis 1. Awareness. The results suggest that the awareness levels for employees are more than that of students. Figure 4 shows plots of results for relative levels of awareness for Employees and Students.

While most students were aware that articles can be created on Wikipedia (71%), there levels of awareness regarding processes and procedures (52%), anonymous editing (51%), minimal contribution (51%) and editing content (61%) were lower. The awareness levels for employees on the other hand were generally higher, with the highest awareness levels related to creating new articles (83%) and adding complementary data (83%), and the lowest being familiarity with processes (70%).

Table 2. Top 5 Contributors and Contributions by Country

Page	Country	Contributors	Contributions
Zambia[a]	United States	44	88
	United Kingdom	17	84
	Zambia	**14**	**204**
	Canada	7	9
	Germany	6	6
History of Zambia[b]	United Kingdom	14	14
	United States	14	14
	Slovakia	2	2
	Canada	1	1
	Germany	1	1
Economy of Zambia[c]	United States	10	10
	Canada	7	7
	United Kingdom	7	7
	Brazil	2	2
	Germany	2	2
Victoria Falls[d]	United States	9	9
	United Kingdom	4	4
	Germany	3	3
	Zambia	**2**	**2**
	Australia	1	1

[a] https://en.wikipedia.org/wiki/Zambia
[b] https://en.wikipedia.org/wiki/History_of_Zambia
[c]https://en.wikipedia.org/wiki/Economy_of_Zambia
[b]https://en.wikipedia.org/wiki/Victoria_Falls

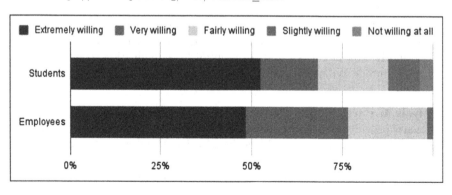

Fig. 5. Survey Participants' Perceived Willingness to Contribute.

Analysis 2. Willingness. Figure 5 shows the relative levels of participants' willingness to contribute content to Wikipedia. The results are very encouraging a significant number of both Students (96%) and Employees (100%) expressed their willingness to contribute content to Wikipedia. Surprisingly enough though, a lot more Students (4%), when compared with Employees (0%) were less willing to contribute content. These findings are further supported by the participants' general comments presented in "Analysis 4. Participants' Remarks" section. The implications of these findings are significant: they suggest that with proper training and awareness, content contribution on and about Zambia on Wikipedia can potentially increase.

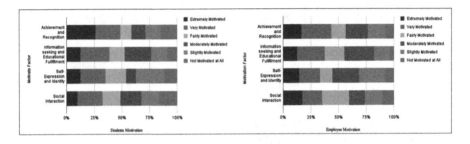

Fig. 6. Survey Participants' Perceived Motivation Factors.

Analysis 3. Motivation. Figure 6 shows the relative levels of motivation for Students and Employees, respectively. Interestingly enough, for both Students and Employees, most of the participants indicated that all the various motivation factors were strong motivation factors. The "Information Seeking and Educational Fullfilment" factor was identified as the most prominent factor for both Students and Employees. Additionally, "Social Interaction" was identified as the least likely motivation factors for both Students and Employees.

These results, and especially findings linked to the "Achievement and Recognition" motivation factor, suggest a potential for gamification to be used an a tool to encourage Wikipedia contributions.

Analysis 4. Participants' Remarks. A thematic analysis of the open-ended comments provided by the participants identified "lack of awareness and knowledge", "willingness to participate", "motivations for contribution", "challenges and concerns", "general perceptions of Wikipedia" and "suggestions for improvement". Some of the remarks provided by the participants are as follows:

> "I was not aware of that one could actually create content and contribute to platforms like Wikipedia. Being able to contribute on such platforms will lead to more innovativeness and enable people to share information and knowledge easily." [Student 7]

"I have not created anything on Wikipedia but am willing to learn on how to do it and would like to express myself with such a platform" [Student 8]

"My enthusiasm on wikipedia platform is there and me knowing that people can contribute and edit articles it gives me a level of understanding were i can't regard wikipedia for my academic writings because some of the information is not clearly explained " [Student 11]

"I wasn't aware, but I would love to create content" [Student 13]

"I'm more than willing to participate in creating content on Wikipedia but the major challenge is I lack knowledge on how to go about the process" [15]

"As a country we are very behind in terms of documenting our story. The collection and preservation of information for posterity is very crucial to enabling future generations to have a fair understanding of what has been in the past. A platform like Wikipedia is the perfect platform to document the history of men and women that have shaped our society and also to give insight into what is and what makes Zambia what it is. Therefore, enhancing the capacity of people to create and add content on Wikipedia is a very big step in the right direction." [Employee 12]

"people aren't even aware that we can edit or even add to wikipedia content" [Employee 27]

"I have little information on content creation on Wikipedia but I am willing to learn once a platform is established. I would love my company to advertise its products and services on Wikipedia." [Employee 45]

4.3   Design, Implementation and Evaluation of WikiMotivate

Figure 7 shows the Web application interface, while Fig. 8 shows a screenshot of the WikiMotivate Facebook public page automatically populated with gamified posts of various Zambian Wikipedia page used during the experiment. The toolkit was successfully integrated with Facebook, with edit histories automatically synchronised from the Wikipedia pages.

The WikiMotivate software was evaluated to determine whether the leaderboard, the badge, or both might capture users' attention, keep it, and inspire them to consistently provide new content to Wikipedia. The majority of the study participants indicated that the WikiMotivate toolkit positively influenced their motivation to contribute content. In addition, the vast majority of participants indicated that combining a leaderboard and badges was more effective that using either leaderboards or badges in isolation. Some interesting participants' general comments were as follows:

"The system was really motivating. I enjoyed seeing my name on the leaderboard" [Participant 3]

"This software has really given me a reason to edit more and more content" [Participant 7].

Both comments from [Participant 3] and [Participant 7] suggest that the software has the potential to be very impactful.

Fig. 7. Screenshot Showing WikiMotivate Leaderboard and Ranking of Top Editors

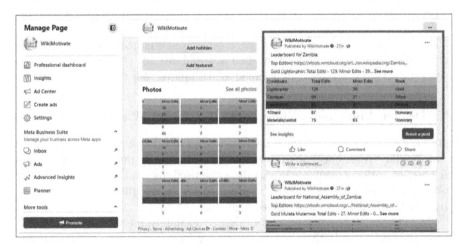

Fig. 8. Screenshot Showing WikiMotivate Top Editors Posted to Facebook WikiMotivate Page

5   Conclusion

This paper presented studies conducted in order to understand the historical contributions of Wikipedia contributions originating from Zambia. While four (4) Wikipedia pages were purposively sampled, the results can arguably generalised, as indicated by the common patterns in the results. Significantly, the quantitative analysis highlights the problem with few Wikipedians from Zambia. The study aimed at determining the awareness, willingness and motivation factors sheds light on the relative levels of awareness, willingness and motivation factors associated with editing content on Wikipedia by potential Zambian Wikipedians; the results suggest that the levels of awareness are significantly low, however, most participants were willing to contribute content. The results further suggest that intrinsic motivation factors have a potential to increase contributions from Zambian Wikipedians. Finally, the implementation and use of the WikiMotivate Facebook plugin demonstrates how software tools and services can potentially be used to encourage contributions to Wikipedia.

Potential future work could involve a large-scale nation-wide survey to further understand how the different demographic factors influence willingness and motivation. In addition, future work could explore the use for more widely used services such as WhatsApp through the use of WhatsApp bots.

References

1. XTools — xtools.wmcloud.org (2008). https://xtools.wmcloud.org. Accessed 03 Apr 2024
2. Alshmemri, M., Shahwan-Akl, L., Maude, P.: Herzberg's two-factor theory. Life Sci. J. **14**(5), 12–16 (2017). https://www.lifesciencesite.com/lsj/life140517/03_32120lsj140517_12_16.pdf
3. Blumler, J.G.: Uses and Gratifications Research. In: The International Encyclopedia of Journalism Studies. pp. 1–8. Wiley, Hoboken (2019). https://doi.org/10.1002/9781118841570.iejs0032
4. Chanda, M., Chirwa, E., Kamanga, M., Kayula, M., Phiri, L.: Factors influencing co-creation of open education resources using learning object repositories. In: Proceedings of the 14th International Conference on Computer Supported Education - Volume 1: CSEDU,. pp. 405–412. INSTICC, SciTePress (2022). https://doi.org/10.5220/0011090300003182
5. Crowston, K., Fagnot, I.: Stages of motivation for contributing user-generated content: a theory and empirical test. In: International Journal of Human-Computer Studies, vol. 109, pp. 89–101 (2018). https://doi.org/10.1016/j.ijhcs.2017.08.005
6. Eisenschlos, J., Dhingra, B., Bulian, J., Börschinger, B., Boyd-Graber, J.: Fool me twice: entailment from wikipedia gamification. In: Toutanova, K., et al. (eds.) Proceedings of the 2021 Conference of the North merican Chapter of the Association for Computational Linguistics: Human Language Technologies, pp 352–365. Association for Computational Linguistics (2021). https://doi.org/10.18653/v1/2021.naacl-main.32
7. Graham, M., De Sabbata, S., Zook, M.A.: Towards a study of information geographies:(im) mutable augmentations and a mapping of the geographies of information. Geo: Geogr. Environ. **2**(1), 88–105 (2015). https://doi.org/10.1002/geo2.8
8. Grigas, A.: Wikimedia wikimedia statistics (2024). https://stats.wikimedia.org/#/all-projects. Accessed 03 Apr 2024
9. Havenga, M., Williams, K., Suleman, H.: Motivating users to build heritage collections using games on social networks. In: Chen, H.H., Chowdhury, G. (eds.) LNCS. LNCS, pp. 279–288. Springer, Heidelberg (2012). https://doi.org/10.1007/978-3-642-34752-8_34
10. Katz, E., Blumler, J.G., Gurevitch, M.: Uses and gratifications research. Public Opinion Q. **37**(4), 509–523 (1973). https://doi.org/10.1086/268109
11. Liu, Y., Cao, J., Liu, C., Ding, K., Jin, L.: Datasets for large language models: a comprehensive survey (2024). https://doi.org/10.48550/arXiv.2402.18041

12. McGregor, D.: The human side of enterprise. In: Readings in Managerial Psychology, pp. 310–321 (1960). https://press.uchicago.edu/ucp/books/book/chicago/R/bo3641132.html. The University of Chicago Press, Chicago. Chapter 5

13. Meta: Graph API - Documentation - Meta for Developers — developers.facebook.com (2024). https://developers.facebook.com/docs/graph-api. Accessed 03 Apr 2024

14. Morschheuser, B., Hamari, J., Koivisto, J.: Gamification in crowdsourcing: a review. In: 2016 49th Hawaii International Conference on System Sciences (HICSS), pp. 4375–4384. IEEE (2016). https://doi.org/10.1109/HICSS.2016.543

15. Naveed, H., et al.: A comprehensive overview of large language models (2024). https://doi.org/10.48550/arXiv.2307.06435

16. Oceja, J., Sierra-Obregón, Á.: Gamifying wikipedia? In: European Conference on Games Based Learning, pp. 504–511. Academic Conferences International Limited (2018). https://dialnet.unirioja.es/servlet/articulo?codigo=6991900

17. OpenAI: Introducing chatgpt (2024). https://openai.com/index/chatgpt. Accessed 03 Apr 2024

18. Ortega Soto, J.F., et al.: Wikipedia: a quantitative analysis. Universidad Rey Juan Carlos, Madrid, Spain (2009). http://hdl.handle.net/10115/11239

19. Pallets: Welcome to Flask — Flask Documentation (3.0.x) — flask.palletsprojects.com (2010). https://flask.palletsprojects.com/en/3.0.x. Accessed 03 Apr 2024

20. Rafaeli, S., Hayat, T., Ariel, Y.: Knowledge building and motivations in Wikipedia: participation as "ba". In: Cyberculture and New Media, pp. 51–67. Brill (2009). https://doi.org/10.1163/9789401206747_004

21. Reagle, J.: Good Faith Collaboration: The Culture of Wikipedia. The MIT Press, Cambridge (2010). https://doi.org/10.7551/mitpress/8051.001.0001

22. Riquelme, F., GonzÃÂąlez-Cantergiani, P.: Measuring user influence on twitter: a survey. Inf. Process. Manag. **52**(5), 949–975 (2016). https://doi.org/10.1016/j.ipm.2016.04.003

23. Royle, M.T., Hall, A.T.: The relationship between McClelland's theory of needs, feeling individually accountable, and informal accountability for others. International journal of management and marketing research **5**(1), 21–42 (2012). https://ssrn.com/abstract=1957209

24. Vroom, V., Porter, L., Lawler, E.: Expectancy theories. In: Organizational Behavior 1: Essential Theories of Motivation and Leadership, pp. 94–113. Routledge, New York, NY (2015). https://www.taylorfrancis.com/chapters/edit/10.4324/9781315702018-9/expectancy-heories-victor-vroom-lyman-porter-edward-lawler. Chapter 7

25. Wahba, M.A., Bridwell, L.G.: Maslow reconsidered: a review of research on the need hierarchy theory. Organ. Behav. Hum. Perform. **15**(2), 212–240 (1976). https://doi.org/10.1016/0030-5073(76)90038-6. Elsevier

26. Xu, B., Li, D.: An empirical study of the motivations for content contribution and community participation in Wikipedia. Inf. Manag. **52**(3), 275–286 (2015). https://doi.org/10.1016/j.im.2014.12.003

27. Yang, H.L., Lai, C.Y.: Motivations of Wikipedia content contributors. Comput. Hum. Behav. **26**(6), 1377–1383 (2010). https://doi.org/10.1016/j.chb.2010.04.011. online Interactivity: Role of Technology in Behavior Change

Empirical Evaluation of Variational Autoencoders and Denoising Diffusion Models for Data Augmentation in Bioacoustics Classification

Charles Herbst[1]📷, Lorène Jeantet[1,2,3]📷, and Emmanuel Dufourq[1,2,3](✉)📷

[1] Stellenbosch University, Stellenbosch, South Africa
[2] African Institute for Mathematical Sciences, Muizenberg, South Africa
{lorene,dufourq}@aims.ac.za
[3] African Institute for Mathematical Sciences - Research and Innovation Centre, Kigali, Rwanda

Abstract. One major challenge in supervised deep learning is the need for large training datasets to achieve satisfactory generalisation performance. Acquiring audio recordings of endangered animals compounds this issue due to high costs, logistical constraints, and the rarity of the species in question. Typically, bioacoustic datasets have imbalanced class distributions, further complicating model training with limited examples for some rare species. To overcome this, our study proposes the evaluation of generative models for audio augmentation. Generative models, such as Variational Autoencoders (VAEs) and Denoising Diffusion Probabilistic Models (DDPMs), offer the ability to create synthetic data after training on existing datasets. We assess the effectiveness of VAEs and DDPMs in augmenting a bioacoustics dataset, which includes vocalisations of the world's rarest primate, the Hainan gibbon. We assess the generated synthetic data through visual inspection and by computing the Kernel Inception Distance, to compare the distribution of the generated dataset to the training set. Furthermore, we investigate the efficacy of using the generated dataset to train a deep learning classifier to identify the Hainan gibbon calls. We vary the size of the training datasets and compare the classification performance across four scenarios: no augmentation, augmentation with VAEs, augmentation with DDPMs, and standard bioacoustics augmentation methods. Our study is the first to show that standard audio augmentation methods are as effective as newer generative approaches commonly used in computer vision. Considering the high computational costs of VAEs and DDPMs, this emphasises the suitability of simpler techniques for building deep learning classifiers on bioacoustic datasets.

Keywords: Bioacoustics · Variational Autoencoders · Diffusion Probabilistic Models

© The Author(s), under exclusive license to Springer Nature Switzerland AG 2024
A. Gerber (Ed.): SAICSIT 2024, CCIS 2159, pp. 45–61, 2024.
https://doi.org/10.1007/978-3-031-64881-6_3

1   Introduction

In recent years, there has been a growing recognition of the significance of environmental preservation. Global environmental challenges, such as climate change [11,13,15] and deforestation [19,32], have emerged as major contributors to the alarming loss of biodiversity and the degradation of ecosystems. Presently, up to 120000 species are listed as endangered on the International Union for Conservation of Nature (IUCN) Red List, with thousands more on the brink of extinction [1,31]. The importance of our natural systems is undoubted; therefore, conservation efforts are increasingly necessary to address the strained relationship between humanity and the environment. To effectively protect and monitor species diversity and habitats, it is crucial to implement robust conservation strategies capable of safeguarding and restoring the natural environment.

Amidst the escalating biodiversity crisis, conservation efforts have increasingly embraced a data-driven approach, facilitated by the deployment of automatic sound recording devices and camera traps. Among these technologies, audio recordings offer a versatile and comprehensive record of natural events [22], providing valuable insights into various biological phenomena. Passive acoustic monitoring (PAM) stands at the forefront of this practice by utilising audio recordings to survey and monitor wildlife and environments [24,27]. PAM enables the estimation of population density [30], the occupancy of species [3], and spatial and temporal trends in animal behaviour [23], among other applications. Notably, PAM achieves these objectives through targeted searches for specific events, such as animal vocalisations.

Traditionally, identifying events of interest within audio recordings required manual review by researchers, who would listen to the recordings and note occurrences. However, advances in machine learning, more specifically deep neural networks, have significantly reduced the need for such manual efforts. Convolutional neural networks (CNNs) have proven to be effective in identifying animal vocalisations from audio datasets [27]. Deep learning has successfully been applied to the detection of vocalisations for various animals, such as bats [35], birds [28,34], primates [6,21], and whales [26], among others. The approach to developing these detection networks often parallels that of computer vision tasks by converting audio from the time domain to 2-dimensional spectrogram images using the short-time Fourier transform. This transformation results in an input format that is similar to a digital image, allowing many of the deep learning techniques and innovations originally developed for computer vision to be used.

A significant hurdle in deep learning PAM applications is the substantial quantity of data required to effectively train neural networks. An inadequate amount of data can lead to models that generalise poorly. This problem becomes particularly acute in the context of audio datasets for endangered species, exacerbated by factors such as limited population sizes, habitats that are difficult to access, and concerns related to conservation. To mitigate these issues, researchers have turned to techniques such as transfer learning [5], and the creation of new audio data by modifying existing data to expand dataset sizes [17]. The latter, also known as audio data augmentation, often includes techniques such as time shifting, masking in both time and frequency domains, introducing additive Gaussian noise, and mixing signals. These have been used in various studies [27]. The objective of these methods is to generate variations of the training data that simulate potential distortions, thereby enhancing the CNN's robustness to variations encountered during testing. Although these approaches produce samples that are unlikely to change the semantic meaning of the audio, they can oversimplify the complexity and may not fully capture the diverse range of real-world natural variations.

Generative modelling is a field that aims to enable machines with the ability to synthesise new data. Within this field, various techniques and models are developed to create new samples from a given distribution. These generative models have been widely applied in the field of computer vision, in which there has been significant progress on image synthesis. Generative models, a class of deep learning models, learn to generate synthetic data after being trained. In this study, we propose a novel learning-driven approach for data augmentation in CNN-based bioacoustic classification. Specifically, by means of a Variational Autoencoder (VAE) [14] and Denoising Diffusion Probabilistic Model (DDPM) [10]. VAEs are conceptually simple models that scale well to complex distributions and large datasets and are relatively easy to train [25] (compared to Generative Adversarial Networks [7]). On the other hand, DDPMs are recently introduced generative models that offer much of the same benefits as VAEs but have emerged as the state-of-the-art generative model.

Our work is motivated by the view that generative models provide another useful tool for data augmentation that can be used to introduce more natural variability and produce synthetic data without limit. In this study, we investigate the efficacy of generative models in augmenting bioacoustic training datasets, in comparison to standard bioacoustic augmentation techniques used to date. We evaluate our methodology using a dataset collected in the Bawangling National Nature Reserve (BNNR), China, for the automated detection of one of the rarest mammals, the Hainan gibbon. To our knowledge, there is currently no existing literature on the use of VAEs and DDPMs for audio data augmentation within the field of biocoustics [27]. This study represents the first attempt to apply generative models for the creation of synthetic animal vocalisations, marking a novel contribution to bioacoustics with potential conservation applications.

2   Methods

2.1   Dataset Description and Preprocessing

The Hainan gibbon dataset was obtained by recording field audio in the BNNR, where audio recorders were placed in close proximity to the known region of the Hainan gibbon population [6]. The raw data comprised a manually annotated subset of 68 .WAV audio files from the original subset, with the duration of each audio file varying from a minimum of 30 min to a maximum of 3.2 h for a total of 61 h. The audio files were manually labelled using two classes by recording the start and stop times of acoustic events, a presence class representing gibbon vocalisations and a negative class representing non-gibbon sounds. The audio files have a sampling rate of 9600 Hz. The dataset was randomly partitioned into independent training and testing subsets, with 28 audio files allocated for training, representing 30% of the total duration, and 40 independent files for testing, constituting 70% of the total duration. The decision to have a larger test set was made to obtain a good estimate of the model's capability on unseen data.

Within PAM research, it is common practice to convert audio into spectrograms and to train CNNs on spectrogram input as opposed to digital audio signals [27]. To preprocess the raw audio data, we extracted 4-s long audio segments based on the annotations. The extraction was carried out by shifting a 4-s window in time, with a 1-s interval. Figure 1 shows a spectrogram with three annotations. The first two are gibbon presence events, and the last is a gibbon absence event. From these annotations, overlapping 4-s window segments can be extracted. Subsequently, each segment underwent Butterworth lowpass filtering, which attenuates frequencies above a selected cutoff frequency of 2000 Hz. Filtering was applied to avoid aliasing issues that might occur from the downsampling step, which is described next. Following this, the segments were downsampled to a new sampling rate of 4800 Hz. This was done since the Hainan gibbon vocalises between 1000 and 2000 Hz and thus higher frequencies are not needed. The value of 4800 Hz was selected based on the Nyquist theorem, which states that the sampling rate must be greater than twice the highest frequency component in the signal to correctly reconstruct it. Next, we applied the short-time Fourier transform (STFT) to each segment, transforming them into 2-dimensional spectrograms. Spectrograms are visual representations which allow us to visualise the change in audio frequencies over time. Additionally, the spectrograms were converted to Mel spectrograms, which are spectrograms whose frequencies have been transformed to the Mel-scale. The Mel-scale more closely resembles the way that humans perceive frequencies, i.e., humans do not perceive frequencies on a linear scale thus the Mel spectrograms take this into account. This representation is commonly used in bioacoustics research [5,6,12,27]. For the STFT transformation, we used a Hanning window, with a window length of 2024 samples, a hop length of 151 samples, and setting the number of Mel frequency bins to 128. These spectrogram parameters were based on previous findings and preliminary experimentation [5,6]. Lastly, the spectrograms were normalised using min-max scaling, resulting in 2-dimensional images of 128 × 128 pixels.

The final preprocessing step involved balancing the number of examples in both classes to prevent potential bias in the model due to the naturally inherent class imbalance within the data. This imbalance was characterised by a considerably larger number of absence class spectrograms compared to the presence class. To achieve this, the majority class was randomly undersampled to obtain an equal class distribution, resulting in a total of 5332 spectrograms, with both classes comprising 2666 spectrograms.

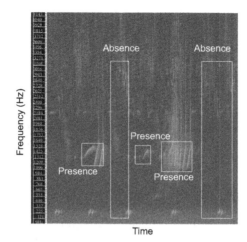

Fig. 1. Examples of manually annotated segments of gibbon vocalisations (presence class) and non-gibbon acoustic events (absence class). Annotations from the absence class were manually selected to include a diverse range of ambient noise such as other animal vocalisations and environmental sounds, typical of the Hainan gibbon biome. It is common that other animals vocalise within the same frequency range as the gibbons.

2.2 Variational Autoencoders

Autoencoders (AEs) are a type of neural network that consists of an encoder and a decoder [33]. The encoder compresses the inputs into a smaller and more compact representation using successive layers, while the decoder reconstructs the input from this representation using an expanding path. The decoder effectively serves as the inverse of the encoder. The ability of the decoder to reconstruct the input depends on the informativeness of the compact representation. Therefore, the encoder and decoder work together and learn the most meaningful and semantic features of the input. The space to which the input is encoded is referred to as the latent space. The latent space of an AE is typically highly irregular and sparse, since the encoded inputs will be structured in a manner that will best allow the AE to perform the reconstruction task.

A VAE is a type of generative model that follows the same structure as an AE, but instead generates a smooth and continuous latent space that is assumed to follow a standard normal distribution, $p(z)$. This is achieved through a probabilistic encoder $q_\phi(z|x)$ that yields two outputs, a vector of means, μ, and a vector of standard deviations, σ, that together define the distribution of $p(z)$. To decode samples, a probabilistic decoder $p_\theta(x|z)$ is used that decodes the distribution defined by μ and σ, and effectively learns new variations associated with a given input. Another consideration when training a VAE is that the distribution produced by the encoder needs to be constrained to be close to a standard normal distribution. Otherwise, the latent space may become sparse, and regions may not correspond to meaningful variations within the data, effectively resulting in an ordinary AE. The loss function for a VAE is given as

$$L(\theta, \phi; x) = -\mathbb{E}_{z \sim q_\phi(z|x)} [\log p_\theta(x|z)] + KL(q_\phi(z|x)||p(z)), \tag{1}$$

where ϕ and θ are the parameters of the encoder and decoder, respectively. The first term on the right-hand side is referred to as the reconstruction error, and KL represents the Kullback-Leibler divergence between the distribution of the encoder and a standard normal distribution. Once the VAE is trained, generating samples from the learned distribution should produce samples that conform to the distribution of the inputs.

2.3   Denoising Diffusion Probabilistic Models

Denoising Diffusion Probabilistic Models (DDPMs) represent a new class of generative models inspired by the physical phenomenon of diffusion, the natural process by which gas molecules move from a high density to a low density. Diffusion models consist of two key aspects; the forward diffusion process and the reverse diffusion process. In the forward diffusion process, an original sample image undergoes gradual degradation through the continuous addition of noise until it becomes pure noise. The mathematical description of the forward diffusion process is given by

$$\mathbf{x}_t = \sqrt{\bar{\alpha}_t} \mathbf{x}_0 + \sqrt{1 - \bar{\alpha}_t} \epsilon, \tag{2}$$

where $\mathbf{x}_t$ represents the noised image after t steps of the forward diffusion process, $\mathbf{x}_0$ denotes the original sample image, ϵ is noise sampled from a multivariate Gaussian distribution, and $\bar{\alpha}_t$ is a hyperparameter obtained by defining $\alpha_t = 1 - \beta_t$ and $\bar{\alpha}_t = \prod_{s=1}^{t} \alpha_s$, and β_t is the variance of the noise added at time step t. In the reverse diffusion process, the model continuously denoises the image by predicting and inferring the noise added during the forward diffusion process. The mathematical description of the reverse diffusion process is given by

$$\mathbf{x}_{t-1} = \frac{1}{\sqrt{\alpha_t}} \left(\mathbf{x}_t - \frac{1 - \alpha_t}{\sqrt{1 - \bar{\alpha}_t}} \epsilon_\theta(\mathbf{x}_t, t) \right) + \sigma_t \mathbf{z}, \tag{3}$$

where $\mathbf{x}_t$ represents the image obtained at time step t, $\epsilon_\theta(\mathbf{x}_t, t)$ is the noise predicted by the model, $\mathbf{z}$ is Gaussian distributed noise, and σ_t denotes the variance at time step t, calculated as follows

$$\sigma_t^2 = \tilde{\beta}_t = \frac{1 - \bar{\alpha}_{t-1}}{1 - \bar{\alpha}_t} \beta_t. \tag{4}$$

To predict the noise added during the forward diffusion process, the model requires training. For this, diffusion models leverage a U-Net-style architecture which are architectures that excel at image denoising tasks [8]. U-Net architecture consists of an encoder, a middle layer, and a decoder. The encoder contracts input data while the decoder expands it. Additionally, U-Net utilises skip connections between the corresponding layers of the encoder and the decoder. The loss function of the network is defined as

$$L = ||\epsilon - \epsilon_\theta(\mathbf{x}_t, t)||^2, \tag{5}$$

where ϵ is the noise that needs to be predicted and $\epsilon_\theta(\mathbf{x}_t, t)$ is the noise predicted by the U-Net model at time step t. The loss function reveals that the model aims to minimize the difference between the noise that was added during the forward diffusion process and the predicted noise. By accurately predicting the noise that was added in the forward diffusion process, the trained U-Net can transform and denoise a sample consisting of pure noise into one that conforms to the original training distribution.

2.4 Standard Data Augmentation

To assess the effectiveness of the generative models, we compared them to standard data augmentation techniques. Our standard data augmentation approach comprised an ensemble of commonly implemented approaches in bioacoustics [27]. We applied these approaches on the spectrograms, and they are detailed as follows:

1. **Time and frequency masking:** the number of masks in both the time and frequency domain is randomly determined, varying from 2 to 4. In frequency masking, masks are applied to the frequency frames $[f_0, f_0 + f)$, where f is the mask width, randomly chosen between 0 and 4, and f_0 represents the starting position of the mask on the frequency axis, randomly selected from $(0, F - f)$, with F being the total number of frequency frames. Similarly, in time masking, masks are applied to the frames $[t_0, t_0 + t)$, where t is the mask width, randomly chosen between 0 and 4, and t_0 represents the starting position of the mask on the time axis, randomly selected from $(0, T - t)$, where T is the total number of time frames.
2. **Additive Gaussian noise:** this is applied by sampling noise from a Gaussian distribution, where the mean is zero and the standard deviation is randomly sampled from the uniform distribution $[0.2, 0.4]$. The resulting noise is then added to the spectrogram image.
3. **Signal mixing:** signal mixing is performed through linear interpolation between two spectrogram images, I_1 and I_2 using the formula, $M = I_1 \times \alpha + I_2 \times (1 - \alpha)$, where M is the mixed image, and the mixing extent α is constrained within the range $[0.25, 0.75]$.
4. **Time shifting:** time shifting is applied on the spectrogram by rolling the pixel values along the time axis by a random amount from the range $[20, 90]$.

The augmentation parameters were chosen to ensure that the resulting distortions were not overly aggressive or ineffective. We randomly sampled images from the training set and distributed them equally among all augmentation techniques. For instance, to create 1000 new images, each technique received 250 images, and each image underwent augmentation once using its respective method.

2.5   Kernel Inception Distance

An effective generative model for data augmentation should be capable of producing a data-generating distribution that closely resembles the actual distribution of the training data. Hence, to assess the similarity between the distribution of the training data and the generated data, we used the Kernel Inception Distance (KID) [2]. The KID is a type of statistical distance measure that uses kernels to measure the discrepancy between two given distributions. The lower the KID, the more similar the two distributions. An InceptionNet model [29], pre-trained on ImageNet, was employed to generate embeddings for each input distribution, from which the KID was calculated as the square of the maximum mean discrepancy (MMD) between the two separate embeddings. Mathematically, it is expressed as

$$
\mathrm{L_{MMD^2}} = \frac{1}{n(n-1)} \sum_{i=1}^{n} \sum_{j=1}^{n} k(x_i, x_j) - \frac{2}{nm} \sum_{i=1}^{n} \sum_{j=1}^{m} k(x_i, y_j)
$$
$$
+ \frac{1}{m(m-1)} \sum_{i=1}^{m} \sum_{j=1}^{m} k(y_i, y_j),
$$

(6)

where $k(x_i, x_j)$ represents the kernel function, m and n represents the number of real and synthetic samples, respectively, and x and y are the two input distributions. Staying consistent with the formulation in [2], the specific kernel function used in this study is a polynomial kernel expressed as $(\frac{a^T b}{d} + 1)^3$, where d is the dimension of the two input distributions a and b.

3   Experiments

To evaluate the generative models, we randomly generated S synthetic spectrograms from the VAE or the DDPM after training them separately for each class. The synthetic spectrograms were then added to the original training set O, comprising the initial 5332 samples, resulting in a larger augmented training set L, where $L = O + S$. To investigate the efficacy of our approach, we trained a binary classifier CNN to detect the Hainan gibbon call on L, and we performed a series of experiments in which we varied the total amount of synthetic data S. Specifically, we considered $S \in \{1000, 2000, 4000\}$, to be added to the training set. For instance, when $S = 1000$, 500 new spectrograms of the presence class and 500 new spectrograms of the absence class were added to O. Additionally, we compared our experiments to a baseline scenario where no augmentation was applied to the initial training set. The implementation of our method is available online at https://github.com/charlesD5herbst/GDBC.

3.1   Model Architectures and Training

VAE. In this study, the encoder consisted of four convolutional layers, with 32, 64, 128, and 256 filters, respectively. Filter size and stride were set to 3×3

and 2×2 for all layers in the encoder, respectively. This was followed by a dense layer that was split in two to form the mean and standard deviation parameters. The final decoder architecture consisted of an initial dense layer with 16384 units and five transposed convolutional layers, with 256, 128, 64, 32, and 1 filter, respectively. Filter size and stride were set to 3×3 and 2×2 for the first four layers in the decoder, respectively, while in the last layer, filter size and stride were set to 1×1 and 2×2. The activation function assigned to all layers was the ReLU activation function, except for the two dense layers comprising the mean and standard deviation. For the training of the VAE, we used the Adam optimisation algorithm with a learning rate initialised to 0.0005. The VAE aimed to minimise the combined sigmoid cross entropy loss function and the KL-divergence. The network was trained on 30 epochs with a batch size of 32.

DDPM. The architecture for the DDPM model used in this study is shown in Fig. 2. Each convolutional block is a residual block comprising two repeating sets of group normalisation, swish activation layer, and convolutional layer. Furthermore, each residual block begins with an initial convolutional layer. The filter size was set to 1×1 for the initial convolutional layer and to 3×3 for all subsequent layers. The number of groups in the group normalisation layers were set to 8. Instead of using time embeddings as in [10], we used sinusoidal embeddings of the noise variance of the forward diffusion process. The embeddings are added to the output of the first set in the residual block. To train the DDPM, the Adam optimisation algorithm was used with an initial learning rate of 0.003. We used the mean square error loss function with weight decay to mitigate overfitting concerns. The network was trained for 50 epochs with a batch size of 32.

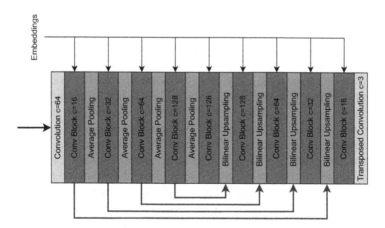

Fig. 2. The architecture of the DDPM, where c represents the number of filters used in a layer.

CNN. For classification, we used ResNet101V2 [9], pre-trained on ImageNet, as the feature extractor for our CNN detection model. Resnet101V2 is a CNN known for its remarkable performance on images [20] and its ability to detect calls in bioacoustic datasets [5]. We adopted our previous research [5], and implemented a transfer learning approach by freezing the network with pre-trained ImageNet weights and fine tuning our own custom classification layers. The classification layers consisted of two fully connected layers. The first layer had 24 units with ReLU activations, while the last output layer consisted of two units with Softmax activations. We used the Adam optimisation algorithm with an initial learning rate of 0.003 to train the CNN. We used the categorical cross-entropy loss function. To mitigate the risk of overfitting, an early stopping condition was implemented, terminating training if the loss did not decrease for three consecutive epochs. The network was trained for 15 epochs with a batch size of 8.

The selection of hyperparameters for the generative models was based on empirical evaluation, specifically by assessing the perceptual quality of the generated synthetic spectrograms. Thus, a targeted exploration of model parameters was prioritised, rather than an exhaustive hyperparameter search. On the other hand, the architecture of the CNN was obtained by performing a random search over the number of layers and filters. Furthermore, separate generative models were trained for each class on the 2666 images to ensure that we could reliably label the images for classification. The models were developed and implemented with TensorFlow 2.0, and the general software pipeline and audio processing was written in Python 3. Spectrograms were created using the Librosa software library [16]. Model evaluations and executions were conducted on the Centre for High-Performance Computing (CHPC), Lengau cluster, using an Nvidia V100 16 GB GPU.

3.2   Inference and Evaluation

During inference, we provided our trained CNN model with a set of test audio files. These files were completely independent from the training audio files and were recorded on separate days. A sliding window approach was used to extract 4-s segments from each test audio file. The windows shift by 1-s in time, until the entire audio file has been traversed. Each extracted segment was processed using the same preprocessing steps applied to the training data, and transformed into Mel spectrograms in the same way as the training spectrograms were created. For each spectrogram, the CNN outputs a pair of softmax probabilities representing the likelihood of a gibbon vocalisation being present (presence class) or absent (absence class). The detection probabilities of the presence class were evaluated against a confidence threshold of 0.5 for classification as a positive detection.

Each test audio file is accompanied with a corresponding manually verified annotation file containing the ground truth start and end times of all the gibbon vocalisations and non-gibbon events, as depicted by the solid black boxes in Fig. 3. Consecutive gibbon presence predictions were merged to represent a single distinct call, as depicted by the solid red boxes in Fig. 3. These predicted gibbon calls, varying in length, were then compared to the ground truth. Specifically, we assessed whether the time interval of the predicted call overlapped with a manually verified presence class (true positive) or absence class (false positive). Overlap is acknowledged only when more than 50% of the predicted call aligns with the manually verified class. Absence intervals with no overlapping prediction were considered as true negatives, and presence intervals with no overlapping prediction were considered as false negatives (Fig. 3). The CNN's final performance was evaluated based on the total number of true positives, false positives, true negatives, and false negatives, using the F_1-score. We averaged the results of 10 independent experimental runs, during which synthetic data was randomly generated, and the weights in the final classification layers of the CNN were re-initialised for each execution.

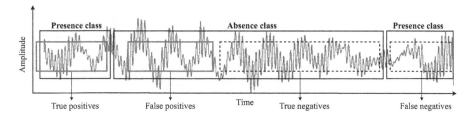

Fig. 3. An illustration of true positives, false positives, true negatives, and false negatives. Each box represents a time interval, where solid black denotes the ground truth, red indicates consecutive segments of positive predictions, and striped lines mark intervals where no predictions were made. (Color figure online)

4   Results

We analysed both the generative capability of the VAE and DDPM, and the classification performance of the proposed methodology. Figure 4 shows some synthetic spectrogram images generated by the VAE and the DDPM. The VAE produced images with noticeable blurriness, lacking in sharpness, and regularly exhibiting an oversmoothed appearance, which resulted in the loss of fine detail. On the other hand, the DDPM produced visually realistic spectrograms, with a more granular appearance in which smaller details were preserved, thus making them perceptually indistinguishable from the real images.

The VAE and DDPM can generate diverse images, encompassing various gibbon vocalisations. These include the one-, two- and three-pulse calls, and notably, the duet call (an example is shown in Fig. 4, real block, row one, column one). The distinction between these calls is determined by the frequency of occurrence of the underlying spectral line in the spectrogram image (see [6] for a detailed description of call types). It was interesting to observe that the DDPM was able to generate the duet call (DDPM block, first row, second column) – which corresponds to overlapping calls from a male and female gibbon – since the duet call can easily be interpreted as a noisy segment. Synthetically generating this call type is important for ensuring robustness, since a classifier may mistakenly classify it as the absence class, leading to an increase in the number of false negatives.

The KID score between the images generated by the VAE and the DDPM are presented in Table 1, and were calculated for a different number of generated spectrograms for each class, to assess the consistency and robustness of generated outputs. For each sample size tested (500, 1000, 1500, 2000, 2500), an equal number of training examples were randomly sampled to compare with the generated spectrograms from the VAE and DDPM and to calculate the KID score. This was repeated five times to obtain an average KID score. Table 1 shows that images generated by the DDPM consistently achieved lower KID scores. This indicates that samples generated by the DDPM are closer to the distribution of the training data than those generated by the VAE. These findings are consistent with the visual samples shown in Fig. 4.

The mean F_1-scores obtained from the 10 independent experimental runs are shown in Table 2. To draw more robust conclusions from the results, a statistical significance test was performed between the different data augmentation methods and their sample sizes. Specifically, we used the Friedman test, which is a non-parametric test to determine if there are differences between groups [4]. By performing this test, we tested the null hypothesis H_o 'there was no significant differences observed in the F_1-scores with the augmented training sets', and the alternative hypothesis H_1 'a significant difference was observed in the F_1-scores with the augmented training sets'. The chosen level of significance for the test was set to $p < 0.05$. We obtained a Friedman test statistic of 6.85, revealing that the null hypothesis was not rejected, and that no statistically significant result was observed.

Table 1. Per-class KID scores for data generated by the VAE and the DDPM indicate that images generated by the DDPM achieved smaller scores, suggesting that they have a higher fidelity to the training data.

Number of images	VAE		DDPM	
	KID_{pres}	KID_{abs}	KID_{pres}	KID_{abs}
500	3.65 ± 0.09	3.17 ± 0.08	1.11 ± 0.04	2.02 ± 0.05
1000	3.57 ± 0.11	3.18 ± 0.10	1.15 ± 0.02	2.01 ± 0.05
1500	3.57 ± 0.08	3.16 ± 0.07	1.14 ± 0.03	2.01 ± 0.03
2000	3.50 ± 0.04	3.15 ± 0.04	1.14 ± 0.02	2.02 ± 0.03
2500	3.52 ± 0.08	3.18 ± 0.06	1.14 ± 0.01	1.99 ± 0.02

Real

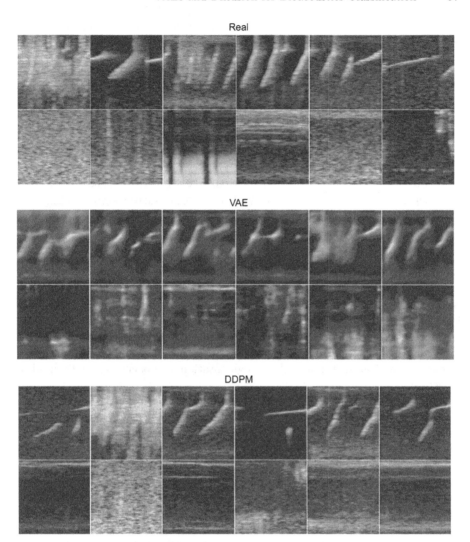

VAE

DDPM

Fig. 4. Examples of synthetic spectrograms generated by the VAE in the middle block, and the DDPM at the bottom block. For reference, we provide some examples of real spectrograms from the training data at the top. The top row of each block includes examples from the presence class, while the bottom row are examples from the absence class.

Table 2. Mean F_1-score obtained over 10 independent classification experiments. In this Table, three distinct data augmentation methods are compared: VAE, DDPM, and standard data augmentation (SAUG), each evaluated against a baseline classification model (ResNet101V2) with no augmentation. Additionally, the amount of data generated by each method is varied three times, progressively increasing.

Number of samples	Augmentation Method			
	BASELINE	SAUG	VAE	DDPM
+0	0.799 ± 0.018	–	–	–
+1000	–	0.821 ± 0.028	0.810 ± 0.026	0.808 ± 0.033
+2000	–	0.812 ± 0.022	0.804 ± 0.029	0.795 ± 0.043
+4000	–	0.798 ± 0.034	0.819 ± 0.035	0.811 ± 0.031

5   Discussion and Conclusion

In this study, we proposed a novel comparison of data augmentation techniques for bioacoustic classification. Inspired from the success of generative models in computer vision, we hypothesised that VAEs and DDPMs could serve as effective tools for this purpose. Thus, our study was driven by the aim to contrast these generative models to standard data augmentation approaches typically used in bioacoustics.

Our experiments show that generative models, such as VAEs and DDPMs, can generate synthetic spectrograms that closely resemble the real training data. Notably, the DDPM demonstrates a superior capability in generating synthetic spectrograms of a higher fidelity than those generated by the VAE. Furthermore, experiments show that the use of generative-based data augmentation is as effective as using standard data augmentation techniques. Moreover, despite the higher quality of the DDPM samples, the VAE augmentation produced the single overall highest F_1-score. We observed that as the contribution of augmentation from standard data augmentation increases, there is a noticeable deterioration in the overall F_1-score, suggesting a practical limit to the extent to which augmentation can be applied. The decline is less noticeable for the VAE or the DDPM, as adding 4000 samples ultimately yields a higher overall F_1-score compared to adding 1000 samples. We hypothesise that this deterioration with SAUG could result from a reduction in the variability of the training data. In this study, SAUG relies on four different methods to incorporate changes of varying degrees into the existing data (see Sect. 2.4), which, beyond a certain threshold of augmented data, here >2000, may result in the creation of relatively similar spectrograms. This decreased variability can lead to models having a reduced ability to generalise to new data, hence the decrease in the F_1-score on the testing dataset. While it is challenging to identify trends with a small amount of data points, further studies are necessary to validate this hypothesis and determine the underlying cause of this decline.

Considering the significant computational burden and specialised expertise associated with training a generative model, their use as an augmentation method may not be needed, particularly when compared to standard data augmentation techniques. For instance, our DDPM model necessitated an average of 383 ± 2.8 seconds per epoch for training, resulting in approximately 5 h of training time per class. It is noteworthy that the scalability of the DDPM may pose significant challenges with an increase in the number of classes or the volume of training data. Conversely, the computational costs associated with the VAE training was considerably lower, with an average of 1.56 ± 0.9 seconds per epoch, requiring a training time of less than a minute per class. Moreover, the standard data augmentation does not require training and samples can be readily produced. On average, performing inference on all test audio files required 22.25 min. In addition, our evaluation indicates that VAEs and DDPMs do not consistently outperform standard data augmentation techniques in terms of efficacy. Therefore, we note that practitioners in bioacoustics may find it more beneficial to resort to well-established standard data augmentation techniques.

While generative models like DDPMs show promise in computer vision applications, they are typically trained on vast datasets comprising hundreds of thousands of examples [18]. In contrast, in bioacoustic applications, particularly those focused on critically endangered species, the amount of data typically has significantly fewer examples available in comparison. The effectiveness of generative models within the context of data augmentation may be closely linked to the quantity of data and the variation within the data that they are trained on. Given the limitations in data availability in bioacoustics, it becomes essential to consider simpler generative methods. Exploring such methods may offer more practical solutions to address data scarcity and improve performance in bioacoustic applications.

This study serves as a stepping stone towards integrating generative models into bioacoustics, highlighting the need for more extensive testing to fully understand their potential and draw more conclusive insights. As future work, it would be interesting to see if a more controlled sampling procedure such as manual inspection or automated validation based on acceptable KID scores, could reduce the variance in the F_1-score and produce more consistent outputs with the VAE and DDPM. Moreover, a further experiment where the classifier is only trained on synthetic data may provide an indication of the relative contribution of the synthetic data. Additionally, it would be valuable to investigate how varying the ratio of real to synthetic training data affects the results, particularly as the proportion of training data decreases. Such an analysis may reveal an increasing utility of synthetic data as the real data becomes more limited. Another interesting exploration would be to compare the different approaches on more challenging bioacoustic datasets that are characterised by a greater complexity and higher variability in the animal's vocalisation.

Acknowledgement. This publication was made possible by a grant from Carnegie Corporation of New York (provided through the AIMS Research and Innovation Centre). The statements made and views expressed are solely the responsibility of the author(s). The authors acknowledge the Centre for High Performance Computing (CHPC), South Africa, for providing computational resources to this research project.

Disclosure of Interests. The authors have no competing interests to declare that are relevant to the content of this article.

References

1. Almond, R.E., Grooten, M., Peterson, T.: Living planet report 2020-bending the curve of biodiversity loss. World Wildlife Fund (2020)
2. Bińkowski, M., Sutherland, D.J., Arbel, M., Gretton, A.: Demystifying MMD GANs. In: International Conference on Learning Representations (2018)
3. Campos-Cerqueira, M., Aide, T.M.: Improving distribution data of threatened species by combining acoustic monitoring and occupancy modelling. Methods Ecol. Evol. **7**(11), 1340–1348 (2016)
4. Demšar, J.: Statistical comparisons of classifiers over multiple data sets. J. Mach. Learn. Res. **7**, 1–30 (2006)
5. Dufourq, E., Batist, C., Foquet, R., Durbach, I.: Passive acoustic monitoring of animal populations with transfer learning. Eco. Inform. **70**, 101688 (2022)
6. Dufourq, E., et al.: Automated detection of Hainan gibbon calls for passive acoustic monitoring. Remote Sens. Ecol. Conserv. **7**(3), 475–487 (2021)
7. Goodfellow, I., et al.: Generative adversarial nets. In: Advances in Neural Information Processing Systems, vol. 27 (2014)
8. Gurrola-Ramos, J., Dalmau, O., Alarcón, T.E.: A residual dense u-net neural network for image denoising. IEEE Access **9**, 31742–31754 (2021)
9. He, K., Zhang, X., Ren, S., Sun, J.: Identity mappings in deep residual networks. In: Leibe, B., Matas, J., Sebe, N., Welling, M. (eds.) ECCV 2016, Part IV. LNCS, vol. 9908, pp. 630–645. Springer, Cham (2016). https://doi.org/10.1007/978-3-319-46493-0_38
10. Ho, J., Jain, A., Abbeel, P.: Denoising diffusion probabilistic models. In: Advances in Neural Information Processing Systems, vol. 33, pp. 6840–6851 (2020)
11. Houghton, J.T., et al.: Climate Change 2001: The Scientific Basis, vol. 881. Cambridge University Press, Cambridge (2001)
12. Jeantet, L., Dufourq, E.: Improving deep learning acoustic classifiers with contextual information for wildlife monitoring. Eco. Inform. **77**, 102256 (2023)
13. Karl, T.R., Trenberth, K.E.: Modern global climate change. Science **302**(5651), 1719–1723 (2003)
14. Kingma, D.P., Welling, M.: Auto-encoding variational bayes. In: 2nd International Conference on Learning Representations (2014)
15. McCarty, J.P.: Ecological consequences of recent climate change. Conserv. Biol. **15**(2), 320–331 (2001)
16. McFee, B., et al.: librosa: audio and music signal analysis in python. In: SciPy, pp. 18–24 (2015)
17. Nanni, L., Maguolo, G., Paci, M.: Data augmentation approaches for improving animal audio classification. Eco. Inform. **57**, 101084 (2020)
18. Nichol, A.Q., Dhariwal, P.: Improved denoising diffusion probabilistic models. In: International Conference on Machine Learning, pp. 8162–8171. PMLR (2021)
19. Paiva, P.F.P.R., et al.: Deforestation in protect areas in the amazon: a threat to biodiversity. Biodivers. Conserv. **29**, 19–38 (2020)

20. Pavithra, K., Kumar, P., Geetha, M., Bhandary, S.V.: Comparative analysis of pre-trained resnet and densenet models for the detection of diabetic macular edema. J. Phys: Conf. Ser. **2571**(1), 012006 (2023)
21. Pellegrini, T.: Deep-learning-based central African primate species classification with MixUp and SpecAugment. In: Interspeech 2021 (2021)
22. Penar, W., Magiera, A., Klocek, C.: Applications of bioacoustics in animal ecology. Ecol. Complex. **43**, 100847 (2020)
23. Putland, R., Constantine, R., Radford, C.: Exploring spatial and temporal trends in the soundscape of an ecologically significant embayment. Sci. Rep. **7**(1), 5713 (2017)
24. Ross, S.R.J., et al.: Passive acoustic monitoring provides a fresh perspective on fundamental ecological questions. Funct. Ecol. **37**(4), 959–975 (2023)
25. Salimans, T., Goodfellow, I., Zaremba, W., Cheung, V., Radford, A., Chen, X.: Improved techniques for training GANs. In: Advances in Neural Information Processing Systems, vol. 29 (2016)
26. Schröter, H., Nöth, E., Maier, A., Cheng, R., Barth, V., Bergler, C.: Segmentation, classification, and visualization of orca calls using deep learning. In: ICASSP 2019-2019 IEEE International Conference on Acoustics, Speech and Signal Processing (ICASSP), pp. 8231–8235. IEEE (2019)
27. Stowell, D.: Computational bioacoustics with deep learning: a review and roadmap. PeerJ **10**, e13152 (2022)
28. Stowell, D., Plumbley, M.D.: Automatic large-scale classification of bird sounds is strongly improved by unsupervised feature learning. PeerJ **2**, e488 (2014)
29. Szegedy, C., Vanhoucke, V., Ioffe, S., Shlens, J., Wojna, Z.: Rethinking the inception architecture for computer vision. In: Proceedings of the IEEE Conference on Computer Vision and Pattern Recognition, pp. 2818–2826 (2016)
30. Thomas, L., Marques, T.A.: Passive acoustic monitoring for estimating animal density. Acoust. Today **8**(3), 35–44 (2012)
31. Tuia, D., et al.: Perspectives in machine learning for wildlife conservation. Nat. Commun. **13**(1), 1–15 (2022)
32. Vijay, V., Pimm, S.L., Jenkins, C.N., Smith, S.J.: The impacts of oil palm on recent deforestation and biodiversity loss. PLoS ONE **11**(7), e0159668 (2016)
33. Vincent, P., Larochelle, H., Lajoie, I., Bengio, Y., Manzagol, P.A., Bottou, L.: Stacked denoising autoencoders: learning useful representations in a deep network with a local denoising criterion. J. Mach. Learn. Res. **11**(12) (2010)
34. Xie, J., Hu, K., Zhu, M., Yu, J., Zhu, Q.: Investigation of different CNN-based models for improved bird sound classification. IEEE Access **7**, 175353–175361 (2019)
35. Zualkernan, I., Judas, J., Mahbub, T., Bhagwagar, A., Chand, P.: A tiny CNN architecture for identifying bat species from echolocation calls. In: 2020 IEEE/ITU International Conference on Artificial Intelligence for Good (AI4G), pp. 81–86. IEEE (2020)

Investigating Markov Model Accuracy in Representing Student Programming Behaviours

Herman Kandjimi[1,2] and Hussein Suleman[1]([✉])

[1] Department of Computer Science, University of Cape Town, School of IT,
Woolsack Drive, Rondebosch, Cape Town 7701, South Africa
kndher001@myuct.ac.za, hussein@cs.uct.ac.za
[2] Faculty of Computing and Informatics, Namibia University of Science
and Technology, 13 Jackson Kaujeua Street, Windhoek, Namibia
https://fci.nust.na/, https://sit.uct.ac.za/

Abstract. Problem-solving skills are an integral component within the computer science field. Due to the diversity brought about by students following different learning and programming behaviours, it is challenging to track and identify when students get overwhelmed while writing programs. When students are overwhelmed, they are unable to complete learning objectives on time and follow prescribed pathways, depriving them of the opportunity to learn new concepts. In this paper, we developed and evaluated the quality of Markov models that encode student programming behaviours based on the evolution of source code submissions during formative practical assignments. In doing so, we use Abstract Syntax Trees (ASTs) extracted from the source code, which are used for clustering similar submissions and tracking students' progressive approaches within the Markov models. An approach based on MinHashLSH is presented that works on AST nodes as input to emphasise structural similarity and related programming approaches. As such, the effectiveness of the Modified MinHashLSH approach is based on the clusters that make up the Markov model.

The research result shows that we can successfully create a high-quality model based on previous data. This model result could be used to inform the development of learning interventions that would move students from their stuck states.

Keywords: Problem-solving · Programming · Markov Model · Source-Code Evolution · Clustering · Model evaluation

A. Gerber (Ed.): SAICSIT 2024, CCIS 2159, pp. 62–78, 2024.
https://doi.org/10.1007/978-3-031-64881-6_4

1   Introduction

Computer Science departments have been flooded with an increase in the number of courses being offered and as the demand for skilled professionals picks up, understanding programming approaches among students is crucial to the overall learning process [25]. This is especially true with introductory courses like Programming 1 mostly registering very large numbers of students. The different backgrounds and experiences that the students have in such courses give rise to diverse approaches in programming and behaviours of learning. Xu et al. [25] state that addressing these challenges requires a student-centric approach that caters to individual learning styles and needs. Assessing students' practical work in such large classrooms is done with the aid of automated grading tools, which allow for continuous student submissions and prompt grading, streamlining the grading process for educators. Figure 1 illustrates the way students would carry out their programming assignments with the aid of an automated grading tool, constantly making changes to their program to improve their grades and complete the tasks within the set deadline. However, complexity in this process is presented by the limited personalized guidance available during practical activities, leaving students stuck in prolonged states of uncertainty [22], unsure of how to proceed, and lacking the resources or feedback needed to clarify their understanding while time to deadlines keeps reducing. Examining the patterns in detail could indicate specific behaviours employed in writing programs and

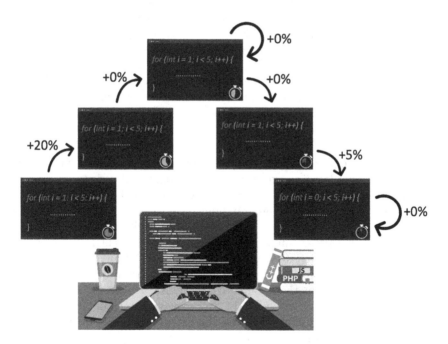

Fig. 1. An overview of student activities during programming assignments.

solving problems by students, offering opportunities and a better understanding of the overall learning process. Classrooms can be enhanced by the richness of perspectives and experiences such diverse student cohorts bring. However, current approaches lack a standard way of evaluating and tracking programming behaviours in student assessment activities, as most studies would only select specific elements in the process and assume relationships to problem-solving behaviours [6,10,23]. Additionally, most teaching and assessment methods often struggle to adapt to the varying paces at which students grasp programming concepts and navigate practical problem-solving tasks [13,20].

The primary focus of this paper is to investigate how we can create and evaluate the quality of Markov models in tracing the programming behaviours of students and expose the underlying patterns discovered within the key states based on the analysis of source code evolutions from programming exercises.

1.1 Motivation

Problem-solving is an essential aspect of programming education, particularly in introductory courses at the university level, ranging from learning outcomes to assessments. The learning outcomes in computing courses are often focused on the development of problem-solving abilities since the skills are imperative to thriving in computing. For example, an outcome may be expressed as, "Students must identify complex problems and create algorithmic solutions, code, test, and debug programs with a focus on correctness and efficiency". Understanding how students approach these kinds of problem-solving tasks in programming is both a complex and crucial component in effective teaching [6,10], which further reflects the importance of problem-solving not just in the classroom but in the general application of computational thinking and handling real-life challenges [24]. By exploring the programming behaviours, this paper aims to shed more light on the complexities of problem-solving and inform teaching pedagogies.

1.2 Research Question

This paper is an important part of a larger project that aims to enhance students' programming learning experiences. Our main objective is to create novel approaches that make use of Markov models by analyzing the evolution of source code collected from formative programming assessments. Through the use of computational methods, our goal is to attempt to address complexities associated with learning programming and promote more efficient learning results. The research question(RQ) that guides this inquiry is: Can we build a high-quality Markov model capable of accurately representing student programming behaviours obtained from their source code evolutions? We highlight the significance of accuracy and reliability in capturing the finer details of student interactions with programming tasks by concentrating on the Markov model's quality using the clustering evaluations.

2 Related Work

Several researchers [11,14,15,17] have studied the problem-solving strategies programmers use to understand their cognitive processes and enhance pedagogical approaches in programming education. While researchers agree that metacognition and scaffolding are important in the problem-solving process, there may be a difference in approach. Margulieux and Catrambone [15] and Loksa and Ko [14] support constructivism, which allows for self-regulated learning, while Hasni [11] emphasizes the importance of a well-structured problem-solving process.

Cabo [4] discovered that students do not use a formal process for developing problem-solving strategies before code writing, and trial-and-error becomes the primary problem-solving strategy. This study underscores the impact of metacognitive awareness and recommends explicit formalization of the development and documentation of problem-solving strategies for computer programming, before code writing. This study complements the categorization of computational practice patterns outlined in [5], encompassing sequential, selective, repetitious, and trial approaches.

Path modelling also referred to as trajectory-based modelling is a way to track the steps taken by students through a specific programming activity, a technique that could serve as a mechanism to help understand the progression of activities of software development that are implemented by the students, as discussed by Fahid [10]. One of the common techniques for path modelling students' approaches in problem-solving is to analyze patterns from source code errors provided by logs on Learning Management Systems (LMSes). Such systems capture students' interaction with programming tasks such as the mistakes they make and how they try to correct them [7]. Another method for discovering problem-solving approaches is through the evolution of source code [18]. This includes how students made iterative changes to their code to overcome any challenges that they faced. Both these methods align with the Knowledge Space Theory(KST), where learning can be considered a multi-dimensional space of knowledge and learner abilities [9].

Markov models have been used in various domains to model problem-solving paths, including in programming. These models enable researchers to capture the dynamic nature of problem-solving processes and analyze the transitions between different states or actions. Mitchell et al. [16] employed a Markov Decision Process (MDP) framework to optimize tutor-student engagement in task-oriented learning environments. Desmarais and Lemieux [8] on the other hand employed hidden Markov models (HMMs) to cluster and visualize problem-solving behaviours based on logs of student interactions with a drill and practice learning environment in college mathematics, revealing distinct patterns in student interactions with learning environments. In particular, the study revealed an unexpected and substantial amount of navigation through exercises and notes without students trying the exercises themselves.

Stefanutti et al. [19] extended Markov modelling by providing a deterministic model for partially ordering individuals, based on their performances in problem-solving tasks and assumed knowledge spaces. The study proposed a Markov model of the solution process of a programming task, that provides a stochastic framework for empirical testing, allowing predictions concerning observable solution processes and underlying knowledge states. This model enables clear connections to be drawn between observable solution processes and the unobservable knowledge state on which these processes are assumed to be based.

3   Methods

3.1   Data Collection

Data for this research was retrieved from a Learning Management System (LMS) of an introductory programming course conducted in Python. Before data collection, students voluntarily consented to the use of their data for research purposes and all their submissions were anonymised before any research analysis was carried out. A total of 73 students' data was retrieved, comprising numerous submissions of source code along with associated scores and comments from the auto-assessment tool integrated into the LMS. Data modelling and analysis were carried out using Google Colab.

The collected submissions were grouped according to the assignments and then later by tasks or problems they addressed, resulting in a total of 501 submissions utilized for the analysis presented in this paper. The raw data extracted is stored in isolated files making it hard to carry out any analysis or usage for modelling. To simplify the process, data from each student's submission is retrieved from the respective files and consolidated into a single comma-separated values(CSV) file for each practical assignment using a Python script.

The consolidated CSV files are then loaded into Google Colab and different Dataframes are created, each storing data for a specific task/problem carried out by the student. A dataframe is a popular data structure in Python that organizes data into a 2-dimensional table of rows and columns, much like a spreadsheet. Within the Dataframes, each submission's source code was then transformed into an Abstract Syntax Tree (AST) - a representation that captures the syntactic structure of the code while abstracting away specific details.

3.2   Similarity Clustering Approach

The consolidated submissions were clustered using a combination of Min-HashLSH and Jaccard similarity algorithm, techniques chosen for their effectiveness in capturing similarities between text documents [12]. In this paper, the text document is a sequence of all the tree nodes from a pre-order walk of the ASTs. Figure 2 illustrates an overview of the MinHashLSH approach adopted from theory on finding similar items in large datasets [12]. MinHashLSH starts with shingling, which is a technique to represent documents as sets using a given set size(k), to identify lexical similarity, and the MinHashing part uses a specific hashing algorithm to transform textual data into vectors for simpler comparisons [12]. Locality-sensitive hashing (LSH) is a method of repeatedly "hashing" data such that more related items will likely end up in the same bucket than different ones.

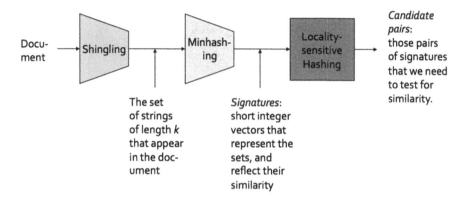

Fig. 2. Overview of MinHash with Local Sensitivity Hashing.

This paper has adjusted the MinHashLSH approach and adapted it to fit the objective of our research while ensuring its effectiveness. Our approach starts with student source codes as input and extends it, by utilising the process output for the clustering of similar source codes based on the structural approach identified from a pre-order walk of the ASTs. Source-code changes are then tracked and represented as transitions within a Markov model, leveraging the relationships between submissions to create a state machine. This model facilitated the visualization of transitions between different problem-solving states. Figure 3 shows the modified MinHashLSH approach with arrows representing key data processes followed by items representing the result of each process. Using the similarity buckets provided by the LSH method, our approach provides an improvement in the clustering time as the comparison is only done on items that are within the identified similarity threshold used by the LSH algorithm.

3.3   Cluster Evaluations

However, the modified approach requires figuring out a few things such as which clustering algorithms to use, what similarity threshold to apply and finally which number of clusters is optimal for the given dataset. Given that our dataset is unlabelled, we decided to carry out a comparative analysis of the clustering scores

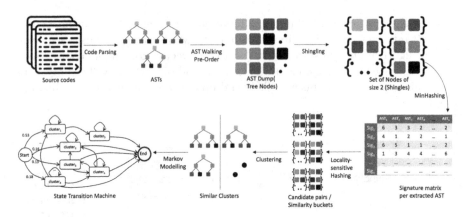

Fig. 3. Modified MinHashLSH for source code modelling.

of three popular clustering algorithms: KMeans, DBSCAN and Agglomerative Clustering [1,21]. Additionally, each of these algorithms was evaluated based on their Silhouette Coefficient, Davies-Bouldin index and Calinski-Harabasz Index [1,2]. These are some of the most common internal methods for evaluating clustering output for unlabelled data based solely on data points within the dataset. To tackle 2 items at once, we varied the threshold values and recorded the clustering scores of each algorithm, allowing us to discover the best algorithm as well as the appropriate threshold to be applied.

The silhouette coefficient measures the cluster's cohesion against separation from other clusters; the value is a measure of how similar a data point is to its cluster compared to the other clusters [1,2,21]. It ranges from -1 to 1, with values closer to 1 indicating well-matched data points within the cluster and a poor relation to neighbouring clusters. A value of 0 means there is no significant distance between the clusters or clusters are indifferent and a negative value means clusters are incorrectly assigned.

The Davies-Bouldin index also measures the separation and compactness of clusters based on the fact that good clusters have low within-cluster variation and high between-cluster separation [1]. It is calculated as the average of the maximum ratio of within-cluster distance and the between-cluster distance for each cluster. The Davies-Bouldin index ranges from 0 to infinity, with a lower value indicating a better clustering solution.

The Calinski-Harabasz Index is also referred to as the Variance Ratio Criterion (VRC); it is another internal evaluation metric that is calculated by the ratio of between-cluster sum squared(Separation) to the within-cluster sum squares(cohesion). Well-defined clusters are hence expected to have a large between-cluster variance and a small within-cluster variance [1,2]. It was combining these 3 evaluation metrics that allowed for a comprehensive look into the clustering algorithms. After a clustering algorithm was picked, we used the elbow method to determine the optimal number of clusters. The Elbow method is one of the most popular ways to find the optimal number of clusters. This method uses the concept of Within Cluster Sum of Squares(WCSS) value, which defines the total variations within a cluster [1]. Therefore, given a range of clusters (e.g. k = 2 to 10) and for each k value centre, we calculate the sum of squared distances from each point to its assigned centre (distortions). The distortions and k values are plotted with a line graph and where the plot bends like an arm the "elbow"(the point of inflection on the curve) indicates the optimal cluster size

4   Results

This section presents the results of a preliminary analysis of student submissions for a practical programming assignment exercise. The unlabelled data from the university's LMS went through basic pre-processing, such as handling missing data and consolidating data formats for uniformity. The first task was to discover the best clustering algorithm to use and with varied similarity thresholds, we were able to get the best algorithm and at which threshold. Figures 4, 5 and 6 illustrate the evaluation results for the Silhouette coefficient, Davies Bouldin index and Calinski-Harabasz Index respectively.

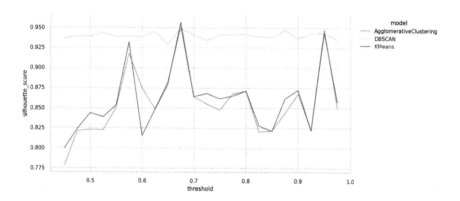

Fig. 4. Silhouette Scores at varied thresholds.

The result in these figures indicated that KMeans was the ideal clustering algorithm and the best threshold was at 0.675. It was further noted that the Agglomerative clustering was quite similar and slightly falling short in some instances; however, the results for DBSCAN are visibly questionable or even low, making it the least favourable choice for our data. In Fig. 5 the inverse value of the Davies Bouldin index is used since lower values in this metric show

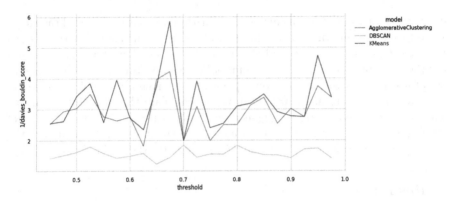

Fig. 5. Inverse of Davies Bouldin Score at varied thresholds.

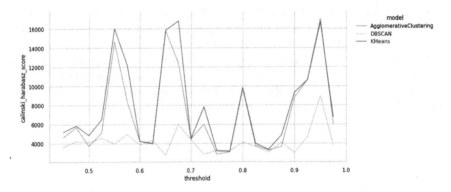

Fig. 6. Calinski-Harabasz score at varied thresholds.

better clustering results, but for consistency in reading the result the inverse was chosen. Knowing that KMeans was the ideal algorithm, made the next job easier and with the elbows method we concluded that 6 clusters were the perfect size. As illustrated in Fig. 7, the line bends right about 6 and the fit time for this cluster size was also low; the fit time represents the time it takes to fit all the points within the given clusters.

Using the discovered cluster size and threshold, our data was then clustered for further analysis and investigation into the students' programming behaviours. A simple look at the clusters in Fig. 8 shows 3 dominant patterns in clusters 1, 3 and 6 respectively, furthermore, the grade distributions within each cluster raise an interesting insight about the student attempts steering toward the idea that each cluster encompasses a comprehensive problem-solving approach.

Figure 8 shows the distributions of student attempts per cluster, covering all grade ranges from 0 to 25% up to 75% to 100%. To explore these data points, a scatter plot was created using Principal Component Analysis(PCA). PCA was

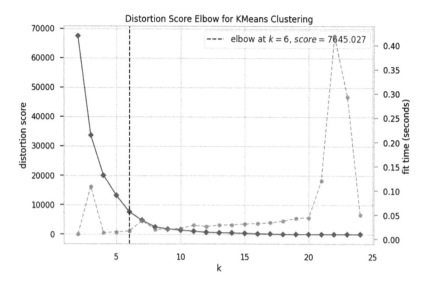

Fig. 7. Optimal Cluster size using Elbow method.

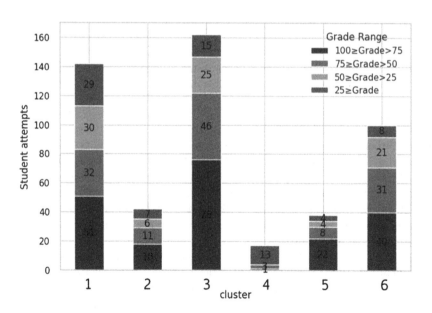

Fig. 8. Grade distribution of student attempts per cluster.

employed as a variable reduction method due to its adaptability in reducing variable data but retaining the essential features; our input variables were based on the similarity matrix of the ASTs and reduced with PCA to retain 95%.

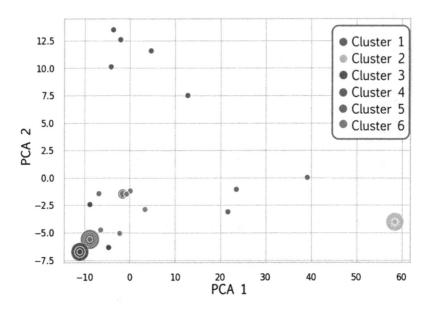

Fig. 9. Scatter plot of student submissions using similarity matrix reduced by 95% using the PCA method and clustered by KMeans algorithm.

The scatter plot shows that some of the clusters are sparsely distributed whereas others are densely distributed around the center points. Clusters such as 2, 3 and 5 can be seen in Fig. 9 with overlapping points hence the enlarged circumference around the points and Cluster 1 seems to be well spread out. The overlapping points within the dense areas could indicate close similarity of student source codes as they evolve within a cluster whereas in other cases, it might mean bigger changes to the source codes but remaining within the cluster or retaining a similar approach.

The above analysis of the cluster points and the grade distributions across the student attempts (Fig. 8 and 9) does not provide a clear relation between the clusters nor does it show us how the students' overall problem-solving process progresses over time. We then employed a Markov model to illustrate the transitions of students' problem-solving processes amongst the respective clusters. Within the model, every student's submission (action) transforms them from one state (cluster) to another and depending on the actual change to the source code submitted this might be transitioning within the same cluster. The transitional process is illustrated in Fig. 10 as a state machine and Fig. 11 shows the corresponding transitional probability matrix.

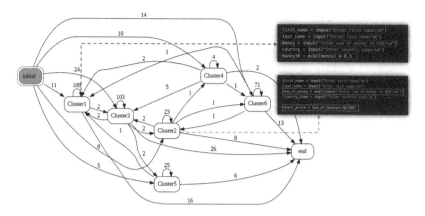

Fig. 10. An overview of the Markov model as a state transitional machine.

	Start	Cluster1	Cluster2	Cluster3	Cluster4	Cluster5	Cluster6	End
Start	0.0	0.152778	0.111111	0.333333	0.138889	0.069444	0.194444	0.000000
Cluster1	0.0	0.858268	0.000000	0.015748	0.000000	0.000000	0.000000	0.125984
Cluster2	0.0	0.000000	0.657143	0.057143	0.028571	0.000000	0.028571	0.228571
Cluster3	0.0	0.014815	0.014815	0.762963	0.000000	0.014815	0.000000	0.192593
Cluster4	0.0	0.142857	0.000000	0.357143	0.285714	0.000000	0.071429	0.142857
Cluster5	0.0	0.031250	0.000000	0.000000	0.000000	0.781250	0.000000	0.187500
Cluster6	0.0	0.011628	0.011628	0.000000	0.000000	0.000000	0.825581	0.151163

Fig. 11. Corresponding transitional probability matrix for Markov model in Fig. 10

The transitional probabilities in the Markov model were calculated to understand student state dependencies. For example, the probability of a student moving to cluster 1 at the beginning of their attempts can be illustrated and calculated as follows :

$$
\begin{aligned}
P\left(\phi \mid C_1\right) &= \frac{Total\ transitions\ from\ \phi\ to\ C_1}{Total\ transitions\ from\ \phi} \\
&= \tfrac{11}{72} = 0.152778 \\
where &: \phi \Rightarrow Initial\ State\ and\ C_1 \Rightarrow Cluster\ 1
\end{aligned}
\tag{1}
$$

Given the transition matrix in Fig. 11, this would be the value where the row labelled Start intersects the column labelled Cluster 1

The typical outcome of the clustered state diagram may appear complex, but it provides valuable insights into the diversity of problem-solving approaches among students. By studying the model further, it becomes possible to identify key elements, such as states where students spend the most time, where they are likely to begin, where student's solutions converge and where they are likely to end up with their attempts.

Figure 12 shows a state machine for all the student attempts within Cluster 3 from Fig. 10. This is a subset of the overall transitional processes when attempts are considered in terms of grade ranges; however, it is worth noting that some of the attempts that start in cluster 3 may change their programming approach and move to another cluster and new students may also join from different clusters.

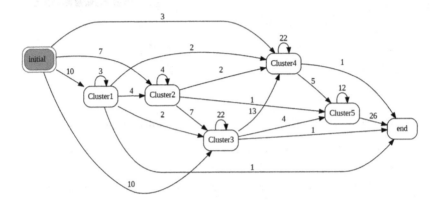

Fig. 12. State transitions within Cluster 3 of Fig. 10 based on 20% grade ranges

Figure 12 acknowledges the notion of comprehensive programming approaches within clusters, as it shows clear incremental progress based on the grade ranges and we could identify the difference in student comprehension, some students may master more than one concept at once allowing them to make big progress, such as going from start to Cluster 4 with grades in the range of 60 and 80; however, others may progress sequentially from 1, 2, 3, 4 up to 5.

5   Discussions

The results and figures presented in the previous section have led us to support as well as come up with our findings on student's problem-solving approaches.

Diversity in Problem-Solving Approaches: given the simplicity of the task tacked for this study, it can be noted that there exist numerous approaches that students would follow as they carry out their programming exercises. This diversity is what most authors have attributed to the increased complexity of problem-solving assessment and tracking in education. From our data, we got 6 clusters(problem-solving approaches) and the number of possible combinations would be approximately the factorial of 6 which is 720 combinations, as this gives us a count of all possible arrangements for the given 6 clusters. These combinations present problems when it comes to instructors and support staff being able to provide personalized guidance.

Similarity in Submission Could Mean the Same Approach: Similarity in student submissions always raises concerns when it comes to plagiarism; however, it is worth noting that despite the diversity in approaches there can only be so many ways to solve the tasks at hand and with students going through the same material it is likely that their approach ends up being similar. This together with the fact that students within clusters do exhibit progress in their grades means that they maintain their approach and make just enough changes to get better grades. It is also possible that some of the approaches do not get the students the maximum possible grades for the task.

Students Change Submission Approaches in No Order: With the assumption that the clusters presented in Fig. 10 are problem-solving approaches, it can be observed that some students change their approaches with time in no particular order. This could be related to the trial-and-error approach practice identified by Chao [5] as computational patterns.

Markov Model Could Help in Tracking the Problem-Solving Process: It is plausible that given additional information associated with the actions of the problem-solving process, we could track students' overall approach and more importantly we might easily link them to knowledge spaces as well as acknowledge their completion of certain learning outcomes. This relation is a crucial aspect in understanding the cognitive process of the students.

6 Conclusion and Future Directions

The findings presented in this paper provide an alternative method of observing and studying how students solve problems in introductory programming classes. Through the use of clustering algorithms and source code evolution analysis, the study was able to identify common beginning points, common transition paths, and possible absorbing states that could be suggestive of comprehensive approaches to problem solutions. In the mathematical theory of probabilities, an absorbing state refers to a state that, once an entity enters into it, the entity cannot exit from it [3]. Traditionally, in models of students' problem-solving approaches, absorbing states mean concepts that students are struggling to grasp.

Our research findings show that we can successfully create a Markov model and an investigation into the absorbing states of the model suggests that these states might be representative of comprehensive approaches to problem-solving. This reinterpretation creates an interesting view for understanding programming conceptual mastery and student advancement. The quality of the model is based on the cluster evaluation metrics as the transition of student activities between clusters is what the Markov model represents. In Fig. 4, the Silhouette Score for the selected clustering algorithm-KMeans was observed at 0.955(Above 95% accuracy), this is a large enough score to conclude that we have a good quality model.

However, it is crucial to recognise the limitations of the research, specifically in the utilization of unlabelled datasets and the relatively low number of consenting students. These constraints may affect the generalizability of the findings and highlight areas for future research.

Moving forward, future studies could explore the application of supervised learning techniques to labelled datasets to validate the findings and compare them against established benchmarks. Additionally, efforts to increase student participation and consent could enhance the robustness of the model and expand the scope of analysis. Moreover, the knowledge gathered from this study can help develop instructional strategies that are specifically aimed at helping students in programming courses enhance their problem-solving abilities. An automated guidance system could provide assistance based on the patterns within a given approach and teachers can create focused interventions to better address misconceptions and scaffold student learning by spotting common patterns and efficient problem-solving techniques.

In conclusion, this study creates a relatively good quality Markov model for understanding how students solve problems when learning programming. Through the reinterpretation of absorbing states as potential identifiers of all-encompassing problem-solving strategies and the application of data-driven methodologies, researchers and educators can achieve a deeper understanding of student learning and improve instructional procedures for better results.

Acknowledgments. This work is financially supported by the Hasso Plattner Institute for Digital Engineering through the HPI Research School in Information and Communications Technology for Development (ICT4D) at the University of Cape Town.

References

1. Ashari, I.F., Nugroho, E., Baraku, R., Yanda, I.N., Liwardana, R.: Analysis of elbow, silhouette, Davies-Bouldin, Calinski-Harabasz, and rand-index evaluation on k-means algorithm for classifying flood-affected areas in Jakarta. J. Appl. Inform. Comput. **7**(1), 89–97 (2023). https://doi.org/10.30871/jaic.v7i1.4947
2. Awong, L.E.E., Zielińska, T.: Comparative analysis of the clustering quality in self-organizing maps for human posture classification. Sensors **23**(18), 7925 (2023). https://doi.org/10.3390/s23187925
3. Bush, K., Kemeny, J.G., Snell, J.L.: Finite Markov chains. Am. Math. Monthly **67**(10), 1039 (1960). https://doi.org/10.2307/2309264
4. Cabo, C.: Developing and documenting problem-solving strategies for computer programming before code writing. In: 2023 IEEE Frontiers in Education Conference (FIE) (2023). https://doi.org/10.1109/fie58773.2023.10343169
5. Chao, P.Y.: Exploring students' computational practice, design and performance of problem-solving through a visual programming environment. Comput. Educ. **95**, 202–215 (2016). https://doi.org/10.1016/j.compedu.2016.01.010
6. Cheng, G., Poon, L.K.M., Lau, W.W.F., Zhou, R.C.: Applying eye tracking to identify students' use of learning strategies in understanding program code. In: ICEMT 2019: Proceedings of the 2019 3rd International Conference on Education and Multimedia Technology (2019). https://doi.org/10.1145/3345120.3345144

7. Deeb, F.A., Kime, K., Torrey, R., Hickey, T.J.: Measuring and visualizing learning with Markov models. In: 2018 IEEE Frontiers in Education Conference (FIE) (2016). https://doi.org/10.1109/fie.2016.7757404
8. Desmarais, M.C., Lemieux, F.: Clustering and visualizing study state sequences. Educ. Data Min. 224–227 (2013). https://www.educationaldatamining.org/EDM2013
9. Doignon, J.P.: Learning spaces, and how to build them. In: Glodeanu, C.V., Kaytoue, M., Sacarea, C. (eds.) Formal Concept Analysis. LNCS, pp. 1–14. Springer, Cham (2014). https://doi.org/10.1007/978-3-319-07248-7_1
10. Fahid, F.M., et al.: Progression trajectory-based student modeling for novice block-based programming. In: UMAP 2021: Proceedings of the 29th ACM Conference on User Modeling, Adaptation and Personalization (2021). https://doi.org/10.1145/3450613.3456833
11. Hasni, T.F., Lodhi, F.: Teaching problem solving effectively. ACM Inroads **2**(3), 58–62 (2011). https://doi.org/10.1145/2003616.2003636
12. Leskovec, J., Rajaraman, A., Ullman, J.D.: Finding Similar Items. Cambridge University Press, Cambridge (2014). https://doi.org/10.1017/cbo9781139924801
13. Lister, R., et al.: A multi-national study of reading and tracing skills in novice programmers. In: ITiCSE-WGR 2004: Working group reports from ITiCSE on Innovation and Technology in Computer Science Education (2004). https://doi.org/10.1145/1044550.1041673
14. Loksa, D., Ko, A.J.: The role of self-regulation in programming problem solving process and success. In: Proceedings of the 2016 ACM Conference on International Computing Education Research (2016). https://doi.org/10.1145/2960310.2960334
15. Margulieux, L.E., Catrambone, R.: Using learners' self-explanations of subgoals to guide initial problem solving in app inventor. In: ICER '17: Proceedings of the 2017 ACM Conference on International Computing Education Research (2017). https://doi.org/10.1145/3105726.3106168
16. Mitchell, C.M., Boyer, K.E., Lester, J.C.: A Markov decision process model of tutorial intervention in task-oriented dialogue. In: Lane, H.C., Yacef, K., Mostow, J., Pavlik, P. (eds.) AIED 2013. LNCS, pp. 828–831. Springer, Heidelberg (2013). https://doi.org/10.1007/978-3-642-39112-5_123
17. Pechorina, Y., Anderson, K., Denny, P.: Metacodenition: scaffolding the problem-solving process for novice programmers. In: ACE 2023: Proceedings of the 25th Australasian Computing Education Conference (2023). https://doi.org/10.1145/3576123.3576130
18. Piech, C., Sahami, M., Koller, D., Cooper, S., Blikstein, P.: Modeling how students learn to program. In: SIGCSE 2012: Proceedings of the 43rd ACM Technical Symposium on Computer Science Education (2012).https://doi.org/10.1145/2157136.2157182
19. Stefanutti, L., De Chiusole, D., Brancaccio, A.: Markov solution processes: modeling human problem solving with procedural knowledge space theory. J. Math. Psychol. **103**, 102552 (2021).https://doi.org/10.1016/j.jmp.2021.102552
20. Stolarek, J., Nowak, P.: A modular, practical test for a programming course. In: SIGCSE 2020: Proceedings of the 51st ACM Technical Symposium on Computer Science Education (2020). https://doi.org/10.1145/3328778.3366886
21. Tan, P.N., Steinbach, M., Karpatne, A., Kumar, V.: Introduction to Data Mining. Addison-Wesley (2019)

22. Ullah, Z., Lajis, A., Jamjoom, M., Altalhi, A.H., Al-Ghamdi, A.A., Saleem, F.: The effect of automatic assessment on novice programming: strengths and limitations of existing systems. Comput. Appl. Eng. Educ. **26**(6), 2328–2341 (2018). https://doi.org/10.1002/cae.21974

23. Whitelock-Wainwright, A., Laan, N., Wen, D., Gašević, D.: Exploring student information problem solving behaviour using fine-grained concept map and search tool data. Comput. Educ. **145**, 103731 (2020). https://doi.org/10.1016/j.compedu.2019.103731

24. Wing, J.: Computational thinking. OECD:Paris (2018). https://doi.org/10.1787/20769679

25. Xu, Y., Ni, Q., Liu, S., Mi, Y., Yu, Y., Hao, Y.: Learning style integrated deep reinforcement learning framework for programming problem recommendation in online judge system. Int. J. Comput. Intell. Syst. **15**(1) (2022).https://doi.org/10.1007/s44196-022-00176-4

A Longitudinal Study on the Effect of Patches on Code Coverage and Software System Maintainability

Ernest Bonginkosi Mamba📧 and Stephen Phillip Levitt$^{(\boxtimes)}$📧

University of the Witwatersrand, Johannesburg, South Africa
stephen.levitt@wits.ac.za

Abstract. Contemporary software development often involves the use of source control repositories which are hosted online and making incremental patches (commits) throughout the development process. Online hosting services facilitate the use of build pipelines and the integration of code coverage services into these pipelines. However, existing research into how incremental patches to software systems affect code coverage has not fully taken advantage of the data that is made available by these coverage services. This paper presents a partial replication of two previous studies on patch coverage, analysing over 50,000 builds from 46 projects obtained from two popular coverage services, Codecov and Coveralls. Data quality issues, such as missing commits, duplicate builds from Cron Jobs, and sudden coverage drops, were identified and addressed, highlighting the need for rigorous data cleaning process when mining data from coverage services. Results indicate that patches are generally either fully covered or entirely uncovered, with a majority achieving full coverage, suggesting that very seldom do engineers opt for partial coverage. There is a weak correlation (correlation coefficient: 0.23) between patch coverage and system coverage, indicating that patch coverage alone cannot be used to predict system coverage evolution. Furthermore, patch testing does not enhance patch maintainability.

Keywords: Patch Coverage · Maintainability · Software System Evolution

1 Introduction

Meir Lehman, a prominent figure in the field of software engineering argued that a software system's enduring utility and success hinge on its ability to evolve continuously; failure to do so leads to a decline in relevance and quality [13,14]. Lehman's laws of evolution posit that a software system's functional capabilities must evolve to maintain user satisfaction, inevitably resulting in an increase in system size and complexity over time with a concurrent decline in system quality unless actively monitored and addressed.

A. Gerber (Ed.): SAICSIT 2024, CCIS 2159, pp. 79–94, 2024.
https://doi.org/10.1007/978-3-031-64881-6_5

Central to the concept of software evolution is the source code, the centre of a multifaceted process that requires the co-evolution of various artifacts, including unit tests (also known as developer tests). These tests, proven effective in identifying bugs [23], play a pivotal role in ensuring the continued proper functioning of a system. One measure of determining how thorough a test suite is, is known as *code coverage*. Code coverage refers to the number of source code lines that are executed when the test suite is run.

There is a delicate relationship between the source code and its tests because as the software evolves even minor code changes and refactoring efforts can disrupt existing tests [20,21] and significantly alter code coverage [6]. This underscores the need for the continued maintenance of tests as the source code, itself, evolves.

Software typically evolves through incremental changes or modifications to source code repositories by means of commits. In this paper, these modifications are termed "patches". A modification refers to the alteration, deletion, or addition of one or more lines within one or more files. A patch can modify source code files (production or test) or non-source files such as a README file. Patch testing specifically evaluates the testing of modified code, focusing on the extent to which the altered code is tested and covered. For the remainder of the study, the terms patch and commit are used interchangeably.

Previous research efforts have extensively investigated the co-evolution of test and source code, however, this has been done through mining multiple, stable *release* versions of systems [24]. While such an approach provides information at stable points in a system's development, it does not provide insights into the development process at day-to-day level. On the other hand, studies using more fine-grained empirical data have predominantly aimed to investigate the synchronous or sequential alteration of production code and test code [15,17,25, 26]. Limited work has been done to understand how test coverage is affected by incremental changes. To date, only two studies from Marinescu *et al.* [16] and Hilton *et al.* [9] have investigated how incremental changes effect test coverage.

As hosting providers have become more sophisticated over time in terms of the services they offer, new opportunities have arisen to study evolution of source code and accompanying tests. GitHub [7], for example, now allows development teams to create flexible build pipelines which can be used to take the source code in a repository through a number of different stages, including unit testing, and ultimately deploy it into production. GitHub also affords tight integration with third-party code coverage services. These services enable the development team to graphically visualise and track their coverage statistics. GitHub's built-in build pipeline functionality, together with the public APIs offered by the third-party coverage services that it integrates with, has both increased the number of open-source projects which generate coverage statistics and made these statistics accessible.

In this paper, the work of Marinescu *et al.* [16] and Hilton *et al.* [9] is extended by considering a different dataset, and specifically making use of code coverage service data, to investigate the maintainability of incremental changes (patches) and the relationship between patch testing and its impact on incremental change maintainability.

2 Related Work

Marinescu *et al.* [16] pioneered the exploration of patch coverage in small incremental changes and subsequently established a formal definition for this concept. To investigate the co-evolution of test and production code, and patch coverage, the authors developed the COVRIG tool and conducted a study involving six open-source software (OSS) projects written in C/C++. The authors selected 250 revisions per project, iteratively checking out each revision, compiling and collecting coverage information from coverage reports. Their findings revealed that patches were either fully covered or not covered at all, with engineers seldom opting for partial patch coverage. Additionally, the study observed that testing appeared to be a *phased* activity for five out of six projects, occurring intermittently after extended periods of development. Hilton *et al.* [9] expanded upon the research conducted by Marinescu *et al.*, introducing an investigation into how covered lines transition between patches and the overall impact of patch coverage. Hilton *et al.* employed a mixed method to collecting coverage information by using coverage service tool Coveralls [18] along with manually compiling code and collecting coverage information. They chose 47 projects spanning different programming languages and utilised 250 revisions for projects hosted on Coveralls. Hilton *et al.* present slightly contradicting results from Marinescu *et al.*, whereby they state that patch coverage is not bimodal, rather, it varies from patch to patch with no-discernible pattern. Notably, Hilton *et al.* identified an intriguing phenomenon termed "flipping", where some patches led to changes in the coverage status of lines, transitioning from previously covered to uncovered in the new modification.

Zaidman *et al.* [25,26] studied whether production and test code co-evolve synchronously at a commit level using two Java projects. The authors observed two patterns of evolution, synchronous - where production and test code are changed together and phased - where production and test code are changed separately. Stanislav *et al.* [15] examined sixty-one projects with a total of 240000 commits to examine the co-evolution of test and production maintenance. Their results showed that, in the majority of cases, production code changes, in particular, code fixes happens solely without modifying test code. Marsavina *et al.* [17], mined five open-source projects and used association rules to identify co-evolution patterns. Their results showed six distinct co-evolution patterns.

3 Research Questions

The study conducted here is a partial replication of the studies conducted by [9,16], and as such the following research questions are the same:

1. What is the distribution of patch sizes? This inquiry aims to assess the total number of lines affected per patch (i.e. magnitude of each patch), potentially unveiling insights into the incremental changes that occur as the system and tests evolve.
2. What is the distribution of patch coverage across the revisions of the system? Analysing patch testing activities could provide insights into testing practices within an open-source environment and help understand why the system coverage is as it appears.
3. How does individual patch coverage affect overall system coverage? The reasonable hypothesis would be that higher patch coverage implies an improved system coverage and vice versa, therefore, this question aims at validating this hypothesis.

Additionally, the following new research question is posed:

4. How maintainable is a typical patch, and how does patch maintainability vary across revisions? Maintainability is measured using the Software Improvement Group's (SIG) maintainability model [12]. This question is investigated because along with patch testing, it is important to understand how maintainability varies at the level of incremental changes.

Aside from the addition of a novel research question, this study adds value by making use of an almost entirely different dataset to the studies that it replicates. Lastly, and importantly, the methodology used here is different in that this work exclusively makes use of commercial coverage services which offer free coverage reporting for open-source projects. Using existing coverage services greatly simplifies the calculation of coverage statistics, enabling a greater breadth of projects to be covered or a more in-depth analysis of individual projects to be conducted, by considering a greater number of project builds.

4   Mining Open-Source Project Builds

Patch and system code coverage are determined by compiling and executing a project's test suite along with the production code being tested, and recording which production code statements have been hit or missed. Downloading and compiling projects can pose significant challenges due to project dependency mismatches and resource requirements, sometimes leading to compile failures for different revisions [25]. Marinescu *et al.* [16] attempted to address this using virtualisation, but acknowledged its continued resource intensity. Hilton *et al.* [9] adopted an approach in which they manually ran the test suites for some projects but used the Coveralls code coverage service for others.

4.1   Dataset Selection

All the projects that were selected for this study are hosted on GitHub [7]. GitHub serves as a central data hub for a huge number of open-source projects due to its openness and licensing nature in contrast to proprietary source control management systems [19].

To identify possible projects, the sampling strategy employed by Pinto *et al.* [22] was adopted. In order for a repository to be considered it needed to be:

1. popular - using number of stars, forks, and contributors as measure of popularity,
2. actively maintained, and
3. stewarded by a well-respected open-source organisation, such as the Apache Foundation, or private company, such as Microsoft.

Repositories meeting the above criteria were then manually inspected to identify README files containing coverage badges from either CodeCov (eg. `codecov 69%`) or Coveralls (eg. `coverage 83%`). These badges indicate that the project in question was submitting data to the respective coverage service (with the badge giving the project's overall code coverage). Projects with diverse range of coverage, and meeting the additional criteria of having a minimum of one hundred builds over a two year period were finally selected. This last criteria ensured that each of the projects chosen has sufficient historical data for longitudinal analysis to be conducted.

It is noted that none of the projects from Marinescu *et al.* study utilised a coverage service; hence, they were excluded. Five projects appearing in the Hilton *et al.* study were selected; however, a larger number of revisions were available for analysis in this investigation.

4.2   Data Cleaning

Data cleaning is essential when there are data issues such as inconsistencies, gaps and misrepresented data. The following issues arose when analysing the data received from the coverage services' APIs:

Missing Commits - Various branching strategies can be adopted when using Git and GitHub, including Gitflow, GiHub flow, and so on. To ensure consistency, data is extracted from all branches. The rationale for mining all branches is that development on all branches will ultimately contribute and affect overall coverage. Additionally, the aim of this investigation is to focus on the incremental contributions towards building a system irrespective of which branches these contributions happen on. These contributions, if incorporated into the trunk (main branch), accurately portray how the system is being built.

However, one of the challenges posed by the various branching workflows discussed above is the issue of dangling commits or short-lived branches, leading to the unavailability of certain commits. A dangling Git commit refers to a commit that is not referenced by any branch or tag. This situation typically arises when a commit is deleted from a branch due to previous actions such as rebase or reset, or when a branch itself is deleted. To address the issue of dangling commits, all commits resulting in a missing commit hash error are skipped.

Additionally, it was observed that Coveralls had a considerable number of builds where the commit hash key was missing, and returned as `null`, while other key statistics were represented correctly. Since a `null` commit hash cannot be checked out, these builds are also excluded from the analysis.

CronJobs/Cron-Builds - These define regular builds on specific branches and dates. CronJobs, which typically build the last commit on a specific branch, are not triggered by either a pull request or a push, and therefore contribute no new coverage and patch statistics because they are merely scheduled jobs. To exclude Cronjobs, builds emanating from unique commit hashes are sought within the build history, and duplicate builds are removed. Occasionally, it was observed that a slight variation in coverage occurs for builds resulting from the exact same commit hash. This is attributed to the dynamic nature of test coverage extraction, as noted by the Coveralls team [3]. Only the first build produced was analysed in situations where duplicate builds emanated from the same commit hash.

Sudden Coverage Drops - The most common data problem observed was either build failures or multi-triggered builds. These issues often lead to the coverage services' API failing to retrieve data from a build. This results in coverage spiking and/or incorrectly reported coverage. In an exchange with the Codecov team [10], it was revealed that sometimes build failures can affect how the API and subsequently the user interface may retrieve and display data from the build. For example, the Apache/libcloud build details as retrieved from Coveralls API in Listing 1 shows two consecutive builds, the first one returns correct data while the second returns 0% coverage. Such a response is highly unlikely and is flagged as a corrupted build in order to maintain the data integrity of the study. Due to these improbable circumstances, a 30% maximum drop in coverage is chosen to filter out the noise in the data. An exponentially-weighted moving average (EWMA) is used to smooth the data from such outliers. Take the example of the Apache Gobblin project in Fig. 1 (top), there are numerous points where the coverage is picked-up as zero. Upon further investigation, it was discovered that these commits contained minimal changes, indicating that they could not have been the sole cause of the significant decrease in coverage from 45% to 0%.

A 30-point EWMA is applied selectively to maintain genuine coverage points, and is calculated only when a coverage value has deviated by a 30% or more from the previous value. The noise reduction that is achieved by adopting this approach can be seen in the bottom graph of Fig. 1.

4.3   Metrics and Measures Computation

Patch Coverage: Marinescu *et al.* [16] define patch coverage as "the ratio between the number of *executed* lines of code added or modified by a patch and the total number of *executable* lines in the patch, measured in the revision

```
 1   [     {"repo_name": "apache/libcloud",
 2           "branch": "trunk",
 3           "commit_sha": "af264fecea1adc8ded707094854a3c64790c3285",
 4           "coverage_change": 36.8,
 5           "covered_percent": 36.791,
 6           "covered_lines": 18742,
 7           "missed_lines": 32199,
 8           "relevant_lines": 50941,
 9           "covered_branches": 0,
10           },
11         {"repo_name": "apache/libcloud",
12           "branch": null,
13           "commit_sha": null,
14           "coverage_change": 0.0,
15           "covered_percent": 0.0,
16           "covered_lines": 0,
17           "missed_lines": 0,
18           "relevant_lines": 0,
19           "covered_branches": 0,
20           },
21         ... # excluded for brevity
22   ]
```

Listing 1: Apache/Libcloud Corrupt Web API Response

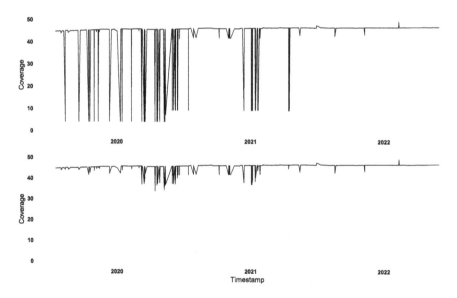

Fig. 1. Apache/Gobblin before data cleaning (top graph) and after data cleaning (bottom graph) with an EWMA

that adds the patch". In other words, unlike system coverage, patch coverage is a far more granular measure focused on newly added code changes [1,11]. Executed lines are lines that are invoked during a test execution whilst executable lines are all "source lines" that have the potential to be invoked, yet may not necessarily be invoked. This definition excludes statements like comments as these are ignored by both interpreters and compilers.

To compute patch coverage for a given commit, the modified files, and the corresponding modified lines, are first identified. Then for each modified line, the line's coverage status is extracted from the code coverage service. The line's coverage status defines whether the line was executed or not. Coveralls represents line coverage status of executable lines as zero (line was not executed during the test run) or $N \in \{1, \ldots, \infty\}$, where N represents how many times the line was invoked during the test run. Codecov represents the line coverage status with a zero or one. Zero denotes lines that are not executed while one represents lines that are run by the tests. Codecov also has the concept of half-covered lines, termed *partial* coverage. Partially covered lines are branches with one or more omitted execution paths, and these are represented with a line coverage status of two. In this context, partially covered lines are not counted as executed (covered) lines and are added to the count of executable lines.

Patch Maintainability: The concept of fine grained maintainability was first explored by Kuipers *et al.* [12] and Heitlager *et al.* [8]. They introduced a maintainability model known as the SIG Maintainability Model (SIG-MM). SIG-MM was developed through the mapping of ISO/IEC-25010 quality characteristics to code properties and ultimately to source code metrics.

To tailor the SIG-MM for incremental changes, Di Biase *et al.* [4] refined this model to focus on patches and called this derivation the Delta Maintainability Model (DMM). Equation (1) presents the mathematical expression to calculate the DMM score of a patch and Fig. 2 depicts the mapping of the ISO/IEC-25010 quality characteristics to the code properties that are used in Eq. (1).

$$DMM\ Score = \frac{DMM\ Size + DMM\ Unit\ Interface + DMM\ Complexity}{No.\ of\ Properties} \quad (1)$$

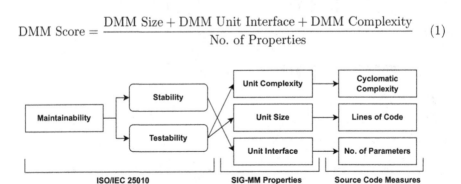

Fig. 2. Relation between SIG Maintainability Model and source code measures and ISO/IEC 25010 quality characteristics

4.4   Compute Infrastructure

Collecting and computing the above metrics required multiple RESTful API calls to the two coverage services. In addition to the API calls, the computation of the maintainability metric and the patch coverage required cloning each project repository in order to iterate over the commit history. Performing all these steps on a local machine can easily become cumbersome and inefficient due to the processing power required. Thus, a virtual machine and containers were utilised to collect and compute all the metrics. A virtual machine hosted on the Microsoft Azure cloud running Ubuntu-20.04 served as the host operating system. The Docker containerisation engine [5] was chosen for its popularity and efficiency. To ensure data collection from the coverage services was conducted in parallel, two containers were deployed with one dedicated to collecting and computing metrics using Coveralls while the other used Codecov.

5   Analyses of Patches and Patch Impacts

5.1   Project Statistics

The study data consists of projects from both Codecov (Table 1) and Coveralls (Table 2). In total 50,666 revisions across 46 projects in 10 programming languages were analysed. Tables 1 and 2 present the projects, along with the time in months denoting the difference between the first and last revision (build) dates, as well as the number of revisions during this period as well as the system coverage as measured for the first and last revisions.

5.2   Typical Patch Size

Hilton et al. [9] argues that smaller patches are easier for engineers to understand, while larger patches may necessitate external strategies for comprehension due to potential complexity. To investigate the size of patches, patches touching non-source files only are excluded from the analysis. This exclusion of non-source files patches led to the exclusion of projects CL{09,18} as their entire build history is based on non-source file patches. The distribution of patch sizes across revisions illustrated by the whisker box in Fig. 3 indicates that the typical size of patch is around 10 lines. It can also be observed that the upper quartile of the distribution indicates that most of the patches contain fewer than 1000 lines of code, suggesting that commits rarely exceed this threshold. These findings align with the work of Hilton et al. but differ slightly from Marinescu et al., who reported a lower number of lines changed, ranging from 4 to 7.

A number of outliers are observed in this distribution, especially project CV10, which has a patch that has close to 100000 lines of code. Upon further examination this patch was revealed to be a merge patch that added just over 62000 lines of code from 3000 files. Further examination of the other outliers revealed that most of the commits of over 1000 LoC are actually merge commits.

Table 1. Project Key Statistics - Codecov

Identifier	Project Name	Language	Time (Months)	Revisions	Coverage (%)	
					Start	End
CV01	codecov/gazebo	Javascript/TypeScript	37	5094	16.67	97.91
CV02	apollographql/apollo-client	TypeScript	61	3034	84.15	95.29
CV03	apollographql/federation	TypeScript	43	354	90.54	68.48
CV04	TNG/property-loader	Java	29	131	86.95	87.81
CV05	alibaba/GraphScope	C++	36	967	77.26	40.91
CV06	jenkinsci/analysis-model	Java	72	2276	88.16	93.09
CV07	jenkinsci/warnings-ng-plugin	Java	62	2796	83.07	81.82
CV08	JabRef/jabref	Java	72	2844	29.68	41.47
CV09	eclipse/kapua	Java	72	2653	52.88	20.64
CV10	eclipse/mosquitto	C	24	117	81.15	80.86
CV11	ARMmbed/continuous-delivery-scripts	Python	33	476	68.81	68.91
CV12	apereo/phpCAS	PHP	41	213	43.77	43.44
CV13	Netflix/Priam	Java	30	441	36.73	47.83
CV14	zxing/zxing	Java	81	209	73.92	79.08
CV15	damianszczepanik/cucumber-reporting	Java	80	252	98.66	97.11
CV16	Netflix/genie	Java	92	1287	89.723	90.750
CV17	Netflix/conductor	Java	31	900	58.03	65.78
CV18	apache/yunikorn-core	Go	44	369	58.06	77.77
CV19	Netflix/titus-executor	Go	36	919	35.42	17.49
CV20	apache/celix	C	43	1276	68.35	88.37
CV21	facebook/metro	Javascript	72	1552	81.32	83.13
CV22	microsoft/superbenchmark	Python	35	513	0.00	85.79
CV23	google/go-github	Go	57	967	33.97	97.72
CV24	apache/apisix-ingress-controller	Go	36	627	58.15	37.24
CV25	kubernetes/ingress-nginx	Go	38	1772	36.61	56.02
CV26	microsoft/responsible-ai-toolbox	TypeScript	24	1196	89.42	89.01

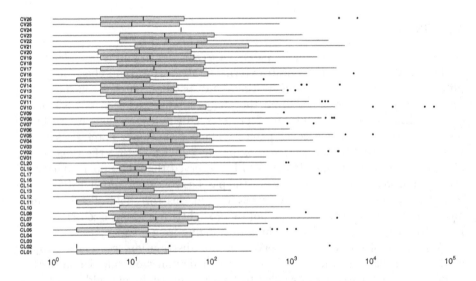

Fig. 3. Distribution of patch size: whisker/box plot representing the minimum, median and maximum patch size of patches modifying source code. The (log scale) x-axis represents the size of a patch in lines of code.

Table 2. Project Key Statistics - Coveralls

Identifier	Project Name	Language	Time (Months)	Revisions	Coverage (%)	
					Start	End
CL01	kubernetes/helm	Go	26	1258	54.579	63.541
CL02	ManageIQ/ui-components	Typescript	64	633	89.744	50.977
CL03	apache/datasketches-cpp	C++	34	180	93.854	98.938
CL04	apache/servicecomb-pack	Java	72	1315	95.278	81.703
CL05	Netflix/repokid	Python	44	171	28.782	56.235
CL06	yahoo/fluxible	Javascript	77	490	90.086	95.749
CL07	facebook/react	Javascript	44	4753	87.115	86.162
CL08	microsoft/botbuilder-python	Python	53	748	74.106	66.985
CL09	F5Networks/f5-adcaas-openstack	Python	29	279	100	94.328
CL10	Microsoft/vscode-mssql	Typescript	28	921	59.322	66.367
CL11	F5Networks/f5-openstack-agent	Python	88	772	28.848	23.441
CL12	Microsoft/sqltoolsservice	C#	42	754	20.158	76.855
CL13	yahoo/react-i13n	Javascript	61	202	86.106	90.342
CL14	HazyResearch/fonduer	Python	24	508	44.844	85.788
CL15	grpc/grpc-node	Typescript	36	514	85.336	73.630
CL16	square/ghostunnel	Go	52	436	90.548	89.655
CL17	square/go-jose	Go	70	397	97.002	90.065
CL18	eBay/ebayui-core	Typescript	36	1096	86.781	83.728
CL19	platinumazure/eslint-plugin-qunit	Javascript	100	465	100	100
CL20	dropwizard/dropwizard	Java	62	1521	55.210	85.738

5.3   Patch Coverage Analysis

To compute the coverage of patches, the definition provided by Marinescu *et al.*
[16], and described earlier, is used. Patch coverage is computed for the entire
build history of changed statements per project. The percentage coverage of
each patch is then binned using the following bins: 0%, (0%–25%], (25%–50%],
(50%–75%], (75%–100%) and 100%. These bins are the same to those of [9].
The 0% and 100% bins are specifically chosen to identify patches that are either
completely uncovered or fully covered. A stacked bar graph is plotted to visualise
the distribution for each project (Fig. 4).

Figure 4 shows that while partial coverage of patches is prevalent in almost
all projects, patches are generally either entirely covered or uncovered, that is,
the largest bins are the 0% or 100% bins in the majority of projects. This finding
corroborates the observations of Marinescu *et al.* [16] and those of Hilton *et al.*
[9].

5.4   Impact of Patches on System Coverage

A patch can either be fully, partially, or not covered. However, the consequence
to the overall system coverage is not known a *priori*. To assess this impact,
a positive influence is defined as an increase in system coverage, negative as a
decrease, and no change (no impact) as neutral. Patches are categorised based on
whether they modify source or non-source files. In answering this question, the
coverage difference between two successive builds is examined. If the net coverage

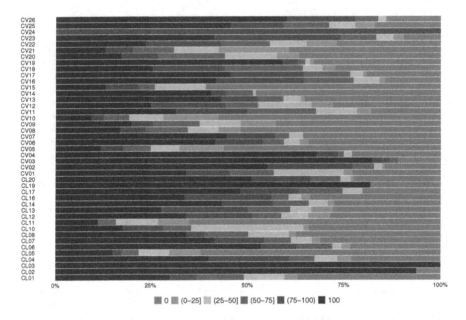

Fig. 4. Distribution of patch coverage for patches touching source files. Each colour represents the range and the size of the bar is the percentage of the patches whose coverage lies within the range.

from b1 (where b1 is the earlier build) to b2 (where b2 is the later build) is less than zero, the patch is said to have decreased (or negatively impacted) coverage, if the difference is greater than zero, the patch is said to have increased (or positively impacted) coverage, and if the difference is zero, the patch is classified as having no impact or change to overall coverage.

The majority of patches depicted in Fig. 5, particularly those altering non-source files, show a significant positive and negative impact. These findings align with Hilton *et al.*'s research [9], who asserted that patches involving non-source files can influence patch coverage. However, it is noted that such magnitudes could also be influenced by the absence of a one-to-one correspondence between commits and builds. Intermediate commits preceding a build-triggering commit may not be fully considered, potentially leading to fluctuations in coverage that are not accurately attributed. Conversely, projects CV{15,16,20,23,24} and CL19 demonstrate behavior deemed as "plausible", wherein patches modifying non-source files exhibit less influence on system coverage. Note in both modification types is the prevalence of patches with no impact/change, which aligns with the distribution of patch coverage. Interestingly, projects CL{09,18}, having build histories in which only non-source code files are modified, have some patches which increase and decrease system coverage. It is suspected that this phenomenon can be attributed to intermediate commits that did not initiate a build, or to the modification of build scripts, such as `Makefile`'s, which could cause coverage changes. To further assess the relationship between patch cov-

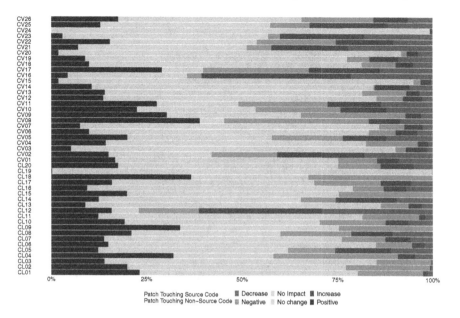

Fig. 5. Distribution of patch impact. Colour represents the range and size represents the percentage of patches whose impact lies within the range.

erage and overall coverage Kendall's coefficient is computed and Cohen's interpretation of correlation strength is employed, revealing a correlation strength of 0.239, classified by Cohen as weak [2].

5.5   Patch DMM Metric

According to Di Biase *et al.* [4], the DMM explores the changes to source code as the "ratio of good changes over the sum of good and bad changes". The resulting value of this ratio is, therefore, between 0 and 1, where zero indicates a "bad" (unmaintainable) change and one indicates "good" (maintainable) change.

Figure 6 illustrates the distribution of DMM score per patch. The DMM bins are split as 0, (0–0.25], (0.25–0.50], (0.50–0.75], (0.75–1.00) and 1.00. As in the case of patch coverage, the bins, 0 and 1.00 are specifically chosen to separate the scores of patches with DMM scores at the extremes, indicating a poor patch and good patch (from a maintainability perspective), respectively. As the DMM score is specifically designed for source code, any patches modifying non-source files will inherently have a DMM score of zero, and therefore, these patches are excluded. Note that the majority of patches have DMM scores either in the (0.50–0.75] bin or 0, which means patches are either "somewhat" maintainable or not maintainable at all. Kendall's coefficient is also computed to assess the influence of testing practices on maintainability. The relationship between patch coverage and DMM is found to be very weak, with a τ value of 0.160.

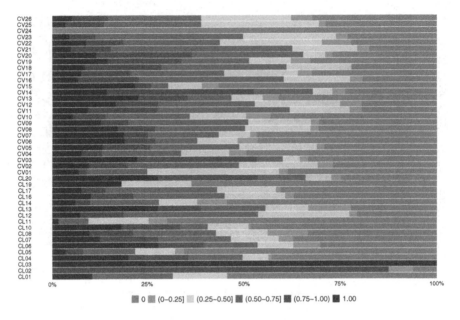

Fig. 6. Distribution of DMM: Each colour represent the range and the size of the bar is the percentage of the patches whose coverage lies within the range

5.6   Threats to Validity

In typical developer workflows, changes to a code repository involve adding/modifying files, staging changes, and pushing to the upstream repository. Developers tend to make multiple commits before pushing upstream. Coverage services are often triggered by pushes or merges to the upstream repository, leading to a lack of one-to-one mapping between commits and coverage reports. This lack of a one-to-one mapping between a commit and coverage service report necessitated using an approach that started from the coverage service end, and gathered all the commits hashes that triggered each build. This means there is no direct one-to-one mapping a between a commit and patch coverage per se. Thus, the patch coverage investigated is patch coverage in the context of triggered builds.

The reliance on coverage service data to analyse patch coverage is a critical factor. The discussion of the Apache/Gobblin data illustrates the potential pitfalls when blindly trusting coverage service data without implementing a rigorous data integrity verification process and employing robust data processing and cleaning methods. To mitigate this, a 30-point EWMA was utilised to smooth the data. Despite the EWMA's effectiveness in filtering out noise, it also introduces a limitation by potentially skewing genuine coverage decreases.

6   Conclusion

A longitudinal study examining testing and maintainability dynamics for small incremental changes is presented. By mining over 50,000 build histories from two popular coverage services, Codecov and Coveralls, it is found that patches are generally either fully covered or entirely uncovered, with rare instances of partial coverage. Patch coverage shows a weak correlation with system coverage, indicating that this metric alone cannot be used to infer the trajectory of system coverage. This, therefore, implies for the development team that patch metrics must be used in conjunction with system metrics for a more thorough understanding of whether the system coverage is improving or not. Patch coverage is also found to have a weak correlation with patch maintainability, suggesting that patch testing may not significantly enhance maintainability. This study contributes to research on fine-grained changes to software systems by replicating two existing studies on an expanded dataset with new projects and by analysing these projects far more comprehensively through processing many more builds. Additionally, the value of leveraging coverage service data for research purposes is emphasised, albeit with a need for data scrutiny and the introduction of data cleaning processes.

References

1. Ben, S.: Patch coverage. https://seriousben.com/posts/2022-02-patch-coverage/. Accessed Feb 2022
2. Cohen, J.: Statistical Power Analysis for the Behavioral Sciences. Lawrence Erlbaum Associates (LEA), 2nd edn. (1988)
3. Coveralls: API returning same commit hash yet different coverage percentage and date (2023). https://github.com/lemurheavy/coveralls-public/issues/1648. (Personal Communication)
4. Di Biase, M., Rastogi, A., Bruntink, M., van Deursen, A.: The delta maintainability model: Measuring maintainability of fine-grained code changes. In: 2019 IEEE/ACM International Conference on Technical Debt (TechDebt), pp. 113–122 (2019). https://doi.org/10.1109/TechDebt.2019.00030
5. Docker: Make better, secure software from the start. https://www.docker.com/. Accessed Aug 2023
6. Elbaum, S., Gable, D., Rothermel, G.: The impact of software evolution on code coverage information. In: Proceedings IEEE International Conference on Software Maintenance. ICSM 2001, pp. 170–179 (2001). https://doi.org/10.1109/ICSM.2001.972727
7. GitHub: Let's build from here: The world's leading AI-powered developer platform. https://github.com/. Accessed Nov 2023
8. Heitlager, I., Kuipers, T., Visser, J.: A practical model for measuring maintainability. In: 6th International Conference on the Quality of Information and Communications Technology (QUATIC 2007), pp. 30–39 (2007). https://doi.org/10.1109/QUATIC.2007.8
9. Hilton, M., Bell, J., Marinov, D.: A large-scale study of test coverage evolution. In: 2018 33rd IEEE/ACM International Conference on Automated Software Engineering (ASE), pp. 53–63 (2018). https://doi.org/10.1145/3238147.3238183
10. Hu, T.: Github issue: Patch coverage formula vs overall coverage ratio. https://github.com/codecov/feedback/issues/55. Accessed Aug 2023
11. Hu, T.: Why patch coverage is more important than project coverage. https://about.codecov.io/blog/why-patch-coverage-is-more-important-than-project-coverage/. Accessed Jan 2024

12. Kuipers, T., Visser, J.: Maintainability index revisited: position paper. In: Special Session on System Quality and Maintainability (SQM 2007) of the 11th European conference on software maintenance and reengineering (CSMR 2007) (2007)

13. Lehman, M.M., Belady, L.A.: Program evolution: processes of software change. Academic Press Professional, USA (1985)

14. Lehman, M.: Programs, life cycles, and laws of software evolution. Proc. IEEE **68**(9), 1060–1076 (1980). https://doi.org/10.1109/PROC.1980.11805

15. Levin, S., Yehudai, A.: The co-evolution of test maintenance and code maintenance through the lens of fine-grained semantic changes. In: 2017 IEEE International Conference on Software Maintenance and Evolution (ICSME), pp. 35–46 (2017). https://doi.org/10.1109/ICSME.2017.9

16. Marinescu, P., Hosek, P., Cadar, C.: Covrig: a framework for the analysis of code, test, and coverage evolution in real software. In: Proceedings of the 2014 International Symposium on Software Testing and Analysis, pp. 93—104. ACM (2014). https://doi.org/10.1145/2610384.2610419

17. Marsavina, C., Romano, D., Zaidman, A.: Studying fine-grained co-evolution patterns of production and test code. In: 2014 IEEE 14th International Working Conference on Source Code Analysis and Manipulation, pp. 195–204 (2014). https://doi.org/10.1109/SCAM.2014.28

18. Merwin, N., Donahoe, L.: Coveralls: deliver better code. https://coveralls.io/. Accessed Nov 2023

19. Midha, V., Palvia, P.: Factors affecting the success of open source software. J. Syst. Softw. **85**(4), 895–905 (2012). https://doi.org/10.1016/j.jss.2011.11.010

20. Moonen, L., van Deursen, A., Zaidman, A., Bruntink, M.: On the interplay between software testing and evolution and its effect on program comprehension. In: Software Evolution, pp. 173–202. Springer, Heidelberg (2008). https://doi.org/10.1007/978-3-540-76440-3_8

21. Nierstrasz, O., Demeyer, S.: Object-oriented reengineering patterns. In: Proceedings of the 26th International Conference on Software Engineering, pp. 734—735. ICSE 2004, IEEE Computer Society, USA (2004)

22. Pinto, L.S., Sinha, S., Orso, A.: Understanding myths and realities of test-suite evolution. In: SIGSOFT FSE (2012). https://api.semanticscholar.org/CorpusID:9072512

23. Runeson, P.: A survey of unit testing practices. IEEE Softw. **23**(4), 22–29 (2006). https://doi.org/10.1109/MS.2006.91

24. Yu, L., Mishra, A.: An empirical study of Lehman's law on software quality evolution. Int. J. Softw. Inform. **7**, 469–481 (2013)

25. Zaidman, A., Rompaey, B., Deursen, A., Demeyer, S.: Studying the co-evolution of production and test code in open source and industrial developer test processes through repository mining. Empir. Softw. Eng. **16**(3), 325–364 (2011)

26. Zaidman, A., Van Rompaey, B., Demeyer, S., van Deursen, A.: Mining software repositories to study co-evolution of production and test code. In: 2008 1st International Conference on Software Testing, Verification, and Validation, pp. 220–229 (2008). https://doi.org/10.1109/ICST.2008.47

Is Transformer-Based Attention Agnostic of the Pretraining Language and Task?

R. H. J. Martin[1]([✉]) [iD], R. Visser[1,2] [iD], and M. Dunaiski[1] [iD]

[1] Computer Science Division, Department of Mathematical Sciences,
Stellenbosch University, Stellenbosch, South Africa
`rivermartin128@gmail.com`, `marceldunaiski@sun.ac.za`
[2] School for Data Science and Computational Thinking, Stellenbosch University,
Stellenbosch, South Africa

Abstract. Since the introduction of the Transformer by Vaswani et al. in 2017, the attention mechanism has been used in multiple state-of-the-art large language models (LLMs), such as BERT, ELECTRA, and various GPT versions. Due to the complexity and the large size of LLMs and deep neural networks in general, intelligible explanations for specific model outputs can be difficult to formulate. However, mechanistic interpretability research aims to make this problem more tractable. In this paper, we show that models with different training objectives—namely, masked language modelling and replaced token detection—have similar internal patterns of attention, even when trained for different languages, in our case English, Afrikaans, Xhosa, and Zulu. This result suggests that, on a high level, the learnt role of attention is language-agnostic.

Keywords: Attention maps · BERT · ELECTRA · Masked language modelling · Replaced token detection · Model interpretability

1 Introduction

The attention mechanism is an integral part of transformer-based natural language models, and in this paper, we focus on the standard attention mechanism implementation as described by Vaswani et al. [23]. Attention is a function that computes updated versions of each of its input embeddings, which are vector representations of tokens from a sequence of text, with information from the other embeddings in the input sequence. For each embedding, the attention function computes a weighted sum of all the input embeddings, with weights specific to the token that will be updated. Transformer-based models use multi-head attention, which applies attention to various representations of the input in parallel, and then aggregates the corresponding contextualized representations of each token. The nested attention functions in multi-head attention are called attention heads, and in this paper we analyse how models trained for different languages use their attention heads. We also show how different pretraining tasks influence the learnt attention heads.

A. Gerber (Ed.): SAICSIT 2024, CCIS 2159, pp. 95–123, 2024.
https://doi.org/10.1007/978-3-031-64881-6_6

The models we consider are based on the Transformer model architecture, which is the foundation of many state-of-the-art language models. Specifically, we pretrain and work with two popular models, namely BERT (Bidirectional Encoder Representations from Transformers) and ELECTRA (Efficiently Learning an Encoder that Classifies Token Replacements Accurately), which are both stacks of Transformer encoder blocks [5,6]. Each encoder block is a multi-head attention unit followed by a feed-forward network. The attention mechanism is used in both encoder and decoder blocks. However, we focus on encoder blocks in this paper because the models we analyse (BERT and ELECTRA) only use encoder blocks.

The main difference between BERT and ELECTRA is that they are pretrained using different tasks as model objectives [5]. BERT is pretrained for masked language modelling, and ELECTRA is pretrained for replaced token detection. Masked language modelling is a pretraining task that involves masking out words randomly and instructing the model to predict the missing words. In contrast, replaced token detection is a pretraining task that requires that the model classify each token in its input as either original or replaced.

Two questions that motivate our work are listed below. The first question is "do differences between the languages used for pretraining affect the attention mechanisms learnt by language models?" and the second is "do models trained for replaced token detection learn the same attention heads as models trained for masked language modelling?" These questions are relevant because it is unknown whether the findings of existing interpretability research are applicable to all languages and to models trained for different pretraining tasks.

Our main finding is that masked language modelling and replaced token detection produce models that use attention in similar ways, independent of which language the models are trained for. Specifically, the models learn to attend strongly to nearby tokens, and to attend slightly more broadly with far less strength. Moreover, they learn to model pairwise relationships between tokens and to use knowledge of these relationships in the calculation of the attention scores. This is evidenced by the results of our experiments, which show empirically that attention maps from ELECTRA models for English, Afrikaans, Xhosa, and Zulu are predictive of pairwise relationships between tokens. One example of such a pairwise relationship is the "object" dependency relation, which the Universal Dependencies contributors [22] describe as relating a verb to the noun phrase that it (the verb) acts on. The relationship is pairwise because it relates two things: the verb and the noun phrase, which is the object that the verb's action is applied to. A specific example of the object relation occurs in the statement "he kicked the ball", where the verb "kicked" is related to the noun phrase "the ball" by the object relation.

We discuss relevant background concepts in Sect. 2, such as multi-head attention and the structure of transformer encoder blocks, which are used by the models in this paper. These concepts are fundamental to this paper because it deals with the intricacies of attention in encoder blocks. After Sect. 2, the rest of this paper is structured as follows: Sect. 3 contains an overview of the analysis of

BERT attention by Clark et al. [4] and an overview of the norm-based approach for analysing language models proposed by Kobayashi et al. [12,13]. In Sect. 4 and Sect. 5, we describe the methodology we followed for our experiments and how we trained our models, as well as our results.

2 Background

2.1 Attention and Multi-head Attention

Multi-head attention is a fundamental component of transformer models.

Vaswani et al. [23] describe attention as a function that maps a query vector and a set of key-value pairs to an output vector. The attention function computes a weighted sum of the value vectors, which is then assigned to the output vector. The weights are determined by the similarity between the query vector and the relevant key vector. In transformer models, scaled dot-product attention is typically used, which applies a scaled dot-product computation on the query and key vectors to represent their similarity. More formally, scaled dot-product attention is defined as

$$\text{Attention}(Q, K, V) = \text{softmax}\left(\frac{QK^T}{\sqrt{d_k}}\right) V \tag{1}$$

where Q, K, and V are matrices whose rows are the query, key, and value vectors, respectively, and d_k is the dimension of the key vectors. The part of Eq. (1) that calculates the attention scores is illustrated in Fig. 1.

Multi-head attention computes attention between multiple representations of the query, key, and value vectors. Learnt projection matrices are used to obtain these representations. Therefore, the attention for the representation i is given as

$$\text{head}_i = \text{Attention}(QW_i^Q, KW_i^K, VW_i^W) \tag{2}$$

where the W_i matrices are the learnt projection matrices. The attention matrices are then concatenated to produce the final output. Finally, multi-head attention is defined by Eq. (3):

$$\text{MultiHeadAttn}(Q, K, V) = \text{Concat}(\text{head}_1, \text{head}_2, \ldots, \text{head}_h)W^O \tag{3}$$

where W^O is another learnt projection matrix that projects the concatenation of the outputs of all the attention heads, which has shape $N \times (hd_v)$, back to the model's internal representation space (the dimension of which is determined by the `embedding_size` parameter). The concatenation and final projection allows the model to aggregate the various representations produced by all the attention heads in a layer.

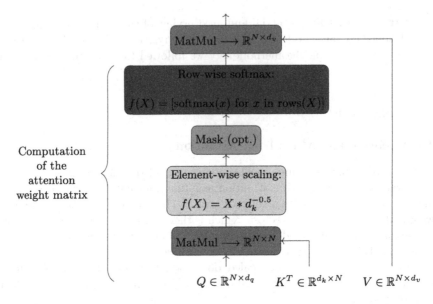

Fig. 1. A flow diagram of the attention weight matrix computation for a single attention head (Adapted from Vaswani et al. [23]). The curly brace indicates the part of the diagram that represents the computation of an attention map. The shapes of the matrices produced by the matrix multiplications are shown to the right of the arrows. The node for the softmax operation shows that the rows of its input are converted to probability distributions. The optional mask operation is not used by the attention mechanisms in BERT and ELECTRA. However, for the sake of completeness, the optional mask operation is used by the extra attention unit in decoder blocks to mask subsequent positions, which restricts attention so that tokens can only attend to themselves or the tokens that occur before them in the sequence. This allows the decoder blocks to perform autoregressive prediction for each position in parallel.

2.2   Transformer Encoder Blocks

The original Transformer encoder was a stack of six identical units, which we call encoder blocks. Each encoder block consists of three components, namely, a multi-head attention unit, a feed-forward neural network, and a normalization function. Each encoder block is organized in accordance with the structure shown in Fig. 2.

The input sequence is fed into the multi-head attention unit, and the output of the unit is fed to a normalization function. Residual connections bypass the multi-head attention unit and add the unprocessed input to the output of the attention unit before normalization. The normalization function is followed by a feed-forward neural network, which again feeds into a normalization function.

The normalization function implements layer normalization [23], which was introduced by Ba, Kiros, and Hinton [2] as a way to speed up training.

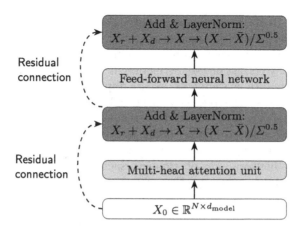

Fig. 2. A diagram of an encoder block (Adapted from Vaswani et al. [23]). X_0 is the input to the encoder block. In the normalization nodes, X_r and X_d represent the direct and residual connections, respectively. Furthermore, $\bar{X}$ and Σ represent the sample mean and a matrix containing the variances of each of the features, respectively. Lastly, the forward slash is used to denote element-wise division, and the exponent of 0.5 should also be applied element-wise.

The gradients with respect to the weights in one layer are very sensitive to changes in the outputs of the preceding layer. Hence, normalizing the outputs of a layer reduces the severity of these changes, which smooths the optimization landscape, thereby facilitating earlier convergence. The layer normalization approach normalizes each element of the input by subtracting the mean and dividing by the standard deviation, where these statistics are computed over the set of input elements that comprise the individual input sequence rather than over the set of input elements for an entire batch of inputs as is done in the batch normalization scheme [2].

2.3 BERT and ELECTRA

BERT (Bidirectional Encoder Representations from Transformers) is a pretrained language model that consists of a stack of transformer encoder blocks [6]. When released, BERT substantially outperformed the best models on all tasks in the General Language Understanding Evaluation (GLUE) benchmark[1]. In this paper, we consider BERT-base, which is a stack of 12 encoder blocks with 12 attention heads in the multi-head attention unit of each block and internal embeddings (which are the internal representations of the tokens) of size 768.

---

[1] Wang et al. [24] introduced the GLUE benchmark, which evaluates natural language understanding through eight text classification tasks (e.g., sentiment analysis of movie reviews) and one regression task (similarity prediction between pairs of sentences).

The input to BERT is a sequence of tokens, which are fundamental units of text. Without going into too much detail, they can be thought of as words or subcomponents of words, such as prefixes, suffixes and individual characters.

A sequence may consist of two distinct segments, which are typically higher-level units of text, such as sentences or paragraphs. In such cases, the segments are separated by a special token ([SEP]) and a learnt representation of the concept of membership in the appropriate segment is added to the internal representation of each token to further distinguish between the two segments.

The segment-pair sequence structure is useful for tasks that require insight into relationships between pairs of segments, such as natural language inference, wherein the model determines whether segment A implies segment B. Moreover, it is useful for framing the next sentence prediction pretraining task, which is a binary classification task whereby the sequence is classified according to whether segment B is a valid continuation of segment A.[2] To facilitate sequence-level classification, i.e. the assignment of a class label to the entire input sequence as a whole (as is required for the next sentence prediction task), another special token ([CLS]) is always prepended to the sequence and the model learns, via pretraining for next sentence prediction or fine-tuning for classification, to encode features of the sequence relevant for sequence-level classification in the representation for this token.

Alternatively, a sequence may comprise only a single segment, with the [CLS] prepended, as is done for every sequence. This sequence structure is useful for downstream tasks that are not framed in terms of pairs of text, such as sentiment analysis and part-of-speech tagging.

For the masked language modelling objective, roughly 15% of the input tokens are masked out, and BERT is tasked to predict their true identities. In other words, BERT is trained to fill in the blank, where the blanks are indicated by a special token ([MASK]).

ELECTRA is a transformer-based model that replaces masked language modelling with a different pretraining approach, and removes the next sentence prediction task entirely[3] [5]. Instead of pretraining for masked language modelling, a pseudo-adversarial approach is used whereby the input sequence is intentionally corrupted, and the model is trained to predict which parts of the input are corrupt.

To corrupt the sequence, approximately 15% of the input tokens are masked out randomly and replaced by predictions made by a smaller model that is designed for masked language modelling, such as BERT. The generator model, which replaces tokens, and the discriminator model, which detects replaced tokens, are trained jointly. In other words, both models are updated in each training step. In comparison, BERT is trained to predict masked out tokens

---

[2] Devlin et al. [6] use the word "sentence" to refer to what we call a "segment" in this paper, which is why we describe "next sentence prediction" in terms of segments, not "sentences".

[3] The motivation behind removing next sentence prediction is explained in Appendix B.

and not to classify tokens as original or replaced [6]. An illustrative example of how masked language modelling and replaced token detection are done when pretraining ELECTRA is shown in Fig. 3.

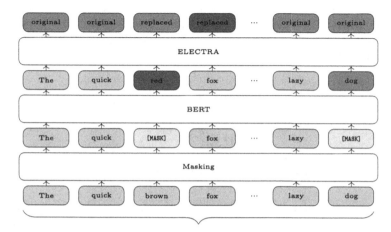

Sequence of input tokens

Fig. 3. An illustrative example of the replaced token detection process [21]. The first two layers represent masked language modelling. The orange rectangles represent original input tokens and the grey rectangles represent tokens that have been masked out at random. BERT makes predictions for the masked out tokens, and they are coloured red if they are incorrect and green if they are correct. BERT's output is then fed to ELECTRA's discriminator model, which classifies tokens as original or replaced. If BERT correctly predicts a masked out token (which is the case for 'dog' in this diagram), we treat it as if it was not masked out when training ELECTRA. Therefore, in this example, if ELECTRA classifies 'dog' as original, it is considered correct.

Clark et al. [5] report that ELECTRA achieves higher GLUE scores than BERT. More precisely, they show that given the same amount of pretraining data, the same amount of compute (the number of floating point operations used for pretraining), and the same internal embedding dimension, ELECTRA achieves higher GLUE scores than BERT. Furthermore, Clark et al. [5] argue that the majority of the improvement of ELECTRA over BERT is due to the loss being defined over the entirety of each training example, rather than just the subset of positions that were masked out, which allows ELECTRA to learn more from each training example. This may be especially important for low-resource languages for which the amount of training text that is available is limited.

2.4   Universal Dependencies

In parts of this paper, we provide evidence for a relationship between attention and pairwise relationships between words, such as dependency relations from the

Universal Dependencies dataset.[4] Hence, we give a brief overview of the Universal Dependencies annotation scheme as it is described by de Marneffe et al. [16].

The Universal Dependencies grammar describes the structure of texts in terms of entities, events, and the words that describe them. Phrases that describe entities are called *nominals* and phrases that describe events are called *clauses*. Subcomponents of nominals and clauses that describe specific attributes are called *modifiers*. Examples of how these terms are used to characterize texts are shown in Fig. 4.

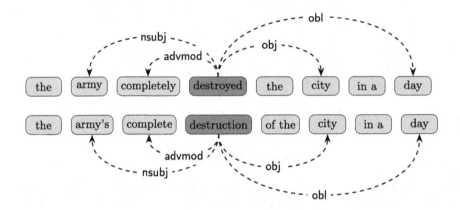

Fig. 4. An example of an annotated nominal (bottom) and an annotated clause (top) (Adapted from de Marneffe et al. [16]). Phrases are structured as trees that stem from a *syntactic head*, which is the core predicate that describes the main idea of the phrase. The other parts of the phrase are *dependents*, which can be nominals, clauses or modifiers. The relationships between the head and its dependents are called dependency relations, of which there are many types. In this example, the object relation (obj) relates the verb "destroy" to the noun "city" that it acts on.

3   Related Work

3.1   Analysis of Attention

Clark et al. [4] analysed BERT attention maps to interpret the behaviour of BERT attention heads. More specifically, they investigated the matrices of attention weights produced by the attention heads, as illustrated in Fig. 2.

They plotted the average attention scores to specific tokens, such as the [CLS] and [SEP] tokens, and calculated the frequencies at which attention heads

---

[4] We use the Universal Dependencies framework because the publicly accessible Universal Dependencies dataset includes annotated Afrikaans texts (specifically, those from [7]), whereas alternatives, such as the Penn treebank which was introduced by Marcus et al. [15] and used by Clark et al. [4] to analyse the attention mechanism of BERT, do not.

attend to the previous token, the current token, and the next token. They found that particular attention heads attend mostly to the previous token or the next token, and that very few attention heads attend mostly to the current token. Additionally, they found that some attention heads often attend almost entirely to the [SEP] token.

Furthermore, Clark et al. [4] trained a probing classifier[5] to predict the syntactic heads of dependency relations using the attention maps as input to the classifier, not token embeddings. They found that specific attention heads specialize in identifying specific dependency relations.

They argued that attention heads attend mostly to [SEP] when their usual role is not required, such as when an attention head that specializes at attending between tokens that are linked by a specific type of dependency relation calculates the attention scores for a token that is not part of a dependency relation of the relevant type. For example, if an attention head specializes in attending between tokens linked by the obj relation, then all the tokens in the sequence that are not parts of nouns and verbs would attend almost entirely to [SEP]. Furthermore, they disregarded the hypothesis that attention to the [SEP] token is used to aggregate segment-level information based on the observation that the attention heads processing [SEP] tokens attend almost entirely to themselves and other [SEP] tokens, instead of broadly across the input sequence.

As a separate experiment, Kobayashi et al. [12] argued that attention-weights alone do not fully describe the relative importance of tokens, because the magnitudes of the vectors that are weighted by attention also affect the contributions of each token to the outputs of the attention mechanism.

In summary, Clark et al. [4] identified and interpreted patterns of attention, and demonstrated that BERT's attention heads are sensitive to dependency relations between tokens and that specific attention heads are sensitive to specific dependency relations.

3.2 Norm-Based Analysis

Kobayashi et al. [12] suggested an alternative to analysing attention weights that accounts for the informativeness of the vectors that are attended to. To explain their approach, they reformulated attention as a weighted sum of transformed vectors, as is shown in Eq. (4):

$$\boldsymbol{y}_{hi} = \Sigma_{j=1}^{N} \alpha_{hij} f_h(\boldsymbol{x}_j) \qquad (4)$$

with $f_h = v_h(\boldsymbol{x}_j) W_h^O$ defining the transformation that produces the transformed vectors used in the weighted sum, where $v_h(\boldsymbol{x}_j)$ produces the value vector representation of $\boldsymbol{x}_j$ for head h, and W_h^O is the part of W^O (from Eq. (3)) that multiplies the output of head h. Using this view of attention, they suggested

---

[5] A probing classifier is a classifier that is used to investigate (probe) a model by showing that some classification problem can be solved using the internal components of the model being investigated (such as attention maps).

using the norm of the weighted transformed vector (i.e. $||\alpha_{hij} f_h(\boldsymbol{x}_j)||$) as a measure of the extent of attention from token i to token j in head h, rather than the weight (i.e. α_{hij}) alone.

Moreover, they showed that tokens that are allocated exceptionally large amounts of attention, such as [SEP], are often associated with transformed vectors (i.e. $f_h(\boldsymbol{x}_j)$) with relatively small magnitudes. In other words, they showed that the norms of the transformed vectors sometimes counteract the effect of scaling by the attention weights. This motivated their analysis of the norms of the weighted transformed vectors, rather than the weights only.

They proceeded to analyse the relationship between the frequencies with which tokens appear in the training text and the norms of their transformed vectors, and found that the norms tend to decrease as the frequency of the tokens increase. More specifically, they found a significant Spearman rank correlation coefficient of 0.75 between the frequencies of tokens and the norms of their transformed vectors (i.e. $||f_h(\boldsymbol{x}_j)||$), and they did not find a significant correlation between the frequencies of tokens and their attention-weights. This shows that BERT learns to decrease the norms of the transformed vectors of highly frequent tokens rather than to decrease the attention weights for such tokens.

4   Methodology

For this paper, we pretrained case-sensitive base-sized ELECTRA models for Afrikaans, Xhosa, and Zulu as well as one BERT[6] model for Afrikaans and one case-insensitive ELECTRA model for English. The Afrikaans, English, Xhosa, and Zulu models were trained, respectively, using 5.1 GB, 1 GB, 158 MB, and 675 MB of text from mC4 [19]. Furthermore, the input texts were tokenized using tokenizer classes from Hugging Face [9,10], which implement the Wordpiece algorithm introduced by Wu et al. [26]. More pretraining details, such as specific hyperparameter values and the number of steps used to pretrain each model, are provided in Appendix C.

For part of our analysis, we executed our trained models on 60 example input sequences and saved the norm matrices for every attention head, where each norm matrix is structured as an attention weight matrix, but contains the norms of the weighted transformed vectors (i.e. $||\alpha_{hij} f_h(\boldsymbol{x}_j)||$). Equation (5) defines the norm matrix from head h on a single example input sequence. The row index of the matrix corresponds to the position of the attending token in the sequence, and the column index corresponds to the position of the attended-to token in the sequence.

$$M = [[||\alpha_{hij} f_h(\boldsymbol{x}_j)|| \text{ for } j \text{ in } 1 \ldots N] \text{ for } i \text{ in } 1 \ldots N] \tag{5}$$

---

[6] We used the same variant of BERT as Clark et al. [5], which differs from the original BERT in that it is not pretrained with next sentence prediction and a different learning rate is used.

We chose to analyse norm matrices instead of attention weight matrices because norm matrices provide more accurate representations of the relative importance of tokens because they take into account the informativeness of the tokens that are attended to.

In order to compare how our models use their attention heads, we compute the mean of the norm matrices for each attention head to produce representations of the typical pattern of attention and then cluster these means using the k-means clustering algorithm. This decision is based on the observation by Clark et al. [4] that five main patterns of attention exist, namely, broad attention, focus on previous token, focus on next token, focus on [SEP], and focus on punctuation, and we wanted to determine whether our models learnt the same patterns. Furthermore, we wanted to determine whether models trained for different languages and different model objectives use their attention heads in different ways or use their attention heads for the same interpretable roles.

We also train probing classifiers that take norm matrices as inputs and predict the presence or absence of known pairwise relationships between tokens. The goal of training and evaluating these classifiers was to find evidence that the models learn these pairwise relationships. Specifically, we predicted the heads of dependency relations with the aim of showing that the models learn the same grammatical relationships between words that humans have identified.

To further establish evidence for the influence of pairwise relationships on attention, we analysed the norms for pairs of tokens that are part of the same named entity, for both BERT and ELECTRA. Specifically, we used the Mann Whitney U test to test the hypothesis that an attention head attends more between such pairs of tokens than between other pairs of adjacent tokens.

5 Experiments and Results

5.1 Norm-Based Characterization of Attention Heads

We extracted the norm matrices from each of our models using input sequences from the Wura dataset introduced by Oladipo et al. [18], which contains unannotated text documents for 16 African languages and was developed by further cleaning mC4 and expanding upon it with additional web-scraping. Specifically, we used the first 60 entries of each of the training sets that our tokenizers tokenize into at least 125 tokens. We represented these inputs with the two segment structure described in Sect. 2.3 by truncating the tokenized input and then adding [CLS] and two [SEP] tokens to get 60 input sequences that each consist of exactly 128 tokens. For each attention head, we then computed the mean norm matrix by averaging over the norm matrices produced using each of these sequences.

Using these norm matrices, we computed the average of the sum of the norms for each attention head and token category considered by Kobayashi et al. [12] (namely, [CLS], [SEP], punctuation, and "other"). The average summed norms for our Afrikaans models are shown in Fig. 5, while the corresponding figures for the English, Xhosa, and Zulu models are shown in the Appendix (Fig. 11). They show that, in agreement with the findings of Kobayashi et al. [12] and in contrast to the findings of Clark et al. [4], none of the attention heads in our models focus intensely on special tokens or punctuation tokens.

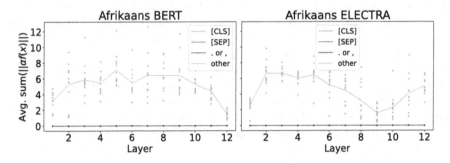

Fig. 5. The average sums of the norms for tokens of different types for our Afrikaans BERT (left) and ELECTRA (right). The dots show the averages for the specific attention heads, and the lines show the average of the averages for the attention heads in each layer. Neither model attends mostly to punctuation tokens or [SEP] tokens.

Subsequently, we used the k-means unsupervised clustering algorithm to partition the attention heads based on their mean norm matrices into three groups. We clustered the attention heads into three groups instead of five because we know that none of our models learn attention heads that attend mostly to [SEP] and punctuation tokens (commas and periods), which eliminates the possibility of two of the patterns observed by Clark et al. [4]. The cluster means for the Afrikaans ELECTRA models are shown in Fig. 6. The clusters for the other models are shown in Appendix E (Figs. 17, 18, 19, and 20). However, k-means produces very similar clusters for all the models.

For additional context, the mean norm matrices that were clustered for the Afrikaans BERT and the Afrikaans, English, Xhosa, and Zulu ELECTRA models can be seen in Appendix E, Figs. 12, 13, 14, 15 and 16, respectively. They are all very similar and show that the clusters found by k-means are reasonable.

The norm values seem to be determined largely by the relative positions of the attending token and the attended-to token. However, in Sect. 5.2 we show that other known pairwise relationships between tokens, such as dependency relations, also influence the norm values. All models tend to focus on tokens that are nearby. In general, it seems that the attention heads either focus a lot on the previous few tokens or the next few tokens, or they focus a little on a relatively broad range of tokens.

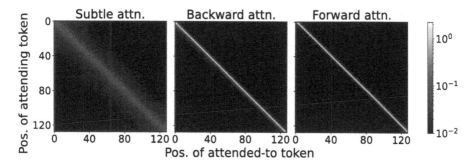

Fig. 6. Heatmaps of the norm matrix cluster means for our Afrikaans ELECTRA model. The clusters were formed by running K-means on the 144 mean norm matrices shown in Appendix E.1, Fig. 13. The cluster on the left (titled "Subtle attn.") attends very slightly to a narrow range of the surrounding tokens. The cluster in the middle (titled "Backward attn.") attends almost entirely to the next token, while the cluster on the right (titled "Forward attn.") attends almost entirely to the previous token.

5.2 Normalized Attention and Known Pairwise Relationships Between Tokens

Using Annotations from the Universal Dependencies Dataset. We used the norm matrices produced by our models to predict the heads of dependency relations between words.[7] To compute the norm matrices (as described in Eq. 5), we used the AfriBooms and English EWT subsets of the Universal Dependencies dataset [7,17]. We reduced the size of the English EWT subset to match that of the AfriBooms subset, and we only used subsamples (the 450 longest example sequences) of each, due to the norm matrices using large amounts of memory and storage space.

We trained the attention-only probing classifiers described by Clark et al. [4] to make the predictions, using information from all attention heads. These classifiers learn the probability distribution $p(i|j)$, which denotes the probability of the i-th word being the syntactic head of a dependency relation between the i-th and j-th words in the input sequence, using only the norm matrices produced by the BERT or ELECTRA model. The q-th word is then predicted to be the head of a dependency relation involving word j, where $q = \arg\max_i p(i|j)$. A more detailed description of these classifiers is provided in Appendix D.

Table 1 show the results of this experiment. Our probing classifiers achieve similar accuracy scores to the 61% observed by Clark et al. [4] for English BERT, and they all substantially out-perform the simple right-branching baseline.

Using Translated Annotations. The Universal Dependencies dataset does not have dependency parse trees for Xhosa and Zulu, so we translated the English dataset into each language. Specifically, we translated the reduced English EWT

---

[7] Dependency relations and their syntactic heads are explained in Sect. 2.4.

Table 1. Accuracy achieved on input sequences from expert-annotated dependency relation data, for each model and language.

Language	Prediction model	Accuracy
Afrikaans	Attn-only probe for BERT	63.2
	Attn-only probe for ELECTRA	58.7
	Right-branching baseline	25.7
English	Attn-only probe for BERT	61.4
	Attn-only probe for ELECTRA	63.6
	Right-branching baseline	29.9

subset of the Universal Dependencies dataset [17] to Afrikaans, Xhosa, and Zulu. We used the Google Translate API to construct translation dictionaries, which we used to produce word-aligned direct translations. Using these translations, we repeated the previous experiment.

For each language, the accuracy is shown in Table 2. The accuracy achieved by the probing classifier for the Afrikaans model is only slightly lower than when it was trained using the norm matrices from the native (not translated) dataset. The probing classifiers associated with the Xhosa and Zulu models also surpass the right-branching baseline. These scores show that known pairwise relationships between tokens influence attention in all of our models.

Table 2. Accuracy achieved by probing classifiers trained on norm matrices generated from direct translations, for each language. This table only shows the result for our ELECTRA models.

Language	Prediction model	Accuracy
All four languages	Right-branching baseline	29.9
Afrikaans	Attn-only probe for ELECTRA	56.3
Xhosa	Attn-only probe for ELECTRA	42.8
Zulu	Attn-only probe for ELECTRA	47.2

It should be noted, that once dependency relation annotations for Xhosa and Zulu are officially incorporated into the Universal Dependencies dataset, our work could be extended by using the higher quality data to repeat this experiment. This would show whether the dictionary-based translations we used can account for the relatively low accuracy scores that we observed for our models of Xhosa and Zulu.

5.3   Norms Between Pairs of Tokens from Named-Entities

We extracted the norm matrices from all our models for the first 1500 entries of one of three annotated datasets for named entity recognition. For the Zulu and

Xhosa models, we used the MasakhaNER2.0 dataset from Adelani et al. [1], and for the Afrikaans and English models, we used the NCHLT and CON-LLPP datasets from Eiselen and Puttkammer [8], and Wang et al. [25] and Sang and De Meulder [20], respectively. All these datasets consist primarily of news articles annotated with named entity tags for categories such as name of person and name of organization, except for NCHLT, which primarily consists of annotated texts from South African government websites. Furthermore, between roughly 11% and 16% of the tokens in each dataset are tagged as being part of a named entity. Lastly, the Zulu and Xhosa subsets of MasakhaNER2.0 comprise roughly 127 thousand tokens each, and the Afrikaans and English training sets of NCHLT and CONLLPP comprise 229 thousand and 203 thousand tokens.

After extracting the norms, we partitioned them according to whether they were between two adjacent tokens that are part of the same named entity, or simply two adjacent tokens. To make the datasets more comparable, we then filtered them based on the named-entity category so that only the labels common between all our datasets were used. The labels from each dataset before and after this filtering are shown in Appendix E, Figs. 9 and 10, respectively.

Subsequently, for each attention head, we used the Mann Whitney U test to test the hypothesis that the norms for adjacent named entity tokens are higher than is typical for adjacent tokens. More specifically, we tested the null hypothesis that $\mu_i \leq \mu_i'$, where μ_i is the mean of the norms associated with adjacent named entities (from the perspective of head i), and μ_i' is the mean of the norms associated with other adjacent tokens. Furthermore, to prevent differences in the statistical power of the tests for each model from biasing our results due to different Type 2 error rates, we sampled $n_{ne} = 3620$ of the norms between adjacent named-entity tokens and $n_{adj} = 36290$ of the norms between other adjacent tokens, for each set of norms.

Figure 7 shows the total number of attention heads from each model that attend significantly more (at significance level $\alpha = 0.05$) to adjacent named entity tokens, and that between 59.7% and 72.9% of the attention heads in each model attend more to named entity tokens. More generally, this shows that whether tokens are part of named entities influences the attention patterns of all the models we considered. A finer-grained visualization that shows the counts for each layer of our models is shown in Appendix E, Fig. 8.

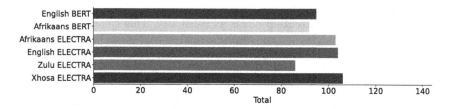

Fig. 7. The total number of attention heads that focus more on named entity tokens than is typical for adjacent tokens. The totals are roughly the same for all the models.

6 Conclusion

All our BERT and ELECTRA models appear to use their attention mechanisms in mostly the same way, irrespective of which language they were trained for. Specifically, their attention-heads typically focus intensely on local context, or attend more broadly over the input sequence with much less intensity. Moreover, interpretable relationships between tokens, such as dependency relations and being part of the same named entity, appear to influence what our BERT and ELECTRA models focus on.

Therefore, our analysis seems to indicate that the projection matrices learned for the attention mechanisms will be transferrable between models for different languages. This complements the work of Chi, Hewett, and Manning [3], which shows that mBERT (a multilingual BERT) learns syntactic features that are common between languages, in explaining how multilingual pretraining results in effective cross lingual transfer learning. Specifically, our findings may help to explain this phenomenon by tentatively suggesting that transferrable parameters for the attention heads can be learned from any monolingual natural language corpus. Furthermore, it may also be possible for models to learn similar transferrable attention head parameters from any sufficiently large and clean multilingual or code-switched natural language corpus.

If this conjecture holds, the cost of pretraining models for low-resource languages could be reduced by fixing the attention head parameters to values learned by architecturally similar existing models of high-resource languages. However, future work that empirically tests whether the attention head parameters are transferrable between models for different languages is needed. Ways to test this conjecture are suggested in Appendix A.

Acknowledgements. This research was supported in part by Google's TPU Research Cloud program, and in part by the National Research Foundation of South Africa (Ref. Number PMDS22111872903).

Appendix A   Suggested Future Work

Subsequent work could test our conjecture by taking the pretrained parameters of the attention heads of an existing model, such as an English ELECTRA model, and then pretraining the other parts of the model "from scratch" while treating the parameters for the attention heads as constants. This could be done for a variety of target languages, and the resulting models could then be benchmarked.

Presumably, the models would achieve results comparable to those from models trained entirely from scratch. Additionally, such a procedure could be done repeatedly with the pretrained parameters from a variety of different languages, and different combinations of languages, to further test whether transferrable attention parameters can be learned from any language or any set of languages.

Appendix B   An Explanation of Why Next Sentence Prediction is No Longer Used

The classification token and the two-segment sequence representation are useful for classification tasks, specifically for expressing downstream tasks for fine-tuning and inference. However, the usefulness of the next sentence prediction task has been disputed and subsequent pretraining methods, such as ELECTRA, introduced by Clark et al. [5], RoBERTa by Liu et al. [14], XLNet by Yang et al. [27], and SpanBERT by Joshi et al. [11], do not involve the task. For example, Yang et al. [27], Liu et al. [14], and Joshi et al. [11] tested their pretraining approaches with and without next sentence prediction for a variety of language understanding benchmarks and did not observe improvements by including the next sentence prediction model objective. Moreover, Joshi et al. [11] found that pretraining for next sentence prediction resulted in worse performance for various language understanding benchmarks, and suggested that the negative examples used for next sentence prediction (i.e., pairs of unrelated texts) add noise to the data that reduces the effectiveness of the other pretraining tasks because the model is forced to condition its predictions on the irrelevant text in the unrelated segment.

Appendix C   Hyperparameter Values Used to Pretrain Our Models

The number of pretraining steps used to train our models are shown in Table 3. The English ELECTRA model was trained for the same number of steps as in Clark et al. [5], i.e. 766 thousand. The other ELECTRA models were trained for more steps than the English model, however, they stopped improving significantly after only 300 thousand steps. Lastly, the other hyperparameters for our models are shown in Table 4.

Table 3. The number of training steps used to train each model. The first and second column specify the model type (BERT or ELECTRA), and the language that the model was trained for. The third column specifies the number of steps used to pretrain a model, which controls the number of times the models parameters are updated at during training. The number of steps used for training is a hyperparameter.

Model	Language	Steps (in thousands)
ELECTRA	English	766
ELECTRA	Afrikaans	1000
ELECTRA	Xhosa	1000
ELECTRA	Zulu	1000
BERT	Afrikaans	1400

Appendix D   Description of Probing Classifiers

The probing classifiers learn the probability distribution described by Eq. (6):

$$p(i|j) \propto \exp\left(\sum_{k=1}^{n} w_k \alpha_{kij} + u_k \alpha_{kji}\right) \tag{6}$$

where $p(i|j)$ denotes the probability of the i-th word being the syntactic head of a dependency relation between the i-th and j-th words in the input sequence, α_{kij} is the attention weight from word i to word j that is produced by the k-th attention head, and u_k and w_k are learnt parameters associated with the k-th attention head. Lastly, the q-th word is predicted to be the head of a dependency relation involving word j, where $q = \arg\max_i p(i|j)$. However, for our experiments, we used the norms of the weighted transformed vectors instead of the attention weights. Moreover, we trained the classifiers using TensorFlow's `AdamOptimizer`, with a learning rate of 0.2%, until the accuracy for the validation set stopped improving.

Appendix E   Additional Results

Figures 9 and 10 show the number of annotations of each type in the named entity datasets before and after filtering. For context, Sang and De Meulder [20] explain that tags of the form "B-XXX" are used to indicate the beginning of a new sequence of tokens of type "XXX" when the new sequence directly follows another sequence of tokens for a different named entity of the same type. In other words, "B-XXX" distinguishes between consecutive named entities of the same type. Furthermore, tags of the form "I-XXX" indicate tokens that are part of (i.e. inside) a named entity of type "XXX".

Table 4. The hyperparameters used to train and run all of our models. This table contains hyperparameter values necessary to load our models correctly for inference and finetuning.

Hyperparameter	Value
attention_probs_dropout_prob	0.1
embedding_size	768
hidden_act	gelu
hidden_dropout_prob	0.1
hidden_size	768
intermediate_size	3072
layer_norm_eps	1e-12
max_position_embeddings	128
num_attention_heads	12
num_hidden_layers	12
position_embedding_type	absolute
summary_activation	gelu
summary_last_dropout	0.1

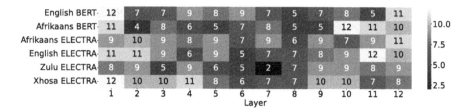

Fig. 8. The number of attention heads, in each layer of our models, that focus more on named entity tokens than is typical for adjacent tokens. The rows are ordered by the size of the dataset used for pretraining the model. There does not seem to be a consistent pattern in how the attention heads that focus more on named entity tokens are positioned in the layers of the model.

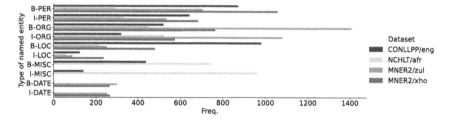

Fig. 9. The frequency of each type of named entity in each dataset. The B-MISC, I-MISC, B-DATE, and I-DATE named entity categories seem to be outliers. Aside from these categories, the datasets seem comparable.

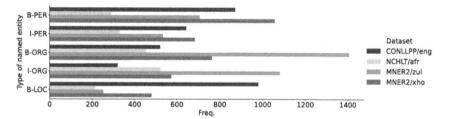

Fig. 10. A visualization of the frequency of each type of named entity after filtering out the named entity types that are not well represented in every dataset (i.e. B-MISC, I-MISC, B-DATE, and I-DATE). These filtered datasets seem comparable.

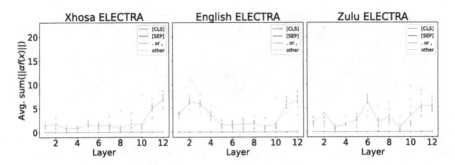

Fig. 11. The average sums of the norms for tokens of different types for our Xhosa (left), English (middle) and Zulu (right) models. The dots show the averages for the specific attention heads, and the lines show the meta-average for each layer (the average of the averages for the attention heads in a layer). None of the models attend mostly to punctuation tokens or [SEP] tokens.

E.1   Mean Norm Matrices

This section contains visualizations of the mean norm matrices associated with each attention head. The colour bars in each figure indicate how the values of the mean of the norms of the weighted transformed vectors (i.e. the mean of $\|\alpha_{hij} f_h(\boldsymbol{x}_j)\|$ from Eq. (4), computed over the values from different input sequences of length 128, as explained in Sect. 5.1) are represented.

Furthermore, each row of a figure in this section represents the attention heads in a layer of a model. The first row contains the attention heads from the first layer of the model, the second row contains the attention heads from the second layer of the model, etc. The position of a head within a layer is arbitrary and inconsequential.

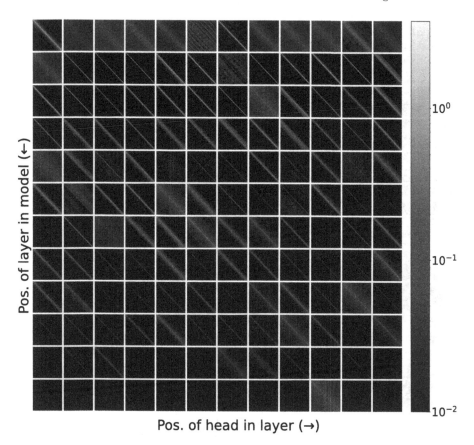

Pos. of head in layer (→)

Fig. 12. Mean norm matrices from Afrikaans BERT. See the introduction to this section (Sect. E.1) for an explanation of the colour bar and how grid positions in the plot are associated with attention heads from the model. These mean norm matrices were clustered with K-means, and the cluster centroids are shown in Fig. 17.

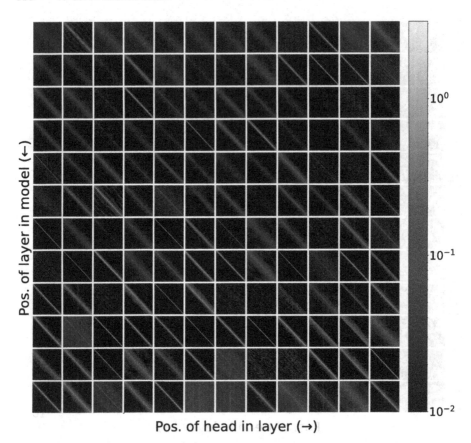

Fig. 13. Mean norm matrices from Afrikaans ELECTRA. See the introduction to this section (Sect. E.1) for an explanation of the colour bar and how grid positions in the plot are associated with attention heads from the model. These mean norm matrices were clustered with K-means, and the cluster centroids are shown in Fig. 6.

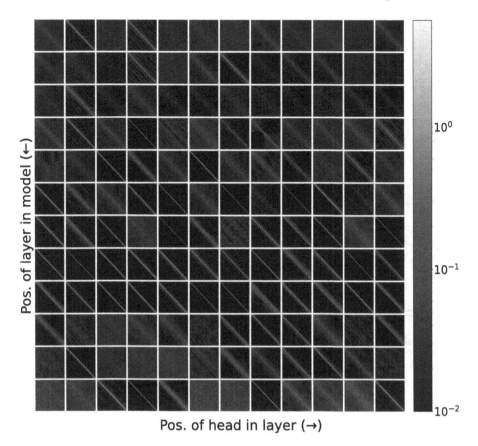

Fig. 14. Mean norm matrices from English ELECTRA. See the introduction to this section (Sect. E.1) for an explanation of the colour bar and how grid positions in the plot are associated with attention heads from the model. These mean norm matrices were clustered with K-means, and the cluster centroids are shown in Fig. 18.

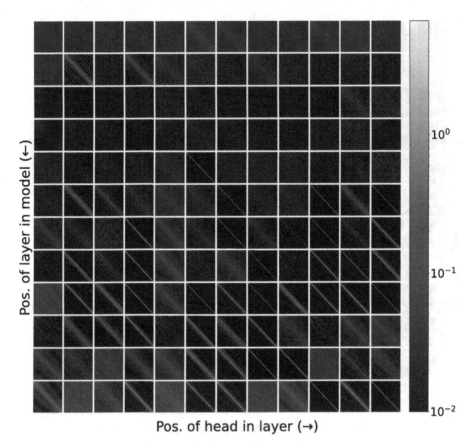

Fig. 15. Mean norm matrices from Xhosa ELECTRA. See the introduction to this section (Sect. E.1) for an explanation of the colour bar and how grid positions in the plot are associated with attention heads from the model. These mean norm matrices were clustered with K-means, and the cluster centroids are shown in Fig. 19.

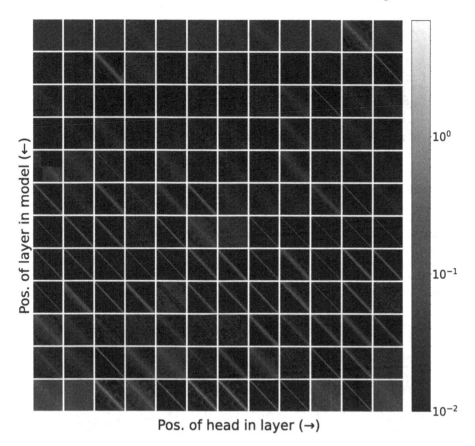

Fig. 16. Mean norm matrices from Zulu ELECTRA. See the introduction to this section (Sect. E.1) for an explanation of the colour bar and how grid positions in the plot are associated with attention heads from the model. These mean norm matrices were clustered with K-means, and the cluster centroids are shown in Fig. 20.

E.2   Norm Matrix Cluster Means

For each model, this section contains a visualization of the cluster centroids produced by clustering the 144 mean norm matrices associated with the model (which are visualized in the relevant Fig. from Sect. E.1), using K-means (with $K = 3$). The colour bars show how the values of the mean of the mean norms (the mean of all the mean matrices that are in the same cluster) are represented.

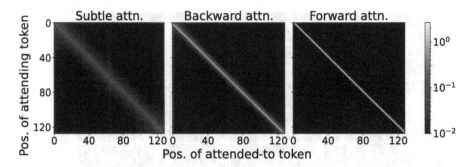

Fig. 17. Heatmaps of the norm matrix cluster means for our Afrikaans BERT model. The clusters were formed by running K-means on the 144 mean norm matrices shown in Fig. 12. The colour bar on the right indicates the value of the mean (computed from matrices in the same cluster) of the mean norm matrices. The cluster on the left (titled "Subtle attn.") attends very slightly to a narrow range of the surrounding tokens. The cluster in the middle (titled "Backward attn.") attends almost entirely to the next token, while the cluster on the right (titled "Forward attn.") attends almost entirely to the previous token.

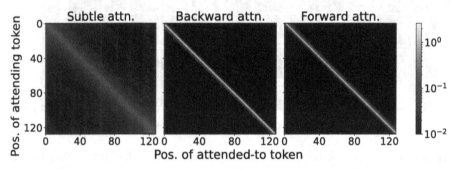

Fig. 18. Heatmaps of the norm matrix cluster means for our English ELECTRA model. The clusters were formed by running K-means on the 144 mean norm matrices shown in Fig. 14. The colour bar on the right indicates the value of the mean (computed from matrices in the same cluster) of the mean norm matrices. The cluster on the left (titled "Subtle attn.") attends very slightly to a narrow range of the surrounding tokens. The cluster in the middle (titled "Backward attn.") attends almost entirely to the next token, while the cluster on the right (titled "Forward attn.") attends almost entirely to the previous token.

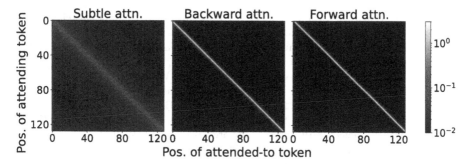

Fig. 19. Heatmaps of the norm matrix cluster means for our Xhosa ELECTRA model. The clusters were formed by running K-means on the 144 mean norm matrices shown in Fig. 15. The colour bar on the right indicates the value of the mean (computed from matrices in the same cluster) of the mean norm matrices. The cluster on the left (titled "Subtle attn.") attends very slightly to a narrow range of the surrounding tokens. The cluster in the middle (titled "Backward attn.") attends almost entirely to the next token, while the cluster on the right (titled "Forward attn.") attends almost entirely to the previous token.

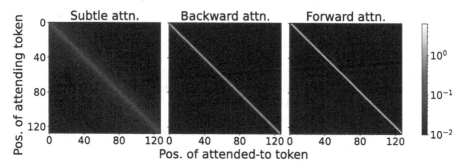

Fig. 20. Heatmaps of the norm matrix cluster means for our Zulu ELECTRA model. The clusters were formed by running K-means on the 144 mean norm matrices shown in Fig. 16. The colour bar on the right indicates the value of the mean (computed from matrices in the same cluster) of the mean norm matrices. The cluster on the left (titled "Subtle attn.") attends very slightly to a narrow range of the surrounding tokens. The cluster in the middle (titled "Backward attn.") attends almost entirely to the next token, while the cluster on the right (titled "Forward attn.") attends almost entirely to the previous token.

References

1. Adelani, D., et al.: MasakhaNER 2.0: Africa-centric transfer learning for named entity recognition. In: Proceedings of the 2022 Conference on Empirical Methods in Natural Language Processing, pp. 4488–4508. Association for Computational Linguistics, Abu Dhabi (2022). https://doi.org/10.18653/v1/2022.emnlp-main.298
2. Ba, J.L., Kiros, J.R., Hinton, G.E.: Layer normalization. arXiv preprint arXiv:1607.06450 (2016). https://doi.org/10.48550/arXiv.1607.06450

3. Chi, E.A., Hewitt, J., Manning, C.D.: Finding universal grammatical relations in multilingual BERT. In: Proceedings of the 58th Annual Meeting of the Association for Computational Linguistics, pp. 5564–5577. Association for Computational Linguistics, Online (2020). https://doi.org/10.18653/v1/2020.acl-main.493

4. Clark, K., Khandelwal, U., Levy, O., Manning, C.D.: What does BERT look at? An analysis of BERT's attention. In: Linzen, T., Chrupała, G., Belinkov, Y., Hupkes, D. (eds.) Proceedings of the 2019 ACL Workshop BlackboxNLP: Analyzing and Interpreting Neural Networks for NLP, pp. 276–286. Association for Computational Linguistics, Florence (2019). https://doi.org/10.18653/v1/W19-4828

5. Clark, K., Luong, M.T., Le, Q.V., Manning, C.D.: ELECTRA: pre-training text encoders as discriminators rather than generators. In: International Conference on Learning Representations. Online (2020). https://openreview.net/forum?id=r1xMH1BtvB

6. Devlin, J., Chang, M.W., Lee, K., Toutanova, K.: BERT: pre-training of deep bidirectional transformers for language understanding. arXiv preprint arXiv:1810.04805 (2018). https://doi.org/10.48550/arXiv.1810.04805

7. Dirix, P., Augustinus, L., van Niekerk, D.: UD afrikaans-afribooms (2017). https://github.com/UniversalDependencies/UD_Afrikaans-AfriBooms. Accessed 16 May 2024

8. Eiselen, R., Puttkammer, M.: Developing text resources for ten South African languages. In: Calzolari, N., et al. (eds.) Proceedings of the Ninth International Conference on Language Resources and Evaluation (LREC 2014), pp. 3698–3703. European Language Resources Association (ELRA), Reykjavik (2014). http://www.lrec-conf.org/proceedings/lrec2014/pdf/1151_Paper.pdf

9. Hugging Face: BERT tokenizer documentation. https://huggingface.co/docs/transformers/model_doc/bert. Accessed 21 Mar 2024

10. Hugging Face: ELECTRA tokenizer documentation. https://huggingface.co/docs/transformers/en/model_doc/electra. Accessed 31 Mar 2024

11. Joshi, M., Chen, D., Liu, Y., Weld, D.S., Zettlemoyer, L., Levy, O.: SpanBERT: improving pre-training by representing and predicting spans. Trans. Assoc. Comput. Linguist. 8, 64–77 (2020). https://doi.org/10.1162/tacl_a_00300

12. Kobayashi, G., Kuribayashi, T., Yokoi, S., Inui, K.: Attention is not only a weight: analyzing transformers with vector norms. In: Webber, B., Cohn, T., He, Y., Liu, Y. (eds.) Proceedings of the 2020 Conference on Empirical Methods in Natural Language Processing (EMNLP), pp. 7057–7075. Association for Computational Linguistics, Online (2020). https://doi.org/10.18653/v1/2020.emnlp-main.574

13. Kobayashi, G., Kuribayashi, T., Yokoi, S., Inui, K.: Incorporating residual and normalization layers into analysis of masked language models. In: Proceedings of the 2021 Conference on Empirical Methods in Natural Language Processing, pp. 4547–4568. Association for Computational Linguistics, Online and Punta Cana (2021). https://doi.org/10.18653/v1/2021.emnlp-main.373

14. Liu, Y., et al.: RoBERTa: a robustly optimized bert pretraining approach. arXiv preprint arXiv:1907.11692 (2019). https://doi.org/10.48550/arXiv.1907.11692

15. Marcus, M.P., Santorini, B., Marcinkiewicz, M.A.: Building a large annotated corpus of English: the Penn treebank. Comput. Linguist. 19(2), 313–330 (1993). https://aclanthology.org/J93-2004

16. de Marneffe, M.C., Manning, C.D., Nivre, J., Zeman, D.: Universal dependencies. Comput. Linguist. 47(2), 255–308 (2021). https://doi.org/10.1162/coli_a_00402

17. Nivre, J., et al.: Universal dependencies (2022). https://universaldependencies.org/

18. Oladipo, A., et al.: Better quality pre-training data and t5 models for African languages. In: Bouamor, H., Pino, J., Bali, K. (eds.) Proceedings of the 2023 Conference on Empirical Methods in Natural Language Processing, pp. 158–168. Association for Computational Linguistics, Singapore (2023). https://aclanthology.org/2023.emnlp-main.11

19. Raffel, C., et al.: Exploring the limits of transfer learning with a unified text-to-text transformer. J. Mach. Learn. Res. **21**(140), 1–67 (2020). http://jmlr.org/papers/v21/20-074.html

20. Tjong Kim Sang, E.F., De Meulder, F.: Introduction to the CoNLL-2003 shared task: language-independent named entity recognition. In: Proceedings of the Seventh Conference on Natural Language Learning at HLT-NAACL 2003, pp. 142–147. Edmonton, Canada (2003). https://aclanthology.org/W03-0419

21. du Toit, J., Dunaiski, M.: Hierarchical text classification using language models with global label-wise attention mechanisms. In: Pillay, A., Jembere, E., Gerber, A.J. (eds.) SACAIR 2023. CCIS, vol. 1976, pp. 267–284. Springer, Cham (2023). https://doi.org/10.1007/978-3-031-49002-6_18

22. Universal Dependencies contributors: Universal dependencies documentation (2023). https://universaldependencies.org/u/dep/obj.html

23. Vaswani, A., et al.: Attention is all you need. In: Guyon, I., et al. (eds.) Advances in Neural Information Processing Systems, vol. 30, pp. 5998–6008. Curran Associates, Inc., Long Beach (2017). https://proceedings.neurips.cc/paper_files/paper/2017/file/3f5ee243547dee91fbd053c1c4a845aa-Paper.pdf

24. Wang, A., Singh, A., Michael, J., Hill, F., Levy, O., Bowman, S.: GLUE: a multitask benchmark and analysis platform for natural language understanding. In: Linzen, T., Chrupała, G., Alishahi, A. (eds.) Proceedings of the 2018 EMNLP Workshop BlackboxNLP: Analyzing and Interpreting Neural Networks for NLP, pp. 353–355. Association for Computational Linguistics, Brussels (2018). https://doi.org/10.18653/v1/W18-5446

25. Wang, Z., Shang, J., Liu, L., Lu, L., Liu, J., Han, J.: CrossWeigh: training named entity tagger from imperfect annotations. In: Inui, K., Jiang, J., Ng, V., Wan, X. (eds.) Proceedings of the 2019 Conference on Empirical Methods in Natural Language Processing and the 9th International Joint Conference on Natural Language Processing (EMNLP-IJCNLP), pp. 5154–5163. Association for Computational Linguistics, Hong Kong (2019). https://doi.org/10.18653/v1/D19-1519

26. Wu, Y., et al.: Google's neural machine translation system: bridging the gap between human and machine translation. arXiv preprint arXiv:1609.08144 (2016). https://doi.org/10.48550/arXiv.1609.08144

27. Yang, Z., Dai, Z., Yang, Y., Carbonell, J., Salakhutdinov, R., Le, Q.V.: XLNet: generalized autoregressive pretraining for language understanding (2020)

Age-Related Face Recognition Using Siamese Networks and Vision Transformers

P. J. Mertens and Mkhuseli Ngxande[(⊠)] [ID]

Stellenbosch University, Stellenbosch, South Africa
pieter.mertens@axxess.co.za, ngxandem@sun.ac.za

Abstract. Face recognition plays a crucial role in various applications, ranging from security to personal convenience. Recent advancements have emphasized the importance of recognizing individuals based on age-related facial features within this domain. This paper presents a comprehensive evaluation of two deep learning architectures for age-based face recognition: Siamese Convolutional Networks (SCNs) and Vision Transformers (ViTs). Convolutional Neural Networks (CNNs), which are critical in modern face recognition, serve as the backbone for Siamese Convolutional Networks (SCNs). SCNs are specifically designed to detect similarities between input pairs by emphasising local features crucial for age-related distinctions. In contrast, ViTs, initially developed for natural language processing, have demonstrated promising performance in image recognition, showcasing their aptitude for capturing global image context. This work investigates the performance of these distinct architectures in discerning age-related variations within facial data features. Performance comparisons were conducted on three established SCN models and two ViT architectures. The results revealed that the optimal SCNs primarily focused on the mouth, nose, and eye regions, indicating their reliance on local features for age estimation. Interestingly, the ViT models achieved superior performance despite lacking explicit feature localization. This suggests that a holistic understanding of the facial context may be more effective than focusing solely on isolated features for age-based recognition.

Keywords: Age-Based Face Recognition · Siamese Networks · Vision Transformers

1 Introduction

Motivated by the recent advancements in deep learning, facial recognition technology has undergone a significant transformation. Applications now encompass a broad spectrum, ranging from user authentication on smartphones to more complex functionalities in security systems, social media platforms, and surveillance [36]. Traditionally, facial recognition pipelines have consisted of three distinct stages: face detection, face alignment, and recognition itself [40]. In this

© The Author(s), under exclusive license to Springer Nature Switzerland AG 2024
A. Gerber (Ed.): SAICSIT 2024, CCIS 2159, pp. 124–143, 2024.
https://doi.org/10.1007/978-3-031-64881-6_7

paper, the face alignment stage is explicitly omitted to reduce complexity. During the training process, the Multi-task Cascaded Convolutional Network (MTCNN) is employed for robust face detection. MTCNN serves a dual purpose: to detect faces and to eliminate any background noise, ensuring that only the significant facial features are subjected to the subsequent recognition process [42].

Early face recognition systems relied on manually engineered feature extraction techniques from facial images for individual identification [19,31]. However, the emergence of deep learning ushered in a new era dominated by deep convolutional neural networks (CNNs), which have since become mainstream in the domain of face recognition [2]. CNNs have emerged as the dominant approach for face recognition tasks due to their exceptional ability to learn discriminative facial features, achieving performance that rivals human-level accuracy on benchmark datasets [30]. However, CNNs are not without their limitations. Their demand for diverse images for each class during training is often a bottleneck, especially when dealing with specialised datasets like age-related, where such comprehensive data might be scarce [11]. To address this challenge, Siamese Convolutional Networks (SCNs), a unique neural network design [14], offer a valuable alternative. SCNs leverage the feature extraction power of CNNs for performing pairwise comparisons, making them particularly well-suited for recognition tasks with limited data availability [11].

CNNs are the dominant approach for face recognition due to their ability to extract localized features through convolutional operations [36]. However, their focus on local information limits their ability to capture global context within images. Vision Transformers (ViTs) [6], a recent advancement, present a compelling alternative to CNNs. ViTs leverage the attention mechanism, originally developed for natural language processing [33], to establish long-range dependencies and capture global relationships within an image, surpassing the localized focus of CNNs. In the context of face recognition, age-based recognition is of growing importance. Recognising individuals based on age-related facial features finds utility in several sectors, such as age-restricted content verification, tailored service provision in retail or health services and targeted marketing. Given the broad-based approach offered by ViTs, they could offer advancements in age-based face recognition, achieving superior accuracy in identifying individuals by effectively interpreting age-related facial features.

This paper compares the efficacy of different neural network architectures for age-related face recognition tasks. Initially, three distinct SCN models are examined, evaluating their performance, interpretability, and robustness. Similarly, evaluation is performed on two pre-trained Vision Transformers. The final segment involves a comparative analysis of the various architectures, delving into their performance metrics and pinpointing the specific facial features each model prioritises.

The remainder of this paper is structured as follows: Sect. 2 delves into a literature review of relevant works in the field. Section 3 discusses the practical aspects of implementing the network architectures. The methodology of experimentation and the fine-tuning of pre-trained models are covered in Sect. 4.

Section 5 is reserved for a discussion of the results and the rationale behind them. The paper concludes with Sect. 6, summarising the findings and drawing relevant conclusions.

2 Literature Survey

Face recognition plays a vital role in numerous applications, including security and personal identification. Its essence lies in its ability to reliably recognise and distinguish individuals based on distinct facial features. An especially significant and challenging subset of this task is age-based face recognition, where individuals are identified based on age-related facial features. Challenges arise due to the dynamic nature of aging, which introduces variability in facial features.

2.1 Face Detection

Existing face recognition systems, as per literature, often show sensitivity to factors such as illumination, pose variations, and occlusion [41]. Despite the capability of deep learning to capture and adjust to these changes, inaccuracies still exist. Aligning and pre-processing images for extracting crucial facial features becomes imperative, especially when many datasets are not inherently clean or pre-processed. Key facial features, particularly the eyes and nose, are critical to age-related recognition tasks, as emphasised in various biological and dermatological studies [29].

However, a recurring limitation observed with Convolutional Neural Networks (CNNs) is their occasional focus on less relevant features such as background elements or changeable facial attributes, such as hair colour. The importance of isolating relevant features becomes even more crucial in images containing multiple faces, requiring algorithms to be robust and scale invariant. Architectures such as CascadeCNN [15] and MTCNN [42], which are cascaded structures with deep convolutional neural networks, have been researched extensively. MTCNN, in particular, has been praised for its high accuracy, especially in datasets with diverse lighting, pose, and age-related facial changes [9]. Meanwhile, algorithms like Faster R-CNN [23] and Single Shot MultiBox Detection [16] are aimed at enhancing the speed of face and feature detection for larger datasets.

2.2 Siamese Networks

Siamese neural networks, commonly termed twin neural networks, employ two input vectors processed through identical networks to produce comparable output vectors [17]. At first glance, these networks appear as dual parallel architectures, as shown in Fig. 1. Yet, this duality is an illusion created by a single network sharing identical weights and parameters [12].

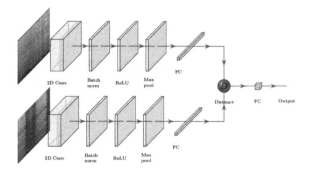

Fig. 1. Architecture of a Siamese neural network.

The dual-input approach of Siamese networks bolsters training speed due to its 1:1 matching, in contrast to CNNs' 1:k matching. The applications of Siamese networks span object detection, visual tracking, and face recognition [22]. When combined with CNNs, Siamese convolutional networks (SCNs) are obtained, which boast simplicity and accelerated training speeds [3]. Over the years, CNNs have set a benchmark in the face recognition domain, with error rates plummeting from 28% in 2010 to a mere 2.3% in 2017 [24]. Despite this, their growing complexity has made them more computationally demanding.

A notable distinction between SCNs and CNNs lies in their operational objectives: while CNNs are trained for specific categorical classification tasks, SCNs aim for binary classification. Further, the output of an SCN is the difference between two input vectors, whereas a CNN provides class probability distributions.

SCNs utilise two identical CNNs, each processing an image and producing an output feature vector. To ascertain the difference or similarity between the two input images, a distance function is applied to the output vectors. While the Euclidean distance and cosine distance are frequently employed in such architectures, diverse distance measures exist, enhancing the model's adaptability to specific tasks or datasets. A notable modification was proposed by Taigman et al. [30]. They introduced an adapted form of the cosine distance, incorporating additional trainable parameters:

$$d(f_1, f_2) = \sum_i \alpha_i \left| f_1[i] - f_2[i] \right| \tag{1}$$

In this equation, α_i represents the trainable parameters, while f_1 and f_2 represent the output feature vectors. By adding these parameters, the distance function can adjust itself based on the unique characteristics of the dataset. This becomes particularly beneficial in scenarios where conventional measures of similarity or dissimilarity are challenging to apply or might not capture the nuances of the data.

The performance of a Siamese network evaluated on age-related images is greatly dependent on the training data [20]. SCNs are trained to minimise the distance between similar entities and maximise the distance between different entities. Aging introduces changes in facial features that could prevent the model from learning accurately. Therefore, it is important that the dataset used for training includes a diverse range of age groups, otherwise, the network may struggle to generalise across various ages, introducing age bias.

2.3   Vision Transformers

Vision transformers (ViT) have witnessed a significant rise in adoption for face recognition tasks in recent times [28]. Originally conceived for natural language processing tasks [33], transformers have since been applied to the field of computer vision. The transformer architecture is based on the self-attention mechanism, as illustrated in Fig. 2. This allows the model to perceive context and interdependencies in the input, irrespective of their positional arrangement.

The preliminary step in ViT involves dividing the input image into a series of non-overlapping patches. Zhong and Deng [43] explored the use of overlapping patches to enhance the representation of inter-patch details, but their results were not conclusively favourable. The image patches undergo a linear transformation to be converted into a sequence of embeddings. A vital element of ViTs is the incorporation of positional embeddings. Since the raw data does not inherently capture the relative positions of patches within an image, these embeddings play a crucial role in retaining that spatial context [6]. The sequence of embeddings then serves as the input for the transformer encoder.

ViTs offer a unique advantage for face recognition – the capability to model long-range interdependencies [26]. While CNNs excel at local feature extraction, they struggle with global variations, especially those linked with aging. In contrast, the self-attention feature in ViTs enables the model to dynamically adjust its focus to different regions of the image based on their significance, making them potentially better suited to handle the broad range of age-related changes that occur in faces. The application of ViTs in age-invariant face recognition

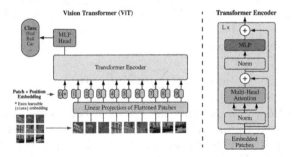

Fig. 2. Representation of a vision transformer for image classification. The depiction of the Transformer encoder was inspired by Vaswani et al. [33]

is an emerging domain, without much research to discover its full potential and limitations. A recent study by Shi et al. [26] combined ViTs with attention-driven convolution with the purpose of estimating age, reporting a performance that surpasses several existing techniques.

2.4   Transfer Learning

In the realm of machine learning, transfer learning has emerged as robust strategy that harnesses pre-trained models to tackle new tasks with limited labeled data. While CNNs have reaped the benefits of this approach, the spotlight is now shifting to its potential in Siamese Convolutional Networks and Vision Transformers for applications like face recognition, image retrieval and one-shot learning.

Transfer learning involves leveraging the knowledge acquired by a model from one task to enhance performance on a distinct, often related, task. The underlying idea is the universality of some features; what a model recognises in one context can be repurposed for another, especially when data for the latter is sparse [21]. The success of transfer learning is dependent on selecting an appropriate source domain. For SCNs, this typically entails a CNN previously trained on large datasets, such as ImageNet. Translating such pre-trained networks to Siamese architectures has yielded encouraging outcomes [11,30]. However, the architectural choice remains dependent on the specific challenge at hand. Commonly adopted architectures include ResNet50 [35], VGG-16 [11], and the Deep-Face CNN [30].

There are diverse strategies for fine-tuning in transfer learning. One approach retains the pre-trained model without the fully connected layers as a static feature extractor, fine-tuning only additional layers to fit the new task. Alternatively, some or all parts of the pre-trained model can be recalibrated with a diminished learning rate. Finally, both of these strategies can be combined by fine-tuning some existing layers and augmenting the existing network. This approach aims to combine the benefits of both methods.

However, transfer learning is not without its complications. The effectiveness of fine-tuning may degrade when source and target domains are too imbalanced [7]. To ensure optimal transfer learning during fine-tuning, the label spaces of the pre-trained network and the target dataset should exhibit a high degree of overlap. Overfitting is also a risk, especially when too many layers are adjusted. The model learns the noise of the small dataset too well, failing to generalise to unseen data from the same domain.

3   Implementation

This paper implements the deep learning models in Python using the Keras library, with the implementation containing approximately 1500 lines of code.

3.1   Network Architecture

This paper implements three distinct SCNs based on different CNN architectures and two ViTs for comprehensive analysis.

DeepFace Based SCN. Recent developments indicate that DeepFace [30] offers superior performance compared to the ResNet architectures. Characterised by its depth, DeepFace contains over 120 million parameters. Therefore, tweaking the final layers of the pre-trained model has the potential to yield augmented performance. The network accepts inputs with dimensions of 152×152, the final fully connected layers are replaced and the first five layers are frozen. A ReLu activation layer with 4096 neurons is appended to the model, along with a dropout layer to mitigate overfitting. Upon traversing these layers, a feature vector is produced for paired images. The cosine difference between the feature vectors is passed through a sigmoid activation layer, producing a value between zero and one, representing the probability that the two images are of a different class.

VGG-16 Based SCN. The architecture for the VGG-16 SCN draws inspiration from the VGG-16 model [27]. The convolutional layers in this network employ 3×3 filters, adhering to a design principle: maintaining consistent filter count for identical output feature map dimensions. When the feature map size reduces by half, the filter count is doubled in order to ensure consistent time complexity across layers. In this Siamese configuration, VGG-16 serves as the twin network. The model undergoes fine-tuning in its final convolutional block, with the final fully connected layers subsequently removed. These final layers are replaced by three fully connected layers, each comprising of 512 neurons and accompanied by ReLu activation [1]. Consequently, the only modifiable weights reside in block five and in the fully connected layers, which are randomly initialised.

ResNet50 Based SCN. ResNet, or Residual Network [10], is a popular convolutional neural network that introduced the concept of residual learning. By employing shortcut connections between its constituent blocks, ResNet effectively counters the vanishing gradient problem, commonly encountered in deeper networks. The ResNet50 variant [39], encompassing 50 convolutional layers, is integrated as the twin network in the Siamese model. The depth of this model, compared to ResNet34, allows for enhanced model capacity, facilitating the extraction of complex feature representations and bolstering performance. ResNet50 undergoes fine-tuning in its terminal convolutional block and the appended fully connected layer with 512 neurons, which aims to reduce overfitting.

ViT 16. The first approach leverages a pre-trained vision transformer, inspired by the architecture proposed by Vaswani et al. [33]. Prior to feeding the input image into the transformer, a learnable embedding, denoted as **x**, is prepended to the sequence. The state of this embedding at the output of the ViT serves as the representative image vector **y**. Following the design of Dosovitskiy et al. [6], a classification head is appended to the image representation after its traversal through the ViT layers. The head facilitates task-specific computations based on the representations learned by the ViT. Furthermore, one-dimensional position embeddings are integrated with the patch embeddings to preserve positional context within the image.

The ViT architecture incorporates a series of alternating multi-headed self-attention (MSA) blocks and multi-layer perceptron (MLP) blocks [33]. The application of Layernorm (LN) precedes every block, and residual connections ensue every block [37]. The pre-trained prediction head is omitted, instead introducing a zero-initialised feedforward layer. For enhancement in fine-tuning performance, the patch size is kept constant while the resolution is elevated. This results in augmented sequence lengths [32], rendering the pre-trained positional embeddings obsolete. To address this, two-dimensional interpolation is employed on the position embedding matrix, similar to pixel value interpolation during image resizing. By incorporating two residual blocks on top of the primary architecture, the efficacy of the model is improved [37]. These additions not only counteract the vanishing gradient problem but also enable deeper, more proficient model training. Furthermore, these supplementary layers have the ability to facilitate superior task-specific feature extraction.

ViT 32. The architectural foundation for the second variant closely mirrors the first, comprising alternating MSA and MLP blocks. However, a distinguishing attribute of the ViT 32, denoted as B32, is its larger patch size of 32. A larger patch size provides the model with a more coarse-grained view of the image, enhancing its ability to detect broader patterns and structures. A smaller patch size, in contrast, can limit the model from capturing more holistic features of the image. Contrasting the ViT 16, the ViT 32 model abstains from the inclusion of additional layers. The final three encoder blocks, in conjunction with the classification head, undergo fine-tuning, initialised with their original weights.

4 Experimentation

4.1 Dataset

The Cross-Age Celebrity Dataset (CACD) [4] is chosen due to its extensive range of ages and diversity in facial features. The CACD dataset comprises 163,446 images of 2,000 different celebrities sourced from the Internet, with ages ranging from 16–62. The images undergo pre-processing for size normalisation and face orientation. This process involves face detection, alignment, normalisation, and pair creation. Classes ranked above five are discarded to eliminate noise. Utilising an excessive number of images is not necessary for fine-tuning. The remaining 18,171 images span 200 classes, with their frequencies depicted in Fig. 3. The images are split into training, validation and testing sets using a percentage

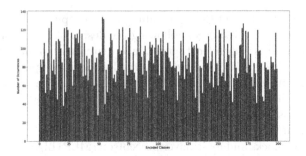

Fig. 3. Distribution of Classes in the Dataset.

split of 75:15:10 respectively. For the SCNs, the division includes 21000 training pairs, 4800 validation pairs and 1000 testing pairs, with an even split between positive (denoted as zero) and negative pairs (denoted as one). Each class has an equal number of positive and negative pairs to maintain consistency. Example pairs are illustrated in Fig. 4. For the ViT, each distinct label corresponds to an integer. This mapping is preserved to ensure consistent interpretation of future predictions.

The use of MTCNN is crucial. Without face cropping, unnecessary background noise persists, potentially distracting the model from the facial features. Cropped images boost processing speed by limiting the information fed to the model, thus enhancing training speeds. Furthermore, cropping ensures that the model consistently receives only the facial region, which is the primary area of interest.

Data augmentation enhances learning capabilities by introducing variance to the training data. Omitting augmentation risks overfitting as the model might memorise noise and outliers in the training data. Augmentation techniques include image flipping and alterations in brightness, saturation, and hue. Image normalisation ensures model efficiency.

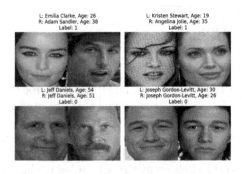

Fig. 4. Pairs fed into the SCN with their associated labels.

4.2   Training

The models are trained using a GPU-backed engine. Key hyperparameters like the learning rate (LR), batch size (BS) and optimiser are tuned manually depending on the problem. The specific parameters for each model are displayed in Table 1. Here, items refer to pairs for SCNs and images for ViTs. Note that the run times are based on non-GPU usage; leveraging a GPU could lead to approximately a tenfold increase in prediction time. The models start with weights initialised using Glorot Uniform initialisation [18] and a zero bias.

The weights yielding the best validation performance are retained as the model's final configuration. Early stopping, depending on the convergence rate of the model, is set with a patience level of either five or eight. While the maximum number of epochs is set at 50, training typically concludes earlier due to early stopping.

Table 1. Hyperparameters and statistics for model training.

Model	LR	BS	Optimiser	Params (M)	Size	(items)/s
DeepFace SCN	0.001	32	ADAM	73.5	156	6.32
VGG-16 SCN	0.0001	128	RMSProp	19.4	128	7.35
ResNet50 SCN	0.0001	128	ADAM	24.6	128	25.64
ViT 16	0.0001	128	ADAM	95.3	224	3.43
ViT 32	0.0001	128	ADAM	87.6	224	16.62

Due to the novelty of age-oriented face recognition using SCNs and ViTs, experimentation is done with various loss functions, optimisers, distance functions and fine-tuned layers. The hyperparameters listed above signify the optimal configurations for each model.

5   Results

5.1   SCN

Table 2 presents the comparative performance of the three SCN models implemented. The models were trained using the hyperparameters from Table 1. The evaluation metrics include test accuracy obtained (Acc.), precision (P), recall

Table 2. SCN Model Performance Comparison

Model	Acc. (%)	Metrics (%)				Loss	Threshold
		P	R	S	F1		
DeepFace	76.40	71.71	87.20	65.6	78.70	0.22	0.11
VGG-16	**83.10**	**76.65**	**95.20**	**71**	**84.92**	**0.17**	0.65
ResNet50	69.50	67.02	76.80	62.20	71.58	0.23	0.42

(R), specificity (S) and F1-Score (F1), contrastive loss calculated on the test set and the optimal distance threshold for distinguishing between negative and positive pairs.

The efficacy of the models without an optimal threshold, utilising a standard threshold of 0.5, is displayed in Table 3. The selection of a threshold demonstrates a significant impact on balancing recall and specificity, particularly evident in the performance of the DeepFace model. With a threshold set at 0.5, the model tends to categorise the majority of pairs as positive, which is an undesirable bias. However, it is important to acknowledge that an "optimal" threshold may not be applicable to all scenarios. For instance, in the case of the VGG-16 SCN, the utilisation of this tailored threshold enables the model to detect 7.8% more true positives at the expense of wrongly classifying an additional 4.6% of true negatives. Such a trade-off, while enhancing overall accuracy, demands consideration in terms of its suitability across different domains, particularly when weighing the consequences of varying error types.

Table 3. SCN Model Performance with a Standard Threshold of 0.5

Model	Acc. (%)	Metrics (%)			
		P	R	S	F1
DeepFace	74.90	67.17	**97.40**	52.40	79.51
VGG-16	**81.50**	**78.18**	87.40	**75.60**	**82.53**
ResNet50	66.90	62.75	83.20	50.60	71.54

Despite high accuracy scores, these models exhibit limitations in negative pair detection, as reflected by their low specificity values. For instance, the VGG-16 SCN demonstrated a strong capability in correctly identifying positive pairs, with a high true positive rate of 95.2%. However, its true negative prediction rate was only 71%. A selection of random predictions made by the model are illustrated in Fig. 5.

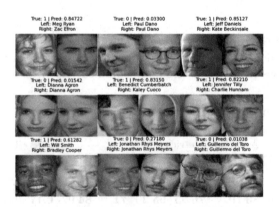

Fig. 5. Random Predictions made by VGG-16 SCN.

The variation in performance between optimal and standard thresholds underscores the importance of customising the decision threshold based on the specific model and application context. Figure 6 showcases incorrect predictions made by the ResNet50 SCN, showcasing struggles with negative pairs of the same gender and diverse skin complexions, suggesting limitations in the diversity of the dataset.

Notably, despite the DeepFace model being originally trained on the SFC dataset for face recognition tasks, it did not emerge as the top performer. The deviation can be attributed to the adaptation of DeepFace as a foundational component of a SCN, diverging from its conventional use as a standalone CNN, and fine-tuning the adapted architecture for an age-related recognition task. Contrarily, the VGG-16 SCN, trained on the more diverse ImageNet dataset, adapts better to both the architectural changes and the new task requirements. This is supported by saliency maps depicted in Fig. 7, which reveal a focus on the central and lower facial areas. This focus contrasts with the emphasis of the other models on peripheral facial features such as outlines, forehead and hair. This distinction underscores the relative insignificance of the upper facial region in age-related face recognition tasks.

Fig. 6. Incorrect Predictions by ResNet50 SCN

Lastly, while ResNet50 SCNs typically employ triplet loss, this paper adopted contrastive loss across all models models for a uniform assessment. This approach significantly impeded the effectiveness of the ResNet50 SCN, as evident from the difficulty in reducing the loss during training, depicted in Fig. 8.

In conclusion, while these SCNs exhibit commendable performance in positive pair identification, their effectiveness is notably reduced for negative pairs. The results underscore the criticality of model-specific threshold optimisation and data diversity in enhancing model accuracy and reliability.

Fig. 7. Saliency Maps of VGG-16 SCN's Final Convolutional Layer

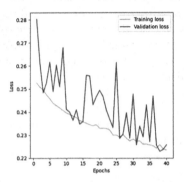

Fig. 8. Training and Validation Loss of ResNet50 SCN

5.2   ViT

The performance of the ViTs, as outlined in Table 4, highlights a significant superiority of the ViT 32 model over the ViT 16 model across all accuracy measures. The ViT 32 model exhibits notably lower loss figures, indicating more effective convergence during training and a better fit to the dataset. The primary distinction between the two models lies in their respective patch sizes, with the larger patch size of ViT 32 enabling it to capture more contextual data per patch. This characteristic is crucial as ViTs, unlike SCNs, leverage self-attention mechanisms to weigh the importance of different patches, rather than focusing on specific features. Depending on the nature of the task and the size of the images, the patch size plays a vital role in determining whether the model prioritises fine-grained details or broader contextual information. The larger patch size in ViT 32 reduces the input sequence length, facilitating more manageable model processing, improved training efficiency, and consequently more opportunities for fine-tuning.

For interpretability, unlike SCNs where methods like grad-cam [25] and saliency maps are effective, ViTs demand alternative approaches due to their lack of convolutional layers. Here, Local Interpretable Model-agnostic Explanations (LIME) [34] are employed. LIME, a technique for approximating the decision-making process of complex models like ViTs, creates a localised, linear surrogate model to interpret individual predictions. The weights of the simple model give an indication of feature importance in the complex model. The application of LIME on the ViT 32 model, as shown in Fig. 9, aligns with SCN findings, pointing to the eyes as key focal points in accurate predictions. This parallel suggests a consistent pattern across different model types in prioritising specific facial features for decision-making.

5.3   Comparative Analysis

The self-attention mechanisms in ViTs demonstrate their adaptability in discerning diverse relationship aspects within data. This flexibility becomes apparent when applied to age-related facial recognition tasks. The capability of ViTs to process global information effectively outstrips the feature-specific approach typical of CNNs and SCNs. In age-related contexts, focusing on less mutable facial features is beneficial, as elements like hair, beards and foreheads are prone to change. This principle is substantiated by the analysis of saliency maps from the ResNet50 SCN, where excessive emphasis on peripheral features results in subpar performance, as illustrated in Fig. 10.

Fig. 9. LIME applied to ViT 32 predictions

Table 4. Comparison of ViT models

Model	Acc. (%)			Metrics (%)			Loss
	All	Top-3	Top-5	P	R	F1	
ViT 16	60.34	77.76	84.21	65.50	60.34	60.23	1.77
ViT 32	**87.23**	**93.87**	**95.42**	**88.74**	**87.23**	**87.27**	**0.55**

Fig. 10. Saliency Maps of the third convolutional layer in the final block of the ResNet50 SCN

The Area Under the Curve (AUC) of the Receiver Operating Characteristic (ROC) curve is a critical metric for assessing classification model performance. The AUC evaluates the proficiency of the model in distinguishing between classes without being dependent on a specific threshold. Figure 11 exhibits the ROC curve and corresponding AUC scores for the models. While an ideal classifier would achieve an AUC score of 1, a score of 0.5 would indicate random classification performance. The VGG-16 SCN, with smaller convolutional filters, is adept at extracting fine-grained details vital for age-related classification. Conversely, the lack of performance of the ResNet50 SCN can be attributed to its broader feature focus, which lacks the specificity required for age-related facial comparisons. The ViTs, with their advanced self-attention mechanisms, proficiently assess the relevance of various image segments, effectively recognising age-related traits spread across the face. The contrasting outcomes between different ViT models highlights the significance of patch size and the final layers of the architectures in model effectiveness.

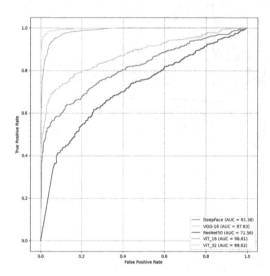

Fig. 11. Receiver Operating Characteristic (ROC) Curve for all models with their respective AUC scores

A comparative analysis of the implemented models with existing implementations, as shown in Table 5, reveals the superior performance of ViT 32 on the CACD dataset. It competes closely with LF CNNs [38] and Human Voting [4]. This outcome reinforces the notion that global contextual understanding, as opposed to local feature detection, is invaluable of age-related facial recognition tasks. Although SCNs show commendable performance, the gap between paired image comparisons and single-image categorical classification is pronounced, with ViTs exhibiting superior effectiveness.

Table 5. Comparative analysis of different methodologies

Method	AUC (%)
High Dimensional LBP [5]	88.8
Hidden Factor Analysis [8]	91.7
Cross Age Reference Coding [4]	94.2
LF CNNs [38]	99.3
Human, Average [4]	94.6
Human, Voting [4]	99.0
DeepFace SCN (Ours)	81.38
VGG-16 SCN (Ours)	87.63
ResNet50 (Ours)	71.56
ViT 16 (Ours)	98.61
ViT 32 (Ours)	99.62

5.4   Observations

Runtimes. The DeepFace SCN exhibits the largest parameters count, primarily attributed to its incorporation of locally connected layers. These layers, by design, do not share weights, leading to a heightened parameter count. This increase manifests as a greater computational demand per forward pass, consequently diminishing throughput. In contrast, models like VGG-16 and ResNet50 do not contain locally connected layers, instead allowing weights to be shared, leading to improved computational efficiency relative to DeepFace. ResNet50 contains skip connections, which establish more direct pathways through the network, expediting computational processing.

A notable distinction in runtime is observed between the ViT models. The ViT 32 model demonstrates superior runtime compared to the ViT 16 model, due to its larger patch size. A 16-sized patch translates to the model handling 196 patches per input, in contrast to the 49 patches necessitated by a 32-sized patch. Given that self-attention mechanisms in transformers possess a quadratic complexity of $O(N^2 \times D)$ [13] with sequence length N and feature dimension D, a model with larger patches enjoys significantly reduced attention computation times. Furthermore, the ViT 16 model is burdened by two additional MLP blocks, adding nearly 10 million extra parameters, thereby impacting runtime. In comparison, ViTs consistently outperform SCNs, particularly when considering input size and parameters count.

Additional Layers. A critical observation is the impact of lacking additional layers in SCNs. This deficiency is seen to constrain the precision and accuracy of the models. Applying a distance function to the outputs of pre-trained models does not suffice to effectively convert them into SCNs via transfer learning. Such models, devoid of additional layers, demonstrate limited adaptability to new tasks during fine-tuning, underscoring the importance of these layers in achieving optimal performance in task-specific applications.

5.5   Discussion and Limitations

The findings suggest that a representative dataset, one devoid of celebrity bias and more reflective of the general population, might improve the performance of image comparison. Furthermore, increasing the number of negative pairs within the training set is recommended to better facilitate the discrimination of distinct features, rather than the models primarily identifying positive correlations.

The focus of many SCN models towards the outer areas of the face, coupled with the dataset examination, signifies that face alignment could be a prospective enhancement. Albeit face alignment has been shown to increase model performance, it necessitates longer pre-processing times [30].

The choice of loss function for the ResNet50 SCN was identified as a constraint that impeded training effectiveness, adversely impacting model performance. Considering the prevalent use of triplet loss in related research, future investigations should explore this avenue to improve the stability of the training loss.

6   Conclusion

This paper sought to conduct a comparative analysis of two different deep learning architectures– Siamese Convolutional Networks (SCNs) and Vision Transformers (ViTs)- within the domain of age-related facial recognition. The proposed system applied image pre-processing using MTCNN, followed by data augmentation and normalisation. The study introduced a suite of models comprising three SCNs and two ViTs, which revealed significant performance variances between the architectures.

The SCNs exhibited a deficiency in specificity for its pairwise comparison. The SCN models struggled to differentiate between negative pairs of the same gender, suggesting that the celebrity-centric dataset employed for fine-tuning failed to provide a comprehensive learning experience across diverse racial and gender demographics. The most proficient SCN model attained a 83.10% accuracy rate, with specificity at a mere 71%. In contrast, ViT models equipped with a larger patch size demonstrated superior performance, achieving an accuracy rate of 87.23%. This advantage is ascribed to the model's capability to incorporate a broader spectrum of information per patch, thus not being constrained to granular, isolated features.

In conclusion, the self-attention mechanisms of the ViTs were observed to surpass the localised, feature-specific approach of SCN models. The outcome of this research underscores the profound potential of ViTs in the realm of age-related face recognition, signifying a preference for categorical classification over pairwise image comparison in datasets characterised by age-related attributes. This research contributes valuable insights into the efficacy of deep learning architectures in facial recognition tasks, advocating for a more global, contextual approach to age-related analysis.

References

1. Agarap, A.: Deep learning using rectified linear units (ReLU). arXiv preprint arXiv:1803.08375 (2019)
2. Alzubaidi, L., et al.: Review of deep learning: concepts, CNN architectures, challenges, applications, future directions. J. Big Data 8(1), 1–74 (2021)
3. Bromley, J., Guyon, I., LeCun, Y., Säckinger, E., Shah, R.: Signature verification using a "siamese" time delay neural network. In: Advances in Neural Information Processing Systems, vol. 6 (1993)
4. Chen, B.-C., Chen, C.-S., Hsu, W.H.: Cross-age reference coding for age-invariant face recognition and retrieval. In: Fleet, D., Pajdla, T., Schiele, B., Tuytelaars, T. (eds.) ECCV 2014, Part VI. LNCS, vol. 8694, pp. 768–783. Springer, Cham (2014). https://doi.org/10.1007/978-3-319-10599-4_49
5. Chen, D., Cao, X., Wen, F., Sun, J.: Blessing of dimensionality: high-dimensional feature and its efficient compression for face verification. In: Proceedings of the IEEE Conference on Computer Vision and Pattern Recognition, pp. 3025–3032 (2013)
6. Dosovitskiy, A., et al.: An image is worth 16×16 words: transformers for image recognition at scale. arXiv preprint arXiv:2010.11929 (October 2020)
7. Ganin, Y., et al.: Domain-adversarial training of neural networks. J. Mach. Learn. Res. 17(1), 2096–2130 (2016)
8. Gong, D., Li, Z., Lin, D., Liu, J., Tang, X.: Hidden factor analysis for age invariant face recognition. In: Proceedings of the IEEE International Conference on Computer Vision, pp. 2872–2879 (2013)
9. Gyawali, D., Pokharel, P., Chauhan, A., Shakya, S.: Age range estimation using MTCNN and VGG-face model. In: Proceedings of the 2020 11th International Conference on Computing, Communication and Networking Technologies (ICCCNT), pp. 1–6 (2020)
10. He, K., Zhang, X., Ren, S., Sun, J.: Deep residual learning for image recognition. In: Proceedings of the IEEE Conference on Computer Vision and Pattern Recognition, pp. 770–778 (2016)
11. Heidari, M., Fouladi-Ghaleh, K.: Using siamese networks with transfer learning for face recognition on small-samples datasets. In: Proceedings of the 2020 International Conference on Machine Vision and Image Processing (MVIP), pp. 1–4 (2020)

12. Johnston, K., Ngxande, M.: Robust facial recognition for occlusions using facial landmarks. In: Proceedings of the 43rd Conference of the South African Institute of Computer Scientists and Information Technologists, vol. 85, pp. 48–61 (2022)
13. Keles, F., Wijewardena, P., Hegde, C.: On the computational complexity of self-attention. In: Proceedings of the International Conference on Algorithmic Learning Theory, pp. 597–619 (2023)
14. Koch, G., Zemel, R., Salakhutdinov, R.: Siamese neural networks for one-shot image recognition. In: Proceedings of the ICML Deep Learning Workshop, vol. 2 (2015)
15. Kouris, A., Venieris, S., Bouganis, C.: CascadeCNN: pushing the performance limits of quantisation in convolutional neural networks. In: Proceedings of the 2018 28th International Conference on Field Programmable Logic and Applications (FPL), pp. 155–1557 (2018)
16. Liu, W., et al.: SSD: single shot multibox detector. In: Leibe, B., Matas, J., Sebe, N., Welling, M. (eds.) ECCV 2016, Part I. LNCS, vol. 9905, pp. 21–37. Springer, Cham (2016). https://doi.org/10.1007/978-3-319-46448-0_2
17. Melekhov, I., Kannala, J., Rahtu, E.: Siamese network features for image matching. In: Proceedings of the 2016 23rd International Conference on Pattern Recognition (ICPR), pp. 378–383 (2016)
18. Mishkin, D., Matas, J.: All you need is a good init. arXiv preprint arXiv:1511.06422 (2015)
19. Mishra, S., et al.: Multivariate statistical data analysis-principal component analysis (PCA). Int. J. Livestock Res. **7**(5), 60–78 (2017)
20. Moustafa, A., Elnakib, A., Areed, N.: Age-invariant face recognition based on deep features analysis. Signal Image Video Process. **14**, 1027–1034 (2020)
21. Pan, S., Yang, Q.: A survey on transfer learning. IEEE Trans. Knowl. Data Eng. **22**(10), 1345–1359 (2009)
22. Ramachandra, B., Jones, M., Vatsavai, R.: Learning a distance function with a siamese network to localize anomalies in videos. In: Proceedings of the IEEE/CVF Winter Conference on Applications of Computer Vision, pp. 2598–2607 (2020)
23. Ren, S., He, K., Girshick, R., Sun, J.: Faster R-CNN: towards real-time object detection with region proposal networks. IEEE Trans. Pattern Anal. Mach. Intell. **28** (2015)
24. Russakovsky, O., et al.: ImageNet large scale visual recognition challenge. Int. J. Comput. Vision **115**(3), 211–252 (2015)
25. Selvaraju, R., Cogswell, M., Das, A., Vedantam, R., Parikh, D., Batra, D.: Grad-CAM: visual explanations from deep networks via gradient-based localization. In: Proceedings of the IEEE International Conference on Computer Vision, pp. 618–626 (2017)
26. Shi, C., Zhao, S., Zhang, K., Wang, Y., Liang, L.: Face-based age estimation using improved swin transformer with attention-based convolution. Front. Neurosci. **17**, 1136934 (2023)
27. Simonyan, K., Zisserman, A.: Very deep convolutional networks for large-scale image recognition. arXiv preprint arXiv:1409.1556 (2014)
28. Sun, Z., Tzimiropoulos, G.: Part-based face recognition with vision transformers. arXiv preprint arXiv:2212.00057 (2022)
29. Swift, A., Liew, S., Weinkle, S., Garcia, J., Silberberg, M.: The facial aging process from the "inside out". Aesthetic Surg. J. **41**(10), 1107–1119 (2021)
30. Taigman, Y., Yang, M., Ranzato, M., Wolf, L.: DeepFace: closing the gap to human-level performance in face verification. In: Proceedings of the 2014 IEEE Conference on Computer Vision and Pattern Recognition, pp. 1701–1708 (2014)

31. Tharwat, A., Gaber, T., Ibrahim, A., Hassanien, A.E.: Linear discriminant analysis: a detailed tutorial. AI Commun. **30**(2), 169–190 (2017)
32. Touvron, H., Vedaldi, A., Douze, M., Jégou, H.: Fixing the train-test resolution discrepancy. In: Advances in Neural Information Processing Systems, vol. 32 (2019)
33. Vaswani, A., et al.: Attention is all you need. In: Advances in Neural Information Processing Systems, vol. 30 (2017)
34. Visani, G., Bagli, E., Chesani, F., Poluzzi, A., Capuzzo, D.: Statistical stability indices for lime: obtaining reliable explanations for machine learning models. J. Oper. Res. Soc. **73**(1), 91–101 (2022)
35. Wang, G., Wang, S., Chi, W., Liu, S., Fan, D.: A person reidentification algorithm based on improved Siamese network and hard sample. Math. Probl. Eng. **2020**, 1–11 (2020)
36. Wang, J., Li, Z.: Research on face recognition based on CNN. In: Proceedings of the IOP Conference Series: Earth and Environmental Science, vol. 170, p. 032110 (2018)
37. Wang, Q., Li, B., Xiao, T., Zhu, J., Li, C., Wong, D., Chao, L.: Learning deep transformer models for machine translation. arXiv preprint arXiv:1906.01787 (2019)
38. Wen, Y., Li, Z., Qiao, Y.: Latent factor guided convolutional neural networks for age-invariant face recognition. In: Proceedings of the IEEE Conference on Computer Vision and Pattern Recognition, pp. 4893–4901 (2016)
39. Wu, H., Xin, M., Fang, W., Hu, H., Hu, Z.: Multi-level feature network with multi-loss for person re-identification. IEEE Access **7**, 91052–91062 (2019)
40. Wu, H., Xu, Z., Zhang, J., Yan, W., Ma, X.: Face recognition based on convolution Siamese networks. In: Proceedings of the 2017 10th International Congress on Image and Signal Processing, BioMedical Engineering and Informatics (CISP-BMEI), pp. 1–5 (2017)
41. Yu, Z., Huang, H., Chen, W., Su, Y., Liu, Y., Wang, X.: YOLO-facev2: a scale and occlusion aware face detector. arXiv preprint arXiv:2208.02019 (2022)
42. Zhang, K., Zhang, Z., Li, Z., Qiao, Y.: Joint face detection and alignment using multitask cascaded convolutional networks. IEEE Signal Process. Lett. **23**(10), 1499–1503 (2016)
43. Zhong, Y., Deng, W.: Face transformer for recognition. arXiv preprint arXiv:2103.14803 (2021)

Sarcasm Detection in Political Speeches Using Recurrent Neural Networks

Mulaudzi Thikho and Sello N. Mokwena(⊠)

Department of Computer Science, University of Limpopo, Sovenga, South Africa
sello.mokwena@ul.ac.za

Abstract. This study investigated the effectiveness of recurrent neural networks (RNN) for the detection of sarcasm in the challenging domain of political speech. Given the inherent nuance of sarcasm, it can be difficult. This study compared three RNN architectures (SimpleRNN, LSTM, and GRU) and demonstrated that ensemble learning techniques (stacking and weighted averaging) further improved accuracy. Pre-trained word embeddings (GloVe) were used to capture semantic cues that signal sarcasm. These embeddings were incorporated by replacing words with their corresponding vector representations. The model was evaluated using standard metrics (accuracy, precision, recall, F1 score). The results showed that the ensembles outperformed individual RNNs, achieving a peak accuracy of 95% and an F1 score of 95% for both sarcastic and nosarcastic classes. Individual RNNs achieved an accuracy of 91%, highlighting the clear benefit of ensemble learning. This improvement suggests that ensembles effectively combine the strengths of different models, leading to more robust and generalisable sarcasm detection in political speech. Furthermore, this research paves the way for the application of similar techniques to sentiment analysis tasks in other complex domains.

Keywords: Sarcasm detection · sentiment analysis · deep learning · RNN's · ensemble · stacking · weighted average

1 Introduction

Political discourse thrives on wit, but deciphering genuine humour from veiled criticism, often delivered through sarcasm, can be challenging. Accurate detection of sarcasm is crucial to understanding the true intent behind political statements [1]. However, current methods that use sentiment analysis often misinterpret sarcastic language, leading to skewed interpretations and hampered communication.

The ability to automatically detect sarcasm in political speech is of great significance [2]. It can improve understanding, combat misinformation, and shape public opinion. Although sentiment analysis tools exist, they often struggle with nuanced language, such as sarcasm, leading to misinterpretations [3, 4]. The challenge lies in capturing context, domain specificity, and data limitations.

To address these challenges, the aim of this study was to develop a robust model to detect sarcasm in political speech using repetitive neural networks (RNN). This study

A. Gerber (Ed.): SAICSIT 2024, CCIS 2159, pp. 144–158, 2024.
https://doi.org/10.1007/978-3-031-64881-6_8

investigated Recurrent Neural Network (RNN) architectures for sarcasm detection. We compared the performance of three models: a basic RNN, long-short-term memory (LSTM), and Gated Recurrent Unit (GRU). To potentially improve accuracy, we explored ensemble learning techniques. Specifically, we examined stacking, which combines predictions from multiple deep learning models, and weighted average ensemble, which leverages the strengths of individual RNN models through a weighted combination of their predictions.

By overcoming the challenges of detecting sarcasm in political speech, this research has the potential to significantly improve our understanding of political discourse, combat misinformation, and shape public opinion in a more informed and nuanced manner. This study is organised as follows: next we deal with literature review, then methodology, results, and lastly conclusion.

2 Literature Review

Sarcasm detection is a major challenge in NLP due to its figurative nature in which words have an opposite meaning [5]. While humans excel at understanding sarcasm, machines struggle. This has significant applications in sentiment analysis and social media monitoring [6]. Recent advances in deep learning, particularly word embeddings, recurrent neural networks (RNN), and convolutional neural networks (CNNs) [7], have shown promise. For example, a word embedding model for tweets achieved state-of-the-art performance, highlighting the potential of deep learning in this domain [8]. In the following section, we review some of the key studies on sarcasm detection.

2.1 Unexpectedness and Contradictory Factor Approach

Reyes et al. in [9] suggested an approach to sarcasm detection based on the idea that sarcastic statements often involve unexpected or contradictory elements. Imagine someone saying 'That's a great idea' in a sarcastic tone, implying the opposite. The method in [10] rules and features to pinpoint such unexpected or contradictory aspects within the text.

Researchers [11] have explored this approach in the analysis of social networks, identifying unexpectedness and contradictions in figurative language expressions to detect irony and sarcasm. For example, some studies measured contextual imbalance by evaluating the similarity and semantic relatedness of concepts. Unexpectedness was viewed as an emotional imbalance between words gauged using external resources such as the American National Corpus [12]. Furthermore, some researchers used classifiers to identify contradictions as features of sarcasm [11].

Although valuable, this approach has limitations. Sarcasm often relies on shared context, and this method might struggle with references, inside jokes, or cultural nuances not explicitly stated. Additionally [13], it might miss noncontradictory sarcasm like deadpan delivery or subtle exaggerations. Furthermore, literal contradictions do not always indicate sarcasm, leading to potential misinterpretations [14].

2.2 Content-Based Approach

The Content-Based Approach combines sentiment analysis, which reveals the emotional tone of a text, with word embedding, which represents words as vectors in a high dimensional space. This combination effectively identifies the sarcasm conveyed through word choice, sentiment, or both [15]. For example, using a positive word in a negative context often suggests sarcasm. Additionally, sentiment classification and emotion detection models can be used as steppingstones for sarcasm detection through learning techniques.

Recent research highlights the importance of contextual signals alongside lexical and syntactic information for sarcasm detection [16]. Studies have explored various features including lexical, pragmatic, implicit, and explicit context incongruity [17]. Explicit incongruity is focused on identifying failed sentimental expectations within the given text [18].

Machine learning plays a crucial role in sarcasm detection. Approaches include Support Vector Machines (SVM) and Random Forest (RF) classifiers, often used in conjunction with feature selection techniques like mutual information (MI), chi-square, and information gain (IG). These techniques help identify the most distinctive characteristics of sarcastic text [19].

Content-based approaches offer valuable information but have limitations. They often rely heavily on explicit markers such as exclamation marks or specific keywords, potentially missing implicit sarcasm. Additionally, they might neglect the broader context or speaker's intent, leading to misinterpretations. However, these approaches also have strengths. By relying on predefined features and rules, they offer objective and consistent detection and can be adapted to specific domains with the inclusion of domain-specific knowledge. Furthermore, its rule-based nature allows automation and integration into larger systems [20].

2.3 Context-Based Approach

The context-based approach tackles sarcasm by analysing the surrounding text. This recognising that sarcasm often relies heavily on context, as a statement might be sarcastic on one situation but not in another. This method is particularly effective at identifying subtle or implied sarcasm compared to approaches that only analyse the content of the text itself.

Several studies highlight the limitations of solely relying on content for sarcasm detection. Research by [21] explored various Long-Short-Term Memory (LSTM) network configurations to model both the conversation context and the potential sarcastic response. Their findings demonstrate that incorporating context significantly improves performance. Another approach by [22] uses a dual-channel convolutional neural network that considers both the meaning and the emotional context of the text.

Linguistic studies have also explored context incongruity as a basis for identifying sarcasm. [23] proposed a context-based feature approach using deep learning models and traditional machine learning, while [24] focused on sarcasm detection in tweets using a combination of hand-crafted features and deep learning techniques.

Although context-based approaches offer significant improvement, they still face challenges [25]. Data dependence is a key weakness, as these models often require large amounts of labelled data with clear context annotations, which can be expensive and time-consuming to collect. Additionally, incomplete context in real-world scenarios can lead to misinterpretations due to missing information, such as cultural references or non-verbal cues. Finally, the same context can be interpreted differently depending on the individual, leading to further ambiguity.

2.4 Deep Learning Approach

Deep learning models are currently leading the way is sarcasm detection, surpassing traditional methods due to their ability to identify complex patterns in text data, crucial for understanding the nuances and context-dependence of sarcasm. Popular examples include Recurrent Neural Networks (RNNs), Long-Short-Term Memory (LSTMs), and Gated Recurrent Units (GRUs) [26].

These models, designed specifically for sequential data like text, process it word-by-word, encoding each word as an embedding representing its meaning. These embeddings are then fed into the network, which updates its internal state at each step, ultimately feeding into a classifier that determines whether the text is sarcastic [27].

Research has explored various deep learning techniques for this task. For example, [28] used LSTMs for Twitter sarcasm detection, while [29] combined RNNs and CNN for Arabic text. Additional studies by [30] demonstrated the effectiveness of combining multiple models (eg., LSTMs, GRUs, and CNNs) with different word embedding models to achieve accuracy rates.

Although deep learning offers powerful tools, it is not without limitations. These models require significant computational resources and training time, which could limit their use for smaller organisations. Additionally, deep learning thrives on large, labelled datasets, and sarcasm's nuanced and subjective nature makes creating such datasets challenging. Finally, models trained on specific data might not perform well on unseen data from different domains or contexts [24].

Despite these limitations, deep learning offers several advantages for sarcasm detection. Deep learning models can analyse large amounts of text to identify subtle patterns and relationships between words, leading to higher accuracy compared to simpler models. Additionally, they can be trained in various data formats such as text, audio, and video, providing a more comprehensive understanding of sarcasm. Their flexibility and scalability allow them to handle massive datasets and continuously improve with new data. Advanced architectures such as LSTM can capture long-range dependencies and context, while deep learning models can be integrated with other features such as sentiment analysis to further improve accuracy [32] (Table 1).

Table 1. Similarities and differences of the approaches

Approaches	Similarities	Differences
Unexpectedness and contradictory factor approach	Relies on linguistic features like negation, exaggeration, and incongruity	Requires manually defined rules and features
Content-Based Approach	Relies on sentiment analysis and word embeddings	May not capture sarcasm that is not expressed through sentiment or word choice
Context-Based Approach	Relies on understanding the context of the text	May require a large amount of training data
Deep learning approach	Uses neural networks to learn complex patterns in text data	Can be computationally expensive

3 Methodology

3.1 Datasets

This study used a dataset of news headlines for the detection of sarcasm [8]. This dataset was collected from Kaggle, and this dataset has advantages over those based on Twitter [33]. It has fewer spelling errors and informal language, making it easier for machine learning models to understand. Additionally, the dataset uses words commonly found in pre-trained language models, boosting model performance. Finally, the headlines are clearly labelled sarcastic (1) or not (0), minimising the noise in the data. The structure and a sample are shown in Figs. 1 and 2. For experiments, it was divided into 80% training and 20% testing data. Each headline has an associated link (Article_link), the headline itself (headline), and a label indicating sarcasm. (Is_sarcastic).

	article_link	headline	is_sarcastic
0	https://www.huffingtonpost.com/entry/versace-b...	former versace store clerk sues over secret 'b...	0
1	https://www.huffingtonpost.com/entry/roseanne-...	the 'roseanne' revival catches up to our thorn...	0
2	https://local.theonion.com/mom-starting-to-fea...	mom starting to fear son's web series closest ...	1
3	https://politics.theonion.com/boehner-just-wan...	boehner just wants wife to listen, not come up...	1
4	https://www.huffingtonpost.com/entry/jk-rowlin...	j.k. rowling wishes snape happy birthday in th...	0

Fig. 1. Snippet of the news headline dataset.

Glove Dataset

This study used a pre-trained word embedding technique called GloVe (Global Vectors). Unlike other methods, GloVe combines two approaches and focusses on statistically relevant words in a large corpus. The specific GloVe used here has embeddings of more than 1.1 million words [34] Fig. 3 shows the flow chart of the methodology.

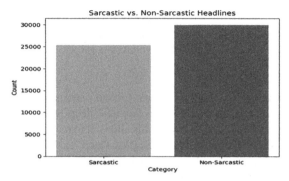

Fig. 2. Distribution of sarcastic and non-sarcastic headlines

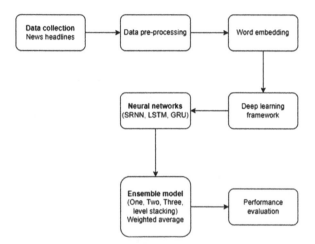

Fig. 3. Methodology flow chat

Data Pre-Processing

To enhance the algorithm's performance, the raw news headlines were subjected to a pre-processing stage using the NLTK library [35]. This involved data cleaning techniques such as removing numbers, non-English characters, punctuation, and special symbols. Additionally, stop words were eliminated, contractions were expanded to their full forms, and lemmatisation was applied to convert each word to its base form, ensuring consistency in the data.

Word Embedding

Traditional methods, such as the bag-of-words model, struggle to capture the relationships between words. Word embeddings address this by converting words into numerical vectors, where similar words have similar representations. This allows models to understand not only the meaning of individual words but also the context in which they are used. Techniques like GloVe (used in this study) achieve this by analysing massive amounts of text data. In our case, the pre-trained GloVe embeddings helped the model identify sarcasm by considering the relationships between words, even if they were not directly next to each other in the sentence. This approach is more efficient than traditional methods and allows a better use of large text datasets [36].

Deep Learning Framework

Deep learning is a powerful technique to find hidden patterns in data [37]. Unlike traditional methods that rely on hand-crafted features, deep learning can automatically discover new features from the data itself. This allows it to build highly accurate models that can even outperform humans in some tasks. Deep learning models are typically made up of many interconnected layers (such as SRNN, LSTM, and GRU) that are trained on large amounts of labelled data.

To detect sarcasm in the news headlines, we employ deep learning techniques. First, the pre-processed text was fed into a word embedding layer, which converted each word into a numerical vector, capturing its semantic meaning and relationship to other words. Then the layers SRNN, LSTM, and GRU were used to analyse the sequence of these vectors. These layers are particularly adept at capturing long-range dependencies within the context, which is crucial for understanding sarcasm. For example, the sentence 'This movie was amazing, not!" might be labelled sarcastic because the negative word 'not' contradicts the positive sentiment of 'amazing', although they are not adjacent words. Finally, the information model condensed the extract from the sequence and used it to classify the headline as either sarcastic or not sarcastic.

Sarcasm Detection

To detect sarcasm, we started by defining an input layer that can handle sequences of varying length. This is followed by the input sequence fed into three separate branches, each containing a different type of recurring neural network (RNN): a SimpleRNN, an LSTM, and a GRU. These branches all have 64 units and use dropout techniques to prevent overfitting. Importantly, they are configured to output fixed-size vectors instead of sequences.

The outputs from these three branches are then merged into a single representation using a concatenate layer. This combines the strengths of each RNN type, allowing the model to capture different aspects of the data. Finally, a dense layer with a single unit and a sigmoid activation function is added. This layer takes the combined output from the RNN branches and predicts the probability of the data belonging to one of two classes (sarcastic or non-sarcastic).

The entire model is then compiled using a binary cross-entropy loss function and the Adam optimiser. Additionally, the accuracy is tracked as a metric to monitor the model's performance during training.

Performance Evaluation

To assess how well sarcasm detection models perform, researchers use metrics such as accuracy, precision, recall, and F1 score. These metrics are based on four key terms:

True Positives (TP): Correctly identified sarcastic cases.
False Positives (FP): Nonsarcastic cases incorrectly classified as sarcastic.

True Negatives (TN): Correctly identified non-sarcastic cases.
False Negatives (FN): Sarcastic cases incorrectly classified as non-sarcastic.

Accuracy measures the overall proportion of correctly predicted cases. Precision focusses on the percentage of positive predictions that were truly sarcastic, while recall looks at the proportion of actual sarcasm that was correctly identified. The F1 score combines precision and recall into a single metric.

4 Results

This section explores the results obtained after data analysis in the above section. All models were trained with the Sigmoid activation function and Adam optimiser. To further improve performance, we fine-tuned the models by adjusting their parameters (details in Table 2).

Table 2. Parameters for training and validation

parameters	values
Kernel	3
Embedding dimensions	100
Epochs	25
Activation function	Sigmoid
Loss	Binary cross entropy
Batch size	32
Word embedding	Glove
Verbose	2
Dropout	0.2
Optimizer	Adam

4.1 Performance Analysis of Individual and Ensemble Models.

Figure 4 shows the trends of training and validation accuracy and training and validation loss of SimpleRNN. The highest training accuracy is around 0.7, while the validation accuracy is around 0.68. The training loss starts around 0.68 and decreases to 0.61, while the validation loss starts around 0.67 and stays relatively flat.

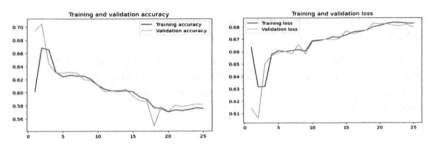

Fig. 4. Training and validation curve for simple RNN.

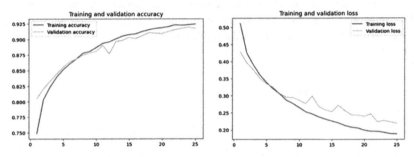

Fig. 5. Training and validation for LSTM.

Figure 5 shows the trends of training and validation accuracy and training loss of LSTM. The highest training accuracy is around 0.925, while the validation accuracy is around 0.90. The training loss starts around 0.5 and decreases to around 0.2, while the validation loss starts around 0.45 and decreases to around 0.25.

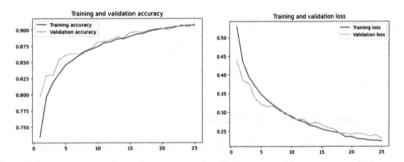

Fig. 6. Training and validation curve for GRU.

Figure 6 shows the trends of training and validation accuracy and GRU training and validation loss. The highest accuracy is 0.9, achieved by the training accuracy. The validation accuracy is around 0.9. The training loss starts around 0.5 and decreases to around 0.2, while the validation loss starts around 0.4 and decreases towards 0.2.

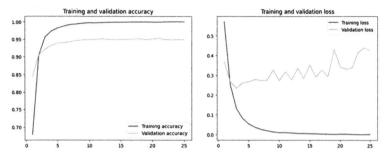

Fig. 7. Training and validation curves for one-level stacking.

Figure 7 shows the trends of training and validation accuracy and training and validation loss of the one-level stacking. The highest accuracy is achieved by the training accuracy, which is around 0.96. The validation accuracy is around 0.92. The training loss starts around 0.6 and decreases to around 0.1, while the validation loss starts around 0.37 and increases towards 0.4.

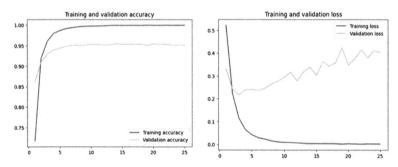

Fig. 8. Training and validation curves for two-level stacking.

Figure 8 shows the trends of training and validation accuracy and training and validation loss two-level stacking. The highest accuracy is achieved by the training accuracy, which is around 0.97. The validation accuracy is around 0.91. The training loss starts around 0.5 and decreases to around 0.1, while the validation loss starts around 0.34 and increases to around 0.4.

Figure 9 shows the trends of training and validation accuracy and training and validation loss. The highest accuracy is achieved by the training accuracy, which is around 0.98. The validation accuracy is around 0.93. The training loss starts around 0.53 and decreases to around 0.1, while the validation loss starts around 0.32 and increases towards 0.4.

Figure 10 shows the trends of training and validation accuracy and training and validation loss. The highest accuracy is achieved by the training accuracy, which is around 0.95. The validation accuracy is around 0.95. The training loss starts around 0.5 and decreases to around 0.1, while the validation loss starts around 0.3 and increases towards 0.5 but decreases towards 0.4.

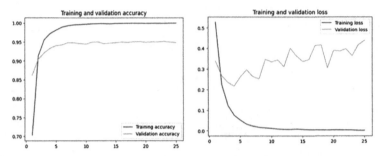

Fig. 9. Training and validation curves for three-level stacking.

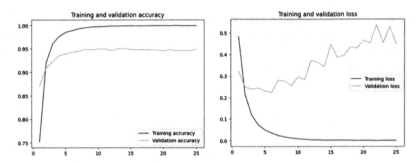

Fig. 10. Training and validation curves for the weighted average ensemble model

Figures 4, 5, 6, 7, 8, 9 and 10 depict the training and validation performance of individual models (SRNN, LSTM, GRU) and ensemble models (one-level, two-level, three-level stacking, and weighted average). Both types exhibit similar trends:

Training accuracy increases over time as the model learns, eventually plateauing.

Validation accuracy initially lags behind, but increases with better generalisation, potentially plateauing, or decreasing slightly due to overfitting.

Training loss decreases, indicating improved predictions in training data.

The validation loss tends to decrease but fluctuates more due to unseen data in the validation set. Figure 3 shows a slight case of overfitting, where the model performs well in training data, but poorly on unseen data.

Ensemble models outperform individual models.

Ensemble models demonstrate faster learning and higher validation accuracy compared to individual models. Although they also exhibit overfitting, the gap between their training and validation accuracy is smaller, suggesting a better generalisation.

The two-level stacking model achieved the best performance (95% accuracy and F1 score for both sarcastic and non-sarcastic classes). This success stems from combining the strengths of individual models (SRNN, LSTM, GRU) and mitigating their weaknesses. In general, ensemble models are more effective in detecting sarcasm than individual models.

See Fig. 8 for detailed performance metrics (accuracy and F1 score) of all models (Fig. 11).

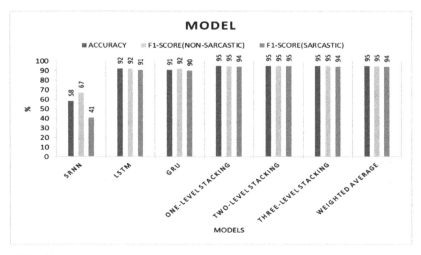

Fig. 11. Accuracy and F1 scores of both non-sarcastic and sarcastic of all models.

4.2 Summary

Section 3 (methodology) discussed the stages for our suggested method, data collection, data preprocessing, deep learning framework, and performance evaluation. The models were implemented using Python programming language due to its libraries such as NLTK, strong community support, and seamless integration with machine learning frameworks, offering simplicity and versatility for developing and implementing NLP tasks.

The results of this study suggest that ensemble models are a promising approach for sarcasm detection. Ensemble models outperformed individual neural network models by a significant margin, suggesting that they can capture more complex patterns in the data and are more resistant to noise.

However, it is important to note that ensemble models can be more complex to train and deploy than simpler models, such as weighted average. Additionally, the performance of different models may vary on different datasets.

5   Conclusion

This research explored ensemble models as a promising approach for detecting sarcasm in political speech. The ensemble models achieved a significant improvement over individual recurrent neural networks (RNNs) such as SimpleRNN, LSTM, and GRU. While the individual RNNs only reached 91% accuracy, the ensemble models attained a peak accuracy of 95% and an F1 score of 95% for both sarcastic and non-sarcastic classes. This enhancement can be attributed to the ensemble's ability to capture more intricate patterns within the data and its increased resilience to noise. Ensemble models function by leveraging the strengths of multiple individual models through combining their predictions. This study found that a two-level stacking model achieved the best performance; however, other techniques like weighted averaging were also demonstrably effective.

Acknowledgements. I express my sincere gratitude to my supervisor, Professor SN Mokwena, ETDP SITA, and my family and friends for their invaluable support throughout this research project.

References

1. Kušen, E., Strembeck, M.: Politics, sentiments, and misinformation: an analysis of the Twitter discussion on the 2016 Austrian Presidential Elections. Online Soc. Netw. Media **5**, 37–50 (2018). https://doi.org/10.1016/j.osnem.2017.12.002
2. Elisabeth: Sarcasm, Pretense, and The Semantics/ Pragmatics Distinction ∗. Nous 1–7 (2011)
3. Wang, H., Can, D., Kazemzadeh, A., Bar, F., Narayanan, S.: A system for real-time twitter sentiment analysis of 2012 U.S. presidential election cycle. In: Proceedings of the Annual Meeting Association Computing Linguistics, no. July, pp. 115–120 (2012)
4. Hussein, D.M.E.D.M.: A survey on sentiment analysis challenges. J. King Saud Univ. – Eng. Sci. **30**(4), 330–338 (2018). https://doi.org/10.1016/j.jksues.2016.04.002
5. Potamias, R.A., Siolas, G., Stafylopatis, A.G.: A transformer-based approach to irony and sarcasm detection. Neural Comput. Appl. **32**(23), 17309–17320 (2020). https://doi.org/10.1007/s00521-020-05102-3
6. Kurniasari, L., Setyanto, A.: Sentiment analysis using recurrent neural network. J. Phys.: Conf. Ser. **1471**(1), 012018 (2020). https://doi.org/10.1088/1742-6596/1471/1/012018
7. Ghosh, A., Veale, T.: Fracking sarcasm using neural network. In: Proceedings of the 7th Workshop Computation Approaches Subjectivity Sentiment Social Media Analysis WASSA 2016 2016 Conference North American Chapter Association Computation Linguistic Human Language Technology, no. April, pp. 161–169 (2016). https://doi.org/10.18653/v1/w16-0425
8. Akula, R.: Interpretable Multi-Head Self-Attention Architecture for (2021)
9. Reyes, A., Rosso, P., Veale, T.: A multidimensional approach for detecting irony in Twitter. Lang. Resour. Eval. **47**(1), 239–268 (2013). https://doi.org/10.1007/s10579-012-9196-x
10. Ghosh, D., Guo, W., Muresan, S.: Sarcastic or Not : Word Embeddings to Predict the Literal or Sarcastic Meaning of Words, pp. 1003–1012. no. September (2015)
11. Reyes, A., Rosso, P., Buscaldi, D.: From humor recognition to irony detection: the figurative language of social media. Data Knowl. Eng. **74**, 1–12 (2012). https://doi.org/10.1016/j.datak.2012.02.005
12. Lucariello, J.: Situational irony: a concept of events gone awry. J. Exp. Psychol.: General **123**(2), 129–145 (1994)
13. Barbieri, F., Saggion, H.: Modelling Irony in Twitter, pp. 56–64 (2014)
14. Buschmeier, K. Cimiano, P., Klinger, R.: An Impact Analysis of Features in a Classification Approach to Irony Detection in Product Reviews, pp. 42–49 (2014)
15. Joshi, A., Sharma, V., Bhattacharyya, P.: Harnessing Context Incongruity for Sarcasm Detection, no. 2003, pp. 757–762 (2015)
16. Amir, S., Wallace, B. C., Carvalho, P., Silva, J.: Modelling Context with User Embeddings for Sarcasm Detection in Social Media, pp. 167–177 (2016)
17. Oraby, S., Harrison, V., Reed, L., Hernandez, E., Riloff, E., Walker, M.: Creating and Characterizing a Diverse Corpus of Sarcasm in Dialogue, no. September, pp. 31–41 (2016)
18. Riloff, E., Qadir, A., Surve, P., De Silva, L., Gilbert, N., Huang, R.: Sarcasm as Contrast between a Positive Sentiment and Negative Situation, no. October, pp. 704–714 (2013)
19. Kumar, H.M.K., Harish, B.S.: ScienceDirect Sarcasm classification: a novel approach by using content based sarcasm classification: a novel approach by using content based sarcasm classification: a novel approach by using content based feature selection method feature selection met. Procedia Comput. Sci. **143**, 378–386 (2018). https://doi.org/10.1016/j.procs.2018.10.409

20. Savini, E., Caragea, C.: Intermediate-task transfer learning with BERT for sarcasm detection. Mathematics **10**(5), 844 (2022). https://doi.org/10.3390/math10050844
21. Ghosh, D., Richard, A., Smaranda, F.: The Role of Conversation Context for Sarcasm Detection in Online Interactions, no. August, pp. 186–196 (2017)
22. Du, Y., Li, T., Pathan, M.S., Teklehaimanot, H.K., Yang, Z.: An effective sarcasm detection approach based on sentimental context and individual expression habits. Cogn. Comput. **14**(1), 78–90 (2022). https://doi.org/10.1007/s12559-021-09832-x
23. Eke, C.I., Norman, A.A., Shuib, L.: Context-based feature technique for sarcasm identification in benchmark datasets using deep learning and BERT model. IEEE Access **9**, 48501–48518 (2021). https://doi.org/10.1109/ACCESS.2021.3068323
24. Razali, M.S., Halin, A.A., Ye, L., Doraisamy, S., Norowi, N.M.: Sarcasm detection using deep learning with contextual features. IEEE Access **9**, 68609–68618 (2021). https://doi.org/10.1109/ACCESS.2021.3076789
25. Wang, Z., Wu, Z., Wang, R., Ren, Y.: Twitter Sarcasm Detection Exploiting a, vol. 9419, pp. 332–336 (2015). https://doi.org/10.1007/978-3-319-26190-4
26. Jaiswal, N.: Neural sarcasm detection using conversation context. In: Proceedings of the Annual Meeting Association Computational Linguistic, pp. 77–82 (2020). https://doi.org/10.18653/v1/P17
27. Baruah, A., Das, K.A., Barbhuiya, F.A., Dey, K.: Context-aware sarcasm detection using BERT. In: Proceedings of the Annual Meeting Association Computational Linguistics, pp. 83–87 (2020). https://doi.org/10.18653/v1/P17
28. Joshi, A., Tripathi, V., Patel, K., Bhattacharyya, P., Carman, M.: Are word embedding-based features useful for sarcasm detection? In: EMNLP 2016 – Conference Empirical Methods Natural Language Processing Proceedings, no. 2013, pp. 1006–1011 (2016). https://doi.org/10.18653/v1/d16-1104
29. Mohammadi, S., Majelan, S.G., Shokouhi, S.B.: Ensembles of deep neural networks for action recognition in still images. In: 2019 9th International Conference on Computational Knowledge Eng. ICCKE 2019, no. Iccke, pp. 315–318 (2019). https://doi.org/10.1109/ICCKE48569.2019.8965014
30. Goel, P., Jain, R., Nayyar, A., Singhal, S., Srivastava, M.: Sarcasm detection using deep learning and ensemble learning. Multimed. Tools Appl. **81**(30), 43229–43252 (2022). https://doi.org/10.1007/s11042-022-12930-z
31. Hochreiter, S., Schmidhuber, J.: Long short-term memory. Neural Comput. **9**(8), 1735–1780 (1997). https://doi.org/10.1162/neco.1997.9.8.1735
32. Patro, J., Bansal, S., Mukherjee, A.: A deep-learning framework to detect sarcasm targets. In: EMNLP-IJCNLP 2019 – 2019 Conference Empirical Methods Natural Language Process. 9th International Joint Conference National Language Processing Proceedings Conference, pp. 6336–6342 (2019). https://doi.org/10.18653/v1/d19-1663
33. Tan, Y.Y., Chow, C.O., Kanesan, J., Chuah, J.H., Lim, Y.L.: Sentiment analysis and sarcasm detection using deep multi-task learning. Wirel. Pers. Commun. **129**(3), 2213–2237 (2023). https://doi.org/10.1007/s11277-023-10235-4
34. Pennington, C.D M.J., Socher, R.: GloVe: Global Vectors for Word Representation. In: Proceedings of the 2014 Conference Empirical Methods Natural Language Processing EMNLP, vol. 19, no. 5, pp. 1532–1543,2(014)
35. Jain, D., Kumar, A., Garg, G.: Sarcasm detection in mash-up language using soft-attention based bi-directional LSTM and feature-rich CNN. Appl. Soft Comput. J. **91**, 106198 (2020). https://doi.org/10.1016/j.asoc.2020.106198
36. Babanejad, N., Davoudi, H., An, A., Papagelis, M.: Affective and contextual embedding for sarcasm detection. In: COLING 2020 – 28th International Conference on Computing Linguistic Proceedings Conference, pp. 225–243 (2020). https://doi.org/10.18653/v1/2020.coling-main.20

37. Elman, J.L.: Finding structure in time. Cogn. Sci. **14**(2), 179–211 (1990). https://doi.org/10.1016/0364-0213(90)90002-E

38. Chung, J., Gulcehre, C., Cho, K., Bengio, Y.: Empirical Evaluation of Gated Recurrent Neural Networks on Sequence Modeling, pp. 1–9 (2014)

39. Lemmens, J., Burtenshaw, B., Lotfi, E., Markov, I., Daelemans, W.: Sarcasm detection using an ensemble approach. In: Proceedings of the Annual Meeting Association Computational Linguistic, pp. 264–269 (2020). https://doi.org/10.18653/v1/P17

40. Fersini, E., Pozzi, F.A., Messina, E.: Detecting irony and sarcasm in microblogs: The role of expressive signals and ensemble classifiers. In: Proceedings of the 2015 IEEE International Conference on Data Science Advertising Analysis DSAA 2015, no. October (2015). https://doi.org/10.1109/DSAA.2015.7344888

Unsupervised State Encoding in Video Sequences Using β-Variational Autoencoders

Stephan Mulder$^{(\boxtimes)}$ and Mathys C. Du Plessis

Nelson Mandela University, Gqeberha, South Africa
stephanmldr@gmail.com

Abstract. Monitoring and providing feedback on the execution of sequential tasks is common in various domains, such as industrial processes for quality control, automated supervision for skill acquisition and even surgical procedures. This research explores the use of a Disentangled β-Variational Autoencoder (β-VAE) to encode different states in video data depicting a sequence of actions being performed on a series of objects without explicit labels. We trained a Disentangled β-VAE on video data of a sequence being performed and evaluated its ability to distinguish between states using visualisations based on similarity metrics. The evaluation was performed using a set of sequences specifically designed to establish the validity and limits of β-VAE's encoding of the states. These sequences included both unseen sequences which were similar to the training data, as well as out-of-distribution sequences which deviate from those seen in training. The results demonstrate that the β-VAE successfully learned to encode distinct states within the sequence, as evidenced by the visualisations. It is shown that β-VAE is capable of detecting states within a sequence. Furthermore, it is demonstrated that these learnt states inherently also have learnt dependencies and relationships regarding the sequence in which they are performed. These findings lay the foundation for the development of an overarching algorithm that monitors a sequence in progress and provides feedback when deviations from the expected sequence occur.

Keywords: State Encoding · VAE · Sequence Modelling

1 Introduction

Sequential video data refers to a series of video frames captured over time, depicting a continuous process or activity. This data is temporal, where the order and timing of the frames carry significant information about the underlying process.

In industrial settings, sequential video data is commonly used for process monitoring and quality control. For example, in manufacturing assembly lines, video cameras can capture the step-by-step assembly process of a product. By analysing this sequential data, manufacturers can identify any deviations or

A. Gerber (Ed.): SAICSIT 2024, CCIS 2159, pp. 159–174, 2024.
https://doi.org/10.1007/978-3-031-64881-6_9

anomalies in the process, enabling early detection of quality issues and facilitating timely interventions.

These video sequences are categorised by the high dimensionality and complexity of the image data contained in each frame [1]. This complexity is not limited to the image data itself, it includes the spatial and temporal dependencies which develop over time. These evolving relationships introduce difficulties in extracting meaningful patterns and insights [2]. This difficulty is further compounded when considering that sequential video data often lacks explicit labels or annotations, requiring unsupervised or weakly-supervised approaches for analysis. Current approaches to state encoding in sequential data analysis face several limitations that hinder their effectiveness and practicality [3]. One of the primary drawbacks is the reliance on manual state labelling and annotation [4]. Supervised learning approaches rely on labeled data for learning, this introduces challenges in the context of state encoding. In many domains, such as industrial processes or surgical procedures, expert knowledge is required to accurately identify and label the different states within a sequence. This manual annotation process is time-consuming, labor-intensive, and subject to human bias and inconsistency [5]. These approaches require a large amount of labeled data [6] to learn the mapping between the input sequences and the corresponding state labels. It becomes increasingly impractical as the volume and complexity of the sequential data grow. Furthermore, supervised learning approaches are limited in their ability to handle novel or unseen states. If a new state emerges in the sequential data that was not present in the training data, the supervised model may not be able to recognise or encode it accurately. This lack of flexibility and adaptability is a significant drawback, especially in dynamic and evolving processes where new states may appear over time [7]. Given these limitations, there is a need for unsupervised methods to handle unlabelled sequential data. Unsupervised approaches aim to learn the underlying structure and patterns in the data without relying on explicit state labels.

Unsupervised methods are more adaptable to changing or evolving processes. As new data is generated, unsupervised models can automatically adapt and update their state representations, ensuring that the encoded states remain relevant and informative over time. This adaptability is relevant in real-world scenarios where the underlying process may undergo gradual or sudden changes [19]. However, unsupervised state encoding also presents its own challenges. Without explicit state labels, evaluating the quality and interpretability of the learned state representations can be difficult [8]. Developing appropriate evaluation metrics and validation strategies is an active area of research in unsupervised learning. Given these factors, the techniques used to approach this problem should be able to handle the high dimensionality, extract meaningful features, and capture the temporal dynamics of the data. Additionally, they should aim to be robust to noise, occlusions, and variations, and operate in an unsupervised or weakly-supervised manner.

The main objective of this research is to explore the use of β-Variational Autoencoders (β-VAE) for unsupervised state encoding in sequential video data.

We aim to develop a novel approach that can automatically discover and encode the distinct states within a sequence without relying on explicit state labels. By leveraging the power of unsupervised learning and the disentanglement capabilities of β-VAE, we seek to overcome the limitations of current approaches and enable more efficient and effective analysis of sequential data.

Disentangled β-VAE is an extension of the standard variational autoencoder (VAE) that introduces a β parameter to control the balance between reconstruction quality and disentanglement in the learned latent representations. By tuning the β parameter, we can encourage the model to learn a more structured and interpretable latent space, where different dimensions capture different factors of variation in the data.

In the context of state encoding, we hypothesise that the disentanglement property of β-VAE can be leveraged to learn a latent space where different states are well-separated and easily distinguishable. By training the disentangled β-VAE on sequential video data, we show the model discovers and encodes the underlying states based on their unique characteristics and temporal dynamics. This unsupervised approach eliminates the need for manual state labelling and enables the analysis of unlabelled sequential data. To evaluate the distinguishability of the states, similarity metrics are used to both quantify and visualise the effectivity of the proposed method.

The remainder is structured as follows, beginning with **Related Work**, the work is proposed in the **Suggest Approach**, with the implementation covered in **Experimental Procedure**, outcomes are shared in **Results** and analysed in **Discussion** and the **Conclusion** summarises the findings.

2   Related Work

In this section, we provide a brief overview of neural networks and delve into the details of VAEs, β-VAEs, and the concept of disentanglement.

2.1   Neural Networks

Neural networks are a class of machine learning models inspired by the structure and function of biological neural networks. They consist of interconnected nodes, or neurons, organised in layers. Each neuron receives input from the previous layer, applies a non-linear activation function, and passes the output to the next layer. Most neural networks are feedforward neural networks, where information flows in one direction from the input layer to the output layer, typically when temporal or contextual understanding is not required. Neural networks learn to approximate complex functions by adjusting the weights of the connections between neurons through a process called backpropagation and an optimisation algorithm such as stochastic gradient descent [9]. To train the NN, input-output pairs are utilised to minimise the error between the expected output and the NN-generated output for a given input. During training the weights of the connections are adjusted using backpropagation and an optimisation algorithm to minimise a loss function that measures the difference between the predicted output and the true output [10]. This process is repeated until the network converges to a solution that generalises well to new, unseen data.

2.2 Variational Autoencoders (VAEs)

Variational autoencoders (VAEs) are a class of generative models in the field of unsupervised learning. VAEs are based on the principles of probabilistic graphical models and neural networks, and they aim to learn a compact and meaningful representation of the input data in a lower-dimensional latent space [13].

The core idea behind VAEs is to model the relationship between the observed data and a set of latent variables that capture the underlying structure and variation in the data. VAEs consist of two main components: an encoder network and a decoder network. The encoder network takes the input data and maps it to a probability distribution in the latent space, typically a multivariate Gaussian distribution. The decoder network then takes a sample from this latent distribution and reconstructs the original input data [11]. The latent space dimensionality determines the compression level of the input data and the capacity of the model to capture the underlying structure of the states. A lower latent dimension results in a more compressed representation, while a higher dimension allows for more information to be preserved. The decoder network takes the latent space representation as input and aims to reconstruct the original image. It starts with a fully connected layer that maps the latent vector to a higher-dimensional space. The resulting tensor is then reshaped and passed through a series of transposed convolutional layers, which gradually increase the spatial dimensions and decrease the number of channels to reconstruct the original image.

The loss function of a VAE consists of two terms: the reconstruction loss $\mathcal{L}_r$ and the regularisation loss $\mathcal{L}_d$ (also known as the Kullback-Leibler (KL) divergence term).

$$\mathcal{L}(\theta, \phi; \mathbf{x}) = \mathcal{L}_r(\theta, \phi; \mathbf{x}) + \mathcal{L}_d(\phi; \mathbf{x}) \tag{1}$$

where: $\mathbf{x}$ is the input data. θ represents the parameters of the decoder network. ϕ represents the parameters of the encoder network.

The reconstruction loss measures the dissimilarity between the original input data $\mathbf{x}$ and the reconstructed data $\hat{\mathbf{x}}$ generated by the decoder:

$$\mathcal{L}_d(\theta, \phi; \mathbf{x}) = -\mathbb{E}_{q_\phi(\mathbf{z}|\mathbf{x})}[\log p_\theta(\mathbf{x}|\mathbf{z})] \tag{2}$$

where: $\mathbf{z}$ is the latent variable $q_\phi(\mathbf{z}|\mathbf{x})$ is the encoder network, which maps the input data $\mathbf{x}$ to the latent space $p_\theta(\mathbf{x}|\mathbf{z})$ is the decoder network, which maps the latent variable $\mathbf{z}$ back to the original data space.

The regularisation loss is the KL divergence between the encoder's distribution $q_\phi(\mathbf{z}|\mathbf{x})$ and a prior distribution $p(\mathbf{z})$, typically chosen to be a standard Gaussian distribution:

$$\mathcal{L}_r(\phi; \mathbf{x}) = D_{KL}(q_\phi(\mathbf{z}|\mathbf{x})||p(\mathbf{z})) \tag{3}$$

This regularisation term encourages the encoder to learn a latent space that follows the prior distribution, which helps to prevent overfitting and promotes a smooth and continuous latent space.

During training, the goal is to minimise the total loss $\mathcal{L}(\theta, \phi; \mathbf{x})$ for the encoder parameters ϕ and the decoder parameters θ. This is typically done using stochastic gradient descent or its variants, such as Adam optimiser.

2.3 β-VAEs and Disentanglement

Disentanglement is a concept in representation learning, particularly in the context of unsupervised learning, which refers to the ability of a model to learn a representation where different dimensions correspond to independent and interpretable factors of variation in the data [12]. In standard VAEs, the latent variables are often entangled, meaning that multiple factors of variation can be encoded in a single latent dimension or that a single factor of variation can be spread across multiple dimensions. This entanglement can hinder the interpretability and controllability of the learned representations [13].

In a disentangled representation, each dimension captures a specific and meaningful aspect of the data, such as colour, shape, or orientation, while being invariant to other factors.

Disentangled representations have several desirable properties, including improved interpretability, controllability, and generalisation. By having a clear understanding of what each dimension in the latent space represents, we can gain insights into the underlying structure of the data and manipulate specific aspects of the generated samples.

β-VAEs are an extension of the standard VAE framework that specifically aims to promote disentanglement in the learned representations. β-VAEs introduce a hyperparameter β that controls the balance between reconstruction quality and disentanglement in the latent space [14]. They modify the standard VAE objective by scaling the regularisation term, which encourages the latent distribution to be close to a prior distribution, typically a standard Gaussian.

$$\mathcal{L}(\theta, \phi; \mathbf{x}) = \mathcal{L}_r(\theta, \phi; \mathbf{x}) + \beta - \mathcal{L}_d(\phi; \mathbf{x}) \tag{4}$$

In β-VAEs, the β-parameter acts as a weight for the regularisation term (Eq. 3) in the VAE objective. By increasing the value of β, the model places more emphasis on the regularisation term, which encourages the latent variables to be more independent and factorised. This increased regularisation pressure forces the model to learn a representation where each dimension captures a distinct factor of variation, leading to improved disentanglement [12]. The loss function provided in Eq. 4 can be further modified to encourage disentanglement [14]. This optimisation requires additional hyperparameters and is expressed in Eq. 5.

$$\mathcal{L}(\theta, \phi; x, z, C) = \mathbb{E}_{q_\phi(\mathbf{z}|\mathbf{x})}[\log p_\theta(\mathbf{x}|\mathbf{z})] - \beta - |D_{KL}(q_\phi(z|x)|p(z)) - C| \tag{5}$$

The hyperparamter C is the target value for the KL divergence, this pressures the divergence to be controllable by adding encoding capacity. The aim is to force the network to learn more factors of variation within the encoder without simply minimising the loss of the objective function as per Eq. 4. Where the standard function might focus on a single differentiable aspect of the data such as object placement, this introduced hyperparameter encourages optimising for other characteristics such as shape or colour for example [14].

2.4   Related Work on Sequence Modelling

Traditional approaches to learning representations from spatio-temporal data, such as 3D Convolutional Neural Networks (CNNs) and Recurrent Neural Networks (RNNs), have shown success in various tasks like action recognition and video classification [15,16]. However, these methods often struggle to effectively disentangle the underlying factors of variation and represent objects independently in multi-object scenes. 3D CNNs learn hierarchical representations by applying convolutions over both spatial and temporal dimensions, but they do not explicitly model the decomposition of scenes into objects or the disentanglement of object properties. Similarly, RNNs can capture temporal dependencies but lack the inherent ability to decompose scenes into objects and represent their properties separately. In recent years, unsupervised representation learning approaches have shown promising results in decomposing and disentangling the underlying factors of variation in complex multi-object scenes. Hsieh et al. proposed the Decompositional Disentangled Predictive Auto-Encoder (DDPAE), a framework that combines structured probabilistic models and deep networks to decompose videos into components and disentangle each component into low-dimensional temporal dynamics for easier prediction [17]. While DDPAE focuses on video prediction tasks and achieves disentanglement through a structured model architecture and learning objectives, Greff et al. introduced IODINE (Iterative Object Decomposition Inference NEtwork), an unsupervised approach that jointly segments and represents objects in multi-object scenes [18]. IODINE leverages iterative refinement of inferred latent representations and learns to decompose scenes into objects and represent them in terms of properties like color, size, position, and material. Although IODINE assumes that objects are placed independently in a scene, the authors suggest that extending the model to handle temporal data and incorporating graph networks to capture relations between objects could be beneficial for modelling physical interactions and tracking objects over time.

3   Suggested Approach

We propose a novel approach to learning the sequence of states contained in video. The goal of the research is to take a sequence of frames from a video and determine if the frames contain the expected sequence of states for a given task. We suggest that this can be achieved by utilising a Neural Network which is trained in an unsupervised manner thereby negating the need to generate any labels regarding the sequence analysed. This can be achieved by taking a set of videos which contain the expected sequence and training a disentangled β-VAE on the frames of these videos.

The proposed approach will leverage the ability of this NN to uniquely encode features of the data to unique dimensions of the latent vector. For sequence learning this will allow the different states and actions of the sequence to be represented by unique dimensions of the latent vector. This will result in repeatable and distinct latent vectors for each state which can then be easily compared using similarity metrics to the latent vector of a reference state which represents the expected states within the sequence. The reference states in the sequence can be extracted by a motion detection algorithm which captures the first frame of every static sequence of frames within another video. The expectation would be for the encoded latent vectors of an unseen sequence to be similar to those of the reference states for the relevant portions of the video if the sequence contained in the video depicts the correct order of states, else the network will either encode the state in the incorrect order, or not encode the state at all, both of which can be used signals that the sequence is incorrect.

By establishing whether a CNN can be trained using a disentangled β-VAE to have unique latent vectors for highly similar images from a sequence of unlabelled data, avenues are opened for leveraging these unique encodings in future works for state prediction and anomaly detection. An encoder proven capable of decoding the states of the sequence could then be combined with temporal neural networks as a more powerful CNN for deciphering highly similar data (Fig. 1).

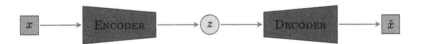

Fig. 1. A simplified diagram of an autoencoder architecture, illustrating the flow from input x through the encoder to produce latent representation z, and then through the decoder to reconstruct $\hat{x}$.

4   Experimental Procedure

The applied method is described here. These were applied for a range of β values to contrast their impact on the results.

4.1   Experiment Outline

The use of a disentangled β-Variational Autoencoder (β-VAE) to learn and encode specific video frame sequences is proposed. The disentangled β-VAE will be trained on synthetic data depicting a particular sequence of actions. To evaluate the model's ability to encode the learned states, we will employ various similarity metric-based visualisations, comparing unseen test footage against the expected learned states extracted from a video sequence of valid sequences using a motion extraction algorithm. The unseen test footage will include videos depicting the same sequence the network was trained on, as well as irregular sequences using the same objects. This approach will allow assessment of the network's capability to detect deviations from the learned sequence. The network's limits will then be evaluated by progressively augmenting frames of an unseen video depicting the same sequence the network was trained on.

4.2   Disentangled β-VAE Architecture

The disentangled β-VAE architecture employed for this research consists of an encoder and decoder network. The encoder network takes an input image of shape (3, 128, 128), representing a frame from the sequential video data. It consists of a series of convolutional layers followed by batch normalisation and ReLU activation. The convolutional layers progressively reduce the spatial dimensions while increasing the number of channels, capturing hierarchical features from the input image. The output of the convolutional layers is flattened and passed through two fully connected layers to obtain the latent space representation. The selection of the latent dimension should balance the trade-off between compression and reconstruction quality, as well as the desired level of disentanglement in the learned representations. For this research, disentanglement is of greater importance than reconstruction, although this should not be entirely sacrificed. The latent space dimension is set to 8, although 16 was also tested and performed similarly for this dataset.

For training a learning rate of $l_r = 10^{-4}$ was utilised. The hyperparameter β was varied to analyse the impact of disentanglement of the encoded states. The following values were used to train the network $\beta = 1, 2, 5, 10, 15, 50, 100$. With $\beta = 1$ being more analogous to a standard VAE and all increased values sacrificing a greater degree of reconstruction ability.

4.3   Video Data and Preprocessing

The simulated video dataset used for training the β-VAE was specifically designed for this research. The synthetic data ensured that the sequence was well-defined and consistent across the dataset and allowed for controlled variations in object appearance and background to improve the network's robustness. It consists of a sequential dataset of frames captured at a frame rate of 12 frames per second. Each frame has a resolution of 600 by 400 pixels and depicts a user moving three distinct shapes (a red circle, a blue rectangle, and a green triangle) into their designated zones. The zones were each a thin-bordered square, approximately ten times the dimension of the shape allowing for variability in placement.

The training dataset comprises 8 videos of the same sequence being performed with slight variations in the path taken to the designated zones, ensuring consistency and variability in the training data. In each video, the shapes are moved to their respective zones in a fixed order, starting with the red circle, followed by the blue rectangle, and finally the green triangle. These states are depicted in Fig. 2. The 4 distinct states for the network to learn are:

- The starting state, where all shapes are lined up and yet to be placed.
- The state where the red circle being placed in its designated zone.
- The state where the blue rectangle being placed in its designated zone.
- The state where the green triangle being placed in its designated zone.

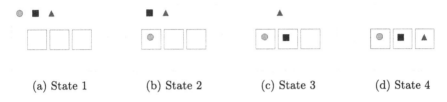

(a) State 1   (b) State 2   (c) State 3   (d) State 4

Fig. 2. Contrasting states (Color figure online)

4.4   Sequence States and Motion Extraction Algorithm

To obtain the expected learned states from the synthetic data, we will employ a motion extraction algorithm. This algorithm will simply identify when the scene is static and no motion is present and capture the first frame as a state. The extracted motion information will serve as the ground truth for evaluating the disentangled β-VAE's ability to encode the learned states.

4.5   Evaluation Data

In addition to the standard training sequence, the dataset also includes multiple testing sequences designed to evaluate the network's ability to capture and encode different states to establish its robustness and usefulness. These testing sequences introduce variations in the order of shape placement, the paths followed by the shapes, and the presence of noise or occlusions. By incorporating these testing sequences, the robustness and generalisation capabilities of the β-VAE can be assessed.

Non-standard Object Paths. The β-VAE was trained on videos with the objects taking the shortest possible route to their designated zones. Irregular object paths video consists of frames of a sequence where the shapes avoid taking this route to their designated zones. This route means the shapes where taken all the way around the designated zones and entered from the bottom rather than simply being placed from the top as before.

Wrong Sequences and Placements. The wrong video sequence video contains frames which depict the incorrect sequence of shapes being placed in the correct designated zones. The blue rectangle is placed before the red circle and lastly the green triangle, hence the states are 1-3-2-4 instead of 1-2-3-4. The wrong placement video sees the objects moved in the same incorrect sequence as the wrong sequence video, but the variation is that now the objects are also placed incorrectly. Hence the blue rectangle is placed first and into the zone of the red circle.

Noisy Images. These augmentations were for random rotation of the image within 10° of the magnitude parameter and transformations of the image appearance. The image adjustments included brightness, contrast, saturation, and hue and are directly proportional to the magnitude.

4.6   Evaluation

Here a brief outline is provided for how the figures used for analysing the results are generated. These figures will be used to establish how the frames of the sequence have been encoded by the network to ascertain if the relationships between the objects have been learnt.

Similarity Heatmap. This figure depicts the magnitude of the similarity of the frames from the video relative to the reference frames of the states. The similarity is determined using Euclidean Distance. This visualisation easily displays whether the states have been successfully encoded differently and if they are in the right sequence. The magnitude of the similarity is returned by the intensity of the colour on the heatmap and easily helps visually differentiate the different states.

Similarity Plot. This is a variation of the heatmap where the magnitudes of the similarity of the reference states are plotted relative to the frames from the video, this allows for visualising the disentanglement and the stability of the encoding of the latent vectors by the similarity of the current state relative to the others.

Averaged Assignments. This visualisation takes the current frame in the video's similarity and averages it with the surrounding four frames to generate a step plot of the assignments over the video. This averaging allows for smoothing any quick mis-assignments which can happen for a single frame and returns a plot which should show the progression of the steps as the video continues.

5   Results

The results consider the similarity of the encodings to the four reference states relative to their place in the sequence as well as the three landmarks within each state as described earlier. Hence the results consider and convey how similar the encoded frame is to the correct reference state as well as the action conveyed by said frame for that portion of the state. It is expected that the similarity will be greatest when the object enters the designated zone and is placed.

5.1 Analysis of Encoded States

When plotting the heatmap of the encoded frame from the sequence relative to the test states (Fig. 3), the relationships between the encoded vectors and hence the learnt representations are easily recognisable. The heatmap shows the degree of similarity between the encoded frames and the reference state. In this case, Euclidean distance is used to measure the similarity and hence the darker blue indicates a greater similarity as the latent vectors are closer together in the latent space relative to the over four vectors. The heatmap reveals that the encodings are less similar relative to the states when the object is in motion (red dashed line to blue dashed line), but the state associated with that shape's movement still tends to be the state with the best similarity, if not second to the preceding state.

The similarity plots reinforce this (Fig. 4). These plot the similarity of each encoded reference state to each encoded video frame. These plots show that the beginning of movement for a shape always signals a dramatic change in similarity, typically seen as a spike that gradually decreases and stabilises by the time the shape reaches the static placement. The milder gradient is usually intersected by the point at which the object enters the designated zone before becoming static, where the slope tends to become even gentler.

Both the similarity plots and the heatmap exhibit four distinct periods corresponding to the four states in the sequence. In the heatmap, these are concentrated blue patches, and in the plot, they are the four periods of low scores and stable gradients that each plot takes, only moving far away from these when the state changes. From the range of β values used in Fig. 3, the impact of increasing β can also be observed, with the quality of the latent vectors for similarity degrading after $\beta = 50$. It can also be observed that $\beta = 15$ has more distinct boundaries between the periods where the object is moving and when it is stationary (the colour change is more abrupt rather than a gradient) whilst retaining a high dissimilarity relative to the other states, it is, therefore, this version of the network which is utilised for subsequent tests.

5.2 Robustness Analysis

To assist in interpreting how the β-VAE has encoded the data to evaluate its effectivity, this section covers the network response to situations not included in, and which in some form deviate from the training data. The network response is analysed using the average assignments plot.

Encoded States for Non-standard Object Paths. The irregular movement (Fig. 5a) is encoded very similarly to the standard data (Fig. 5b, with the first

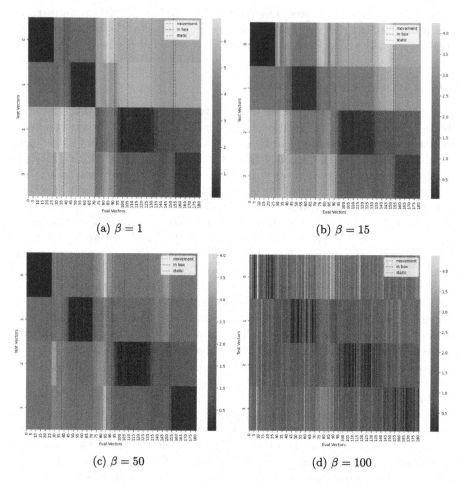

(a) $\beta = 1$ (b) $\beta = 15$

(c) $\beta = 50$ (d) $\beta = 100$

Fig. 3. Contrasting similarity heatmaps for a standard sequence for a range of β values (Color figure online)

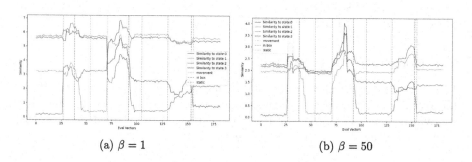

(a) $\beta = 1$ (b) $\beta = 50$

Fig. 4. Contrasting similarity plots for a standard sequence

movement triggering a state change, as can be seen with the state assignment plots (blue and green) relative to the reference plot (orange). This differs from the second state, which changes when the object enters the designated zone As with the plot for the standard data, the irregular data. The two differ for the final states where the green triangle is placed with the irregular data being assigned to the state once the object moves. Also visible here is the difference between a small window for averaging the assignments. The green plot is the averaged assignments for a window of 5 frames. Whereas the blue plot is the averaged assignments for a window of 10 frames. The result for this data is that the larger window reacts slower to the change in state.

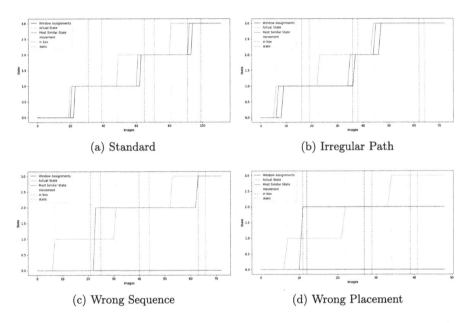

(a) Standard   (b) Irregular Path

(c) Wrong Sequence   (d) Wrong Placement

Fig. 5. Contrasting the Average State Assignments on different sequence types, all for the same model trained with $\beta = 15$ (Color figure online)

Encoded States for Incorrect Placements and Sequences. When analysing the averaged assignment plot for the smaller window (green) for the wrong sequence data (Fig. 5c) we begin to understand how the β-VAE has encoded and learnt the relationships between the objects as well as the sequence. The plot shows the encoded states of 0-2-3. The state associated with the red circle (s1) is never assigned as the blue rectangle moves first in this data. The state associated with placing the blue rectangle (s2) is only assigned just before the object is stationary and remains there as the red circle is placed and only changes once the green triangle is placed.

For the wrong placement dataset (Fig. 5d), where objects are moved to the wrong places and in the wrong sequence, the averaged assignments clearly detect the wrong sequence. The frames for this sequence depict the blue circle moving first to the zone dedicated to the red circle, that is two say states 2 and 1 are inverted in both placements. Unlike before where the incorrect object was heading to the correct zone, when the blue rectangle is placed its state (s2) is assigned, but the subsequent placement of the red circle in the wrong zone and the green triangle in the correct zone do not trigger a change in state.

When analysing the averaged assignments for window size of 10 frames (blue plot) it can be seen that the state never changes, indicating that the incorrect sequence has great variability in its encoding when the sequence is not respected. This shows that the networks can successfully encode the differences between states as well as deviations from the expected sequence as the placement of all three objects has not been respected.

Network Performance on Noisy Data. To begin to asses how the network might perform on real-world data, it is tested on noise-injected data. This data depicted the standard validation sequence with Gaussian noise, random rotations, and hue changes added to the images. A scaling factor of m was used to control these image augmentations. For small values of m ($m => 0.1$), it was shown to have minimum no effect for this average assignment, but variations from the degree of similarity from frame to frame could be seen in the heatmap for this data. When m begins to be relatively sizeable $m = 0.4$ the results (Fig. 6a) show the encoder can no longer successfully discern the states. Globally, a vague correct sequence can be identified, but the degree of noise on the plot is indicative of the inability of the network to decipher the states from the added noise.

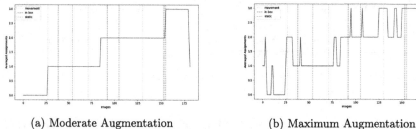

(a) Moderate Augmentation   (b) Maximum Augmentation

Fig. 6. Contrasting Average State Assignments for varying amounts of image noise for $\beta = 15$

6   Discussion

Interpretation of Results. The experiments demonstrate that the β-VAE learns to encode distinct states within sequential data without explicit labels. The results show that the network can distinguish between different states based on the position and movement of objects in the sequence. The similarity metrics and evaluation protocols established in this research provide a framework for validating the β-VAE's ability to detect states in video data. The disentangled β-VAE's success in training a CNN to encode disentangled representations of states suggests that it can be utilised for analysing and understanding sequences without the need for manual labelling. The patterns observed, such as the network's ability to recognise the correct sequence of object placements, its sensitivity to deviations from the expected sequence and the inferred relationships between states, highlight the potential of the proposed approach for monitoring and providing feedback in various applications. These show that the CNN is capable of detecting errors. The learned disentangled representations provide interpretable and meaningful insights into the underlying states of the sequence, enabling better understanding and analysis of the data without the need for explicit labels. All labels included in these results are for visualisation and validation and were not included in the training of the network. These results were achieved by training with just 8 examples of the sequence at less than 80 frames each. However, the proposed approach also has some limitations. The performance of the β-VAE may be sensitive to the choice of hyperparameters. In cases where the sequential data is highly complex or contains a large number of states, it would be suspected that the network may struggle to capture all the relevant information. To mitigate these limitations and improve the robustness of the approach, several strategies can be explored. Incorporating techniques such as data augmentation can enhance the network's ability to handle variations and generalise to new sequences.

7   Conclusion and Future Work

This research explores the use of a β variational autoencoder (VAE) for unsupervised state encoding in sequential data. The key findings demonstrate that the β-VAE is capable of learning disentangled representations of distinct states within a sequence as well as anomalies, without the need for explicit labels. The proposed approach, along with the established evaluation protocols and similarity metrics, provides a framework for validating the network's ability to detect and encode states in video data.

References

1. Li, J., Li, B., Lu, Y.: Deep contextual video compression. In: Advances in Neural Information Processing Systems, vol. 34, pp. 18114–18125 (2021)

2. Chen, C.-F.R., et al.: Deep analysis of CNN-based spatio-temporal representations for action recognition. In: Proceedings of the IEEE/CVF Conference on Computer Vision and Pattern Recognition, pp. 6165–6175 (2021)

3. Liu, H., et al.: Learning to identify critical states for reinforcement learning from videos. In: Proceedings of the IEEE/CVF International Conference on Computer Vision, pp. 1955–1965 (2023)

4. Wang, L., et al.: Temporal segment networks: towards good practices for deep action recognition. In: Leibe, B., Matas, J., Sebe, N., Welling, M. (eds.) ECCV 2016. LNCS, vol. 9912, pp. 20–36. Springer, Cham (2016). https://doi.org/10.1007/978-3-319-46484-8_2

5. Rangineni, S.: An Analysis of data quality requirements for machine learning development pipelines frameworks. Int. J. Comput. Trends Technol. **71**(9), 16–27 (2023)

6. Wang, L., Qiao, Y., Tang, X.: Action recognition with trajectory-pooled deep-convolutional descriptors. In: Proceedings of the IEEE Conference on Computer Vision and Pattern Recognition, pp. 4305–4314 (2015)

7. Qi, G.-J., Luo, J.: Small data challenges in big data era: a survey of recent progress on unsupervised and semi-supervised methods. IEEE Trans. Pattern Anal. Mach. Intell. **44**(4), 2168–2187 (2020)

8. Lipton, Z.C.: The mythos of model interpretability: in machine learning, the concept of interpretability is both important and slippery. Queue **16**(3), 31–57 (2018)

9. Goodfellow, I., Bengio, Y., Courville, A.: Deep Learning. Adaptive Computation and Machine Learning. MIT Press (2016)

10. LeCun, Y., Bengio, Y., Hinton, G.: Deep learning. Nature **521**(7553), 436–444 (2015). https://doi.org/10.1038/nature14539

11. Kingma, D.P., Welling, M.: Auto-encoding variational bayes. arXiv preprint arXiv:1312.6114 (2013)

12. Higgins, I., et al.: Beta-VAE: learning basic visual concepts with a constrained variational framework. In: International Conference on Learning Representations (2016)

13. Liu, W., et al.: Towards visually explaining variational autoencoders. In: Proceedings of the IEEE/CVF Conference on Computer Vision and Pattern Recognition, pp. 8642–8651 (2020)

14. Burgess, C.P., et al.: Understanding Disentangling in β-VAE. arXiv preprint arXiv:1804.03599 (2018). https://doi.org/10.48550/arXiv.1804.03599

15. Tran, D., Bourdev, L., Fergus, R., Torresani, L., Paluri, M.: Learning spatiotemporal features with 3D convolutional networks. In: 2015 IEEE International Conference on Computer Vision (ICCV), pp. 4489–4497. IEEE, Santiago (2015). https://doi.org/10.1109/ICCV.2015.510

16. Donahue, J., et al.: Long-term recurrent convolutional networks for visual recognition and description. In: Proceedings of the IEEE Conference on Computer Vision and Pattern Recognition, pp. 2625–2634 (2015)

17. Hsieh, J.-T., Liu, B., Huang, D.-A., Fei-Fei, L.F., Niebles, J.C.: Learning to decompose and disentangle representations for video prediction. In: Advances in Neural Information Processing Systems, vol. 31 (2018)

18. Greff, K., et al.: Multi-object representation learning with iterative variational inference. In: International Conference on Machine Learning, pp. 2424–2433. PMLR (2019)

19. Gama, J., Žliobaitė, I., Bifet, A., Pechenizkiy, M., Bouchachia, A.: A survey on concept drift adaptation. ACM Comput. Surv. (CSUR) **46**(4), 1–37 (2014)

User Centred Design and Implementation of Useful Picture Archiving and Communication Systems for Effective Radiological Workflows in Public Health Facilities in Zambia

Andrew Shawa[1], Elijah Chileshe[1], Brighton Mwaba[3], John Mwanza[3], Wilkins Sikazwe[3], Ernest Obbie Zulu[2], and Lighton Phiri[3](✉)

[1] Department of Computer Science, University of Zambia, Lusaka, Zambia
{andrew.shawa,elijah.chileshe}@cs.unza.zm
[2] Department of Radiology, Adult Hospital, University Teaching Hospitals, Lusaka, Zambia
obbiernest@gmail.com
[3] Department of Library and Information Science, University of Zambia, Lusaka, Zambia
{2018218409,2018171968,2018215311}@student.unza.zm, lighton.phiri@unza.zm

Abstract. Radiological workflows in public health facilities in The Republic of Zambia are performed using manual processes. With a broad spectrum of stakeholders—physicians, radiographers and radiologists involved in radiological workflows, the efficiency of health service provision is drastically reduced, subsequently compromising clinical care. While there are a number of software platforms that are used in radiological workflows, Picture Archiving and Communication System platforms are important as they are primarily used to store, manage and facilitate access to Medical Images. This paper outlines the user-centred design and implementation of a Picture Archiving and Communication System for storing, managing, and facilitating access to medical images in public health facilities in Zambia, in order to demonstrate the feasibility of automating manual medical imaging workflows in public health facilities. Semi-structured interviews were conducted with two (2) radiologists and four (4) radiographers in order to understand medical imaging workflows in public health facilities. A Picture Archiving and Communication System was designed and implemented using Dicoogle as the base platform and, subsequently evaluated—using the TAM 2 questionnaire— in order to assess its perceived usability and usefulness. The interviews conducted provide insight into the extent towards which manual workflows are employed, with Change to Digital Imaging and Communications in Medicine (DICOM) Viewers used as the main technology in the workflow. The implementation and evaluation of the Picture Archiving and Communication System demonstrates the feasibility of implementing these platforms in public health facilities and their potential usefulness, respectively.

© The Author(s), under exclusive license to Springer Nature Switzerland AG 2024
A. Gerber (Ed.): SAICSIT 2024, CCIS 2159, pp. 175–189, 2024.
https://doi.org/10.1007/978-3-031-64881-6_10

Keywords: Enterprise Medical Imaging · Medical Images · Picture Archiving and Communication System · Radiological Workflows

1 Introduction

The automation of radiological workflows, such as through implementation of Picture Archiving and Communication System (PACS)—software tools used to store, manage and access medical images such as X-rays—and Radiology Information System (RIS)—software tools used to manage radiological workflow processes as requests for patients to be examined, has undoubtedly proved valuable at improving the productivity and efficiency of radiology departments. Although the implementation of PACS systems often result in increased workload for some individual stakeholders—such as radiologists, gains are ultimately realised through the resultant time efficiency and enhanced image storage, access, management and transfer.

However, the lack of PACS has been identified as the critical missing element for international radiology development in resource constrained countries [13]. In The Republic of Zambia, public health facilities lack this important software platform and as such, radiological workflows are currently performed using manual processes. For instance, historical medical images are stored on optical discs and external hard drives. Coupled with other confounding challenges including the critical shortage of radiologists, low utilisation of technology among stakeholders and the broad spectrum of stakeholders involved in the radiological workflows, this drastically reduces the efficiency of the radiological services thereby compromising clinical care. Zulu and Phiri [18] highlighted challenges and opportunities associated with the implementation of Enterprise Medical Imaging (EMI) strategies, whose important infrastructure components are PACS platforms.

Open source PACS platforms are increasingly becoming available and offer multiple advantages for PACS platform implementation to resource-limited institutions, including relative cost-effectiveness, flexibility for customisation to meet local users' imaging needs and interoperability with other existing and future software systems within the domain of electronic health record systems.

This paper outlines the design, implementation and subsequent evaluation for usefulness, of a prototype user-centered PACS platform aimed at demonstrating the feasibility of designing and implementing potentially cost-effective PACS platforms for use in public health facilities in Zambia.

The remainder of this paper is organised as follows: Sect. 2 describes relevant literature related to this work; Sect. 3 outlines the methodological approach employed to conduct this study; Sect. 4 describes and interprets the results associated with the study and, finally, Sect. 5 presents concluding remarks and potential future work.

2 Related Work

2.1 Radiological Workflow Challenges

The challenges associated with access to radiological services in Low and Middle Income Countries (LMICs) are extensively documented in literature. Hricak et al.

report that a global assessment of medical imaging revealed significant shortages of human resource and equipment in LMICs [11]. Frija et al. further emphasise seriousness of these challenges and highlight the importance of access to imaging services in LMICs due to the rise in cases of non-communicable diseases [9]. Zambia faces a challenge of not having enough radiology workers countrywide, a situation that slows down the process of delivering radiological findings to support medical diagnosis and decision making, with a recent study reporting the existence of only nine (9) radiologists in public health facilities, servicing a population of 18 million [6].

In one of our most recent work [18] aimed at identifying potential ways of addressing radiological workflow challenges in public health facilities in Zambia, a SWOT analysis conducted revealed challenges and potential opportunities that exist through the use of Enterprise Medical Imaging—"a set of strategies, initiatives, and workflows implemented across a healthcare enterprise to consistently and optimally capture, index, manage, store, distribute, view, exchange, and analyze all clinical imaging and multimedia content to enhance the electronic health record" [16]. While EMI strategies involve the use of various technological infrastructures, PACS platforms are considered a important technological infrastructure. This study focused on early attempts at designing and implementing PACS platforms to be used in public health facilities in Zambia.

2.2 Free and Open Source Picture Archiving and Communication System Platforms

In the recent past, a number of Free and Open Source Software (FOSS) PACS platforms have been designed and implemented, focused on facilitating the storage of medical images.

ClearCanvas is an open source PACS platform and archive that conforms to the Digital Imaging and Communications in Medicine (DICOM) standard. It offers features such as storage, compression, retrieval of objects and a single user login for secure access [7]. It provides a solution for managing medical image data and organisation of studies. It also offers several plugins that add additional features to the system.

Dicoogle is a PACS archive platform based on a modular architecture, allowing for quick development of auxiliary functionalities [14,15]. The Dicoogle design enables for the automated information extraction, indexing and storage of metadata associated with medical images, addressing limitations with DICOM-compliant query services.

Orthanc functions as a standalone PACS server aimed at providing relatively easy implementation with ease of installation, configuration, running and integration [12]. Orthanc's design focuses on improvement of DICOM workflows in health facilities and is reported to have a design that hides the complexities of the DICOM format and protocol in order for users to focus on the content of medical images.

DCM4CHEE is a widely used PACS platform used to archive and manage images. It offers a modular architecture and allows for system customization and flexible data flow configuration [3]. It contains utilities developed in Java for performance and portability, with a strong focus on adherence to the DICOM standard, providing robust and scalable services for healthcare enterprise applications.

EasyPACS is a PACS server that incorporates an online DICOM viewer. It utilises the DCM4CHE API tools, rewritten using modern frameworks such as Spring Boot and Gradle Build Environments. The server accepts DICOM files, generating entity data representing patients, studies, series, equipment and instances which are stored in a relational database management system [2]. It also offers affordable PACS server capabilities and the flexibility to customise the system according to the workflow logic of different health facilities.

While the design and implementation considerations and approaches are different, the vast majority of FOSS PACS platforms are integrated with basic features necessary to store, manage and access medical images. As part of this study, a systematic comparative analysis—outlined in Sect. 3.3—was done by focusing on crucial feature offerings.

3 Methodology

This section explores the methodology used to understand current challenges, design a potential solution, and evaluate its user acceptance.

A mixed-method approach was used as the basis for conducting this research, combining the use of guided interview sessions and questionnaires.

Ethical clearance was granted by The University of Zambia Biomedical Research Ethics Committee (Reference Number: 2731-2022) and The National Health Research Authority (Reference Number: NRHA000024/10/05/2022), to conduct this study at two (2) public health facilities—University Teaching Hospitals (UTHs) and Levy Mwanawasa University Teaching Hospital (LMUTH). In addition, formal permission was granted from the two (2) facilities.

3.1 Research Design

The primary aim of this study is to understand current challenges in radiological workflows, design a potential solution in the form of a PACS platform, and evaluate its user acceptance in public health facilities in Zambia. Sections 3.2 to 3.4 provide details about the radiological workflow challenges, the implementation of the PACS platform and the evaluation details of the PACS platform, respectively.

3.2 Medical Image Workflows

To gain insights into existing challenges associated with storage, management and access to medical images, in medical image workflows, semi-structured interviews were conducted with two (2) key stakeholder groups: radiologists and radiographers. Radiographers are technicians who perform imaging examinations on patients and generate medical images in various modalities. Radiologists, on the other hand, are medical professionals who interpret these images and report their findings.

This study was conducted at two (2) large referral hospitals in Zambia: UTHs and LMUTH. The target population for the study included trainee radiologists and radiographers working at these public health facilities. Convenience sampling was employed to select participants from this population.

The audio data collected during the interview sessions were transcribed and thematically analysed to identify recurring themes and pain points related to image storage, management, and access.

3.3   Design and Implementation of Picture Archiving and Communication System Platform

Picture Archiving and Communication System Frameworks Feature Evaluation. An evaluation of the identified FOSS PACS Platforms—ClearCanvas [7], Dicoogle [14], DCM4CHEE [3], EasyPACS [2] and Orthanc [4] was carried out to assess the suitability and effectiveness of the platforms. The evaluation involved the assessment of the PACS platforms considering the following factors which were systematically arrived at during experimentation:

- Base Programming Language—Programming language used as the foundation for implementing the PACS platform
- Extensibility—PACS platform's ability to easily be extended with additional functionalities
- Extension Languages—Programming languages supported during development of plugins or extensions
- Operating System Support—Operating system software supported by the platform
- Database—Database management systems used by the PACS platform
- Search Service—Search service integrated with the PACS platform to facilitate effective searching and browsing
- Authentication Support—Platforms used to support authentication
- DICOM compliance—Ability to adhere to the DICOM standard
- DICOM Modality Worklist—Ability of PACS platform to support the DICOM Modality Worklist
- API Support—API support used by the PACS platform
- Scalability—Ability to handle increased workloads
- Relative Adoption—Level of adoption and usage of the PACS platform
- Community Support—Free support including documentation, forums and user-communities

Table 1 is a feature matrix, showing a summary of the results of the evaluation exercise conducted to assess the various FOSS PACS platforms. Ultimately, the Dicoogle platform was chosen as the base framework to be used to implement the PACS Server.

Table 1. Free and Open Source Picture Archiving and Communication Systems Software Evaluation Matrix

Feature	Dicoogle	DCM4CHEE	EasyPACS	ClearCanvas	Orthanc
Base Programming Languages	Java	Java	Java	C#	C++
Extensibility	High	High	High	Medium	High
Extensibility Programming Languages	Java	Java	Java, Python, Ruby	C++, VB.NET	C++, Python
Operating System Support	Windows, Linux, MacOS	Windows, Linux, MacOS	Windows, Linux, MacOS	Windows, Linux, MacOS	Windows, Linux, MacOS
Database Support	NoSQL	Apache Derby, Postgre SQL, MySQL, Oracle	MySQL	PostgreSQL	NoSQL
Search Service	Lucene	Lucene	Lucene	PostgreSQL	SQLite
Authentication Support	Local Auth	LDAP	LDAP, SSO, 2FA	OAuth 2.O	Local Auth
DICOM Compliance	Yes	Yes	Yes	Yes	Yes
DICOM Modality Worklist	Yes	Yes	Yes	Yes	Yes
API Support	RESTful	RESTful	RESTful	.NET	RESTful
Scalability	High	High	High	Low	High
Relative Adoption	Low	High	Medium	Low	High
Community Support	Yes	Yes	Yes	No	Yes

Picture Archiving and Communication System Design and Implementation. Using input from the interactions with key stakeholders—outlined in Sect. 3.2—and the systematic comparative analysis of existing FOSS platforms—outlined in Sect. 3.3—an appropriate base PACS framework was identified as the basis for the design and implementation of the UTHs PACS prototype platform.

The design and implementation of the PACS platform necessitated the development of two (2) software components—the PACS Server/Archive and a corresponding PACS Client:

- PACS Server/Archive—responsible for the storage and retrieval of medical images

– PACS Client—used to ingest/deposit medical images into the PACS Server. In essence the medical images are deposited into one of many storage locations integrated with the PACS Server.

Figure 1 shows the Context diagram, illustrating how the various external entities interact with the two (2) software components comprising the PACS platform ecosystem. Radiographers would ideally use the PACS Client to ingest/deposit medical images after performing an examination with an applicable modality, while Radiologists and Physicians would primarily use the PACS server to retrieve medical images

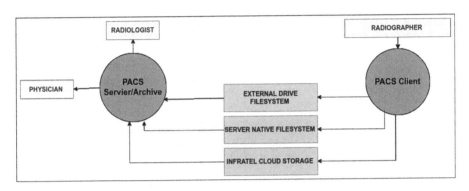

Fig. 1. Context Diagram Outlining High-Level Elements of the Picture Archiving and Communication System Platform

Radiographers would ideally use the PACS Client to ingest/deposit medical images after performing an examination with an applicable modality, while radiologists and physicians would primarily use the PACS server to retrieve medical images.

As stated in Sect. 3.3, the Dicoogle FOSS toolkit was used as the base platform framework for the implementation of the UTHs PACS Server. Specifically, extensive changes were made to the front-end and, additionally, the platform was modified in order to facilitate password authentication. Furthermore, the feasibility of utilising cloud storage services was explored by using Amazon Web Services [1] as a case example.

The PACS Client is a standalone thin client implemented to facilitate seamless upload of DICOM images to the appropriate storage services associated with the PACS Server. The Python Flask [5] Web framework was used to implement the PACS Client.

3.4   Prototype Usability Evaluation

Table 2. Study Design Experiment Tasks

INPUTS	PACS URL: pacs.xxxxx.zm:8081
	Login details: (username = xxxxx, password = xxxxx)
	Patient Full Name
	Patient Last Name
	Patient ID
STEPS	1. Insert website URL "pacs.xxxxx.zm:8081" in address bar
	2. Login into PACS platform using username "xxxxx" and password "xxxxx"
	3. Go to the search bar and search an image by:
	– Patient Full Name: Shankalu Lazarous
	– Patient Last Name: Shankalu
	– Patient ID: US222
EXPECTED DURATION	10 min

The PACS platform, implemented as outlined in Sect. 3.3, was evaluated in a controlled environment in order to assess relative potential to being adopted into a typical public health facility in Zambia. Radiology Registrars from UTHs were recruited, using convenience sampling, in order to participate in the controlled study which involved interacting with the deployed PACS prototype platform and subsequently completing a questionnaire.

Participants were required to perform a series of predefined tasks, outlined in Table 2, which involved searching and browsing for a medical image stored in the PACS platform. Participants were then required to complete a TAM 2 based questionnaire comprising of a section to capture participants' demographics, TAM 2 construct items—TAM 2 helps explain perceived usefulness and usage intentions in terms of social influence and cognitive instrumental processes [17]—and a questionnaire item for participants to provide general comments about the PACS platform and the study in general. TAM 2 instrument comprises questionnaire items—measured on a 7-point likert scale—associated with constructors that helped in the assessment of the perceived usefulness and usage intention for the PACS platform. The TAM 2 constructors are interpreted as follows:

– Perceived Usefulness—Extent of PACS platform in enhancing participants' job performance

- Perceived Ease of Use—Extent towards which PACS platform will be free of effort
- Result Demonstrability—Extent to which PACS produces observable benefits or outcomes
- Output Quality—Quality and reliability of PACS output
- Job Relevance—Extent to which PACS will be relevant and beneficial to a user's job
- Subjective Norm—Pressure or influence from others regarding the acceptance and use of PACS
- Voluntariness—User's freedom and autonomy in deciding whether or not to adopt the PACS
- Intention to Use—User's personal inclination or readiness to adopt and use the PACS platform.

4 Results and Discussion

The findings of this research on improving radiological workflows in Zambian public health facilities are presented, exploring the challenges of current practices, showcasing the prototype PACS platform designed to address these challenges, and analysing the user evaluation of the prototype.

4.1 Workflow Challenges

Guided interviews were conducted with six (6) participants—four (4) radiographers and two (2) trainee radiologists. All the participants had more than four (4) years experience with radiological workflows. Table 3 shows a summary of the interview responses.

Interactions with radiographers focused on determining challenges associated with image storage and management. The results indicate that medical images are primarily stored in both analog and digital formats, with a combination of compact discs (CDs), external hard drives and storage rooms used as primary storage techniques. Interestingly enough, there was reference to patients being given physical copies of their medical images on film (such as X-rays) to carry and go home with for safe keeping. This practice might be used to ensure that medical images are available to referring physicians when needed. Expectedly, the main themes linked to challenges with medical image storage were largely associated with retrieval of existing medical images and storage capacity.

The interviews with radiologists were primarily aimed at determining challenges associated with accessing medical images during the interpretation process. The main issue raised is associated with long-term preservation of medical images. For instance, [Radiologist 1] emphasised that follow-ups with patients are difficult as images are typically given to patients and will generally be unreadable, making it difficult to determine the progression of diseases. [Radiologist 2] echoed this point by highlighting that films will frequently be discarded in order to reclaim space for recent medical images. Interestingly enough, [Radiologist 2]

Table 3. Summary of Interview Responses

Participants	Facility	Experience	Storage Mediums	Image Formats	Challenges Themes
Radiographer 1	UTHs	5+ Years	Hard Drive · Basement	Analog · Digital	Retrieval Challenges
Radiographer 2	UTHs	5+ Years	Imaging Machine Computer · Store Room	Analog · Digital	Retrieval on Patients' Request
Radiographer 3	UTHs	5+ Years	Hard Drive · Films · Patients	Analog · Digital	Storage Capacity Challenges
Radiographer 4	UTHs	7+ Years	CDs · Films	Analog · Digital	Difficulties Accessing Images
Radiologist 1	LMUTH	11+ Years	–	Analog · Digital	Image Preservation · Follow Ups
Radiologist 2	UTHs	4+ Years	–	Analog · Digital	Limited Space · Images Discarded

made mention of the importance of preservation of medical images in order to further research.

The research illustrates several key principles, relationships, and generalizations. Centralising and digitalising image storage is crucial for addressing retrieval and long-term preservation challenges, effectively resolved by a PACS platform. While issues related to storage capacity may not be directly addressed by PACS alone, these can be mitigated through proper policies, procedures, and management investment in storage infrastructure. The study reveals a clear relationship between PACS deployment and the resolution of image retrieval issues, emphasising the need for organizational commitment to address storage capacity. Generalizations from user feedback indicate a positive perception of PACS, suggesting that mandatory organizational policies are essential for consistent usage. Continuous improvement and expert involvement are also necessary for refining a production-quality PACS platform.

4.2 Prototype Picture Archive and Communication System Platform

As earlier mention in Sect. 3.3, the Dicoogle was ultimately used as the base platform for the implementation of the PACS. Figure 2 shows a search result page rendered using the final version of the PACS Server high fidelity prototype that was designed and implemented. Once successfully logged into the PACS Server, a physician or radiologist can search for medical images using open ended text queries corresponding to metadata linked to the medical image.

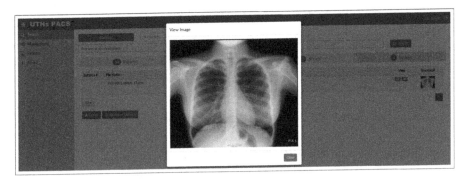

Fig. 2. Screenshot of the Prototype Picture Archiving and Communication System

Using the content rendered on the search result page, the user can then browse to the desired medical image using the DICOM hierarchy [8], making it possible for patient, study, series and image data to be accessed. The access to specific images associated with a Study Series has a provision for users to view thumbnails of medical images.

While the current basic discoverability features would be sufficient for physicians and radiologists to engage with the platform, further enhancements are required to implement vital functionalities, including the downloading of DICOM formatted medical images and seamless integration with other platforms prevalent in public health facilities. This iterative process aligns with the principles of continuous refinement and advancement to achieve a production-quality PACS platform. Notably, the prototype's implementation serves as a pivotal step in probing and refining requirements, illustrating the relationship between iterative development and meeting evolving clinical needs. This underscores the generalization that continuous improvement is essential for optimising the platform's utility and effectiveness within healthcare settings.

4.3   Usability Evaluation Using TAM 2 Questionnaire

Participants Demographics. A total of eight (8) radiology registrars (trainee radiologists), from UTHs, at different levels of training participated in the study. Table 4 shows a summary of demographic factors for the study participants. Most of the study participants were females, with those at higher levels of training having had prior exposure to other training sites besides the study site (UTHs). In addition, most of the participants had "1–5 years" medical practising experience. Furthermore half of the participants had no experience using PACS platforms.

Analysis 1. TAM 2 Constructs. The TAM 2 questionnaire items for each of the constructs described in Sect. 3.4 were aggregated and average score computed. Figure 3 is a radar chart that illustrates average scores for the TAM 2 constructs.

Table 4. Participants' Demographic Factors

Demographic Factors		Radiology Residency Year				
		1st	2nd	3rd	4th	5th
Gender	Male	0	1	0	1	0
	Female	1	1	1	2	1
Experience in Practising	1–5 Years	0	2	0	1	0
	5–10 Years	1	0	1	2	1
Prior Experience Using PACS	Yes	0	0	1	2	1
	No	1	2	0	1	0

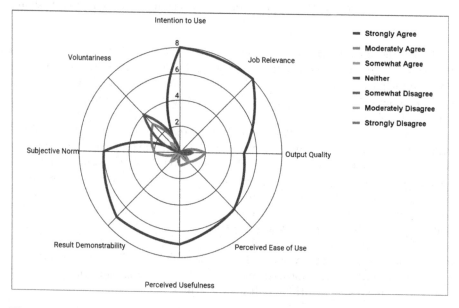

Fig. 3. Spider/Radar Chart Illustrating Average Ratings for the Eight (8) TAM 2 Constructs

The results indicate that most of the participants felt positive about "Intention to Use," "Job Relevance," "Perceived Usefulness," and "Result Demonstrability." This positive feedback suggests that participants recognized the clear benefits of using a PACS platform compared to the manual workflows currently in use. Comments made by [Radiologist 1] and [Radiologist 2] during the interview sessions, as outlined in Table 3 in Sect. 3.2, support this assertion, underscoring the principle of streamlining radiological workflows through centralized digital platforms. However, the lower ratings for "Output Quality," "Perceived Ease of Use," and "Subjective Norm" likely reflect the prototype's limited features and the study's brief duration, highlighting the relationship between platform functionality and user perception. Notably, the low ratings for "Voluntariness" suggest the need for organizational policies mandating PACS adoption to ensure its integration into radiological practices.

Analysis 2. Participants Remarks. The general comments provided by study participants mostly consisted of suggestions on how to improve the PACS platform. The general comments suggest a need to further involve experts during the refinement of requirements as the production-quality PACS platform is being designed and implemented.

Some open ended general comments specified by the study participants are as follows:

"Integration to an online patient clinical records would significantly enhance patient care" [Participant 1]

"It's a step in the right direction" [Participant 2]

"Suggestions are that it should be a multimodality platform and should have a provision for reporting images" [Participant 3]

"Incorporating a DICOM viewer (digital imaging and communication in medicine) would help to large data sets (CT scans and MRI Scans)" [Participant 4]

"There is supposed to be free access to the internet in the department." [Participant 5]

"IT WOULD ADD A LOT OF VALUE IF IMAGES WERE EXPORTABLE." [Participant 6]

"Order of metadata should prioritise patient pertinent details as opposed to technical lingo" [Participant 8].

5 Conclusions and Future Work

This paper outlined a study conducted to design, implement and evaluate a prototype PACS platform. The research aimed to demonstrate the feasibility of designing and implementing cost-effective PACS platforms for use in public health facilities, particularly in resource-limited settings like Zambia. The results from the usability study conducted with Radiology Registrars suggest that deploying a PACS at the UTHs has the potential to improve radiological workflows, primarily due to the fact that medical imaging workflows currently utilise manual processes. Deploying a PACS platform has the obvious potential of facilitating efficient and effective medical imaging workflows. The study is aligned with existing study focused on PACS evaluation, such as the study by Hasani et al., in which improvements of mean reporting time and utilisation of CT scans were reported [10].

This work contributes to the growing body of research on affordable healthcare IT solutions. By focusing on a prototype with limited functionalities, we aimed to establish a foundation for developing PACS platforms that are both functional and mindful of budgetary constraints. Additionally, the emphasis on interoperability during the prototype's development aligns with theoretical considerations for future healthcare IT systems, where various software platforms need to seamlessly interact.

Presently, ongoing work is focused on implementing production-quality PACS platforms informed by the learnings from the prototype. These platforms are expected to significantly improve image management workflows within public health facilities. Furthermore, efforts are underway to explore the potential of using machine learning techniques to automatically classify medical images once ingested into PACS. This integration has the potential to further streamline workflows and potentially assist healthcare professionals in diagnosis.

PACS platforms typically operate within a complex ecosystem of heterogeneous software platforms. As such, interoperability was a key consideration during the development process. While current efforts are confined to well-resourced public health facility settings in Zambia, there is a need for PACS that can function effectively in settings with limited bandwidth, common in remote locations. Potential future work could explore the design and implementation of tools for devices with significantly small form factors to cater to such settings. Additionally, further research could focus on developing strategies to ensure that future PACS platforms are interoperable with a wide array of software platforms used in public health facilities.

Acknowledgments. This study was conducted as part of a much larger "Enterprise Medical Imaging in Zambia" project. The project is funded through generous grants from Google Research, Data Science Africa and The University of Zambia. We are very appreciative of this funding.

References

1. Cloud computing services - amazon web services (AWS). https://aws.amazon.com/. Accessed 25 Sept 2023
2. Easy PACS. http://mehmetsen80.github.io/EasyPACS. Accessed 25 Sept 2023
3. Open source clinical image and object management. https://www.dcm4che.org. Accessed 25 Sept 2023
4. Orthanc - DICOM server. https://www.orthanc-server.com. Accessed 25 Sept 2023
5. Welcome to flask—flask documentation (2.3.x). https://flask.palletsprojects.com. Accessed 25 Sept 2023
6. Bwanga, O., Sichone, J.M., Sichone, P.N., Kazuma, Y.B.: Image interpretation and reporting by radiographers in Africa: findings from the literature review and their application to Zambia. Med. J. Zambia **48**(2), 125–135 (2021). https://doi.org/10.55320/mjz.48.2.40
7. ClearCanvas Open Source Project (2023). http://clearcanvas.github.io. Accessed 19 June 2023
8. DICOM Standards Committee: PS3.3: DICOM PS3.3 2023b - information object definitions (2023). https://dicom.nema.org/medical/dicom/current/output/html/part03.html. Accessed 18 June 2023
9. Frija, G., et al.: How to improve access to medical imaging in low- and middle-income countries? EClinicalMedicine **38**, 101034 (2021). https://doi.org/10.1016/j.eclinm.2021.101034

10. Hasani, N., Hosseini, A., Sheikhtaheri, A.: Effect of implementation of picture archiving and communication system on radiologist reporting time and utilization of radiology services: a case study in Iran. J. Digit. Imaging **33**(3), 595–601 (2020). https://doi.org/10.1007/s10278-019-00314-z

11. Hricak, H., et al.: Medical imaging and nuclear medicine: a lancet oncology commission. Lancet Oncol. **22**(4), 136–172 (2021). https://doi.org/10.1016/S1470-2045(20)30751-8

12. Jodogne, S.: The Orthanc ecosystem for medical imaging. J. Digit. Imaging **31**(3), 341–352 (2018). https://doi.org/10.1007/s10278-018-0082-y

13. Kesselman, A., et al.: 2015 RAD-AID conference on international radiology for developing countries: the evolving global radiology landscape. J. Am. Coll. Radiol. **13**(9), 1139–1144 (2016). https://doi.org/10.1016/j.jacr.2016.03.028

14. Lebre, R., Pinho, E., Jesus, R., Bastião, L., Costa, C.: Dicoogle open source: the establishment of a new paradigm in medical imaging. J. Med. Syst. **46**(11), 77 (2022). https://doi.org/10.1007/s10916-022-01867-3

15. Lebre, R., Pinho, E., Silva, J.M., Costa, C.: Dicoogle framework for medical imaging teaching and research. In: 2020 IEEE Symposium on Computers and Communications (ISCC). IEEE (2020). https://doi.org/10.1109/ISCC50000.2020.9219545

16. Roth, C.J., Lannum, L.M., Persons, K.R.: A foundation for enterprise imaging: HIMSS-SIIM collaborative white paper. J. Digit. Imaging **29**(5), 530–538 (2016). https://doi.org/10.1007/s10278-016-9882-0

17. Venkatesh, V., Davis, F.D.: A theoretical extension of the technology acceptance model: four longitudinal field studies. Manag. Sci. **46**(2), 186–204 (2000). https://doi.org/10.1287/mnsc.46.2.186.11926

18. Zulu, E.O., Phiri, L.: Enterprise medical imaging in the global south: challenges and opportunities. In: 2022 IST-Africa Conference (IST-Africa), pp. 1–9. IEEE (2022). https://doi.org/10.23919/IST-Africa56635.2022.9845508

Single Matrix Block Shift (SMBS) Dense Matrix Multiplication Algorithm

Daniel Ohene-Kwofie[1,2]([⊠]) [iD] and Scott Hazelhurst[1,3] [iD]

[1] School of Electrical and Information Engineering, University of the Witwatersrand, Johannesburg, South Africa
{daniel.ohene-kwofie,scott.hazelhurst}@wits.ac.za
[2] School of Public Health, University of the Witwatersrand, Johannesburg, South Africa
[3] Sydney Brenner Institute for Molecular Bioscience, University of the Witwatersrand, Johannesburg, South Africa

Abstract. Many scientific and numeric computations rely on matrix-matrix multiplication as a fundamental component of their algorithms. It constitutes the building block in many matrix operations used in numeric solvers and graph theory problems. Several algorithms have been proposed and implemented for matrix-matrix multiplication, especially, for distributed-memory systems, and these have been greatly studied. In particular, the Cannon's algorithm has been implemented for distributed-memory systems, mostly since the memory needs remain constant and are not influenced by the number of processors employed. The algorithm, however, involves block shifting of both matrices being multiplied. This paper presents a similar block-oriented parallel algorithm for matrix-matrix multiplication on a 2-dimensional processor grid, but with block shifting restricted to only one of the matrices. We refer to this as the *Single Matrix Block Shift (SMBS) algorithm*. The algorithm, we propose, is a variant of the Cannon's algorithm on distributed architectures and improves upon the performance complexity of the Cannon and SRUMMA algorithms. We present analytic as well as experimental comparative results of our algorithm with the standard Cannon's algorithm on 2-dimensional processor grids, showing over *4X* performance improvement.

Keywords: Parallel algorithms · Matrix multiplication · Computational efficiency · Scalability · Speedup

1 Introduction

Distributed computing combines computational resources to solve problems that are too complex to be solved by a single system. In general, for computationally demanding problems, exploiting parallelism is key to computing the solution within a reasonable time. Matrix-matrix and matrix-vector multiplications

A. Gerber (Ed.): SAICSIT 2024, CCIS 2159, pp. 190–206, 2024.
https://doi.org/10.1007/978-3-031-64881-6_11

are two essential linear algebra operations in numerous scientific and numerical computations. Operations involving very large matrices are computationally intensive and need several memory resources as well as processing power.

In the past few decades, a variety of algorithms have been implemented for multiplying the matrix **A** and the matrix **B**, to produce the **C** matrix, particularly, for parallel systems with distributed-memory. This operation is generally expressed as

$$\mathbf{C} = \alpha(\mathbf{A} \times \mathbf{B}) + \beta\mathbf{C}$$

where α and β represent some constants.

Some of the widely known algorithms are the Shared and Remote-memory based Universal Matrix Multiplication Algorithm (SRUMMA) [12], the Scalable Universal Matrix Multiplication Algorithm (SUMMA) [24], the Parallel Universal Matrix Multiplication Algorithm (PUMMA) [5], and the Cannon algorithm [14]. Several studies have been conducted on distributed algorithms regarding matrix-matrix multiplication [8,9,11,15-18,20,25]. These algorithms are most effective when implemented on processor grids where the matrices **A** and **B**, have been decomposed into blocks of vertical and horizontal chunks, and distributed across the processors. A typical advantage of this method is that the small blocks can leverage data locality on individual processors. These sub-blocks are transferred into the fast local memory of the nodes, and their elements can then be repeatedly used. Usually, these algorithms are implemented using one- and two-dimensional block-cyclic partitioning. Such data partitioning, however, results in increased performance improvement if the data is reused several times and data movement is minimised.

We present another scalable parallel algorithm for dense matrix-matrix multiplication which is best suited for a 2D grid of processors. Our algorithm is a variation of the Cannon's matrix algorithm that enhances the performance complexity by restricting block shifting to only one matrix, thus taking advantage of data locality by minimising the amount of data movements. We present an analytic and an experimental comparative analyses of our algorithm with the Cannon's routine over a 2D grid of processors.

The principal contribution being presented is the development of the SMBS algorithm for computing the matrix-matrix multiplication on systems with distributed-memory, which leverages data locality to enhance performance. The primary results being shown include:

i the technique adopted to develop and implement the blocked parallel algorithm for performing dense matrix-matrix multiplication for distributed-memory systems.

ii the analyses and experiments conducted to assess the algorithmic efficiency of SMBS compared to the Cannon and SRUMMA matrix-matrix multiplication routines.

The organization of the paper is as follows: The section (Sect. 2) that follows provides a short background of various matrix-matrix multiplication algorithms which are best suited for systems with distributed-memory. Particularly, we discuss the Cannon's routine for matrix-matrix multiplication. Detailed description and practical implementation of our algorithm, including the analysis of its performance, is highlighted in Sect. 3. We discuss the results from the experiments conducted with our algorithm compared to the Cannon's method in Sect. 4. Finally, Sect. 5 summarises the work presented and provides directions for future work.

2   Background

More than 30 years ago, Gupta et al. [10] showed that parallel matrix-matrix multiplication algorithms perform differently under various conditions. A number of techniques for parallelising such algorithms on distributed architectures have been developed and extensively studied [9,11,18,25]. Current advanced computer architectures feature hierarchical memory systems, where accessing data from the levels up the hierarchy provides faster performance compared to accessing data in the lower levels. Efficient techniques to take advantage of the power of such systems include the development of algorithms that maximise the top levels of the memory hierarchy. Thus, limiting the costly accesses to the levels at the lower hierarchy. In dense linear algebraic operations, for instance, the technique of using block-partitioned algorithms has been extensively explored. The technique involves recasting the algorithms into expressions that utilise operations on sub-matrices, which could thus exploit the memory's hierarchy to improve performance. This technique has been employed in diverse forms in many matrix-matrix multiplication routines implemented for distributed-memory systems.

A typical example of such an algorithm is the *Shared and Remote-memory based Universal Matrix Multiplication Algorithm (SRUMMA)* [12], developed for both systems with distributed-memory and shared memory parallel systems. Consider the computation of the multiplication solution for $\mathbf{C} = \mathbf{A} \times \mathbf{B}$; each process in SRUMMA is allocated the relevant blocks from matrices $\mathbf{A}$ and $\mathbf{B}$, performs their multiplication, and stores the outcome in a locally managed section of the matrix, $\mathbf{C}$. The processors access non-local blocks based on whether they are stored in other shared memory or in the same locations [12]. SRUMMA utilizes *Remote Memory Access (RMA)* to independently retrieve matrix blocks, eliminating the need for coordination with the processors that own those blocks. However, it involves an initial running-time cost from sorting a task list (including of recording) to assess and optimize the data locality references [19].

The Scalable Universal Matrix Multiplication Algorithm (SUMMA) is another well-established matrix multiplication routine which is currently used in the Scalable Linear Algebra PACKage (ScaLAPACK) [3,22] and other related parallel libraries. The ScaLAPACK library consists of a subgroup of the LAPACK [2,23] methods, which have been optimised for multiple instruction multiple data (MIMD) systems with distributed-memory. The matrix $\mathbf{A}$ and the matrix $\mathbf{B}$ in SUMMA, are decomposed into various columns and various rows of fixed-size blocks, respectively. The column chunks of matrix $\mathbf{A}$ multiply the respective row chunks of matrix $\mathbf{B}$ till the final column chunk of $\mathbf{A}$ is multiplied with the final row chunk of $\mathbf{B}$ [23].

Choi [4] proposed the *Distribution-Independent Matrix Multiplication Algorithm (DIMMA)* as an alternative to SUMMA. Unlike SUMMA, DIMMA employs an adapted pipelined communication strategy to effectively overlap communication and computation. Consequently, this approach exploits the least common multiple (LCM) block idea to attain the optimised block sizes for maximum performance. The fundamental concept of the LCM approach is to concurrently process multiple tiny columns of **A** blocks and an equivalent number of tiny rows of **B** blocks. This allows the processors to multiply several tiny matrices from **A** and **B** concurrently to achieve optimal performance [4]. Rather than distributing a one column strip of matrix **A** and a one row strip of matrix **B**, the approach ensures that a column of processors broadcasts multiple columns of **A** along the corresponding row of processors, with the distance between these blocks being determined by the LCM in the column direction [4].

The Cannon algorithm is a popular matrix-matrix multiplication algorithm which is well suited for distributed-memory systems. One significant benefit of the Cannon algorithm is the memory efficiency. It is founded on a $\mathbf{P} \times \mathbf{P}$ logical or physical grid of processors using a blocked data distribution approach where every processor handles a many consecutive data blocks. The Cannon algorithm is well suited for homogeneous 2D grids, but does present some difficulties when extending the algorithm to heterogeneous 2D grids. In Cannon's algorithm, given a two-dimensional processor grid, the processor P_{ij} $(0 \leq i, j \leq P - 1)$, has the elements or blocks in position ij $(0 \leq i, j \leq P-1)$ of matrices A, B and C. From this data distribution, the matrices **A** and **B** blocks are skewed or reassigned such that given the 2D grid of $\mathbf{P} \times \mathbf{P}$ processors, the element or sub-matrix **A** in row i and column $(j+i)$ mod P, i.e., $a_{i,(j+i)}$ mod P, and also the element or sub-matrix of **B** in row $(i+j)$ mod P and column j, i.e., $b_{(i+j)}$ mod P,i, are allocated to the processor P_{ij}. Specifically, each data of row i, for $(0 \leq i \leq P - 1)$, of the sub-matrices of **A** is shifted i times towards the left processors, while each data or column j, for $(0 \leq j \leq P - 1)$ of the elements or sub-matrices of **B** is transferred j times towards upper processors.

The Fig. 1a shows the initial block assignment, and Fig. 1b the initial relocation (skewing of the **A** and **B** blocks), imposed by Cannon's Algorithm. This initialisation stage impacts the algorithmic performance.

Generally, matrix-matrix multiplication for distributed-memory systems involves significant data movement, making it challenging to minimize synchronization overhead among the nodes. Thus, the efficiency of these distributed algorithms typically depends on how efficient data is distributed and the parallel organisation of the processors. It is therefore not surprising that the state-of-the-art linear algebra routines, like the LaPACK [1] and ScaLAPACK [13], experience performance degradation on some multi-socket systems of multicore processors. This is because some of the algorithms are unable to fully make use of thread-level parallelism and data locality. Exploiting data locality is possible if data is reused several times, which further enhances cache hits and the overall algorithmic performance.

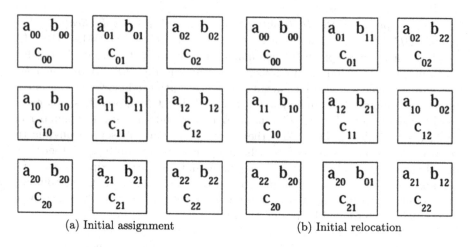

(a) Initial assignment   (b) Initial relocation

Fig. 1. Data Allocation for Cannon's Algorithm on 3×3 Grid

The next section gives a detailed discussion of our proposed algorithm, which is a variant of the Cannon method. But, unlike the Cannon's routine, where blocks of matrix **A** and matrix **B** are re-aligned logically onto neighbouring processors in the *2D* grid, our approach limits block shifts to just a single matrix, thus exploiting data locality and also avoids the initial block skews. In addition, we attain algorithmic efficiency by overlapping computations with communication. The reduced need for sender-receiver synchronisation for either of the **A** or **B** matrices (such as in Cannon's algorithm) contributes greatly to the overall algorithmic efficiency.

3   The Single Matrix Block Shift (SMBS) Algorithm

Given the matrices

$$A_{M,K} = \begin{pmatrix} a_{1,1} & a_{1,2} & \cdots & a_{1,K} \\ a_{2,1} & a_{2,2} & \cdots & a_{2,K} \\ a_{3,1} & a_{3,2} & \cdots & a_{3,K} \\ \vdots & \vdots & \ddots & \vdots \\ a_{M,1} & a_{M,2} & \cdots & a_{M,K} \end{pmatrix} \text{ and } B_{K,N} = \begin{pmatrix} b_{1,1} & b_{1,2} & \cdots & b_{1,N} \\ b_{2,1} & b_{2,2} & \cdots & b_{2,N} \\ b_{3,1} & b_{3,2} & \cdots & b_{3,N} \\ \vdots & \vdots & \ddots & \vdots \\ b_{K,1} & b_{K,2} & \cdots & b_{K,N} \end{pmatrix}$$

we consider the matrix-matrix product

$$C \leftarrow A \times B, \text{where } c_{i,j} = \sum_{k=1}^{K} a_{i,k} b_{k,j}$$

where A, B and C are dense matrices.

In principle, we can compute $c_{i,j}$ of matrix $\mathbf{C}$ in parallel by taking the dot product of each row i of matrix $\mathbf{A}$ and column j of matrix $\mathbf{B}$ on a processor. However, this technique does not scale well since as many as MN processes are expected to evaluate all sub-products, $c_{i,j} \in \mathbf{C}$.

Given that there are $m \times n$ 2D processor grids, the block sizes of the $\mathbf{A}$, $\mathbf{B}$ and $\mathbf{C}$ matrices are $\dfrac{M}{m} \times \dfrac{K}{k}$, $\dfrac{K}{k} \times \dfrac{N}{n}$ and $\dfrac{M}{m} \times \dfrac{N}{n}$ respectively. The process $P_{i,j}$ evaluates all $c_{i,j}$ in block $C_{i,j}^{+}$, with C^{+} representing a block in the $\mathbf{C}$ matrix. In a similar fashion, the blocks in matrix $\mathbf{A}$ are denoted as A^{+}, and those in $\mathbf{B}$ are denoted as B^{+}. Our approach is similar to that of the Cannon's algorithm with some major differences. Unlike the Cannon's algorithm, we block matrix $\mathbf{A}$ column-wise and $\mathbf{B}$ row-wise or vice versa. Additionally, our algorithm is not limited to a square grid of processors. For the purposes of this presentation, we limit our discourse to the case where matrix $\mathbf{A}$ is blocked column-wise and $\mathbf{B}$ row-wise. Given the dense matrices $\mathbf{A}$ and $\mathbf{B}$ blocked into 4×4 matrices (depicted in Fig. 2). The SMBS algorithm proceeds as follows:

1. Divide matrix $\mathbf{A}$ and matrix $\mathbf{B}$ into $m \times n$ blocks. Distribute $\mathbf{A}$ column-wise and $\mathbf{B}$ row-wise such that $A_{0,0}^{+}$ and $B_{0,0}^{+}$ are located on processor $P_{0,0}$, $A_{0,1}^{+}$ and $B_{1,0}^{+}$ on processor $P_{0,1}$, etc. The blocks are distributed such that the columns count of matrix $\mathbf{A}$ is the same as the rows count of matrix $\mathbf{B}$. Figure 3 illustrates the data distribution strategy.
2. Create a row communicator for each row of the 2D grid. This helps to aggregate the final $C_{i,j}^{+}$ per iteration.
3. The algorithm then enters the main computational loop to perform local block multiplication $m-1$ times. For a square grid, where $m = n$, the routine executes in $O(\sqrt{m^2 - 1})$ time.
4. For each step in the computation loop, call **Reduce** on the row communicator to get the sum of all the partial sums, i.e. $\sum_{j=0}^{col\_size} c_{i,j}$. This results in the final $C_{i,j}^{+}$ block of $\mathbf{C}$. We compute the rank of the processor $P_{i,j}$ which will hold the $C_{i,j}^{+}$ as follows:

$$(i + row) \mod col\_size.$$

where i is the i-th iteration, row is the row number, and col_size is the total number of columns per row.
5. Each block of $\mathbf{B}$ is shifted one step up with wrap-around. Unlike the Cannon algorithm, matrix $\mathbf{A}$ is not shifted, thus enhancing data locality and reuse, which enhances the overall performance.
6. Perform next block multiplication: **Reduce** the partial result per row, repeat $m - 1$ times.

The routine is formally depicted in Algorithm 1.

Considering the dense matrices $\mathbf{A}$ and $\mathbf{B}$ blocked into 4×4 matrices as illustrated in Fig. 2, the matrices are distributed on the 2D 4×4 processor grid as

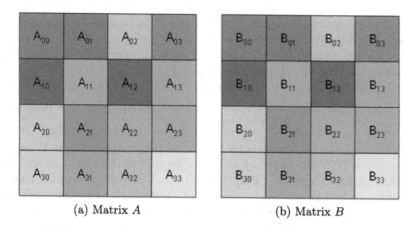

(a) Matrix A (b) Matrix B

Fig. 2. Block of Matrices A and B

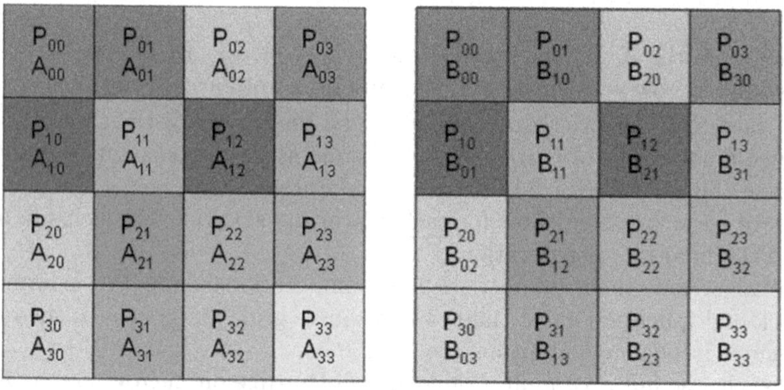

(a) Distribution of **A**   (b) Distribution of **B**

Fig. 3. Block Distribution of Matrices A and B

shown in Fig. 3. We distribute A and B such that the processor $P_{i,j}$ has blocks $A_{i,j}^{+}$ and $B_{j,i}^{+}$ at the initialisation stage of the algorithm. The product of $A_{i,j}^{+}$ and $B_{j,i}^{+}$ is computed per processor, and a reduction per-row results in the final $C_{i,j}$. Figure 4d illustrates the $C_{i,j}$ blocks produced for each i_{th} iteration. In our 4×4 example, the per row reduction results in the diagonal matrix $C_{i,i}$ on processors $P_{i,i}$ where $i \longleftarrow \{0, 1, 2, 3\}$ during stage 1 of the algorithm. Similarly, the per row reduction in the 2nd iteration produces the $C_{0,1}^{+}, C_{1,2}^{+}, C_{2,3}^{+}, C_{3,0}^{+}$ on the $P_{0,1}, P_{1,2}, P_{2,3}, P_{3,0}$ processors respectively. It should be noted that all processor rows perform this reduction at the same time. This reduction step is overlapped with the shifting of the B matrix blocks as illustrated in Figs. 4b and 4c, thus resulting in a better performance.

We note that each i-th iteration results in the final $C_{i,j}^{+}$ in the $P_{i,k}$ processor of that row where $k = (i + row) \mod col\_size$. Thus, a total of $C_{i,j}^{+}$ blocks is

---

Algorithm 1: SMBS

    Data: $A[M][K], B[K][N]$, gridsize $m \times n$

    Result: $C[M][N]$

1 **begin**

2   Distribute A column-wise and B row-wise across the $m \times n$ grid

3   **for** $r \leftarrow 0$ **to** $m - 1$ **do**

4          $.\ matMult(A_{i,k}, B_{k,j}, C_{i,j}^+)$

5   ** $reduceMatMultPerRow(\ C_{i,j}^+, C_{i,j}\ )$

6          $j \longleftarrow (row + r) \mod p$

7          $C_{r,j} \longleftarrow \sum_{j=0}^{p-1} C_{r,j}^+$

8   Up-circular-shift each column of B by 1, so that $B_{i,j}$ is overwritten by $B_{i,(j+1)\ \mod\ p}$

9   **end**

10   **return** C

11 **end**

---

the total number of row blocks produced per iteration. This becomes very significant in some image processing applications, for instance, where portions of the final image are required during processing. The completed blocks could be asynchronously collected for further processing while the other iterations continue. Such overlapping further provides a performance advantage over existing algorithms.

3.1 Non-blocking SMBS Algorithm

The SMBS algorithm presented, reduces the amount of data block shifts by half in the Cannon's algorithm. Further enhancements to the algorithm are achieved by implementing non-blocking message passing to overlap computation and communication. For large matrices and large applications for that matter, it is unusual for communication to contribute more than half the total latency in a distributed system. Application performance is therefore significantly improved if algorithms are redesigned to overlap communication and computation.

We implement non-blocking SMBS (NB-SMBS) in the primary computational loop of the SMBS algorithm depicted in Algorithm 1. We leverage the non-blocking point-to-point communication of the Message Passing Interface (MPI) *(Isend, Irecv)* to send and receive block buffers of matrix B in this case before the *matMult* computation. Note that the block shifts in this case, unlike

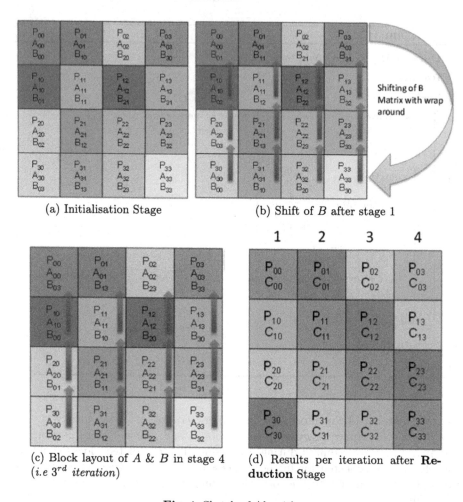

(a) Initialisation Stage

(b) Shift of B after stage 1

(c) Block layout of A & B in stage 4 (*i.e* 3rd *iteration*)

(d) Results per iteration after **Reduction** Stage

Fig. 4. Sketch of Algorithm

Cannon's, are on only one matrix. The trade-off, in the non-blocking operation as usual, is the provision of extra buffers to hold the in-coming blocks. The non-blocking SMBS leverages the Remote Direct Memory Access (RDMA) capabilities of the underlying inter-node communication and thus provides significant performance improvement. Preliminary results presented indicate about 5× performance gains over blocking SMBS.

3.2   Analysis of the Algorithm

It is interesting that a seemingly simple algorithm, expressed as a single statement and three nested loops (such as matrix-matrix multiplication), has garnered significant research interest over the past few decades. This is because matrix-matrix multiplication is a foundational routine in numerous scientific applications. Since it has $O(N^3)$ algorithmic complexity, the scientific and numeric applications depending on them often allocate significant computation time (resources) to complete operations. A number of research efforts have been undertaken to minimise the $O(N^3)$ time complexity of matrix-matrix multiplication routines. The Strassen's algorithm [7, 21] is the pioneering and widely adopted fast routine that reduces operational complexity from $O(N^3)$ to $O(N^{2.81})$ operations. The Coppersmith and Winograd's algorithm [6] further reduced this to attain $O(N^{2.38})$. Nevertheless, these routines sacrifice numerical stability as they attain the reduced operational complexity by performing extra operations.

Given the matrix-matrix product routine $C \longleftarrow AB$, where A, B, and C are $M \times K$, $K \times N$, and $M \times N$ matrices respectively, we denote

t_s the cost for initialisation
P the number of available processors
$p \times q$ the size of the 2D processor grid, i.e. $p \times q = P$
T_{trans} data transfer (shift) latency
n_i number of iterations $= \sqrt{P} - 1$, i.e. the number of column blocks of matrix A

For simplicity, we also assume that A, B and C are dense square matrices, and that we have a 2D processor grid with the matrices distributed as illustrated in Fig. 3. Each processor is assigned a block from the $A, B,$ and C matrices of sizes:

$$\frac{M}{p} \times \frac{K}{q}, \frac{K}{q} \times \frac{N}{p}, \text{ and } \frac{M}{p} \times \frac{N}{q} \text{ respectively.}$$

The total running-time for the algorithm, T_{total} is given by:

$$T_{total} = \text{Time per iteration} + \text{startup cost}$$
$$T_{total} = T_{row} \times n_i + t_s$$

where

$$T_{row} = T_{trans} + \text{compute-time, and}$$
$$T_{compute} = \left(\frac{M}{p} \times \frac{K}{q} \times \frac{N}{p} \right) \times t_c$$

Let $M = K = N$, and $p = q$ then

$$T_{compute} = \left(\frac{N}{q} \times \frac{N}{q} \times \frac{N}{q} \right) \times t_c$$
$$= \frac{N^3}{q^3} t_c = \frac{N^3}{P^{\frac{3}{2}}} t_c, |P = q^2$$

where $t_c =$ cost factor for computing.

T_{trans} can be a relatively much smaller value since data is shifted in blocks concurrently. For the non-blocking implementation of SMBS, which overlaps the transfer with the computation, $T_{trans} \approx 0$ and so:

$$T_{row} = T_{trans} + \frac{N^3}{P^{\frac{3}{2}}} \times t_c$$

$$T_{total} = \left(T_{trans} + \frac{N^3}{P^{\frac{3}{2}}} \times t_c \right) \times \left(\sqrt{P} - 1 \right) + t_s$$

$$= \left(\frac{N^3}{P} \right) t_c - \left(\frac{N^3}{P^{\frac{3}{2}}} \right) t_c + T_{trans}\sqrt{P} - T_{trans} + t_s \tag{1}$$

assuming a network with sufficient bandwidth, and $t_s \approx 0$

$$T_{total} = O\left(\frac{N^3}{P} \right) - O\left(\frac{N^3}{P^{\frac{3}{2}}} \right) + O\left(\sqrt{P} \right) \tag{2}$$

Equation 2 indicates that our algorithm has performance comparable to well-known algorithms such as SRUMMA, and Cannon. However, unlike SRUMMA which has latencies bounded by $O\left(\frac{N^3}{P} \right) + O\left(\frac{N^2}{\sqrt{P}} \right) + O\left(\sqrt{P} \right)$, our analysis of the SMBS algorithm shows a further reduced theoretical bound, especially at some increasing workloads, resulting in much higher operational throughput and lower latencies.

4 Preliminary Results

We assessed the performance of our algorithm using both blocking and non-blocking variants of the Cannon Algorithm on the Edison cluster of the National Energy Research Scientific Computing Center (NERSC). We evaluated the algorithms using up to 2500 cores of the cluster. Each selected cluster node has two sockets, each having a 12-core Intel Ivy Bridge 2.4 GHz processor, a total of 24 cores and 64 GB DDR3 1866 MHz memory (four 8 GB DIMMs per socket) per node. The nodes are interconnected with the Cray Aries in a Dragonfly topology. All the codes were written in C and compiled using Intel MPI. Each of the experiments was conducted using synthetic double-precision floating-point numbers. The Intel MPI 5.0 library and the Global-Array toolkit GA-5.2 were used.

We performed several experiments, primarily to assess the efficiency of SMBS compared to that of the Cannon algorithm. Both blocking and non-blocking implementations were evaluated. In the initial set of evaluations, we increased the matrix sizes ($N \times M$) from 900×900 through to, $10,800 \times 10,800$ while keeping the number of nodes and processor cores constant. We set $N = M$ in all experiments and therefore both matrices A and B have sizes $N \times N$. The time to compute the solution $C \longleftarrow A \times B$ for our algorithm was compared with that of the Cannon Algorithm. The objective in these runs was also to evaluate the effect of distributing across several nodes, in which case inter-node latencies will affect the computational times. We conducted the additional set of experiments to assess the scalability of our algorithm with differing cores and workloads.

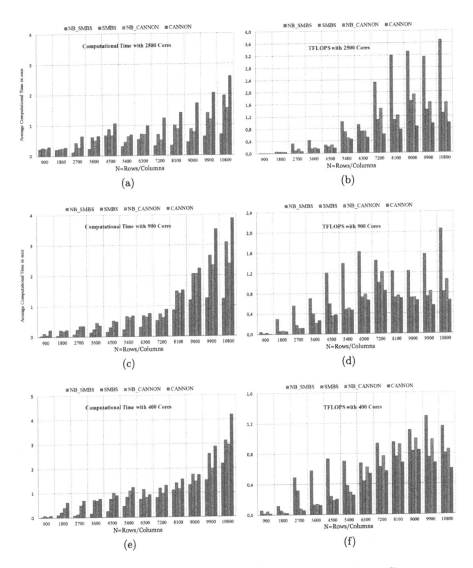

Fig. 5. Computational time and FLOPs with varying Matrix Sizes

Figures 5a, 5c and 5e show the average computation times (over three repetitions), while Figs. 5b, 5d and 5f show the corresponding operational throughput in teraflops (TFLOPS). The actual matrix sizes are the squares of N (e.g., 900 corresponds to a 900×900 matrix).

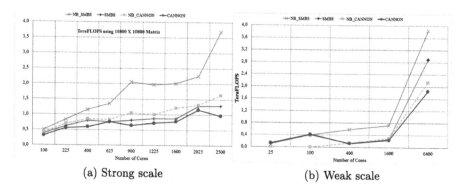

(a) Strong scale   (b) Weak scale

Fig. 6. Evaluation of algorithms' scalability. In the strong scale test, we kept a fixed problem size of 10800×10800 and increased the number of processors from 100 to 2500 cores. In the weak scale test, we increased matrix sizes from 60×60 to 14400×14400 and increased the processors from 25 to 6400 cores

Figure 5a shows the time to compute the solution as the sizes of the matrices increase for the varying the algorithms. As the sizes of the matrices increase, more work is required by each processor as the block size per core also increases. This results in more communication and computation between nodes, as well as increased latency. SMBS performs better than Cannon since it does fewer data movements and hence less inter-node communication. The non-blocking SMBS (which we will refer to as NB_SMBS) shows a much better performance improvement compared to the non-blocking Cannon Algorithm.

As the sizes of the matrices increase, the rate of increase in the latency is far slower in the SMBS than Cannon's Algorithms. We refer to the non-blocking implementation of the Cannon's Algorithm as NB_CANNON. Both non-blocking algorithms have significantly lower latencies as expected, with NB_CANNON growing much faster in terms of the worst latency. This is primarily due to the fact that as the matrix sizes increase, so do the block sizes, and there is a subsequent increase in the time to perform block shifts. Even though we overlap computation with data movement, the overhead cost incurred is obvious from the experiment. NB_SMBS does not incur much latency in data movement since data movement is limited to only a single matrix while employing latency hiding by overlapping the data communication with the computation and hence the better performance recorded. Further, unlike the NB_CANNON, NB_SMBS takes advantage of data locality since the A matrix is not shifted during the data shifting steps. This naturally translates into the higher FLOP values as shown in Figs. 5b, 5d and 5f. Generally, more cores will result in fewer blocks per core and therefore faster computations and effectively lower latencies.

The next set of experiments were conducted to determine the scaling efficiency (scalability) of SMBS, especially the non-blocking SMBS as compared to the Cannon Algorithm. In the strong scaling test, we evaluate how the computational time of a fixed-size matrix changes when the processor resources increase. The goal of the strong scaling test is to assess the efficiency of the algorithm when additional computational resources are allocated. The weak scaling test, on the other hand, measures how the time to compute the product varies with processor count with a fixed system size per processor.

In the strong scaling test, we maintained a fixed problem size (workload) of 10800×10800 while increasing the processing cores. Processor cores were increased from 100 to 2500 cores, and the FLOPS for 3 runs computed. Figure 6a shows the graph for the strong scaling efficiency test. As the number of processor cores increase, less work is required by each core and therefore the computational time reduces, and the operational throughput for that matter increases. The operational throughput generally increases as the core count is increased. We, however, note a slow increase in the blocking algorithms. This could be attributed to an increase in inter-process communication latencies which is, however, overlapped with computation resulting in good scaling efficiency for the non-blocking algorithms.

Figure 6b shows the results of the operational throughput in TFLOPS for the weak scaling test in which the workload (matrix sizes) is increased from 60×60 to 14400×14400 while increasing the processor cores from 25 to 6400. The test shows a general increase in performance as both cores and problem sizes increase. Performance gains increased at a much higher rate when $P = 1600$ (corresponding to matrix size of 3600×3600) in most cases, though there was a gradual increase from the initial cases. NB_SMBS did outperform Cannon's Algorithm as the processor/load increased.

5 Summary and Future Work

We have discussed a Single-Matrix-Block Shift distributed matrix-matrix multiplication algorithm which scales well with increasing number of cores and provides a better performance to the existing Cannon's algorithm by some order of magnitude with theoretical bounds comparatively to a highly tuned SRUMMA algorithm. SMBS achieves higher performance by limiting the number of block shifts and essentially does half of the data movement (Shifts) in the traditional Cannon algorithm. SMBS presents an elegant approach to obtain final block results per computational loop unlike Cannon's and other well-known algorithms like SRUMMA, LaPACK, etc., which present partial results until the final reduction step is complete. SMBS eliminates the final reduction step as the final results become available per iteration. This makes SMBS very applicable to image processing applications, for instance, which require several portions of the final product while the process continues.

SMBS consequently reduces the amount of communication and data movement during computation, and since communication has been identified to contribute more than a half of the total latency in large distributed algorithms, a technique to minimise data movement and inherently exploit data locality is much desirable. Matrix-matrix multiplication is a foundational routine in numerous scientific applications. These, therefore, can leverage the performance enhancement shown by SMBS for further performance gains and processing throughput. We have also presented non-blocking SMBS which leverages non-blocking point-to-point messaging to overlap communication with computation and provides significant performance gains of over $5X$ compared to the blocking SMBS. The algorithm, however, works best with dense matrices.

Future work will exploit non-blocking collectives as well as Partition Global Address Space (PGAS) paradigm and GPU implementations with real-world matrix datasets to evaluate the performance of the algorithm. PGAS is a parallel programming model involving a global memory address space abstraction from logically aggregated random access memory (RAM) of multiple nodes, where a portion is local to each process or node. This, we anticipate, will further leverage data locality, and enhance the overall algorithmic performance. Further experiments on locality and cache efficiency, are also anticipated.

Acknowledgement. Special thanks to the National Energy Research Scientific Computing Center (NERSC), Berkeley, USA, for providing access to their computing infrastructure to run these experiments.

In memoriam: We would like to acknowledge the invaluable contributions of the late Prof Ekow Otoo who inspired and made invaluable contributions to this work. We are both in his intellectual debt. Our thoughts are with his family, friends, and colleagues during this time of reflection.

References

1. Anderson, E., et al.: LAPACK Users' Guide, 3rd edn. Society for Industrial and Applied Mathematics, Philadelphia (1999)
2. Anderson, E., et al.: LAPACK: a portable linear algebra library for high-performance computers. In: Proceedings of the ACM/IEEE Conference on Supercomputing, Supercomputing 1990, Los Alamitos, CA, USA, pp. 2–11. IEEE Computer Society Press (1990)
3. Blackford, L.S., et al.: ScaLAPACK Users' Guide. Society for Industrial and Applied Mathematics, Philadelphia (1997)
4. Choi, J.: A new parallel matrix multiplication algorithm on distributed-memory concurrent computers. In: High Performance Computing on the Information Superhighway, HPC Asia 1997, pp. 224–229 (1997). https://doi.org/10.1109/HPC.1997.592151
5. Choi, J., Walker, D.W., Dongarra, J.J.: Pumma: parallel universal matrix multiplication algorithms on distributed memory concurrent computers. Concurr. Pract. Exp. **6**, 543–570 (1994). https://doi.org/10.1002/cpe.4330060702
6. Coppersmith, D., Winograd, S.: Matrix multiplication via arithmetic progressions. J. Symb. Comput. **9**(3), 251–280 (1990). https://doi.org/10.1016/S0747-7171(08)80013-2

7. D'Alberto, P., Nicolau, A.: Adaptive Strassen's matrix multiplication. In: Proceedings of the 21st Annual International Conference on Supercomputing, ICS 2007, pp. 284–292. ACM, New York (2007). https://doi.org/10.1145/1274971.1275010

8. D'Amore, L., Laccetti, G., Lapegna, M.: Block matrix multiplication in a distributed computing environment: experiments with NetSolve. In: Wyrzykowski, R., Dongarra, J., Meyer, N., Waśniewski, J. (eds.) PPAM 2005. LNCS, vol. 3911, pp. 625–632. Springer, Heidelberg (2006). https://doi.org/10.1007/11752578_75

9. Fawzi, A., et al.: Discovering faster matrix multiplication algorithms with reinforcement learning. Nature **610**(7930), 47–53 (2022). https://doi.org/10.1038/s41586-022-05172-4

10. Gupta, A., Kumar, V.: Scalability of parallel algorithms for matrix multiplication. In: International Conference on Parallel Processing - ICPP 1993, vol. 3, pp. 115–123 (1993). https://doi.org/10.1109/ICPP.1993.160

11. Huang, H., Chow, E.: CA3DMM: a new algorithm based on a unified view of parallel matrix multiplication. In: SC22: International Conference for High Performance Computing, Networking, Storage and Analysis, pp. 1–15 (2022).https://doi.org/10.1109/SC41404.2022.00033

12. Krishnan, M., Nieplocha, J.: SRUMMA: a matrix multiplication algorithm suitable for clusters and scalable shared memory systems. In: 18th International Parallel and Distributed Processing Symposium, 2004 Proceedings, p. 70- (2004). https://doi.org/10.1109/IPDPS.2004.1303000

13. Kurzak, J., Ltaief, H., Dongarra, J., Badia, R.M.: Scheduling dense linear algebra operations on multicore processors. Concurr. Pract. Exp. **22**(1), 15–44 (2010). https://doi.org/10.1002/cpe.v22:1

14. Lee, H.J., Robertson, J.P., Fortes, J.A.B.: Generalized Cannon's algorithm for parallel matrix multiplication. In: Proceedings of the 11th International Conference on Supercomputing, ICS 1997, pp. 44–51. Association for Computing Machinery, New York (1997). https://doi.org/10.1145/263580.263591

15. Li, K.: Scalable parallel matrix multiplication on distributed memory parallel computers. J. Parallel Distrib. Comput. **61**(12), 1709–1731 (2001). https://doi.org/10.1006/jpdc.2001.1768

16. Li, K.: Fast and highly scalable parallel computations for fundamental matrix problems on distributed memory systems. J. Supercomput. **54**(3), 271–297 (2010). https://doi.org/10.1007/s11227-009-0319-0

17. Li, W., Chen, Z., Wang, Z., Jafar, S.A., Jafarkhani, H.: Flexible distributed matrix multiplication. IEEE Trans. Inf. Theory **68**(11), 7500–7514 (2022). https://doi.org/10.1109/TIT.2022.3204488

18. Lu, H.C., Su, L.Y., Huang, S.H.: Highly fault-tolerant systolic-array-based matrix multiplication. Electronics **13**(9), 1780 (2024). https://doi.org/10.3390/electronics13091780

19. Nimako, G., Otoo, E.J., Ohene-Kwofie, D.: Fast parallel algorithms for blocked dense matrix multiplication on shared memory architectures. In: Xiang, Y., Stojmenovic, I., Apduhan, B.O., Wang, G., Nakano, K., Zomaya, A. (eds.) ICA3PP 2012. LNCS, vol. 7439, pp. 443–457. Springer, Heidelberg (2012). https://doi.org/10.1007/978-3-642-33078-0_32

20. Solomonik, E., Demmel, J.: Matrix multiplication on multidimensional torus networks. In: Daydé, M., Marques, O., Nakajima, K. (eds.) VECPAR 2012. LNCS, vol. 7851, pp. 201–215. Springer, Heidelberg (2013). https://doi.org/10.1007/978-3-642-38718-0_21

21. Strassen, V.: Gaussian elimination is not optimal. Numer. Math. **13**(4), 354–356 (1969). https://doi.org/10.1007/BF02165411

22. University of Tennessee and University of California, Berkeley and University of Colorado, Denver and NAG Ltd.: ScaLAPACK - Scalable Linear Algebra PACKage (2022). https://www.netlib.org/scalapack/. Accessed 10 May 2024
23. University of Tennessee and University of California, Berkeley and University of Colorado, Denver and NAG Ltd.: LAPACK - Linear Algebra PACKage (2024). https://www.netlib.org/lapack/. Accessed 10 May 2024
24. Van De Geijn, R.A., Watts, J.: SUMMA: scalable universal matrix multiplication algorithm. Concurr. Pract. Exp. **9**(4), 255–274 (1997)
25. Williams, V.V., Xu, Y., Xu, Z., Zhou, R.: New bounds for matrix multiplication: from alpha to omega (2023)

Automatic Supervision of Online Assessments Using System Process Information and Random Photography

Malia Sekokotoana[1]⬨, Siyabonga Mhlongo[1(✉)]⬨, and Abejide Ade-Ibijola[2]⬨

[1] Department of Applied Information Systems, University of Johannesburg,
Johannesburg, South Africa
216059089@student.uj.ac.za, siyabongam@uj.ac.za
[2] Research Group on Data, Artificial Intelligence, and Innovations for Digital
Transformation, JBS Innovation Lab, Johannesburg Business School,
University of Johannesburg, Johannesburg, South Africa
abejide@jbs.ac.za

Abstract. Recently, online teaching and learning have seen a notable
uptrend in adoption, subsequently increasing interest in conducting
online assessments. The limitation of remote online assessments lies in
the challenge of supervising the individual being assessed. For this reason, many consider human supervision a superior method for maintaining the integrity of assessments. This paper introduces algorithm-driven
techniques for the automated supervision of online assessment-takers by
analysing system processes on their devices and conducting random pho-
tographic monitoring. These techniques, along with their associated algorithms, have been encapsulated into a proof of concept tool. The approach aims to deter assessment-takers from accessing unauthorised files
on their devices during assessments and to instil a sense of being monitored. The system is built around two primary components: one that
monitors process activity and another that analyses images captured
through the assessment-taker's device webcam. Data collected through
these methods are further analysed using facial recognition and additional algorithms to detect behaviours potentially indicative of cheating
during the assessment. Initial testing of the proposed tool achieved a
96.3% accuracy rate in image analysis for identifying cheating behaviour.
Moreover, university lecturers' evaluations strongly support the tool's
potential to deter cheating, its effectiveness in detection, and its role in
maintaining the integrity of online assessments. Future research is recommended to address the challenges identified with the proof of concept
tool, with the objective of enhancing both the accuracy and the overall
effectiveness of the proposed techniques.

Keywords: Online proctoring · Online assessments · Proctoring
systems · Facial recognition · Image processing · Process monitoring

© The Author(s), under exclusive license to Springer Nature Switzerland AG 2024
A. Gerber (Ed.): SAICSIT 2024, CCIS 2159, pp. 207–226, 2024.
https://doi.org/10.1007/978-3-031-64881-6_12

1 Introduction

There has been a rapid increase in e-learning (online learning) over the last two decades, and it has become a critical part of many education systems around the world [25,30]. This is because of the increase in the abilities and capabilities of modern technology [32]. Examples of e-learning platforms include virtual learning environments (VLEs), massive open online courses (MOOCs), and learning management systems (LMSs). Advantages of such platforms include the ability for students to access global resources anytime and seamlessly track their progress [6,16]. In addition to the already growing e-learning domain, the Coronavirus Disease 2019 (COVID-19) pandemic accelerated efforts by educational institutions to extensively use online learning platforms and techniques due to limited contact learning during the pandemic [12,28,29,34].

While e-learning is changing the ways in which educational institutions teach and students learn, it continues to face the challenge of reliably assessing online assessments and limiting cheating [9]. One of the measures that institutions have taken to ensure academic integrity in online assessments is the use of online proctoring. Online proctoring, also referred to as remote proctoring, is the supervision of online assessments through the use of a webcam, microphone, screen-sharing, and other technology means over the internet [13]. The main goal of online proctoring is to ensure that these assessments are fair and honest, by detecting and discouraging cheating [9,13].

There is a prevalent problem of cheating in online assessments [9]. In on-site assessments, students cheat by sneaking in notes, whispering, exchanging papers, and so on [37]. This can be detected by an invigilator and necessary disciplinary action will be taken. Cheating in online assessments on the other hand can be in the form of students receiving help from other people in the same room and texting or using other material such as books or online resources during the assessment. Regardless of the form, cheating is generally referred to as a type of academic dishonesty [14]. Disadvantages of cheating are that it deprives students of true learning opportunities and educators become unaware of their true learning progress.

Online proctoring is the main way in which educational institutions try to detect and discourage cheating in online assessments. Techniques that are typically used are one or a combination of: (i) a webcam to monitor the student's actions; (ii) their computer's microphone to monitor speech levels; (iii) screen-sharing to monitor students' activities on the computer; and (iv) preventing the students from some functionalities such as opening new tabs or exiting the browser or program that is used to take the assessment [4,13,16]. The implementation may be in real-time, where the students are monitored live by remote invigilators or the data gathered from the assessment session can be later reviewed by the invigilator to determine whether any of the students had been cheating or not. Some programs such as *Proctotrack* automatically analyse identification, video and audio data to determine cheating behaviour [21]. Dendir and Maxwell found that students being proctored in online assessments tend to be more compliant to the rules stipulated [9].

Our proposed solution leverages these facts and combines them with the benefits of evidence from online proctoring to develop a hybrid technique for automatically proctoring online assessments. It adds to the body of knowledge of different techniques in automatic online proctoring. The proposed solution is the development of an online assessment tool that monitors the running processes on the assessment-takers' computers, takes photos at random intervals during the assessment, and analyses these photos to detect and discourage cheating.

The contribution of this paper is as follows. We have:

(i) reviewed the background, history and previous tools that have been implemented in online proctoring;
(ii) developed a proof of concept for an online assessment tool that uses a hybrid method of online proctoring, combining process monitoring, random photography, and photo analysis;
(iii) tested and analysed the efficacy of the tool; and
(iv) evaluated the effectiveness of using the tool.

The remainder of this paper is structured as follows: The next section offers a background and reviews related literature on online proctoring. Following that, the paper outlines the design of the online assessment tool, with a detailed description of its implementation in the subsequent section. This leads to the presentation of testing and evaluation results. The paper concludes with a discussion, summarising the findings, drawing conclusions, and suggesting avenues for future research.

2 Background and Related Work

This section provides a background on academic dishonesty in general, and more specific to online assessments. Furthermore, it provides a brief background on online proctoring, some of the current tools that are used in the problem area, as well as previous work that is related to the problem domain of this research.

2.1 Academic Dishonesty in Online Assessments

Research shows that there has been an increase in various forms of online teaching and learning, so has been the need for online assessments [11,31]. While it has been helpful in ensuring students continue to receive education during periods of limited contact learning, some disadvantages include the difficulty of monitoring activities such as cheating by students [40]. Furthermore, online learning may be vulnerable to plagiarism and inappropriate copying and pasting of answers during an assessment [40]. Adkins *et al.* suggest that these activities constitute academic dishonesty [1]. This is also emphasised by [33], who described academic dishonesty as cheating on a test, plagiarism, fabrication, unfair advantage, aiding and abetting, falsification of records, and access to unauthorised material during an assessment.

It is quite easy for students to practice academic dishonesty [1]. Therefore, the use of online assessments is a potential enabler for learners to practice academic dishonesty. For example, in a study which surveyed over 1000 students from six Romanian universities, the results found that roughly 95% of the students who participated in the survey had done one or more forms of violation of academic integrity during online examinations [18].

The main idea behind the proctoring of online assessments is to preserve the integrity of the assessments and the institutions that offer them. Research indicates that students tend to perform better on online assessments that are timed but not invigilated, compared to those with traditional in-person invigilation [8,23,36].

This evidence suggests that the integrity of online assessments may be compromised to some extent, and it is where the use of technology is involved to try to counter this, as pointed out by [22] and [38].

2.2   Online Proctoring

Foster and Layman compared eight popular services that are currently in use for online invigilation [13]. All these services have a way of trying to prevent the assessment-taker from performing any form of infringement while taking the assessment. An observation from their analysis is that they have grouped the features of these services into three groups:

(i) Lockdown features: These features are a form of limiting the assessment-taker from performing any form of infringement during the assessment. This can be achieved through limiting the assessment-taker's ability such as navigating in a browser or right-clicking on their mouse to copy and paste answers [24].
(ii) Authentication options: These options pertain verifying that the person sitting for the examination is the right one. Examples to achieve this include the use of fingerprint identification [19].
(iii) Webcam use and other features: Most of these online proctoring services rely on the use of a webcam and a microphone for assessment-takers to be invigilated [26]. Video footage or images taken using webcams are analysed for suspected behaviour, which can hint at cheating.

There are other features that are provided by these services. For instance, the *Kryterion* system can detect cheating behaviour by analysing inappropriate keystrokes and audio levels to determine if there is any cheating [13,26].

2.3   Current Tools

There are three general types of online proctoring [16]. The first one is live proctoring, where an actual invigilator is monitoring students that are taking the assessment virtually online. The invigilator monitors them through video and sometimes also audio and looks out for any suspicious activities. These could include suspicious eye movements, someone in the room assisting the student, or someone else taking the assessment for the student. If the invigilator suspects any form of cheating from a student, they can give a warning through video conferencing [10,16].

The second type of online proctoring is recorded proctoring. This is where footage and audio of the assessment-taker are recorded during the assessment and then reviewed later by an invigilator. The advantage here is that it reduces the ratio of student-to-invigilator during the assessment, however, any infringement cannot be dealt with in real-time [9,16].

The third type of online proctoring is advanced automated proctoring [20]. Here, instead on the proctor monitoring live or reviewing like the previously discussed methods, the invigilation system analyses information from the assessment in order to determine whether there was any infringement [2,7]. For example, the system uses the student's webcam, and through artificial intelligence, determines whether the student is wandering or is being assisted during the assessment. It could also be used for authentication purposes to determine whether the person taking the exam is the right one [16,39].

Table 1. Summary of existing online proctoring tools.

Tool	Summary of Features
Proctorio [35]	It locks down the assessment-taker's browser, disabling opening of new tabs, printing, clipboard and right-clicking the mouse to prevent copying and pasting
Respondus [15]	The customised browser opens in full screen and cannot be exited or minimised until the assessment is over. Screen capture, messaging, screen-sharing, virtual machine, and network monitoring applications are blocked from running. All recorded data is then sent to instructors for review
Kryterion [5]	It allows instructors to gain access to real-time video and audio of assessment-takers in order for them to detect suspicious behaviour. Each session can also be reviewed at a later stage based on the captured data
ProctorU [27]	The student and the surrounding environment are recorded during the entire exam and instructors can quickly review details of the assessment, and even watch the recorded video

From Table 1, the highlighted existing online proctoring systems all either lock down the student's abilities with their device, or monitor their environment using their webcam or microphones to determine whether they are cheating or not. None of them incorporate currently running processes in the student's devices during the assessment.

2.4   Related Work

Automated Online Proctoring. Atoum *et al.* present a multimedia analytics system that performs continuous and automatic online examination proctoring [3]. They introduce a multimedia analytics system designed for online exam proctoring. The system focuses on maintaining academic integrity in e-learning environments and is described as affordable and convenient for assessment-takers, requiring only two inexpensive cameras and a microphone. One of the cameras and the microphone are built into the assessment-taker's computer while the other camera is worn or attached to eyeglasses to capture the field of view of the assessment-taker. The system extracts low-level features from six basic components: (i) user verification; (ii) text detection; (iii) speech detection; (iv) active window detection; (v) gaze estimation; (vi) and phone detection. These features are then processed further to obtain high-level features used for cheating detection. According to their results, the system's capabilities were validated using a database of 24 assessment-takers, representing real-world behaviours in online assessments. The results showed a segment-based detection rate of nearly 87% across all types of cheating behaviours.

Automated Cheating Detection in Online Assessments via Webcam Image Processing. Jalali and Noorbehbahani propose a two-method approach to online supervision [19]. In the first method, differences between two images are detected through pixel subtraction. For implementation, the system measures the distance between an image and a reference image. If this distance surpasses a specified threshold, the image is deemed indicative of cheating. In the second method, a clustering algorithm groups 50 pre-assessment images of students. The clustering algorithm uses the same distance function as utilised the first method. Subsequently, images of students taken during the assessment are compared with the centre of their nearest clusters. If the distance to all cluster centres falls below the threshold level, the image is classified as normal. Conversely, if the distance exceeds the threshold, the image is identified as indicative of cheating.

The results of the study indicate that both suggested methods for cheating detection in online assessments were implemented with 10 new students as participants. The mean accuracies for a threshold of 8.8 and 9 were compared, showing that the proposed method of cheating detection for a threshold of 9 achieved higher accuracy. Specifically, the average accuracy for the first method at a threshold of 9 was 0.78, while the second method had an average accuracy of 0.68. Furthermore, the study found that the proposed methods could detect empty seats due to students leaving exam chairs with 100% accuracy. However, the study noted challenges in detection accuracy related to clothing colour and background. When students wore light-coloured clothes against a light-coloured background, detection accuracy decreased. Similarly, if a student held a paper sheet in front of a white wall, cheating could not be detected effectively.

Cheating Detection in Online Examinations. Kasliwal proposes a tool designed to monitor student browser activity and changes during exams [24].

This tool can detect cheating by tracking visits to either blacklisted or whitelisted websites, as defined by a pre-established list. Blacklisted websites contain information relevant to exam answers, whereas whitelisted sites are deemed acceptable. This approach is suitable for exams where internet use is permitted. The study conducted multiple test cases using a support vector machine (SVM) algorithm, and observed accuracy rates based on different sizes of training and testing datasets. It found that accuracy increased sharply from 60% to around 90% but then plateaued, showing stable accuracy near 90% even with larger training datasets. The study noted challenges in detecting certain cheating methods, like using Remote Desktop Protocol (RDP) for web browsing, communication through encrypted channels like Google Hangouts, and sharing encrypted messages through email. It was also noted in the study that cheating methods, like using personal laptops with stored materials, or asking answers directly, were undetectable.

Webcam Proctoring to Prevent Online Examination Misconduct. Hylton *et al.* aimed to investigate whether misconduct during online exams could be deterred using a webcam for remote proctoring, and whether this method could enhance the integrity of online exams [17]. Their methodological approach involved a true experimental design with participants randomly assigned to treatment (monitored) and control (non-monitored) groups. The study used an online proctoring tool called Computer Aided Proctored Assessments (CAPA), which monitored participants via webcam during exams. Participants were allowed to take exams from various locations, and webcams were provided if needed. The results indicated significant differences between the monitored and non-monitored groups. The non-monitored participants took longer to complete exams and scored higher than monitored participants. Furthermore, the non-monitored participants perceived greater collaboration opportunities than monitored participants, and perceived greater opportunities to utilise unauthorised resources compared to monitored participants. The monitored participants felt a greater level of deterrence to engage in misconduct compared to non-monitored participants. Overall, these findings indicate a reduced likelihood of cheating amongst students aware of being monitored, which was also supported by other studies [18,36].

3 Design

This section presents the different design components of the proposed automatic online assessment supervision tool.

3.1 Design Overview

Figure 1 provides a high level view of the flow of the automatic supervision tool from the beginning to the end of an assessment.

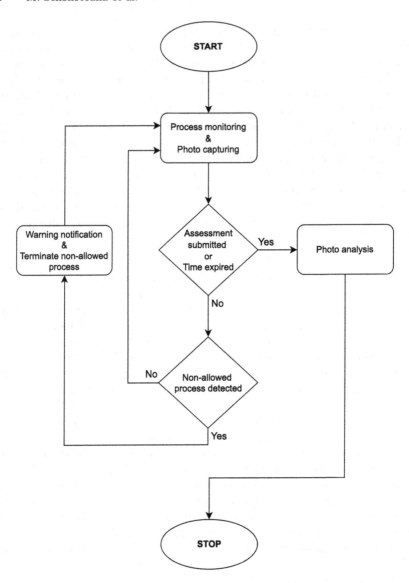

Fig. 1. Design overview of the online assessment monitoring tool.

In the proposed solution, when the assessment is started, all processes that are running in the assessment-taker's computer are monitored. Simultaneously, photos are captured at random intervals using the computer's webcam. The process monitoring and photo capturing continues until either the assessment is submitted, or the assessment time expires. During the assessment, should any non-allowed process run, the assessment-taker is given a warning notification, and the non-allowed process is terminated. After the assessment, all the captured photos are analysed using facial recognition to determine if the assessment-taker was alone, not receiving help from other people, and not copying from other sources.

3.2 Process Monitoring

Algorithm 1 presents the algorithm for process monitoring. At the onset, the database is populated with the names and unique identifiers of processes that are not allowed to run during an assessment, including those associated with applications such as web browsers (for example, Microsoft Edge, or Google Chrome), document readers (for example, Adobe Acrobat), and office productivity applications (for example, Microsoft Word, PowerPoint, or Excel).

Algorithm 1: Process monitoring

Data: nonallowed_processes[ ], running_processes[ ],issues[ ]
Result: $Warning\_notification$
$issues[\ ] \leftarrow nonallowed\_processes \cap running\_processes$;
if $issues[\ ].count() > 0$ **then**
    foreach $nonallowed\_process$ in $issues$ **do**
        | $nonallowed\_process.Kill()$
    end
    return $Warning\_notification$
else
    | do nothing;
end

When the assessment begins, the system collects the names and unique identifiers of the processes currently running on the assessment-taker's computer. These are then continuously compared to the list of prohibited processes using their unique identifiers. Should any non-allowed process be detected, a pop-up warning is displayed to the assessment-taker, and the non-allowed process is terminated. This monitoring then continues until the assessment-taker submits the assessment, or the allocated assessment time runs out.

3.3 Random Photography

Algorithm 2 presents the algorithm for random photography. Before starting an assessment, the application detects all webcams connected to the assessment-taker's computer. If no webcam is detected, an error message is displayed, preventing the start of the assessment. If one or more webcams are detected, the primary one is selected for random photography. When the assessment starts, a video stream is initiated, and photos are captured from this stream at random intervals.

The intervals for taking photographs are randomly determined as follows: As the assessment begins, a random number between 1 and 120 inclusive is selected.

Algorithm 2: Random photography

Data: current_time, previous_time, max_range, min_range,
        countdown_timer, interval

$max\_range \leftarrow 120$;

$min\_range \leftarrow 0$;

while $countdown\_timer > 0$ **do**

    $interval \leftarrow Rand(min\_range, max\_range)$;

    $capture\_photo()$ at $interval$;

    $countdown\_timer \leftarrow countdown\_timer - (current\_time - previous\_time)$;

    $previous\_time \leftarrow current\_time$;

end

This serves as the number of seconds between one picture being taken and the next. This process repeats until the assessment is submitted, or the allocated assessment time expires. Limiting the number of seconds to 120 ensures that at least one photo of the assessment-taker is captured every two minutes, while also randomising the total number of photos taken within that time frame.

3.4 Photo Analysis

The photo analysis that is conducted at the end of an assessment is presented in Algorithm 3. When an assessment is submitted, or the allocated assessment time expires, the photos captured during the assessment are examined to ascertain the presence of a face, and to determine the number of faces present in each of the photos. Flags were created and designed to activate under two conditions: (i) if no face is detected; or (ii) if more than one face is detected. These flags indicate potential instances where the assessment-taker is away from their computer, or receiving assistance from others.

Algorithm 3: Image analysis

Data: captured_photos[], face_landmarks[], faces_detected[]

Result: Flag

foreach $photo$ in $captured\_photos[]$ **do**

    $face\_predictor \leftarrow Deserialize(face\_landmarks)$;

    SEND $request$ to API;

    $faces\_detected \leftarrow$ RESPONSE;

    if $faces\_detected.count() > 1$ **then**

        $Flag \leftarrow True$;

    else

        $Flag \leftarrow False$;

    end

    Return $Flag$;

end

---

4   Implementation

The system is implemented as a Windows Presentation Foundation (WPF) application, developed using the Visual Studio Integrated Development Environment (IDE). It is a Windows desktop application installed on the assessment-taker's computer, with the assessment accessible through the application's interface. Figure 2 illustrates the user interface; in this instance, Microsoft PowerPoint is open during the examination but is automatically closed, followed by the display of a pop-up warning.

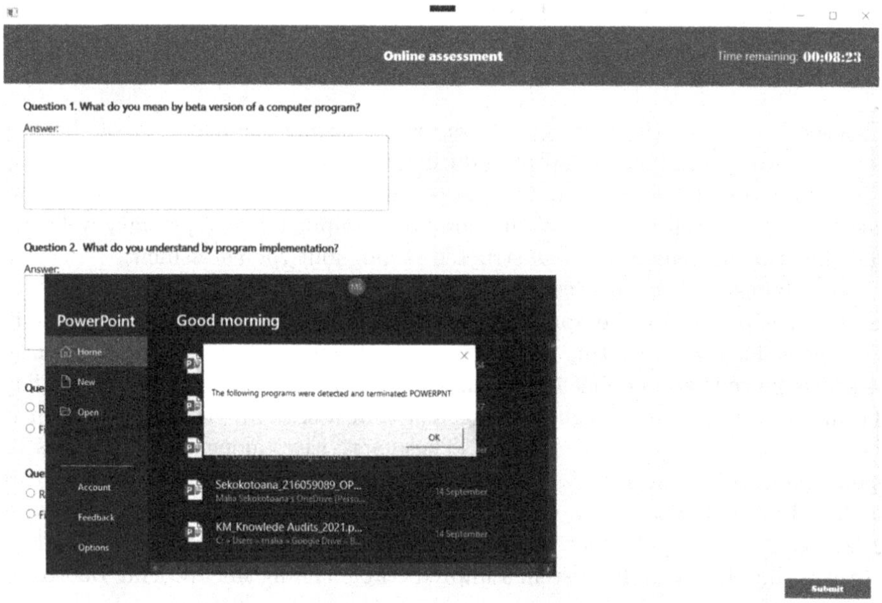

Fig. 2. Interface

The system's implementation relied on two primary technologies: (i) the Dlib[1] application programming interface (API); and (ii) the AForge.NET[2] library. The Dlib API was instrumental in the image analysis component of the tool, primarily for face detection. It works by first scanning input images to identify any that contain a face. The Dlib FrontalFaceDetector employs a face detector specifically optimised for frontal faces, while the Deserializer loads an OpenCV[3] configuration file for a deep neural network trained in face recognition. This network detects faces by identifying five key landmarks on the human

---

[1] See: http://dlib.net/.
[2] See: https://www.aforgenet.com/framework/.
[3] See: https://opencv.org/.

face. To enhance accuracy, a face predictor module is incorporated, ensuring that faces are detectable even when not all landmarks are visible. This module is particularly effective at recognising faces at challenging angles, or when only a portion of the face is visible within the frame.

For the image capturing functionality of the assessment tool, the `AForge.NET` library was utilised. It is tasked with identifying camera devices on the assessment-taker's computer. Once the primary camera is detected, it initiates a video stream, capturing images at randomly determined intervals throughout the assessment period.

5   Testing and Evaluation

5.1   Face Detection Testing and Results

This section details the testing process for evaluating the accuracy of the face detection feature in images captured during assessments with the proposed tool. The foundational assumptions for the testing process include the assessment-taker being in a well-lit room, their computer equipped with a primary webcam, and the webcam remaining unobstructed throughout the assessment.

To demonstrate this process, Fig. 3 displays the analysis results of two images randomly captured by the application during an assessment. In Image 33, only one face is detected, resulting in the image not being flagged. In contrast, Image 34 shows more than one face detected, leading the system to automatically flag the image. Should any image be flagged within a session, the entire session is then considered suspect for cheating. These activities, along with attempts to open unauthorised applications, are recorded in a log file. A snippet of this log file is presented in Fig. 4, documenting an attempt to open Microsoft Word at 22:14:30. The log further indicates that images were captured at random intervals, highlighting the system's unpredictable timing in capturing photos.

Image: 33.jpg
Faces detected: 1
Flag: False

Image: 34.jpg
Faces detected: 2
Flag: True

Fig. 3. Illustration of photo analysis technique and results.

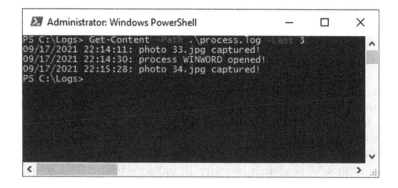

Fig. 4. Sample log file illustrating process events.

To comprehensively evaluate the photo analysis module and its underlying algorithms, a series of tests were conducted on a batch of 100 photos, each containing between one to three faces. These photos were taken under consistent bright room lighting conditions. The test dataset intentionally included scenarios where some faces were not directly facing the webcam, some were partially occluded, some were in close proximity, some were lined up in a row, and some varied in distance from the webcam. The precise count of faces in these photos was determined through manual counting. These photos were then analysed by the photo analysis module, allowing for a comparison between the module's face detection results and the manual count. This comparison facilitated the calculation of the tool's accuracy. The results of this evaluation are summarised in Table 2.

Table 2. Face detection testing parameters and results.

Parameter	Results
Total number of photos	100
Actual number of faces manually counted	217
Detected number of faces	209
Accuracy (%)	96.3

The results indicate a 96.3% accuracy rate in identifying the number of faces in a photo, assuming compliance with the predefined conditions. This high accuracy suggests that the algorithm has been implemented robustly. However, notable limitations include the algorithm's inability to recognise faces in suboptimal lighting conditions or when the assessment-taker is wearing a facial covering, such as a mask. Addressing these challenges could potentially enhance the accuracy further.

5.2   Tool Evaluation

A survey was carried out with 31 university lecturers through Google Forms to gather insights into their perceptions of implementing and utilising the proposed techniques for online assessments. Participants were provided with a link to a short video demonstration of the tool operating in a live assessment scenario, along with evaluation statements on a 5-point Likert-type scale. The objective was to understand lecturers' views on several aspects, including whether the use of this monitoring technique would deter cheating in online assessments, its effectiveness in identifying cheating incidents, and whether they believe such a tool could uphold academic integrity in online settings. The responses are detailed in Table 3 and in Figs. 5, 6 and 7.

Table 3. Statistical results of tool evaluation.

| | Mode | Median | CI[a] on Median | | IQR | CI[a] on IQR | |
			Lower	Upper		Lower	Upper
DET	4[b]	4	4	4	1	1	1
EFF	4	4	4	4	1	1	1
INT	5	4	4	5	1	1	1

[a] Bootstrap results are based on 5000 bootstrap samples.
[b] Multiple modes exist. The smallest value is shown.
Notes: CI: BCa 95% Confidence Interval; IQR: Interquartile Range; DET: Deterrent;
EFF: Effectiveness; INT: Academic Integrity; Likert scale response anchors: 5 = Strongly
Agree/Very Effective; 1 = Strongly Disagree/Not at all Effective;

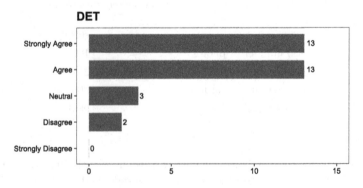

Note: DET: Deterrent;

Fig. 5. Perceptions of the deterrent effect of monitoring on cheating in online assessments using the proposed techniques.

Figure 5 summarises the university lecturers' perceptions on the effectiveness of the proposed monitoring technique in deterring cheating during online assessments, based on a 5-point Likert-type scale evaluation. With 26 out of 31 respondents expressing agreement or strong agreement to the statement that the technique would deter cheating in online assessments, the results underscore a significant endorsement of the method's potential. The analysis revealed a bimodal distribution of responses, with modes at both 4.0 (*'Agree'*) and 5.0 (*'Strongly Agree'*), indicating that the most frequent responses leaned towards agreement.

Furthermore, the median value, determined to be 4.0 (*'Agree'*), along with a BCa 95% confidence interval (CI) of [4.0, 4.0], reinforces the strong central agreement amongst respondents. This suggests a robust belief in the monitoring technique's deterrent effect. The interquartile rage (IQR), computed to be 1.0 with a BCa 95% CI of [1.0, 1.0], points to a tight clustering of responses within the middle 50% of the data, indicating minimal variability in lecturers' perceptions. This tight dispersion, paired with the certainty provided by the CIs, denotes a cohesive and strong endorsement of the technique's deterrent effect across the academic community.

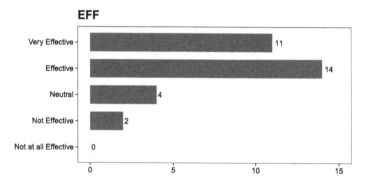

Note: EFF: Effectiveness;

Fig. 6. Perceptions of the effectiveness of the proposed techniques in detecting cheating in online assessments.

Figure 6 illustrates the responses of university lecturers to the effectiveness of the proposed techniques in detecting cheating during online assessments, evaluated using a 5-point Likert-type scale. The responses reveal that 14 out of 31 participants deemed the technique to be *'Effective'*, while another 11 viewed it as *'Very Effective'*. This distribution of opinions strongly suggests that, from their perspective, the lecturers consider these techniques to be effective in combating cheating in online settings. The mode being computed at 4.0 (*'Effective'*) further underscores the prevailing belief amongst the respondents that the technique is indeed effective.

The analysis further finds solid support in the median value, determined to be 4.0 (*'Effective'*), accompanied by a BCa 95% CI of [4.0, 4.0]. This underscores a strong belief in the proposed techniques' ability to identify cheating in online assessments. The IQR, calculated to be 1.0 with a BCa 95% CI of [1.0, 1.0], underscores the concentrated nature of the responses. Such a tight clustering within the central 50% of the dataset signifies a uniformity in the lecturers' opinions. This consistency, together with the certainty provided by the CIs, reflects a unified approval of the techniques' capability to uphold academic integrity through effective detection of cheating behaviours.

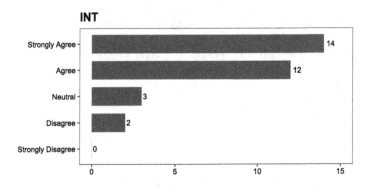

Note: INT: Academic Integrity;

Fig. 7. Perceptions of academic integrity preservation with the use of the proposed techniques in online assessments.

Figure 7 depicts university lecturers' levels of agreement or disagreement, measured on a 5-point Likert-type scale, with the statement question: *'To what extent do you agree or disagree that this tool can help preserve academic integrity in online assessments?'* Analysis of the data shows that 12 out of 31 participants agreed, while 14 out of 31 strongly agreed, highlighting a consensus that a tool like this can significantly contribute to upholding academic integrity in online assessments. The mode, computed at 5.0 (*'Strongly Agree'*), amplifies this collective endorsement.

Furthermore, the median value of 4.0 (*'Agree'*), coupled with a BCa 95% CI of [4.0, 5.0], signals a robust central agreement amongst the lecturers. The IQR, also calculated to be 1.0 with a BCa 95% CI of [1.0, 1.0], points to a tight grouping of responses, indicating a homogeneous view amongst the respondents regarding the tool. These statistical indicators suggest a strong agreement within the academic community that employing such monitoring techniques can be crucial in maintaining the integrity of online assessments.

6   Discussion, Conclusion, and Future Work

This study embarked on an exploration of online proctoring, motivated by the growing shift towards online teaching, learning, and assessment modalities. In addressing this digital transition, the research reviewed and analysed existing proctoring approaches, resulting in the development of a proof of concept tool for online assessments. This tool integrates a hybrid online proctoring methodology, encompassing process monitoring, random photography, and photo analysis. It was then evaluated to assess its deterrent effect, effectiveness, and overall appropriateness in safeguarding academic integrity within the context of online assessments.

Based on the evaluation results, it is clear that university lecturers perceive the proposed tool, and its underlying techniques and algorithms, as both effective and indispensable for preserving academic integrity in online assessments. The data reveal a strong consensus amongst lecturers on several key aspects. Firstly, the tool's monitoring capabilities are believed to potentially deter cheating amongst students. Secondly, its techniques are perceived to be very effective for detecting cheating occurrences. Lastly, lecturers view the tool as playing a crucial role in promoting honesty and fairness within online assessment environments.

The results highlight the academic community's endorsement of the tool as a valuable asset for administering and monitoring online assessments. Lecturers regard the tool not merely as a means of detecting cheating, but as a proactive measure to deter misconduct, thereby contributing to a culture of integrity. This broad acceptance suggests that such technological interventions are viewed by lecturers as crucial in transitioning to more digitally focused teaching and assessment methods, thereby fostering more conducive learning environments. The unified support for the tool's effectiveness, and its potential role in upholding academic standards, underscores the potential for wider adoption in educational institutions aiming to navigate the challenges posed by online assessments.

Specific tests on the accuracy of the face detection module confirmed its effectiveness in identifying individuals present in front of the computer during live assessment sessions. Similarly, the functionality for flagging and terminating non-permitted applications demonstrated that the underlying techniques operate in alignment with their algorithms. Notwithstanding, several limitations and areas for future research have emerged from the implementation and testing phases. The first concern involves the face detection module, which does not perform optimally under sub-optimal lighting conditions, or when the assessment-taker is wearing facial coverings, such as masks. The second issue relates to the detection of non-permitted processes, which relies on predefined names and process identifiers; consequently, new, unknown, or modified applications may evade detection. The third challenge involves the possibility of students receiving external assistance undetected, especially if the helper stays out of the camera's view. This includes scenarios where students might use mobile phones, textbooks, or notes as unauthorised reference materials. The fourth and final limitation pertains to the evaluative scope, which was somewhat limited by the proof of concept nature of this implementation. The identified challenges highlight the need for continuous improvement, and underscore the tool's potential for further development.

Future research efforts should aim to explore strategies for overcoming these identified challenges, with the goal of further improving the accuracy and effectiveness of the proposed techniques. Additionally, incorporating techniques such as capturing and analysing short video snippets could further enhance the robustness and credibility of the evidence in cheating cases. It is essential that these approaches be evaluated in broader contexts, including real-world settings, to fully assess their practicality and impact. The outcomes of such investigations hold the potential to significantly refine and advance the capabilities of online proctoring tools, contributing to more secure and integrity-driven online assessment environments.

References

1. Adkins, J., Kenkel, C., Lim, C.L.: Deterrents to online academic dishonesty. J. Learn. High. Educ. **1**(1), 17–22 (2005)
2. Arnò, S., Galassi, A., Tommasi, M., Saggino, A., Vittorini, P.: State-of-the-art of commercial proctoring systems and their use in academic online exams. Int. J. Distance Educ. Technol. **19**(2), 55–76 (2021). https://doi.org/10.4018/ijdet.20210401.oa3
3. Atoum, Y., Chen, L., Liu, A.X., Hsu, S.D.H., Liu, X.: Automated online exam proctoring. IEEE Trans. Multimedia **19**(7), 1609–1624 (2017). https://doi.org/10.1109/tmm.2017.2656064
4. Bergmans, L., Bouali, N., Luttikhuis, M., Rensink, A.: On the efficacy of online proctoring using Proctorio. In: Csapó, B., Uhomoibhi, J. (eds.) Proceedings of the 13th International Conference on Computer Supported Education, vol. 1, pp. 279–290. SciTePress (2021). https://doi.org/10.5220/0010399602790290
5. Cai, H., King, I.: Education technology for online learning in times of crisis. In: Mitsuhara, H., et al. (eds.) 2020 IEEE International Conference on Teaching, Assessment, and Learning for Engineering (TALE), Takamatsu, Japan, pp. 758–763. IEEE (2020). https://doi.org/10.1109/tale48869.2020.9368387
6. Callan, V.J., Bowman, K.: Sustaining e-learning innovations: a review of the evidence and future directions. Government report TD/TNC 102.739, Australian Flexible Learning Framework, Australia (2010)
7. Choudhury, S., Pattnaik, S.: Emerging themes in e-learning: a review from the stakeholders' perspective. Comput. Educ. **144**, 103657 (2020). https://doi.org/10.1016/j.compedu.2019.103657
8. Daffin Jr, L.W., Jones, A.A.: Comparing student performance on proctored and non-proctored exams in online psychology courses. Online Learn. J. **22**(1), 131–145 (2018). https://doi.org/10.24059/olj.v22i1.1079
9. Dendir, S., Maxwell, R.S.: Cheating in online courses: evidence from online proctoring. Comput. Hum. Behav. Rep. **2**, 100033 (2020). https://doi.org/10.1016/j.chbr.2020.100033
10. Eisenberg, A.: Keeping an eye on online test-takers. Online News Article (2013). The New York Times. https://immagic.com/eLibrary/ARCHIVES/GENERAL/GENPRESS/N130302E.pdf

11. Favale, T., Soro, F., Trevisan, M., Drago, I., Mellia, M.: Campus traffic and e-learning during COVID-19 pandemic. Comput. Netw. **176**, 107290 (2020). https://doi.org/10.1016/j.comnet.2020.107290

12. Ferdig, R.E., Baumgartner, E., Hartshorne, R., Kaplan-Rakowski, R., Mouza, C. (eds.): Teaching, Technology, and Teacher Education During the COVID-19 Pandemic: Stories from the Field. Association for the Advancement of Computing in Education (AACE) (2020). https://www.learntechlib.org/p/216903

13. Foster, D., Layman, H.: Online proctoring systems compared (2013). https://caveon.com/wp-content/uploads/2013/03/Online-Proctoring-Systems-Compared-Mar-13-2013.pdf

14. Gamage, K.A., de Silva, E.K., Gunawardhana, N.: Online delivery and assessment during COVID-19: safeguarding academic integrity. Educ. Sci. **10**(11), 301 (2020). https://doi.org/10.3390/educsci10110301

15. Gilbert, L., Nunez-Argote, L., Hunter, K., Smith, C.: Prevention of digital cheating with respondus monitor. Clin. Lab. Sci. **30**(2), 88 (2017)

16. Hussain, M., Zhu, W., Zhang, W., Abidi, S.M.R.: Student engagement predictions in an e-learning system and their impact on student course assessment scores. Comput. Intell. Neurosci. **2018**, 1–21 (2018). https://doi.org/10.1155/2018/6347186

17. Hylton, K., Levy, Y., Dringus, L.P.: Utilizing webcam-based proctoring to deter misconduct in online exams. Comput. Educ. **92–93**, 53–63 (2016). https://doi.org/10.1016/j.compedu.2015.10.002

18. Ives, B., et al.: Patterns and predictors of academic dishonesty in Romanian university students. High. Educ. **74**(5), 815–831 (2017). https://doi.org/10.1007/s10734-016-0079-8

19. Jalali, K., Noorbehbahani, F.: An automatic method for cheating detection in online exams by processing the student's webcam images. In: 3rd Conference on Electrical and Computer Engineering Technology (E-Tech 2017), Tehran, Iran (2017)

20. Jefferies, A., Barton, K., Meere, J., Peramungama, S., Pyper, A., Yip, A.: Trialling online proctoring for e-assessments: early outcomes from the Erasmus+ OP4RE project. In: Mesquita, A., Peres, P. (eds.) 16th European Conference on e-Learning (ECEL 2017), pp. 221–228. Academic Conferences International Limited, Porto (2017)

21. Joyner, D.A.: Building purposeful online learning: outcomes from blending CS1301. In: Madden, A.G., Margulieux, L., Kadel, R.S., Goel, A.K. (eds.) Blended Learning in Practice: A Guide for Practitioners and Researchers, pp. 69–96. The MIT Press (2019). https://doi.org/10.7551/mitpress/11352.003.0008

22. Kamble, K.P., Ghorpade, V.R.: Video interpretation for cost-effective remote proctoring to prevent cheating. In: Patil, V.H., Dey, N., Mahalle, P.N., Shafi Pathan, M., Kimbahune, V.V. (eds.) Proceeding of First Doctoral Symposium on Natural Computing Research. LNNS, vol. 169, pp. 259–269. Springer, Singapore (2021). https://doi.org/10.1007/978-981-33-4073-2_25

23. Karim, M.N., Kaminsky, S.E., Behrend, T.S.: Cheating, reactions, and performance in remotely proctored testing: an exploratory experimental study. J. Bus. Psychol. **29**(4), 555–572 (2014). https://doi.org/10.1007/s10869-014-9343-z

24. Kasliwal, G.: Cheating detection in online examinations. Master's Projects, 399. San Jose State University (2015). https://doi.org/10.31979/etd.y292-cddh

25. Kentnor, H.E.: Distance education and the evolution of online learning in the United States. In: Flinders, D.J., Moroye, C.M. (eds.) Curriculum and Teaching Dialogue, vol. 17, pp. 21–34. Information Age Publishing, Charlotte (2015)

26. Maat, K.: Determining efficient shot boundary detection on screen-recorded video's of digital exams. Research report, University of Amsterdam (2018)

27. Milone, A.S., Cortese, A.M., Balestrieri, R.L., Pittenger, A.L.: The impact of proctored online exams on the educational experience. Curr. Pharm. Teach. Learn. **9**(1), 108–114 (2017). https://doi.org/10.1016/j.cptl.2016.08.037

28. Mpungose, C.B.: Emergent transition from face-to-face to online learning in a South African university in the context of the coronavirus pandemic. Humanit. Soc. Sci. Commun. **7**(1), 113 (2020). https://doi.org/10.1057/s41599-020-00603-x

29. Mpungose, C.B.: Lecturers' reflections on use of Zoom video conferencing technology for e-learning at a South African university in the context of coronavirus. Afr. Identities **21**(2), 266–282 (2023). https://doi.org/10.1080/14725843.2021.1902268

30. Power, T.M., Morven-Gould, A.: Head of gold, feet of clay: the online learning paradox. Int. Rev. Res. Open Distrib. Learn. **12**(2), 19 (2011). https://doi.org/10.19173/irrodl.v12i2.916

31. Rafique, G.M., Mahmood, K., Warraich, N.F., Rehman, S.U.: Readiness for online learning during COVID-19 pandemic: a survey of Pakistani LIS students. J. Acad. Librariansh. **47**(3), 102346 (2021). https://doi.org/10.1016/j.acalib.2021.102346

32. Raja, R., Nagasubramani, P.C.: Impact of modern technology in education. J. Appl. Adv. Res. **3**(Suppl. 1), S33–S35 (2018). https://doi.org/10.21839/jaar.2018.v3iS1.165

33. Stuber-McEwen, D., Wiseley, P.A., Hoggatt, S.: Point, click, and cheat: frequency and type of academic dishonesty in the virtual classroom. Online J. Distance Learn. Adm. **12**(3), 1–10 (2009)

34. Subedi, S., Nayaju, S., Subedi, S., Shah, S.K., Shah, J.M.: Impact of e-learning during COVID-19 pandemic among nursing students and teachers of Nepal. Int. J. Sci. Healthc. Res. **5**(3), 68–76 (2020)

35. Swauger, S.: Our bodies encoded: algorithmic test proctoring in higher education. In: Stommel, J., Friend, C., Morris, S.M. (eds.) Critical Digital Pedagogy: A Collection, pp. 51–66. Hybrid Pedagogy Inc., Washington, DC (2020). https://hybridpedagogy.org/our-bodies-encoded-algorithmic-test-proctoring-in-higher-education/

36. Varble, D.: Reducing cheating opportunities in online test. Atlantic Mark. J. **3**(3), 131–149 (2014)

37. Witherspoon, M., Maldonado, N., Lacey, C.H.: Undergraduates and academic dishonesty. Int. J. Bus. Soc. Sci. **3**(1), 76–86 (2012)

38. Yekefallah, L., Namdar, P., Panahi, R., Dehghankar, L.: Factors related to students' satisfaction with holding e-learning during the COVID-19 pandemic based on the dimensions of e-learning. Heliyon **7**(7), e07628 (2021). https://doi.org/10.1016/j.heliyon.2021.e07628

39. Zhang, Z., Zhang, M., Chang, Y., Esche, S.K., Chassapis, C.: A virtual laboratory system with biometric authentication and remote proctoring based on facial recognition. Comput. Educ. J. **7**(4), 74–84 (2016)

40. Zhao, P., Sintonen, S., Kyanäslahti, H.: The pedagogical functions of arts and cultural-heritage education with ICTs in museums - a case study of FINNA and Google Art Project. Int. J. Instr. Technol. Distance Learn. **12**(1), 3–15 (2015)

Iterative Approximation of Nash Equilibrium Strategies for Multi-agent Systems

Nils Timm[(✉)][iD] and Kyle Smith[iD]

Department of Computer Science, University of Pretoria, Pretoria, South Africa
ntimm@cs.up.ac.za, u20435992@tuks.co.za

Abstract. We present a technique for approximating Nash equilibrium strategies for multi-agents systems for resource allocation (MRAs). Agents in MRAs seek to maximise the frequency of reaching their resource allocation goals, which can be measured by means of a pay-off. A strategy is an ϵ-approximation of a Nash equilibrium if no agent can multiply its pay-off by more than ϵ via unilateral deviation, where ϵ is a rational number. For small ϵ's approximate Nash equilibria are practically useful and stable strategies since agents will only have a small incentive to change their strategic behaviour. Our technique is based on encoding the strategy synthesis problem in propositional logic with weighted 'pay-off' clauses and solving it via weighted maximum satisfiability solving. In our approach we initially synthesise a collectively optimal strategy and determine for each agent the *improvement potential*, which is the pay-off increase that can be achieved via unilateral deviation. We seek to iteratively reduce the improvement potentials of synthesised strategies: The weights of the 'pay-off' clauses associated with agents get adjusted such that agents with a currently high improvement potential will be favoured when solving the weight-adjusted strategy synthesis problem in the subsequent iteration. We show that our approach facilitates the synthesis of ϵ-equilibrium strategies with small ϵ's.

1 Introduction

Multi-agent systems for resource allocation (MRAs) are a concept for modelling competitive resource allocation problems in distributed computing [5]. An MRA is composed of a set of agents and a set of resources. Agents have access to a subset of the overall set of resources. Moreover, each agent has a goal in terms of the amount of resources to accumulate. Particular resources can be allocated by means of request actions. Further types of actions are release and idle. MRAs run in discrete rounds. In each round each agent selects an action, and the tuple of selected actions gets executed in a simultaneous manner. Once an agent has achieved its goal, it releases all accumulated resources and starts to allocate them again. Agents may pursue to achieve their goals once-off or repetitively. Since resources are generally shared, the achievement of goals is a competition between agents. Several practically relevant scenarios of resource allocation can be modelled as a multi-agent system for resource allocation.

A. Gerber (Ed.): SAICSIT 2024, CCIS 2159, pp. 227–243, 2024.
https://doi.org/10.1007/978-3-031-64881-6_13

For MRAs (or more specifically, for the scenarios that they model) it is typically of importance that they are designed such that resource goals can be achieved in an optimal way. For instance, once-off goals shall be achieved as early as possible and repetitive goals shall be achieved as frequently as possible. These forms of goal-achievement optimality can be measured by means of a pay-off. Ensuring optimality in MRAs is associated with the strategy synthesis problem. A strategy for a multi-agent system is a mapping between states of the system and actions to be taken by the agents in these states. A strategy is collectively optimal if following the strategy guarantees that each agent achieves its goal at least once and additionally the overall pay-off gets maximised. The synthesis of collectively optimal strategies can be reduced to the maximum satisfiability problem (Max-SAT) [20]. For this, the MRA under consideration and the goal-achievement properties to be optimised get encoded in propositional logic such that a Max-SAT solver can determine a max-satisfying truth assignment from which a collectively optimal strategy can be immediately be derived.

A collectively optimal strategy only ensures optimality with regard to the overall system but not necessarily with regard to each individual agent. For scenarios where just the overall system performance is of importance such a solution will be sufficient. But for strictly competitive scenarios a collectively optimal strategy that favours certain agents over others may not be acceptable. For such scenarios a Nash equilibrium strategy can be an adequate solution. A Nash equilibrium of an MRA is a strategy that ensures that: 1. Each agent will achieve its individual goal at least once. 2. No agent can increase its individual pay-off by deviating from the strategy with alternative strategic decisions, assuming that the remaining agents still adhere to the strategy. Hence, a Nash equilibrium is a strategy on which even competing agents may agree.

Algorithms for solving the 2EXPTIME-complete Nash equilibrium synthesis problem have been theoretically defined [1], but due to the high complexity the development of efficient synthesis techniques is still an open problem. Further challenges with regard to the Nash equilibrium synthesis are that for several scenarios Nash equilibria may not exist at all or that a discovered Nash equilibrium may be far away from optimality. An example for the latter is the well-known prisoner's dilemma.

In this paper, we present an iterative algorithm for approximating Nash equilibrium strategies for multi-agent systems. Our approach is based on the synthesis of ϵ-equilibria, which are strategies that approximately satisfy the condition of an exact Nash equilibrium. In an ϵ-equilibrium no agent can multiply its individual pay-off by more than ϵ by deviating from the strategy with alternative strategic decisions, assuming that the remaining agents still adhere to the strategy. For small ϵ-values such an approximate Nash equilibrium is typically still an acceptable and practically useful solution due to the status quo bias. Besides the reduced computational costs in comparison to the exact Nash equilibrium synthesis our approach has the advantage that it can synthesize approximate solutions for scenarios where no exact equilibrium exists and that it enables to find a balanced trade-off between equilibrium and optimality.

Our algorithm encodes the synthesis problem in propositional logic. The encoding contains weighted 'pay-off' clauses that characterise states where an individual agent achieves its goal. In the initial iteration all weights are set to 1. Via weighted Max-SAT solving the algorithm searches for a truth assignment that maximises the sum of weights of the satisfied 'pay-off' clauses and translates the assignment into a corresponding strategy. For this strategy we compute for each agent how much it could multiply its individual pay-off, assuming that the other agents keep their strategic decisions unchanged. We call this multiplier the *improvement potential* of an agent. The current strategy is an ϵ-equilibrium where ϵ is the maximum improvement potential out of the potentials of all agents. In the subsequent iteration, the weights of the 'pay-off' clauses get adjusted proportionally to the improvement potential: The higher the improvement potential of an agent, the larger the weight that will be assigned to its 'pay-off' clauses. The intention behind the weight-adjustment is that pay-off preference will be given to agents that previously had a high improvement potential, and consequently, the maximum improvement potential, i.e., ϵ decreases. The algorithm continues with Max-SAT-based strategy synthesis, the computation of the improvement potentials and weight-adjustment for a number of specified iterations and keeps track of the minimal ϵ-value and the corresponding ϵ-equilibrium strategy that can be obtained.

We have implemented our ϵ-equilibrium synthesis technique on top of the Max-SAT solver OPEN-WBO [16]. Experiments show promising results in terms of synthesising close approximations of Nash equilibrium strategies.

2   Related Work

The synthesis of Nash equilibrium strategies for multi-agent systems has been studied in several works on *rational verification* [9,12,21]. In rational verification the objectives of agents are qualitative in the sense that agents only have a once-off goal. In contrast, our approach focusses on quantitative goal objectives: Agents seek to achieve their goals as frequently as possible. Only quantitative objectives allow to synthesise ϵ-equilibria.

Nash equilibria with regard to quantitative aspects have been considered in [1,3,11]. In [1] the authors propose the temporal logic LTL[$\mathcal{F}$] that allows to specify quantitative objectives. Nash equilibrium synthesis is reduced to model checking, whereas our approach reduces the synthesis to maximum satisfiability solving. The authors of [11] introduce multi-agent systems in which agents have a primary goal that is qualitative and a secondary goal that is quantitative. It is proven that if the qualitative goals are Büchi conditions, then an *NP*-algorithm for solving the corresponding Nash equilibrium synthesis problem exists. Another framework for reasoning about systems where agents have both quantitative goals is proposed in [3]. The authors augment multi-agent systems with transition pay-offs and introduce a quantitative extension of the logic ATL*. The contributions of the above works are predominantly of theoretical nature and focus on establishing general complexity results of the proposed synthesis problems, whereas our work also comprises tool support and experimental results. A further difference to our work is that the above-mentioned approaches solely consider the synthesis of exact Nash equilibria.

To the best of our knowledge, our technique is the first Max-SAT-based approach to the synthesis of ϵ-equilibrium strategies. In related fields, Max-SAT has been employed to find optimal coalitions of agents [15], to synthesise optimal controllers [6], and to model check quantitative hyper-properties [7].

The synthesis of approximate Nash equilibria is considered in [8,10,13,18]. In [10] it is shown that if the goals of agents are linear temporal logic properties then the ϵ-equilibrium synthesis problem for a given ϵ is 2EXPTIME-complete. The authors of [18] propose a construction method for ϵ-Nash equilibrium strategies for non-zero-sum differential games. The approach is based on solving differential equations. It is restricted to two-agent scenarios and it assumes that ϵ is a given constant. The theoretical work of [13] proves that for any Nash equilibrium of a continuous game, and any sequence of perturbations of that game, there exists a corresponding sequence of ϵ-equilibria converging to the given equilibrium of the original game, with the ϵ converging to zero. A different notion of approximate Nash equilibria is considered in [8]. The authors introduce the concept of *local equilibria* in multi-agent systems. A local equilibrium is an approximation of an exact equilibrium in the sense that only a subset of the overall agents may be in equilibrium. In contrast to our approach, none of the above works is based on an iterative search for the smallest detectable ϵ-equilibrium.

3   Multi-agent Systems for Resource Allocation

In our approach we focus on *multi-agent systems for resource allocation* (MRAs), originally introduced in [5].

Definition 1 (Multi-agent System for Resource Allocation)
A multi-agent system for resource allocation is a tuple $M = (Agt, Res, d, Acc)$ where

- $Agt = \{a_1, \ldots, a_n\}$ *is a finite set of agents,*
- $Res = \{r_1, \ldots, r_m\}$ *is a finite set of resources,*
- $d : Agt \to \mathbb{N}$ *is a demand function that defines the number of resources that each agent needs to accumulate in order to achieve its individual goal,*
- $Acc : Agt \to 2^{Res}$ *is an accessibility function that defines the subset of resources that each agent can access.*

Example. The graph on the right describes an MRA M consisting of the agents a_1, a_2 and the resources r_1, r_2, r_3. The edges of the graph characterise the accessibility function. Moreover, we assume that the demand function of M is defined as follows: $d(a_1) = 2, d(a_2) = 2$.

Each agent has the goal to gradually accumulate a number of resources such that its demand is finally satisfied. The actions that can be performed for this are as follows.

Definition 2 (Actions)
Given an MRA M, the set of actions Act is the union of the following types of actions:

- *request actions:* $\{req_r^a \mid a \in Agt, r \in Acc(a)\}$
- *release actions:* $\{rel_r^a \mid a \in Agt, r \in Acc(a)\}$
- *release-all actions:* $\{rel_{all}^a \mid a \in Agt\}$
- *idle actions:* $\{idle^a \mid a \in Agt\}$

Hence, an agent can request a particular resource, release a particular resource that it currently holds, release all resources that it currently holds, or just idle. The fact that agents may hold certain resources gives rise to the notion of *states* of an MRA, which we subsequently define. An MRA runs in discrete rounds where in each round each agent chooses its next action. In a round the tuple of chosen actions, one per agent, gets executed simultaneously. The execution of actions leads to an evolution of the system between different states over time.

Definition 3 (States)
A state of an MRA M is a function $s : Res \to Agt^+$ where $Agt^+ = Agt \cup \{a_0\}$ and a_0 is a dummy agent. If $s(r) = a_0$ then resource r is unallocated in state s. If $s(r) = a_i$ and $i > 0$ then r is allocated by agent a_i in s. We denote by s_0 the initial state of M, where $s(r) = a_0$ for each $r \in Res$, i.e., initially all resources are unallocated. We denote by S the set of all possible states of M. If we want to express that resource r is currently allocated by agent a_i but the current state is not further specified, then we simply write $r = a_i$.

Hence, states describe the current allocation of resources to agents. An agent may not be able to observe the entire state of the MRA. We assume that agents can only observe the (state of the) resources they have access to.

Definition 4 (State Observations)
Let M be an MRA, let $a_i \in Agt$ and let $s \in S$. Then the observation of agent a_i in state s is a function $s_{a_i} : Acc(a_i) \to Agt^+$ such that $s_{a_i}(r) = s(r)$ for all $r \in Acc(a_i)$. We denote by S_{a_i} the set of all possible state observations of a_i.

In each state only a subset of actions may be available for execution by an agent, which we call the protocol:

Definition 5 (Action Availability Protocol)
The action availability protocol is a function $P : S \times Agt \to 2^{Act}$ defined for each $s \in S$ and $a \in Agt$:

1. *if $|s^{-1}(a)| = d(a)$ then $P(s, a) = \{rel_{all}^a\}$;*

2. *otherwise:*

   (a) $rel_{all}^a \notin P(s, a)$;

(b) $req_r^a \in P(s,a)$ iff $s(r) = a_0;$

(c) $rel_r^a \in P(s,a)$ iff $s(r) = a;$

(d) $idle^a \in P(s,a).$

Thus, if an agent has reached its goal, it has to release all of its allocated resources. Otherwise, an agent can request an accessible resource that is currently unallocated, an agent can release a resource that it currently holds, and an agent can idle.

Definition 6 (Action Profiles)
An action profile in an MRA M is a mapping $ap : Agt \to Act$. AP denotes the set of all action profiles. We say that a profile ap is executable in a state $s \in S$ if for each $a \in Agt$ we have that $ap(a) \in P(s,a)$.

Based on action profiles we can formally define the evolution of an MRA.

Definition 7 (Evolution)
The evolution of an MRA is a relation $\delta \subseteq S \times AP \times S$ where $(s, ap, s') \in \delta$ iff ap is executable in s and for each $r \in Res$:

1. *if $s(r) = a_0$ then:*
   (a) if $\exists a : ap(a) = req_r^a \wedge \forall a' \neq a : ap(a') \neq req_r^{a'}$ then $s'(r) = a;$
   (b) otherwise $s'(r) = a_0.$
2. *if $s(r) = a$ for some $a \in Agt$ then:*
   (a) if $ap(a) = rel_r^a \vee rel_{all}^a$ then $s'(r) = a_0;$
   (b) otherwise $s'(r) = a.$

If an action profile is executed in a state of an MRA M, this leads to a transition of M into a corresponding successor state, i.e., a change in the allocation of resources according to the actions chosen by the agents. According to the evolution, the request of a resource r by an agent a will only be successful if a is the only agent that requests r in the current round. If multiple agents request the same resource at the same time, then none of the agents will obtain it.

4 Strategies

We are interested in solving strategy synthesis problems with regard to multi-agent systems for resource allocation. A strategy is defined as follows:

Definition 8 (Strategy)
A strategy of an agent $a \in Agt$ in an MRA is an injective function $\alpha_a : S_a \to Act$. A strategy can also be denoted by a relation $\alpha_a \subseteq S_a \times Act$ where $\alpha_a(s_a, act^a) = true$ iff $\alpha_a(s_a) = act^a$. A joint strategy is a tuple of strategies $\alpha_{Agt} = (\alpha_a)_{a \in Agt}$, one for each $a \in Agt$.

A strategy determines which action an agent will choose under which observation. A strategy is uniform if the following holds: Each time that an agent makes the same observation, it will perform the same action according to the strategy. The outcome of a strategy α_{Agt} in a state s is a path of length k where k is the number of rounds for which the MRA is running.

Definition 9 (Outcome of a Strategy)
Let M be an MRA, s a state of M and k the number of rounds. Moreover, let α_{Agt} be a joint strategy of Agt. Then the outcome of α_{Agt} in state s is a path

$$\pi(s, \alpha_{Agt}) = s_0 \ldots s_k \mid s_0 = s \wedge \forall 0 \leq t < k :$$
$$\left(s_t, \left(\alpha_{a_1}((s_t)_{a_1}), \ldots, \alpha_{a_n}((s_t)_{a_n}) \right), s_{t+1} \right) \in \delta$$

where $(s_t)_a$ denotes the observation of agent a in state s_t.

We use a temporal strategy logic for specifying strategic goal-achievability properties of agents in MRAs.

Definition 10 (Strategy Logic Syntax)
Let M be an MRA. Then strategy logic formulas $\langle\!\langle Agt \rangle\!\rangle \varphi$ over M are defined as follows:

$$\varphi := a.goal \mid \neg\varphi \mid \varphi \vee \varphi \mid \varphi \wedge \varphi \mid \mathbf{G}\varphi \mid \mathbf{F}\varphi$$

where $a \in Agt$ and $a.goal$ is an atomic proposition that expresses that agent a has reached its goal, i.e., $s(a.goal) = true$ iff $|s^{-1}(a)| = d(a)$ for $s \in S$.

Here $\mathbf{G}$ refers to 'globally' and $\mathbf{F}$ refers to 'finally'. The definition of the strategy logic semantics is as follows:

Definition 11 (Strategy Logic Semantics)
Let M be an MRA and let $s \in S$ be a state of M. Then the evaluation of a strategy logic formula $\langle\!\langle Agt \rangle\!\rangle \varphi$ on the state s, written $[M, s \models \langle\!\langle Agt \rangle\!\rangle \varphi]$, is inductively defined as:

$$\begin{aligned}
[M, s \models \langle\!\langle Agt \rangle\!\rangle \varphi] &\equiv \exists \alpha_{Agt} : [M, \pi(s, \alpha_{Agt}) \models \varphi] \\
[M, \pi \models a.goal] &\equiv |\pi[0]^{-1}(a)| = d(a) \\
[M, \pi \models \mathbf{G}\varphi] &\equiv \forall 0 \leq t \leq k : [M, \pi[t] \models \varphi] \\
[M, \pi \models \mathbf{F}\varphi] &\equiv \exists 0 \leq t \leq k : [M, \pi[t] \models \varphi]
\end{aligned}$$

where $\pi[t]$ denotes the t-th state of the path π. Moreover, Boolean operators $\neg, \vee, \wedge$ are interpreted with the usual semantics.

The basic goal-achievability formula that we consider in our approach is

$$\varphi = \bigwedge_{a \in Agt} \left(\mathbf{F} a.goal \right).$$

Hence, each agent shall achieve its goal at least once in a run of an MRA. We call a strategy that ensures φ a winning strategy.

Definition 12 (Winning Strategy)
Let M be an MRA with initial state s_0 and let φ be a goal-achievability formula. Moreover, let α_{Agt} be a joint strategy of Agt. Then α_{Agt} is a winning strategy if $[M, \pi(s, \alpha_{Agt}) \models \varphi]$ holds.

4.1 Collectively Optimal Strategies

The basic goal-achievability formula characterises a purely qualitative objective. In order to also consider optimality and equilibria in strategy synthesis, we introduce an additional quantitative objective: Goals shall be achieved as frequently as possible. Optimality with regard to this quantitative objective can be measured by means of a pay-off, which we define for states and paths.

Definition 13 (State Pay-Off)
Let M be an MRA and let $a \in Agt$ be an agent. Then the pay-off for agent a in states $s \in S$ of M is a function $\rho_a : S \to \{0, 1\}$ where

$$\rho_a(s) = \begin{cases} 1 & if \ |s^{-1}(a)| = d(a), \\ 0 & otherwise. \end{cases}$$

Hence, the pay-off of an agent is 1 in exactly the states where the demand of the agent is satisfied, i.e., the individual resource allocation goal is achieved. Assuming that we want to maximise the frequency of reaching the goal, the pay-off function can be extended to paths as follows:

Definition 14 (Path Pay-Off)
Let M be an MRA, let $a \in Agt$ be an agent, and let k be the number of rounds. Moreover, let π be a path of M. Then the path pay-off for agent a on π is

$$\rho_a(\pi) = \sum_{t=0}^{k} \rho_a(\pi[t])$$

where $\pi[t]$ denotes the t-st state along π. The collective path pay-off of all agents in Agt is

$$\rho_{Agt}(\pi) = \sum_{a \in Agt} \rho_a(\pi).$$

Thus, a winning strategy can be regarded as collectively optimal with regard to frequency if following the strategy results in an execution path for which the collective pay-off is maximal. We can now formally define collectively optimal strategies:

Definition 15 (Collectively Optimal Strategy)
Let M be an MRA, let k be the number of rounds, and let φ be a goal-achievability formula. Moreover, let α_{Agt} be a joint strategy and let $(\rho_a)_{a \in Agt}$ be a tuple of pay-off functions, one for each $a \in Agt$. Then α_{Agt} is a collectively optimal strategy with regard to $(\rho_a)_{a \in Agt}$ if the following conditions hold:

1. $[M, \pi(s_0, \alpha_{Agt}) \models \varphi]$

2. $\neg \exists \alpha'_{Agt}$ with $[M, \pi(s_0, \alpha'_{Agt}) \models \varphi]$ and $\rho_{Agt}(\pi(s_0, \alpha'_{Agt})) > \rho_{Agt}(\pi(s_0, \alpha_{Agt}))$.

Hence, a winning strategy α_{Agt} is collectively optimal if there does not exist an alternative winning strategy α'_{Agt} that results in a greater collective pay-off. We denote the collectively optimal strategy synthesis problem of an MRA M with goal-achievability formula φ by $[M, s_0 \models \langle\!\langle Agt \rangle\!\rangle \varphi]_{Opt}$.

A collectively optimal winning strategy ensures that each agent achieves its goal at least once (Condition 1) and it additionally maximises the *overall* pay-off (Condition 2), but it does not necessarily optimise the pay-off of each individual agent in Agt. Thus, such a strategy may favour certain agents while disadvantaging others.

4.2   Nash Equilibrium Strategies

In competitive scenarios it may be practically more useful and fair to synthesise a strategy that is a *Nash equilibrium* [19] rather than just being collectively optimal. In a joint Nash equilibrium strategy $\alpha_{Agt} = (\alpha_a)_{a \in Agt}$, no agent can increase its individual pay-off by deviating from α_{Agt}, assuming that all other agents keep following their local strategies α_a prescribed by α_{Agt}.

Definition 16 (Nash Equilibrium Strategy)
Let M be an MRA, let k be the number of rounds, and let φ be a goal-achievability formula. Moreover, let α_{Agt} be a joint strategy of all agents and let $(\rho_a)_{a \in Agt}$ be a tuple of path pay-off functions, one for each $a \in Agt$. Then α_{Agt} is a Nash equilibrium strategy if the following conditions hold:

1. $[M, \pi(s_0, \alpha_{Agt}) \models \varphi]$

2. $\forall a \in Agt \; \neg \exists \alpha'_a$ with

$[M, \pi(s_0, \alpha_{Agt}[\alpha_a \leftarrow \alpha'_a]) \models \varphi]$ and $\rho_a(\pi(s_0, \alpha_{Agt}[\alpha_a \leftarrow \alpha'_a])) > \rho_a(\pi(s_0, \alpha_{Agt}))$

where $\alpha_{Agt}[\alpha_a \leftarrow \alpha'_a]$ is the substitution of α_a by α'_a in α_{Agt}.

Hence, a joint strategy α_{Agt} is a Nash equilibrium if it ensures that the collective goal will be achieved (Condition 1) and no agent can improve its individual pay-off by deviating from α_{Agt} with an alternative strategy α'_a, assuming that all other agents keep following their strategies prescribed by α_{Agt} (Condition 2). We denote the Nash equilibrium synthesis problem of an MRA M with goal-achievability formula φ by $[M, s_0 \models \langle\!\langle Agt \rangle\!\rangle \varphi]_{Nash}$.

An ϵ-Nash equilibrium strategy is an approximation of an exact Nash equilibrium in the sense that no agent can multiply its individual pay-off by more than ϵ via deviation where ϵ is a rational number. It is formally defined as follows:

Definition 17 (ϵ-Nash Equilibrium Strategy)
Let M be an MRA, let k be the number of rounds, and let φ be a goal-achievability formula. Moreover, let α_{Agt} be a joint strategy of all agents, let $(\rho_a)_{a \in Agt}$ be a tuple of path pay-off functions, one for each $a \in Agt$, and let $\epsilon \in \mathbb{Q}$. Then α_{Agt} is an ϵ-Nash equilibrium strategy if the following conditions hold:

1. $[M, \pi(s_0, \alpha_{Agt}) \models \varphi]$

2. $\forall a \in Agt \; \neg \exists \alpha'_a$ with

$[M, \pi(s_0, \alpha_{Agt}[\alpha_a \leftarrow \alpha'_a]) \models \varphi]$ and

$\rho_a(\pi(s_0, \alpha_{Agt}[\alpha_a \leftarrow \alpha'_a])) > \epsilon \cdot \rho_a(\pi(s_0, \alpha_{Agt}))$

where $\alpha_{Agt}[\alpha_a \leftarrow \alpha'_a]$ is the substitution of α_a by α'_a in α_{Agt}.

Figure 1 depicts an instance of an ϵ-Nash equilibrium strategy and the resulting execution path for the MRA example provided in Sect. 3. The states along the path consist of tuples (x, y, z) where x, y and z characterise the current allocation of the resources r_1, r_2 and r_3, respectively. Within the tuples, 0 indicates an unallocated resource, 1 indicates a resource allocated by agent a_1 and 2 indicates a resource allocated by a_2. The transitions are labelled with pairs of actions $\langle act, act' \rangle$ where act is the action performed by agent a_1 and act' is the action performed by a_2. Hence, all actions along the path form the joint strategy of the agents. The number of rounds is 6. Along the path agent a_1 achieves its goal in the states at rounds 2 and 6, whereas a_2 achieves its goal in the state at round 4. For agent a_1 the joint strategy is individually optimal, i.e., the agent cannot increase its pay-off via unilateral deviation. However, a_2 can increase its pay-off from 1 to 2 by changing its strategic decision in the initial state from requesting resource r_3 to requesting resource r_2. This unilateral deviation doubles a_2's pay-off. Thus, the strategy is an ϵ-equilibrium with $\epsilon = 2$.

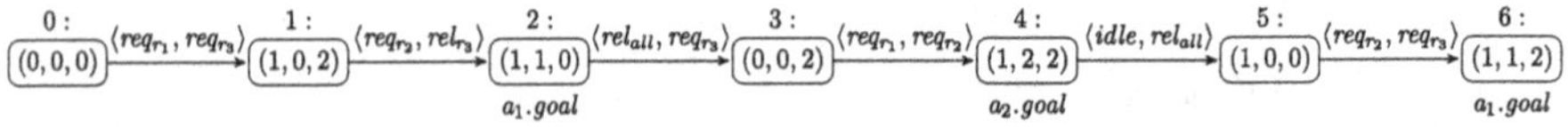

Fig. 1. ϵ-Nash equilibrium strategy and resulting path.

For small ϵ's an ϵ-Nash Equilibrium is typically still a useful strategy. This particularly holds for scenarios where no exact equilibrium exists. In our approach we propose an algorithm that iteratively searches for the smallest detectable ϵ and corresponding ϵ-Nash Equilibrium strategy for a given scenario. Our approach is based on maximum satisfiability solving.

5 Max-SAT-Based Strategy Synthesis

Given a multi-agent system for resource allocation M and a goal-achievability formula φ, the corresponding collectively optimal strategy synthesis problem can be encoded in propositional logic and solved via maximum satisfiability solving [20]. Here we show how this approach can be extended to synthesise approximations of Nash equilibrium strategies. The encoding is a propositional logic formula in weighted conjunctive normal form:

Definition 18 (Weighted Conjunctive Normal Form (WCNF))
*Let Var be a set of Boolean variables. A propositional logic formula $\mathcal{F}$ over Var
in weighted conjunctive normal form is a conjunction of weighted clauses $(\mathcal{C}, w_{\mathcal{C}})$
where $\mathcal{C}$ is a standard clause and $w_{\mathcal{C}} \in \mathbb{N}_{\infty}$ is its weight. A clause $(\mathcal{C}, w_{\mathcal{C}})$ with
$w_{\mathcal{C}} \in \mathbb{N}$ is called a soft clause and a clause $(\mathcal{C}, \infty)$ is called a hard clause.*

For the sake of simplicity we typically just write $\mathcal{C}$ for hard clauses $(\mathcal{C}, \infty)$. Each
WCNF formula $\mathcal{F}$ can be written as a conjunction $\mathcal{H} \wedge \mathcal{S}$ where $\mathcal{H}$ are the hard
clauses and $\mathcal{S}$ are the soft clauses of $\mathcal{F}$.

For WCNF formulas the following optimisation problem has been defined [2]:

Definition 19 (Maximum Satisfiability Problem)
*Let $\mathcal{F} = \mathcal{H} \wedge \mathcal{S}$ over Var be a propositional logic formula in weighted conjunctive
normal form where $\mathcal{H}$ are the hard clauses and $\mathcal{S}$ are the soft clauses. The
maximum satisfiability problem with regard to $\mathcal{F}$ is the problem of finding a
truth assignment $\alpha : Var \to \{\mathbf{0}, \mathbf{1}\}$ that maximises*

$$\sum_{(\mathcal{C}, w_{\mathcal{C}}) \in \mathcal{S}} \alpha(\mathcal{C}) \cdot w_{\mathcal{C}}$$

subject to the condition that $\alpha(\mathcal{H}) = 1$ holds.

Hence, the solution of the maximum satisfiability problem with regard to $\mathcal{F}$
is a truth assignment α that *maximises* the sum of weights of the satisfied
soft clauses, under the condition that *all* hard clauses are satisfied. If no such
assignment exists, then the maximum satisfiability problem has no solution.

For WCNF formulas $\mathcal{F} = \mathcal{H} \wedge \mathcal{S}$ over a set of variables Var and assuming that
$\mathcal{A}(Var)$ is the set of all possible truth assignments over Var we define maximum
satisfiability as the function

$$\textbf{max-sat}(\mathcal{F}) = \begin{cases} nil & \text{if } \textbf{sat}(\mathcal{H}) = \mathbf{0}, \\ \underset{\alpha \in \mathcal{A}(Var)}{\arg\max}\left(\alpha(\mathcal{H}) \cdot \big(\sum_{(\mathcal{C}, w_{\mathcal{C}}) \in \mathcal{S}} \alpha(\mathcal{C}) \cdot w_{\mathcal{C}}\big)\right) & \text{otherwise.} \end{cases}$$

Hence, $\textbf{max-sat}(\mathcal{F})$ returns nil if the problem has no solution. Otherwise it
returns the truth assignment satisfying all hard clauses that maximises the sum
of weights of the satisfied soft clauses.

In our Max-SAT-based approach there is a one-to-one correspondence
between the path pay-off resulting from following a strategy α_{Agt} and the sum of
weights of soft clauses satisfied by an assignment α. Therefore, we also define the
pay-off as a function ρ on truth assignments α and WCNF formulas $\mathcal{F} = \mathcal{H} \wedge \mathcal{S}$:

$$\rho(\alpha, \mathcal{F}) = \alpha(\mathcal{H}) \cdot \big(\sum_{(\mathcal{C}, w_{\mathcal{C}}) \in \mathcal{S}} \alpha(\mathcal{C}) \cdot w_{\mathcal{C}}\big).$$

As it can be seen, the pay-off of assignments α that do not satisfy all hard clauses
$\mathcal{H}$ will be always 0, and the pay-off of assignments that satisfy all hard clauses
will be the sum of weights of satisfied soft clauses.

The encoding of the collectively optimal strategy synthesis problem $[M, s_0 \models \langle\!\langle Agt \rangle\!\rangle \varphi]_{Opt}$, as introduced in [20], is a WCNF formula

$$\mathcal{F}_{Agt} = [\langle\!\langle Agt \rangle\!\rangle] \wedge [M] \wedge [\varphi] \wedge [Opt_{Agt}]$$

where $[\langle\!\langle Agt \rangle\!\rangle]$ encodes the condition that all agents must adhere to the protocol, $[M]$ encodes all paths of the system that start in the initial state, and $[\varphi]$ is a constraint that restricts the paths to those that satisfy φ. Moreover, $[Opt_{Agt}]$ encodes all possibilities of agents being in a state where their individual goal is achieved, i.e., states in which their pay-off is 1. The sub-formula $[\langle\!\langle Agt \rangle\!\rangle] \wedge [M] \wedge [\varphi]$ consists of hard clauses whereas $[Opt_{Agt}]$ consists of soft 'pay-off' clauses with a weight of 1 each. If $\mathbf{max\text{-}sat}(\mathcal{F}_{Agt}) = \alpha$ and α_{Agt} is the joint strategy corresponding to α then α_{Agt} is a collectively optimal strategy, i.e., a strategy that maximises the overall pay-off.

In order to determine whether a joint strategy α_{Agt} is an equilibrium or not, it is necessary compute for each agent a whether it can follow an alternative individual strategy α'_a that increases its pay-off, assuming that the remaining agents still adhere to α_{Agt}. The problem of whether such an alternative strategy α'_a exists for an agent a can be encoded as a slight variant of the encoding $\mathcal{F}_{Agt}$:

$$\mathcal{F}_{a|\alpha_{Agt \setminus a}} = [\langle\!\langle a \rangle\!\rangle] \wedge [\alpha_{Agt \setminus a}] \wedge [M] \wedge [\varphi] \wedge [Opt_a]$$

Here $[\langle\!\langle a \rangle\!\rangle]$ encodes that agent a must adhere to the protocol, $[\alpha_{Agt \setminus a}]$ encodes that all agents besides a follow the strategy α_{Agt}, $[M]$ and $[\varphi]$ are defined as before, and $[Opt_a]$ encodes all possibilities of agent a being in a state where it receives a pay-off.

Solving $\mathbf{max\text{-}sat}(\mathcal{F}_{a|\alpha_{Agt \setminus a}})$ yields a truth assignment from which we can derive a strategy α'_a that is optimal for agent a assuming that the remaining agents follow α_{Agt}. This facilitates to determine whether a joint strategy is an exact Nash equilibrium or an ϵ-equilibrium: If we can show for a joint strategy $\alpha_{Agt} = (\alpha_a)_{a \in Agt}$ that for each agent $a \in Agt$ the individually optimal strategy α'_a derived from $\mathcal{F}_{a|\alpha_{Agt \setminus a}}$ does not increase a's pay-off in comparison to α_a, then we can conclude that α_{Agt} is an exact Nash equilibrium. Moreover, if we can show that for each $a \in Agt$ the individually optimal strategy α'_a does not multiply a's pay-off by more than ϵ in comparison to α_a, then α_{Agt} is an ϵ-equilibrium. In the next section, we present an algorithm that utilises these properties of $\mathcal{F}_{a|\alpha_{Agt \setminus a}}$ in a search for a minimal ϵ and corresponding ϵ-equilibrium strategy.

6 ϵ-Nash Equilibrium Synthesis Algorithm

Algorithm 1 facilitates the synthesis of close approximations of Nash equilibrium strategies for multi-agent systems for resource allocation.

Algorithm 1: *Approximate Nash-Equilibrium-Strategy-Synthesis($\mathcal{F}_{Agt}$)*

---

1 $\alpha_{Agt}^{0} := \textbf{max-sat}\left(\mathcal{F}_{Agt}\right)$ ▷ $\mathcal{F}_{Agt}$ is the initial encoding where the weights ω_a
   of each agent a are set to 1

2 **if** $\left(\alpha_{Agt}^{0} = nil\right)$ **then**

3 | **return** 'no winning strategy exists'

4 **for** $i = 0$ **to** *number_of_iterations* **do**

5 | **for each** $a \in Agt$ **do**

6 | | $\alpha_a^{i+1} := \textbf{max-sat}\left(\mathcal{F}_{a|\alpha_{Agt\backslash a}^{i}}\right)$

7 | $IP^i := \left(\rho(\alpha_a^{i+1}, \mathcal{F}_{Agt})/\rho(\alpha_a^{i}, \mathcal{F}_{Agt})\right)_{a \in Agt}$ ▷ improvement potential vector

8 | $\epsilon^i := \textbf{max}(IP^i)$

9 | $IP_N^i := \textbf{normalise}(IP^i)$

10 | $\mathcal{F}_{Agt}^{W} := \mathcal{F}_{Agt}[\omega_a \leftarrow IP_N^i(a)]_{a \in Agt}$ ▷ create weight adjusted encoding
   | where the weights are updated according to the normalised vector IP_N^i

11 | $\alpha_{Agt}^{i+1} := \textbf{max-sat}\left(\mathcal{F}_{Agt}^{W}\right)$ ▷ synthesise collectively optimal strategy for the
   | weight adjusted encoding

12 **return** $\textbf{min}(\epsilon^i)_{0 \leq i < number\_of\_iterations}, \alpha_{Agt}^{i}$

The algorithm takes the encoding $\mathcal{F}_{Agt}$ of the strategy synthesis problem for a given MRA as an input and employs Max-SAT to initially synthesise a collectively optimal strategy α_{Agt}^{0} if existent (line 1). In each iteration i for each agent a an individual strategy α_a^{i+1} is synthesised that is optimal for a assuming that all other agents follow the collective strategy α_{Agt}^{i} (line 6). Based on these individually optimal strategies, the *improvement potential* of each agent is computed, which is the quotient of the pay-off under the strategy α_a^{i+1} and the pay-off under the strategy α_a^{i}. The improvement potentials are stored in the vector IP^i (line 7). The maximum improvement potential in IP^i is the ϵ-value of the collective strategy α_{Agt}^{i} synthesised in the current iteration (line 8). The improvement potentials are the basis of a weight adjustment of the encoding: Since weights are required to be integers, the fractional improvement potentials are scaled up and stored in a normalised vector IP_N^i, preserving the relative differences (line 9). The algorithm then constructs the weight-adjusted encoding $\mathcal{F}_{Agt}^{W}$ where the weights of the pay-off clauses of each agent are set according its current (normalised) improvement potential (line 10). While $\mathcal{F}_{Agt}$ encodes the *actual* strategy synthesis problem, the weight-adjusted encoding $\mathcal{F}_{Agt}^{W}$ represents a *virtual* problem. A collectively optimal strategy α_{Agt}^{i+1} for the virtual problem is synthesised (line 11) and used in the subsequent iteration to re-compute the improvement potentials. Since the weight-adjusted encoding favours agents who previously had a high improvement potential, this approach facilitates to lower the improvement potentials, and consequently, to decrease ϵ. The algorithm terminates after the number of predefined iterations and returns the smallest detected ϵ^i and corresponding ϵ^i-Nash equilibrium strategy α_{Agt}^{i} (line 12).

In the subsequent section we report on experimental results using Algorithm 1 for the synthesis of approximate Nash equilibria for several MRA scenarios.

7   Experimental Results

We developed the tool SATMAS[1] that implements Algorithm 1. SATMAS is written in Python and supports ϵ-Nash equilibrium strategy synthesis for MRAs. It takes an MRA M and a bound k as input. The associated strategy synthesis problem is then encoded in propositional logic, converted to WCNF and written to a DIMACS file. The tool utilises the Max-SAT solver OPEN-WBO [16] which takes the DIMACS file as input. The solver generates a satisfying truth assignment from which a corresponding strategy is derived. SATMAS then follows the steps of Algorithm 1 in order to iteratively improve the strategy with regard to the ϵ-value.

In an experimental evaluation we considered MRAs with up to 11 agents and 9 resources. In each experiment the bound on the number of rounds that was used was 16 and we let the algorithm run for 10 iterations. The results in terms of the initial and smallest detected ϵ as well as the runtime of the algorithm are depicted in Table 1. The Scenario column indicates the number of agents in Agt and the number of resources in Res. Moreover, $\mathcal{D}$ is the interval from which the demand of each agent was randomly selected, and $\mathcal{ACC}$ is the interval from which number of accessible resources of each agent was randomly selected. The experiments were conducted on a 4.05 GHz Apple M3 system with 8 GB.

Table 1. Experimental results.

Scenario	Initial ϵ	Smallest ϵ	Runtime
$|Agt| = 4$, $|Res| = 6$, $\mathcal{D} = [1,3]$, $\mathcal{ACC} = [1,4]$	1.3	1.25	728 s
$|Agt| = 5$, $|Res| = 7$, $\mathcal{D} = [1,3]$, $\mathcal{ACC} = [1,4]$	1.3	1.3	345 s
$|Agt| = 6$, $|Res| = 8$, $\mathcal{D} = [1,3]$, $\mathcal{ACC} = [1,4]$	1.3	1.0	651 s
$|Agt| = 7$, $|Res| = 9$, $\mathcal{D} = [1,3]$, $\mathcal{ACC} = [1,4]$	2.0	1.0	954 s
$|Agt| = 8$, $|Res| = 10$, $\mathcal{D} = [1,3]$, $\mathcal{ACC} = [1,4]$	1.6	1.0	1234 s
$|Agt| = 9$, $|Res| = 11$, $\mathcal{D} = [1,3]$, $\mathcal{ACC} = [1,4]$	4.0	1.0	2324 s

As it can bee seen, for larger scenarios with more than 6 agents our iterative algorithm allows to significantly decrease ϵ in comparison to the ϵ-value obtained for the strategy synthesised in the initial iteration. Surprisingly, our approach was even able to synthesise 1.0-equilibrium strategies, which are de facto *exact* Nash equilibrium strategies, for the majority of the considered scenarios. Solely for the scenarios with 4 and 5 agents where the initial ϵ was already very small

---

[1] available at https://github.com/TuksModelChecking/Satmas/tree/epsilon-nash.

the algorithm could achieve only minor or no reduction, respectively, in the ϵ-value. Our conjecture is that for these scenarios the initially synthesised strategy is already (very close to) the best possible approximation of a Nash equilibrium strategy.

8 Conclusion and Future Work

We presented a technique for approximating Nash equilibrium strategies for multi-agents systems for resource allocation (MRAs). Agents in MRAs seek to maximise the frequency of reaching their resource allocation goals, which can be measured by means of a pay-off. A strategy is an exact Nash equilibrium if no agent can increase its individual pay-off by unilaterally deviating from the strategy. Moreover, a strategy is an ϵ-approximation of a Nash equilibrium if no agent can multiply its pay-off by more than ϵ via unilateral deviation, where ϵ is a rational number. For small ϵ's approximate Nash equilibria are practically useful and stable strategies since agents will only have a small incentive to change their strategic behaviour. Moreover, ϵ-equilibria may be the best possible solution for scenarios where no exact equilibrium exists.

Our technique is based on encoding the strategy synthesis problem in propositional logic with weighted 'pay-off' clauses and solving it via weighted Max-SAT. In our approach we initially synthesise a collectively optimal strategy and determine for each agent the *improvement potential*, which is the pay-off increase that can be achieved via unilateral deviation. The collectively optimal strategy is already an ϵ-equilibrium where ϵ is the maximum improvement potential out of the potentials of all agents. However, ϵ-equilibria with smaller ϵ's may still exist. We iteratively search for the smallest detectable ϵ and corresponding ϵ-equilibrium strategy: For this the weights of the 'pay-off' clauses associated with agents get adjusted such that agents with a currently high improvement potential will be favoured when solving the weight-adjusted strategy synthesis problem in the subsequent iteration. The weight adjustment facilitates to iteratively lower the improvement potentials, and consequently, to decrease ϵ. In an experimental evaluation, we demonstrated that our iterative approach allows to significantly decrease ϵ in comparison to the initially obtained ϵ. For several MRA scenarios our approach was even able to synthesise ϵ-equilibrium strategies with $\epsilon = 1$, which are in fact *exact* Nash equilibria.

Multi-agent systems for resource allocation are a general and versatile concept for modelling resource allocation problems. The operational model of MRAs can be adjusted such that concrete practical problems can be represented. As future work we plan to consider real-world scenarios such as resource allocation in distributed operating systems [14], wireless sensor networks [17] or clouds [4] and to demonstrate that our approach allows to synthesise ϵ-equilibrium strategies for these scenarios. Max-SAT-based strategy synthesis is still a computationally hard problem. Therefore, we intend to utilise parallelisation in our algorithm. The synthesis of the individually optimal strategies for all agents in each iteration can be conducted in parallel. This may enable to speed up the synthesis process and to allow the consideration of significantly larger MRA scenarios. Our current approach to weight adjustment in the synthesis algorithm is very straightforward but quite effective according to our experimental results. In the future we plan to evaluate more differentiated weight adjustment heuristics with the goal to find the best possible ϵ-equilibria within fewer iterations.

References

1. Almagor, S., Kupferman, O., Perelli, G.: Synthesis of controllable Nash equilibria in quantitative objective game. In: IJCAI, vol. 18, pp. 35–41 (2018)
2. Bacchus, F., Järvisalo, M., Martins, R.: Maximum satisfiability. In: Handbook of Satisfiability, pp. 929–991. IOS Press (2021)
3. Bulling, N., Goranko, V.: Combining quantitative and qualitative reasoning in concurrent multi-player games. AAMAS **36**(1), 1–33 (2022)
4. Chang, F., Ren, J., Viswanathan, R.: Optimal resource allocation in clouds. In: 2010 IEEE 3rd International Conference on Cloud Computing, pp. 418–425. IEEE (2010)
5. De Masellis, R., Goranko, V., Gruner, S., Timm, N.: Generalising the dining philosophers problem: competitive dynamic resource allocation in multi-agent systems. In: Slavkovik, M. (ed.) EUMAS 2018. LNCS (LNAI), vol. 11450, pp. 30–47. Springer, Cham (2019). https://doi.org/10.1007/978-3-030-14174-5_3
6. Dimitrova, R., Ghasemi, M., Topcu, U.: Reactive synthesis with maximum realizability of linear temporal logic specifications. Acta Informatica **57**(1), 107–135 (2020)
7. Finkbeiner, B., Hahn, C., Torfah, H.: Model checking quantitative hyperproperties. In: Chockler, H., Weissenbacher, G. (eds.) CAV 2018. LNCS, vol. 10981, pp. 144–163. Springer, Cham (2018). https://doi.org/10.1007/978-3-319-96145-3_8
8. Gutierrez, J., Harrenstein, B., Steeples, T., Wooldridge, M.: Local equilibria in logic-based multi-player games. Autonomous Agents and Multi-Agent Systems (AAMAS 2018) (2018)
9. Gutierrez, J., Harrenstein, P., Wooldridge, M.: From model checking to equilibrium checking: reactive modules for rational verification. Artif. Intell. **248**, 123–157 (2017)
10. Gutierrez, J., Murano, A., Perelli, G., Rubin, S., Steeples, T., Wooldridge, M.: Equilibria for games with combined qualitative and quantitative objectives. Acta Informatica **58**(6), 585–610 (2021)
11. Gutierrez, J., Murano, A., Perelli, G., Rubin, S., Wooldridge, M.: Nash equilibria in concurrent games with lexicographic preferences. In: Proceedings of the Twenty-Sixth International Joint Conference on Artificial Intelligence, IJCAI-17, pp. 1067–1073 (2017). https://doi.org/10.24963/ijcai.2017/148
12. Gutierrez, J., Najib, M., Perelli, G., Wooldridge, M.: On computational tractability for rational verification. In: Proceedings of the Twenty-Eighth International Joint Conference on Artificial Intelligence, IJCAI-19, pp. 329–335. International Joint Conferences on Artificial Intelligence Organization, July 2019. https://doi.org/10.24963/ijcai.2019/47
13. Jackson, M.O., Rodriguez-Barraquer, T., Tan, X.: Epsilon-equilibria of perturbed games. Games Econ. Behav. **75**(1), 198–216 (2012)
14. Kurose, J.F., Simha, R.: A microeconomic approach to optimal resource allocation in distributed computer systems. IEEE Trans. Comput. **38**(5), 705–717 (1989)

15. Liao, X.: Maximum Satisfiability Approach to Game Theory and Network Security. Ph.D. thesis, Kyushu University (2014)
16. Martins, R., Manthey, N., Terra-Neves, M., Manquinho, V., Lynce, I.: Open-WBO@ MaxSAT evaluation 2020. MaxSAT Evaluation **2020**, 24 (2021)
17. Mukherjee, A., Goswami, P., Yan, Z., Yang, L., Rodrigues, J.J.: ADAI and adaptive PSO-based resource allocation for wireless sensor networks. IEEE Access **7**, 131163–131171 (2019)
18. Mylvaganam, T., Sassano, M., Astolfi, A.: Constructive ϵ-Nash equilibria for nonzero-sum differential games. IEEE Trans. Autom. Control **60**(4), 950–965 (2015)
19. Nash, J.F., Jr.: Equilibrium points in n-person games. Proc. Natl. Acad. Sci. **36**(1), 48–49 (1950)
20. Timm, N., Botha, J., Jordaan, S.: Max-SAT-based synthesis of optimal and Nash equilibrium strategies for multi-agent systems. Sci. Comput. Program. **228**, 102946 (2023). https://www.sciencedirect.com/science/article/pii/S016764232300028X
21. Wooldridge, M., Gutierrez, J., Harrenstein, P., Marchioni, E., Perelli, G., Toumi, A.: Rational verification: from model checking to equilibrium checking. In: Proceedings of the AAAI Conference on Artificial Intelligence, vol. 30 (2016)

A Comparison of Text Representation Techniques and Encoder-Decoder Implementations in a Deep Neural Network for Converting Natural Language into Formal Logic Formulas

Kade Devan Tissink[ID] and Mathys Cornelius du Plessis[✉][ID]

Nelson Mandela University, Gqeberha, South Africa
{s217272479,mc.duplessis}@mandela.ac.za

Abstract. Semantic parsing is the task of extracting a structured machine-interpretable representation from natural language utterance. This representation can be used for various applications such as question answering, information extraction, and dialogue systems. However, semantic parsing is a challenging problem that requires dealing with the ambiguity, variability, and complexity of natural language. This paper investigates neural parsing of natural language (NL) sentences to first-order logic (FOL) formulas. FOL is a widely used formal language for expressing logical statements and reasoning. FOL formulas can capture the meaning and structure of NL sentences in a precise and unambiguous way.

FOL parsing is approached as a sequence-to-sequence mapping task using both long short-term memory (LSTM) and transformer encoder-decoder architectures for character-, subword-, and word-level text tokenisation. These models are trained on NL-FOL datasets with supervised learning and evaluated using various metrics. Previous solutions to neural FOL parsing differ dramatically in training approaches and scale. As such, there is no comprehensive comparison of models for different methods of text representations or encoder-decoder architectures.

The main contributions of this paper are: the formation of a complex NL-FOL benchmark that includes algorithmically generated and human-annotated FOL formulas, evaluation of 15 sequence-to-sequence models on the task of neural FOL parsing for different text representations and encoder-decoder architectures, and an in-depth analysis of the strengths and weaknesses of these models.

Keywords: semantic parsing · first-order logic · natural language processing · artificial intelligence

1 Introduction

Extracting machine-interpretable first-order logic (FOL) representations from natural language (NL) sentences is a challenging and time-consuming task that

A. Gerber (Ed.): SAICSIT 2024, CCIS 2159, pp. 244–260, 2024.
https://doi.org/10.1007/978-3-031-64881-6_14

requires an understanding of both the mathematical structure and logical elements of FOL, as well as the ability to identify entities, objects, and their relationships in NL sentences. NL-FOL translation is a skill that is usually learnt at higher-level education. There are great benefits in expressing NL as structured formulas, including the ability to apply automated theorem proving to a FOL knowledge base. As such, there is impetus to automate the FOL parsing process. This research presents neural FOL parsing solutions constrained to problems where a single NL sentence is translated to a single FOL formula.

FOL parsing is a subtask of semantic parsing. An NL sentence of arbitrary length must be processed to an arbitrary length FOL sequence. There have been rule-based solutions proposed to tackle FOL parsing [2], but these are limited to examples that match hand-crafted templates and often fail to interpret the intricacies of NL. More recently, researchers have investigated using deep neural methods for the task of FOL parsing [10,12,16,20], specifically using sequence-to-sequence models [3] that are capable of handling the variable length source and target sequences. The use of deep learning methods was motivated by the success seen in similar natural language processing (NLP) problems, like machine translation, and even other semantic parsing problems [4,10,16].

Previous works have investigated neural FOL parsing, however, there is no direct comparison between model architectures and implementations in similar training environments. Most of the results from previous works are achieved on invented datasets and do not compare to other research, but even if comparisons are made, there are such drastic differences in model sizes and even training approaches (reinforcement learning vs. supervised learning, fine-tuned vs. trained from scratch) that the comparisons are not fair. Additionally, with regard to representation techniques, researchers have tended to investigate only one approach that is either chosen with little motivation or is inherited from a language model that is being fine-tuned. Consequently, there is insufficient evidence to suggest that any one representation technique and encoder-decoder architecture is optimal for neural FOL parsing.

This research investigates neural FOL parsing models for a selection of different text representations and encoder-decoder architectures. These solutions approach FOL parsing as generic sequence-to-sequence tasks, without incorporating any FOL-specific modifications. Results from model evaluations are used to perform a comprehensive analysis of the individual components under equal conditions. Tests compare encoder-decoder architectures and representation techniques on two FOL parsing benchmarks. Furthermore, some models include text representation methods that have yet to be explored for FOL parsing.

2 Background

Semantic parsing is the task of extracting a structured meaning representation from NL utterance. For this research, the target meaning representations are logical forms, specifically FOL. Successfully translating NL to logical representations allows machines to understand the unstructured text and redundancies we as humans use. This enables problems such as question answering, robot navigation, database querying, reasoning, etc., to be solved by machines through NL communications [16].

The essential elements of FOL are variables, constants, predicates, quantifiers, and logical connectives. Predicates are functions that take objects (variables or constants) as inputs and return either true or false. Predicates can be combined using logical connectives to create complex formulas. Quantifiers declare variables, distinguishing whether information is relevant to all instances of the variable (universal quantifier) or only that there exist instances for which the statements hold (existential quantifier). FOL is sufficiently expressive to represent knowledge concisely and capture complex relationships between entities. Automated theorem proving can be applied to information expressed in FOL. Many deductive systems for FOL are sound and complete.

As an example, the sentence "Everyone enrolled for the AI course is clever" can be expressed in FOL as:

$$\forall x : \text{enrolled}(x, \text{AI}) \implies \text{clever}(x),$$

where "$\forall$" is the universal quantifier, "x" is a variable, "enrolled" is a binary predicate, "AI" is a constant, " $\implies$ " is a logical connective, and "clever" is a unary predicate.

Early semantic parsers were predominantly rule-based, relying on high-quality lexicons, predefined templates, and manually designed features to map NL templates to meaning representations. Most modern semantic parsers model the parsing of NL sentences into meaning representations as sequence-to-sequence transduction tasks.

The encoder-decoder architecture was proposed as a solution to sequence-to-sequence problems by [3]. These initial implementations were recurrent neural network (RNN)-based, and were applied to neural machine translation tasks. Encoder-decoder implementations were iteratively improved from these initial solutions and applied to other sequence-to-sequence problems in NLP and other domains. Notable improvements were the use of bidirectional RNNs for the encoder and, most importantly, the introduction of the attention mechanism [1,13]. In 2017, [19] proposed the transformer encoder-decoder, which has since become one of the most prominent neural network (NN) architectures in artificial intelligence (AI), particularly NLP.

Previous works in the domain of neural FOL parsing have investigated both RNN and transformer architectures. [16] use an LSTM-based encoder-decoder with word-level representations of tokens on their synthetic dataset which has yet to be publicised. [10] apply character-level models with several RNN encoder-decoder architectures on a dataset they created. [5] evaluate (transformer-based) large language models with subword text representation and hundreds of billions of parameters on their newly-presented, human-annotated dataset. [20] adapt a different large language model (7 billion parameters) with subword representations. Finally, [12] fine-tuned yet another transformer (300+ million parameters) with a different method of subword representations using dual reinforcement learning.

3   Implementation Details

Figure 1 presents the sequence-to-sequence model for FOL parsing. This model is comprised of representation modules, an encoder-decoder, and a linear classifier. The implementations of these components are discussed in this section.

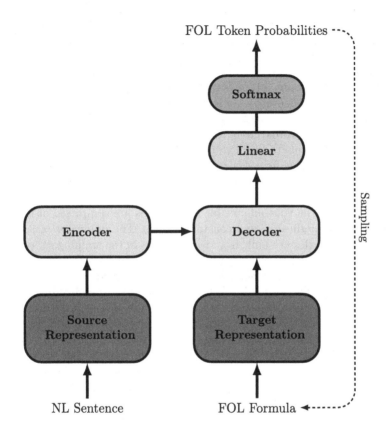

Fig. 1. Sequence-to-sequence model for neural first-order logic parsing.

3.1   Text Representation

Text representation modules use tokenisers, vocabularies, and a vectorisation technique to convert text into vector inputs that can be processed by a NN. Text sequences are split into tokens using the tokenisers. Tokens are then mapped to unique vocabulary IDs, with any out-of-vocabulary tokens being mapped to the ID of a default unknown token. Finally, the unique IDs can be encoded or replaced with vector representations. Source representation modules represent NL text as vector inputs for encoders and target representation modules encode FOL formulas for decoders.

There are seven text representation modules defined for this research:

One-hot Char One-hot character encoding uses a character vocabulary and the one-hot encoding technique to generate representations for text at a character level. The module is used with the exact (uncased) vocabularies from [10] to recreate their results, as well as a dataset-agnostic (cased) vocabulary that consists of all *printable* characters from Python's string library.

Char emb The character embeddings module represents the cased vocabulary of characters using dense embeddings that are randomly initialised and trained alongside the other network parameters.

Subword emb Randomly initialised embeddings are used to represent tokens of the RoBERTa-base [11] subword vocabulary for both source and target sequences. The embeddings are learned within the training process.

NL word emb For NL source sequences, a word-level vocabulary is constructed as a subset of all words in the training sets of benchmarks with frequency greater than or equal to five. Pre-trained GloVe [14] word vectors are used to initialise embeddings for tokens where available; otherwise, vectors are randomly initialized. All word embeddings are then fine-tuned/learned during model training.

FOL word emb The vocabularies for FOL tokens are comprised of FOL notation symbols, predicates, and constant tokens. The predicate/constant subsets of vocabularies are built from word tokens in the training set of an associated benchmark dataset. These vocabularies are used to represent tokens with randomly initialised embeddings that are learned.

Char-Word emb The idea behind character-based word embeddings is to represent each word as a sequence of character embeddings, and then combine these character embeddings to obtain a word-level embedding [9,15]. NL sentences are tokenised into words and then further decomposed into individual characters. The character-based word embedding module uses the cased character vocabulary with dense character-level embeddings. Character embeddings are processed into word-level embeddings using a BiLSTM [9].

Composite NL emb The composite embedding module annotates character-based word representations with part-of-speech (POS) embeddings for source sequences. A vocabulary of fine-grained POS tags[1] is defined such that this additional linguistic knowledge can be provided as input to models. POS tags are predicted using spaCy's pre-trained *en_core_web_trf* model and these tags are mapped to randomly initialised embeddings. Character-word representations are hypothesised to be sufficient for the syntactic representation of words. POS embeddings then provide semantic and contextual meaning derived from a high-accuracy pre-trained model.

3.2   Encoder-Decoder

There are two encoder-decoder implementations investigated for this research. The first architecture is a more traditional LSTM-based encoder-decoder with a

---

[1] See https://machinelearningknowledge.ai/tutorial-on-spacy-part-of-speech-pos-tag ging/.

bidirectional LSTM encoder, unidirectional LSTM decoder, and Luong attention mechanism [13]. The specific implementation is a generalisation of [10]'s LSTM-based encoder-decoder for more than one encoder and decoder layer. This LSTM architecture is investigated for both single-layer (SL LSTM) and multi-layer (ML LSTM) variants. LSTM encoder-decoder architectures have historically achieved good results on sequence-to-sequence tasks, including neural FOL parsing [10,16].

The second architecture is the transformer [19] encoder-decoder. The transformer is a powerful architecture that uses attention mechanisms to calculate long-term dependencies between vector embeddings. Implementations in this research substitutes the ReLU activation function in feedforward networks with the GELU [6] activation function. GELU is a more modern activation function and smooth approximation of ReLU, meaning it is differentiable across its entire domain.

3.3   Linear Classifier

Linear classifiers, when combined with a sampling algorithm, convert the processed outputs of an NN back into sequences of tokens. A linear classifier is comprised of a single linear layer with a softmax[2] activation function. The linear layer maps the output of a decoder to the length of a target vocabulary and the softmax activation converts the result to probabilities. The output from the linear classier is then a probability distribution over each token in the target vocabulary, with each element of the output representing a probability for a corresponding token ID. Target tokens are sampled from these probability distributions.

4   Experimental Setup

This section describes the experimental setup for the study. The investigated sequence-to-sequence models are explicitly listed. Next, the two benchmarks used to train and evaluate the performance of these models are briefly discussed. The main topics for discussion of models are outlined. Lastly, the performance metrics used to measure model performance are defined.

4.1   Parsing Models

Experiments in this research are designed to evaluate models with matching source and target tokenisation granularities. There are 15 candidate sequence-to-sequence models which are listed in Table 1 with unique identifiers and their component modules.

---

[2] Softmax is a non-linear activation function that normalises the values of a vector to the interval $[0, 1]$, with the sum across the output vector equating to 1. Therefore, softmax essentially converts a vector to a probability distribution.

Table 1. Text representation modules, encoder-decoder architectures and linear classifier vocabulary combinations for neural first-order logic parsing models.

Model	Identifier	Source Representation	Target Representation	Encoder-Decoder Architecture	Classifier Vocabulary
1	Text2Log uncased	One-hot Char	One-hot Char	SL LSTM	Char
2	Text2Log cased	One-hot Char	One-hot Char	SL LSTM	Char
3	Text2Log optimised	One-hot Char	One-hot Char	SL LSTM	Char
4	One-hot Enc LSTM	One-hot Char	One-hot Char	ML LSTM	Char
5	SL Char LSTM	Char emb	Char emb	SL LSTM	Char
6	Char LSTM	Char emb	Char emb	ML LSTM	Char
7	Subword LSTM	Subword emb	Subword emb	ML LSTM	Subword
8	Word LSTM	NL word emb	FOL word emb	ML LSTM	FOL word
9	Char-Word LSTM	Char-Word emb	FOL word emb	ML LSTM	FOL word
10	Composite LSTM	Composite NL emb	FOL word emb	ML LSTM	FOL word
11	Char Transformer	Char emb	Char emb	Transformer	Char
12	Subword Transformer	Subword emb	Subword emb	Transformer	Subword
13	Word Transformer	NL word emb	FOL word emb	Transformer	FOL word
14	Char-Word Transformer	Char-Word emb	FOL word emb	Transformer	FOL word
15	Composite Transformer	Composite NL emb	FOL word emb	Transformer	FOL word

4.2   Benchmarks

Experimental results are obtained for the models on two benchmark datasets:

Benchmark 1: A slightly modified version of [10]'s NL-FOL dataset with minor corrections and a new split of the data using a ratio of 8:1:1. Benchmark 1 is adapted from [10] with existing results for comparison. However, this benchmark is algorithmically generated and therefore lacking in structural diversity. The benchmark also includes duplicate patterns and other inconsistencies. The dataset contains 93,333 patterns.

Benchmark 2: A new Collective Logic dataset (CLD) that merges and standardises notation of NL-FOL pairs presented in literature [5,10,18,20] and manually scraped from online sources – predominantly university lecture notes. Benchmark 2 is larger (154,193 patterns), more complex, more diverse in terms of NL sentence and FOL formula structures, has richer vocabularies, and includes both algorithmically generated and human-annotated patterns. Benchmark 2 ensures uniqueness of patterns.

4.3   Experiment Goals

The training and testing of the sequence-to-sequence models across both benchmarks are designed to:

1. Recreate existing results with a one-hot encoding character-level LSTM-based encoder-decoder and extend the testing to the additional benchmark. Model 1 is most similar to [10]'s highest performing implementation. Model 2 updates the vocabulary of Model 1 to use a dataset-agnostic character vocabulary.

Finally, Model 3 further extends the cased variant by changing the hyperparameters, most notably, the number of training epochs.

2. Replace one-hot encoding representations with the more advanced technique of dense embeddings. Model 5 implements a single-layer LSTM-based encoder-decoder with dense character embeddings.

3. Investigate the effect of additional depth in the LSTM-based encoder-decoder. Models 4 and 6 investigate the effect in models with one-hot encoding and dense embedding representations, respectively.

4. Compare the performance of different text representation modules for the task of FOL parsing. Models 5 to 10 implement combinations of representation modules with LSTM encoder-decoders, and Models 11 to 15 compare representations for transformers.

5. Compare the LSTM-based encoder-decoder architecture to the transformer architecture for different text representations. Encoder-decoder architectures maintain similar scales in terms of parameters for the sake of fair comparison.

Discussions of model results surrounding these goals are structured into sections for character-level LSTM models, representation comparisons, and lastly LSTM and transformer comparisons.

4.4   Performance Metrics

The prediction abilities of models are evaluated using several metrics, detailed below.

- **Sequence accuracy (SeqAcc).** Sequence accuracy is an exact match metric that measures the percentage of correctly predicted sequences. A sequence is considered correct if every token in that sequence is correct. Sequence accuracies can be compared across tokenisation vocabularies.
- **Syntactic validity (SynVal).** Syntactic validity is a metric used by [5] that measures the percentage of predicted FOL formulas that can be successfully parsed. This metric requires formulas to use correctly paired brackets, follow the appropriate notation, and appropriately declare variables.
- **Structure accuracy (StructAcc).** This metric evaluates the formula structures of predictions, where predicates and constants are replaced with generic type tokens. The structure accuracy is the percentage of predicted FOL structures that are exactly equal to the true target structures. Variable identifiers are not required to match, as long as their usage is consistent.
- **Predicate and constant similarity (P&C Similarity).** Predicate and constant similarity measures whether predicted and true predicates and constants are similar, but not necessarily identical. This metric requires predictions to maintain reasonable naming of predicates and constants but allows for some flexibility.

Sequence accuracy of a model is used as an overview of model performance, while the other metrics provide more detail on different aspects of FOL parsing.

5   Training

All models are implemented in Python using PyTorch and trained using supervised learning. Models are trained for a maximum of 100 epochs on each benchmark. Additional details of model training are discussed below.

5.1   Hyperparameters

Table 2 presents the hyperparameters used for models. Models 1 and 2 follow the exact hyperparameter choices of [10].

The embedding dimension, n_x, is the length of vectors used to represent vocabulary tokens and determines the size of hidden state vectors in encoder-decoder architectures. The batch size, $\mathcal{N}$, is the number of patterns input simultaneously to a model during training. P_{drop} is a probability used in dropout [17] layers, as discussed in Sect. 5.4. $\mathcal{D}_E$ and $\mathcal{D}_D$ define the number of layers in the encoder and decoder, respectively. $\mathcal{F}$ is the size of intermediary hidden vectors calculated in transformer feedforward sub-layers. Transformer multi-head attention mechanisms are composed of $\mathcal{H}$ attention heads. Finally, learning rates for transformers are linearly increased from zero, reaching a maximum after $\mathcal{W}$ warm-up steps.

Learning rates were found to have the greatest impact on model performance during hyperparameter optimisation. As such, models are trained with slightly different learning rates to aim for the best possible versions of each model. However, most learning rates are around 8×10^{-4}.

5.2   Optimisation Algorithms

One-hot LSTM models are optimised using RMSProp [7] to conform to the findings of [10]. All other models are optimised using the Adam optimisation algorithm [8] with $\beta_1 = 0.9$, $\beta_2 = 0.999$, $\epsilon = 1 \times 10^{-8}$, and weight decay $= 0$. Adam is the choice optimisation algorithm for many NLP models [5,11,16,19].

Table 2. Encoder-decoder network hyperparameters.

Hyperparameter	Symbol	SL LSTM	ML LSTM	Transformer
Embedding dimension	n_x	50	50	50
Batch size	$\mathcal{N}$	32	32	32
Dropout	P_{drop}	0.1	0.1	0.1
Encoder layers	$\mathcal{D}_E$	1	3	3
Decoder layers	$\mathcal{D}_D$	1	3	3
Feedforward dimension	$\mathcal{F}$	—	—	512
Attention heads	$\mathcal{H}$	—	—	5
Warm-up steps	$\mathcal{W}$	—	—	4000

5.3 Scheduled Learning Rates

Transformer-based models are trained with a cosine learning rate schedule and 4,000 warm-up steps. A learning rate schedule is not applied in the training of LSTM-based models as neither [10] nor [16] use warm-up or scheduled decay in neural FOL parsing tasks with LSTM architectures.

5.4 Dropout

Dropout [17] layers are incorporated into encoder-decoder architectures to mitigate overfitting during training. For bidirectional LSTM encoders, dropout is applied to the outputs of each encoder layer, except the last. LSTM-based decoder layers apply dropout to the outputs of LSTMs and attention blocks for every decoder layer. Transformer architectures follow the use of dropout in [19].

6 Results

The test results for models on the two benchmarks are provided and discussed in this section. Decoders auto-regressively predict probability distributions until the end-of-sequence token is sampled. Decoding also terminates after 1,000 steps, to avoid infinite looping. Token sampling from decoder probability distributions is done using a beam search with a beam width of 10.

6.1 Benchmark 1

Table 3 provides the test set performance metrics for models on Benchmark 1. Overall, models can accurately predict FOL sequences from the test set of Benchmark 1. The high syntactic validity metrics of Table 3 show that, in the vast majority of cases, models learn to predict FOL formulas with correct bracket pairing and variable declarations. Discrepancies lie in the abilities of models to predict FOL formula structures and semantically similar predicates and constants compared to the true test targets.

Table 3. Test set performance metrics for models on Benchmark 1.

Model	SeqAcc (%)	SynVal (%)	StructAcc (%)	P&C Similarity (%)
Text2Log uncased	89.810	99.914	92.002	99.358
Text2Log cased	90.836	99.872	93.146	99.251
Text2Log optimised	92.868	99.840	94.910	99.312
One-hot Enc LSTM	94.162	99.904	95.370	99.554
SL Char LSTM	91.136	99.850	93.541	99.127
Char LSTM	**94.621**	99.957	**95.787**	**99.674**
Subword LSTM	76.550	99.016	90.986	91.226
Word LSTM	77.427	99.444	93.809	91.663
Char-Word LSTM	71.236	99.262	91.756	89.264
Composite LSTM	70.477	99.251	92.397	88.357
Char Transformer	89.917	**100**	92.162	99.596
Subword Transformer	73.086	99.615	92.536	92.308
Word Transformer	80.357	99.818	95.199	94.060
Char-Word Transformer	83.298	99.872	94.750	95.500
Composite Transformer	84.068	99.872	95.006	95.907

Character-Level LSTM Models. The *Text2Log uncased* model achieves a sequence accuracy of 89.81% on Benchmark 1, compared to the 89.54% reported by [10], but with a different data split and dropout implementation. The cased variant of this model provides a slight improvement in accuracy while increasing parameter count. *Text2Log optimised* provides a more substantial improvement, benefiting from additional training epochs. These three Text2Log models provide strong baselines and successful extensions to [10]'s findings.

Next, *SL Char LSTM* substitutes one-hot character encodings with dense character embeddings, and achieves similar performance to the Text2Log models while using fewer parameters. However, *Text2Log optimised* betters *SL Char LSTM* in terms of sequence accuracy.

Both *Text2Log optimised* and *SL Char LSTM* see performance increases for additional depth. *Char LSTM* provides a substantial increase in performance across all test metrics compared to the single layer equivalent, culminating in the best-performing model on the benchmark. *One-hot Enc LSTM* also sees performance gains across the board, but not to the degree seen in the dense embedding alternative. Moreover, *Char LSTM* uses fewer parameters at 557,609 compared to 591,809.

Comparing Representations. Character-level models achieve significantly greater performance than other representations. Character models exceed 99% in P&C similarities for both encoder-decoder architectures, while the other representations are considerably lower. In word-level models, this partly stems from the fact that the target word vocabulary is missing tokens necessary to test set predictions. These target word vocabularies are also detrimental to the performance of

Char-Word and *Composite* models. For Benchmark 1, about 8% of the patterns in the test set requires predicate or constant tokens not contained in the word vocabulary. So, it is outright impossible for word-level models to correctly predict these sequences, but even words that are included in the target vocabulary are difficult to correctly predict unless they see sufficient use during training. Moreover, there is a significant increase in parameter count for word and subword models, with the majority of parameters being allocated to the representation modules and linear classifiers.

However, the sequence accuracies in training for models with word-level target vocabularies are far greater than validation and test set sequence accuracies despite the inclusion of dropout during training. Additionally, the structure accuracies of Table 3 show that word models are competitive with character LSTM models when only considering the FOL formula structure. So, there is potential in these word-level models provided they have the capacity to predict all necessary tokens and sufficient training data to learn appropriate embeddings. Furthermore, *Char-Word* and *Composite* representation models achieve similar performance to regular word representation models using a fraction of the source representation parameters, but the target representation module and linear classifier still account for a majority of the model parameters. A final advantage word models have over character models is the reduced sequence length. A shorter sequence results in faster training/inference times and reduced memory requirements.

Subword representations are a mix between word and character representations, but end up performing worse than both individual parts. There may be insufficient training data to effectively harness the potential of subword representations. A solution to improve their efficacy is to fine-tune an existing model for FOL parsing.

LSTM vs. Transformer. A major advantage of transformers is the global self-attention in the encoder and decoder which can learn the long-range dependencies within a sequence, whereas LSTM networks are biased towards their most recent inputs. From a human perspective of character-level representations, there is very little relation between two arbitrary characters in a sentence. Rather, the meaning of a sentence is obtained by sequentially combining local characters into words. In this sense, the recurrent LSTM processing of characters with a strong focus on other nearby characters seems to be a boon rather than a hindrance. Moreover, LSTMs can learn more complex functions for relating these sequences of characters, while transformer architectures are fixed with the attention function. Table 3 supports this intuition with the *Char LSTM* model reaching greater results than transformer equivalents. That being said, the transformer architectures are still able to find meaning in long-range character relationships, achieving competitive syntactic validity and P&C similarity scores.

The transformer outshines the LSTM architecture for word-level representations. In particular, the *Char-Word* and *Composite* transformer models reach greater metrics than even the *Word Transformer*. The *Char-Word* and *Composite* models incorporate the strengths of LSTMs and transformers in character and word-level processing, respectively.

6.2   Benchmark 2

The test set performance metrics for Benchmark 2 are provided by Table 4. The results of models are considerably lower for Benchmark 2. However, this is expected for the more complex benchmark, and the larger differences in performance metrics serve to highlight strengths and weaknesses of models.

A maximum sequence length of 256 tokens was introduced to account for the longer sequences in Benchmark 2. This change truncated a small number of character-tokenised patterns in the training and validation sets. During testing, the maximum sequence length was not necessary, but the inherent weakness of long sequences associated with character-level models is noteworthy nonetheless.

Table 4. Test set performance metrics for models on Benchmark 2.

Model	SeqAcc (%)	SynVal (%)	StructAcc (%)	P&C Similarity (%)
Text2Log uncased	48.565	72.703	54.653	69.496
Text2Log cased	70.742	93.519	76.540	90.583
Text2Log optimised	72.587	95.537	78.552	92.796
One-hot Enc LSTM	75.450	96.769	80.596	94.571
SL Char LSTM	70.542	94.087	76.823	90.876
Char LSTM	**75.488**	96.724	**80.647**	94.508
Subword LSTM	41.601	88.038	71.548	68.935
Word LSTM	42.555	88.399	70.884	68.276
Char-Word LSTM	40.730	90.185	76.075	66.806
Composite LSTM	40.201	93.074	76.798	67.608
Char Transformer	71.555	**99.716**	77.913	**96.086**
Subword Transformer	35.984	98.865	74.902	73.334
Word Transformer	44.186	97.556	76.894	75.416
Char-Word Transformer	43.709	98.291	77.333	75.355
Composite Transformer	45.935	97.640	79.055	76.176

Character-Level LSTM Models. Findings for character models are consistent with those of Benchmark 1, only at lower accuracies. The test set metrics show that the multi-layer character models are more adept at predicting syntactically and semantically accurate FOL formulas than their single-layer counterparts, whereas on Benchmark 1 these differences were negligible. Both one-hot and dense embedding approaches offer similar performance at a depth of three with neither consistently outperforming the other across all test metrics.

Comparing Representations. As with Benchmark 1, models with character representations reach greater accuracies than word- or subword-level models. The discrepancies in performance are even more drastic for Benchmark 2. Character models again benefit from high P&C similarities, which is clearly a significant flaw in other representations.

The limiting factor of the word target vocabulary is exacerbated in Benchmark 2 with almost 27% of test patterns requiring tokens not included in the target word vocabulary. The redeeming qualities of word models include the shortened sequences, and competitive syntactic validity and structure accuracies. Additionally, the character-word and composite source representation modules appear to be suitable alternatives for the source word embeddings. The inclusion of POS embeddings in *Composite Transformer* provides the desired benefits over the character-word representations.

Unfortunately, the subword models continue their trend of disappointing performance from Benchmark 1 with few discernible advantages over other models.

LSTM vs. Transformer Encoder-Decoder. The LSTM encoder-decoder again has greater sequence and structure accuracy for character-level representations than the transformer. However, Benchmark 2 reveals that the character-level transformers have notably greater syntactic validity and P&C similarity. The *Char-Word* and *Composite* transformer models achieve sufficiently greater performance metrics compared to the LSTM alternatives.

7   Sample Prediction Analysis

Table 5 presents interesting sample predictions made during testing of the (a) *Char LSTM* and (b) *Composite Transformer*, trained on Benchmark 2. The analysis of sample predictions demonstrates weaknesses in parsing models, drawbacks of supervised learning, and imperfections with the exact match metrics for FOL formula evaluation. Samples from these two models are selected because they are the highest-performing character- and word-level models, respectively.

Errors in FOL formulas are highlighted in red. Text is highlighted in blue to indicate differences between the true target and prediction. The right column of Table 5 uses symbols to indicate how the true target and prediction compare. Table 6 is the key for interpreting these symbols.

Sample 1 is a trivial NL-FOL translation typical to the LogicNLI [18] dataset. The *Char LSTM* predicts the expected target with an expectedly high probability considering the simplicity of the problem. However, the *Composite Transformer* fails to predict the correct FOL formula because the name "Archibald" is missing from the FOL word vocabulary for Benchmark 2. All word-level models are faced with many similar problems. Despite lacking the correct name, the model does a decent job of finding an alternative in "Reginald".

Table 5. Test set prediction samples from Benchmark 2 for (a) *Char LSTM* and (b) *Composite Transformer.*

Sample	1	
Source	Archibald is not bitter.	
True Target	not(_bitter(F_Archibald))	
Prediction (a)	not(_bitter(F_Archibald))	✓
Confidence (a)	99.965%	
Prediction (b)	not(_bitter(F_**Reginald**))	✗
Confidence (b)	42.086%	
Sample	2	
Source	A dessert is either cold or hot, but not both.	
True Target	exists x0: (_dessert(x0) and ((_cold(x0) and not(_hot(x0))) or (not(_cold(x0)) and _hot(x0))))	
Prediction (a)	all x0: (_dessert(x0) => (_cold(x0) xor _hot(x0)))	✓✓
Confidence (a)	90.516%	
Prediction (b)	all x0: (_dessert(x0) => (_cold(x0) xor _hot(x0)))	✓✓
Confidence (b)	96.292%	
Sample	3	
Source	All prices include Breakfast.	
True Target	all x0: (_price(x0) => exists x1: ((x1 = F_Breakfast) and _include(x0,F_Breakfast)))	
Prediction (a)	all x0: (_price(x0) => exists x1: ((x1 = F_Breakfast) and _include(x0,F_Breakfast)))	✗
Confidence (a)	85.154%	
Prediction (b)	all x0: (_price(x0) => exists x1: (_breakfast(x1) and _include(x0,x1)))	✓✗
Confidence (b)	99.647%	

Table 6. Sample prediction result key.

✓	Prediction and true targets are identical, and both are correct
✓✓	Prediction and true targets are not identical, but both are correct
✓✗	Prediction is correct, but the true target is incorrect
✗	Prediction is incorrect

For Sample 2, the *Char LSTM* and *Composite Transformer* models produce the same prediction. These predicted formulas are acceptable alternatives to the true target. Firstly, the true target makes use of the existential quantifier which is possibly the more accurate approach, considering the indefinite article "A". However, the universal quantifier seems reasonable for this specific problem. Secondly, the predicted FOL formula is more concise than the true target, exploiting the exclusive disjunction operator that logically equates to the expansion used in the true target. This example demonstrates the shortcomings of the exact match metrics used in evaluations. The FOL models are heavily penalised for this example by the exact match metrics despite the precision of the outputs.

In Sample 3, the mistake is in the true target generated by a rule-based semantic parser. The word "Breakfast" is considered a constant in the true target, likely due to its capitalisation. However, the inaccuracy of the target is the declaration of an unused variable "x1". The *Char LSTM* learnt to match the incorrect label. The prediction for *Composite Transformer* in this case is accepted over the true target. This example again highlights the problems with the exact match metrics, as well as weaknesses of supervised learning for neural FOL parsing.

8 Conclusion

This paper detailed the training of sequence-to-sequence models for neural FOL parsing. Experimental results were found for models on two benchmark datasets and were used to contrast the benefits and drawbacks of different text representation techniques and encoder-decoder implementations using detailed performance metrics. Lastly, the paper provided analysis of sample predictions made by select trained models.

In summary, the experimental results show that character-level representation models with the LSTM-based encoder-decoder achieve the overall greatest performance. However, character-level tokenisation artificially inflates sequence lengths, limiting this class of models to problems with very short sentences. Word-level transformer models are a viable alternative; though, the limited target FOL word vocabulary is restrictive in predictions.

The analysis of sample errors highlighted weaknesses in the exact match metrics and supervised training of FOL parsing models. However, the aim of comparing representations and encoder-decoder architectures is achieved and is a relevant contribution to the field of neural FOL parsing.

References

1. Bahdanau, D., Cho, K., Bengio, Y.: Neural machine translation by jointly learning to align and translate. ArXiv **1409** (September 2014)
2. Bansal, N.: Translating natural language propositions to first order logic, May 2015. https://www.cse.iitk.ac.in/users/karkare/MTP/2014-15/naman2015logica.pdf
3. Cho, K., et al.: Learning phrase representations using RNN encoder–decoder for statistical machine translation. In: Proceedings of the 2014 Conference on Empirical Methods in Natural Language Processing (EMNLP), pp. 1724–1734. Association for Computational Linguistics, Doha, Qatar (2014). https://doi.org/10.3115/v1/D14-1179, https://aclanthology.org/D14-1179
4. Dong, L., Lapata, M.: Language to logical form with neural attention. In: Proceedings of the 54th Annual Meeting of the Association for Computational Linguistics (Volume 1: Long Papers), pp. 33–43. Association for Computational Linguistics, Berlin, Germany (2016). https://doi.org/10.18653/v1/P16-1004, https://aclanthology.org/P16-1004
5. Han, S., et al.: FOLIO: natural language reasoning with first-order logic. arXiv preprint arXiv:2209.00840 (2022). https://arxiv.org/abs/2209.00840
6. Hendrycks, D., Gimpel, K.: Gaussian error linear units (GELUs) (2016). https://doi.org/10.48550/ARXIV.1606.08415, https://arxiv.org/abs/1606.08415
7. Hinton, G., Srivastava, N., Swersky, K.: Neural networks for machine learning (2018). https://www.cs.toronto.edu/~tijmen/csc321/slides/lecture_slides_lec6.pdf
8. Kingma, D., Ba, J.: Adam: a method for stochastic optimization. In: International Conference on Learning Representations, December 2014
9. Lample, G., Ballesteros, M., Subramanian, S., Kawakami, K., Dyer, C.: Neural architectures for named entity recognition. In: Proceedings of the 2016 Conference of the North American Chapter of the Association for Computational Linguistics: Human Language Technologies, pp. 260–270. Association for Computational Linguistics, San Diego, California, June 2016. https://doi.org/10.18653/v1/N16-1030, https://aclanthology.org/N16-1030

10. Levkovskyi, O., Li, W.: Generating predicate logic expressions from natural language. In: SoutheastCon 2021, pp. 1–8 (2021). https://doi.org/10.1109/SoutheastCon45413.2021.9401852

11. Liu, Y., et al.: RoBERTa: a robustly optimized BERT pretraining approach. arXiv preprint arXiv:1907.11692 (2019)

12. Lu, X., et al.: Parsing natural language into propositional and first-order logic with dual reinforcement learning. In: Proceedings of the 29th International Conference on Computational Linguistics, pp. 5419–5431. International Committee on Computational Linguistics, Gyeongju, Republic of Korea (2022). https://aclanthology.org/2022.coling-1.481

13. Luong, T., Pham, H., Manning, C.D.: Effective approaches to attention-based neural machine translation. In: Màrquez, L., Callison-Burch, C., Su, J. (eds.) Proceedings of the 2015 Conference on Empirical Methods in Natural Language Processing, pp. 1412–1421. Association for Computational Linguistics, Lisbon, Portugal (2015). https://doi.org/10.18653/v1/D15-1166, https://aclanthology.org/D15-1166

14. Pennington, J., Socher, R., Manning, C.D.: Glove: global vectors for word representation. In: Empirical Methods in Natural Language Processing (EMNLP), pp. 1532–1543 (2014). http://www.aclweb.org/anthology/D14-1162

15. Santos, C.D., Zadrozny, B.: Learning character-level representations for part-of-speech tagging. In: Xing, E.P., Jebara, T. (eds.) Proceedings of the 31st International Conference on Machine Learning. Proceedings of Machine Learning Research, vol. 32, pp. 1818–1826. PMLR, Bejing, China, 22–24 June 2014. https://proceedings.mlr.press/v32/santos14.html

16. Singh, H., Aggrawal, M., Krishnamurthy, B.: Exploring Neural Models for Parsing Natural Language into First-Order Logic. arXiv e-prints arXiv:2002.06544 (2020)

17. Srivastava, N., Hinton, G., Krizhevsky, A., Sutskever, I., Salakhutdinov, R.: Dropout: a simple way to prevent neural networks from overfitting. J. Mach. Learn. Res. **15**(1), 1929–1958 (2014)

18. Tian, J., Li, Y., Chen, W., Xiao, L., He, H., Jin, Y.: Diagnosing the first-order logical reasoning ability through LogicNLI. In: Proceedings of the 2021 Conference on Empirical Methods in Natural Language Processing, pp. 3738–3747. Association for Computational Linguistics, Online and Punta Cana, Dominican Republic (2021). https://doi.org/10.18653/v1/2021.emnlp-main.303, https://aclanthology.org/2021.emnlp-main.303

19. Vaswani, A., et al.: Attention is all you need. In: Proceedings of the 31st International Conference on Neural Information Processing Systems, pp. 6000–6010. NIPS'17, Curran Associates Inc., Red Hook, NY, USA (2017)

20. Yang, Y., Xiong, S., Payani, A., Shareghi, E., Fekri, F.: Harnessing the power of large language models for natural language to first-order logic translation. ArXiv **abs/2305.15541** (2023). https://api.semanticscholar.org/CorpusID:258888128

Information Systems Track

Leveraging Environmental Data for Intelligent Traffic Forecasting in Smart Cities

Oluwaseyi O. Alabi[1]([⊠]) [iD], Sunday A. Ajagbe[2] [iD], Olajide Kuti[3] [iD],
Oluwaseyi F. Afe[4] [iD], Grace O. Ajiboye[5] [iD], and Mathew O. Adigun[2] [iD]

[1] Department of Mechanical Engineering, Lead City University, Ibadan, Nigeria
`alabi.oluwaseyi@lcu.edu.ng`
[2] Department of Computer Science, University of Zululand, Kwadlangezwa 3886, South Africa
[3] Data Science Department, University of Salford, Salford, UK
[4] Department of Computer Science, Lead City University, Ibadan, Nigeria
[5] Department of Computer Science, Precious Cornerstone University, Ibadan, Nigeria

Abstract. This research revolves around the intersection of environmental data and smart city infrastructure to develop an innovative approach for forecasting traffic patterns. In an era of urbanization and the proliferation of smart cities, managing traffic congestion is a critical challenge. This research explores the utilization of air pollution data, a readily available environmental metric, to intelligently predict traffic patterns and improve urban mobility. The study will delve into the potential correlations between air pollution levels and traffic congestion, considering factors such as vehicular emissions, weather conditions, and geographical attributes. By harnessing the power of big data analytics and machine learning techniques, this research aims to develop a predictive model that leverages real-time air pollution data for traffic forecasting. The K-Nearest Neighbors (KNN) model performs better than all other regression models evaluated in this study, according to our findings. The KNN model considerably lowers the error rate in traffic congestion prediction by more than 28%, according to experimental results.

Keywords: Artificial intelligence · Traffic prediction · Air pollution · Environmental metrics · Error Rate · Regression Techniques

1 Introduction

The rapid expansion of the global economy and the continuous increase in population density have resulted in heightened road congestion. This congestion, as highlighted by research from the Harvard School of Public Health, has severe repercussions for the health of urban residents [1]. The Harvard School of Public Health further reports that annually, more than 22,000 fatalities are attributed to air pollution stemming from congested roads, incurring a staggering $18 billion in healthcare costs. This issue is prevalent in urban areas across 83 different countries. In addition to being a time and fuel drain, traffic congestion exacts a significant economic toll. According to Bloomberg, it can lead to an increase in commute times by as much as 35 to 37 h per year, negatively

A. Gerber (Ed.): SAICSIT 2024, CCIS 2159, pp. 263–278, 2024.
https://doi.org/10.1007/978-3-031-64881-6_15

impacting job growth [2]. Urban areas, in particular, face significant air pollution due to vehicular traffic, which contributes to a range of health and environmental problems. In the United Kingdom and other industrialized nations, it is regarded as a serious threat to clean air. The harmful compounds emitted by road traffic, including carbon monoxide (CO), sulfur dioxide (SO_2), nitrogen dioxide (NO_2), and others, have detrimental health effects [3].

The World Health Organization (WHO) claims that the main factors contributing to the higher-than-average death rates in large cities' metropolitan regions are pollution and deteriorating air quality, predominantly driven by traffic congestion [4]. Within the European Union (EU), the 115 largest cities, home to approximately 40 million people, face the challenge of meeting strict air quality standards. To address this issue, many cities are implementing sensor networks along roadways to monitor both traffic flow and air pollution levels resulting from congestion. Prolonged traffic congestion leads to vehicles consuming a higher proportion of gasoline, thereby escalating emissions of carbon dioxide (CO_2), carbon monoxide (CO), hydrocarbons (HC), and other pollutants, including nitrogen dioxide (NO_2) [5]. These emissions are known to contribute to a spectrum of health problems, ranging from lung cancer and cardiovascular conditions to various respiratory ailments and infections. Equally concerning, traffic jams can be mitigated if drivers receive advance information about uncongested routes or adjusted travel times, which, in turn, has the potential to reduce air pollutants and foster improved health outcomes.

Numerous studies have delved into the prediction and simulation of air quality through the analysis of traffic data, by [6]. The primary methodology employed in this research was the utilization of long short-term memory (LSTM) techniques, noted for their expedited performance in contrast to several other Deep Learning (DL) models. These LSTM models were instrumental in estimating the concentrations of vital pollutants, including O_2, PM2.5, NO_2, and CO_2 [4]. In the course of the study, a range of five distinct combinations was investigated, integrating various metrics and components such as weather conditions, vehicle emissions, pollution levels, and traffic statistics. It's worth noting, however, that the study did not account for the influence of high traffic volume. The critical value of traffic awareness for a traveler's convenience and reduced stress is underscored, emphasizing that traffic control systems represent a pivotal component of smart cities [5]. The facet of smart mobility, a cornerstone of comprehensive traffic management services, stands as particularly paramount. In numerous major urban centers, traffic congestion is not only a nuisance but also a catalyst for various health-related issues, besides causing considerable time loss [4]. The implementation of well-managed strategies to divert individuals onto less congested routes, coupled with lower air pollution levels, is pivotal in mitigating the adverse health effects of traffic-related air pollution. Predicting traffic flow effectively and efficiently has become a formidable challenge due to the intricate interactions within the dynamic nature of road systems. The deployment of intelligent congestion reduction systems directly impacts mobility, travel convenience, and the evolution of urban areas, all integral aspects of traffic management in smart cities. This research underscores the pivotal role of air quality data in predicting traffic intensity, demonstrating that air pollution information can indeed serve as a valuable tool for accurate road traffic forecasting a shift from prior studies that primarily utilized transportation data for air pollution predictions.

Within the realm of Machine Learning (ML), there exists a diverse range of subfields, and Deep Learning (DL) stands as a prominent one. DL is an integral facet of artificial intelligence (AI) that hinges on algorithms designed to refine their performance through experiential learning. In contrast to the relatively simpler principles that govern ML, Deep Learning leverages Artificial Neural Networks (ANN) as its foundation. These ANNs emulate the cognitive processes of human thinking and learning, bearing a striking resemblance to the workings of the human brain. Advancements in computational power and the advent of Big Data tools have ushered in the era of intricate and multifaceted neural networks. This transformative development has empowered computers with the capability to recognize patterns, learn from them, and expedite the resolution of complex problems, often outperforming human capabilities. Deep Learning has brought about significant enhancements in areas such as speech recognition, language translation, and image classification, among others. In a multitude of domains, including speech recognition, image categorization, and pattern recognition, Deep Learning has spearheaded advancements without human intervention. At the heart of the ANN lie multiple layers, each harnessing the prowess of Deep Learning. Deep neural networks (DNN) represent a specific category of networks in which each layer has the capacity to decipher intricate patterns, whether they pertain to textual information or image analysis. An increasing number of businesses are embracing this groundbreaking technology to develop innovative models in the rapidly expanding field of machine learning.

Predicting or alleviating traffic congestion has been a topic of limited academic exploration, with the majority of studies overlooking the forecasting of congestion density. Additionally, they approached this problem using conventional statistical methods while modern neural networks are better equipped to tackle such issues with greater. The substantial presence of vehicles stands as the predominant factor behind the heightened concentration of air pollutants observed during traffic congestion. Consequently, one approach to gauging road congestion involves predicting the volume of vehicles through the analysis of air pollution statistics. Given the considerable traffic volume on modern roadways, leading to elevated air pollution levels, the analysis of air pollution data offers a viable means of anticipating the number of vehicles on these roads.

The application of Long Short-Term Memory (LSTM) technology plays a pivotal role in crafting models capable of recognizing sequential patterns, a utility that extends to challenging scenarios such as speech recognition and machine translation. LSTMs represent a sophisticated subfield within Deep Learning (DL) [7]. In reference to [8–10], the authors harnessed DL techniques to extract traffic-related features, employing temporal attributes and graph convolution through LSTM cells. It's important to note that this work did not factor in air pollution data; instead, it relied on GPS (sparse trajectory) data sourced from Didi services in the Chinese cities of Chengdu and Xi'an. Notably, the authors introduced a novel model known as the Residual Graph Convolution Long Short-Term Memory (RGC-LSTM), which was applied to spatial–temporal data for prediction at ten-minute intervals. Data were drawn from two primary sources: traffic flow data from the Caltrans Performance Measurement System (PeMS) and data from

Shanghai, China. However, the model's performance was limited by the use of fewer features and the absence of air pollution data [11–13].

Zolfaghari et al., (2021) [14], employed a Stacked Bidirectional and Unidirectional LSTM (SBU-LSTM) network architecture as a foundational element in devising a neural network strategy for traffic status prediction. The linchpin of this strategy is the utilization of LSTM, with a specific focus on bidirectional LSTM (BDLSM) for spatiotemporal data, which assists in capturing both forward and backward temporal dependencies. Addressing the issue of missing values within spatial–temporal data, the authors introduced a data imputation method, named LSTM-I, derived from the LSTM structure. This method was implemented to construct an imputation unit, reducing data gaps and facilitating traffic prediction. A segment of LSTM-I, adapted to function in a bidirectional manner, was seamlessly integrated into the SBU-LSTM architecture. Experimental validation was conducted using real-world datasets encompassing network-wide traffic conditions, and the results were made publicly available to contribute to advancements in traffic forecasting research. Different multi-layer LSTM and BDLSTM model types were assessed, with particular attention given to the two-layer BDLSTM network, which informed the development of the SBU-LSTM system. While it demonstrated strong performance in network-wide traffic prediction, it was associated with somewhat higher Mean Absolute Error (MAE) and Root Mean Square Error (RMSE) values. In another approach [15], the authors leveraged the graph attention method to extract spatial relationships among road segments, complemented by the utilization of an LSTM network to capture temporal characteristics. It's noteworthy that this study harnessed data from the California Department of Transportation's PeMSD7 dataset but did not factor in air pollution data.

The primary objective of this research is to evaluate the effectiveness of the proposed approach in mitigating traffic congestion and achieving the desired outcomes. Furthermore, it aims to assess the success of the models utilized in this study and their potential to reduce the reliance on diverse types of traffic sensors deployed on roadways. The maintenance and operation of these sensors entail substantial resource consumption. If it becomes feasible to predominantly rely on commonly used sensors designed for complex urban traffic scenarios, it may open the door to the possibility of a traffic forecasting model that relies solely on air pollution data, rendering the complex network of traffic sensors largely redundant.

2 Methodology

2.1 Prediction of Traffic Flow

In Fig. 1, we illustrate the prediction of traffic flow through the application of machine learning and deep learning. Machine learning constitutes one of the diverse subfields within the realm of artificial intelligence (AI). ML techniques encompass an array of models and algorithms designed to emulate human decision-making by adapting and learning from the data they are exposed to. These ML models progressively acquire new capabilities and enhance their learning capacity over time, in response to the data they are trained on.

A Naive Bayes classifier is employed to categorize feature instances into labels based on feature value vectors, with labels drawn from a finite set of class values. In a previous study [16], a Naive Bayes classifier system was successfully utilized to model causal relationships. This approach leveraged data from a field survey and the Python Scikit-learn module to establish connections between variables. Subsequently, both test and training datasets were derived from the data. The suggested model exhibited an accuracy of 72.25% in the training set and 85.03% in the testing set. The model's Root Mean Square Error (RMSE) stood at 0.46, and its Mean Absolute Error (MAE) at 0.28. The results of the Naive Bayes classifier model underscore its strong performance in ascertaining the impact of weather on traffic conditions. This strategy was devised to establish an Advanced Traveler Information System (ATIS) and an Advanced Traffic Management System (ATMS) for the city of Dhaka, affording vehicles the flexibility to select less congested routes, thereby effectively mitigating traffic congestion.

The K-Nearest Neighbors (KNN) approach, a supervised learning technique, addresses classification and regression challenges by assuming that similar objects are proximate to each other. In [17], the authors tackle the problem of rigid model architectures that lack clarity regarding both spatial and time-dependent interactions. They introduce an Adaptive Space and Time-based K Nearest-Neighbor model (Adaptive-STKNN) for short-term traffic flow prediction. This model comprehensively considers the spatial variations in urban traffic by incorporating elements like spatiotemporal weights, adaptive spatial neighbors, and time intervals. The initial phase involves determining the size of geographical neighbors and the duration of time windows for each road segment using cross-correlation and autocorrelation functions, to assess traffic impact. Subsequently, adaptive spatiotemporal weights are integrated into the distance functions to enhance the efficiency of candidate neighbor search methods. This process culminates in the creation of an adaptive spatiotemporal model, featuring numerous potential neighbors and a weighting variable within the prediction module, thereby reflecting real-time changes in traffic conditions. In [18], the Kernel KNN scheme was proposed, focusing on time series data about road traffic conditions. The approach entailed gathering traffic flow statistics on roads and utilizing reference sequences to establish the dynamic characteristics of road traffic. A kernel module was developed to analyze time series data related to road traffic conditions, comparing and matching data sequences from reference and current data. The emphasis lay on vehicular transportation.

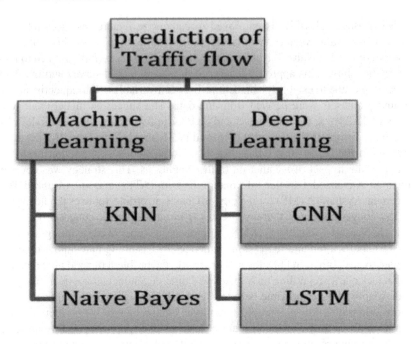

Fig. 1. An illustration of traffic movement predictions made using various methods.

2.2 Data Gathering

The most important task in any methodology is data collection and processing, and the performance of the model depends heavily on it. The dataset used in this study was a sizable one that was obtained in real-time from the city pulse Aarhus, Denmark, and is openly accessible. Essentially, two datasets were used: the traffic intensity dataset and the data for pollution [19]. The city has several sensors installed, and information was acquired on the passing automobiles every five minutes using these devices. The air dataset contains information about the air pollutants, including CO, (SO_2), ozone (O_3), and particle matter, which were released by these vehicles (PM). Datasets for traffic, vehicle density, and pollution covered a period of more than a year. It has 96,000 instances and includes features like (O_3), PM, (CO_2), (SO_2), and (NO_2) in addition to a vehicle count and a timestamp to record when a vehicle arrived. Traffic flow and pollution statistics were provided separately since they were used to predict one another. Data on both pollution levels and vehicular flow were sourced from the Aarhus, Denmark website and subsequently merged by aligning the timestamps found in both datasets. This study utilized real-time data recorded through publicly accessible, open-source sensor datasets, which provide valuable insights into the city's dynamic pulse in Aarhus.

The datasets utilized in the experiments encompassed both traffic data, incorporating information on traffic intensity, and pollution data, encompassing NO_2, CO, SO_2, O_3, PM, latitude, longitude, and details on the distance between two sites. To explore the interrelationships among the dataset's attributes, a correlation matrix graph, depicted in

Fig. 2, was employed. This graph aids in discerning the degree of correlation among the various attributes.

This study did not directly employ vehicle data from the traffic dataset. Instead, vehicle data was integrated separately based on their respective timestamps into the pollution dataset. These two datasets were combined because the data collection sensors were positioned along the same route. Moreover, there exists a strong correlation between the number of vehicles and pollution emissions, with an increase in emissions of NO_2, CO, and SO_2 corresponding to heavier traffic conditions. To reduce the infrastructure costs associated with traffic flow assessment, the study primarily relies on pollutant data, providing a model suitable for broader urban monitoring rather than focusing on fine-grained details. This approach offers an economical advantage by minimizing the need for specialized sensors, and instead, making generalized predictions using the pollution dataset, thereby reducing the overall number of sensors used. A sample of the dataset can be found in Table 1, and a correlation matrix is illustrated in Fig. 2. Predictions can be made, lowering the number of sensors utilized. Table 1 includes a sample of the dataset, and Fig. 2 includes a correlation revealing patterns, such as clusters of correlated variables or outliers, which can inform data preprocessing, feature selection, or model specification.

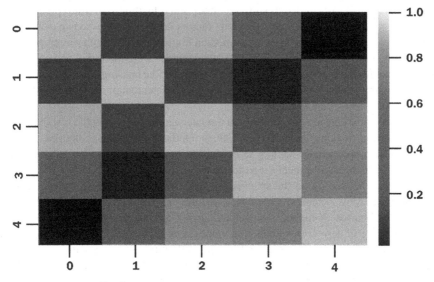

Fig. 2. The Correlation Matrix for the used dataset.

Table 1. A sample of the dataset.

Ozone	Particular Matter	Carbon Monoxide	Sulfur Dioxide	Nitrogen Dioxide
66	48	33	53	83
65	39	31	55	80
60	42	28	52	83
58	38	29	57	81
51	40	31	53	80
50	38	28	53	80
46	41	25	58	82

2.3 Data Pre-processing

This stage involves the completion of data processing, which is a critical step in effectively establishing the connection between input and output variables. The data needed to be transformed into a format compatible with the model, addressing challenges like missing values, outliers, and other data issues. Several strategies were employed to prepare the data, making it suitable for input to the models and facilitating further processing.

Missing values can arise due to various factors such as survey non-responses and data entry errors. To address this, a mean/median imputation technique was employed to populate missing values. In this process, missing values were identified and eliminated using the pandas library. The specific column containing the missing data was pinpointed, and the missing values were replaced with the mean of the remaining values within that column.

In essence, outliers are data points that deviate significantly from the rest of the data within a dataset, making them atypical values. Outliers can pose challenges in statistical analysis by potentially leading tests to miss important discoveries or by skewing the results, which can ultimately lead to false conclusions. The approach to handling outliers varies depending on the specific context. In this study, outliers were detected and managed using Z-scores, which measure the deviation of a data point from the mean of the dataset. A higher Z-score indicates a greater deviation from the mean, while a Z-score of zero corresponds to a value equal to the mean. The SciPy package was employed to calculate Z-scores and subsequently filter out values with Z-scores less than 3, thus effectively removing outliers. Data underwent cleansing and standardization to ensure compatibility with algorithms like K-Nearest Neighbors (KNN), which rely on comparing distances between data points. To achieve this, the Min–Max Scaler and normalization pre-processing tools from the Scikit-Learn library were employed. Data pre-processing is instrumental in maintaining the integrity of the data used for model training, ensuring it can be effectively utilized as input for Machine Learning (ML) or Deep Learning (DL) models [20]. Data normalization is particularly vital when the features within a dataset exhibit wide-ranging values. For instance, a dataset may encompass traffic density values ranging from 0 to 50, while values for attributes like CO_2 and NO_2 span from 0 to 4.2 and 0 to 300, respectively. Such discrepancies in scale can adversely impact the performance of models [21]. Data normalization addresses these challenges by bringing the various scales within the dataset into alignment. This, in turn, contributes to more efficient model training and performance. Various data normalization methods are available, including min–max normalization, median normalization, and Z-score decimal scaling, among others. For this study, the widely recognized min–max normalization method was applied in the experiments [22].

2.4 Building Regression Models by Ensemble

Within this phase, an ensemble model, as depicted in Fig. 3, was crafted through a three-stage process. Initially, the data was partitioned into multiple samples of size 'B,' known as bootstrap samples, by randomly selecting 'B' observations from a starting dataset of size 'N.' Subsequently, further steps were taken as follows.

$$A^n b = a^1 1, a^1 2, \ldots a^1 B, \ldots a^2 1, a^2 2, \ldots a^2 B, \ldots .a^3 1, a^3 2, \ldots a^3 B. \tag{1}$$

After using bootstrapping, N independent weak learners were fitted on each dataset in the following phase.:

$$W^L = w^1, w^2, w^3, \ldots, W^L, \tag{2}$$

The results of all N independent weak models were combined after fitting to create an ensemble model with low variance using the following equation:

$$A^N = 1/n \sum_{i=1}^{N} W^L \tag{3}$$

A^N was an aggregated result after the ensemble.

This study employed various bagging ensemble techniques, integrating multiple models to enhance prediction accuracy. The final model harnessed the insights from several weaker models to refine its predictions. The workflow of this model can be summarized as follows: the dataset was initially divided into multiple 'B'-sized samples using the bootstrap technique. Various weak models were then concurrently trained on distinct samples from the original dataset. Lastly, the predictions produced by these weak models were aggregated using techniques such as averaging to yield final results.

The study utilized three bagging ensemble combinations:

- KNN ensemble
- Random forest ensemble
- Multi-layer perceptron ensemble

Among these three models, the KNN ensemble emerged as the top performer, boasting the lowest error rate.

2.5 Evaluation Metrics

We utilized well-known metrics to assess the models. Relative absolute error (RAE), mean absolute error (MAE), R-squared (R-SQR), and RMSE (root mean square error) are four of the most popular evaluation metrics that were used.

$$MAE = \frac{1}{n} \sum_{i=1}^{n} |G_i - GP_i| \tag{4}$$

$$MAE = \frac{1}{n} \sum_{i=1}^{n} (G_i - GP_i)^2 \tag{5}$$

$$RSME = \sqrt{\frac{1}{n} \sum_{i=1}^{n} (G_i - GP_i)^2} \tag{6}$$

$$ME = Max|G_i - GP_i| \tag{7}$$

$$R_{Squared} = 1 - \frac{SS_{regression}}{SS_{total}} \tag{8}$$

3 Results and Discussion

3.1 The Evaluation of Different Regression Techniques

This section conducts a comparative analysis of the various regression models employed in the experiment. Multiple regression models are utilized to determine which model offers the most effective performance in traffic forecasting, specifically concerning the prediction of traffic flow or the number of vehicles. These models employ various evaluation metrics, including MAE, RMSE, RAE, and R-Square as shown in Fig. 3. R-SQR values for the different models. R-SQR reflects the variance in the response variable that the regression model has captured. The ideal R-SQR value is 1, indicating almost no differences between the observed and fitted data values. A higher R-SQR value is essential for a more accurate data fit. In this context, KNN has achieved the highest R-SQR value. Figure 4 displays the RAE (Relative Absolute Error) values, which are represented as a ratio comparing the mean error (residual) to the errors produced by a simple or naive model. Effective models yield a ratio lower than one. The x-axis of Fig. 4 indicates the RAE values, while the y-axis lists the models used. Both KNN and MLP exhibit the lowest RAE values, as evident from the graph. A comprehensive chart displaying RMSE, MAE, R-SQR, and RAE can be found in Fig. 4.

Two common error measures for assessing the performance of regression models were utilized in Fig. 5 to compare the model's results with those of various baseline models. RMSE and MAE values were examined to gauge a model's error rate, which reflects the disparity between the model's predicted and actual values. Lower RMSE and MAE values indicate more effective model learning, while higher values suggest significant errors. As Fig. 5 illustrates, the model outperforms other baseline models, achieving the lowest error across all of them. This study also compared its findings with the base paper [21]. The experiments demonstrated that using a bagging ensemble, as opposed to the boosting ensemble employed in [21], reduced the error rate by over 30%. Since both studies used the same dataset and addressed the same problem, they are comparable. The initial stage of data pre-processing is typically consistent across most machine learning projects. Some machine learning models, such as ANN and Decision Tree, were common to both studies. Although [21] did not employ these methods, the KNN and Elastic Net models were used. Figure 5 includes the findings of the base paper for reference in the comparison of the proposed approach's performance with another research.

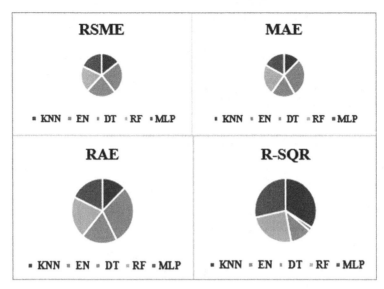

Fig. 3. A comparative analysis of the various regression models employed in the experiment.

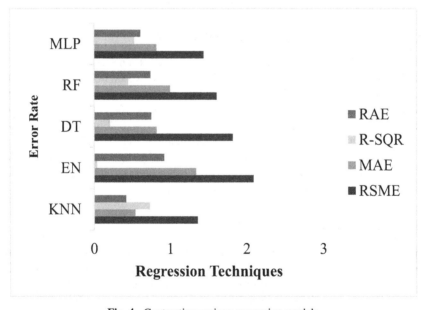

Fig. 4. Contrasting various regression models.

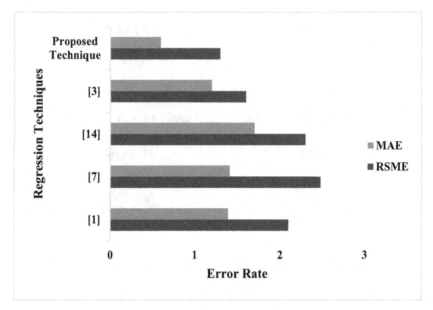

Fig. 5. Performance comparison between proposed model and other baseline models.

3.2 Comparison of Models on Different Dataset Sizes

The best-performing model, the bagging KNN model, was trained and tested on a dataset with 96,000 instances. Subsequently, a random subset of 20,000 instances was selected from the dataset, and models were trained on this smaller dataset to assess whether the model's performance remained robust with fewer instances. The model was then tested, and the individual results are presented in Figs. 6 and 7 96,000 instances and 20,000 instances respectively. The findings demonstrate that the model's performance remains consistent even when presented with a smaller dataset. Any slight variation in the results can be attributed to the model's capacity to learn new patterns as it processes additional data, thereby enhancing its performance.

3.3 Threat to Validity

At present, only data from Aarhus City have been utilized in this analysis. While the number of electric vehicles on the road is increasing, which is expected to lead to a substantial reduction in pollution levels in and around major cities, it's essential to recognize that the transition to electric vehicles will not occur overnight. During this transitional phase, the model may adapt to new patterns. The adoption of electric vehicles is gaining momentum worldwide due to concerns about air pollution. For instance, some countries have set ambitious targets for the sale of over seven million electric vehicles annually beginning in 2020 [23]. The replacement of conventional vehicles with electric ones will be a gradual process, which could pose a challenge to the long-term effectiveness of the strategy presented in this study, given its reliance on the pollution emitted by these vehicles.

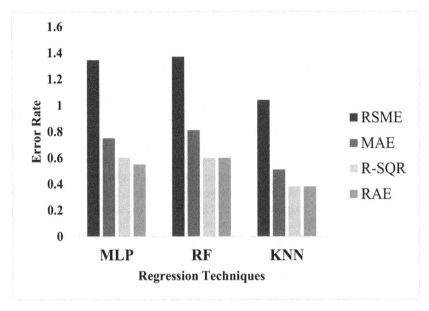

Fig. 6. Comparative of different bagging KNN model of 96,000 instances datasets

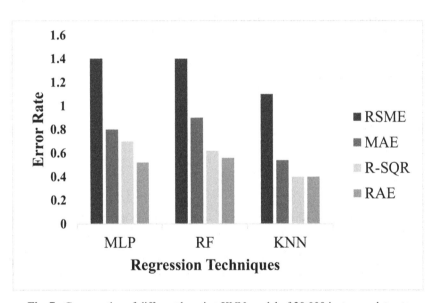

Fig. 7. Comparative of different bagging KNN model of 20,000 instances datasets

4 Conclusion

The primary objective of smart cities is precise traffic flow prediction, which can significantly enhance journey management for drivers. In this study, traffic and pollution data from Aarhus, Germany, were integrated to create an accurate traffic flow estimation. Various conventional machine learning algorithms were applied to the dataset to identify the most accurate one, with KNN exhibiting the lowest MAE and RMSE values. After assessing the results of conventional methods, bagging and stacking ensemble techniques were employed to improve MAE and RMSE values. The dataset was divided into samples through bootstrapping with replacement, and these samples were used to train various homogeneous models. The output of these models was combined to create a robust bagging ensemble model. Among all the bagging and stacking ensemble combinations, the KNN bagging ensemble model emerged as the most accurate. KNN's superior performance can be attributed to its proficiency in handling non-linear data. However, KNN can underfit when the number of nearest neighbors (K) is too low and overfit when it is too high. Comparing this experimental study to prior research using boosting for traffic flow prediction in smart cities, the proposed bagging ensemble approach was found to reduce error rates by 28%.

Author Contribution.   All the authors meet the ICMJE criteria.

Funding Statement.   The authors received no funding for this study.

Data Availability Statement.   Not applicable.

References

1. Shahid, N., Shah, M.A., Khan, A., Maple, C., Jeon, G.: Towards greener smart cities and road traffic forecasting using air pollution data. Sustain. Cities Soc. **72**, 103062 (2021). https://doi.org/10.1016/j.scs.2021.103062
2. Bhardwaj, A., Iyer, S.R., Ramesh, S., White, J., Subramanian, L.: Understanding sudden traffic jams: from emergence to impact. Dev. Eng. **8**, 100105 (2023). https://doi.org/10.1016/j.deveng.2022.100105
3. Patella, V., et al.: Urban air pollution and climate change: 'The Decalogue: Allergy Safe Tree' for allergic and respiratory diseases care. Clin. Mol. Allergy **16**(1), 1 (2018). https://doi.org/10.1186/s12948-018-0098-3
4. Affolder, N.: Transnational environmental law's missing people. Transnatl. Environ. Law **8**(3), 463–488 (2019). https://doi.org/10.1017/S2047102519000190
5. Jereb, B., Stopka, O., Skrúcaný, T.: Methodology for estimating the effect of traffic flow management on fuel consumption and co2production: a case study of Celje, Slovenia. Energies **14**(6), 1–18 (2021). https://doi.org/10.3390/en14061673

6. Abdurrahman, M.I., Chaki, S., Saini, G.: Stubble burning: Effects on health & environment, regulations and management practices. Environ. Adv. **2**(September), 100011 (2020). https://doi.org/10.1016/j.envadv.2020.100011

7. Adekunle, T.S., et al.: An intrusion system for internet of things security breaches using machine learning techniques. Artif. Intell. Appl. (2024). https://doi.org/10.47852/bonviewAI A42021780

8. Akhtar, M., Moridpour, S.: A review of traffic congestion prediction using artificial intelligence. J. Adv. Transp. (2021). https://doi.org/10.1155/2021/8878011

9. Jiang, W., Luo, J.: Graph neural network for traffic forecasting: A survey. Expert Syst. Appl. (2022). https://doi.org/10.1016/j.eswa.2022.117921

10. Adekunle, T.S., Alabi, O.O., Lawrence, M.O., Ebong, G.N., Ajiboye, G.O., Bamisaye, T.A.: The use of ai to analyze social media attacks for predictive analytics. J. Comput. Theor. Appl. **2**(2), 170–178 (2024). https://doi.org/10.62411/jcta.10120

11. Khan, A., Fouda, M.M., Do, D.T., Almaleh, A., Rahman, A.U.: Short-term traffic prediction using deep learning long short-term memory: taxonomy, applications, challenges, and future trends. IEEE Access **11**(September), 94371–94391 (2023). https://doi.org/10.1109/ACCESS. 2023.3309601

12. Alabi, O.O., Adeaga, O.A., Ajagbe, S.A., Adekunle, E.O., Adigun, M.O.: Design and implementation of an alcohol detection driver system. Int. J. Reconfigurable Embed. Syst. **13**(2), 278–285 (2024). https://doi.org/10.11591/ijres.v13.i2.pp278-285

13. Chen, X., et al.: Traffic flow prediction by an ensemble framework with data denoising and deep learning model. Phys. A Stat. Mech. its Appl. **565**, 125574 (2021). https://doi.org/10.1016/j.physa.2020.125574

14. Zolfaghari, M., Golabi, M.R.: Modeling and predicting the electricity production in hydropower using conjunction of wavelet transform, long short-term memory and random forest models. Renew. Energy **170**, 1367–1381 (2021). https://doi.org/10.1016/j.renene.2021. 02.017

15. Nunez, I., Nehdi, M.L.: Machine learning prediction of carbonation depth in recycled aggregate concrete incorporating SCMs. Constr. Build. Mater. **287**, 123027 (2021). https://doi.org/10.1016/j.conbuildmat.2021.123027

16. Barua, S.: A Naïve bayes classifier approach to incorporate weather to predict congestion at intersections. World Academics J. Eng. Sci. **7**(June), 72–76 (2020). https://www.academia.edu/download/64308303/10-WAJES-03550.pdf

17. Khan, N.U., Shah, M.A., Maple, C., Ahmed, E., Asghar, N.: Traffic flow prediction: an intelligent scheme for forecasting traffic flow using air pollution data in smart cities with bagging ensemble. Sustainability **14**(7), 4164 (2022). https://doi.org/10.3390/su14074164

18. Xu, Wei, C., Peng, P., Xuan, Q., Guo, H.: GE-GAN: A novel deep learning framework for road traffic state estimation. Transport. Res. Part C: Emerg. Technol. **117**, 102635 (2020). https://doi.org/10.1016/j.trc.2020.102635

19. Wilding, M., et al.: Exploring the Structure of High Temperature, Iron-bearing Liquids. Mater. Today Proc. **2**, S358–S363 (2015). https://doi.org/10.1016/j.matpr.2015.05.050

20. Ma, Q., Yang, Y.: Analysis of ecological environment evaluation and coupled and coordinated development of smart cities based on multisource data. J. Sensors **2022**, 1–9 (2022). https://doi.org/10.1155/2022/5959495

21. Vafaei, N., et al.: Normalization techniques for multi-criteria decision making: analytical hierarchy process case study. In: Camarinha-Matos, L.M., Falcão, A.J., Vafaei, N., Najdi, S. (eds.) Technological Innovation for Cyber-Physical Systems: 7th IFIP WG 5.5/SOCOLNET Advanced Doctoral Conference on Computing, Electrical and Industrial Systems, DoCEIS 2016, Costa de Caparica, Portugal, April 11–13, 2016, Proceedings, pp. 261–269. Springer International Publishing, Cham (2016). https://doi.org/10.1007/978-3-319-31165-4_26

22. Velliangiri, S., Karthikeyan, P., Arul Xavier, V.M., Baswaraj, D.: Hybrid electro search with genetic algorithm for task scheduling in cloud computing. Ain Shams Eng. J. **12**(1), 631–639 (2021). https://doi.org/10.1016/j.asej.2020.07.003

23. Nimesh, V., Sharma, D., Reddy, V.M., Goswami, A.K.: Implication viability assessment of shift to electric vehicles for present power generation scenario of India. Energy **195**, 116976 (2020). https://doi.org/10.1016/j.energy.2020.116976

Understanding Limited Enterprise Systems Benefits in Government: An African Case

Musani Butale and Lisa F. Seymour[(⊠)] [iD]

Department of IS, University of Cape Town, Rondebosch 7700, South Africa
BTLMUS001@myuct.ac.za, lisa.seymour@uct.ac.za

Abstract. Enterprise systems (ES) are increasingly being used in government. Yet the benefits being realized are lower than anticipated and rarely match the level of investment. Post-implementation is when, through usage, benefits are realized and yet it is the ES phase researched the least. Hence there is little understanding of why benefits are limited in government departments. Therefore, this study aimed to answer the question 'Why are limited ES benefits realized in government?' The case studies chosen were in the government of an African developing country. Data included semi-structured interviews and secondary data. The explanatory model, inductively derived, reveals no ES benefits management processes in the cases. Low usage and limitations in their ES were predominantly due to the limited IT support post-implementation although limitations with the initial implementation project were raised. The root causes of limited benefits are organizational constraints within the government departments and poor consultant knowledge transfer.

Keywords: ERP · Enterprise Systems · Africa Government · Benefits Realization

1 Introduction

An enterprise system (ES) is a standard packaged or customized business software solution integrating processes from various business functions across an organization [1]. This integration enables access to information in real time by utilizing shared and integrated databases and workflow standardization [1]. ES have evolved to integrate later technologies and are core to digital transformation [2]. The ES market is the fastest growing segment in the IT industry, with 2022 experiencing a 7% annual increase, the Enterprise Resource Planning Systems (ERP) market sub-segment accounts for $95 billion in revenue [3]. The budget for ES maintenance and upkeep is substantial [4] with ES making up the largest part of most organizations' Information Technology (IT) budgets [5]. Before organizations commit resources to ERP implementations, business cases are developed, detailing the expected benefits [5]. Despite the business cases produced, the actual benefits realized by organizations are lower than anticipated and rarely match the level of investment [6]. IT projects in the public sector, in particular, have experienced poor results [7]. It is known that after an ES has been implemented, benefits need managing for them to be realized [1, 8]. However, it is not clear why limited ES benefits

A. Gerber (Ed.): SAICSIT 2024, CCIS 2159, pp. 279–294, 2024.
https://doi.org/10.1007/978-3-031-64881-6_16

are realized in government. Which is what this study sought to answer. There is a call for more IS researchers to return to the socio-technical roots of their discipline which considers the technical artifacts and the social contexts and sees outcomes emerging from the interaction between the two [9]. In this study we derive a socio-technical model in which limited ES benefits emerge from the interactions between social themes and the ES and its limitations as the technical artifact.

2   Related Research: ES Benefits Realization in Government

The ES lifecycle is commonly described across literature as three phases of pre-implementation, implementation and post implementation [10]. During post-implementation the realization of benefits occurs [1, 4]. ES post implementation activities include maintenance and support, measurement and evaluation, change management, user training, process optimization, upgrades and reimplementation [4, 11]. Organizations can encounter various challenges with benefits realization in post implementation ES, such as communication challenges, functionality errors, workarounds and the complexity of the system [1, 12] which ES post implementation activities are meant to avert. However, post implementation activities are often not carried out [4, 13]. For example ES failures have been blamed on inadequate post-implementation maintenance and support [4]. However, the research literature explains little on how organizations manage ES post implementation activities [1].

2.1   Benefit Realization

Benefit management involves designing, organizing and managing activities undertaken by an organization to ultimately realize potential benefits [14, 15]. Benefits need to be actively managed throughout an ES lifecycle through a deliberate benefit realization management approach or process [15, 16]. In the ES context, benefit realization focuses on identifying, classifying, planning and measuring benefits to ensure that ES implementations deliver business benefits [1, 8]. There are a multitude of potential ES benefits that have been researched [17, 18]. ERP benefit realization research attributes benefits to building better business cases and benefit realization plans, identifying and classifying benefits, identifying benefit owners and measurements, defining organization change management, communication, risk management strategies, project governance and ensuring that critical success factors are in place [19–21]. In addition, post implementation ERP benefits are achieved through education, training and support, efficient and effective use, business process improvement, and availing financial and human resources for future ERP implementations and improvements [11, 17, 18]. Benefits management models and frameworks include the Cranfield Benefits Management Model, Active Benefit Realization, and Model of Benefits Identification [22]. Yet these are of minimal effect if relevant stakeholders do not embrace and adopt them [22]. Research indicates that organizations often don't have robust benefit management approach or practices in place [1, 23].

2.2 ES in Government and in Developing Countries

Digitally transforming the public sector is seen as crucial to streamline service delivery [24]. Given the rising demand of accountability and the potential strategic and operational benefits from the utilization of ES, governments are adopting ES as part of their public governance reforms and digital transformation initiatives [2, 25]. Governments seek to increase returns from their ES by streamlining internal processes and through effective provision of services to the public [2, 26]. Therefore ES form an important platform for e-government [27]. IT projects have experienced poorer results in public sector when compared to private sector and ERP project follow the same trend, it seems a large percent of government ERP implementations are classified as failures [7]. This is attributed to public sector organizations having significant differences to private sector that influence ES success [26] such as external regulations, available resources, siloed and complex structures, outsourced IT, and internal culture [24, 27]. Government departments have other differences, for instance, top level management in government tend to be political appointees who are likely to be less supportive towards the implementation of new IT than professional middle managers in government [26]. Other differences include public interest, accountability, political sensitivity, whole-of-government ecosystem, budget cycle complexity, information exchange, regulating society, and machinery of government changes [28, 29].

The public sector is the largest employer in developing countries, hence developing countries public sector organizations have become a major target market for ES vendors [25]. ES market saturation in developed countries and improving economic growth in developing nations has also helped fuel the consequent increase in ES adoption in developing countries [30]. However, ES implementations in developing countries are high risk and experience high failure rates [25, 31]. Effective ICT adoption requires infrastructure such as stable electricity grid, computers, internet with sufficient bandwidth, data centers, and telecommunications [31]. Yet, organizations in developing countries lack sufficient funds and expertise to procure up to date technologies and evaluate return on ES investment [31]. African developing nations, just as much as most developing countries, have their own context characterized by low economic capacities, limited infrastructures, limited skills and expertise, and a certain culture [32]. In addition, organizations in Africa are governed by specific laws and regulations, and have a business culture different from other continents [32]. These characteristics or differences are likely to cause misalignments or misfits between ES designed around developed nations best practices and practices in the African context [31]. For instance, some African countries have a hierarchically inclined culture that creates a power distance contrary to certain developed nation's culture that assumes information sharing among employees [30, 32].

2.3 Barriers to ES Usage and ES Benefits

Continuous usage of an ES is a significant factor for realizing and sustaining benefits [33–35]. If users are reluctant to use a system and use workarounds, expected benefits would be negatively impacted even though the system has been implemented successfully from a technical perspective [35]. Yet the individual adoption decision has limited impact in the case of an ES where usage is mandated [30]. Given the importance of ES utilization to benefit realization, literature proposes various theoretical frameworks for investigating usage barriers during the post implementation phase including the Absorption Capacity Theory, Task Technology Fit Theory, and the DeLone and McLean IS Success model [35]. Even broader IT adoption models at organization level include the Rogers diffusion of innovation (DOI) model and the Depietro et al. technology, organization and environment (TOE) model [36]. Yet with organizational IT adoption models the focus is often on variables influencing an adoption decision or the rate of diffusion [37] but not why or how organizational adoption and its benefits are challenged which we wanted to answer. The Staehr, et al. [17] ERP business benefits explanatory framework is useful. The framework has nine categories leading to benefits from ERP systems. Yet there is a call for more post-implementation as well as more context-aware research into ES adoption [38] and existing frameworks don't explain why benefits are not achieved in government contexts.

Another approach to IT adoption is the Alter systems theory of IT innovation, adoption and adaption or work system approach [39] which is argued to be the natural unit of analyzing the adoption of socio-technical systems in organizations [40]. A work system comprises processes and activities; participants; information; and technology. The work system produces products and services; serves customers; and is impacted by the internal and external organizational environment (including culture), strategies and infrastructure [39]. All these elements can be drivers or obstacles to IT innovation and its impact. Barriers to ES benefit are broader than ES usage and include barriers to the ES benefit management process. In the post implementation phase of ES systems, organizations can experience various challenges with ES benefits realization such as insufficient management practices, people, culture, communication challenges, workarounds and the complexity of the system [1, 12, 20, 41].

2.4 Summary of Literature

Existing ES literature focuses more on pre-implementation and implementation phases of ERPs, and less on post implementation [1, 4]. Furthermore, existing ERP research focuses more on private sector organizations and enterprises, and less on public sector or governments [27]. Moreover, most public sector research was undertaken in public sector organizations of developed countries [27]. The most common research topics on ES in the public sector or government is the identification of success factors related to system implementation and assessing the impact of ES on organizations that implemented it [27]. Davison, et al. [40] refer to the 'curious omission' of research on inadequate technology, such as the case of ES not providing value. Our review of related literature looked broadly at benefits realization, benefits management, ES usage and barriers to benefits realization. We noted a gap in the literature on barriers to ES benefit realization in governments. In particular, the African context is under studied and is a context that can least afford limited benefits from their investments. Journals have called for 'fundamental empirical studies' as well as specific domain knowledge so that benefits and shortcomings could be better understood [42]. Most theories and models reflect the minority Western, Industrial and Rich (WIR) worldview, hence the IS community has been challenged to expand the spread of IS research sites to developing countries [43].

Hence, our empirical study within an African context to understand why limited ES benefits are realized in government.

3   Research Method

To understand the limited ES benefits in government, we followed an interpretive research stance that advocates that social reality is determined, or constructed by different human experiences and social contexts [44]. We adopted a qualitative multiple case study strategy with an inductive approach to theory development. We chose two cases of ES implementations in different departments (Org A and B) of the government of an African developing country as they are recent ES implementations and limited benefits have been realized. Data was collected in 2022, mainly through interviews, supplemented with six documents obtained from the project manager of OrgA. We obtained ethics clearance from the University in line with the institution's ethics policies. Management and individual consent were obtained from organizations and participants prior to any data collection. Participants were emailed a copy of the interview transcripts for their confirmation and feedback as a member checking strategy [45]. Table 1 lists documents D1-D6. Table 1 lists the 13 participants of the in-depth face-to-face semi-structured interviews (10 from OrgA and three from OrgB). The participants selected because of their experience in working on government ES projects. Codes RA1 to RB3 were given to respondents where the second digit indicates the organization. Organizations and interviewees were kept anonymous by excluding any personally identifiable information from the findings and not adding codes to the table.

Table 1.   List of research participants and secondary documents.

Org	Role	Org	Role	ID	Document Description
A	Consultant – Support Engineer	A	System user	D1	Current Situation Analysis Report
A	System user & Manager Admin Accounts	A	IT Officer	D2	Systems Requirement Specification Document
A	Consultant – Lead Project Engineer	A	System key user	D3	System support and upgrade report
A	System user/Process owner	B	IT Manager	D4	Go-Live Report 2017
A	System user	B	Project Manager	D5	Project Closure Report
A	Project Manager	B	System user	D6	Training evaluation form

Case 1 is an ES implementation at a department (OrgA) tasked with constructing and maintaining the national road network. OrgA's strategic plan of 2009, documented in the Current Situation Analysis Report (D1), identified the 'lack of developed IT infrastructure to enhance effective and efficient service delivery as well as improve communication to internal and external stakeholders' as one of the major constraints the department was facing. Therefore, OrgA initiated a project to design, develop and implement an integrated road management system (ES-A) with comprehensive functionality to adequately support its business processes across all divisions. ES-A went live in July 2017 and is used by regions and depots across the country.

Case 2 is a systems implementation at a different department (OrgB) of the same African developing country's government as Case 1. OrgB is responsible for the procurement, maintenance, and disposal of the government's entire fleet. To better carry out its mandate, OrgB embarked on a systems development project of a fleet management and maintenance system (ES-B). The ES aims to improve vehicle tracking, fuel management and maintenance monitoring of the government fleet from acquisition to disposal. The implementation was completed in 2012. ES-B is an Oracle ERP application based on 12c application and 11g database. The technology is very old.

The phases of inductive thematic analysis included data preparation and organization, initial immersion, coding, categorizing and theming, and interpretation [46]. Initial immersion and reading of the text was performed prior to coding. All data sources were then imported into NVivo, and the first author did initial coding by finding patterns and themes recuring in the data. Themes were then categorized. As part of peer examination, the second author reviewed the codes and categories through multiple cycles. Interpretation involved looking for meaning and links between the different categories and themes and the outcome was an explanatory model. The final model went through multiple refinements by both authors. In qualitative case studies, credibility, transferability, dependability and confirmability are used to assess research rigor and quality [45]. To improve credibility of analysis, we performed member checking, triangulation, and peer debriefing. To improve transferability, we provided thick descriptions and sampled purposively. For dependability, we kept an audit trail of the coding and performed triangulation and peer examination.

4 Findings and Discussion

The cases were selected due to the limited benefits that they had achieved from their ES. This section first describes their state of benefits realization and then describes reasons for their limited benefits. Due to page constraints quotes for all themes could not be included. This section then explains the relationships between themes and presents an explanatory model. Both cases lack an ES benefit management process and aren't carrying out the required post implementation activities.

4.1 The Lack of an ES Benefit Management Process

Benefit realization is a continuous process of five stages starting with identifying and understanding the expected benefits [21]. Participants can identify and understand the expected benefits from their ES implementations, in line with the first stage. For instance, one participant stated, *'Benefits I think here in my case, my own understanding would mean such like you know like operational efficiency.' (RA3)*. However, participants had difficulty speaking to the benefit management process followed in their government. The following quote indicates that there is no standard or formal ES benefit management process following initially identifying benefits. *'it's a new concept to manage benefits realization of systems. We don't do that' (RA3).*

ES benefits are achievable through building better business cases and benefit realization plans [19–21]. From interviews and secondary data, we note that business cases are not common, benefit plans seem not to exist, and benefits are not quantified. *'A business case is not a document that is common in government.' (RB1).*

4.2 ES Limitations

Low usage of, and the actual nature of the ES, negatively impacted realization of benefits. Beliefs that the introduction of an ES reduces user's power and authority and puts jobs in risk create resistance and barriers to ES benefit realization [47]. In this study quotes show **low usage of the ES** and that post implementation employees are still skeptical and resistant to using the ES which they believe threatens their jobs. *'The users, especially the outside users like the ministries, they didn't accept it indefinitely... this system was automating most of their processes, if not all. Then they were thinking that, oh this type of work that I'm doing, maybe I'm going to be irrelevant, maybe in the future' RB2.*

Excessive customization of an ES usually leads to a complex system and introduces difficulties in software maintenance and upgrades, further complicating benefits identification and realization [1, 4]. Excessive customization of an ES post-implementation was found in case 2. *'OK, let me start with the ES-B... it's overly customized and it has been condemned by Oracle... the customizations have caused, or rather have hindered the patching, the upgrades... So, the over customizations have hindered the full benefits that would be getting from a standard Oracle ERP' (RB1).*

Task technology fit refers to the extent to which an ES assists a user in performing their portfolio of tasks [35]. This study revealed that not all tasks were catered for in the systems available. If the gap between the requirements of a task and the functionalities of an ES widens, individual and organizational performance drops thus affecting realization of benefits [35].

4.3 Implementation Project Limitations

While many of the reasons for reduced benefits were due to the current situation, some of the blame for a lack of benefits realization was found to stem from the initial ES implementation project. The findings reveal **inadequate initial requirements gathering** emanating from the lack of coordination between stakeholders which affected the final ES product and realization of benefits. *'the actual users of the system were not engaged during requirements engineering and after implementation we did realize that some of the detailed processes were missed out in the actual process flow. As such, the final product did not address all the process tasks' (RA2).*

Improvements in organizational performance through ES, require reengineering of organizational business processes [48]. In both cases there was **insufficient process reengineering and automation of processes**. *'The challenge that we have, number one is reengineering of processes is lacking in government.' (RB1).*

The research findings reveal that the **ES build was incomplete** and had dysfunctional modules. Employees that are expected to use an incomplete ES get demotivated and lose confidence in the systems.

Successfully achieving ES benefits requires implementing the corresponding organizational changes that enable benefits [11]. However, there was a **lack of organizational change management** in government ES implementation projects.

4.4   IT Infrastructure and Support Limitations

Technical resources are needed post-implementation that can either enable or constrain the desired results of the ES investment [33–35]. Many of these limitations could be present in any organization but are more dominant in developing countries. Organizations in developing countries, including Africa, have been reported to have limited skills and expertise to procure up to date technologies and evaluate returns on ES investments [31]. This research found that, there are **low skills and ES expertise within government IT** to manage ES projects. *'we as IT don't provide advice because we're not knowledgeable on the matter at hand' (RB1).*

Access and support should be adequate to prevent users from inventing manual workarounds that could be detrimental to benefit realization efforts [17]. In this case there was **inadequate IT support** to address system issues that arise lead to delays and demotivation to use the ES.

The findings reveal **poorly drafted ES support contracts.** Some contracts had unfavorable clauses that hinder government from engaging different consultants for maintenance and support. *'when we tried to get a different consultant on site, we realized that the previous contract that we had signed had some other binding clauses that were hindering us from getting a different consultant' (RB1).*

Participants identified **outdated IT infrastructure** as a barrier to ES benefit realization in line with prior literature that attributes poor deployment of software packages in developing countries to poor infrastructure [31]. *'Our infrastructure … it's old and those systems they're upgraded to run on new machines.' (RA8).*

ES implementations require stable network connectivity, and sufficient bandwidth to run successfully [31, 35]. However, in this study, the **intermittent network with insufficient bandwidth** is confirmed by quotes and secondary data *'we find that the system is not running because of the network' (RA9). 'the speed of the internet. So, that's the one which sometimes demotivate people to use government systems' (RA6).*

Participants highlighted **insufficient IT equipment**. In certain instances, government employees must share computers which results in delays and affects productivity. *'The government… It's not even providing enough equipment for the IT.' (RA9).*

ES implementation requires technical resources [35]. Participants indicate that government struggles with timely adoption of technology due to bureaucracy, red tape, and long procurement processes. The **slow IT projects** cause post-implementation project delays and affects timely upgrades. *'The government is a slow adopter in terms of technology' (RA2). 'In government is there is a hierarchical barrier because you'd find out that there's a lot of channels that have to be followed in terms of approvals and process flows' (RA2).*

Successful ES benefit realization requires a systematic and communicative approach amongst post implementation ERP stakeholders [1] without which undesirable delays and user resistance occurs [12]. The participant quotes show **poor communication and collaboration between IT and business** stakeholders.

4.5 Organizational Constraints

Organizational constraints emanate from aspects such as culture, management, structures, and policies of the government departments that are perceived to impact poor realization of ES benefits. Four themes that appear unique to the government context, include the slow and lengthy procurement processes, the employee culture, the structures and top management support.

One of the conditions to be met before benefits are realized is the allocation of resources to post-implementation ES improvements [11]. In this study, **limited financial resources were allocated to ES improvements**. *'these IT systems, you know, they are classified as supporting structures to the overall mandate of an organization. So, they're not given that much priority' (RA6)*. These findings are in line with literature that found that improvements of ES implementations in government are compromised by complex budgetary processes [29].

In both cases, there was a **lack of comprehensive risk management**. *'What I want to say is that government or state government departments, they never they are nowhere near risk management.' (RA3)*. Yet a lack of business case development has been reported across many sectors. A global CIO survey noted that only 36% of organizations had a well-defined IT investment process and business case template [49].

The post implementation phase demands efficient and effective use, therefore this phase requires more competencies, skills and knowledge than other ES phases [17]. Literature identifies adequate education and training, as one of the critical success factors of ES post implementation benefits realization [18] and a frequently mentioned challenge [50]. In this study, **inadequate education and training on ES systems** left users unable to effectively use the systems. *'Insufficient training whereby you find that people who are actually using the systems are not well trained.' (RA7)*.

Respondents complained about **slow and lengthy procurement processes** that exist in government departments. They attributed their inability to achieve IT benefits to this process. *'If there's a delay in procurement, obviously you find that by the time the government manages to buy, those who can buy quickly are already advanced' (RA7)*.

Benefits from ES projects can only be realized if there is an appropriate organizational culture and lack of motivation and interest among government employees, has been reported to impact the realization of ES benefits [22]. In this study the **unmotivated employee culture** with a lack of urgency impacted the realization of ES benefits. *'On the end users there is lack of interest in adopting those.' (RA6)*. *'IT officers in the government industry are a bit I'd say relaxed. And they're not that willing to improve on whatever they have' (RA1)*.

ES benefit management initiatives should strive to transform an organization's structures and attitudes to ensure a good synergy between the organization and new ES implementations [41]. In this study the government **organizational structures don't support ES**. *'But where there isn't proper organizational structures some of such projects just* *die a natural death' (RA4). 'I think the biggest challenge that comes in now it is the bureaucratic arrangements or the way we are arranged,' (RA3).* The silo-ed nature of government is a known constraint to IT projects [24, 27].

Top management support is one of the factors that enable ES success [27]. Top level management in government tend to be political appointees who are reported to be less supportive towards the implementation of new IT than professional middle managers in government [26]. This is unique to government. In this study, it is apparent that post-implementation, **inadequate top management buy-in and support** results in ES not being given the necessary priority thus affecting the flow of benefits. *'...there is no buy in from or support from top management. Hence the rest of the support staff are reluctant to use the systems.' (RA6).*

4.6 Environmental Constraints

Environmental constraints that reduce ES benefits include legislation and consultant's approach. The findings from both cases indicate that legislation affects ES benefit realization. Existing legislation prescribes old processes, which are incompatible with the latest ES provisions. Hence the **legislation prevents process improvements**. Changing legislation to suit new developments takes time, and negatively affects ES benefit realization. *'you find that the authority has not changed its existing process to follow best industry standards. Then I'll be forced to follow the current legislation that is being used to carry out a certain process that was brought about by legislation... We have to first prompt for a change in legislature' (RB1).*

Consultants have been reported to have a conflict of interest as they are driven by increasing their market share and revenue at the expense of delivering service to their clients [51]. The research findings show that ES consultants' approach can be a barrier to ES benefit realization. Consultants seek long term or permanent relationships with government entities; therefore, they adopt approaches that hinder knowledge and skills transfers to government employees. As **consultants don't transfer knowledge** there is an over reliance on consultants by government which and negatively affects ES benefit realization because of the high cost and the problem if the relationship breaks down. Case 1 did refer to a relationship breakdown. *'...our consultants at times become a little bit stingy. It's like they were reluctant to have the IT team to be trained to provide the proper administration of the system such that we can sustain ourselves, because they wanted to always be on site to provide support and maintenance. I think that that also led to the fallout that we had with the consultant' (RA10).*

4.7 Resultant Explanatory Model

The resultant socio-technical explanatory model for limited ES benefits in the government of an African developing country is shown in Fig. 1. In our model the technical artifact is the ES and its limitations, the other themes represent the social and what emerges from their interactions is limited ES benefits. The limited ES benefits experienced are attributed to the limitations of the resultant ES and the lack of having a benefits management process. Evidence for the other inductively derived relationships is now provided.

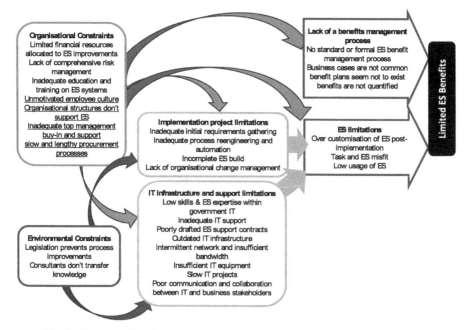

Fig. 1. Understanding limited ES benefits in the government of an African country.

The initial implementation **project contributed to the existing ES limitations**. Inadequate requirements gathering, and inadequate process reengineering resulted in task and ES misfits and over customization of the ES post-implementation. *'the actual users of the system were not engaged during requirements engineering … As such, the final product did not address all the process tasks.' (RA2).*

The **limitations with the ES** were also caused by **limitations in IT infrastructure and support**. Unavailability of systems due to intermittent networks and inadequate infrastructure reduces ES usage and causes resistance and adoption of workarounds by employees. *'when the networks are slow or unstable… the users of the systems tend to become demoralized and revert back revert to the manual processes thereby not using the systems and realizing the benefits fully.' (RA2).*

Organizational constraints in the form of limited financial resources allocated to ES improvement and the slow and lengthy procurement process increase the IT infrastructure and support limitations as well as implementation project limitations. They cause deferments or delays in the renewal of support and maintenance contracts, upgrades, trainings, and equipment replacements. *'For example, the procurement process, long as it is.' (RA3). 'limited funds to undertake IT projects as well as to finance the post implementation activities such as user trainings.' (RA2).*

Organizational constraints also contribute to **ES limitations** directly. Inadequate education and training and inadequate top management buy-in result in low usage of the ES. Employees who are inadequately trained resist using the ES system and adopt workarounds. *'The users of the system… they lack that training and motivation.' (RA8).*

"limited management buy-in… they don't ensure that their subordinates fully utilize the systems." (RA2).

Research participants indicated the need for and **the lack of an ES benefit management process,** but little has been done so far to achieve that. Participants attribute the slowness to **organizational constraints** in the form of limited resources. *'So, the plans are that these systems that we have within the organization should be fully utilized so that they do the functions as planned…' (RA6).*

Environmental constraints also influenced **the project and IT infrastructure and support limitations.** Existing legislation impacted the re-engineering of processes. *'the authority has not changed its existing process to follow best industry standards' (RB1).* Amendments in legislature are necessary before re-engineered processes can be adopted and automated. Consultants not transferring knowledge also resulted in low ES expertise within government IT. *'they were reluctant to have the IT team to be trained to provide the proper administration of the system such that we can sustain ourselves' (RA10).*

Yet all models and theories are bounded by their contextual applicability [43]. Interpretive case studies are made generalizable by drawing relationships and by providing rich insight [52]. To generalize from empirical finding to a model requires that one abstracts from the particular instances and that the model applies beyond the domain observed [53]. The question is then if this model and its relationships hold true in other clearly defined settings [53]. Many of the themes on our model could be generalizable to any context even within the private sector and that has been noted in the findings. Yet some of the themes (underlined in Fig. 1) appear unique to government and many other themes appear to be more dominant in developing countries. We argue that any organization with the limitations and constraints found in the government departments studied would end up with limited ES benefits and hence the relationships should hold true in most cases.

4.8   Limitations

This study has limitations. Data saturation was not approached, and it is possible that many themes were missed. The interviewees were in management roles and a richer picture might have been obtained if more employees from different ranks were interviewed. The study was cross-sectional at a particular point in time after their initial implementation which potentially reduced the number of themes that respondents could remember. Getting frank responses from government employees is not easy and bias in answers is a high risk. Participant bias is common when there is a threat to job security, and in organizations that have an authoritarian management style [44] such as in government. The research was also limited to a single African developing country government. Furthermore, the research was limited to two case studies from central government, yet government comprises local government and parastatals. So, generalization is limited as the findings may not hold true for other contexts.

5 Conclusion

The objective of this research is to explain the limited ES benefits in government. The findings regarding ES benefit realization practices are that there is no standard or deliberate benefits management process accompanying ES implementations in the African government department studied. The main challenges include limited funding, lack of top management support, and consultants not transferring knowledge. ES consultants, to secure long-term contracts, are reluctant to impart the requisite ES support skills and knowledge to government employees. In the resultant explanatory model of barriers to ES benefit realization in the government of an African developing country, organizational constraints had a strong influence. Lack of resourcing of the post-implementation phase, misaligned organizational structures, unmotivated employee culture and inadequate top management support plague the government departments.

From a practical perspective, it is expected that through this explanatory model, governments of African developing countries will be able to appreciate the underlying barriers to ES benefit realization as they plan for future ES implementations and maintenance. Awareness of potential constraints and limitations would enable them to mitigate them. From a theoretical perspective this research contributes to filling the research gaps in ES post implementation, especially in the context of ES in government and in African developing countries.

Yet this study has limitations. The authors suggest more similar studies in other developing nations in the African context to enhance these research findings. Further research involving more case studies, and a larger sample size across government would help validate and extend the findings. Longitudinal studies could identify how value is derived at various stages post implementation. In addition, action research studies could focus on methods to improve ES benefits realization.

References

1. Hietala, H., Päivärinta, T.: Benefits realisation in post-implementation development of ERP systems: a case study. Procedia Comput. Sci. **181**, 419–426 (2021). https://doi.org/10.1016/j.procs.2021.01.186
2. Pittaway, J.J., Montazemi, A.R.: Know-how to lead digital transformation: the case of local governments. Gov. Inf. Q. **37**, 101474 (2020)
3. Vailshery, L.: Enterprise software total worldwide expenditure 2009–2023, Statista. https://www.statista.com/statistics/203428/total-enterprise-software-revenue-forecast/. Last accessed 5 Nov 2023
4. Amado, A., Belfo, F.P.: Maintenance and support model within the ERP Systems lifecycle: action research in an implementer company. Procedia Comput. Sci. **181**, 580–588 (2021)
5. Johansson, B., Karlsson, L., Laine, E., Wiksell, V.: After a successful business case of ERP – what happens then? Procedia Comput. Sci. **100**, 383–392 (2016). https://doi.org/10.1016/j.procs.2016.09.173
6. Janssens, G., Kusters, R., Martin, H.: Expecting the unexpected during ERP implementations: a complexity view. Int. J. Inform. Syst. Project Manag. **8**(4), 68–82 (2021). https://doi.org/10.12821/ijispm080404
7. FreeBalance. ERP Failures in Government, FreeBalance, https://freebalance.com/en/blog/government-digital-transformation/erp-failures-in-government. Last accessed 3 Nov 2021

8. Badewi, A., Shehab, E.: The impact of organizational project benefits management governance on ERP project success: neo-institutional theory perspective. Int. J. Project Manage. **34**, 412–428 (2016). https://doi.org/10.1016/j.ijproman.2015.12.002

9. Sarker, S., Chatterjee, S., Xiao, X., Elbanna, A.: The sociotechnical axis of cohesion for the IS discipline: its historical legacy and its continued relevance. MIS Q. **43**(3), 695–719 (2019). https://doi.org/10.25300/MISQ/2019/13747

10. Hasibuan, Z.A., Dantes, G.R.: Priority of key success factors (KSFS) on enterprise resource planning (ERP) system implementation life cycle. J. Enterp. Resour. Planning Stud. **2012**, 1–15 (2012). https://doi.org/10.5171/2012.122627

11. Hawking, P., Stein, A., Foster, S.: Revisiting ERP systems: benefit realisation. In: Proceedings of the 37th Hawaii International Conference on System Sciences, Hawaii (2004). 10.11.96.387

12. Osnes, K.B., Olsen, J.R., Vassilakopoulou, P., Hustad, E.: ERP systems in multinational enterprises: a literature review of post-implementation challenges. Procedia Comput. Sci. **138**, 541–548 (2018). https://doi.org/10.1016/j.procs.2018.10.074

13. Markus, M.L., Tanis, C.: The enterprise systems experience-from adoption to success. In: Zmud, W.R. (ed.): Framing the Domains of IT Management: Projecting the Future Through the Past. Pinnaflex Educational Resources, pp. 173–207 (2000)

14. Mohamad, M., Sultan, A.: ERP performance triangle: exploring the interplay between benefits realisation management, project governance, and project success. In: British Academy of Management 2018 Conference Proceedings, Manchester: University of Salford (2018). http://usir.salford.ac.uk/id/eprint/48515/

15. Peppard, J., Ward, J., Daniel, E.: Managing the realization of business benefits from IT investments. MIS Q. Exec. **6**, 12 (2007)

16. Williams, S.P., Schubert, P.: Benefits of enterprise systems use. In: 43rd Hawaii International Conference on System Sciences, pp. pp. 1–9. IEEE, Hawaii (2010) https://doi.org/10.1109/hicss.2010.82

17. Staehr, L., Shanks, G., Seddon, P.: An explanatory framework for achieving business benefits from ERP systems. J. Assoc. Inform. Syst. **13**(6), 424–465 (2012). https://doi.org/10.17705/1jais.00299

18. Slabbert, B., Seymour, L., Schuler, J.: Business benefits and challenges of a multiple ERP landscape. In: International Conference on Information Resources Management, Cape Town, South Africa. (2016). http://aisel.aisnet.org/confirm2016/60

19. Al-Twairesh, N., Al-Mudimigh, A.S.: Business cases for ERP implementations. J. Theor. Appl. Inf. Technol. **25**, 43–49 (2011)

20. Einhorn, F., Marnewick, C., Meredith, J.: Achieving strategic benefits from business IT projects: the critical importance of using the business case across the entire project lifetime. Int. J. Project Manage. **37**, 989–1002 (2019). https://doi.org/10.1016/j.ijproman.2019.09.001

21. Ward, J., Daniel, E., Peppard, J.: Building better business cases for IT investments. MIS Q. Exec. **7**, 1–20 (2007)

22. Hesselmann, F., Mohan, K., Where are we headed with Benefits Management Research? Current shortcomings and avenues for future research. In: European Conference on Information Systems Tel Aviv, Israel, pp. 1–17 (2014)

23. Anaya, L.: To what extent is it viable to apply benefits management approach for ERP systems? Procedia Comput. Sci. **164**, 33–38 (2019). https://doi.org/10.1016/j.procs.2019.12.151

24. Thunes, J., Kempton, A.: Achieving digital transformation in the public sector through targeted insourcing, in *ECIS 2023 Research Papers*, Kristiansand, Norway, p. 279 (2023). https://aisel.aisnet.org/ecis2023_rp/279

25. Primeau, M.-D., Leroux, M.-P.: ERP Systems in public sector organization: critical success factors in african developing countries. Int. J. Adv. Syst. Measur. **12**, 279–290 (2019)

26. Alves, M.C., Matos, S.I.A.: ERP adoption by public and private organizations – a comparative analysis of successful implementations. J. Bus. Econ. Manag. **14**(3), 500–519 (2012). https://doi.org/10.3846/16111699.2011.652979

27. Roztocki, N., Strzelczyk, W., Weistroffer, H.R.: Driving forces in enterprise systems implementation in the public sector: a conceptual framework. In: 13th Annual AIS SIG GlobDev Pre-ICIS Workshop, Austin, USA (2021). https://aisel.aisnet.org/globdev2021/5

28. Mpanga, D.: Understanding public sector enterprise resource planning system implementation in developing countries: a literature review. IFIP Adv. Inform. Commun. Technol. **558**, 255–273 (2019). https://doi.org/10.1007/978-3-030-20671-0_18

29. Tregear, R., Jenkins, T.: Government Process Management: a review of key differences between the public and private sectors and their influence on the achievement of public sector process management. BP Trends (2007) 1 0.11.226.1110

30. Talasi, T., Seymour, L.F., Understanding the value of enterprise resource planning (ERP) systems: a lesotho study. In: Jones, M. (ed.), Proceedings of InSITE 2022: Informing Science+ IT Education Conference, p. 026 (2022). https://doi.org/10.28945/4983

31. Bitsini, N.: Investigating ERP misalignment between ERP systems and implementing organizations in developing countries. J. Enterp. Resour. Plann. Stud. (2015). https://doi.org/10.5171/2015.570821

32. Tobie, A.M., Etoundi, R.A., Zoa, J.: A literature review of ERP implementation in African countries. Electron. J. Inform. Syst. Dev. Countries **76**, 1–20 (2016)

33. Deng, X., Chi, L.: Understanding postadoptive behaviors in information systems use: a longitudinal analysis of system use problems in the business intelligence context. J. Manag. Inf. Syst. **29**, 291–326 (2014). https://doi.org/10.2753/mis0742-1222290309

34. Nwankpa, J.K.: ERP system usage and benefit: a model of antecedents and outcomes. Comput. Hum. Behav. **45**, 335–344 (2015). https://doi.org/10.1016/j.chb.2014.12.019

35. Urus, S.T., Mat, T.Z.T., Nazri, S.N.F.S.M., Fahmi, F.M.: ERP sand clock barriers and antecedents model: from the lens of task technology fit theory. J. Soc. Sci. Res. (2018). https://doi.org/10.32861/jssr.spi5.970.983

36. Oliveira, T., Martins, M.F.: Literature review of information technology adoption models at firm level. Electron. J. Inform. Syst. Eval. **14**, 110 (2011)

37. Jeyaraj, A., Rottman, J.W., Lacity, M.C.: A review of the predictors, linkages, and biases in IT innovation adoption research. J. Inf. Technol. **21**, 1–23 (2006). https://doi.org/10.1057/palgrave.jit.2000056

38. Saxena, D., McDonagh, J.: Factors influencing enterprise systems procurement in public service organisation: a socio-technical case study. In: ECIS 2018 Proceedings, Portsmouth, UK (2018). https://aisel.aisnet.org/ecis2018_rp

39. Alter, S.: A systems theory of IT innovation, adoption, and adaptation. In: European Conference on Information Systems (ECIS), Portsmouth, UK (2018). https://aisel.aisnet.org/ecis2018_rp/26

40. Davison, R.M., Wong, L.H., Alter, S., Ou, C.: Adopted globally but unusable locally: What workarounds reveal about adoption, resistance, compliance and non-compliance. In: European Conference on Information Systems (ECIS), Stockholm & Uppsala, Sweden (2019). https://aisel.aisnet.org/ecis2019_rp/19/

41. Coombs, C.R.: When planned IS/IT project benefits are not realized: a study of inhibitors and facilitators to benefits realization. Int. J. Project Manage. **33**, 363–379 (2015). https://doi.org/10.1016/j.ijproman.2014.06.012

42. Gray, J., Rumpe, B.: How to write a successful SoSyM submission. Softw. Syst. Model. **15**, 929–931 (2016). https://doi.org/10.1007/s10270-016-0558-5

43. Osei-Bryson, K.-M., Brown, I., Meso, P.: Advancing the development of contextually relevant ICT4D theories – from explanation to design. Eur. J. Inf. Syst. **31**, 1–6 (2022). https://doi.org/10.1080/0960085x.2022.1994119

44. Saunders, M., Lewis, P., Thornhill, A.: Research Methods for Business Students, 7th edn. Pearson Education Limited, Harlow, England (2016)
45. Anfara, V.A., Brown, K.M., Mangione, T.L.: Qualitative analysis on stage: making the research process more public. Educ. Res. **31**, 28–38 (2002)
46. Leavy, P.: Research design: Quantitative, Qualitative, Mixed Methods, Arts-Based, and Community-Based Participatory Research Approaches. Guilford Publications, New York (2017)
47. Aladwani, A.M.: Change management strategies for successful ERP implementation. Bus. Process. Manag. J. **7**, 266–275 (2001). https://doi.org/10.1108/14637150110392764
48. Somers, T.M., Nelson, K.G.: A taxonomy of players and activities across the ERP project life cycle. Inform. Manag. **41**, 257–278 (2004). https://doi.org/10.1016/s0378-7206(03)00023-5
49. Briggs, B., Lamar, K., Kark, K., Shaikh, A.: Follow the money 2018 global CIO survey, chapter 3. Deloitte Insights (2018)
50. Obwegeser, N., Danielsen, P., Hansen, K.S., Helt, M.A., Nielsen, L.H.: Selection and training of super-users for ERP implementation projects. J. Inform. Technol. Case Appl. Res. **21**, 74–89 (2019)
51. Lederer, A.L.: Decision support systems unfrastructure: the root problems of the management of changing IT. Decis. Support Syst. **45**, 833–844 (2008)
52. Walsham, G.: Interpretive case studies in IS research: nature and method. Eur. J. Inf. Syst. **4**, 74–81 (1995)
53. Seddon, P.B., Scheepers, R.: Generalization in IS research: a critique of the conflicting positions of Lee & Baskerville and Tsang & Williams. In: Willcocks, L.P., Sauer, C., Lacity, M.C. (eds.) Formulating Research Methods for Information Systems, pp. 179–209. Palgrave Macmillan UK, London (2015). https://doi.org/10.1057/9781137509857_8

Gender Perceptions of Software Developers' Job Satisfaction

Margaret Cullen[1]([⊠]) [iD], Andre P. Calitz[2] [iD], and Nico Claassen[1] [iD]

[1] Nelson Mandela University Business School, Port Elizabeth, South Africa
`Margaret.Cullen@Mandela.ac.za, Nico@S4.co.za`
[2] Department of Computing Sciences, Nelson Mandela University, Port Elizabeth, South Africa
`Andre.Calitz@Mandela.ac.za`

Abstract. In a competitive market, Information Technology (IT) organisations must retain their most valuable assets, namely the IT employees, specifically software developers. Employee job satisfaction is important for organisations because it influences employee motivation, productivity and commitment to the organisation. The link between gender and job satisfaction has been extensively researched, however limited research has been conducted in the IT industry in South Africa. It is therefore necessary to understand the factors that influence job satisfaction in the IT industry for each gender. Evaluating the career satisfaction of software developers and their intent to remain in their current positions are important for IT organisations.

The literature review for this study focused on motivating and hygiene factors that influence job satisfaction and the intention to resign in the IT industry. This research study used a positivistic approach and a quantitative survey. The study established that statistically significant differences regarding gender exist for different factors influencing job satisfaction and the intention to resign at a large South African IT organisation. Gender related statistical differences were found for the factors Career Development, Career Advancement, Leadership, Working Environment – Onsite, Working Environment – Home, Corporate Culture, Company Reputation, Rewards, Purpose, Job Security and Intention to Resign. However, for the factors Job Satisfaction and Organisational Commitment no statistical significant differences were found between male and female software developers. The study is the first study investigating gender differences on job satisfaction and intention to resign in the IT industry in South Africa.

Keywords: IT Industry · Gender differences · Job Satisfaction · Intention to Resign

1 Introduction

The employee is the most valuable asset in a software development organisation [1]. To meet the organisation's ultimate objectives and achieve success, retention of these valuable assets through keeping employees satisfied and loyal [2] and leveraging their collective knowledge is critical [3]. Researchers have approached the concept and definition of job satisfaction from many different perspectives. Recent definitions of job satisfaction reflect the various degrees of emotional and psychological health involved [4], however Frutos-Bencze et al. [4] indicate that job satisfaction is the extent to which people like their jobs. Males dominate the information technology (IT) and software development profession, however both genders have experienced different treatment in their work environment and different factors affect their job satisfaction and intention to resign [5].

The link between gender and job satisfaction has been extensively researched and is especially intriguing due to the so-called gender paradox. It is argued that women generally receive lower pay, benefits and less opportunities for career advancement, yet they have reported higher levels of job satisfaction [4]. Males and females are not completely identical in terms of the factors influencing their job satisfaction [6].

In a study on job satisfaction in the IT industry in India, the researchers found a weak correlation between age and job satisfaction ($r = 0.363$) and gender and job satisfaction ($r = 0.358$) [7]. A study conducted in the IT industry in Serbia reported that women are less satisfied with their jobs than men [8]. The study showed that women employed in the private IT sector were more dissatisfied with certain aspects of work, specifically job security [8]. It is therefore necessary to understand the various factors of job satisfaction for each gender separately because the value or weight genders attribute to these factors may vary. The two categories of factors impacting job satisfaction levels of IT employees are (i) Job content factors (depends on the individual) (ii) Job context factors (depends on the organisation) [7].

The aim of this paper was to report on the gender perceptions on job satisfaction and intention to resign of male and female software developers at a large software development organisation in South Africa. The organisational factors that have an effect on the intention to resign and a persons' job satisfaction are Career Development, Career Advancement, Leadership, Working Environment, Corporate Culture, Company Reputation and Rewards. The personal factors that strongly influence IT employees are a Sense of Purpose, Job Security, Career Satisfaction and Organisational Commitment [9].

The layout of the study is as follows. In Sect. 2, the research problem and research questions being investigated are introduced. Section 3 provides a literature review, which focuses on the factors affecting job satisfaction in the IT industry. The results of the study are discussed in Sect. 4. The study is concluded in Sect. 5, where limitations and future research are also presented.

2 The Research Problem and Research Design

Determining the factors affecting the job satisfaction of IT employees in an organisation is a difficult task. A number of instruments to measure job satisfaction have been developed, for example the Job Satisfaction Survey (JSS), which examines global job satisfaction as well as its dimensions [4]. Previous research has found significant gender differences in job satisfaction [4]. Researchers found a weak correlation between gender and job satisfaction ($r = 0.358$) in the IT industry in India [7] and a study conducted in Serbia reported that women are less satisfied with their jobs than men [8].

Modern literature on job satisfaction and retention clearly define general success strategies [10, 11]. However, these strategies do not cater exclusively for the challenges encountered by software development organisations. The COVID-19 pandemic and the resulting worldwide lockdown came with existential and economic uncertainties and increased adoption of new working environment dynamics, such as working from home [12]. Remote work has resulted in numerous new job opportunities for software developers [1] and the quest for purpose in life and alignment with their beliefs are contributing to "The Great Resignation" [13].

The software development industry is experiencing a considerable increase in demand for software development resources and relatively limited qualified candidates are available [14]. The problem statement for this paper is that the gender differences for the factors related to employee retention at a large IT software development organisation have not been determined. The research objective of the paper is to determine the gender perceptions regarding the factors that affect job satisfaction and intention to resign at a large IT organisation in South Africa.

Factors that affect job satisfaction include job security, motivation, career growth and participation opportunities, working conditions, salary structure, flexible working hours, working-from-home, specifically during the Covid-19 pandemic, leadership and easy communication with management [15]. A questionnaire for software developers was compiled using similar questionnaires used in previous studies [10, 16]. The survey was anonymous and the questionnaire consisted of the sections listed in Table 1.

Table 1. Questionnaire Framework

Factor	Purpose
Demographics	The items target the collection of data about the respondents' demographics
Career Development	The statements focus on the respondents' opinions about career development opportunities
Career Advancement	The statements focus on the respondents' opinions about career advancement
Leadership	The statements seek to gather the opinion on leadership
Working Environment	The statements aim to collect information on the respondents' working environment at the office and at home
Corporate Culture	The statements seek to find the respondents' opinion on corporate culture
Company Reputation	The statements focus on the opinion on the reputation of the IT organisation
Rewards	The statements seek information about the respondents' opinion on rewards such as recognition, remuneration and other rewards
Purpose	The statements aim to gather information on the respondents' feelings on their sense of purpose

(*continued*)

Table 1. (*continued*)

Factor	Purpose
Job Security	The statements examine the respondents' sense of job security
Career Satisfaction	The statements aim to collect information on their career satisfaction
Organisational Commitment	The statements examine the organisational commitment
Intention to Resign	The statements will gather information on the intention of respondents to resign

The findings presented in this paper focus on the gender differences for the factors included in the main study [9]. The main study focused on developing a model for IT employee retention, based on the independent factors *Career Development, Career Advancement, Leadership, Working Environment, Corporate Culture, Company Reputation, Rewards, Sense of Purpose, Job Security, Career Satisfaction and Organisational Commitment* and the dependent factor *Intention to Resign*.

A five-point Likert rating scale (1 = Strongly disagree to 5 = Strongly agree) was used to gather data from software developers, regarding the motivating and hygiene factors that influence their job satisfaction. The questionnaire was captured using an on-line survey tool, QuestionPro. The data were statistically analysed using Statistica. Ethics clearance approval was obtained from the University Ethics Committee.

3 Literature Review

3.1 Theoretical Models

The Herzberg Motivation-Hygiene Theory, also known as the Herzberg Two-Factor Theory [17], was developed in 1959, taking influence from Maslow's hierarchy of needs [18]. Motivating factors and hygiene factors are the two types of factors that lead to job satisfaction and dissatisfaction. The first category includes motivators associated with growth and self-actualisation that employees manage within their work contexts. Growth factors such as the work itself, responsibility, achievement, recognition and potential for future growth increase job satisfaction, with their absence resulting in no job satisfaction. In addition to being complex and subjective, motivators are intrinsic and are often difficult to measure [18].

The second category describes hygiene factors commonly associated with minimising discomfort. Hygiene factors, such as working conditions, company administration and policies, salary, interpersonal relationships and relationships with management are extrinsic and not within the employee's control [18]. Hygiene factors can reduce job dissatisfaction but do not act as motivating factors [17]. Once hygiene factors fall below a level deemed acceptable by the employee, they will become dissatisfied [18]. The motivating factors and hygiene factors for this study are discussed in Sects. 3.3 and 3.4.

3.2   Employee Job Satisfaction and Software Developers

Employee job satisfaction represents a fundamental construct that gauges employee job satisfaction and impacts employee turnover [2, 16]. Job satisfaction is the reaction of a person who enjoys and does their work well, revealing qualities of fulfilment and pride based on various aspects of an individual's general attitude toward their job [2]. Males and females have similar levels of general job satisfaction across a large number of countries. However, there are still differences in terms of which factors affect their job satisfaction, thus indicating that males and females are not completely identical in terms of the factors influencing their job satisfaction [6]. Statistically insignificant differences in job satisfaction were found in the engineering industry relating to the factors meaninglessness of work, experiencing happiness at work and the satisfaction with the relationship with supervisors [19]. A study conducted in the IT industry in Serbia showed that women were more dissatisfied with their job compared with men [8]. The findings are contradictory to most of studies that reported that women have more job satisfaction than men [16].

3.3   Motivating Factors

Five motivating factors were identified, namely Purpose, Career Success, Career Growth Prospects, Learning and Development Opportunities and Job Security. A discussion of each motivating factor is presented in this sub-section.

Purpose
Chilton, Hardgrave and Armstrong [21] highlight the importance of workplace relationships for software developers as they can strongly influence job satisfaction and the perception of doing meaningful work. Since their work environment strongly influences a person's sense of purpose, in the long run, the positive influence on job-related successes by career adaptability will result in greater life satisfaction [20]. Employees having challenging daily demands in the workplace encourage independent work motivation by increasing employees' perceived enjoyment, interest and purpose in their job. Software developers perform best in demanding, dynamic work environments as these situations encourage them to stay engaged and committed [21].

Career Success
Career success is an interpretative concept and its appraisal varies depending on who does the appraisal [22]. Individuals may make appraisals of their career success, but others may also judge it. The basis of other people's perceptions and assessment of one's career success is objective using observable indicators, such as promotions and remuneration [22]. Therefore, it is known as objective career success and defined as visible career achievements judged against promotional and remuneration measures or the broader definition of a favourable psychological or employment-related outcome or accomplishment resulting from one's professional experiences [22].

Career Growth Prospects

Career prospects become important when people consider joining organisations for extended periods as a career. If opportunities for development and advancement within the company over a long period exist, joining the organisation might be an incentive to stay with it [23]. Previous research identified remuneration and promotion as crucial factors in organisational commitment. Weng, McElroy, Morrow and Liu [24] indicated that career growth is a viable means for organisations to rekindle and maintain organisational commitment. Employees evaluate their career decisions based on the progress toward their career goals, whereas professional skill development is the foundation for long-term career success [23].

Learning and Development Opportunities

The development of employees through training is vital in building knowledge and an essential strategy for employee retention [25]. There is a much higher chance of employees committing to stay with an organisation where a secure, supportive and safe environment of existing rules and procedures and a culture of learning and appreciation exists. The absence of these qualities increases the probability of employees leaving [25]. Employees who work on complicated tasks are happier and more intrinsically motivated than those who work on menial tasks [26]. Software developers enjoy challenges and employers need to carefully align any learning and development with the individual employees' appetite for knowledge and ambition and recognise and appreciate the individual effort in improving skills [27].

Job Security

Job security is the probability that an individual will keep their job. Many factors threaten job security, including globalisation, outsourcing, downsizing, recession and the introduction of new technologies. Job security influences organisational behaviours, such as productivity, change resistance and employee turnover. Job security appears prominently as a factor influencing employees' intention to stay in an organisation's service [28]. Significant predictors of career change are high levels of job insecurity and dissatisfaction and additional characteristics such as openness to experiences and extraversion.

3.4 Hygiene Factors

Six hygiene factors were identified, namely Remuneration and Rewards, Working Environment, Corporate Culture, Leadership, Social Work Relationships and Company Reputation. A discussion of each hygiene factor is presented in this sub-section.

Remuneration and Rewards

Karanja, Kinyili and Namusonge [29] identified four reward categories: individual, transactional, relational and communal. Individual rewards include base salary, incentive pay, contingent pay, bonuses, profit sharing and shares, while transactional rewards are perks, leave, flexibility, pension plans and medical aid plans. Career development is a relational reward and communal rewards include recognition, organisational values, the individuals' voice, achievement and leadership [29]. IT professionals continually look for better opportunities, both internally in the organisation and in the external market [10].

Rewards can affect employees' feelings, attitudes and behaviour and rewards offered by other organisations affect turnover [29].

Working Environment

Software developers spend most of their time in the office, where the physical environment influences work productivity, performance, physical and emotional well-being and job satisfaction. Workplace digitalisation has accelerated through the combined effects of the Fourth Industrial Revolution and the COVID-19 pandemic, shifting toward remote working and e-commerce, generating a surge in work-from-home arrangements and new job opportunities [1]. Conflicting benefits and disadvantages of working from home exist for software developers [30]. Remote work is not "one size fits all", citing the combination of high task interdependence, low autonomy and technology stressors that may result in technostress, leading to a loss in job satisfaction [30].

Corporate Culture

Many leaders today believe that organisational culture is a critical component of an organisation's success and is more important than strategy and leadership [31]. Corporate culture consists of beliefs, shared values and behaviours that define us as individuals within our organisations, evolving through experience, new ideas and changes in management styles [32]. Corporate culture plays a vital role in creating an organisation's brand, which is strengthened by employees joining an organisation for reasons such as wanting to be there, making them feel good at their workplace and increasing employee productivity. Good corporate culture is an effective strategy for strengthening organisational commitment. A good fit between perceived and actual values positively influences this commitment [32].

Leadership

Leaders and leadership styles remain vital in employee retention in organisations [3, 26]. However, the importance of leadership is not limited to organisational commitment and employee turnover, but also employee performance, stress and job commitment and satisfaction [33]. Brian Joo and Lim [26] highlight the importance of transformative leadership in career satisfaction, finding a strong positive link between perceived transformational and psychological empowerment, favourably impacting career satisfaction. Fedirko and Campo [3] conclude that transformational leadership is most effective for employee motivation and retention in the IT industry.

Social Work Relationships

Chilton, Hardgrave and Armstrong [21] highlight the link between work stress, satisfaction with co-worker relationships and their link to career satisfaction for software developers. Colleagues, mentors, support personnel, supervisors and managers are examples of co-workers [34]. Colbert et al. [34] identified five co-worker relationship support types that contribute to employee career development, namely task assistance, emotional, friendship, personal growth and career advancement. Sunardi and Putri [35] make two important observations. Firstly, even though employees can trust their peers, their career satisfaction will suffer if a positive reciprocal interaction does not match that trust. Secondly, when leaders and their subordinates have a good relationship, they will help each other achieve career satisfaction [35].

Company Reputation

Company reputation is the perceived appeal of a company to all of its stakeholders compared to other notable competitors formed by prior actions and future possibilities [36]. This perception of how others regard one's employer is the perceived corporate reputation and plays a pivotal role in decision-making when deciding on an organisation as a viable employer [37]. Group membership and association with an organisation shape one's social identity and self-concept. Due to the link between an employee's self-concept and an organisation's reputation, perceived corporate reputation should impact employee self-esteem and pride in their affiliation with the organisation [37]. Pride and job satisfaction boost productivity and employees are more willing to participate in activities that help the organisation achieve its objectives [37].

4 Results

The biographical details of the respondents will be provided, followed by the reliability of the research instrument. A detailed discussion is provided for each of the factors regarding differences between gender perceptions.

4.1 Descriptive Statistics

Table 2 details an almost equal distribution of respondents' age in the years '21–25' and '26–30' with 43% and 42% respectively. Eighty-five per cent of the respondents are under the age of 31 (n = 106) and 15% are over the age of 31 (n = 30). Regarding gender, 81% of respondents were 'Male' and 19% indicated 'Female'. The majority of respondents, 94%, reported their highest qualification as a degree or higher, with 6% indicating another type of qualification. The distribution of responses in Table 2 shows that 65% of respondents have been employed between one and two years, with 31% employed between three and four years and 13% for five years or longer.

Table 2. Demographic Profiles (n = 136)

Highest Qualification	3-Year Diploma/Degree	4-Year Diploma/Degree	Master's Degree	Other
	58 (43%)	48 (35%)	22 (16%)	8 (6%)
Working Experience	0–2	3–4	5–7	8 +
	60 (44%)	35 (26%)	25 (18%)	16 (12%)

(*continued*)

Table 2. (*continued*)

Highest Qualification	3-Year Diploma/Degree	4-Year Diploma/Degree	Master's Degree	Other
	58 (43%)	48 (35%)	22 (16%)	8 (6%)
Years Employed	**1–2**	**3–4**	**5 +**	
	88 (65%)	31 (23%)	17 (13%)	
Age	**21–25**	**26–30**	**31 +**	
	59 (43%)	57 (42%)	20 (15%)	
Gender	**Male**	**Female**	**Total**	
	109 (81%)	27 (19%)	136 (100%)	

The results show that most of software developers were of Generation Z and the minority from the Millennial generation. The overwhelming majority are well-educated with tertiary qualifications. A large contingent of software developers have been with the company for under two years.

4.2 Reliability

The results in Table 3 indicate that the Cronbach alpha coefficient values were all above 0.80, indicating excellent reliability [7, 38]. The highest mean score of $\mu = 4.30$ was reported for the responses for the Organisational Commitment factor. The lowest mean score of $\mu = 2.17$ was reported for the response for the Intention to Resign factor. Apart from Career Satisfaction ($\sigma = 1.01$), the standard deviation is comparatively small for all factors ($0.60 \leq \sigma \leq 0.84$), suggesting that responses among respondents did not vary greatly. The aggregate mean and standard deviation were $\mu = 3.90$ and $\sigma = 0.72$, respectively.

Table 3. Cronbach's Alpha Coefficient, Mean and Standard Deviation for the Factors (n = 136)

Factor	Cronbach's Alpha	Internal Reliability	Mean	S.D
Career Development	0,87	Excellent	3,83	0,71
Career Advancement	0,90	Excellent	4,03	0,60
Leadership	0,91	Excellent	4,19	0,61
Working Environment – Onsite	0,88	Excellent	4,17	0,64
Working Environment – Home	0,89	Excellent	3,91	0,83

(*continued*)

Table 3. (*continued*)

Factor	Cronbach's Alpha	Internal Reliability	Mean	S.D
Corporate Culture	0,92	Excellent	3,98	0,67
Company Reputation	0,87	Excellent	4,16	0,62
Rewards	0,94	Excellent	3,74	0,71
Purpose	0,91	Excellent	4,18	0,68
Job Security	0,90	Excellent	3,81	0,80
Career Satisfaction	0,92	Excellent	3,67	1,01
Organisational Commitment	0,93	Excellent	4,30	0,65
Intention to Resign	0,85	Excellent	2,71	0,84

4.3 ANOVA Results Regarding Gender Perceptions

Career Development

Weng, McElroy, Morrow and Liu [24] propose a four-factor career development model. According to this model, four factors affect career development: (i) achieving one's career objectives, (ii) improving one's professional skills, (iii) earning promotions and (iv) remuneration appropriate to one's capabilities. Employees evaluate their career decisions based on the progress toward their career goals, whereas professional skill development is the foundation for long-term career success [23].

A two-sample t-test determined that *Career Development* (F-value = 11,36; $p < 0.001$; Cohen's d = 1.00; n = 136) is statistically significant with large practical significance. Male respondents were less positive ($\mu_1 = 3.68$) than female respondents ($\mu_2 = 4.33$), indicating a difference in how male and female respondents perceive *Career Development*. The results suggest that female software employees experience better career development than their male counterparts.

Career Advancement

According to Weng et al. [24], there is a link between career progression and organisational loyalty. Career advancement options are a primary predictor of employee-organisational relations. When organisations include career goal achievement and progression support strategies in workplace relations, they can provide the conditions required for overall career satisfaction. The literature review established that career advancement options are a primary predictor of employee-organisational relations and organisations that offer options for career growth establish a mutual investment relationship with employees [24].

A two-sample t-test determined that *Career Advancement* (F-value = 8,67; $p < 0.004$; Cohen's d = 0.97; n = 136) is statistically significant with large practical significance. The ANOVA result for *Career Advancement* showed that male respondents were less positive ($\mu_1 = 3.90$) than female respondents ($\mu_2 = 4.45$), suggesting that female software employees experience better career advancement than male software developers.

Leadership

Leaders and leadership styles continue to play a vital role in employee retention in organisations [26]. Leadership significantly impacts employee commitment to remain with their organisation [3], as well as employee performance, stress and job commitment and satisfaction [33]. The literature review established that leaders and leadership styles play a vital role in employee retention. Leadership significantly impacts employee commitment, performance, stress, job commitment and satisfaction [33].

A two-sample t-test determined that *Leadership* (F-value $= 6,83$; $p = 0.010$; Cohen's $d = 0.81$; $n = 136$) is statistically significant with large practical significance. The ANOVA result for Leadership showed that male respondents were less positive ($\mu_1 = 4.06$) than female respondents ($\mu_2 = 4.53$), suggesting that female software developers associate better with the organisation's leadership or management than their male counterparts.

Working Environment – Onsite

Software developers spend most of their time in the office, where the physical environment influences work productivity, performance, physical and emotional well-being and job satisfaction. Ayoko and Ashkanasy [39] note that Generation X and Millennial employees prefer chaotic workplace environments, while older generations prefer the calm and quiet environments of private offices. However, multiple studies have since confirmed concerns with the open-plan environment and noted an increase in employee dissatisfaction when moving to an open-plan office [40].

A two-sample t-test determined that *Working Environment – Onsite* (F-value $= 5,86$ $p = 0.017$; Cohen's $d = 0.81$; $n = 136$) is statistically significant with large practical significance. The ANOVA result for *Working Environment – Onsite* showed that male respondents were less positive ($\mu_1 = 4.05$) than female respondents ($\mu_2 = 4.55$), suggesting that female software developers associate better with the onsite working environment than male software developers.

Working Environment – Home

Work-from-home refers to an employment practice where workers do not neces-sarily need to be physically present at their workplace during working hours [32]. Remote working allows employees to be flexible in where they choose to work, giving them the freedom to work wherever they want; however, it has also created significant challenges for workers' well-being [1]. The literature review reveals many complexities regarding working from home. From an employee perspective, digitalisation and the COVID-19 pandemic have generated a surge in work-from-home arrangements and new opportunities [1]. The perception exists that flexible work hours boost productivity, job happiness, employee retention, loyalty and dedication and are essential to a family-friendly workplace, all factors that appeal to Millennial employees [39].

A two-sample t-test determined that *Working Environment – Home* (F-value $= 7,88$; $p = 0.006$; Cohen's $d = 0.81$; $n = 136$) is statistically significant with large practical significance. The ANOVA result for *Working Environment – Home* showed that male respondents were less positive ($\mu_1 = 3.76$) than female respondents ($\mu_2 = 4.40$), suggesting that female software developers are more likely to associate with the option to work from home compared to their male counterparts.

Corporate Culture

Corporate culture consists of beliefs, shared values and behaviours that define us as individuals within our organisations [32] and plays a vital role in making employees feel good at their workplace and increasing employee productivity [31]. A two-sample t-test determined that *Corporate Culture* (F-value = 10,53; p = 0.002; Cohen's d = 1.01; n = 136) is statistically significant with large practical significance. The ANOVA result for *Corporate Culture* showed that male respondents were less positive ($\mu_1 = 3.83$) than female respondents ($\mu_2 = 4.45$), suggesting that female software developers associate better with the corporate culture than male software developers.

Company Reputation

Company reputation is the perceived appeal of a company to all of its stakeholders compared to other notable competitors formed by prior actions and future possibilities [36]. Employees appreciate working for recognised companies and the perception of how others regard one's employer plays a pivotal role in deciding on an organisation as a viable employer [37]. The literature review reveals that employees appreciate working for recognised companies and company reputation is a primary consideration for employment [2]. Due to the link between an employee's self-concept and an organisation's reputation, perceived corporate reputation impacts employee self-esteem and pride, boosts productivity and the willingness of employees to participate in activities that help the organisation achieve its objectives [37].

A two-sample t-test determined that *Company Reputation* (F-value = 6,71; p = 0.011; Cohen's d = 0.83; n = 136) is statistically significant with large practical significance. The ANOVA result for *Company Reputation* showed that male respondents were less positive ($\mu_1 = 4.04$) than female respondents ($\mu_2 = 4.52$), suggesting that female software developers have a more favourable impression of the organisation's reputation as than male software developers.

Rewards

One of the most significant aspects of the employer-employee relationship is re-wards. According to Weng et al. [24], promotion and rewards provide employees with a measure of how the organisation views them and play a crucial role in employees' turnover intention. Classically, the discussion around rewards or remuneration focused on salaries. Rewards are considered to include basic salaries, incentives, bonuses and retirement and medical benefits [10]. The challenge for employers is that IT professionals are continually looking for better opportunities, both internally in the organisation and in the external market [10].

A two-sample t-test determined that *Rewards* (F-value = 9,47; p = 0.003; Cohen's d = 0.95; n = 136) is statistically significant with large practical significance. The ANOVA result for *Rewards* showed that male respondents were less positive ($\mu_1 = 3.58$) than female respondents ($\mu_2 = 4.20$), suggesting that female software developers are happier with the rewards offered by the organisation than male software developers.

Purpose

The literature review reveals that meaning in life works as a buffer between career uncertainty and anxiety, improves well-being and equips people to deal with adversity [20]. Since the work environment strongly influences software developers' sense of purpose, it results in greater life satisfaction in the long term [21]. Employees should engage in their workplace and the organisation must recognise employee achievements and that providing clear expectations, feedback, guidance and rewards for good performance is the key to retaining Millennial employees.

A two-sample t-test determined that *Purpose* (F-value = 7,30; p = 0.008; Cohen's d = 0.82; n = 136) is statistically significant with large practical significance. The ANOVA result for *Purpose* showed that male respondents were less positive ($\mu_1 = 4.04$) than female respondents ($\mu_2 = 4.57$), suggesting that female software developers perceived a greater sense of purpose in their work at the IT organisation than their male counterparts.

Job Security

Job security guarantees employment after the employee and employer have signed a legal employment contract and is a prominent factor influencing employees' intention to stay in an organisation's employ [28]. Job insecurity and dissatisfaction are significant predictors of an employee's intent on a career change. A two-sample t-test determined that *Job Security* (F-value = 4,08; p = 0.046; Cohen's d = 0.72; n = 136) is statistically significant with medium practical significance. The ANOVA result for *Job Security* showed that male respondents are more positive ($\mu_1 = 3.96$) than female respondents ($\mu_2 = 3.43$), suggesting that male software developers perceive a greater sense of job security than female software developers.

Job/Career Satisfaction

A career is a position held by a person in an organisation for the duration of their employment. The term "career success" is widely used to describe an individual's sense of achievement and fulfilment in their career. Career satisfaction is a subjective indicator of career success since it reflects an individual's activity in their profession according to their perception and represents a fundamental construct that impacts employee turnover [2]. A two-sample t-test determined that *Career Satisfaction* (F-value = 3,81; p = 0.053; Cohen's d = n/a; n = 136) indicated no statistically significant difference between male and female software developers regarding job satisfaction.

Organisational Commitment

Organisations offering a supportive atmosphere conducive to positive outcomes benefit employee career development, satisfaction and organisational commitment. Besides career satisfaction, the employee's commitment to the organisation is vital since organisations require psychologically engaged employees for optimal organisational performance [37]. Employees and organisations gain value from reciprocating employment relations that provide prospects for professional advancement and critical individual and organisational results. A two-sample t-test determined that *Organisational Commitment* (F-value = 2,84; p = 0.094; Cohen's n/a; n = 136) indicated no statistically significant differences between male and female software developers.

Intention to Resign

Employees are an organisation's most valuable assets and play an essential role in contributing to organisational performance based on their job performance [35]. Employee turnover costs (including hiring costs and productivity loss) are a concern as replacement costs typically account for 2.5 times an individual's income. In order to meet the organisation's ultimate objectives and achieve success, employees must be satisfied and remain loyal [2]. A two-sample t-test determined that *Intention to Resign* (F-value = 5,30; p = 0.023; Cohen's d = 0.85; n = 136) is statistically significant with large practical significance. The ANOVA result for the factor *Intention to Resign* showed that the mean score were less (μ_1 = 2.56) for male respondents than female respondents (μ_2 = 3.35), suggesting that female software developers are more likely to resign than their male counterparts.

5 Conclusions, Limitations and Future Research

Talent acquisition, talent management and retaining talent have become the biggest concerns for the IT industry in the present times [7]. Determining the level of job satisfaction of software developers is important in the highly competitive IT industry. It is important to regularly determine the main factors related to job satisfaction, specifically factors relating to working conditions, work, the workplace, as well as the personal perceptions and evaluations by the employees about the work environment [15]. Job satisfaction is mainly affected by job insecurity [15], therefore employers must provide a secure job environment, specifically for females. Female employees who were satisfied with their jobs were more likely to pursue career advancement opportunities [5].

Andrade et al.'s [6] research found that there are not consistent statistically significant gender differences in job satisfaction levels across countries. However, they indicated that males and females are not completely identical in terms of the factors influencing their job satisfaction [6]. The authors indicated that "The fact that women and men are similar in their satisfaction levels at work, shows that gender differences are becoming less relevant" [6]. Statistically significant gender-related differences in job satisfaction were found in the engineering industry [19].

The results of this study showed that female software developers experience better career development than their male counterparts. Female software employees experience better career advancement and associate better with the organisation's leadership than their males. Female software developers associate better with the onsite working environment, however they preferred the option to work from home more compared to the male software developers. Female software developers have a more favourable impression of the organisation's reputation and were more satisfied with the rewards offered by the organisation than males. Female software developers perceived a greater sense of purpose than the male software developers.

Regarding job security, female software developers did not perceive a greater sense of job security, indicating that females were less confident in holding their current position. No statistical differences were found for the factors *Job security* regarding male and female software developers. Finally, female software developers' *Intention to Resign* were more likely than their male counterparts.

The findings suggest that IT organisations establish more formal programmes for employees to further their education. They must cultivate a positive leadership culture and building the next generation of transformational leaders. They should consider re-introducing private workspaces to alleviate noise, stress and a lack of privacy [30]. In addition they should consider a hybrid working arrangement for software developers. Finally, management of software developers must develop employees, provide continuous training and education, improve work-life balance, conduct regular job satisfaction studies to increase organisational and professional commitment, strengthening organisational support and providing satisfactory remuneration.

The limitation of this study is that it was conducted at one large software development national organisation with a limited female sample size. Future research will encourage similar organisations to repeat the study and to conduct a follow-up study after addressing and implementing recommendations from the study. This study is the first recent study to investigate gender perceptions on job satisfaction at a large software development organisation in South Africa.

References

1. Schwab, K.: The Future of Jobs Report 2020. In World Economic Forum. (2020) https://www3.weforum.org/docs/WEF_Future_of_Jobs_2020.pdf
2. Moro, S., Ramos, R.F., Rita, P.: What drives job satisfaction in IT companies? Int. J. Product. Perform. Manag. 70(2), 391–407 (2021). https://doi.org/10.1108/IJPPM-03-2019-0124
3. Fedirko, R., Campo, S.S.: Leadership in IT, Employees' Motivation and Retention. Blekinge Institute of Technology (2018). https://www.diva-portal.org/smash/record.jsf?pid=diva2:1221874
4. Frutos-Bencze, D., Sokolova, M., Zubr, V., Mohelska, H.: Job satisfaction during Covid-19: industry 5.0 as a driver of sustainable development and gender equality. Technol. Econ. Dev. Econ. 28(5), 1527–1544 (2022)
5. Enriquez, K.N.B., Hidalgo, A.M.S., Quina, R.F.T., Valencia, N.J.L., Buzon, J.R.M.: Productivity, and career progression of female IT and software professionals. Millennium J. Hum. Soc. Sci. 4(1), 1–26 (2023)
6. Andrade, M.S., Westover, J., Peterson, J.: Job satisfaction and gender. J. Bus. Divers. 19(3), 22–40 (2019)
7. Sudershana, S., Satpathy, I., Patnaik, B.C.M.: Impact of age, gender and job satisfaction on employee engagement in the IT sector. Int. J. Innov. Technol. Explor. Eng. 9(2), 4841–4845 (2019)
8. Dašić, M., Mihajlov, N., Mihajlov, S.: The gender-job satisfaction paradox: the evidence of Serbia. J. Sustain. Bus. Manag. Solutions Emerg. Econ. (2023). https://doi.org/10.7595/management.fon.2023.0003
9. Claasen, N.: A Model for the retention of IT personnel at a selected firm in Gqeberha. MBA Treatise, Business School, Nelson Mandela University, Gqeberha, South Africa (2022)
10. Farooq, H., Janjua, U.I., Madni, T.M.: Identification and analysis of factors influencing turnover intention of Pakistan IT professionals: an empirical study. IEEE Access 10, 64234–64256 (2022). https://doi.org/10.1109/ACCESS.2022.3181753
11. van Nguyen, P., Trieu, H.D.X., Ton, U.N.H., Dinh, C.Q., Tran, H.Q.: Impacts of career adaptability, life meaning, career satisfaction, and work volition on level of life satisfaction and job performance. Human. Soc. Sci. Lett. 9(1), 96–110 (2021). https://doi.org/10.18488/journal.73.2021.91.96.110

12. Hadapad, M.R., Battur, A.: A Study on Work Life Balance of Information Technology Employees Working from Home During Covid-19. Sdmimd. Ac. In, pp. 1–11 (2020). https://www.sdmimd.ac.in/incon_cd_2020/papers/HR329.pdf

13. Vyas, D., Hyman, L., Freedman, E., Hasenoehrl, C.: Another Great Resignation Record (2022). https://www.kornferry.com/insights/this-week-in-leadership/another-great-resignation-record?utm_campaign=01-06-22-twil&utm_source=marketo&utm_medium=email&mkt_tok=NDk0LVZVQy00ODIAAAGBzZzRT0ArK0fAq-Uku_s2HG13iPDN8kn84Pqka7tlCLM-rQE-YTXIG9Tvzkq34haUG_tZj9O7

14. Kolding, M., Sundblad, M., Alexa, J., Stone, M., Aravopoulou, E., Evans, G.: Information management – a skills gap? Bottom Line **31**(3–4), 170–190 (2018). https://doi.org/10.1108/BL-09-2018-0037

15. Ipşirli, M., Namal, M.K.: Main factors that influence job satisfaction. Yönetim ve Ekonomi Araştırmaları Dergisi **21**(1), 205–223 (2023). https://doi.org/10.11611/yead.1231706

16. Lee, T.J.: Relationship Between Intrinsic Job Satisfaction, Extrinsic Job Satisfaction, and Turnover. Walden Dissertations and Doctoral Studies Walden, pp. 1–165 (2017)

17. Alshmemri, M., Shahwan-Akl, L., Maude, P.: Herzberg's two-factor theory. Life Sci. J. **14**(5), 12–16 (2017). https://doi.org/10.7537/marslsj140517.03

18. Atan, A., Ozgit, H., Silman, F.: Happiness at work and motivation for a sustainable workforce: evidence from female hotel employees. Sustainability **13**(14), 7778 (2021). https://doi.org/10.3390/su13147778

19. Živčicová, E., Masárová, T., Gullerová, M.: Job satisfaction in the light of gender in the engineering sector in Slovakia. Probl. Perspect. Manag. **20**(2), 1–9 (2022). https://doi.org/10.21511/ppm.20(2).2022.01

20. Yuen, M., Yau, J.: Relation of career adaptability to meaning in life and connectedness among adolescents in Hong Kong. J. Vocat. Behav. **91**, 147–156 (2015). https://doi.org/10.1016/j.jvb.2015.10.003

21. Chilton, M.A., Hardgrave, B.C., Armstrong, D.J.: Person-job cognitive style fit for software developers: the effect on strain and performance. J. Manag. Inf. Syst. **22**(2), 193–226 (2005). https://doi.org/10.1080/07421222.2005.11045849

22. Judge, T.A., Cable, D.M., Boudreau, J.W., Bretz, R.D.: An empirical investigation of the predictors of executive career success. Pers. Psychol. **48**(3), 485–519 (1995). https://doi.org/10.1111/j.1744-6570.1995.tb01767.x

23. Coetzee, M., Bester, M.S.: Exploring the reciprocal correspondence among workplace relationships, career goal instrumentality, career satisfaction, and organisational commitment. South African J. Psychol. **51**(1), 81–94 (2021). https://doi.org/10.1177/0081246320948366

24. Weng, Q., McElroy, J.C., Morrow, P.C., Liu, R.: The relationship between career growth and organizational commitment. J. Vocat. Behav. **77**(3), 391–400 (2010). https://doi.org/10.1016/j.jvb.2010.05.003

25. Govaerts, N., Kyndt, E., Dochy, F., Baert, H.: Influence of learning and working climate on the retention of talented employees. J. Work. Learn. **23**, 35–55 (2011). https://doi.org/10.1108/13665621111097245

26. Brian Joo, B.K., Lim, T.: Transformational leadership and career satisfaction: the mediating role of psychological empowerment. J. Leadersh. Organ. Stud. **20**(3), 316–326 (2013). https://doi.org/10.1177/1548051813484359

27. Li, P.L., Ko, A.J., Zhu, J.: What makes a great software engineer? Proc. – Int. Conf. Softw. Eng. **1**, 700–710 (2015). https://doi.org/10.1109/ICSE.2015.335

28. Frederiksen, A.: Job satisfaction and employee turnover. German J. Hum. Res. Manag. / Zeitschrift Für Personalforschung **31**(2), 132–161 (2017). https://www.jstor.org/stable/26905380

29. Karanja, K., Kinyili, J., Namusonge, G.: Role of remuneration and career advancement practices on the retention of employees in organizations: evidence from research. Int. J. Adv. Res. Manag. Soc. Sci. **4**(7), 254–279 (2015)

30. Charalampous, M., Grant, C., Tramontano, C., Michailidis, E.: Systematically reviewing remote e-workers' well-being at work: a multidimensional approach. Eur. J. Work Organ. Psy. **28**, 1–23 (2018). https://doi.org/10.1080/1359432X.2018.1541886

31. Kaul, A.: Culture vs strategy: which to precede, which to align? J. Strateg. Manag. **12**(1), 116–136 (2019). https://doi.org/10.1108/JSMA-04-2018-0036

32. Fiordelisi, F., Renneboog, L., Ricci, O., Lopes, S.S.: Creative corporate culture and innovation. J. Int. Finan. Markets. Inst. Money **63**, 101137 (2019). https://doi.org/10.1016/j.intfin.2019. 101137

33. Yukl, G.: Managerial leadership: a review of theory and research. J. Manag. **15**(2), 251–289 (1989). https://doi.org/10.1177/014920638901500207

34. Colbert, A.E., Bono, J.E., Purvanova, R.K.: Flourishing via workplace relationships: moving beyond instrumental support. Acad. Manag. J. **59**(4), 1199–1223 (2016). https://doi.org/10. 5465/amj.2014.0506

35. Sunardi, I., Putri, V.W.: Career satisfaction based on trust and proactive personality. Manag. Anal. J. **9**(1), 35–45. (2020) https://doi.org/10.15294/maj.v9i1.36882

36. Eckert, C.: Corporate reputation and reputation risk: definition and measurement from a (risk) management perspective. J. Risk Financ. **18**(2), 145–158 (2017). https://doi.org/10.1108/JRF-06-2016-0075

37. Helm, S.: Employees' awareness of their impact on corporate reputation. J. Bus. Res. **64**(7), 657–663 (2011). https://doi.org/10.1016/j.jbusres.2010.09.001

38. Collis, J., Hussey, R.: Business Research: A Practical Guide for Undergraduate and Postgraduate Students. Palgrave Macmillan, Basingstoke (2014)

39. Ayoko, O.B., Ashkanasy, N.M.: The physical environment of office work: future open plan offices. Aust. J. Manag. **45**(3), 488–506 (2020). https://doi.org/10.1177/0312896220921913

40. Chacon Vega, R.J., Gale, S.P., Kim, Y., Hong, S., Yang, E.: Does an open-plan office actually work? A workplace gap analysis: importance and perceived support of key activities. J. Corp. Real Estate **22**(4), 261–277 (2020). https://doi.org/10.1108/JCRE-03-2020-0014

Understanding Farmer Perceptions: Impacts on Agricultural IoT Adoption in Western Cape, South Africa

Andrew Kent and Zainab Ruhwanya

University of Cape Town, Cape Town, South Africa
kentand001@myuct.ac.za

Abstract. The Internet of Things (IoT) is a transformative technology with applications in various fields, such as medicine, manufacturing and agriculture. Within agriculture, IoT has been shown to improve food security and profitability while saving costs and resources. Further, studies relating to social aspects of IoT, such as user perspectives and adoption, are limited. The Western Cape's agricultural sector is vulnerable to challenges such as food insecurity and the effects of climate change. Despite this, the adoption of agricultural IoT is uneven within this sector. This study interviewed 17 farmers to gain insights into farmers' perceptions of agricultural IoT, focusing on how these perceptions influence the adoption of IoT within the Western Cape. Pertinent literature was used to construct a combined framework of potential reasons for and against the adoption of IoT within the Western Cape. This research followed a deductive approach by comparing the combined framework with feedback provided by farmers during the interviews. Farmers within the Western Cape cited multiple reasons that influenced their decision to adopt IoT. Farmers reported IoT to be easily accessible while providing a relative advantage over previous systems. Farmers that had not adopted IoT expressed various reasons for doing so. For smaller farming operations, the complex nature of deriving sufficient benefits from IoT did not necessarily justify the costs. Other factors included the cultural change required to adopt new technology and external factors such as insufficient data coverage and governmental support.

Keywords: Internet of Things (IoT) · Agricultural IoT · Farm

1 Introduction

The Internet of Things (IoT) has revolutionised numerous sectors. The application of IoT has radically affected multiple industries, including healthcare, energy, manufacturing, production, agriculture, education and transport. The introduction of IoT is predicted to foster rapid innovation, as it enables machines, devices or things to communicate with other devices via an internet connection [1]. The world is on the cusp of a new era of innovation, as technology that connects machines with the internet enables communication networks between devices [2]. IoT is a logical progression of the internet, as it integrates machine-to-machine communication via sensors [3]. The use of IoT and sensors in agriculture offers benefits in precision farming, which include real-time crop monitoring, soil monitoring, water management and weather forecasting [4].

© The Author(s), under exclusive license to Springer Nature Switzerland AG 2024
A. Gerber (Ed.): SAICSIT 2024, CCIS 2159, pp. 312–330, 2024.
https://doi.org/10.1007/978-3-031-64881-6_18

The application of IoT in creating smart farms in South Africa is a promising prospect, as sensors could improve water management and automation of production and distribution logistics. In recent years, the Western Cape region of South Africa has been severely affected by droughts; accordingly, efficient use of water and other resources is vital [5]. Further extreme weather events such as droughts threaten both food security and economic growth within the Western Cape [6]. The Western Cape's agricultural sector plays a crucial role in South Africa's economy, contributing 14.68% to the national Gross Value Added (GVA) in 2022, with agriculture providing 24% of national agriculture employment and 14% of national formal employment [7]. In addition, the Western Cape is more dependent on horticultural production than the rest of South Africa [7, 8]; horticulture is one area of agriculture that is said to benefit from smart farming with sensors and IoT [4]. Thus, it is essential to ensure the Western Cape's agricultural sector remains economically competitive and resilient to extreme weather by encouraging the adoption of efficient technologies such as IoT.

Despite the potential and benefits of achieving digital transformation, the Western Cape's agricultural sector is limited in its adoption of related IoT technologies. Regarding the countrywide adoption of agricultural IoT, there are issues that are unique to the South African context. These difficulties include unequal racial distributions of IoT technology, the threat of criminal interference, the effect of education level and age on the willingness to adopt IoT, and the possibility of IoT automating jobs, increasing unemployment [9]. Nevertheless, South Africa's agricultural sector has shown a degree of readiness to adopt IoT [5, 9]; however, farmers' perceptions of this technology require further analysis. As farmers are the end users of agricultural IoT, their firsthand experiences may confirm or refute the difficulties of IoT adoption in South Africa and provide a point of departure for addressing such challenges. Therefore, this study's aim is *to investigate how the perceptions of farmers influence the adoption of agricultural IoT in the Western Cape, South Africa.*

This research paper is structured as follows. Section 2 reviews the literature, Sect. 3 discusses the research methodology. Section 4 presents the analysis and findings, Sect. 5 presents the discussion, and the conclusion is presented in Sect. 6.

2 Literature Review

2.1 Perceptions of Technology in South Africa's Agricultural Sector

South Africa's agricultural sector is defined by a dual environment of commercial and small-scale subsistence farmers, who empower many people by providing opportunities for employment and entrepreneurship [7, 10]. However, approximately three decades after the introduction of democracy in South Africa, this sector is still riddled with complexities. The farming industry is still suffering from a broad spectrum of socioeconomic, political, cultural, and racial divisions between commercial and subsistence farmers [11]. The gap within this disparate sector is so severe that it stands out as a uniquely unequal industry even when compared to agricultural sectors in other countries. In most agricultural sectors, it is standard for a range of different sized farms to coexist [12]. Despite some small-scale farmers joining commercial supply chains, the racial and economic division remains entrenched [13].

The adoption of advanced digital technologies, such as IoT, is predicted to empower small-scale farmers to improve efficiency and production [14]. IoT and other technologies commonly associated with the fourth industrial revolution (4IR) certifiably improve production efficiency [15]. However, the nature of this division impacts almost all aspects of this sector, including farmers' attitudes towards adopting technology. Well-resourced commercial farmers in South Africa are aware of the benefits of introducing agricultural technology [14]. Accordingly, they are often quick to adopt and implement the latest technology to improve production [14]. This suggests that commercial farms positively perceive technologies such as IoT and are likely to implement IoT-based devices. However, the perception of technology amongst small-scale farmers may differ significantly from commercial farms.

In addition, in a South African context, there are concerns that such implementations may exacerbate this divide in the agricultural setting and affect technology adoption [9]. These concerns include the threat of IoT automation causing unemployment, potentially prompting farmers to avoid the adoption of IoT [9]. South Africa's skills shortage also plays a role, as farmers may be unable to source the required technical knowledge to implement and maintain IoT devices. These factors, combined with a lack of governmental support and insufficient infrastructure, indicate there may be conflicting perceptions of IoT [14]. There is also the consideration of expensive IoT devices being stolen [9]. In small-scale farming, where there is vulnerability to food insecurity and poverty, farmers would often practice a conservative and low-risk attitude to preserve their livelihoods. For farmers in a position to implement IoT, their perceptions could be positive, while others, particularly in rural areas affected by multiple challenges, may perceive it as an unobtainable resource [14]. Accordingly, the commonly expensive implementation of advanced digital technologies is an arduous barrier to adoption for farmers.

South Africa is defined by multiculturalism as it is home to a population with numerous religions, cultures, languages and beliefs. Considering South Africa's magnitude of cultural systems and societal dynamics, perceptions of technology within these groups often differ [15, 16] as some cultures do not utilise agriculture for commercial purposes [16]. For example, rearing livestock within the Zulu community often relates to prestige as the community merits farmers based on their livestock and not necessarily their commercial outcomes [16]. In such an example, encouraging members of this community to utilise IoT for production and efficiency could potentially contradict their beliefs. Undermining cultural practices may lead to negative perceptions of technology and other conflicts; thus, respecting and accommodating beliefs is crucial.

Education and age play a role in forming perceptions. Well-educated farmers tend to show more willingness to adopt technology such as IoT, while less educated farmers may lack the required exposure to understand its benefits [9]. Age is relevant in forming perceptions as younger farmers are potentially more technically inclined and often show a greater willingness to adopt agricultural technologies such as IoT [9].

Furthermore, the Western Cape is subject to the dual nature of South Africa's agricultural economy and the subsequent factors that may determine the perceptions of technology adoption. Most small-scale farmers in the Western Cape's rural areas operate with inadequate infrastructure, ensuring limited access to digital technology [17]. However, the Western Cape differs from the rest of South Africa as it is increasingly exposed to the requirements of its foreign export market in Europe [7, 17, 18]. In addition, the Western Cape is particularly vulnerable to natural resource scarcity, such as land and water shortages, due to population growth and climate change [6, 7, 17].

2.2 Adoption of Climate-Smart Agriculture (CSA)

Climate-smart agriculture (CSA) refers to various environmental agricultural practices that sustainably improve production and encourage resilience to climate change [19]. Given the European influence on South African agriculture, many regulations require agricultural sectors to be more environmentally friendly, and CSA technologies can be a solution. IoT is a central CSA technology [20]. Long et al. [19] conducted a study using qualitative, semi-structured interviews with farmers to examine the challenges of CSA technology adoption in Switzerland, the Netherlands, France, and Italy. Further, a theoretical framework was developed that highlighted the most common barriers [19] (Table 1)

Table 1. Barriers to the Adoption of CSA Technology, as reported by European Farmers, adapted from [19]

Reported Barriers to Adoption from [19]
• Insufficient awareness of CSA and technical language barriers
• High initial costs of CSA implementation and the lengthy period before the return on investment (ROI) is realised
• Uncertainty regarding the impact of implementing CSA
• Challenges with Regulatory or Policy requirements
• Difficulties in contacting and upskilling farmers
• Research, development and policies differing from the actual requirements or nuances of adopting CSA
• Financial Impact on the farmer's customers
• Farmers not receiving the benefits of CSA, as they may instead reach other parties in the supply chain

In comparing the perceptions of CSA technologies in Europe, several factors may be mirrored in markets and sectors like the South African agricultural sector [14, 19]. In applying the lens of this framework to South Africa's agricultural sector, many similar challenges are evident, except magnified by South Africa's dual agricultural system. These factors include CSA technology's expensive nature. Technical language barriers are also worsened in South Africa by a skills shortage [14, 21]. Many technology-focused, sustainable agricultural practices are disseminated using complex, academic terminology limiting accessibility to uneducated farmers [21]. South African subsistence farmers in rural areas are likely to have insufficient awareness of agricultural technologies and a limited financial budget to invest in any non-essential equipment [14].

However, the above framework used to analyse perceptions in Europe is limited, as it focuses on developed economies and barriers to adoption as opposed to positive perceptions or benefits [19]. Given the limitations of this framework, there is a need to supplement it with research that includes both positive and negative perceptions of agricultural technology adoption in a developing economy. In terms of comparative emerging economies, India's agricultural sector has similarities with South Africa, which may provide useful insights [22].

2.3 Behavioural Reasoning Theory and the Adoption of IoT

The behavioural reasoning theory (BRT), analyses people's beliefs, reasons or motives and the subsequent influence such motives have on one's behaviour [23]. The all-encompassing proposition of BRT "states that reasons serve as important linkages between people's beliefs, global motives (e.g., attitudes, subjective norms, and perceived control), intentions, and behaviour" [22. p. 115]. The BRT provides adoption and resistance reasons and has been utilised in the adoption of IoT in different sectors, including healthcare [24] and agriculture [25]. Reasons relate to the perceptions used to justify and explain one's behaviour [23–25]. Pillai & Sivathanu [25] surveyed farmers in India to analyse the reasons for and against adopting IoT within this agricultural sector. Using BRT, the *reasons for* agricultural IoT adoption in India are "*relative advantage, social influence, perceived convenience, and perceived usefulness*", while the *reasons against* it are "*image barrier, technological anxiety, perceived price, and perceived risk*" [24. p. 136].

Reasons For. Relative advantage refers to a new technology's advantage over an incumbent system. Social influence refers to the influence of peers and competitors in forming a perception. Peers and competitors may encourage the adoption in the Western Cape, as utilising the latest technology often ensures a competitive edge [17]. Perceived usefulness and perceived convenience may also play a role, as commercial farmers in the Western Cape have historically been early adopters of useful technology [15, 17]. In this context, perceived usefulness refers to the extent to which an IoT system is user-friendly [25].

Reasons Against. Technological anxiety refers to the belief that the technical aspects of using IoT may be too advanced to implement [24, 25]. Perceived risk also negatively influences the adoption of agricultural IoT as farmers feel the use of IoT may result in consequences such as having sensitive data leaked [24, 25]. In a South African context, the skills shortage may encourage technical risk and anxiety, potentially leading to a negative perception of IoT [9, 14]. The image barrier of IoT refers to potential users' perceptions that IoT is ineffective in providing value to operations [25]. In a South African context, in areas where there is limited digital infrastructure, an image barrier has the potential to further establish the perception of IoT as being unobtainable. The perceived price of IoT is also a potential factor in a South African context. For example, subsistence farmers who face food insecurity and poverty may not have the financial resources to adopt expensive technologies such as IoT [14]. Global Motives, Intentions and Behaviour.

2.4 Combined Theoretical Framework

The two studies that utilised BRT in India and CSA in Europe helped in identifying key factors that can be applied in analysing farmers' perceptions in the Western Cape. However, neither of the frameworks could solely account for the unique aspects of South Africa's agricultural sector, such as its dual nature and cultural influences. Further, the study done in Europe [19] only included negative perceptions or barriers to IoT adoption. The study done in India by [25] included both positive and negative factors but only in the form of a survey, where nuanced feedback by the farmers was not provided.

Therefore, considering these limitations, a combined theoretical framework will be utilised using BRT (reasons for and reasons against) and other factors from the literature review that influence the perceptions of agricultural IoT in India, South Africa and Europe. This framework serves as a benchmark for analysing and comparing feedback provided by farmers in the Western Cape through qualitative semi-structured interviews (Table 2).

Table 2. Combined Reasons for and Against Adopting Agricultural IoT in South Africa.

Reasons For	Reasons Against
• Relative Advantage • Social Influence • Perceived Convenience • Perceived Usability	• Lack of Value or Benefit to the particular Situation of the Farmer • Insufficient Technical Skills or Knowledge of IoT • Financial or Cost Implications of IoT • Governmental or Policy Issues & Insufficient Digital Infrastructure • Threat of IoT Creating Unemployment • Threat of Crime or IoT devices being stolen • Cultural Reasons

3 Methodology

The research utilised a deductive approach to theory [27], drawing on the combined framework from the BRT and CSA. Qualitative data was gathered through semi-structured interviews, allowing for nuanced insights into the reasons for and against adopting agricultural IoT. Two sampling methods, stratified sampling and judgment sampling, were employed to ensure a broader representation of the population [28]. The use of judgment sampling targeted knowledgeable farmers, such as senior leaders from agricultural groups, a commercial farmer with 12 years of industry experience, and a subsistence farmer who operates as an agricultural community advisor. Data was collected from 17 participants. Participants were stratified into small, medium, and large-scale farms in the Western Cape, as shown in Table 3.

Table 3. Participants details

Farming Purpose	Commercial			Subsistence	
Scale	Large	Medium	Small	Medium	Small
No. of farms that have Adopted IoT	5	1	–	–	–
No. of farms that have not Adopted IoT	1	4	3	1	2

4   Data Analysis and Findings

Data were analysed using thematic analysis [29]. The details of each farmer have been formatted into pseudonyms, including the initials of their farm's scale and purpose. Farmers that have adopted IoT have the number "1" signified in parenthesis in their pseudonyms, while farmers that have not adopted IoT are assigned a "2", as displayed in Table 4.

Table 4. Pseudonyms of Participants.

Pseudonym	Explanation
Participant 1 (L, C, 1)	Large-scale, commercial farmer that has adopted IoT
Participant 1 (S, S, 2)	Small-scale, subsistence farm that has not adopted IoT

Famers Who Have Adopted IoT. IoT is used for farming purposes in the following ways: Crop or plant health monitoring via drones and sensors; Smart irrigation systems; Cold room temperature monitoring; Packing, Quality and Employee management information for packhouses; A smart silo for poultry farming; Weather stations that provide predictive data on the weather, insects and diseases; Plant weight monitoring scales; Harvesting assistant systems that transport produce that has been picked, automatically tracking the productivity of each farm worker.

Type of Farming. Among all farmers interviewed, the types of farming produce included fruit (citrus, wine, berries), poultry, cattle, pork, sheep, vegetables (olives, spinach, onion, pumpkins, celery, parsley), beekeeping, and wheat.

4.1   Reasons for the Adoption of Agricultural IoT

Farmers that have adopted IoT cited reasons that fell between two main themes. These themes refer to reasons external to the farmer's operations, such as the advice of peers or internal reasons, such as improving their business operations. "In our group, it's (IoT) absolutely essential. I couldn't see us being able to continue farming without it." Participant 6 (L, C, 1).

Internal Reasons

Decision making, *Control and Automation.* When participants described the advantage IoT held over previous systems, their answers were divided between three main factors. Namely, these factors referred to improved decision-making, control and the automation of manual processes. The participants explained that the data IoT provides is essential for making informed decisions. "IoT has provided the ability to see the matrix of important matters that make it viable to keep your business going. It provides an integrated view of everything that matters. This includes fuel levels, productivity and level of mechanisation in the packhouse." Participant 1 (L, C, 1). In addition, participants stated that IoT provides data and functionality that enhances their level of control. "On the production side, we can turn pumps off and on, and monitor fertiliser going into a field. In this case, it's not only monitoring but also controlling systems." Participant 1 (L, C,1). Participants also frequently mentioned that IoT automated many manual processes. "Before, we would weigh and measure everything manually. The sensors have made our jobs far easier. Initially, you needed four to five people working the chicken house. With this technology, we now need only one person to oversee 25 000 hens. Everything is automated through these sensors." Participant 4 (M, C, 1).

Perceived Convenience and Usability. Most participants who had adopted IoT expressed that they benefited from its accessible nature. In particular, they found IoT to be easy and convenient to use. This participant cited the convenience of remotely controlling their operation as crucial. "the moment your operation grows and functions in various broad environments, managing it remotely via IoT becomes crucial. If you diversify the operations in geographic locations, the need for IoT becomes very important... I need to be able to view and analyse the marketing information of our farms directly." Participant 1 (L, C, 1). In terms of usability. The participants referred to the straightforward nature of accessing their IoT devices. "once it's set up, it's a friendly app on your phone." Participant 5 (L, C, 1). "it needs to be simple and uncomplicated for farmers to use it successfully." Participant 2 (L, C, 1).

External Reasons

Most participants spoke positively about IoT's direct impact on their operation. However, some were primarily or initially influenced by external factors in their decision to adopt IoT. These factors are divided between the social influence of peers and meeting customer or compliance needs. "IoT is important for the retailers that we sell to" Participant 3 (L, C, 1).

Social Influence. The Recommendation from Peer; Three of the six farmers stated that members of their community, such as farming associations, friends, business partners and other farmers, influenced their decision to adopt IoT. "Other farmers and business partners informed us about IoT... We needed this information about internet and cloud-based irrigation systems because you can't farm blueberries without it." Participant 5 (L, C, 1). Participants that were not influenced by any external parties to adopt IoT stated that they independently researched IoT before deciding to adopt it. "We see ourselves as ahead of the pack in this perspective... Essentially we focused on implementing IoT due to our own research more than we did from the recommendations of others." Participant 6 (L, C, 1).

Compliance or Third-Party Requirements. Ensuring Compliance and Quality Assurance; Two of the six farmers stated that IoT helped ensure they met regulatory and legal requirements, especially in exporting products to foreign markets. "The overseas markets require audits of the suppliers where they ensure we are in compliance and producing goods according to their standards… We couldn't supply all the required information for these audits without proper programs." Participant 4 (L, C, 1). Some participants were encouraged to adopt IoT due to its ability to assist with ensuring the quality of produce, as per the requirements of their clients. "If the client accuses us of selling them rotten meat… We can use the readings and stored data to illustrate the temperatures the meat has been stored and prove the fault is not on our side." Participant 3 (L, C, 1).

4.2 Reasons Against the Adoption of Agricultural IoT

Cost versus Benefit

Cost and financial implications were the most commonly referenced reasons against adopting agricultural IoT by the participants. When asked to expand on the details of such financial implications, most participants would qualify the costs in relation to the value or benefit that IoT could provide their operation. "I'd have to calculate a cost to benefit from this technology. I'm not going to spend R100 000 on something that I'm never going to get back. One has to weigh up; over what time frame will this thing pay for itself? There has to be a sufficient benefit to using it. Cost to benefit would always be a consideration…" Participant 4 (L, C, 2).

Of the farmers that had adopted IoT but still wished to share negative feedback, one participant explicitly expressed that the challenges of adopting were worth the provided benefits. "While I have some major concerns, the value IoT adds makes it worth utilising." participant 1 (L, C, 1).

Financial or Cost Implications Initial or Purchase Cost. Several small-scale farmers expressed that the purchase costs excluded them from being able to adopt IoT. "It's only the initial costs that prevent me from using it. This is normally true for smaller farmers like myself. However, I think the return on investment will be high enough over the long term for the purchase to be worth it." Participant 7 (M, C, 2).

Operational Costs. Participants who either had attempted to adopt IoT or had shown a level of adoption of IoT were concerned with the varied operational costs required to run an IoT system. "…the capital required to use IoT may be more expensive than leaving the process in its manual form… Every system that you use will have a cost. When you layer each system together, it becomes expensive." Participant 1 (L, C, 1). These costs include ensuring that infrastructure can sustain IoT. "I also don't have either internet or power at most sections of the farm. There's an additional cost to getting your infrastructure ready to have IoT devices." Participant 2 (M, C, 2).

Service Provider Costs. Three participants shared their experience of attempting to hire external service providers specialising in building IoT systems. These participants found the service providers to be costly while providing limited tailor-made solutions to fit the participant's unique requirements. "If you want to implement any IoT setup and you go to a commercial company, they will charge a lot of money… Sometimes the commercial guys are not specific enough to cater for my needs, which means I'll pay a lot of money for services I don't actually need." Participant 2 (M, C, 2).

Lack of Value or Benefit

Adding Complexity to an Established System. Seven of the eleven participants felt that IoT would be beneficial to their operations if adopted. However, several of these participants stated they did not have a specific need to adopt IoT, as their current system functions adequately. "In my specific situation, I don't have a need for IoT devices." Participant 4 (L, C, 2). This farmer provided examples of how adopting IoT may complicate their established system. "I always try to look at things holistically. I'm not looking just at the cost factor of purchasing alone because if I looked only at the cost factor, I'm pretty sure I would be able to justify it. However, I'm looking not only at the cost but, I'm also looking at the security (the cost of replacing stolen devices) and I'm looking at the nuisance factor. I have to take all of these things, put them together and say, which is simpler for me? It's the whole problem of installing, maintaining and ensuring the physical security of IoT, not the single problem of cost. It becomes a security risk, it becomes an economic risk." Participant 1 (M, C, 2).

IoT is More Suited to Larger Operations. Several small-scale farmers questioned the need for IoT within their operations, as they were able to use non-digital means to monitor their farms. "I often walk the fields. It's a small enough farm to do so, and the best feedback I've received is from field walks... Our field is small enough that I could look at an area and tell it's not growing well." Participant 5 (S, C, 2). "It's not that it is not beneficial. It's that our farm is too small to justify the cost." Participant 6 (S, C, 2).

IoT Service Providers Offer Insufficient Solutions. Several participants expressed that the service offerings of companies that provided agricultural IoT solutions did not meet the required standards. In particular, the participants felt the service providers did not understand their unique needs. "The resistance to IoT, in my mind, is the challenge of real-world application and the disconnect of service providers. They do not have a full idea of what is happening on the farm... IoT Service providers aren't generally agricultural experts. They don't know basic agronomist principles. IoT may be more suited to larger commercial farmers that can employ agrologists and other agri-experts." Participant 6 (S, C, 2). "I've found that some people sit on computers but don't have any experience on farms in the real world. I don't trust IoT or these service providers most of the time unless they can show me the data of what they've done. They provide half-developed systems hoping to use the data to improve and refine the system. However, we're paying for their system to learn, which is irritating and a waste of money." Participant 2 (L, C, 1). However, one farmer felt their service provider sufficiently met expectations. "Any system we struggle to use evolves quickly with the help of a service provider. All of our IoT service providers are constantly upgrading and fine-tuning and even tailor-making IoT applications to suit our needs." Participant 1 (L, C, 1).

Personal or Organisational Factors

Culture was only directly mentioned as a consideration by four of the eleven participants that had not adopted IoT. However, the participants often mentioned factors related to culture in determining their perspectives on IoT. This included elements such as habits, personal beliefs, trust of technology, expertise and awareness. "With the adoption of new technologies, you'll need to upskill employees and create new habits. This can take anywhere from one to five years. I suppose there is a huge barrier to entry into the agricultural space related to habits. I know of a group from America who changed to a new IoT system and it was a mess. The company almost went down because they underestimated the culture that is required for the system to operate. When IoT is adopted, there is a culture change and there is an expertise change." Participant 1 (L, C, 1).

Awareness or Knowledge of IoT. Five of the eleven participants that had not adopted IoT expressed that they were reasonably familiar with IoT within agriculture. Two of the participants that expressed a lack of familiarity also mentioned that they were uncertain as to how or where they could gain such knowledge. "I have limited knowledge of IoT. I don't get exposed to it... Although I haven't investigated IoT thoroughly. It is possible that I don't know where to look. Unless you go into the type of places that work with technology, you won't be exposed to it. I don't know what's available." Participant 4 (L, C, 2).

Insufficient Technical Skills

Belief that the Technical Skills are Obtainable. Most participants felt undeterred by the technical skills required to utilise IoT. While they were not certain of the required skills, they felt confident that these skills could be ascertained. "I wouldn't say that I've very tech savvy, but I have faith that I could figure it out." Participant 5 (S, C, 1). "I'm not daunted by anything practical. In my mind, it's just like big boys Lego for me... It's purely a step-by-step for me. It's very logical." Participant 4 (L, C, 2).

Technical Skills: Software Engineering and Cybersecurity Skills. Several participants stated that technical skills such as software engineering and cybersecurity are considerations towards the use of IoT. "...For our requirements there are programming skills required to tailor-make the sensor or app for our needs. My skills are lagging regarding programming." Participant 2 (M, C, 2). "Hackers can take down your internet-based devices for two, three, or four days. If your system is too integrated without overriding mechanisms, where you can go manual, your business can quickly go underwater. Cybersecurity within IoT should never be underestimated." Participant 1 (L, C, 1).

Trust

Privacy Concerns and Mistrust of Technology. Several participants stated that the interconnected nature of IoT exposes them to the possibility of privacy violations. "This technology is very useful but it can be dangerous and exploited by other humans with bad intentions. What's private to me should remain private to me..." Participant 3 (L, C, 1). Further, one participant felt that they minimised their reliance on external systems by not relying on internet technology. "...By not relying on traditional systems and operating off the grid, we can produce food self-sufficiently. Should there be a shutdown of any form, we'd be able to carry on." Participant 2 (M, S, 2). Multiple participants questioned the efficacy of solely relying on IoT as a source of information within their operation. In particular, these participants expressed concern that IoT devices may relay data inaccurately. "...There needs to be a balance between using the internet of things and actually getting your feet on the ground on the farm. I'll still need to check these problem areas in person and take my own soil sample or reading to confirm the data. I wouldn't rely on just sitting in my office, hoping for the best and trusting the data without getting out there myself" Participant 2 (L, C, 1).

Culture

Traditional Practices or Ancestral Knowledge. One farmer stated that their considerable generational knowledge potentially provided more value than adopting IoT. "...We've farmed this land for five generations. We gathered information over the years about the soil and crops... When we do decision-making, we already have generations worth of information to help us." Participant 6 (S, C, 2). Another felt that traditional methods of agriculture do not necessarily combine well with the use of IoT. "There's a lot of tradition with soil and ancestry... much of the land has been left by great-great-grandfathers" Participant 3 (S, S, 2).

Preference for Organic Methods. Three participants expressed a preference for natural methods of farming over the use of technology. "I have a very strong belief in organic processes and keeping technology out of the processes." Participant 2 (M, S, 2). "I love to go and feel and touch my soil. It's the contact between me and the soil. Culturally I need to go and touch the soil. If I had IoT, I might not spend that much time with the soil..." Participant 3 (S, S, 2).

Organisational Culture Change. Several participants expressed that employees within an organisation can be challenged by the cultural change required to adopt IoT. "...There are still staff members in our operation that don't see the full potential of what they gain by using these systems. They aren't resistant to IoT, but they're also not fully aware of how much easier IoT can make their lives." Participant 6 (L, C, 1). "We work with employees that have either basic or no education that have to use a phone or higher-grade software and devices to perform certain tasks. IoT requires extra effort to teach." Participant 2 (L, C, 1).

External Factors

While cost versus benefit and personal or organisational factors were top of mind for most participants; they also expressed concern for external factors. These factors are generally outside of the participants direct control, such as data coverage and power outage within their area or governmental issues. The following farmer had a degree of IoT adoption within their operation; however, several external concerns prevented comprehensive adoption. "We won't be able to use IoT unless we have full WiFi installed around the farm. How will these things be powered? What if Eskom [Eskom is the South African national electricity power supplier supplier] goes down? If Eskom goes down, then the data is lost." Participant 3 (L, C, 1).

Governmental or Policy Issues. When participants were asked to expand on their views toward the government's role in their adoption of agricultural IoT, their statements were majority negative. "There is no attitude towards government. They do nothing for farming. There's no subsidisation or any assistance. They are grossly inefficient..." Participant 8 (M, C, 2). However, one farmer shared an experience where the government was instrumental in promoting agricultural Technology. "While I was studying at Elsenburg, the Western Cape Government tried to promote technology... They worked hard to promote it." Participant 7 (M, C, 2).

Insufficient Digital Infrastructure. Multiple participants are based in areas with limited data coverage. These participants explained that attempting to use IoT within an area with limited coverage is challenging. "It's one of the key issues. If you've got no cellphone coverage, you're wasting your time. That's the bottom line. ...This is a very significant limiting factor for me." Participant 1 (M, C, 2).

Threat of IoT Creating Unemployment. None of the participants viewed the possibility of IoT automating processes and creating unemployment as a current factor that prevented the adoption of IoT. "I think the technology isn't quite there yet in terms of automating manual jobs entirely. The fruit on our farms still actually needs to be picked by a person... I think it's a while to go before workers are pushed out of the fields by machines... As of now, I don't see it as a risk to employment." Participant 6 (L, C, 1). Several participants stated that the efficiency of IoT would allow them to grow employment opportunities within their operations. "We'd simply become more efficient as the company grows and ultimately employ more people." Participant 3 (S, C, 2). One participant stated that IoT had played a role in automating some positions, causing unemployment within their operation. However, this participant also explained that most employees had been accommodated. "Over the last 20 years, we've changed from manual processes to automating 60\% of the operation. Fortunately, the business grew so we could accommodate most employees; however, some were made redundant." Participant 1 (L, C, 1).

Threat of Crime or IoT Devices Being Stolen. Several farmers in exposed areas expressed concern regarding the possibility of having their IoT devices stolen. "This would be the biggest problem. It would be stolen the day after being implemented. The area we farm in is very high risk. Any equipment we use is at risk of being stolen." Participant 1 (S, S, 2).

5   Discussion

The following section discusses the identified relationships between farmers' perceptions and the adoption of agricultural IoT in the Western Cape. This section also explains why these relationships exist and their subsequent boundaries. These relationships and findings are discussed comparatively to the criteria found in the combined framework and existing literature.

5.1   Reasons for the Adoption of Agricultural IoT in the Western Cape

Internal Factors
Relative Advantage. Large-scale farmers within the Western Cape are internationally competitive, often depending on the latest technology to ensure a competitive edge [17]. The participants stated that IoT provides a relative advantage over the previous systems

by significantly improving decision-making and control while automating manual processes. The participants positively described this relative advantage as a clear incentive to adopt agricultural IoT.

Accessibility. Perceived convenience and usability were initially separate concepts within the combined framework. However, participant feedback regarding these factors overlapped to the point of being combined into one factor of accessibility. Large-scale farms are defined as farms that are larger than 100 ha [30]. Most farmers that adopted IoT met this criteria and further described their operations as multifaceted or complex. For commercial farmers that operate over large geographic areas, the convenience of remotely managing their operations is crucial. In terms of usability, the participants supported this factor by describing IoT as to easy to use once it had been set up.

External Reasons
Social Influence. Multiple participants stated that the recommendations of friends, business partners and farming associations positively contributed to their decision to adopt agricultural IoT.

Compliance or Third-Party Requirements. Large-scale commercial farms within the Western Cape are significantly impacted by the regulations and requirements of their export markets [17]. Accordingly, the participants in this study confirmed that IoT is beneficial in assisting farms to meet these requirements. Specifically, IoT is useful in providing data for auditing purposes and quality assurance of produce.

5.2   Reasons Against the Adoption of Agricultural IoT in the Western Cape

Cost versus Benefit
Financial or Cost Implications. The expensive nature of digital technology is a challenging obstacle to adoption for small-scale farmers [14]. The participants strongly supported this notion, as cost was frequently mentioned as a concern in their consideration of adopting agricultural IoT. However, small-scale farmers are not the only affected party, as medium and large-scale participants also shared concerns about the varied costs of IoT. Most large-scale commercial participants were able to tolerate the cost of IoT. However, the majority of the medium to small-scale farmers found IoT not to be a financially viable option.

Lack of Value or Benefit. Given the expensive nature of IoT, participants, frequently questioned the benefit they would receive from its adoption. Several farmers doubted whether the benefit was worth the complexity of digitising an established and functional system. Smaller farmers challenged the value of IoT in their operations as they were comfortable with non-digital means of monitoring. Further, these farms found that IoT service providers offered solutions that were too generic to add value to their unique operations. One large-scale farmer explained that the challenges of adopting IoT were worth overcoming to enjoy the benefits. Essentially well-resourced, large-scale farmers are more likely to require IoT within their operations. Accordingly, they will overcome the challenges in cost or complexity to ensure they adopt IoT. Contrastingly, smaller farms with limited resources must carefully consider if the costs are worth the benefit, often preventing the adoption of agricultural IoT.

Personal or Organisational Factors

Culture. South Africa's population is characterised by multiculturalism and is home to people with various religions, cultures and beliefs [15]. Perceptions of technology between such cultural groups often differ. The findings supported such sentiments as participants described several cultural factors in their decision to avoid adopting IoT. Participants who were small-scale or subsistence farmers often preferred organic or natural agricultural processes and generally limited their use of technology. Several farmers mentioned the traditions and knowledge passed down by previous generations as deterrents in their consideration of IoT. Cultural factors also affect larger or medium-sized commercial farms. Multiple participants spoke of the challenge of organisational culture change. Specifically, for established farms, employees may be hesitant to change or require training when IoT is introduced into the operation.

Awareness. South African subsistence farmers that operate in rural areas are more likely to have a limited awareness of new technology [14]. Multiple participants expressed a general lack of familiarity and awareness of IoT. These participants were not limited to small-scale subsistence farmers but also included medium to large-scale commercial farms. Two participants stated they were uncertain how or where they could gain suitable information regarding IoT and how to implement it in their operations. Their feedback suggests that knowledge and awareness of IoT is a consideration that is not limited to only subsistence farmers.

Trust. Trust was not included directly in the combined framework or explicitly noted within the literature review. However, the participants frequently mentioned matters relating to trust in their consideration of adopting agricultural IoT. IoT is a data-centric technology that gathers potentially private or sensitive user data [31]. Accordingly, trust and privacy are essential elements for consumers considering the adoption of IoT [31]. Participants from every sub-population, including commercial and subsistence farmers, shared concerns regarding trust and privacy. Several farmers expressed concern regarding the threat of malicious actors breaching digital IoT systems and accessing sensitive data. One farmer expressed general mistrust of digital technology and wished to operate without relying on technical systems.

Technical Skills. Agriculture within the Western Cape is generally limited by a lack of technical skills and expertise [17]. Most participants felt undeterred by the technical skills required to adopt agricultural IoT. However, these participants were usually unsure of the exact skills required to use IoT but stated that they were confident in their abilities to acquire these skills. Several participants who had experience in either successfully adopting or attempting to adopt IoT expressed that the required skillset should not be underestimated. This skillset included software engineering capabilities to construct specialised IoT solutions and cybersecurity skills to ensure the privacy and information security of the operation. The participants that mentioned these skills felt that learning or applying them in practice is complicated and should not be underestimated.

External Factors

Government or Policy Issues. South Africa's government has an established reputation for corruption [9]. Accordingly, financial or policy support for farmers looking to implement new technologies may be significantly limited [9, 32]. The participants supported such assertions as they expressed overly negative views towards South Africa's government. Small and medium-scale participants frequently mentioned they would not risk relying on government assistance, as they were unlikely to receive any benefit. In cases where farmers may require assistance regarding knowledge or financial factors, this perception towards the government limits the adoption of agricultural IoT.

Insufficient Digital Infrastructure. Farmers that operate in rural or remote areas endure limited access to infrastructure such as electricity and data coverage [14]. Multiple participants shared this experience. Further, they stated that the complication of ensuring consistent internet access is a limiting factor in their consideration of adopting agricultural IoT.

Threat of IoT creating Unemployment. The vast majority of participants felt that the possibility of IoT automating jobs within their operation was not a factor in determining their adoption of IoT [9]. Technological innovations within the agricultural sector may cause unemployment over the short term. However, over extended periods, the benefits of such innovation may ensure that farmers can remain competitive and ultimately employ more people as their business grows [9]. Participants were able to give examples of this sentiment. Participants who had adopted IoT explained that despite the automation of manual processes, most tasks still require a degree of human interaction. Further, they felt that IoT is crucial in managing their operations, ultimately ensuring the creation of jobs. Most small or medium-scale farmers stated that IoT has the potential to grow their operations or increase efficiency. These participants felt their employees would be accommodated to perform other tasks, and new employees would be hired as the business grew.

Threat of Crime or IoT Devices Being Stolen. Expensive IoT devices may often operate in exposed areas and are vulnerable to theft [9]. Several participants cited crime as a consideration in their adoption of not only IoT but any expensive technology that may be subject to theft. One participant stated that the possibility of theft is their primary concern regarding adopting IoT, as they are located in an area highly exposed to crime.

6 Conclusion

This section combines the above findings and discussions to answer the primary research question. Specifically, to explain how farmers' perceptions influence the adoption of agricultural IoT within the Western Cape. The dual nature of South Africa's agricultural sector plays a central role in shaping farmers' perceptions. For example, well-resourced commercial farmers perceive technology differently from smaller or subsistence farmers. Large-scale commercial farms in the Western Cape are competitive internationally, operating over vast geographic locations. Accordingly, large-scale farms have prioritised adopting IoT as it provides a relative advantage, enabling these farms to maintain their competitive edge. Further, the accessibility of IoT is essential in seamlessly and remotely managing complex and large agricultural operations.

External factors also encourage the adoption of agricultural IoT within the Western Cape. This includes positive recommendations or social influence from a farmer's community. Commercial farms within the Western Cape are significant exporters and must adhere to their customers' regulatory or product requirements. Commercial farmers accordingly adopt IoT, as its data tracking capabilities assists in meeting compliance standards and performing quality assurance. Farmers within the Western Cape commonly perceive cost or financial implications as a consideration before adopting IoT. Smaller farmers that are not well-resourced are immediately excluded from being able to adopt expensive IoT devices. Farms that are well-provisioned may still be deterred from using IoT, as deriving value from its systems is not a simple process. Farmers may have to consider the complexity and suitability of adopting IoT within their operations. Even well-provisioned large-scale commercial farmers listed multiple challenges in adopting and using IoT. The role of personal or organisational factors also influences the adoption of IoT within the Western Cape. South Africa is home to a range of cultural and traditional beliefs. Accordingly, perceptions of technologies between cultures often differ. Specifically, smaller and subsistence farms often prefer traditional or organic methods over technology such as IoT. Some employees within farming organisations are hesitant to embrace IoT within their established system.

As IoT is a data-reliant technology, farmers within the Western Cape are reluctant to adopt it due to privacy concerns. Further, cybersecurity skills are required to ensure an IoT system's privacy. Farmers attempting to implement specialised IoT solutions within their operations may also need to acquire software engineering skills. Essentially, several unique and challenging skills are required to adopt agricultural IoT. Multiple external factors may further limit the adoption of agricultural IoT within the western Cape. Namely, limited digital infrastructure, such as poor data coverage in remote areas, discourages farmers from being able to implement internet-based technology. Farmers that operate in areas at risk of crime cannot use expensive IoT devices that may quickly be stolen. Further, farmers within the Western Cape hold a generally pessimistic view towards governmental assistance or policies. Accordingly, farmers believe they are unlikely to receive any benefits, such as training or funding, from the government that could assist in the adoption of agricultural IoT.

The limitation of this study is in the use of qualitative data, which may limit its ability to generalise. Additionally, the small sample size of only 17 farms may not be fully representative of all farmers in the Western Cape. The thematic analysis approach, while flexible, can also introduce inconsistencies in the research process. To address this limitation, we followed a six-step process developed by Nowell et al.[33]. The researchers' subjective judgment in selecting codes and themes could also introduce potential bias into the data analysis.

For future research, we recommend combining qualitative and quantitative analyses to provide a more comprehensive overview of the findings. We also recommend focusing on a single sub-population, such as small-scale farmers, to gain additional insights specific to those farmers. This study exclusively focused on the perceptions of farmers towards agricultural IoT adoption. Other experts may also have valuable information on what factors currently influence the adoption of agricultural IoT. Therefore, future research could focus on the adoption of agricultural IoT from the perspectives of technical experts such as IoT service providers or engineers.

References

1. Islam, N., Marinakis, Y., Majadillas, M.A., Fink, M., Walsh, S.T.: Here there be dragons, a pre-roadmap construct for IoT service infrastructure. Technol. Forecast. Soc. Chang. **155**, 119073 (2020)
2. Edquist, H., Goodridge, P., Haskel, J.: The Internet of Things and economic growth in a panel of countries. Econ. Innov. New Technol. **30**, 262–283 (2021)
3. Abdalgawad, N., Sajun, A., Kaddoura, Y., Zualkernan, I.A., Aloul, F.: Generative deep learning to detect cyberattacks for the IoT-23 dataset. IEEE Access. **10**, 6430–6441 (2021)
4. Rajak, P., Ganguly, A., Adhikary, S., Bhattacharya, S.: Internet of Things and smart sensors in agriculture: scopes and challenges. J. Agric. Food Res. **14**, 100776 (2023). https://doi.org/10.1016/j.jafr.2023.100776
5. Botha, E., Malekian, R., Ijiga, O.E.: IoT in Agriculture: enhanced throughput in South African farming applications. In: 2019 IEEE 2nd Wireless Africa Conference (WAC). pp. 1–5. IEEE (2019)
6. Zwane, E.M.: Impact of climate change on primary agriculture, water sources and food security in Western Cape, South Africa. Jàmbá: J. Disaster Risk Stud. **11**, 1–7 (2019)
7. Maseko, S., Mrwebi, B.: 2024 Sustainable Agriculture Market Intelligence Report – GreenCape. Greencape (2024)
8. Morokong, T., Sibulali, A., Murdoch, J.: Western Cape Agricultural Sector Profile: 2022. Western Cape Department of Agriculture (2022)
9. Soeker, I., Lusinga, S., Chigona, W.: Readiness of the South African Agricultural Sector to Implement IoT. arXiv preprint arXiv:2108.10081. (2021)
10. STATS SA: Agricultural survey, 2022 (2023)
11. Pienaar, L., Traub, L.: Understanding the smallholder farmer in South Africa: Towards a sustainable livelihoods classification (2015)
12. Kirsten, J.F., Van Zyl, J.: Defining small-scale farmers in the South African context. Agrekon **37**, 551–562 (1998)
13. Sihlobo, W., Kirsten, J.: How to narrow the big divide between black and white farmers in South Africa. He Conversation **3**, 30 (2021)
14. Nkambule, T.B., Agholor, A.I.: Information Communication Technology as a tool for agricultural transformation and development in South Africa: a review. Turkish Online J. Qual. Inquiry (TOJQI) (2021)
15. Nkosi, M., Agholor, A.I.: The fourth industrial revolution and its implication for agricultural advisory services in South Africa: a review. Turkish Online J. Qual. Inquiry (TOJQI) (2021)
16. Adeyemo, A.A., Silas, E.: The Role of Culture in Achieving Sustainable Agriculture in South Africa: Examining Zulu Cultural Views and Management Practices of Livestock and Its Productivity. Regional Development in Africa, p. 183 (2020)
17. USB: The Future of the Western Cape Agricultural Sector in the Context of the Fourth Industrial Revolution. University of Stellenbosch Business School (2017)
18. Van Niekerk, J.B.S., Brent, A.C., Musango, J.K., De Kock, I.H.: Implications for the agriculture sector of a green economy transition in the Western Cape Province of South Africa: a system dynamics modelling approach to food crop production. S. Afr. J. Ind. Eng. **28**, 133–144 (2017)

19. Long, T.B., Blok, V., Coninx, I.: Barriers to the adoption and diffusion of technological innovations for climate-smart agriculture in Europe: evidence from the Netherlands, France, Switzerland and Italy. J. Clean. Prod. **112**, 9–21 (2016)
20. Biró, K., Szalmáné Csete, M., Németh, B.: Climate-smart agriculture: sleeping beauty of the hungarian agribusiness. Sustainability **13**, 10269 (2021)
21. Myeni, L., Moeletsi, M., Thavhana, M., Randela, M., Mokoena, L.: Barriers affecting sustainable agricultural productivity of smallholder farmers in the Eastern Free State of South Africa. Sustainability **11**, 3003 (2019)
22. Mbatha, M.W.: The Agricultural Sector in Improving the Country's Economy. J. African Foreign Affairs. **7**, 77–93 (2020)
23. Westaby, J.D.: Behavioral reasoning theory: identifying new linkages underlying intentions and behavior. Organ. Behav. Hum. Decis. Process. **98**, 97–120 (2005). https://doi.org/10.1016/j.obhdp.2005.07.003
24. Hajiheydari, N., Delgosha, M.S., Olya, H.: Scepticism and resistance to IoMT in healthcare: application of behavioural reasoning theory with configurational perspective. Technol. Forecast. Soc. Chang. **169**, 120807 (2021)
25. Pillai, R., Sivathanu, B.: Adoption of internet of things (IoT) in the agriculture industry deploying the BRT framework. Benchmarking Int. J **27**, 1341–1368 (2020)
26. Sahu, A.K., Padhy, R.K., Dhir, A.: Envisioning the future of behavioral decision-making: a systematic literature review of behavioral reasoning theory. Australas. Mark. J. **28**, 145–159 (2020). https://doi.org/10.1016/j.ausmj.2020.05.001
27. Azungah, T.: Qualitative research: deductive and inductive approaches to data analysis. Qual. Res. J. **18**, 383–400 (2018). https://doi.org/10.1108/QRJ-D-18-00035
28. Bhattacherjee, A.: Social Science Research: Principles, Methods, and Practices. University of South Florida (2012)
29. Braun, V., Clarke, V.: Using thematic analysis in psychology. Qual. Res. Psychol. **3**, 77–101 (2006)
30. Jayne, T.S., et al.: Africa's changing farm size distribution patterns: the rise of medium-scale farms. Agric. Econ. **47**, 197–214 (2016)
31. AlHogail, A.: Improving IoT technology adoption through improving consumer trust. Technologies **6**, 64 (2018)
32. Waeterloos, E.: State-led agrarian reform in South Africa: policy incoherencies and the concern for authoritarian populism. Can. J. Dev. Stud./Revue canadienne d'études du développement. **41**, 399–416 (2020)
33. Nowell, L.S., Norris, J.M., White, D.E., Moules, N.J.: Thematic analysis: striving to meet the trustworthiness criteria. Int. J. Qual. Methods **16**, 160940691773384 (2017). https://doi.org/10.1177/1609406917733847

POPIA Compliance in Digital Marketplaces: An IGOE Framework for Pattern Language Development

Mmaphefo Octavia Kumalo⬥ and Reinhardt A. Botha(✉)⬥

Center for Research in Information and Cyber Security, Nelson Mandela University,
Gqeberha 6001, South Africa
{s220013292,ReinhardtA.Botha}@mandela.ac.za

Abstract. The rapidly growing digital marketplace landscape presents a unique challenge: reconciling the increased demand for consumer privacy with the innovative spirit and economic benefits these platforms offer. This tension is particularly acute in South Africa, where the Protection of Personal Information Act (POPIA) imposes stringent data privacy regulations. Striking a balance between these competing forces requires a nuanced approach that prioritises both consumer privacy and the continued growth of the digital marketplace ecosystem. This paper proposes a novel approach to navigating this complex landscape by leveraging the power of Pattern Languages. We utilize the IGOE framework (Inputs, Guides, Outputs, Enablers) to develop a POPIA compliance pattern language specifically tailored for digital marketplaces.

Keywords: Privacy · Digital Marketplaces · POPIA · IGOE Framework · Pattern Language

1 Introduction

Arguably, whilst the advent of the Internet has brought with it new innovations, new intelligence and new ways of doing things and has ultimately disrupted the traditional way in which we communicate, transact, socialise and live life in general [1–4]. It has also brought stakeholder contentions, between business, consumers and regulators due to the superficial understanding of how digital services and platforms work [5] especially with regards to data management practices. The Internet era has manifested in traditional corporates transforming and digitising their, *inter alia*, business models, operations, processes, products, and customer engagements, driven by the advantages and benefits of digitalisation versus the old ways of doing business [6]. Enter the growth of the digital marketplaces, where goods and services are exchanged by users through software enabled transactions [4]. Digital marketplaces match buyers and suppliers, facilitate transactions, maintain institutional infrastructure [7] and create value for consumers by co-creating value adding services with ecosystem complementors [8, 9]. Digital marketplace sales account for 62% of the global online retail sales and in 2020 alone, about $2.67 trillion was spent on the world's top 100 marketplaces [10].

A. Gerber (Ed.): SAICSIT 2024, CCIS 2159, pp. 331–346, 2024.
https://doi.org/10.1007/978-3-031-64881-6_19

Digital marketplaces have provided benefits for consumers by offering diverse products and services, often personalised to individual preferences [11] at competitive prices, increasing accessibility for consumers [12]. The collection, processing, exchange, and storage of data drives the innovation, customisation, and personalisation of these marketplaces [3, 11]. Data as the 'new oil' of the twenty first century [13] fuels the progressive collection of vast amounts of user data, including demographics, preferences, locations, consumer browsing and behaviour to profile individuals and extract predictive information [14, 15]. This data is processed, analysed, and often shared with third parties to generate insights for innovation, personalisation, and targeted advertising [16, 17].

For the consumer, the benefits provided by participating in marketplaces although very valuable come at some kind of cost and risk [15, 18]. Consumers inadvertently give up certain freedoms and rights [19] with regards to their privacy [18, 20, 21] however, they are increasingly concerned about data privacy, particularly regarding collection, use, and potential misuse [11, 21, 22]. The increasing privacy concerns have necessitated regulators stepping in to provide the legal tenets and frameworks for responsible processing of personal data [11] *inter alia*, the General Data Protection Regulation (GDPR)[1] of the European Union and the Protection of Personal Information Act (POPIA)[2] in South Africa. Regulators try to ensure that consumer information and data is protected from exploitation from business and that there is fairness and justification for certain practices [11, 15, 23, 24].

There is a lack of transparency on the data lifecycle management practices[3] of personal information acquired by businesses whether knowingly or un-knowingly by consumers which leads to privacy and trust issues [24, 25]. The conditions of lawful processing of personal information as articulated in POPIA are principles and guidelines which organisations need to comply with. This is, however, a difficult feat considering the balance between data-driven innovation and user privacy for these digital marketplaces [26]. The evolution of digital marketplaces themselves into either multi-sided marketplaces, large aggregator platforms or even "super platforms" serving many different use cases and buyer markets has increased data and information flows through various entities [6] hence the complexity of lawfully handling customer data.

A proposed solution for digital marketplace operators to comply with data privacy regulations, building trust and transparency with consumers whilst also balancing innovation [4, 24] can be achieved through leveraging the power of Pattern Languages. The pattern language would provide modular, reusable patterns that address specific privacy concerns related to data management practices in the digital marketplace ecosystem,

---

[1] General Data Protection Regulations. This Regulation lays down rules relating to the protection of natural persons regarding the processing of personal data and rules relating to the free movement of personal data.

[2] POPIA, promotes the protection of personal information processed by public and private bodies; and introduces certain conditions to establish minimum requirements for the processing of personal information.

[3] This term encompasses the entire spectrum of activities involved in handling data from its initial collection through its processing, exchange, storage, and eventual disposal. The term encapsulates the definition of 'processing' defined in Chapter 1 of POPIA and emphasises the holistic approach to handling data throughout its lifecycle, encompassing various activities such as data collection, processing, sharing, and retention.

thus eliminating unnecessary efforts and inappropriate scope. Furthermore, the pattern language explicitly acknowledges the inherent tension and trade-off between privacy and innovation [4], offering guidance on how to strike a balance that satisfies consumers and digital marketplace stakeholders.

This paper proposes a novel approach to navigating the complexities of developing the pattern language specifically tailored for digital marketplaces by utilising the IGOE framework (Inputs, Guides, Outputs, Enablers), originally introduced by Roger Burlton in 2001 and extended by Harmon in 2010 [27]. Complex analysis and comprehension of the pattern language's components are necessary for the development of a POPIA compliance pattern language; thus, the paper is organised as follows: first, a concise explanation of privacy as a multifaceted concept is provided; second, the significance of pattern languages as an innovative resolution is established; third, a comprehensive outline of the IGOE for pattern language development is presented; and finally, the paper concludes with a discussion of future endeavors and recommendations.

2 Privacy as a Complex Concept

While there is no universally accepted definition of privacy due to its intricate and multifaceted nature [18, 28, 29], data privacy, which is a subset of privacy, is unquestionably a subject of public interest given the exponential growth of processed and exchanged data resulting from technological advancements which is reported at 328.77 million terabytes per day [30]. The introduction describes how concerns regarding data privacy have prompted the implementation of numerous data privacy laws and regulations across the globe. As evidenced by the top ten data breaches and subsequent fines in 2023, where millions of users' personal information was compromised, resulting in financial losses and reputational harm, improper management of personal information can have severe repercussions. The most notable cyberattack of 2023, in terms of data exposure, occurred at Microsoft. Perpetrators unlawfully obtained access to the company's online exchange data, which comprised millions of records [31]. As of January 2024, the largest fine for GDPR violations was imposed on Meta Platforms Inc., the proprietors of Facebook, in May 2023. This fine was set at 1.2 billion euros and was a result of improper compliance with EU regulation regarding the transmission of personal data to the United States [32].

The theoretical underpinnings of data privacy encompass a multifaceted examination of ethical considerations, legal frameworks, and global perspectives as posited by philosophists and scholars [28, 29, 33]]. Literature in this domain highlights the evolving nature of privacy concerns, from the traditional notions of personal space to the intricate web of online interactions [18]. Data privacy extends beyond legal compliance to ethical considerations, emphasising the responsible handling of personal and sensitive data [29].

It is argued that individuals relinquish their privacy– also referred to as privacy paradox [19] – when they choose to use and interact with platforms, applications, devices, and services. The challenge that individuals have is with regards to the lack of transparency provided by companies and service providers on the collection, processing, analysis, and exchange of their personal data [34].

Within the context of digital marketplaces, four distinct data privacy concepts emerge as particularly relevant. The first, *decisional privacy*, emphasises freedom from interference in personal choices and decisions based on data analysis [24]. This concept is violated when algorithms mine personal data to influence product recommendations or purchasing behaviours without individual consent. This can lead to concerns about manipulation and a lack of agency.

The second concept, *informational privacy*, focuses on individual control over the flow of personal information, their ability to exert influence and autonomy over decisions and freedom from unsolicited marketing communications [35, 36]. This encompasses control over collection, use, disclosure, and retention of data. In marketplaces, these manifests when individuals lack control over how their data is shared with third-party vendors or used for marketing purposes beyond the initial transaction. This can lead to feelings of unease and a loss of personal autonomy.

Moving beyond individual-centric perspectives, privacy as *social context, norms, and values* recognizes that privacy expectations and violations are shaped by social norms and situational contexts [29]. This concept highlights how the appropriateness of information sharing and the potential for privacy violations vary depending on factors such as the type of information, the actors involved, and the purpose of the interaction. For example, sharing personal information on social media carries different privacy implications than sharing the same information with a close friend.

Finally, privacy as *affordances and design* emphasizes the role of technology design in shaping privacy expectations and behaviours [37]. This concept acknowledges that the features and functionalities of technology platforms, such as the ability to delete messages or control data access settings, influence how individuals perceive and manage their privacy. Ideally, privacy principles should be proactively incorporated into the design of systems to minimize the potential for privacy violations and empower users to make informed choices [38].

These privacy concepts highlight the privacy requirements that need to be considered within the context of the digital marketplace and serve as guiding principles to consider and incorporate into data management practices.

3   A Pattern Language as a Solution for Privacy Compliance

The balance between innovation; data lifecycle management practices; data monetisation and privacy is challenging in digital marketplace ecosystems and with the addition of data privacy regulation requirements it becomes even more difficult. Efforts in data regulation compliance are often hindered by issues related to amongst others, the interpretation of the regulations; resource allocation; documentation and monitoring [25]. A POPIA compliant pattern language for digital marketplaces is proposed as a solution which will provide reusable, proven solutions [39] in the form of patterns, thus allowing the organisations to navigate the ever-changing landscape of data regulations.

Patterns can address common data privacy requirement challenges like user consent flows, data minimisation techniques, and transparent privacy notices through a shared vocabulary. This fosters collaboration and ensures consistent privacy practices across the organisation, streamlining compliance efforts and ultimately allowing innovation to flourish within a privacy-respecting framework.

The pattern language for digital marketplaces draws upon several key frameworks to inform its design from theoretical privacy frameworks to legal foundations such as POPIA. The POPIA compliance pattern language for digital marketplaces should prioritise a fair balance between the rights, needs, and obligations of the involved parties, namely the data subjects and the responsible parties or data processors. These parties have conflicting interests, and it is crucial to consider both the commercial and innovation needs of the responsible party while ensuring compliance with legislation and building trust with data subjects [40] through transparent data lifecycle management practices. Thus, the POPIA compliance pattern language for digital marketplaces will be the blueprint that enables and supports the network to be compliant, support ease of use, comprehension, and extensibility, using a few natural classification properties which provide a roadmap to implementation [18]. It can thus be reasonably argued that the pattern language approach is a viable solution for creating a data privacy compliant framework for digital marketplaces.

4   IGOE Framework as a Pattern Language Development Tool

The development of the POPIA compliant pattern language for digital marketplaces requires a novel approach to navigating the complexities of the pattern language. The IGOE framework which proposes the understanding, analysis and use of Inputs, Guides, Outputs, Enablers to enable and support the pattern language is the proposed approach to navigating the complexities of developing the compliance pattern language. Through this innovative approach, we aim to contribute to a more sustainable and responsible digital marketplace landscape in South Africa, one that prioritises both consumer privacy and the continued growth of this dynamic sector.

4.1   The IGOE Framework

The IGOE Framework, previously known as the Burlton Process Scope Diagram, emerged as an extension of the US Air Force's Integrated DEFinition (IDEF) methodology [27]. The framework has continuously evolved, transitioning from capturing manufacturing processes to encompassing service-oriented processes [41]. This versatility positions it as a suitable framework for understanding and analysing the process of developing the POPIA compliance pattern language. Furthermore, the framework aligns with the desired outcome of this research – the development of the POPIA compliance pattern language.

The framework facilitates the implementation of a process which is triggered by an event, governed by rules, executed by individuals, and facilitated by technology and infrastructure [42]. This aligns perfectly with the components of the IGOE framework: Inputs, Guides, Outputs, and Enablers. The fundamental difference between inputs, guides, and enablers can be understood based on what they offer within a process or activity, whereas inputs provide the building blocks or raw materials needed to initiate and complete a process. The guides offer the rules, principles, or best practices that steer the process towards its desired outcome. The enablers provide the tools, infrastructure, or capabilities that facilitate the transformation of inputs into desired outputs. The line between inputs and guides can be blurry, however, the key differentiators between inputs and guides are enforceability: inputs are enforceable, while guides are not. In terms of specificity: inputs are specific requirements, while guides offer broader recommendations.

Inputs Are transformed elements within a process [41] and they are essential and mandatory for the process to function. in the context of developing the popia pattern language, inputs are the requirements as set out by the information regulator, the privacy needs and concerns of consumers, and the marketplace-specific data flows and processing activities.

Guides Govern the process execution, encompassing elements like business rules, stakeholder expectations, standards, and compliance constraints [27, 41, 42]. The guides provide direction and recommendations, not absolute requirements and can be adapted or adjusted based on specific circumstances. In this case, guides could include POPIA regulations, industry standards, and ethical considerations related to data privacy.

Outputs Are the desired outcomes of the process [27, 41]. In this context, the output would be the comprehensive and effective POPIA compliance pattern language together with its supporting considerations such as a data classification and taxonomy reference model or the privacy patterns identified.

Enablers Are the resources facilitating the transformation of inputs into outputs. The enablers support the execution of the process but aren't directly consumed by it and can include human expertise, technologies, tools, facilities, and systems [27, 41, 42].

Utilising the IGOE Framework and its well-defined elements, this study acquires a systematic methodology to examine and comprehend the POPIA compliance pattern language development process. This paradigm offers useful insights into the different components, their relationships, and their impact on the intended result (see Fig. 1).

The components illustrated are unpacked further to provide context to the POPIA compliant pattern language for digital marketplaces.

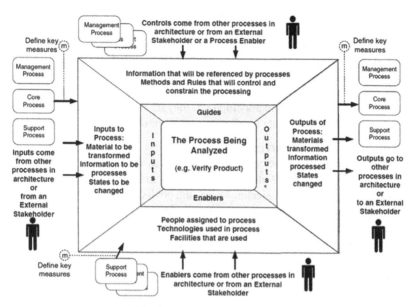

Fig. 1. IGOE Framework [27].

4.2 Applying the IGOE Components to the POPIA Pattern Language

The POPIA [43] compliance pattern language for digital marketplaces must find a middle ground between the marketplace operators' duties and the innovative services provided to consumers facilitated by the data lifecycle practices of personal information, whilst also protecting consumers' data privacy concerns. The pattern language aims to standardise POPIA compliance across data types, transaction types, and data lifecycle and processes. To advance the pattern language, the IGOE framework necessitates the identification, recognition, and analysis of the framework's various components, including but not limited to compliance obligations imposed by the Information Regulator; data sharing practices and requirements among participants in digital marketplaces; consumer data privacy concerns; marketplace operators' legal responsibilities; and prevalent practices and scenarios associated with data collection. To fully comprehend and analyse these components, one must carefully evaluate the delicate balance between them.

The components outlined within the framework play a crucial role in the guidance towards effective compliance strategies tailored to the intricacies of digital marketplace operations. The elements of the framework ensure that the resultant pattern language (1) is legally sound and user-centric by addressing the legal obligations and user needs; (2) provides a solid foundation and adaptability by considering the various guides in the form of privacy patterns, standards, policies and frameworks; (3) provides practical solutions (4) adapts to evolving context by considering industry best practices and addressing emerging privacy issues provided by academic discourse and finally (5) can be a source of competitive advantage for marketplaces as it makes compliance more efficient.

Pattern Language Inputs

The inputs are the elements which provide the context and requirements from various stakeholders who have a concern or a need to be considered.

The requirements are from the Information Regulator as the custodian of POPIA; the data lifecycle management practices within the marketplace ecosystem; the legal obligations placed upon marketplace operators for privacy; the consumer data privacy concerns and their rights and responsibilities.

These are essential and mandatory inputs as they form the foundation for understanding regulatory expectations, data handling responsibilities, and privacy considerations.

Information Regulator Requirements

The information regulator as the custodian of POPIA, as articulated in Sect. 40 of the Act has a legal obligation amongst other responsibilities to issue compliance notices, conduct research on data processing technologies, and publish reports on its findings. Within the ambit of the compliance pattern language, the information regulator requires digital marketplace operators to comply with the requirements as set out in the Act. The requirements in POPIA serve as the fixed and mandatory input requirements based on the Act's provisions and the Regulator's interpretations. They represent enforceable obligations for digital marketplace operators. Examples include amongst others, data minimization principles (Sect. 11); lawful processing grounds (Sect. 6); security safeguards (Sect. 12); data subject rights procedures (Sect. 27), etc.

By considering the information regulator's requirements we ensure that the foundation to the entire process is solid as they define the mandatory legal obligations that the pattern language must adhere to, ensuring enforceable compliance. By aligning organisational practices with these requirements, digital marketplaces can ensure adherence to the regulatory framework established by POPIA.

Marketplace Operators Data Flows and Legal Obligations

The marketplace-specific data flows and processing activities as inputs to the compliance pattern language play a crucial and essential role by assisting in the identification of potential areas of non-compliance. Mapping these flows against legal obligations helps pinpoint where personal information is processed, stored, or transferred, enabling the identification of necessary safeguards and controls. The identification of the types of data collected, used, and shared within the marketplace context informs the data handling aspects of the pattern language. This also provides a view of the different legal justifications for processing. Different data types require different legal justifications for processing (Sect. 6 of POPIA). Different data types require different levels of security protection based on their sensitivity and potential harm if compromised (Sect. 12 of POPIA). Different data types also have implication for enabling data access, rectification, and deletion (Sect. 27 of POPIA).

Thus, understanding the marketplace operator's data flows and processing activities shapes the functionalities and mechanisms within the patterns to address the unique data handling needs of the digital marketplaces while fulfilling its legal responsibilities.

Consumer Privacy Concerns and Rights

Consumers have concerns about data collection, i.e., what information is collected, how it's used, and who has access to it [44]; they also have concerns about the perceived constant monitoring and profiling which raise concerns about loss of control and autonomy [26]. Consumers fear personal information leaks and misuse due to cyberattacks and vulnerabilities [21, 45]. While some appreciate tailored experiences, others find them intrusive and privacy invasive [22]. Furthermore, consumers often struggle to understand complex privacy policies and feel they lack control over their data [17].

From these various concerns consumers want clear explanations of data lifecycle management practices and the logic behind algorithms; granular control over data sharing and opt-out options; privacy settings that consider the context of data collection and use and call for more stringent data protection laws and effective enforcement mechanisms [17, 21, 46].

These concerns have been codified in regulations such as POPIA to give consumers affordances in the form of certain privacy rights that they can exercise. These rights amongst others such as the right to access (Sect. 23) or the right to correction of personal information (Sect. 24) provide necessary input to the POPIA compliance pattern language.

Therefore, integrating user privacy considerations from the outset fosters trust and transparency. This input ensures that the pattern language respects user rights (data access, rectification, deletion) and addresses the consumers' evolving privacy concerns whilst mitigating the risk of regulatory penalties and reputational damage for marketplace operators.

Pattern Language Guides

The pattern language guides govern and influence the pattern language. These are the components which provide the direction and recommendations but not necessarily the mandatory requirements. They serve as invaluable resources in navigating the complexities of POPIA compliance and provide valuable insights and frameworks for developing a robust compliance strategy.

Information Regulator Perspectives

The recommendations and best practices issued by the Regulator offer guidance on implementing POPIA's principles but are not strictly enforceable. They may evolve based on the Regulator's evolving interpretations and industry practices and examples include guidance notes on data breach notifications; industry-specific best practices endorsed by the Regulator, etc.

The recommendations offered by the information regulator provide valuable insights into the Regulator's expectations and interpretations of the Act. By considering this perspective, the pattern language aligns with the spirit and letter of the law, reducing the risk of non-compliance issues.

POPIA Perspectives

POPIA guides help with the interpretation and implementation of the law but do not directly translate to legal obligations. They provide flexibility for adapting the pattern language to specific marketplace contexts.

A comprehensive understanding of POPIA requirements is essential for developing tailored compliance measures. By leveraging insights into POPIA's provisions, the marketplace operators can proactively address compliance gaps and mitigate associated risks. Similarly, as with the information regulator by combining these perspectives the pattern language will align with the law reducing risks of non-compliance.

Policies, Standards, Frameworks and Best Practices

Privacy policies, industry standards, frameworks and guidelines provide structure and direction by setting the general principles and requirements, outlining boundaries, and guiding overall design choices for example National Institute of Standards and Technology (NIST) Privacy Framework. They also assist in ensuring compliance which builds trust, and often provide best practice advice and recommend approaches that enhance privacy protections, informing specific functionalities and mechanisms within the patterns. They offer guidance and recommendations for implementing privacy principles effectively which inform the design and functionalities of the pattern language (e.g., data retention policies, user consent mechanisms).

Incorporating industry-recognised best practice advice and recommendations in the pattern language ensures that the patterns are effective, efficient, and address contemporary privacy challenges.

Common Data Lifecycle Management Practices

Understanding and analysing existing data lifecycle management practices together with their various practice methods and techniques e.g., Secure File Transfer Protocols (SFTP) for data exchanges, helps define what data is typically collected, used, and shared, influencing the pattern design. Benchmarking against common practices offers efficient solutions and show potential pitfalls to avoid as these common practices highlight the importance of managing data from its inception to its eventual disposition.

Thus, for the pattern language it is important to identify common data lifecycle management practices prevalent within the industry to facilitate the development of a standardised compliance framework tailored to specific digital marketplace operational contexts. Leveraging common practices streamlines compliance efforts and fosters interoperability among the marketplace ecosystem stakeholders.

It's worth noting that there are also common specific data practices as they relate to privacy. These practices such as data encryption, access controls and authentication, data minimisation, etc. are also practices which will guide the resultant pattern language and are considered in the process.

Existing Data Privacy Patterns

Existing privacy patterns offer pre-designed solutions for handling specific data operations, saving time and ensuring consistency, whilst also providing examples on how to embed privacy considerations into design elements, offering concrete ideas for implementation. Building on existing patterns fosters interoperability and facilitates adoption within the wider data privacy community.

By considering existing data privacy patterns, the pattern language benefits from the practical guidance on implementing effective controls and safeguards and capitalises on the proven solutions. This expedites the development of the pattern language and reduce implementation risks.

Academic Discourse on Privacy Concepts and Theories

The pattern language design benefits from engaging in academic discourse as it enriches the understanding of underlying privacy principles and their practical implications. Integrating theoretical insights into the pattern language adds a principled approach to data protection that transcends regulatory requirements.

These guides are crucial in guiding the design of the pattern language and help with the structure, classification, and abstraction of the privacy patterns for the pattern language.

Pattern Language Outputs

The ultimate result of the process will be a POPIA compliance pattern language for digital marketplaces. However, to get to the pattern language overall data requirements will be produced from the various analyses and requirements gathering; and individual privacy patterns will be written either from existing privacy patterns or new pattern formulated. The resulting pattern language will be supported by training material and guidelines for utilisation. The outputs offer tangible deliverables tailored to digital marketplaces that will help in structuring compliance efforts effectively.

POPIA Data Classification and Taxonomy Reference Model

Establishing a standardised data classification and taxonomy reference model facilitates consistent data governance practices, enhances data visibility, and structures and organises data in alignment with regulatory requirements. By categorising data based on sensitivity and risk, the reference model can guide the prioritisation of resource allocation and implementation of targeted security measures. Through providing data handling guidelines, the data classification and taxonomy reference model aids how different types of data should be processed, stored, and shared to comply with POPIA regulations.

POPIA Data Requirements

Documenting POPIA-specific data requirements ensures alignment with regulatory mandates and facilitates ongoing compliance monitoring. By clearly articulating data handling expectations, the digital marketplaces can promote accountability and transparency throughout the data lifecycle.

POPIA Privacy Patterns

Developing POPIA-specific privacy patterns offers reusable solutions to common compliance challenges, streamlining implementation efforts and reducing compliance overhead. By codifying best practices into actionable patterns, the digital marketplaces can accelerate compliance initiatives and improve operational efficiency.

Training Guides

Providing comprehensive training guides equips the digital marketplace employees with the knowledge and skills necessary to support POPIA compliance objectives. By investing in employee education and awareness, the marketplaces can foster a culture of compliance and empower individuals to make informed decisions regarding data handling practices.

Pattern Language Enablers

The pattern language enablers are those reusable resources or assets that support the development thereof. These enablers identified for the pattern language development such as process and data flow analysis, expert panels for quality assurance, process mapping tools, and requirements analysis play a critical role in facilitating the implementation of compliance measures by providing necessary support and validation.

Process and Data Flow Analysis

The digital marketplace operational processes and data flows will be mapped and analysed to ascertain data elements, types and data flow requirements which are mapped against the privacy regulatory requirements from POPIA.

Conducting process and data flow analysis of the digital marketplaces enables the identification of compliance risks and vulnerabilities inherent in their operations. By systematically assessing the data lifecycle management practices, compliance gaps and data protection controls are identified.

People

There are two outcomes envisaged from a people perspective. Firstly, merchant operators from identified case study digital marketplaces will be interviewed to confirm the process and data flow analysis. The second outcome is to conduct expert panels with subject matter experts in various disciplines, i.e., legal, compliance, architecture, marketplaces, and user experience design to assure the quality, comprehensiveness, utility, relevance, and appropriateness of the pattern language.

The interviews with digital marketplace service providers to confirm the results of the process and data flow analysis is a validation step of the findings which ensures accuracy and completeness of compliance assessments.

Leveraging expert panels for quality assurance provides independent validation of the pattern design, compliance measures and recommendations. By tapping into diverse expertise, the pattern language benefits with the robustness and effectiveness of their expert opinions and guidance.

Tools

Various technologies such as process and data mapping tools will be used to support the drawing and analysis of the business process and data flow diagrams. Requirements mapping and analysis will be done using a data analysis tool where different views will be explored to guide the required patterns.

Utilising process and data mapping tools streamlines the assessments and facilitates visualisation of data flows and the various requirements outcomes.

When thoroughly analysed and understood, the components will form a complete and accurate pattern language for digital marketplaces that complies with POPIA. By leveraging these resources effectively, the pattern language can assist them in navigating the complexities of data protection regulations, mitigate compliance risks, and uphold consumer trust in an increasingly data-driven ecosystem. The modified diagram from Harmon [27] demonstrates the integration of the framework components. The components will ensure a thorough comprehension and precision of the resulting pattern language (Fig. 2).

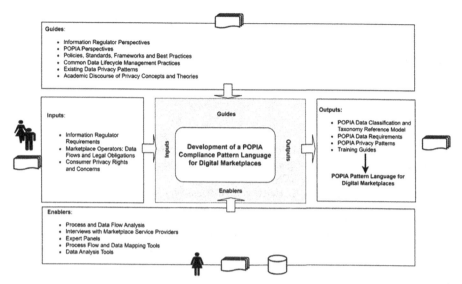

Fig. 2. The IGOE Framework for POPIA Compliance Pattern Language for Digital Marketplaces

5 Conclusion and Further Discussion

Whilst the development of the POPIA compliance pattern language is still in progress, the IGOE framework serves as a guide for the pattern language to be accurate and comprehensive. The components identified as IGOE's in the development framework will all be looked at during the process of developing the pattern language.

Future work on the development of the POPIA pattern language for digital marketplaces includes the analysis, understanding and requirements resulting from the other components of the IGOE framework, *inter alia* understanding the data types and flows in the marketplace ecosystems; understanding the compliance requirements from POPIA; understanding the guidelines from data privacy policies, standards and frameworks; figuring out the POPIA specific data privacy patterns and how to depict them, whilst trying to ensure that the patterns are balanced towards the needs of all stakeholders involved.

The immediate future work is to create a digital marketplace POPIA data classification and taxonomy reference model, by utilising inputs from the information regulator; with guidance from data privacy industry – best practices, standards and frameworks and academic discourse and enabled by a digital marketplace process and data flow analysis. The data reference model will assist with the identification and structural framework of the patterns and pattern language.

The utility, comprehensiveness, completeness, and quality assurance of the resultant pattern language must also be tested as part of the final research activity. The IGOE framework provides a simplified, structured approach to developing the pattern language, however there may be legal nuances, technical requirements and organisational considerations that may not be fully captured by this framework. These limitations might potentially be identified when the pattern language is tested through the envisaged expert panel review. The expert panel review will consist of experts in Enterprise Architecture, Data Architecture, Design Thinking, Privacy Law, and e-Commerce.

Disclosure of Interests. The author has no competing interests to declare that are relevant to the content of this article.

References

1. Flyverbom, M., Deibert, R., Matten, D.: The governance of digital technology, big data, and the internet: new roles and responsibilities for business. Bus. Soc. **58**, 3–19 (2019). https://doi.org/10.1177/0007650317727540
2. Kozyreva, A., Lewandowsky, S., Hertwig, R.: Citizens versus the internet: confronting digital challenges with cognitive tools. Assoc. Psychol. Sci. **21**, 103–156 (2020). https://doi.org/10.1177/152910062094670
3. Lee, S.U., Zhu, L., Jeffery, R.: Data governance for platform ecosystems: critical factors and the state of practice. In: Twenty First Pacific Asia Conference on Information Systems. Langkawi: Pacific Asia Conference on Information Systems (2017)
4. Lenard, T.M., Rubin, P.H.: In defense of data: information and the costs of privacy. Policy Internet **2**, 149–183 (2010). https://doi.org/10.2202/1944-2866.1035
5. Kulhari, S.: Building-Blocks of a Data Protection Revolution: The Uneasy Case for Blockchain Technology to Secure Privacy and Identity. Nomos Verlagsgesellschaft mbH & Co. KG (2018)
6. McAfee, A., Brynjolfsson, E.: Machine, Platform, Crowd: Harnessing Our Digital Future. W.W. Norton & Company, New York, NY, USA (2017)
7. Bakos, Y.: The emerging role of electronic marketplaces on the Internet. Commun. ACM **41**, 35–42 (1998). https://doi.org/10.1145/280324.280330
8. Hein, A., et al.: Digital platform ecosystems. Electron. Mark. **30**, 87–98 (2020). https://doi.org/10.1007/s12525-019-00377-4
9. Barns, S.: Negotiating the platform pivot: from participatory digital ecosystems to infrastructures of everyday life. Geogr. Compass. **13**, (2019). https://doi.org/10.1111/gec3.12464
10. Spryker Systems: Everything You Need to Know about Starting a Marketplace, spryker.com (2021)
11. Salazar, J.: Whose data? information economics, digital privacy, and the right to be forgotten. In: Austrian Stud. Sch. Conf. (2021)
12. Saberian, F., Amirshahi, M., Ebrahimi, M., Nazemi, A.: Linking digital platforms' service dimensions to customers' purchase. Bottom Line. **33**, 315–335 (2020). https://doi.org/10.1108/BL-01-2020-0001
13. Zahid, R., et al.: Secure data management life cycle for government big-data ecosystem: design and development perspective. Systems **11**, 380 (2023). https://doi.org/10.3390/systems11080380
14. Mantelero, A.: The EU Proposal for a General Data Protection Regulation and the roots of the 'right to be forgotten.' Comput. Law Secur. Rev. **29**, 229–235 (2013). https://doi.org/10.1016/j.clsr.2013.03.010
15. Fuller, C.S.: The perils of privacy regulation. Rev. Austrian Econ. **30**, 193–214 (2017). https://doi.org/10.1007/s11138-016-0345-0
16. Chen, C.: Storey: business intelligence and analytics: from big data to big impact. MIS Q. **36**, 1165 (2012). https://doi.org/10.2307/41703503
17. Ohm, P.: The rise and fall of invasive ISP surveillance. Univ. Ill. Law Rev. (2009)

18. Knijnenburg, B.P., Page, X., Wisniewski, P., Lipford, H.R., Proferes, N., Romano, J. (eds.): Modern Socio-Technical Perspectives on Privacy. Springer International Publishing, Cham, Switzerland (2022)
19. Bandara, R., Fernando, M., Akter, S.: The privacy paradox in the data-driven marketplace: the role of knowledge deficiency and psychological distance. Proc. Comput. Sci. **121**, 562–567 (2017). https://doi.org/10.1016/j.procs.2017.11.074
20. Pentina, I., Zhang, L., Bata, H., Chen, Y.: Exploring privacy paradox in information-sensitive mobile app adoption: a cross-cultural comparison. Comput. Hum. Behav. **65**, 409–419 (2016). https://doi.org/10.1016/j.chb.2016.09.005
21. Acquisti, A., Grossklags, J.: Privacy and rationality in individual decision making. IEEE Secur. Priv. Mag. **3**, 26–33 (2005). https://doi.org/10.1109/MSP.2005.22
22. Acquisti, A., Taylor, C., Wagman, L.: The economics of privacy. J. Econ. Lit. **54**, 442–492 (2016). https://doi.org/10.1257/jel.54.2.442
23. Bandara, R., Fernando, M., Akter, S.: Addressing privacy predicaments in the digital marketplace: a power-relations perspective. Int. J. Consum. Stud. **44**, 423–434 (2020). https://doi.org/10.1111/ijcs.12576
24. Solove, D.J.: Conceptualizing privacy. Calif. Law Rev. Inc. **90**, 1087–1155 (2022)
25. Billgren, P., Ekman, L.W.: Compliance challenges with the general data protection regulation. Lund Univ. Sch. Econ. Manag. Dep. Inform. (2017)
26. Bruns, H., Perino, G.: The role of autonomy and reactance for nudging — Experimentally comparing defaults to recommendations and mandates. J. Behav. Exp. Econ. **106**, 102047 (2023). https://doi.org/10.1016/j.socec.2023.102047
27. Harmon, P.: The scope and evolution of business process management. In: Brocke, J.V., Rosemann, M. (eds.) Handbook on Business Process Management 1, pp. 37–81. Springer, Berlin Heidelberg, Berlin, Heidelberg (2010)
28. Moor, J.H.: Towards a theory of privacy in the information age. ACM SIGCAS Comput. Soc. **27**, 27–32 (1997). https://doi.org/10.1145/270858.270866
29. Nissenbaum, H.: Privacy as contextual integrity. Wash. Law Rev. **79**, (2004)
30. Duarte, F.: Amount of Data Created Daily (2024). https://explodingtopics.com/blog/data-generated-per-day
31. Orange Cyberdefense: Security_Navigator_2024.pdf. Orange Cyberdefense (2023)
32. Petrosyan, A.: Fines issued for General Data Protection Regulation (GDPR) violations as of May 2023, by type of violation. https://www.statista.com/statistics/1172494/gdpr-fines-by-type-violation/
33. Katzav, G.: Compartmentalised data protection in South Africa: the right to privacy in the Protection of Personal Information Act. South Afr. Law J. **139**, 432–470 (2022). https://doi.org/10.47348/SALJ/v139/i2a8
34. Pavlou: State of the information privacy literature: where are we now and where should we go? MIS Q. **35**, 977 (2011). https://doi.org/10.2307/41409969
35. Westin, A.F.: Privacy and freedom. Wash. Lee Law Rev. 25, (1968)
36. Gabisch, J.A., Milne, R.G.: The impact of compensation on information ownership and privacy control. J. Consum. Mark. **31**, 13–26 (2014). https://doi.org/10.1108/JCM-10-2013-0737
37. Friedman, B., Kahn, P.H., Borning, A., Huldtgren, A.: Value sensitive design and information systems. In: Doorn, N., Schuurbiers, D., Van De Poel, I., Gorman, M.E. (eds.) Early Engagement and New Technologies: Opening up the Laboratory, pp. 55–95. Springer, Netherlands, Dordrecht (2013)
38. Cavoukian, A.: Privacy by Design The 7 Foundational Principles
39. Alexander, C., Ishikawa, S., Silverstein, M., Jacobson, M., Fiksdahl-King, I., Angel, S.: A Pattern Language. Oxford University Press, London (1977)

40. Hine, C.: Privacy in the marketplace. Inf. Soc. **14**, 253–262 (1998). https://doi.org/10.1080/019722498128700

41. Long, K.A.: IGOE — Guides from policy to business rules. https://www.brcommunity.com/articles.php?id=b661

42. Wangen, G., Snekkenes, E.A.: A comparison between business process management and information security management. In: Presented at the Federated Conference on Computer Science and Information Systems , Warsaw 29 Sep. 29 (2014)

43. Michalsons: Protection of Personal Information Act 4 of 2013. https://popia.co.za/. (2022)

44. Barocas, S., Selbst, A.D.: Big data's disparate impact. SSRN Electron. J. (2016). https://doi.org/10.2139/ssrn.2477899

45. Dinev, T., Hart, P.: An extended privacy calculus model for e-commerce transactions. Inf. Syst. Res. **17**, 61–80 (2006). https://doi.org/10.1287/isre.1060.0080

46. Ananny, M., Crawford, K.: Seeing without knowing: limitations of the transparency ideal and its application to algorithmic accountability. New Media Soc. **20**, 973–989 (2018). https://doi.org/10.1177/1461444816676645

Educators' Cybersecurity Vulnerabilities in Marginalised Schools in South Africa

Caroline Magunje[(✉)] ⓘ and Wallace Chigona ⓘ

University of Cape Town, Cape Town, South Africa
caroline.magunje@uct.ca.za

Abstract. Schools are experiencing an increased adoption and use of technology in curriculum delivery, administrative tasks, and community engagement. This was reinforced by the COVID-19 pandemic. The increased adoption has amplified exposure of schools to cyberattacks, as cyber criminals are finding opportunities such as deploying ransomware, stealing information, and extorting money from schools. Their positioning in a school setting makes educators paramount to cybersecurity in schools since cyber criminals can create a breach in the security system by targeting people, not computers. Schools in most Sub-Saharan Africa countries are, to an extent, defenceless to cyberattacks as the region faces various challenges such as limited financial resources, lack of or weak cybersecurity policies and comprehensive cyber safety initiatives, and limited cybersecurity knowledge and skills by educators. These challenges leave educators, the school and various stakeholders vulnerable to cyber-attacks which may compromise the security of the entire school information systems. This study aims to answer the question: What are the cybersecurity vulnerabilities of educators in marginalised schools in South Africa? The study employed a qualitative exploratory methodology using case studies of four schools located in marginalised schools in the Western Cape and Limpopo provinces of South Africa. We collected the data via semi structured interviews of educators. We analysed the data using thematic analysis based on the threat and coping appraisal constructs of the Protection Motivation Theory. The findings suggest that educators' cybersecurity vulnerabilities emanate from a limited cybersecurity knowledge and skills which lead to compromised perception of threat severity, threat vulnerability, and misguided cybersecurity self-efficacy among educators. The study contributes to cybersecurity in education by emphasising the need for cybersecurity policies, interventions and initiatives for schools that can address the vulnerability and susceptibility of educators to cybersecurity threats.

Keywords: Cybersecurity in Education · Marginalised Schools · Protection Motivation Theory

1 Introduction and Background

Schools play a crucial role in the digital age as they are centrally positioned in community development in their role of teaching learners' essential information communication technology (ICT) skills as well as providing guidance to parents on internet usage at home [1]. Further, digitisation entails that schools are custodians of huge amounts of data comprising personal information of various stakeholders including learners, parents, educators, and administrative staff [2]. Nonetheless, the cyberspace has created an asymmetric, low-risk environment for cybercriminals with malicious intentions that can disrupt schools [3]. Cybercriminals tend to target humans as they are regarded as the weakest link in cybersecurity [4–6]. Thus, there has been calls for cybersecurity diligence within school contexts particularly among educators since they are centrally positioned and have access to sensitive data of learners and parents. A cyber-attack caused by poor cyber hygiene practices of educators would have a devastating effect on the school system [7]. Educators' cybersecurity vulnerabilities pose as a great source of potential risk to schools through their cybersecurity decision making and behaviours as they use the internet, whether with intent or through negligence [2].

For both their professional and personal life, educators, like all internet users, should be well informed on how to identify potential cyberthreats and take appropriate action against these threats [10]. Regrettably, most African nations have not prioritised cybersecurity capacitation; they consider it as a luxury, not a necessity. As a result, most internet users on the continent are not technologically competent and lack the required skills to protect themselves from rapidly rising cyber-threats [11].

Schools, in particular, have not prioritised cybersecurity to the same levels as corporate businesses and industries. Schools, find themselves ill-prepared to deal with cyberthreats [12]. Marginalised schools in developing contexts face a myriad of resource constraints and are, therefore, much less prepared to deal with cyberthreats and attacks as they use ICTs in their daily practices [13]. Nonetheless, cybersecurity training awareness initiatives should be prioritised as they are the only way to build trustworthy systems and protect users as they use the cyberspace [14, 15]. Subsequent paragraphs, however, are indented.

We define marginalised schools as schools that operate with limited resources that do not meet all their needs to provide an adequate wholesome teaching and learning experience for learners. In the South African context, marginalised schools generally operate under frugal financial conditions as a result they might not have the resources to have cybersecurity interventions to capacitate the various stakeholders in the school [16]. Inevitably, educators from marginalised schools were unable to continue teaching and learning during the enforced lock down periods during the COVID-19 pandemic [17].

Educators in resource-constrained schools might be vulnerable and susceptible to cyberattacks and cyberthreats as they use various online platforms for school or personal use. Their positioning and close connections with administration, parents, and learners in a school context, increases their potential to expose the whole school to cyberattacks. Highlighting educators' vulnerabilities in the cyberspace is, therefore, important as knowledge of educator's cybersecurity vulnerabilities can inform appropriate cybersecurity interventions and awareness for marginalised schools. This study seeks to answer the question:

What are the cybersecurity vulnerabilities of educators in marginalised schools in South Africa?

The objective of the study is to explore the cybersecurity vulnerabilities of educators in marginalised schools in South Africa. The findings of the study may pave way for cybersecurity interventions for educators in marginalised schools that will cultivate a cyber safety culture for the various stakeholders in these schools. The study explores how educators in marginalised schools respond to cyberthreats and how they evaluate the threats so they can protect themselves as they use the cyberspace. The distinct economic disparity of South Africa, which is a result of its apartheid legacy makes the country an appropriate context for this study. In addition, South Africa has deliberately sought to integrate ICTs and implement government policies to provide ICTs in schools [18]. The Western Cape Province and Limpopo provinces where the schools used in this study are drawn from, represents an affluent and economically challenged province respectively.

2 Literature Review

2.1 Cybersecurity and Human Cybersecurity Vulnerabilities

The cyberspace covers "the entire spectrum of networked information and communication technologies and systems worldwide as well as the physical hardware," including various manifestations of ICTs [3]. In the digital age individuals must access and use the cyberspace in their work and personal life as the internet has infiltrated every facet of life. However, through cyberattacks, cybercriminals make the cyberspace an unsafe environment. Cyberattacks are actions taken with the intent to jeopardize a technical or socio-technical system's confidentiality, availability, and integrity [3].

In the South African context, 86% of the population regularly use online platforms. This has attracted cyber criminals who consider the country's cyber environment to be a low-hanging fruit [11]. Increased use of online platforms during the COVID-19 pandemic led to a 57% increase in phishing attacks in South Africa [19]. The low levels of cybersecurity awareness increase the vulnerability of individuals to cyberattacks. In a school context, these attacks may aim to access and manipulate sensitive information of the school and extort money from various stakeholders such as parents, educators, administrative staff, and the schools trading partners.

Cybersecurity is a security mechanism which upholds the confidentiality, availability, and integrity of digital information [20]. Humans play a huge role in cybersecurity, either through upholding it or compromising it through human errors and risk factors which increases cybersecurity vulnerabilities to cyberattacks and threats [21]. Cyber criminals exploit the vulnerabilities of individuals' minds with broad tactics that include phishing and social engineering [20]. Susceptibility to cyberthreats have, however, been attributed to individual tendencies to trust and help others whereof malicious actors will take advantage [22]. These malicious actors take advantage of the "naive" nature of individuals and exploit their vulnerabilities to access confidential information [10]. Thus, without malicious intent to cause harm, internet users make up the bulk of cybersecurity breaches that organisations suffer [15].

Human errors in cybersecurity inevitably remain an inherent limitation in risk mitigation entailing the importance of considering individuals decision-making processes online [23]. Cybersecurity education, training and awareness are therefore important to ensure cyber safety in schools as they reduce educators' cybersecurity vulnerabilities and the risk of cyber-attacks and threats [15]. However, most countries in sub-Saharan Africa, cannot implement such initiatives as they require huge amounts of financial resources [24]. For organisations educating employees about cybersecurity is quite expensive and time and labour intensive, the situation for marginalised schools is therefore much dire [25].

2.2 Marginalised Schools in South Africa

In the South African context marginalised schools are generally found in rural areas and low-income urban suburbs. These schools which were segregated against during apartheid were classified as "non-white schools" and they were not prioritised in resource allocation. In the ever-expanding digital age of the 21st century, these schools are still on the downside of the digital divide as they are forced to operate with limited ICTs resources, knowledge, and skills [26]).

Educators in most South African schools are not digitally competent, and this negatively affects their use of technology for work and personal use [27]. Thus, educators in most South African schools have limited cyber safety knowledge and skills [28]. The vulnerability of educators to cyber threats in marginalised schools can, however, put schools at risk leading to unintended consequences which can be multiplied many times within short timeframes due to the interconnectedness of the cyber environment [29]. Despite the efforts of the government to redress the inequalities of the apartheid era through several initiatives, former "non-white" schools in rural areas, former townships and informal settlements remain marginalised and under-resourced [30]. The government's efforts to uplift the schools include providing ICTs and enabling educators to use them in their teaching. The digital age and the COVID-19 pandemic, in particular, has reinforced the use of ICTs in schools, including marginalised schools, resulting in increased use of ICTs and a growing number of learners using cell phones, tablets, and computer labs [31].

The Department of Basic Education, Quintile System determines the state of a school being regarded as marginalised [32]. The quintile system classifies schools into five categories, ranging from the poorest (Quintile 1) to the least poor (Quintile 5). Government financial support is allocated based on the quintiles. Quintile 1 schools receive the highest allocation per learner and Quintile 5 receive the lowest [33]. Schools in rural and low-income high-density suburbs usually fall between Quintile 1 and Quintile 3. Learners in schools in Quintiles 1 to 3 are often not required to pay tuition fees.

Due to their limited resources, marginalised schools have limited exposure to cyber-security initiatives and are, therefore, more vulnerable to cyber-attacks than their affluent counterparts [13, 34]. Thus, educators in marginalised schools in South Africa are vulnerable to cyberthreats and cyber-attacks as they lack the resources, knowledge, and skills to ensure cybersecurity in schools [28]. The cybersecurity vulnerabilities of educators can have devastating effects not only on themselves but for the school and its various stakeholders in the event of a cybersecurity breach. To ensure their safety as they use the internet educators should be able to acknowledge that they are vulnerable to cyber threat, and they must perceive that they are able to protect themselves and others in the cyberspace [35].

3 Theoretical Framework

We employed the Protection Motivation Theory (PMT) as a theoretical underpinning for the study. The framework can be used in a variety of risky situations where threats are of personal, social, and economic nature [36, 37]. PMT posits that environmental factors and personal factors combine to pose a potential threat where two cognitive processes: threat appraisal and coping appraisal are initiated from the threat [38]. The framework assumes that a threat appraisal is a prerequisite in evaluation of the coping [39]. In the context of cybersecurity, an educator's threat appraisal arises when they perceive themselves to be vulnerable as they use the cyberspace and considers the results of falling victim to a cyber-attack.

Threat appraisal refers to an individual's susceptibility to a threat, for instance, how susceptible an individual is to the possibility of being a cyber-attack victim such as phishing [35]. An individual's perception of a threat depends on a range of factor such as sources of information or antecedents, observational learning and how vulnerable individuals perceive themselves to being targeted by cyberattacks [7, 40]. The individual must believe that their vulnerability to a cyber threat is severe, and that they can defend themselves against it [36]. Coping appraisal assesses the various factors that are likely to ensure that an individual engages in recommended responses and responds in a way that is mainly preventive [35]. In the context of cybersecurity this would include an educator not opening emails being sent from a suspicious email address.

Based on PMT, individuals assess the threat by perceiving that they are vulnerable to the threat, and it is severe enough. Through coping appraisal, they acknowledge the cost of carrying out the suggested action to comply with the recommended behaviour [37, 39]. Threat appraisals consist of:

- threat vulnerability- (the probability of the threat)
- threat severity-the severity of the consequences if the threat is manifested [36].

The coping appraisal process evaluates an individual's capacity to cope with and avoid the risk (self-efficacy and response efficacy) [41]. Coping appraisal consist of:

- self-efficacy-the perceived ability of an individual to enact a protective response.
- response efficacy-the perception about the effectiveness of that response in averting a threat.

Figure 1 illustrates PMT, and its sub-constructs as used in this study.

Figure 1 shows the constructs of PMT arranged in two pathways: the threat appraisal pathway and the coping appraisal pathway, which are linked to perceptions about behaviour. PMT integrates cognitive process with information, knowledge, and attitudes to behaviours [42].

Fear appeals are regarded as a source of information in addition to prior experience, observational learning, and personality [36]. Protection motivation refers to the intention to perform a behaviour and is a positive linear function. Of note is how protection motivation, threat and coping appraisal may lead to maladaptive coping responses which include denial, avoidance, fatalism, and hopelessness [42]. Threat appraisal can, therefore, be correlated with maladaptive coping responses, highlighting that high threat perceptions makes one likely to adopt either adaptive or maladaptive coping responses

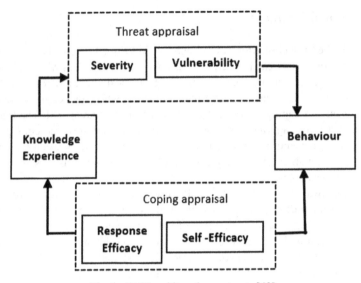

Fig. 1. PMT and its sub-constructs [48]

[43]. PMT enabled us to highlight how perceptions about cyberthreats and available coping strategies are important determinants of cybersecurity behaviour as educators use ICTs in marginalised schools [44].

4   Research Methodology

In this study we used an interpretive approach, which is deductive, qualitative, and cross-sectional. To ensure the reliability of the findings, we employed a multiple case study methodology and an exploratory qualitative study design to detect patterns in various complex situations [45]. We used purposive sampling of four schools chosen evenly from rural and low-income high density urban schools from Limpopo and Western Cape provinces. The sample for the study consists of 20 educators from the four selected schools. Data was collected through semi-structure in-depth interviews from consenting participants between the period April and September 2023. Using NVivo 14 software, we analysed the data through qualitative thematic analysis using a deductive approach by applying themes from PMT and literature to identify instances that match the predefined themes [46].

We obtained ethical clearance for the study from the researchers' institution as well as permission from the respective departments of education. To maintain confidentiality and anonymity, we employed pseudonyms for the four schools in the study. The schools from the Western Cape are identified as WC1 and WC2; the schools from Limpopo are identified as LMP1 and LMP2. The respondents are identified by a code which represents their school and an alphabetical letter representing a respective serial number.

5 Case Description

Table 1 summarises the information about the sampled schools. All the schools in the sample are non-tuition fee paying; meaning they depend on government for financial support.

Table 1. Summary of the statistics of the sampled schools

Province	School	Location	No. of learners	No. of educators	ICTs
Western Cape	WC1	Urban	1600	48	Internet connection, Computer lab (35 Computers) 14 laptops School Management system
	WC2	Rural	1500	44	Internet connection, Computer lab (17 Computers) 11 laptops 4 staff computers School Management system
Limpopo	LMP1	Urban	1188	34	Internet connection 8 laptops School Management system
	LMP2	Rural	1100	29	Internet connection, 4 computers School Management system

WC1 is located in a high-density suburb that is overwhelmed by a sprawling informal settlement. The settlement is characterised by poverty, high crime and unemployment rates, and substance abuse. WC2 is located in a rural farming area that is characterised by high unemployment and illiteracy rates, poverty, and substance abuse.

LMP1 is an urban school located in a low-income high-density suburb characterised by high crime and unemployment rates, substance abuse and poverty. LMP2 is a rural school located in a community bedevilled by various challenges including high unemployment and illiteracy rates and poverty.

6   Empirical Analysis and Discussions

6.1   Vulnerabilities Based on Limited Information on Cyberthreats

The respondents showed a limited understanding of cyberthreats and consequently, mis-informed coping appraisal. In general, the respondents recognised that, *"it's not that safe especially Facebook maybe your profile picture is not really protected. I heard stories of people who are doing this, asking money on behalf of someo*ne" (WC1A).

Most of the information they had on the topic was based on what they had gathered from people within their environment: "*I heard from friends and many people that you must not open some links for safety reasons*" (LMP2D) In most cases the information was not adequate for them to recognise the severity of the cyberthreats. Therefore, they could not make comprehensive threat appraisals: "*I don't have a proof, but there's a lot that we do not understand*" (WC1D).

Although most respondents recognised threat vulnerability when using online plat-forms, they lacked comprehensive cybersecurity knowledge and skills that would allow them to perform the required coping appraisals to protect themselves from cyber threats. "*We know Facebook is not good but there is a lot of stuff we do not know*" (LMP1A). The respondents had a low self-efficacy and lacked response efficacy which increased their cybersecurity vulnerabilities to cyberthreats as they lacked threat appraisal skills "*we just don't know which is a dangerous link or a fishy phone call" (WC1B)*.

6.2   Fear-based Vulnerabilities

Cybersecurity vulnerability among some respondents emanated from fear. In most cases the fear emanated from observations and hearing accounts of cyber victims in their environment. This entails that the respondents had a certain appreciation of cyberthreat vulnerability and recognised their susceptibilities to cyber threats:

"*I'm scared of the internet and online things. I don't want to use my details online*" (LMP2B).

"*Although I have never experienced any cyber harm, I fear the various threats and risks I hear about the internet. I fear losing money*" (WC1C)

In some cases, the respondents recognised the severity of the threat and that they were vulnerable. However, the respondents had limited cybersecurity knowledge and skills, hence they were not equipped to apply coping appraisals against the cyber threats. Their self-efficacy was low; therefore, they could not practice any coping appraisal and because of the limited digital skills, they could not apply recommended responses. "*I am not comfortable with the internet because I am not trained on how to use it*" (WC2B). Their low levels of cybersecurity and digital knowledge and skills increased their cybersecurity vulnerability due to low self-efficacy and hopeless maladaptive behaviour: "*I'm so scared that if I press any button, I will be answering into some other things*" (LMP1C).

Some respondents demonstrated a positive threat appraisal. They acknowledged being vulnerable online and could recognise the severity of cyberthreats. However, their coping appraisal was misinformed. For example, one respondent indicated that they "… *always put a black dark tape on my computer camera when I use it, because I feel like these hackers can see me*" (LMP1A). The respondent had a positive threat appraisal; acknowledged being vulnerable online and could recognise the severity of cyberthreats. However, their coping appraisal was misinformed. The respondent's cybersecurity vulnerability is enhanced as they acted on the misconception that their action of physically covering their computer camera can effectively protect them from cyber threats.

6.3   Vulnerabilities Based on Misguided Self-efficacy

Some respondents demonstrated a false sense of confidence caused by limited cybersecurity knowledge. Consequently, they were not cautious as they used the internet and ICT devices.

> *"These days there's no point of hiding a password, I don't feel a threat at our level because I'm working with educators. They do not have that high technology know-how; how can they rob or do whatever"* (WC1E).

In this case, the respondent recognised that sharing password was risky, however, they failed to appreciate the true nature of the threat and the consequences. Their vulnerability and susceptibility to cyberthreats is increased because of their misinformed trust, as cyber criminals can easily take advantage of their gullibility [22]. Misguided self-efficacy among respondents is manifested when they fail to recognise that their practices increased their cybersecurity vulnerabilities, *"I always share my phone, laptop and my passwords at school and at home"* (WC2A). Respondents had no perception of cyberthreat vulnerabilities or the severity of threats that might occur because of their sharing behaviour as they use ICTs, since did not consider any protective behaviour.

The misguided self-efficacy of the respondents exacerbated their vulnerability to cyberthreats as they *"feel very safe on the internet"*. In some instances, the self-efficacy rose from their high use of the internet *"because day and night we are on the internet"* (LMP1B). Further, they were of the perception that only those that are naive can fall victim to cyberattacks and adopted avoidance maladaptive as their coping appraisal, *"I can say that it is up to an individual to be unsafe on the internet, remember you are the one that will click on the link, if you just ignore the link, you are safe* (LMP2C). The respondent showed how they are increasingly susceptible to cyberthreats and cyberattacks, *"I go like for an hour without using my cell phone, so I feel safer* (LMP2B), as they expressed their maladaptive avoidance behaviour which they perceived as an appropriate coping appraisal due to misguided self-efficacy and limited cybersecurity knowledge.

6.4   Vulnerabilities Based on Limited Resources

Whilst some respondents were aware of the severity of cyber threats, they recognised that their environment increased their cybersecurity vulnerabilities;

"We struggle to participate safely on the internet because of lack of funds, we are forced to share laptops with family and colleagues because they have a work or university deadline. It's not like the person wants to watch a movie or something" (LMP1D).

The limited number of ICT devices in the respondents' environment entailed that they must share the devices. This exposed them to cyber threats and increased their vulnerabilities to cyberattacks. Whilst they perceived that they were vulnerable and identified the severity of threats because of behaviours and practises, they were not equipped to ensure appropriate coping appraisals and to apply recommended responses where individuals must share devices. Respondents recognised their cybersecurity vulnerabilities as they acknowledged that the marginalised context exposed them to cyber threats:

"I don't feel safe on the school computer because of viruses. We don't have money to buy an antivirus program ... Unfortunately we can't ... we are a no fee-paying school" (WC2D)

The respondent was knowledgeable that an antivirus would be an appropriate coping mechanism against virus-related cyber threats. However, the resource-constrained environment of the school meant the school could not afford to acquire the software thereby increasing the cybersecurity vulnerability of the whole schools as they could easily fall victim to cyberattacks.

6.5 Experience and Knowledge as Tools to Minimise Cybersecurity Vulnerabilities

Respondents who had previously fallen victim to cyberattacks tended to realise their cybersecurity vulnerability and to recognise the severity of threats. *"I was scammed when I was in college. I logged onto the website and my money was gone* (WC2E). The cyberattack experience made the respondent aware of the severity of cyber threats. Consequently, the respondent adopted the required coping appraisals and applied recommended responses to ensure protection from cyberthreats *"I protect my email, my Facebook I am careful wherever I use personal information".* (WC2E).

As a result of a previous cyber bullying attack, a respondent is highly aware of the severity of cybersecurity threats. *"When I was younger, I experienced a lot of traumas with social media. I had stalkers and the worst thing is, I was being harassed, by my so-called friends"* (LMP2A). Thus, respondents who had been victims of cyber-attacks could assess the threat appraisal as they acknowledged their threat vulnerabilities and adapted the recommended coping appraisals;

"I value safety, I only have the people that I know on Facebook and, if I see something, which seems like bullying, if I know the person, I communicate with him and tell him remove it because it's not relevant" (LMP1E).

Perceptions of severity and vulnerability informed by the respondents' prior experiences influenced their intentions to adopt and adhere to recommended cybersecurity responses and actions (Nam, 2019).

Respondents with cybersecurity knowledge and skills, however, proved to be able to protect themselves and ensure cyber safety;

"I doubt [that] I will share (my laptop). I believe some information is meant for school only, the sharing might put the integrity of the school at risk (LMP1A)

I pay for Norton firewall as a security. It will block these funny pop ups." (WC2C).

The respondents had a high cybersecurity self-efficacy and could perform cybersecurity threat appraisal as they applied appropriate coping appraisal to protect themselves and the school from possible cyber threats.

"I do not share my password with people even my partner. I keep my password to myself, and I change it after some time. You must protect yourself by getting yourself an anti-virus to make sure the internet doesn't just push in anything malicious" (LMP2E)

The respondent was aware of the dangers and severity of cyberthreats and acknowledged their vulnerability in the cyberspace. Because they were acting from an informed position, they had the capabilities to perform effective threat appraisals and apply the required coping appraisals and recommended responses. Respondents, therefore, had a high self-efficacy and response-efficacy and practiced cyber hygiene to protect themselves, even though they are in marginalised contexts.

7 Conclusion

As ICTs become part of schools, educators in marginalised schools find themselves exposed to cyberthreats and cyber-attacks [13]. Education authorities have prioritised the use of ICTs for curriculum delivery and administration purposes without taking into consideration the technological and cybersecurity skills of educators increasing their vulnerabilities to cyberthreats. The study revealed the economic disparity between the Western Cape and Limpopo provinces, with the schools in the former having more access to ICTs than the latter. However, the two provinces face similar challenges in as far as the cybersecurity vulnerability of educators is concerned.

Since most educators in marginalised schools have not received any formal training on cybersecurity, they depend on hearsay piecemeal information on the dangers of the internet. In most cases this leads to low cybersecurity self-efficacy amongst the educators. Further, the educators can neither gauge the severity of cyberthreats nor understand how they can protect themselves to ensure cyber safety. Educators become fearful of using online platforms as a result they adopt inappropriate and ineffective preventive behaviours against cyberthreats, further increasing their vulnerability.

Limited cybersecurity knowledge may engender misguided self-efficacy among educators in marginalised schools. Educators' cybersecurity vulnerability is enhanced by a false sense of security, as they fail to recognise the global nature of the cyberspace and believe they can behave negligently on the internet without consequences. Because of limited cybersecurity knowledge, the educators based their security on the internet on gullible ineffective actions and behaviours [22]. Their naivety increases their cybersecurity vulnerability as cybercriminals depend on such exploitable tendencies to feed their malicious activities in the cyberspace.

The resource-constrained environment of marginalised schools exposes the educators to cyber risks from multiple fronts. First, they are forced to operate without basic preventive technologies such as antivirus software [47]. Second, they must share limited ICT devices. In addition, they must share personal devices with family and colleagues without knowledge on how they can protect themselves to guarantee their cyber safety in such circumstances, enhancing their cybersecurity vulnerability.

The study has, however, shown that educators in marginalised schools with cybersecurity knowledge and skills can safely navigate the cyberspace. These educators are capacitated to realise that individuals are vulnerable online, and they have the skills to identify cyberthreats and to practice appropriate cybersecurity behaviours to ensure cyber safety. We, therefore, recommend that cybersecurity training and digital literacy should be a precursor of the provision of ICTs in schools as governments in Sub-Saharan Africa seek to ensure the inclusion of everyone in the digital age. Cybersecurity trainings should be part of educators' continuous professional development given the dynamic nature of ICTs. Furthermore, pre-service teacher training should include a comprehensive cybersecurity curriculum to adequately prepare educators as they join the technology enhanced teaching profession. Future studies should use more case studies and a larger sample size.

Acknowledgement. The authors would like to acknowledge the financial contribution of the National Research Foundation (NRF) in conducting this study as part of the research project entitled Cybersecurity framework for rural and disadvantage schools in South Africa.

Disclosure of Interests. The authors have no competing interests to declare that are relevant to the content of this article.

References

1. Rahman, T., Rohan, R., Pal, D., Kanthamanon, P.: Human factors in cybersecurity: a scoping review. In: Proceedings of the 12th International Conference on Advances in Information Technology (1–11) (2021)
2. Richardson, M.D., Lemoine, P.A., Stephens, W.E., Waller, R.E.: Planning for cyber security in schools: the human factor. Educational Planning 27(2), 23–39 (2020)
3. Nam, T.: Understanding the gap between perceived threats to and preparedness for cybersecurity. Technology in Society 58 (2019)
4. Anwar, M., et al.: Gender difference and employees' cybersecurity behaviours. Computers in Human Behavior **69**, 437–443 (2017
5. Aldawood, H., Skinner, G.: Reviewing cyber security social engineering training and awareness programs-pitfalls and ongoing issues. Future Internet **11**(3) (2019)
6. Frauenstein, E.D., Flowerday, S.: Susceptibility to phishing on social network sites: a personality information processing model. Comput. Secur. **94**, 101862 (2020)

7. Coleman, C.D., Reeder, E.: Three reasons for improving cybersecurity instruction and practice. In: Society for Information Technology & Teacher Education International Conference, pp. 1020–1025 (2018)
8. Tunggal, A.T.: Cybersecurity Vulnerability? Does a Vulnerability Become, access to a computer system. https://www.upguard.com/blog/vulnerability#:~:text=Abi. Last accessed 13 April 2024
9. Williams, E.J., Hinds, J., Joinson, A.N.: Exploring susceptibility to phishing in the workplace. Int. J. Hum. Comput. Stud. **120**, 1–13 (2018)
10. Papatsaroucha, D., Nikoloudakis, Y., Kefaloukos, I., Pallis, E., Markakis, E.K.: A Survey on Human and Personality Vulnerability Assessment in Cyber-security: Challenges, Approaches, and Open Issues (2021)
11. Kshetri, N.: Cybercrime and Cybersecurity in Africa. In: Journal of Global Information Technology Management, vol. 22, Issue 2, pp. 77–81. Taylor and Francis Inc. (2019)
12. Goldsborough, R.: Protecting yourself against ransomware. Teach. Libr. **43**(4), 70 (2016)
13. Kritzinger, E.: Improving cybersafety maturity of South African schools. Information (Switzerland) **11**(10), 1–17 (2020)
14. Schneider, F.B. From the editors Cybersecurity Education in Universities (2013). http://com putingnow.computer.org
15. Mabece, T., Futcher, L., Thomson, K.-L.: South African Computing Educators' Perspectives on Information Security Behaviour 121–132 (2017)
16. Chigona, W., Mudavanhu, S.L., Siebritz, A., Amerika, Z.: Domestication of free Wi-Fi amongst people living in disadvantaged communities in the Western Cape Province of South Africa. ACM International Conference Proceeding Series, 26–28-Sept. (2016)
17. Dube, B.: Rural Online Learning in the Context of COVID-19 in South Africa: Evoking an Inclusive Education Approach **10**(2), 135–157 (2020)
18. Dzansi, D.Y.: Integrating ICT into Rural South African Schools: Possible Solutions for Challenges. Int. J. Edu. Sci. **06**(02) (2014)
19. Smith, C.: Move aside malware, the rising threat is stalkerware. Fin24 (2021). https://www.news24.com/fin24/companies/ict/move-aside-malware-the-rising-threat-isstalkerware-202 10501. Last accessed 2 April 2024
20. Alsharif, M., Mishra, S., AlShehri, M.: Impact of human vulnerabilities on cybersecurity. Comput. Syst. Sci. Eng. **40**(3), 1153–1166 (2021)
21. Wang, Z., Zhu, H., Sun, L.: Social engineering in cybersecurity: effect mechanisms, human vulnerabilities, and attack methods. IEEE Access **9**, 11895–11910 (2021)
22. Conteh, N.Y., Royer, M.D.: The rise in cybercrime and the dynamics of exploiting the human vulnerability factor. Int. J. Comp. **201**, 1–12 (2016)
23. Debb, S.M., Mcclellan, M.K.: Perceived vulnerability as a determinant of increased risk for cybersecurity risk behavior. Cyberpsychol. Behav. Soc. Netw. **24**(9), 605–611 (2021)
24. Chibanda, R., Kabanda, S.: Towards an African cybersecurity community of practice. In: Proceedings of 43rd Conference of the South African Institute of Computer Scientists and Information Technologists, vol. 85, pp. 1–14 (2022)
25. McGettrick, A., Cassel, L.N., Dark, M., Hawthorne, E.K., Impagliazzo, J.: Toward curricular guidelines for cybersecurity. In: SIGCSE 2014 - Proceedings of the 45th ACM Technical Symposium on Computer Science Education 0, pp. 81–82 (2014)
26. Gunzo, F., Dalvit, L.: A survey of cell phone and computer access and use in marginalised schools in South Africa. In: Proceedings of M4D 2012 28–29 February 2012 New Delhi, India **28**(29), 232 (2012)
27. Nkula, K., Krauss, K.E.M.: Proceedings of the 8th international development informatics association conference. ICTs for Inclusive Communities in Developing Societies **8**, 241–261 (2014)

28. Scholtz, D., Kritzinger, E., Botha, A.: Cyber safety awareness framework for South African schools to enhance cyber safety awareness. In: Applied Informatics and Cybernetics in Intelligent Systems: 9th Computer Science On-Line (2020)
29. Liang, N., Biros, D., Luse, A.: Taxonomy of malicious insiders: a proof of concept study. AMCIS 2016: Surfing the IT Innovation Wave - 22nd Americas Conference on Information Systems, 2005, pp. 1–10 (2016)
30. Du Toit, N.B., Forster, D., Roux, E.L., Weber, S.: Born free? South African young adults, inequality, and reconciliation in Stellenbosch. Int. bulletin Miss. Res. 46(2), 200–210 (2022)
31. Shambare, B., Simuja, C., Olayinka, T.A.: Educational technologies as pedagogical tools: perspectives from teachers in rural marginalised secondary schools in South Africa. Int. J. Info. Commun. Technol. Edu. (IJICTE) 18(1) (2022)
32. White, C.J., Van Dyk, H.: Theory and practice of the quintile ranking of schools in South Africa: A financial management perspective. S. Afr. J. Educ. 39(Supplement 1), s1-19 (2019)
33. CAPS 123: Understanding School Fees and Quintiles in South African Public Schools (2023)
34. Kortjan, N., Von Solms, R.: Cyber Security Education in Developing Countries: A South African Perspective. In: LNICST, vol. 119 (2013)
35. Bada, M., Nurse, J.R.: The social and psychological impact of cyberattacks. In: Emerging cyber threats and cognitive vulnerabilities, pp. 73–92. Academic Press (2020)
36. Rogers, R.W.: Cognitive and physiological processes in fear appeals and attitude change: a revised theory of protection motivation. Social psychology: A source book, pp. 153–176 (1983)
37. Rogers, R.W., Prentice-Dunn, S.: Protection motivation theory. In: Gochman, D. (ed.) Handbook of health behaviour research: Vol. 1. Determinants of health behaviour: Personal and social, pp. 113–132. Plenum (1997)
38. Arthur, D., Quester, P.: Who's afraid of that ad? Applying segmentation to the protection motivation model. Psychol. Mark. 21(9), 671–696 (2004)
39. Floyd, D.L., Prentice-Dunn, S., Rogers, R.W.: A meta-analysis of research on protection motivation theory. J. Appl. Soc. Psychol. 30(2), 407–429 (2000)
40. Iuga, C., Nurse, J.R., Erola, A.: Baiting the hook: factors impacting susceptibility to phishing attacks. HCIS 6, 1–20 (2016)
41. Khan, N.F., Ikram, N., Murtaza, H., Javed, M.: Evaluating protection motivation based cybersecurity awareness training on Kirkpatrick's Model. Computers and Security 125 (2023)
42. Milne, S., Sheeran, P., Orbell, S.: Prediction and intervention in health-related behavior: a meta-analytic review of protection motivation theory. J. Appl. Soc. Psychol. 30(1), 106–143 (2000)
43. Abraham, C.S., Sheeran, P., Abrams, D., Spears, R.: Exploring teenagers' adaptive and maladaptive thinking in relation to the threat of HIV infection. Psychol. Health 9(4), 253–272 (1994)
44. Dodel, M., Mesch, G.: Cyber-victimization preventive behavior: a health belief model approach. Comput. Hum. Behav. 68, 359–367 (2017)
45. Hollweck, T.: Case Study Research Design and Methods, 5th ed., p. 282. Sage, Thousand Oaks, CA. The Canadian Journal of Program Evaluation 108–110 (2016)
46. Fereday, J., Muir-Cochrane, E.: Demonstrating rigor using thematic analysis: a hybrid approach of inductive and deductive coding and theme development. Int. J. Qual. Metho. 5(1), 80–92 (2006)
47. Milne, A.: The rising cost of cyber security expertise. Field Effect (2021). https://fieldeffect.com/blog/rising-cost-cyber-security-expertise/. Last accessed 23 March 2024
48. Xiao, H., et al.: Protection motivation theory in predicting intention to engage in protective behaviours against schistosomiasis among middle school students in rural China. PLoS Neglected Tropical Diseases 8(10) (2014)

Cautious Optimism: The Influence of Generative AI Tools in Software Development Projects

Takura Mbizo, Grant Oosterwyk[✉] ⓘ, Pitso Tsibolane ⓘ,
and Popyeni Kautondokwa ⓘ

Commerce Faculty, Department of Information Systems, University of Cape Town, Cape Town,
South Africa
takura.mbizvo@alumni.uct.ac.za, {grant.oosterwyk,
pitso.tsibolane}@uct.ac.za, ktnpop001@myuct.ac.za

Abstract. Generative artificial intelligence has emerged as a disruptive technology with the potential to transform traditional software development practices and methodologies. This study examines the implications of integrating AI tools in software development projects, focusing on potential benefits, challenges, and perceptions of the broader software development community. The study employs a qualitative methodology that captures the sentiments and personal adaptive measures from a diverse group of industry professionals who integrate generative AI tools such as ChatGPT and GitHub's Copilot in their software development projects. Findings suggest that generative AI tools aid developers in automating repetitive tasks, improve their workflow efficiency, reduce the coding learning curve, and complement traditional coding practices and project management techniques. However, generative AI tools also present ethical limitations, including privacy and security issues. The study also raises concerns regarding the long-term potential for job elimination (insecurity), over-reliance on generative AI assistance by developers, generative AI lack of contextual understanding, and technical skills erosion. While developers are optimistic about the positive benefits of generative AI use within project environments in the short term, they also hold a pessimistic view in the longer term. There is a need for the software development projects community to critically assess the use of generative AI in software development projects while exploring how to retain the critical aspect of human oversight and judgment in the software development process in the long term.

Keywords: Generative AI · Development Projects · ChatGPT

1 Introduction

Generative artificial intelligence (AI) tools have been predicted to cause a significant shift in how software is developed [24]. AI is a branch of technology that enables computers to perform tasks in a human-like manner and trains computers to simulate human behaviors like judgment and decision-making [7]. A significant advancement in AI technology is the evolution of reinforcement learning models [11], which, when coupled with deep learning techniques, have empowered AI to interpret and learn from unstructured

A. Gerber (Ed.): SAICSIT 2024, CCIS 2159, pp. 361–373, 2024.
https://doi.org/10.1007/978-3-031-64881-6_21

data, leading to the creation of sophisticated Large Language Models (LLMs) [23]. The underlying architecture of LLMs has brought about the creation of generative AI tools. Generative AI systems are LLMs that have been trained on massive datasets to generate content in response to user prompts. ChatGPT is an example of a language mode that utilizes explicitly the Generative Pre-training Transformer (GPT) architecture developed by OpenAI [17]. With its capability to generate human-like conversational text, ChatGPT has found applications in language translation, essay writing, code generation, debugging, and testing [1].

Generative AI tools have been embraced in different domains. They are used to carry out various tasks, from writing text to generating code used within software development projects [13]. Platforms like GitHub's Copilot easily integrate into well-known programming environments like Visual Studio Code, Neovim, and JetBrains IDEs, just a few examples of these technologies' innovation in software development [8]. The paper also highlights how tools like Tabnine stand out in code completion and adherence to open-source principles and reiterates that AI-driven augmentation in software development is not just limited to code completion. Tasks like testing, debugging, and deployment are being automated, potentially reducing development cycles and overheads [8].

However, the reception of these tools has been met with a wide variety of contrasting opinions in the software development community [18, 21, 22]. This research study examines the perceived influence of generative AI tools in software development projects, posing the first research question: *How does generative AI shape the landscape of software development projects?* The paper further aims to understand the benefits and the challenges of its integration into the software development process, thereby formulating the second research question: **What benefits and challenges are associated with integrating Generative AI in software development projects?**

The rest of the paper is organised as follows. Section 2 is a literature review on Generative AI in software development. Section 3 describes the methodological framework of the paper. Section 4 focuses on the data analysis, while Sect. 5 discusses the paper's findings. Section 6 concludes the paper with recommendations and future implications.

2   Literature Review

Generative AI tools like Copilot and ChatGPT have gained popularity with their ability to generate human-like conversation and advanced software code generation, attracting over a million users within a few days [14]. This section explores the role, perceptions and ethical concerns regarding using Generative AI in software development projects.

2.1   Perceived Roles of Generative AI in Software Development

Research suggests potential benefits beyond entertainment. Studies exploring ChatGPT in medical education found it performing moderately well at the level of a third-year medical student [10]. However, its application in software development education, specifically undergraduate software testing, yielded fewer promising results [15]. This highlights the potential for generative AI to be a transformative tool in specific contexts while requiring careful evaluation for suitability in others.

2.2 Perceptions of Generative AI Tools in Software Development Integration and Application

The ability to automate tasks and provide solutions quickly has rendered generative AI tools useful in the field of software development, yet there remain concerns about their effectiveness and accuracy, along with the consequences of such implications. [15] specifically delved into ChatGPT's performance in an undergraduate software testing course, finding its capabilities to be somewhat lacking in accuracy when it came to answering textbook questions. [20] reinforced this finding by noting that while Chat-GPT could automate software bug fixing, the cost of verifying its generated solutions potentially outweighed the benefits of using it. In their editorial opinion, [7] praised ChatGPT specifically for improving work productivity, further insinuating that it could be instrumental in completing tasks and ensuring quality output. It is also clear that software developers are not just experimenting with generative AI tools but are actively integrating them into their software projects, mainly to ease and automate redundant tasks.

Negative Perceptions Towards the Implications of Automation
Adopting these technologies has been criticized professionally, specifically with the long-standing reservation that automation potentially leads to job displacement. Generative AI's prowess to efficiently automate repetitive tasks unsurprisingly poses a threat to many professionals and their respective professions. While tools like ChatGPT are good at generating, refactoring, and optimizing code at exceptional speeds, their reliability is questionable. Professionals who have worked with ChatGPT have often reported encountering misleading responses, errors, and even security vulnerabilities [6]. Drawing parallels to the introduction of calculators in the 1970s, [7] discuss how AI tools should complement rather than replace human intellect and skill.

Concerns Regarding the Accuracy and Quality of Output (Hallucination)
Launched by GitHub in collaboration with OpenAI, Github Copilot is another example of a generative AI tool specifically known for its real-time collaborative capabilities and termed the 'AI pair programmer' [16]. A focused assessment was set up where GitHub Copilot was tested using LeetCode programming challenges across four languages: JavaScript, C, Java, and Python. The results of the experiment revealed high accuracy scores in code suggestions from the AI tool, with Java achieving the highest and JavaScript the lowest. Further, Copilot's output displayed low complexity across all languages. While Copilot can save developers time and provide insightful information, it is essential to consider all its recommendations carefully as the tool could provide incorrect answers while stating them boldly, a phenomenon known as hallucination. For the most part, Copilot will aid developers in solving programming problems and, at the very least, give them a satisfactory starting point [16].

Project and Software Development Life Cycle
Beyond the mainstream ChatGPT, [18] found that generative AI tools have the potential to improve the Software Development Life Cycle (SDLC) significantly. Their research suggests that these AI solutions could efficiently analyze past Agile projects by identifying their trends and patterns, which can primarily facilitate future project planning.

Further, this assists in managing the workload and velocity of the new project based on the performance of previous cycles. By offering grammatical checks, code formatting, and debugging, amongst other intricate software use cases, AI can swiftly turn system designs into code, improving code optimization and ensuring the efficient utilization of resources [18]. The anticipated result is that these advancements will enhance developers' productivity, potentially realizing the benefits of this improvement at the project outcome level.

Augmentation Software Development Processes
Generative AI tools have shown their capability to augment various aspects of software development, and the literature shows how this has propelled researchers to examine their use cases and possible implications within the field [22]. Examining ChatGPT's prompt patterns for improving code quality, refactoring, and designing software revealed the chatbot's capabilities in enhancing these processes. In a similar way, [21] investigated ChatGPT's potential impact on code generation and software development jobs, noting that while ChatGPT could automate specific tasks and improve the efficiency of traditional software development processes, it is not a direct replacement for human expertise. His counter-argument was that ChatGPT should rather be seen as a tool that can complement and supplement the abilities of software developers. The key suggestion was that generative AI tools like ChatGPT can be used wisely to carry out repetitive tasks, provide relevant suggestions, and facilitate problem-solving [21]. The integration of ChatGPT in this manner could lead to a more productive and streamlined workflow, allowing developers to focus on more complex and creative aspects of their work.

Potential of Generative AI in Software Education
The use cases of generative AI tools are likewise examined in the educational sector, where ChatGPT's performance in software testing education, its ability to teach software testing concepts and its capabilities to provide personalized feedback to the students were assessed [15]. The findings revealed how ChatGPT could effectively supplement the teaching process as it could give more tailored explanations to the individual's needs. In this outcome, generative AI tools can transform the educational landscape of some aspects of software development, with the main emphasis being their ability to provide a personalized learning experience [15].

2.3 Ethical Concerns in Generative AI Tools in Software Development

Cybersecurity Concerns
Beyond their potential applications in education, generative AI tools have been shown to be highly useful in cybersecurity, as noted by Author(s) [13], who highlights the inherent drawbacks of these tools. Cybercriminals can use these tools as digital weapons to launch phishing attacks, social engineering schemes, and more complex security breaches. On the contrary, these same tools can enhance tasks by improving threat intelligence, securing code production, and automating vulnerability detection [13]. While tools like ChatGPT can expedite the analysis of threats, their misuse can also inadvertently leak sensitive data, as observed in an incident at Samsung. In an effort to utilize ChatGPT to write and debug code, Samsung employees fed the model confidential

company information, which accidentally got leaked. Privacy concerns are a significant concern, given the potential of these AI tools to store and utilize personal data, possibly in conflict with privacy laws such as the European Union's General Data Protection Regulation (GDPR). This concern is exacerbated by tools such as Google Bard, which is suspected of using users' activity for training purposes [13].

Privacy and Security Challenges

Generative AI (GenAI) tools, especially prominent ones like ChatGPT, have become deeply embedded in users' daily lives. Their convenience and capabilities make them very useful to people. However, the usefulness of these AI tools comes at the significant cost of users' personal data, as a large amount of it is needed to train these machines [9]. This puts individuals at risk of data leaks and makes them vulnerable to system errors. Like many AI agents, a vast amount of personal data is needed to train the tools as effectively as possible. Generative AI tools are not exempted from this principle, so they require the similar personal information in their training data, posing a threat to privacy [19]. The study identified various challenges related to the use of GenAI tools, summarizing other additional issues that must be considered in the rapidly changing field of generative AI [9].

Over-Reliance on Generative AI

These tools differ from traditional search engines that provide multiple sources of information, often requiring users to rationalize a couple of them. Generative AI responses are very convenient because they give specific answers to users' questions. While this may appear harmless, users may habitually accept AI-generated answers without rationalizing or critiquing them [19].

There are grounds for concern that users of generative AI tools may become overly reliant on them, particularly for software development practices. Software coding is a multi-faceted practice, and there are many steps and procedures to follow when designing good-quality applications. Some of these tasks tend to be tedious and challenging, with the essential skill being the art of problem-solving [5].

The Perpetuation of Bias

[19] highlight that the outputs of Generative AI tools are only as good as the data on which they are trained. The datasets AI machines are trained on are, unfortunately, filled with human biases. Expectedly, when AI tools are trained on data that has biases, they learn from them and perpetuate them in their output. This raises questions about systemic biases like racial and gender biases, which show up in actual real-world applications [19]. While integrating tools like ChatGPT offers many advantages in domains such as software development and education, it is essential to recognize their assumptive limitations. A study of ChatGPT [14] identified that the AI chatbot occasionally produces biased or inaccurate responses, possibly leading to unintentional harm or misinformation for users.

Ethical Implications of Reinforcement Learning in Generative AI

The personalisation of individual users' experiences and interpersonal interactions with

Generative AI machines comes with the concern of unethical data collection. This threatens personal autonomy as AI can subtly sway a user's choice, posing the risk of users being manipulated without their awareness [12]. This covert influence on decisions raises questions about individuals' degree of autonomy and independence when interacting with AI-enhanced platforms. [3] highlighting the potential for errors and biases in AI responses, which can be consequential in professional contexts like software development.

3 Research Methodology

The inductive qualitative approach was found to be fitting for the exploratory nature of this research [2]. With generative AI tools being an emergent technology, their role and influence on software development practices are yet to be fully understood. Thematic analysis offers a systematic yet flexible framework for uncovering patterns and gaining deeper insights into the data [4]. By facilitating the interpretation of various aspects of the research topic, thematic analysis will further enable a deeper understanding of software developer perceptions regarding generative AI tools [4].

4 Data Analysis

The data was collected through semi-structured interviews with ten participants (see Table 1). Transcripts were securely stored in a licensed cloud storage. Data analysis was performed through a thematic analysis approach, given its strengths in identifying and organizing patterns within qualitative data in detail [4].

Table 1. Demographics of Participants in the study.

Participant	Position	Type of Firm	Experience
P1	Manager: Machine Learning	Broadcast Media Production	**10 years**
P2	Graduate Software Developer	Financial Services	**1 year**
P3	Machine Learning Specialist	Broadcast Media Production	**3 years**
P4	Junior Software Engineer	IT Services and IT Consulting	**2 years**
P5	Junior Software Engineer	IT Services and IT Consulting	**1 years**
P6	Infrastructure and Security Engineer	Computer and Network Security	**8 years**
P7	Graduate Data Engineer	Broadcast Media Production and Distribution	**1 years**
P8	Product Engineer	Computer and Network Security	**4 years**
P9	Junior Software Engineer	IT Services and IT Consulting	**1 years**
P10	Product Owner	Information Technology & Services Agency	**3 years**

4.1 Findings

The data analysis phase produced five overarching emergent themes regarding generative AI (GenAI) in software development projects, namely: A) the role of GenAI, B) the influence of GenAI, C) the benefits of GenAI, D) the ethical challenges of GenAI use, and E) professional perceptions of GenAI use. The themes and sample interview extracts, are presented in Table 2.

Table 2. The thematic analysis structure includes the relevant sub-themes, themes, and interview extracts

Codes with Sample Interview Extracts	Themes - Generative AI in Software Development Projects
Code Generation Capabilities *"ChatGPT can generate a code file in just a few seconds, provided you know what's needed"* (P4) *"Speed means quicker return on investment. They don't always require perfect solutions; they need usable and functional solutions that can be iterated upon."* (P1) **Project Structuring** *"... particularly beneficial for tasks like creating boilerplate or scaffolding. When extensive setup is required, you could even request it to design a framework template."* (P4) *".. Saves you a lot of time because most of the time is spent scaffolding parts and so that's already like 30% of the code."* (P2) **Code and Language Assistant** *"So I'll often be on a call and we will be trying to figure out something or debug something and it'll be a let's just check with ChatGPT." P10* *"So I use it a lot for my emails also having to admit that English is not my first language, so I love the fact that it makes it a lot more concise and professional sounding." P10*	*Role of GenAI*
Efficiency and Productivity *"... gives the engineer in charge essentially more time to focus on tougher problems, problems that are more difficult to solve that can't be solved by generative AI"* (P9) *"Why would you want to spend so much time trying to do maths? All that maths in your head when you could be having something to do that for you and you could then focus your time and attention on something that would be more useful?"* (P3) *"Maybe it takes me half a day to implement something and ship it for review. It takes you 10 min to pick up the discrepancies... then I get your comments so I can implement the small changes and we're good to go."* (P8) **Reskilling and Learning New Coding Approaches** *"I was one of those who would use Stack Overflow for many of these sorts of things and have transitioned to kind of going to ChatGPT first, and then if I can narrow down my question, I'll maybe look for human input later."* (P8) **Reducing the Software Development Learning Curve** *"Yeah, it just lowers the barrier to kind of access that ability. So usually if you want to achieve something in a particular framework, you need to go learn the framework and like run through the tutorials and then only then can you start to actually do the thing you had to do. Now you can go, you can sketch out the problem and start right away, get an example, and then go from there."* (P8)	*Influence of GenAI*

(continued)

Table 2. (*continued*)

Codes with Sample Interview Extracts	Themes - Generative AI in Software Development Projects
Generative AI as a Collaborative Knowledge Assistant *"In general, I would have thought about something, try and figure it out in my head, try and ask a colleague, but now it's just so easy to get the information that's relatively accurate."* (P10) *"So, I'll often be on a call and we will be trying to figure out something or debug something and it'll be a let's just check with ChatGPT"* (P8) *"So, I use it a lot for my emails also having to admit that English is not my first language, so I love the fact that it makes it a lot more concise and professional sounding. So even if I would just type out the bullet points or meeting minutes...as I have a meeting with the clients, I capture just in bullet points, the meeting minutes, that we've discussed, and I'll push that to ChatGPT."* (P10) *"I'll check that it works and then...I might just even ask it back and saying, hey, like, what does that line do? And then maybe running a Google search myself off the stuff that it spits out."* (P8) **Generative AI for Content Creation and Workflow Automation** *"I'll push that to ChatGPT and then it would curate a list of...accurate the minutes and I'll send that through to the client which helps me a lot just to fast track that"* (P10) *"And then beyond that, as I mentioned, for our internal processes or setting up like onboarding documentation or any learning documentation...there's a really cool way of embedding AI in notion... if I'd have to curate a paragraph for a client that might be specific to them, or it might just be specific to our processes...I'd also just back slash type in the prompt and it would curate the paragraph."* (P10)	*Benefits of GenAI*
Limitations in Grasping Contextual, Long-Term Organisational Objectives *"I don't think an AI tool would, at least not in its current form, is going to be very good at it because it just needs the wider context. It doesn't have good information to go on whereas someone who has been working at a company for five or ten years and knows what the next six months look like is in a much better place to say."* (P8) *"But I wanted to do a specific thing and I searched that on ChatGPT and did give me a way and it worked. But then when we submitted that code for review, it said that the code was lacking some stuff. There were deprecated libraries and couldn't be allowed to pass to production because of quality purposes obviously."* (P7) *"It doesn't have that kind of background context for what this function is doing or where it should sit, and so you might be given a perfect function that you can kind of copy, paste and drop into the code base, but it violates a bunch of the standards or structure that surrounds that part of the code."* (P8) **Limited Creativity and Authenticity In AI-Generated Output** *"It goes through the internet, goes through different sources of information, and learns how to code way better than you."* (P1) *"At the moment, it's not as great, especially when you go through the creative side of things... There is a sort of synthetic aspect to how AI generates the theme music, for example, comparable to how a human would."* (P1) *"... or even something like an email. Can we present that as our own words to clients?"* (P10) **AI-Generated Hallucinations and Bias** *"I asked it to do something which there's no way of doing actually, but it will. It will inject its own solution into it, which actually won't work."* (P6) *"There's bias based on the data it's trained on. I noticed when you ask it something more South African based, it's trickier than if you ask about the US."* (P1) **Data Privacy Concerns** *"Normally, you're uploading code, not personal data. But there is a concern about uploading code that our clients pay for. If others could access and reuse that code without paying, it poses issues."* (P4) *"there's a paid feature by open AI so that they don't store your data. If you pay them for that particular feature."* (P6) *"Contracts and like the APIs and stuff generally provide enough security for integration. I know a lot of companies actually end up rolling out their own localized versions of these language models so that they don't have to communicate with open AI directly."* (P9)	*Ethical Challenges of GenAI*

(*continued*)

Table 2. (*continued*)

Codes with Sample Interview Extracts	Themes - Generative AI in Software Development Projects
Potential Negative Impact on Junior Developer Roles *"I learned more about problem solving through having to go through all these documentations and having to go through Stack Overflow. I feel sad for this new generation that won't be able to go to Stack Overflow due to everything being given to them."* (P2) *"...sometimes you now stumble across different issues when you're reading through forums. You see different ways of thinking where people say, OK, I tried doing it this way, but I failed because of this."* (P2) *"You don't want to lose that skill of thinking or really wrestling with the problem yourself. I'm not against the technological advancement, but it should be approached with caution."* (P3) *"For repetitive tasks, perhaps there's a case to be made about junior engineers or interns being substituted by ChatGPT."* (P4) **Professional Stigma (negative) associated with GenAI use** *"I think obviously like on a more on a professional level like it's not advised. Like you wouldn't openly disclose that you are using ChatGPT to do your work because then it makes it seem like you're not actually doing your work yourself."* (P7) *"Yeah. Definitely. Like...What? You don't just open your ChatGPT tab like on your screen... cause it's like, why did they hire you then...they could have searched that on ChatGPT themselves."* (P7) **Concern over Potential Loss of Core Skills** *"But now there is an argument to be made that you're missing out on the important learning aspect of, yes it would have taken you longer, but now you understand more... But you will never progress as an engineer if you don't learn the fundamentals and understand everything."* (P4) *"...Maybe as a junior that's fine but you will never get to a senior level without that learning and that understanding. You will never be able to progress, because when your roles change as you move up the ranks, you are expected to be able to implement best practices or be able to code review."* (P4) **Guarded Optimism and Acceptance** *".. we're still determining its full range, with numerous systems now being developed based on generative AI. It can create images and manage presentations, among other tasks."* (P1) *"we still don't know how far this thing can go and we're finding new things. And most systems are being developed on this principle of generative AI right now. This bot generates images, things that can reach high potential and can do presentations and everything else, right?"* (P10)	*Professional Perceptions of GenAI use*

5 Discussion

This section summarizes the findings from Sect. 4 above.

A: The Role of Generative AI in Software Development Projects

The role of generative AI in software development projects encompasses three key sub-themes. Firstly, the 'code generation capabilities' of tools like ChatGPT enable rapid code generation, significantly reducing development time and effort. This facilitates a quicker return on investment and allows for creating usable and functional solutions that can be iteratively improved upon. Secondly, 'project structuring' is enhanced through the automation of tasks such as creating boilerplate code and scaffolding, thereby streamlining the initial setup phase and saving considerable time. Finally, generative AI tools' 'code and language assistant' function provides valuable support during debugging sessions and aids in language refinement, particularly for non-native English speakers. These sub-themes collectively highlight the efficiency gains and workflow improvements brought about by integrating generative AI tools into software development projects.

B: The Influence of Generative AI in Software Development Projects

The influence of generative AI in software development projects comprises three main sub-themes. Firstly, 'efficiency and productivity' are enhanced as generative AI tools streamline tasks, allowing developers to focus on more challenging problems in software development projects. Secondly, 'reskilling and learning new coding approaches' are facilitated as developers transition from traditional learning methods to generative AI for coding assistance. Finally, the 'software development learning curve' is reduced, enabling quicker access to problem-solving and implementation within specific frameworks. These sub-themes collectively illustrate the transformative impact of generative AI on software development practices, improving efficiency and accelerating learning processes.

C: The Benefits of Generative AI in Software Development Projects

The benefits of generative AI in software development projects comprise two main sub-themes. Firstly, generative AI serves as a 'collaborative knowledge assistant,' facilitating quick access to accurate information and aiding in tasks such as debugging and email composition. Users leverage its capabilities to streamline communication and enhance productivity within team settings. Secondly, generative AI enables 'content creation and workflow automation,' which allows for the rapid generation of activities such as meeting minutes, client-specific documentation, and other content. This automation accelerates workflow processes and contributes to overall efficiency in software development projects.

D: The Ethical Challenges Associated with Generative AI Use in Software Development Projects

The ethical challenges of integrating generative AI in software development projects encompass several sub-themes. Firstly, limitations in 'grasping contextual, long-term organisational objectives' are evident, as AI tools lack the nuanced understanding of organisational realities and future implications, potentially leading to suboptimal solutions. Secondly, concerns arise regarding the 'limited creativity and authenticity' in AI-generated output, particularly in creative endeavours like music composition or email writing, where the synthetic nature of AI-generated content may undermine authenticity. Thirdly, AI-generated 'hallucinations and biases' pose significant risks. AI systems may inject erroneous solutions or exhibit biases based on the data they are trained on, raising concerns about the reliability and trustworthiness of AI-generated output. Finally, 'data privacy concerns' emerge, including issues related to the security of uploaded code, potential data breaches, and the need for enhanced privacy measures to safeguard sensitive information.

E: The Professional Perceptions of Generative AI Use Among Software Developers

The professional perceptions of generative AI use among developers in software development projects reflect various attitudes and concerns. Firstly, there's apprehension regarding the potential negative impact on junior developer roles, with fears that reliance on GenAI tools may diminish opportunities for skill development and problem-solving. Secondly, there's a professional stigma associated with GenAI use, with concerns that openly relying on such tools may undermine perceptions of individual competence and autonomy. Thirdly, there's concern over the potential loss of core skills among developers, particularly junior engineers, who may miss out on essential learning experiences.

Despite these reservations, there's also guarded optimism and acceptance, acknowledging the evolving nature of GenAI technology and its potential to revolutionise various aspects of software development, from image creation to presentations, suggesting a cautious embrace of its capabilities while recognising the need for ongoing evaluation and adaptation.

6 Conclusion

This research examined the impact of integrating generative AI tools into software development project environments. It specifically explored how developers perceive the influence of these tools. The first research question, "How does generative AI influence software development projects?" is addressed by themes A and B. The paper further aimed to understand the benefits and challenges of integrating generative AI. The second research question, "What benefits and challenges are associated with integrating Generative AI in software development projects?" is addressed by themes C and D. Theme E, which emerged from the data, explores the perceptions of software professionals about generative AI. This theme highlights an important factor in discussing generative AI's implications for software development. In conclusion, while the short-to medium-term outlook for generative AI in software development appears optimistic, the identified professional and ethical drawbacks necessitate caution in the long term.

6.1 Limitations and Recommendations for Future Research

Limitations
This study has limitations. The findings are grounded in the perspectives of a select group of participants. The professional backgrounds of these participants are diverse but skewed towards a subset of software developers who are relatively in the infancy of their careers. Therefore, this sample size might not fully capture the range of opinions within the larger software development community. Additionally, the geographical scope of the research was confined to specific regions and organisations. This geographic limitation potentially overlooks nuances tied to cultural, economic, or regional variations in the adoption and perception of generative AI tools.

Recommendations for Future Research
Future research studies in this area can benefit from a few recommendations. First, a broader participant base would be useful in capturing a more holistic view of the industry's stance on generative AI tools. This would ideally encompass professionals from different geographical, cultural, and economic backgrounds. Secondly, longitudinal studies that periodically engage with the same set of participants can better track changing perceptions and challenges over time.

References

1. Ahmad, A., et al.: Towards Human-Bot Collaborative Software Architecting with ChatGPT. Paper presented at the Proceedings of the 27th International Conference on Evaluation and Assessment in Software Engineering, pp. 279–285 (2023)
2. Bhattacherjee, A.: Social Science Research: Principles, Methods, and Practices (2012)
3. Borji, A.: A Categorical Archive of ChatGPT Failures. arXiv. Cornell University (2023)
4. Braun, V., Clarke, V.: Using thematic analysis in psychology. Qual. Res. Psychol. **3**(2), 77–101 (2006)
5. Cooper, K.: Problem-Solving in Software Engineering: An Inside Look. Springboard Blog (2022). https://www.springboard.com/blog/software-engineering/problem-solving-in-software-engineering-an-inside-look/
6. Davis, J.C., Lu, Y., Thiruvathukal, G.K.: Conversations with ChatGPT about C Programming: An Ongoing Study. Figshare (2023)
7. Dwivedi, Y.K., et al.: So what if ChatGPT wrote it? Multidisciplinary perspectives on opportunities, challenges and implications of generative conversational AI for research, practice and policy. Int. J. Inf. Manage. **71**, 102642 (2023)
8. Ebert, C., Louridas, P.: Generative AI for Software Practitioners. IEEE Softw. **40**(4), 30–38 (2023). https://doi.org/10.1109/MS.2023.3265877
9. Fui-Hoon Nah, F., Zheng, R., Cai, J., Siau, K., Chen, L.: Generative AI and ChatGPT: Applications, challenges, and AI-human collaboration. J. Info. Technol. Case and Applicat. Res. **25**(3), 277–304 (2023)
10. Gilson, A., et al. How does ChatGPT Perform on the Medical Licensing Exams? The Implications of Large Language Models for Medical Education and Knowledge Assessment. medRxiv (Cold Spring Harbor Laboratory) (2022)
11. Gozalo-Brizuela, R., Garrido-Merchan, E.C.: ChatGPT is not all you need. A State of the Art Review of large Generative AI models (2023). arXiv Preprint arXiv:2301.04655
12. Greene, T., Shmueli, G., Ray, S.: Taking the Person Seriously: Ethically-aware IS Research in the Era of Reinforcement Learning-based Personalization (2022)
13. Gupta, M., Akiri, C., Aryal, K., Parker, E., Praharaj, L.: From ChatGPT to ThreatGPT: Impact of Generative AI in Cybersecurity and Privacy, pp. 80218–80245. IEEE Access (2023)
14. Haque, M.U., Dharmadasa, I., Sworna, Z.T., Rajapakse, R.N., Ahmad, H.: I think this is the most disruptive technology": Exploring Sentiments of ChatGPT Early Adopters using Twitter Data (2022). arXiv Preprint arXiv:2212.05856
15. Jalil, S., Rafi, S., LaToza, T.D., Moran, K., Lam, W.: ChatGPT and Software Testing Education: Promises & Perils. arXiv (Cornell University) (2023)
16. Nguyen, N., Nadi, S.: An empirical evaluation of github copilots code suggestions. In: Paper presented at the Proceedings of the 19th International Conference on Mining Software Repositories, pp. 1–5
17. OpenAI: Introducing ChatGPT (2022). https://openai.com/blog/chatgpt
18. Pothukuchi, A.S., Kota, L.V., Mallikarjunaradhya, V.: Impact of Generative AI on the Software Development Lifecycle (SDLC). Int. J. Creat. Res. Thoug. **11**(8) (2023)
19. Siau, K., Wang, W.: Artificial intelligence (AI) ethics: ethics of AI and ethical AI. J. Datab. Manage. (JDM) **31**(2), 74–87 (2020)
20. Sobania, D., Briesch, M.S., Hanna, C., Petke, J.: An analysis of the automatic bug fixing performance of ChatGPT. arXiv (Cornell University) (2023)
21. Taecharungroj, V.: What Can ChatGPT Do? Analyzing Early Reactions to the Innovative AI Chatbot on Twitter. Big Data and Cognitive Computing **7**(1), 35 (2023)
22. White, J., Hays, S., Fu, Q., Spencer-Smith, J., Schmidt, D.C.: ChatGPT Prompt Patterns for Improving Code Quality, Refactoring, Requirements Elicitation, and Software Design. arXiv (Cornell University) (2023). https://doi.org/10.48550/arxiv.2303.07839

23. Zhang, C., Lu, Y.: Study on artificial intelligence: The state of the art and future prospects. J. Ind. Inf. Integr. **23**, 100224 (2021)
24. Oosterwyk, G., Tsibolane, P., Kautondokwa, P., Canani, P.: Beyond the hype: a cautionary tale of ChatGPT in the programming classroom. In: Online Proceedings of 52nd Annual Conference of the Southern African Computer Lecturers' Association (SACLA 2023) (2023). Available Online: https://arxiv.org/abs/2406.11104

Cybersecurity as a Competitive Advantage for Entrepreneurs

Nangamso Mmango[1](✉) and Tapiwa Gundu[2] (iD)

[1] University of South Africa, Pretoria, South Africa
nangamso.mmango@yahoo.com
[2] Nelson Mandela University, Gqeberha, South Africa

Abstract. This paper presents a systematic literature review focused on exploring the strategic role of cybersecurity as a competitive advantage for entrepreneurs. In the contemporary digital landscape, where cyber threats loom large, the ability to effectively manage and leverage cybersecurity practices has become a pivotal factor distinguishing successful entrepreneurial ventures. The review synthesizes existing research to identify actionable strategies through which cybersecurity can be transformed from a mere operational necessity into a significant competitive differentiator. Key findings from the literature underscore that robust cybersecurity measures enhance customer trust and loyalty, enable market differentiation, integrate seamlessly with strategic business objectives, foster innovation, and ensure compliance with regulatory standards. Strategies such as transparent communication about cybersecurity efforts, development of customized security solutions, integration of cybersecurity risk assessments into strategic planning, and investment in cybersecurity research and development are highlighted as effective means to leverage cybersecurity for competitive advantage. The review further elucidates the importance of adopting ethical data practices and staying abreast of regulatory compliance as mechanisms for reinforcing customer trust and navigating the complex legal landscape surrounding digital business operations. Through the analysis of selected case studies and best practices, the paper demonstrates practical applications of these strategies in real-world entrepreneurial contexts, illustrating how businesses can secure a competitive edge by prioritizing cybersecurity. Conclusively, the paper argues that cybersecurity, when strategically managed, offers entrepreneurs a unique opportunity to fortify their market position, enhance customer relationships, and drive sustainable business growth. It calls for a paradigm shift in how cybersecurity is perceived within the entrepreneurial ecosystem, advocating for its integration into the very fabric of business strategy development and execution.

Keywords: Entrepreneurship · Competitive Advantage · Cybersecurity · Strategic and Business Planning

1 Introduction

In an era dominated by digital transformation, cybersecurity has transcended its traditional role as a technical safeguard, emerging as a critical element in shaping the competitive landscape for entrepreneurs [1]. The ubiquity of digital technologies and

© The Author(s), under exclusive license to Springer Nature Switzerland AG 2024
A. Gerber (Ed.): SAICSIT 2024, CCIS 2159, pp. 374–387, 2024.
https://doi.org/10.1007/978-3-031-64881-6_22

the internet in business operations has not only catalyzed innovation and market expansion but has also introduced a myriad of cybersecurity threats capable of compromising customer trust, financial assets, and the overall integrity of business ventures [2]. This evolving scenario necessitates a reassessment of cybersecurity, not merely as a cost of doing business but as a potential competitive advantage that can be strategically leveraged for business growth and sustainability.

The concept of cybersecurity as a competitive advantage is predicated on the notion that effective cybersecurity measures can enhance customer trust, enable market differentiation, foster innovation, and ensure compliance with an increasingly stringent regulatory environment [3]. In the digital age, where data breaches and cyber-attacks frequently make headlines, consumers are becoming more discerning, prioritizing businesses that demonstrate a commitment to protecting personal and financial information [2]. This shift in consumer priorities underscores the potential of cybersecurity to serve as a unique selling proposition (USP) that distinguishes entrepreneurs in the crowded digital marketplace.

Despite its significance, the strategic integration of cybersecurity into business operations remains an underexplored area within the entrepreneurial literature [4]. While existing research has extensively documented the technical aspects of cybersecurity and its role in mitigating risks, there is a paucity of scholarly work investigating how entrepreneurs can harness cybersecurity to create value and achieve competitive differentiation. This gap in the literature motivates the current study, which seeks to systematically review existing research to identify actionable strategies that entrepreneurs can employ to leverage cybersecurity as a competitive advantage. It explores how cybersecurity can enhance customer trust and loyalty, serve as a basis for market differentiation, integrate with strategic business goals, and stimulate innovation. Additionally, the paper contributes to a deeper understanding of cybersecurity's strategic potential and offers guideline for entrepreneurs to capitalize on this underutilized asset in their quest for market leadership and business excellence.

The remainder of this paper is organized into several key sections to systematically explore the role of cybersecurity in entrepreneurship. The Related Literature section reviews existing studies, setting the groundwork for our analysis. In the Methodology section, we describe our approach to the systematic literature review, including selection criteria and analytical methods. The Results section presents our findings, identifying key competitive advantages of cybersecurity. The Discussion interprets these findings, offering practical strategies for entrepreneurs and suggesting areas for further research. Finally, the Conclusion summarizes the paper's main insights, emphasizing the importance of cybersecurity as a strategic asset and highlighting future research directions to advance understanding in this vital area.

2 Related Literature

2.1 Entrepreneurship

An entrepreneur is fundamentally an individual who identifies an opportunity in the market, devises an innovative solution, and takes the initiative to transform this concept into a tangible business venture [5]. Entrepreneurs are characterized by their willingness to embrace risk and navigate the uncertainties inherent in starting and growing a business. They are visionaries, often seeing potential where others see obstacles, and are relentless in the pursuit of their goals, demonstrating resilience in the face of setbacks and failures [6].

Entrepreneurs play a multifaceted role in the economy and society. They are innovators, introducing new products or services that can alter consumer behaviors, improve lives, and drive technological and social progress. As risk-takers, they are not deterred by the possibility of failure, instead viewing it as an opportunity to learn and evolve [7]. This attitude is crucial for fostering a dynamic and resilient economy, where experimentation and failure are seen as necessary steps in the path to success.

The entrepreneurial journey typically involves several key stages, beginning with the identification of a market need or problem. Entrepreneurs then engage in the development of a business model that outlines how the venture will create, deliver, and capture value. This stage is followed by the mobilization of resources, including capital, talent, and technology, to launch and scale the business [8]. Throughout this process, entrepreneurs must exhibit strategic leadership to navigate challenges, adapt to changing market conditions, and sustain the growth of the venture.

Entrepreneurs differ from traditional business managers in their focus on innovation and value creation through new venture creation. While managers may concentrate on optimizing existing operations within established organizations, entrepreneurs seek to disrupt and redefine markets by introducing novel solutions [6]. This distinction highlights the entrepreneur's role in driving economic renewal and advancing societal change.

Moreover, entrepreneurs contribute significantly to economic development by fostering innovation, creating jobs, and stimulating competition [9]. Through their ventures, they introduce new competition into existing markets, compelling incumbents to innovate and improve, which benefits consumers through better products and services and more competitive prices. Additionally, by creating new employment opportunities, entrepreneurs contribute to job creation and economic diversification, further underscoring their importance to both the economy and society [10].

2.2 Competitive Advantage

A competitive advantage is a condition or circumstance that places a company in a favourable or superior business position compared to its competitors [11]. It arises from unique attributes, resources, strategies, or capabilities that allow an organization to outperform its rivals in the market. These advantages can stem from a wide range of sources, including product innovation, cost leadership, superior customer service, brand strength, proprietary technology, and efficient processes, among others. The essence of a competitive advantage lies in its ability to create significant value for a firm value that is distinctive, defensible, and sustainable over time.

2.2.1 Types of Competitive Advantage

According to [9] Competitive advantages can be broadly categorized into two types:

Cost Advantage: This occurs when a company can deliver the same services or products as its competitors but at lower costs. Cost leadership can be achieved through economies of scale, more efficient production techniques, or lower input costs, enabling the company to either price more competitively or enjoy higher profit margins.

Differentiation Advantage: A company achieves a differentiation advantage when it provides products or services perceived as unique or superior in the market, allowing it to command premium pricing. Differentiation can be based on product quality, brand, customer service, or technological innovation.

Cybersecurity offers a competitive edge by enabling cost advantages through mitigating financial losses, improving compliance efficiency, and ensuring operational continuity [12]. It also fosters differentiation advantages by enhancing brand trust and loyalty, providing innovative security features, and elevating customer service [13]. These aspects not only protect the business but also position it distinctively in the market, contributing to both cost savings and the potential for premium pricing.

2.2.2 Characteristics of a Sustainable Competitive Advantage

According to [14], for competitive advantage to be sustainable, it must be:

Valuable: It should provide significant value to the company, either by opening new markets, enhancing profitability, or improving efficiency.

Rare: The resources or capabilities providing the advantage should not be easily accessible to competitors.

Inimitable: Competitors should find it difficult to replicate or substitute the advantage due to complexity, unique culture, brand identity, or proprietary technology.

Non-substitutable: There should be no immediate substitutes that competitors can use to achieve a similar benefit.

Cybersecurity stands as a sustainable competitive advantage primarily due to its intrinsic value in safeguarding against financial and reputational damage from data breaches, thus directly enhancing a company's profitability and efficiency [15]. Its rarity stems from customized strategies that blend advanced technologies and specialized personnel, elements not readily available to all competitors. The complexity and specialized knowledge required for effective cybersecurity implementation render it inimitable, with unique organizational cultures and proprietary technologies raising barriers against replication. Furthermore, in the digital age, there are no effective substitutes for comprehensive cybersecurity measures. The indispensable role of cybersecurity in protecting against a wide array of digital threats and ensuring business continuity makes it a non-substitutable asset, solidifying its position as a key competitive advantage in today's business landscape [16].

2.2.3 Strategic Implications

The concept of competitive advantage is central to strategic planning and execution. Companies strive to identify, develop, and sustain competitive advantages to achieve long-term success and market leadership [3]. Doing so requires continuous innovation, strategic foresight, and investment in key areas that contribute to the company's unique strengths. Moreover, maintaining a competitive advantage necessitates constant monitoring of the competitive landscape and adapting to changes in market dynamics, consumer preferences, and technological advancements.

2.3 Cybersecurity

In the evolving landscape of digital business operations, cybersecurity has transitioned from a peripheral concern to a central strategic pillar for entrepreneurial ventures [17]. As businesses increasingly rely on digital platforms, networks, and data, the importance of safeguarding these digital assets has never been more critical. Cybersecurity, in this context, refers to the collective measures, technologies, processes, and practices designed to protect networks, computers, programs, and data from attack, damage, or unauthorized access [18]. This paper positions cybersecurity not merely as a technical necessity but as a distinctive competitive advantage that can significantly influence an entrepreneur's success in the digital economy.

The integration of cybersecurity as a competitive advantage aligns with the broader shift towards recognizing the strategic value of trust, reliability, and brand integrity in the digital marketplace. In an era where data breaches and cyber threats are increasingly common, a robust cybersecurity posture can differentiate a business from its competitors, building customer trust and loyalty by ensuring the confidentiality, integrity, and availability of data [19]. This trust becomes a crucial asset, as it enhances customer engagement, fosters brand loyalty, and potentially leads to a premium positioning in the market.

Moreover, cybersecurity's role extends beyond risk mitigation. It encompasses a proactive approach to creating value within the entrepreneurial ecosystem [20]. For instance, compliance with international cybersecurity standards can open new market opportunities, particularly in sectors where data security is paramount. Similarly, innovative cybersecurity solutions can offer unique selling propositions, enabling entrepreneurs to capture niches that value privacy and security. However, the strategic incorporation of cybersecurity into business operations presents unique challenges and opportunities for entrepreneurs. On the one hand, the resource-intensive nature of developing and maintaining a comprehensive cybersecurity framework can be daunting [2], especially for startups and SMEs with limited financial and technical capabilities [21]. On the other hand, the increasing demand for secure digital experiences presents a fertile ground for entrepreneurs who can adeptly navigate the cybersecurity landscape to establish a competitive edge.

3 Methodology

3.1 Review Objectives and Scope

The primary objectives were twofold: first, to substantiate the assertion that cybersecurity acts as a competitive advantage in the entrepreneurial landscape, and second, to formulate a strategies that embeds cybersecurity within business operations. The scope included studies from the past decade, focusing on sectors where digital technology plays a critical role in business operations.

3.2 Literature Search and Selection

Google Scholar was used to access a variety of databases, including IEEE Xplore, ScienceDirect, and specialized journals focusing on cybersecurity and entrepreneurship. The search strategy involved keywords such as "cybersecurity," "competitive advantage," "entrepreneurship," "business," and "strategy." The inclusion criteria were designed to select studies that directly connected cybersecurity practices with entrepreneurial success, market differentiation, and strategic business outcomes. Through a meticulous two-step screening process, which began with reviews of titles and abstracts before progressing to full-text evaluations, we ensured the relevance and quality of the selected studies. Initially, 128 sources were identified as potentially relevant. However, after applying our exclusion criteria, which filtered out studies based on their relevance to the specific intersection of cybersecurity and entrepreneurship, along with the rigor and recency of the research, only 18 studies met our stringent requirements for inclusion in the final analysis. This rigorous selection process was instrumental in distilling the essence of how cybersecurity serves as a competitive advantage in the entrepreneurial domain.

3.3 Data Extraction and Synthesis

The data extraction and synthesis process were carefully structured to derive meaningful insights from the 18 studies that fulfilled our selection criteria, focusing on the dual themes of competitive advantages conferred by cybersecurity and the strategies entrepreneurs can follow to integrate cybersecurity into their business practices.

3.3.1 Data Extraction

In reviewing the selected studies, critical data points were carefully extracted, emphasizing the nature of cybersecurity's competitive advantages and the actionable strategies for cybersecurity integration highlighted within the entrepreneurial context. This involved cataloguing the types of competitive advantages identified, such as trust enhancement, market differentiation, and innovation facilitation alongside specific cybersecurity strategies recommended for entrepreneurs. A standardized data extraction template ensured uniformity in gathering information across all articles, including details on the research methodology, industry focus, key cybersecurity practices, outcomes related to competitive advantage, and the strategic recommendations for entrepreneurs.

3.3.2 Synthesis

The synthesis phase involved a thematic analysis of the extracted data, aimed at distilling common themes around competitive advantages and strategic recommendations for incorporating cybersecurity. This process allowed for the construction of a comprehensive narrative that bridges theoretical insights with actionable guidance, illustrating both the importance and the means of leveraging cybersecurity in entrepreneurial ventures.

4   Results

The results of the systematic literature review conducted in this research show the profound impact of cybersecurity on entrepreneurship, revealing eight distinct competitive advantages. This comprehensive analysis sifted through an extensive corpus of literature to uncover how cybersecurity, far from being a mere technical requirement, acts as a strategic lever that entrepreneurs can pull to gain a competitive edge. These advantages span various dimensions of business strategy and operations, highlighting the multifaceted role of cybersecurity in not only safeguarding digital assets but also in enhancing market presence, building customer trust, driving innovation, and more. The findings underscore the significance of integrating cybersecurity into the entrepreneurial ethos, illustrating its potential to transform business prospects in the increasingly interconnected and digitally reliant business landscape.

4.1   Cybersecurity Competitive Advantages

The competitive advantages discussed in this section highlight how a robust approach to cybersecurity can transcend traditional defensive roles, becoming a multifaceted strategic asset that underpins trust, compliance, resilience, innovation, and supply chain integrity. For entrepreneurs, leveraging these aspects of cybersecurity can significantly enhance their competitive positioning, enabling them to navigate the digital landscape with confidence and integrity.

    I. *Cybersecurity as a Market Differentiator* [13, 22, 23]

    Transactions, interactions, and data sharing are increasingly conducted online and cybersecurity has emerged as a pivotal market differentiator for entrepreneurs. This differentiation stems from the growing consumer awareness and concern over data privacy, security breaches, and identity theft. As a result, businesses that proactively address these concerns by integrating robust cybersecurity measures not only safeguard their operations but also significantly enhance their market appeal and competitive positioning.

   II. *Cybersecurity as a Trust Signal* [11, 24]

   For consumers and businesses alike, trust is a fundamental concern in the digital ecosystem. A company's ability to demonstrate its commitment to cybersecurity can serve as a powerful trust signal, reassuring customers that their data is handled securely and responsibly. This trust is particularly crucial in industries dealing with sensitive information, such as finance, healthcare, and e-commerce, where the potential damage from breaches can severely impact consumer confidence and loyalty. Therefore, entrepreneurs who prioritize cybersecurity can leverage this focus as a core element of their value proposition, differentiating their offerings in a crowded market.

  III. *Innovation and Customer-Centric Security Solutions* [25–27]

  Entrepreneurial ventures have the unique opportunity to innovate in the realm of cybersecurity, developing tailored solutions that address specific market needs or niches. By embedding cybersecurity seamlessly into their products and services, entrepreneurs can create a differentiated customer experience that emphasizes security as a key feature. This innovation can extend to the use of advanced technologies such as blockchain, artificial intelligence, and machine learning to enhance security measures, providing a clear competitive edge in markets where such technological sophistication is highly valued.

Building Trust: How robust cybersecurity measures can serve as a signal of reliability to customers, enhancing trust and loyalty.

IV. *Cybersecurity as a Compliance Advantage* [28, 29]

In a world where regulatory requirements around data protection are becoming increasingly stringent, cybersecurity compliance becomes a competitive advantage. Businesses that not only meet but exceed these regulatory standards can differentiate themselves by showcasing their commitment to data protection and privacy. This compliance is especially critical in industries like finance, healthcare, and services that handle personal data, where failure to comply with regulations can result in significant fines and damage to reputation. Entrepreneurs who proactively adopt and communicate their compliance with standards such as GDPR, HIPAA, or CCPA can thus gain a competitive edge, appealing to privacy-conscious consumers and partners.

V. *Enhanced Operational Resilience* [30, 31]

Cybersecurity contributes to the operational resilience of a business, allowing it to withstand and quickly recover from cyber incidents. In an environment where such incidents can disrupt operations, lead to loss of revenue, and damage brand reputation, resilience becomes a key competitive advantage. Businesses that demonstrate an ability to maintain operations in the face of cyber threats not only reassure customers and investors but also position themselves as reliable and stable partners in the business ecosystem. This resilience can open doors to new business opportunities and partnerships, as reliability becomes a deciding factor in vendor and partner selection processes.

VI. *Leveraging Cyber Insurance as a Competitive Advantage* [32, 33]

The strategic use of cyber insurance can also serve as a competitive advantage. By securing comprehensive cyber insurance, businesses not only protect themselves from the financial implications of cyber incidents but also demonstrate to their customers and partners that they are taking proactive steps to manage risk. This can enhance customer trust and satisfaction, as stakeholders recognize that the business is prepared to address potential cyber threats and their consequences effectively. Entrepreneurs can leverage their investment in cyber insurance as a testament to their commitment to cybersecurity and risk management, distinguishing their business in the competitive landscape.

VII. *Cybersecurity as a Catalyst for Business Growth* [9, 34, 35]

Far from being just a protective measure, effective cybersecurity strategies can also act as a catalyst for business growth. By enabling safe and secure digital transformation initiatives, businesses can explore new markets, adopt innovative technologies, and offer new services without the looming threat of cyber incidents stifling innovation. This secure foundation for growth allows businesses to experiment and innovate with confidence, knowing that their cybersecurity measures are robust. Entrepreneurs who communicate this secure base for innovation to their customers can create a perception of a forward-thinking, dynamic business that values both growth and security.

VIII. *Supply Chain Security as a Competitive Differentiator* [36, 37]

As businesses become increasingly interconnected, the security of the supply chain becomes a critical concern. Entrepreneurs who ensure that their supply chains are secure not only protect themselves from third-party risks but also become more attractive to larger companies that are meticulous about their vendors' cybersecurity posture. By implementing and demanding stringent cybersecurity measures across their supply chain, businesses can stand out to potential partners who prioritize security in their vendor selection criteria. This supply chain security becomes a significant competitive differentiator, particularly in sectors where the integrity of the supply chain is vital to operational success and compliance.

5   Discussion

For entrepreneurs intrigued by the benefits highlighted in the results section and looking to harness the competitive advantages of cybersecurity, the discussion section lays out five key strategies for effective implementation. These strategies are designed to guide entrepreneurs through the integration of cybersecurity into their business operations, ensuring they can fully leverage its potential to safeguard their ventures and gain a significant edge in the digital marketplace. From establishing a robust cybersecurity framework to fostering a culture of security awareness within their organizations, these strategies provide a roadmap for entrepreneurs to not only protect their digital assets but also enhance their market position, innovate, and build lasting trust with their customers. This section serves as a practical guide for those ready to embark on the journey of transforming cybersecurity from a defensive measure into a core component of their business strategy.

5.1   Recommended Strategies

I. *Risk-Based Cybersecurity Strategy*

This strategy prioritizes cybersecurity efforts based on the identification, assessment, and prioritization of cyber risks that pose the greatest threat to the business [38]. It involves mapping out potential cybersecurity risks against the critical assets and operations of the business, allowing for a targeted allocation of resources.

Implementation Steps:

1. conduct a comprehensive cyber risk assessment to identify vulnerabilities within the business infrastructure.
2. Prioritize risks based on their potential impact on critical business operations and assets.
3. Allocate resources to mitigate high-priority risks, implementing protective measures tailored to these key areas.
4. Regularly review and update the risk assessment to adapt to new threats and changes in the business environment.

II. *Cybersecurity-First Culture*

Developing a cybersecurity-first culture involves fostering awareness, responsibility, and proactive behavior towards cybersecurity across all levels of the organization

[17]. This cultural shift ensures that cybersecurity considerations are embedded in every business decision and operation.

Implementation Steps:

1. Initiate ongoing cybersecurity training and awareness programs for all employees, emphasizing the role each individual plays in maintaining security.
2. Incorporate cybersecurity performance metrics into employee evaluations and incentives to encourage proactive security behaviors.
3. Leadership should model cybersecurity best practices, demonstrating the organization's commitment to security from the top down.
4. Promote an open environment where employees feel comfortable reporting security concerns or incidents without fear of reprisal.

III. *Strategic Alignment of Cybersecurity and Business Objectives*

This framework ensures that cybersecurity initiatives are directly aligned with overarching business goals [17], enabling cybersecurity to drive rather than hinder business growth and innovation.

Implementation Steps:

1. Integrate cybersecurity considerations into the strategic planning process, ensuring that security initiatives support and enhance business objectives.
2. Foster collaboration between cybersecurity teams and other business units to ensure that security measures complement and facilitate business operations.
3. Leverage cybersecurity initiatives to explore new business opportunities, such as entering markets with stringent data protection regulations.

IV. *Agile Cybersecurity Innovation*

Emphasizes continuous innovation in cybersecurity measures to stay ahead of evolving threats and leverage new technologies for competitive advantage [2]. This approach involves adopting agile methodologies to rapidly develop, test, and deploy cybersecurity solutions.

Implementation Steps:

1. Establish a dedicated cybersecurity innovation team tasked with exploring and implementing new security technologies and practices.
2. Adopt agile development methodologies, allowing for the rapid iteration and deployment of cybersecurity solutions.
3. Encourage partnerships with cybersecurity startups, research institutions, and technology providers to gain access to cutting-edge security innovations.

V. *Customer-Centric Cybersecurity*

This strategy focuses on integrating cybersecurity measures that directly enhance the customer experience, using security as a value proposition to build trust and loyalty among the customer base [27].

Implementation Steps:

1. Design and implement user-friendly security features that enhance rather than complicate the customer experience, such as seamless authentication processes.
2. Communicate clearly about the cybersecurity measures in place to protect customer data, using this transparency as a marketing point.
3. Involve customers in the cybersecurity feedback loop, using their insights to refine security measures and address customer concerns proactively.

6 Conclusion

In conclusion, this paper has illuminated the multifaceted role of cybersecurity as a significant competitive advantage in the entrepreneurial landscape. As digital transformation accelerates across industries, the imperative for robust cybersecurity measures has transitioned from a mere operational necessity to a strategic asset that can distinguish businesses in a competitive marketplace. The exploration within this paper underscores that cybersecurity is not just about safeguarding data and systems; it is a critical element that can enhance market differentiation, build consumer trust, drive innovation, ensure compliance, and foster operational resilience.

Cybersecurity's emergence as a market differentiator reveals the growing consumer awareness and concern over data privacy and security. Businesses that proactively integrate sophisticated cybersecurity measures can significantly enhance their market appeal, establishing themselves as trusted entities in a landscape fraught with threats. This trust, particularly vital in sectors handling sensitive information, can be a linchpin for customer loyalty and long-term business success.

Moreover, the opportunity for innovation within the realm of cybersecurity presents entrepreneurs with a pathway to create unique, customer-centric solutions. By embedding cybersecurity seamlessly into products and services, entrepreneurs can offer differentiated experiences that prioritize security, appealing to a market that increasingly values digital safety. The adoption of advanced technologies such as blockchain and artificial intelligence further amplifies this advantage, allowing businesses to stay ahead in markets where technological sophistication is a benchmark for excellence.

Compliance with international cybersecurity standards not only mitigates the risk of penalties but also serves as a strategic tool for market entry and expansion. Businesses that navigate these regulatory landscapes with agility can leverage compliance as a competitive edge, appealing to a global customer base that demands high standards of data protection.

Operational resilience, bolstered by effective cybersecurity measures, ensures that businesses can withstand and swiftly recover from cyber incidents. This resilience is crucial for maintaining continuous operations and protecting the bottom line, attributes that are indispensable in today's fast-paced business environment. Furthermore, the strategic use of cyber insurance emerges as a prudent approach to managing cyber risks, offering an additional layer of protection and confidence for both the business and its stakeholders.

The integration of cybersecurity into supply chain management highlights the importance of end-to-end security in today's interconnected business ecosystems. Entrepreneurs who champion supply chain security not only safeguard their operations but also enhance their attractiveness to potential partners who value rigorous cybersecurity standards.

This paper advocates for a paradigm shift where cybersecurity is viewed through the lens of strategic business planning rather than as a technical or compliance issue. Entrepreneurs who embrace this perspective, integrating cybersecurity into the core of their strategic initiatives, stand to gain a significant competitive advantage. In doing so, they not only protect their ventures from the myriad of cyber threats but also position their businesses for sustainable growth, innovation, and success in the digital age.

Cybersecurity, therefore, should be at the heart of entrepreneurial strategy, driving value creation and competitive differentiation in an increasingly digital world.

Looking ahead, the future beckons with opportunities for adaptive cybersecurity frameworks, development of clear metrics linking cybersecurity to business performance, exploration of sector-specific strategies, initiatives for cybersecurity talent development, international collaboration on cybersecurity standards, and the integration of privacy-enhancing technologies. These avenues promise to enrich the strategic integration of cybersecurity within business operations, emphasizing its value beyond risk mitigation to a fundamental driver of competitive differentiation and innovation. Entrepreneurs who adeptly incorporate these insights into their strategic planning will not only safeguard their ventures but also position themselves at the forefront of the evolving digital marketplace.

References

1. Gharbaoui, O.E., Boukhari, H.E.: Navigating the digital landscape: a roadmap to competitive advantage: theoretical overview. African J. Bus. Fina. **1**, 63–73 (2023)
2. Gundu, T., Mmango, N.: A Cybersecurity Collaborative model: best practices sharing among south african tourism and hospitality businesses. ICTR **7**, 222–231 (2024). https://doi.org/10.34190/ictr.7.1.2159
3. Jebril, I., Almaslmani, R., Jarah, B., Mugableh, M., Zaqeeba, N.: The impact of strategic intelligence and asset management on enhancing competitive advantage: The mediating role of cybersecurity. Uncertain Supply Chain Manage. **11**, 1041–1046 (2023)
4. Panteleev, D.N.: Cybersecurity for the stimulation of entrepreneurship development in the digital economy markets. In: Popkova, E.G., Sergi, B.S. (eds.) Anti-Crisis Approach to the Provision of the Environmental Sustainability of Economy, pp. 263–271. Springer Nature, Singapore (2023). https://doi.org/10.1007/978-981-99-2198-0_28
5. Filion, L.J.: Defining the entrepreneur. In: World Encyclopedia of Entrepreneurship, pp. 72–83. Edward Elgar Publishing (2021)
6. Ramoglou, S., Gartner, W.B., Tsang, E.W.K.: "Who is an entrepreneur?" is (still) the wrong question. J. Bus. Ventur. Insights **13**, e00168 (2020). https://doi.org/10.1016/j.jbvi.2020.e00168
7. Stanworth, J., Stanworth, C., Granger, B., Blyth, S.: Who becomes an entrepreneur? Int. Small Bus. J. **8**, 11–22 (1989). https://doi.org/10.1177/026624268900800101
8. Klonek, F.E., Isidor, R., Kauffeld, S.: Different stages of entrepreneurship: lessons from the transtheoretical model of change. J. Chang. Manag. **15**, 43–63 (2015). https://doi.org/10.1080/14697017.2014.918049
9. Davidsson, P., Delmar, F., Wiklund, J.: Entrepreneurship as growth: growth as entrepreneurship. In: Strategic Entrepreneurship, pp. 328–342. John Wiley & Sons, Ltd. (2017). https://doi.org/10.1002/9781405164085.ch15
10. Astebro, T.B., Tåg, J.: Entrepreneurship and Job Creation (2015). https://papers.ssrn.com/abstract=2576044
11. Wen-Cheng, W., Chien-Hung, L., Ying-Chien, C.: Types of competitive advantage and analysis. IJBM. **6**, p100 (2011). https://doi.org/10.5539/ijbm.v6n5p100
12. Gundu, T., Modiba, N.: Building competitive advantage from ubuntu: an african information security awareness model. In: ICISSP. pp. 569–576 (2020)
13. Kosutic, D., Pigni, F.: Cybersecurity: investing for competitive outcomes. J. Bus. Strateg. **43**, 28–36 (2020). https://doi.org/10.1108/JBS-06-2020-0116

14. Coyne, K.P.: Sustainable competitive advantage—What it is, what it isn't. Bus. Horiz. **29**, 54–61 (1986). https://doi.org/10.1016/0007-6813(86)90087-X

15. Gundu, T.: Towards an information security awareness process for engineering SMEs in emerging economies (2013)

16. Gundu, T.: Big Data, Big Security, and Privacy Risks. J. Info. Warf. **18**, 15–30 (2019)

17. Gundu, T., Maronga, M.I., Boucher, D.: Industry 4.0 business perspective: fostering a cyber security culture in a culturally diverse workplace. In: Proceedings of 4th International Conference on the, pp. 85–94 (2019)

18. Craig, J.: Cybersecurity research—essential to a successful digital future. Engineering **4**, 9 (2018). https://doi.org/10.1016/j.eng.2018.02.006

19. Anisetti, M., Ardagna, C., Cremonini, M., Sessa, J., Costa, L.: Security Threat Landscape. Security Threats (2020)

20. Sun, N., et al.: Cyber threat intelligence mining for proactive cybersecurity defense: a survey and new perspectives. IEEE Commun. Surv. Tutor. **25**, 1748–1774 (2023). https://doi.org/10.1109/COMST.2023.3273282

21. Mitrofan, A.-L., Cruceru, E.-V., Barbu, A.: Determining the main causes that lead to cybersecurity risks in SMEs. Bus. Excell. Manage. **10**, 38–48 (2020)

22. Knight, G., Moen, Ø., Madsen, T.K.: Antecedents to differentiation strategy in the exporting SME. Int. Bus. Rev. **29**, 101740 (2020). https://doi.org/10.1016/j.ibusrev.2020.101740

23. Zhang, Y., Wang, H., Zhou, X.: Dare to be different? conformity versus differentiation in corporate social activities of chinese firms and market responses. AMJ. **63**, 717–742 (2020). https://doi.org/10.5465/amj.2017.0412

24. Chui, K.T.: Building Digital Trust: Challenges and Strategies in Cybersecurity **5** (2022)

25. Fornell, C., Iii, F.V.M., Hult, G.T.M., VanAmburg, D.: The Reign of the Customer: Customer-Centric Approaches to Improving Satisfaction. Springer Nature (2020)

26. Muktar, B.G., Idrissa, Y.L., Orifah, M.O., Nwachukwu, I.M.: Innovation centric extension services and information communication technologies benevolence: implications for local innovation generation and agripreneurial promotion for sustainable food systems. J. Agricult. Extens. **27**, 26–37 (2022)

27. Saeed, S.: A customer-centric view of e-commerce security and privacy. Appl. Sci. **13**, 1020 (2023). https://doi.org/10.3390/app13021020

28. Chen, X., Wu, D., Chen, L., Teng, J.K.L.: Sanction severity and employees' information security policy compliance: Investigating mediating, moderating, and control variables. Info. Manage. (2018). https://doi.org/10.1016/j.im.2018.05.011

29. Chua, H.N., Wong, S.F., Low, Y.C., Chang, Y.: Impact of employees' demographic characteristics on the awareness and compliance of information security policy in organizations. Telematics Inform. **35**, 1770–1780 (2018). https://doi.org/10.1016/j.tele.2018.05.005

30. Mmango, N., Gundu, T.: Cyber resilience in the entrepreneurial environment: a framework for enhancing cybersecurity awareness in SMEs. In: 2023 International Conference on Electrical, Computer and Energy Technologies (ICECET), pp. 1–6 (2023). https://doi.org/10.1109/ICECET58911.2023.10389226

31. Sharma, S., Rautela, S.: Entrepreneurial resilience and self-efficacy during global crisis: study of small businesses in a developing economy. J. Entreprene. Emerg. Econ. **14**, 1369–1386 (2021). https://doi.org/10.1108/JEEE-03-2021-0123

32. Jiang, N.N., Loukas, A., Wang, P., Wu, H.: Sometimes Less is More: Risk Aversion, Balanced Growth, and the (sub) Optimality of Entrepreneurial Insurance. pp. 1–21 (2023)

33. Negrutiu, C., Vasiliu, C., Enache, C.: Sustainable entrepreneurship in the transport and retail supply chain sector. J. Risk and Fina. Manage. **13**, 267 (2020). https://doi.org/10.3390/jrfm13110267

34. Miroshnychenko, I., De Massis, A., Miller, D., Barontini, R.: Family business growth around the world. Entrep. Theory Pract. **45**, 682–708 (2021). https://doi.org/10.1177/104225872091 3028
35. Wright, M., Stigliani, I.: Entrepreneurship and growth. Int. Small Bus. J. **31**, 3–22 (2013). https://doi.org/10.1177/0266242612467359
36. Cortes, A.F., Lee, Y., Cortes, J.D., Liñan, I.: Entrepreneurial orientation in supply chain management: a systematic review. Int. J. Entreprene. Knowl. **9**, 127–143 (2021). https://doi.org/10.37335/ijek.v9i1.127
37. Ketchen, D.J., Craighead, C.W.: Research at the intersection of entrepreneurship, supply chain management, and strategic management: opportunities highlighted by COVID-19. J. Manag. **46**, 1330–1341 (2020). https://doi.org/10.1177/0149206320945028
38. Cai, S., et al.: Security risk intelligent assessment of power distribution internet of things via entropy-weight method and cloud model. Sensors **22**, 4663 (2022). https://doi.org/10.3390/s22134663

Factors Affecting User Participation in the Design of Governmental Digital Services in South Africa

Namfezeko Ntika[✉] [iD] and Wallace Chigona[iD]

University of Cape Town, Cape Town, South Africa
ntknom002@myuct.com

Abstract. User participation in the design of governmental digital services remain a latent policy stance in South Africa despite its benefits to address public service challenges in the country. Consequently, the country is marked by destructive service delivery protests due to government services that fail to meet the needs of the citizens. Citizens, as users of public services, may help improve the quality and quantity of public services by identifying problems with the existing digital services and suggesting new solutions that may better address their needs thereby improving user experience, satisfaction, and trust. This study, therefore, aimed to systematically identify and critically review relevant literature to provide insights into factors that affect user participation in the design of governmental digital service in South Africa. This study adopted a qualitative strategy and deductive approach and is underpinned by the revised IAP2 'spectrum of public participation' as the theoretical framework. Sixteen articles, published from 2019–2024, from credible online databases, were included in this study. Findings show that factors that affect user participation in the design of governmental digital services include lack of trust in government, poor implementation of good governance, digital exclusion, to name but a few factors. Findings also show that the negative economic growth of the country has eroded government capacity to fully embrace inclusive governance. The study intended to broaden the understanding of factors that affect user participation in the design of governmental digital services in South Africa and to shape policies intended to address these factors.

Keywords: User Participation · Digital Services · Government · South Africa

1 Introduction

The Information and Communication Technology (ICT) has enabled the government to complement and replace the traditional public services with digital services. Digital services are public services that are accessed online through websites, portals and mobile devices [1]. Globally, governments appreciate the potential benefits offered by digital services, evidenced by 193 United Nations' member states that have launched national portals to publish government information, 47% of which have launched online services [2]. The ICT facilitates fast transmission of information between humans and computers,

© The Author(s), under exclusive license to Springer Nature Switzerland AG 2024
A. Gerber (Ed.): SAICSIT 2024, CCIS 2159, pp. 388–403, 2024.
https://doi.org/10.1007/978-3-031-64881-6_23

making digital services more efficient and effective than traditional services [2]. The South African government has made commendable strides in developing the digital services to improve the efficiency of government. Such digital services include e-filing, e-Natis, e-recruitment, eHome Affairs [3]. Despite these strides, challenges exist that render government services inefficient, resulting in perpetual destructive service delivery protests [2, 4]. As a result, some citizens feel that the governmental digital services have brought more problems than solutions [5]. User participation in the design of digital service design is recognized as part of the solution to solve persistent challenges with service delivery, as it creates a shared space for collaboration and engagement [6]. To this end, the South African government has been increasingly leveraging the ICT infrastructure to support SMS, emails, voice calls, e-petition and social media to enable real-time and cost-effective engagement with government [6].The provision of multiple channels of user engagement is pivotal if the objective of achieving inclusive participation, of all social groups, is to be achieved [2].

Citizens, as users of public services, may help to improve the quality and quantity of public services, and identify problems with the existing digital services thereby improving user experience and satisfaction [7]. The common practice to public services design is to automate the existing services and processes which are decided upon at the national government and filtered down to provincial and local government, without inputs of the citizens [4]. This practice has been found to be fundamentally flawed, as it imposes the worldviews of government officials and politicians on citizens, no wonder 80% of governmental digital initiatives fail to meet their objectives in the developing countries like South Africa [8, 9].

This study aimed to systematically identify and critically review relevant literature and provide insights into factors that affect user participation in the design of governmental digital service in South Africa. The study aims to answer the research question: What are the factors that affect user participation in the design of governmental digital service in South Africa?

2   Background and Context of the Study

South Africa is a middle-income country with a young democracy that was attained in 1994 [10]. South Africa is a formidable player in the African economy, with public service being the biggest contributor to the Gross Domestic Product (GDP) (Trading Economics, 2023). South Africa is one of the technologically advanced countries in the African continent, with advanced mobile infrastructure and more than 50% internet users, as a percentage of the population [11].

The South African constitution of 1996 demands equal right to knowledge and information. To this end, the Electronic Act of 2005, the Electronic Transaction Act of 2005, the Broadband policy, the Thusong Service Centre Framework were developed to ensure digital inclusion, of all citizens, in the country, regardless of their backgrounds and limitations [12]. The South African government has achieved commendable successes in implementing these inclusive governance frameworks, as a result, the United Nations (UN) e-Government survey (2022), a benchmarking tool for comparative assessment of e-Government of UN Member states, reported that South Africa is among five countries in Africa that offer 20–21 online public services to the public. Despite South Africa's position and influence in the African continent, the South African government has been struggling to improve the economic outlook of the country. As a result, the country is plagued by high level of unemployment, poor education outcomes and lack of digital skills, all of which render the citizens unable to participate in, and benefit from the digital economy [10, 13].

The advent of governmental digital services, as the extension of public services, was meant to overcome the challenges faced by government by improving efficiency and effectiveness of the public services. However, instead, the digital services have inherited the existing challenges in government services [14]. These perpetual challenges are attributed to government tendency of designing public services without input from the citizens' who are the targeted users of the government services. Consequently, the digital services tend to reflect the assumptions and perceptions of the decision-makers, resulting in failure to meet the needs and solve the problems of the citizens [15, 16].

2.1 Conceptualization of User Participation

Although the subject of user participation has preoccupied researchers for decades, it still suffers from conceptual inconsistency as there is no universally accepted definition. Literature provides various definition of user participation as illustrated in Table 1. Drawing on these various definitions, this study defines user participation as the coordinated engagement process between government and citizens in the design of governmental digital services, through multiple channels of engagement, to address the needs and solve the problems of the citizens to achieve public value. The term user participation and citizen participation are used interchangeably depending on the context.

Table 1. Conceptualization of user participation

Conceptualization of user participation	Definition	Source
Co-creation	Co-creation is the involvement of all relevant stakeholders in the development cycle of public services	[15]
Co-design	Co-design is the collaborative approach between the users of governmental digital services and the providers of such services to understand and deliver the government services that meet the user expectation and needs	[17]

(continued)

Table 1. (*continued*)

Conceptualization of user participation	Definition	Source
Citizen participation	Citizen participation is the involvement of citizens as individual or groups in the decision-making process to address the needs of disadvantaged communities	[18]
Inclusive governance	Inclusive governance refers to the deliberate centering of public engagement in government innovation	[19]

2.2 Conceptualization of Governmental Digital Services

Literature is laden with various definitions of governmental digital services from various domains, indicating conceptual inconsistency of this concept. However, the application of internet differentiates between traditional and digital services, making digital services more standardized, transparent and efficient than tradition public services [20]. Table 2 shows definitions of government's digital services form the literature. Drawing on these various definitions, this study defines governmental digital services as online public services that are developed with user requirements in mind to address the needs of the citizens, and to empower citizens with abilities to participate in the digital economy.

Table 2. Conceptualization of Governmental Digital Services

Conceptualization of governmental digital service	Definition	Source
e-services	e-services are public online services that re delivered by the government agencies to the citizens to reduce operational costs, improve government efficiency and satisfy the needs of the citizens	[21]
E-Government	E-Government refers to the incorporation of ICT into processes and transactions to improve efficiency, accountability, and transparency of the public services	[22]

(*continued*)

Table 2. (*continued*)

Conceptualization of governmental digital service	Definition	Source
Digital government	Digital government is the modernization of public administration to provide online public services for the purpose of improving efficiency of public services and trust between government and its stakeholders	[23]
Smart government	Smart government is the citizen-centric approach that utilizes smart applications to better understand the requirements and needs of the citizens to deliver services that address those needs	[24]

2.3 Gaps in Literature

User participation is advocated as the legitimate and effective mechanism to achieve the citizens-centricity as it break the boundary between government and citizens by promoting accountability, responsiveness, transparency and legitimacy of public policy thereby improving trust in government [6, 25]. Furthermore, user participation ensures a better understanding of citizens' needs and preferences, from the citizen perspective thereby increasing user satisfaction and uptake [25].Despite the substantial research attention paid to user participation, gaps still exist in the literature. The existing literature mostly focused on the role of user participation, evaluation of user participation strategies, relationship between user participation and user satisfaction. The existing research is most concentrated in developed and other developing countries, with minimal research attention paid to understanding factors that affect user participation in the design of governmental digital services in South Africa, which may help to solve the challenge of low uptake of the digital services and the persistent service delivery challenges in the country. This study therefore aims to close this gap in the literature.

2.4 Theoretical Framework

The user participation activities are intended to create opportunities and platforms for citizens to engage and influence public policy [26]. A significant number of frameworks have been used to understand the theoretical foundations for user participation. Such frameworks include Stakeholder inclusive approach [27], Community-based participatory approach [28], Social capital [29], e-participation scoping framework [30], IAP2 spectrum of public participation [31], participatory approach [32] and theory of systems change [33].

This study adopted the revised International Association for Public Participation (IAP2) spectrum of public participation presented in Fig. 1, which was originally developed by the international association for public participation, to assist the public organizations to incorporate user participation in the decision-making processes [31]. The IAP2 spectrum of public participation posits that if the users of the government services are to influence public policies, they must be given a level of authority over decision. Thus, involving citizens early enough in the decision-making process strengthens the credibility and legitimacy of user engagement activities (Bonzon et al., 2024). The spectrum of public participation provides five levels of user engagements, goal of user participation at each level and the promise to the public, as users of government services.

The inform level is considered as the basic level of user participation where government utilizes one-way communication platforms such as websites, radio and tv, newspapers, to keep the citizens informed. Language used to inform citizens is the vital aspect in this level to ensure inclusivity of the governmental digital services. The consult, involve and collaborate are argued to involve the same level of engagement depending on the purpose and goals of engagement. These levels require high level of trust to achieve their goals and objectives [31]. To ensure inclusivity, government must employ multiple channels of engagement such as polls, surveys, social media, community meetings, written submissions.

Unlike the preceding levels, empowerment is a method by which government handover power to the people to take control of their lives and to change their socio-economic circumstances. At this level, government must be led by citizens to understand their needs

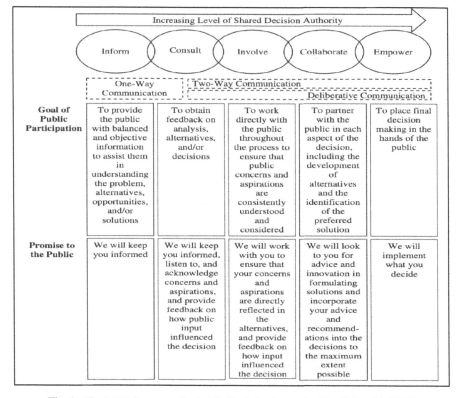

Fig. 1. The IAP2 Spectrum for Public Participation revised by Nabatchi (2012)

and aspirations and therefore implements the decisions taken by the citizens [34]. To achieve the objectives of this framework, government must provide tools and support to all social groups and ensure access to the required skills, information and infrastructure to participate effectively in the design of governmental digital services [33]. Users of the government services are more likely to accept decisions of which they took part and which reflect their worldviews [35].

3   Methodology

3.1   Philosophical Paradigm

The research philosophy provides the starting point for the research process. It indicates the researcher's assumptions regarding the development of knowledge and nature of that knowledge. It consist of Ontology, which is concerned with the nature of reality and Epistemology, which is concerned with the nature of knowledge and how that knowledge is acquired [36–38]. This study adopted a constructive ontology and interpretive epistemology to examine and analyse factors that affect user participation in the design of governmental digital services in South Africa. Constructive ontology and Interpretive epistemology are suitable for the qualitative research method adopted in this study.

3.2   Systematic Literature (SLR) Protocol

Knowledge advancement must be built on the existing knowledge in order to understand its strengths and weaknesses, and therefore to identify gaps to be explored [39]. To answer the research question, this study adopted the SLR as the research method, following the guidelines of [39] on conducting a qualitative SLR for Information Systems research. This study included peer-reviewed articles extracted from Google Scholar, Web of Science, and IEEE Xplorer. The literature search used the following key words "User participation in governmental digital service in South Africa", "Citizen participation in eGovernment in South Africa", "Public participation in smart government in South Africa". To ensure that this study was grounded on the recent and relevant literature, the search was limited to articles published between 2019 and 2024 whose focus was on South Africa three spheres of government. The adapted PRISMA flowchart, in Fig. 2, presents the literature inclusion and exclusion processes followed.

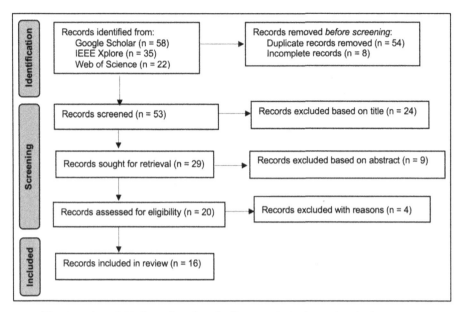

Fig. 2. Adapted PRISMA flowchart for literature inclusion and exclusion process

3.3 Data Analysis Protocol

The thematic data analysis was adopted as the guideline for interpretation of findings and conclusion [40]. Thematic data analysis was chosen for its ability to produce reliable and insightful findings [41]. A total of 16 records that were included in the review were analysed following a five-step approach, which included familiarisation with the data, coding, generation of themes, review of themes and write up. The thematic data analysis process yielded twelve persistent factors that affect user participation in the design of governmental digital services in South Africa, as depicted in Fig. 3.

4 Findings and Discussion

Figure 3 shows the distribution of factors that affect user participation in the design of governmental digital services in South Africa. Due to page restriction of the conference paper, only the top four findings will be discussed.

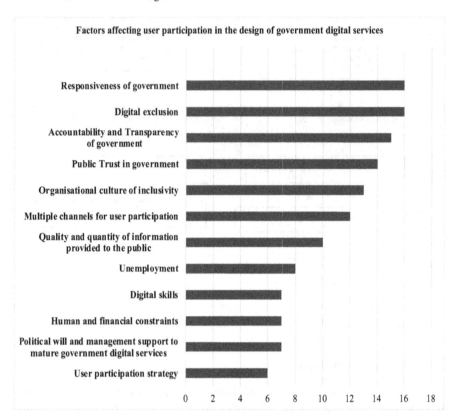

Fig. 3. Distribution of factors affecting user participation in the design of governmental digital services.

4.1 Public Trust in Government

Public trust refers to the perception that government will implement good governance principles to protect, serve and empower citizens [42]. Public trust is the expectation that government will allocate public funds responsibly and ethically to solve the problem of the citizens and to serve their needs [43]. Globally, trust in government has declined in the past few years, due to corruption, poor service delivery and poor implementation of good governance [44]. In South Africa, the decline of trust is evidenced by poor voter turnout and the number of destructive service delivery protests [4]. Government offices that operate in rural communities are characterized by outdated information on government websites, slow email transmission, poor citizen service, poor ICT infrastructure, ineffective communication platforms, all of which erodes public trust in government [29, 30, 45, 46]. The advent of governmental digital services was meant to address public service inefficiency. However, due to lack of user participation in the design of these services they often do not meet user expectation, resulting in low uptake and further decline of public trust [47].

Over the years, the South African government has been refreshing the ICT infrastructure and adopting emerging technologies to improve user participation and trust in government [45]. Such efforts include leveraging Artificial intelligence, Analytics, SMS, voice notes, online petition, and social media [6]. The user participation mechanisms, used effectively, has the potential to address the service delivery challenges in the country, by adopting the principle of 'user participation by design' to ensure that citizens' input find expression in the decision-making process thereby improving public services and trust in government[45]. When public trust fails, citizens become disengaged and uninterested in government affairs, leading to a disjuncture between citizens' needs and government services [42]. Consequently, the country is plagued with destructive service delivery protests and lawlessness [42].

4.2 Digital Exclusion

Digital exclusion refers to the disparities in the distribution of, and access to, ICT between urban and rural communities, driven by slow information transmission to the rural areas, poor ICT infrastructure, poor digital literacy [12]. The UN 2030 Sustainable Development Goals (SDG) demands that no one be left behind [12]. The South African constitution of 1996 demands equal right to knowledge and information. To this end, the Electronic Act of 2005, Electronic Transaction Act of 2005, Broadband policy, The Thusong Service Centre Framework, have been to drafted to close the digital gap in the country [12].

Government has achieved some successes in the implementation of these frameworks, evidenced by the United Nations (UN) e-Government survey (2022), which has reported that South Africa is among five countries in Africa that offer 20–21 online public services. While the UN e-Government survey report provides indication of the progress made by South Africa, from the global perspective, it fails to provide insights into the progress made at local government level where public services are delivered directly to the citizens [20].

Despite the progress made in addressing the digital exclusion in the country, government has been struggling to improve the socio-economic circumstances of the citizens as anticipated at the dawn of democracy. There are the high levels of unemployment, poor levels of education and digital skills, high number of people depending on social grant to survive. These challenges are pronounced in rural settings and are perpetuated by digital exclusion [13].

Government, as the biggest economy and the custodian of the public value, has the moral obligation to ensure that people are empowered to participate in, and benefit from, the digital economy [48]. To this end, the South African government is increasingly repurposing the public facilities such as libraries and Thusong Services centers by refreshing the IT infrastructure, providing access to reliable internet, upskilling, and staffing these facilities [12]. These initiatives have made a remarkable difference in closing the digital divide, however, more still needs to be done to strengthen these initiatives if the objectives of the UN Sustainable developmental Goal 2030 and South African constitution are to be achieved.

4.3 Accountability and Transparency

Accountability and transparency refer to the commitment of government to use the public resources, lawfully and ethically, to serve citizens and to regularly report its achievements against goals [43]. The benefits of transparency and accountability include perceived legitimacy of government and increased trust in government [49].

In South Africa transparency and accountability are the basic principles of good governance and are mandated by the Constitution of the Republic of South Africa of 1996, to prevent corruption and abuse of power. The Constitution of the Republic of South Africa has provided for the establishment of the Chapter 9 institutions and accountability committees, all of which are aimed at facilitating and fostering public accountability. Such institutions include Public Service Commission, National Prosecuting Authority, Auditor General, Public Protector and Standing Committee for Public Account [50]. While transparency is the cornerstone for accountability, it is citizen participation and engagement that enforced accountability [51].

In the past era, citizen participation was conducted through traditional methods such as community engagements and public hearings, however, in the digital era these methods have been criticized for being ineffective, inefficient and for lacking the accountability layer, as government seldom going back to the communities to report back on the public services and associated expenditure [6]. Hence, the South African government, in some spheres of government, has been increasingly adopting the inclusive smart governance whereby a broad range of stakeholders, as users of governmental digital services, participate in the policy decision-making process and the design of governmental digital services. In inclusive smart governance, emerging digital platforms, such as social media, censors, artificial intelligence, robotics, Internet of Things, open government portals, are utilized to collect big data for data-led decision-making, and to improve accountability and transparency [27, 46].

These emerging platforms have ushered in new ways of decentralizing the information production process by enabling citizens to become active producers of real-time data, making transparency and accountable possible [52]. Despite the available avenues for user participation to encourage transparency and accountability, South Africa has been plagued by increasing levels of corruption and 'state capture' [50]. State capture refers to activities undertaken to subvert the principles of good governance [53]. The digital technologies have received a warm reception from all social groups and scholars; they have been criticized for increasing the inequality as some citizens lack access and skills to use technology [51]. Furthermore, there are increasing concerns about data privacy, cyber security, and national security associated with the increased adoption of emerging digital technologies [54].

To overcome lack of transparency and accountability, the South African government must strengthen the capacity and capability of the accountability and legal institutions, cultivate an inclusive culture by embedding the design principle of user engagement, and provide adequate support to the marginalized social groups to ensure that government services reflect the aspirations and worldviews of all citizens. Furthermore, government must improve the quality and quantity of information provided to the public regarding government service so that citizens could be able judge government performance and hold the official accountable for poor service delivery [32, 45, 51]. Lack of accountability weakens the democracy and renders government activities illegitimate. Without effective and efficient transparency systems, accountability remains elusive [51].

4.4 Responsiveness of Government

Responsiveness refers to the government's ability to respond swiftly to dynamic demands and queries of the citizens [55]. The effective responsiveness and inclusive user participation are underpinned by the availability of multiple channels of engagement, reliable internet connectivity and trained government employees to maintain engagement and to resolve citizens' queries online [46]. Government has recognized the importance of adopting the user-centered approach to the design of government services, hence, the increased investment in citizen-facing digital services to improve user participation [56]. Globally, governments are increasingly adopting social media as the two-way, real-time and low-cost mass-communication platform to improve responsiveness and to promote public participation [57]. Social media is the internet-based application that enables users to participate in the real-time creation and sharing of information through smart technologies. Popular Social media applications include Twitter (X), Facebook, YouTube, Instagram [58].

Statistics shows an upward trend of social media subscription in South Africa, with 10.1 million subscribers on WhatsApp, 9.1 million active users on Facebook, 4.7 million active users on Twitter (X), 9 million active subscriptions on YouTube and 3.7 million subscription on LinkedIn [30]. Despite social media's ability to meet citizens where they are, and its collaborative power, the South African government has not been capitalizing on these platforms as they are merely used for public announcements and information broadcasting [30]. This failure is due to lack of skilled employees to handle user engagement online, inadequate budget to mature the digital services and aging government ICT infrastructure. Citizens lack digital skills and access to reliable ICT infrastructure as the public Wi-Fi, which is the wireless internet provided by government to the public, is unstable to maintain meaningful engagement online [30, 46].

Social media has not always been used ethically and for good intentions. It has been criticized for facilitating widespread of fake news, misinformation, and cybercrimes, resulting in diminished trust in trust in digital services. It has also been used to manipulate the governance processes by tampering with the election databases and voting systems [59]. Despite the challenges with the user participation platforms, government, as the custodian of the public value, has a mandate to ensure that efforts are made to improve responsiveness of government to encourage user participation and to build trust in government to close the digital gap, and to solve the service delivery challenges in the country [60].

5 Conclusion

The aim of this research was to synthesize literature and critically analyze it to provide insights into factors that affect user participation in the design of governmental digital services in South Africa. The UN SDG 2030 and the constitution of the Republic of South Africa are the overarching imperatives whose objectives are to enforce inclusive governance for sustainable socio-economic and human development. To this end, the South African government has taken commendable policy positions to achieve inclusive governance, despite the persistent challenges with service delivery which are attributed to the top-down approach in the design of governmental digital services, resulting in public services that do not solve the problems of citizens. To overcome this challenge, the South African government must adopt the principle of 'user-participation by design' to ensure that inputs from citizens are incorporated early enough in the design of governmental digital services. Users of the government services are more likely to accept decisions of which they took part, and which reflect their worldviews.

6 Implications of the Study

This study intended to make a practical contribution by providing government with research-based findings that may be used as an input into the policies and processes intended to improve user participation in the design of governmental digital services, which may increase public trust and uptake of the digital services in South Africa. This study also intended to make a theoretical contribution by broadening the understanding of the factors that affect effective and legitimate user participation in the design of governmental digital services in South Africa, and providing guidance on the ways in which these factors could be addressed.

7 Limitations and Future Recommendations

The findings should be interpreted considering the limitations of the study which suggest a future direction. First, the researchers relied on secondary data collected in previous studies therefore this study assumed ethicality, quality, and reliability of prior studies. However, quality and eligibility of articles that were included in the review were ensured by critically reviewing the title, abstract, keywords and the full-text of peer-reviewed articles from reputable publishers [39]. Second, this study focused on South Africa government, a future study may consider a comparative study across different countries in Africa to get a holistic view of factors that affect user participation in the design of governmental digital services in Africa. Finally, future studies could conduct a similar study using quantitative methods to increase reliability and generalizability of findings.

Acknowledgments. This study was not funded by any institution or individual.

Disclosure of Interests..   The authors have no competing interests to declare that are relevant to the content of this article.

References

1. Mergel, I.: Digital service teams in government. Gov. Inf. Q. **36**(4), 101389 (2019)
2. Chan, F.K., et al.: Service design and citizen satisfaction with e-government services: a multidimensional perspective. Public Adm. Rev. **81**(5), 874–894 (2021)
3. Blom, P., Uwizeyimana, D.: Assessing the effectiveness of e-government and e-governance in South Africa: During national lockdown 2020 (2020)
4. Osah, J., Pade-Khene, C.: E-government strategy formulation in resource-constrained local government in South Africa. J. Inform. Tech. Polit. **17**(4), 426–451 (2020)
5. Mesa, D.: Digital divide, e-government and trust in public service: the key role of education. Front. Sociol. **8**, 1140416 (2023)
6. Bouzguenda, I., Alalouch, C., Fava, N.: Towards smart sustainable cities: a review of the role digital citizen participation could play in advancing social sustainability. Sustain. Cities Soc. **50**, 101627 (2019)
7. Ma, L., Wu, X.: Citizen engagement and co-production of e-government services in China. J. Chinese Governa. **5**(1), 68–89 (2020)
8. Seadira, B.: Bridging the digital divide: Critical analysis of the South African broadband policy. North-West University (South Africa) (2019)
9. Pérez-Morote, R., Pontones-Rosa, C., Núñez-Chicharro, M.: The effects of e-government evaluation, trust and the digital divide in the levels of e-government use in European countries. Technol. Forecast. Soc. Chang. **154**, 119973 (2020)
10. Swilling, M., Musango, J., Wakeford, J.: Developmental states and sustainability transitions: prospects of a just transition in South Africa. J. Environ. Plan. Policy Manage. **18**(5), 650–672 (2016)
11. Donati, D.: Mobile internet access and political outcomes: evidence from South Africa. J. Dev. Econ. **162**, 103073 (2023)
12. Adedokun, T.A., Zulu, S.P.: Towards digital inclusion in South Africa: the role of public libraries and the way forward. Interdiscipl. J. Econo. Bus. Law **11**(4) (2022)
13. Pasara, M.T., Garidzirai, R.: Causality effects among gross capital formation, unemployment and economic growth in South Africa. Economies **8**(2), 26 (2020)
14. Lee-Geiller, S., Lee, T.D.: Using government websites to enhance democratic E-governance: A conceptual model for evaluation. Gov. Inf. Q. **36**(2), 208–225 (2019)
15. Khan, A., Krishnan, S.: Citizen engagement in co-creation of e-government services: a process theory view from a meta-synthesis approach. Internet Res. **31**(4), 1318–1375 (2021)
16. Demirdoven, B., Cubuk, E.B.S., Karkin, N.: Establishing relational trust in e-Participation: A systematic literature review to propose a model. In: Proceedings of the 13th International Conference on Theory and Practice of Electronic Governance (2020)
17. Nusir, M.: Government Digital Service Co-design: Concepts to Collaboration Tools. In: ICETE (3) (2020)
18. Rosilawati, Y., et al.: Citizen participation for the effectiveness of local governance system: a quantitative study of local health and sanitation sectors. J. Public Aff. **22**(4), e2653 (2022)
19. Macnaghten, P., Guivant, J.S.: Narrative as a resource for inclusive governance: a UK–Brazil comparison of public responses to nanotechnology. J. Respons. Innov. **7**(sup1), 13–33 (2020)
20. Mayedwa, M.: Towards the implementation of a fully-fledged electronic service for citizens: the case for local government in South Africa (2023)
21. Alabdallat, W.I.M.: Toward a mandatory public e-services in Jordan. Cogent Business & Management **7**(1), 1727620 (2020)
22. Othman, M.H., Razali, R., Nasrudin, M.F.: Key factors for e-government towards sustainable development goals. Int. J. Adv. Sci. Technol **29**(6), 2864–2876 (2020)

23. Aftab, M., Myeong, S.: An analysis of foreign residents' perceptions and behaviors regarding digital government portal services in the Republic of South Korea. Int. Rev. Administr. Sci. **19** (2022)

24. Alqaryouti, O., et al.: Aspect-based sentiment analysis using smart government review data. Appl. Comp. Info. **20**(1/2), 142–161 (2024)

25. He, A.J., Ma, L.: Citizen participation, perceived public service performance, and trust in government: Evidence from health policy reforms in Hong Kong. Public Perform. Manag. Rev. **44**(3), 471–493 (2021)

26. Reynante, B., Dow, S.P., Mahyar, N.: A framework for open civic design: Integrating public participation, crowdsourcing, and design thinking. Digital Govern. Res. Pract. **2**(4), 1–22 (2021)

27. Shava, E., Vyas-Doorgapersad, S.: Inclusive participation in information and communication technologies (ICTs) processes for smart services in the city of Johannesburg. Insights into Regional Development **5**(1), 26–40 (2023)

28. Brush, B.L., et al.: Success in long-standing community-based participatory research (CBPR) partnerships: A scoping literature review. Health Educ. Behav. **47**(4), 556–568 (2020)

29. Khumalo, M.: The effect of information and communications technologies deployment on citizen engagement in a South African metropolitan municipality. University of the Witwatersrand (2022)

30. Fashoro, I., Barnard, L.: Assessing South African government's use of social media for citizen participation. The African J. Info. Sys. **13**(1), 3 (2021)

31. Maliwichi, P., et al.: Does mobile phone ownership matter? Insights on engagement in mHealth and e-government interventions from Southern Africa. Int. J. Heal. Promot. Edu. 1–22 (2021)

32. Mziba, M.: The role of public participation in service delivery: A case of a selected township in the Cape Metropolitan Area, South Africa. Cape Peninsula University of Technology (2020)

33. Galushi, L.T., Malatji, T.L.: Digital public administration and inclusive governance at the south african local government: in depth analysis of E-government and service delivery in musina local municipality. Acade. J. Interdiscipl. Stud. **11**(6), 116–126 (2022)

34. Lokaimoe, P.L., Bartocho, E., Omillo, F.O.: Refocusing public participation for a new management era in kenya: insights from literature. African J. Edu. Sci. Technol. **6**(2), 24–39 (2021)

35. Bonzon, M.-L., Roberts, J.J., Wright, J.: Research Brief: Public Participation in Net Zero Policymaking for Rural Regions in the UK (2024)

36. Bleiker, J., et al.: Navigating the maze: qualitative research methodologies and their philosophical foundations. Radiography **25**, S4–S8 (2019)

37. Muhaise, H., et al.: The research philosophy dilemma for postgraduate student researchers. Int. J. Res. Sci. Innov. **7**(4), 2321–2705 (2020)

38. Al-Ababneh, M.M.: Linking ontology, epistemology and research methodology. Science & Philosophy **8**(1), 75–91 (2020)

39. Xiao, Y., Watson, M.: Guidance on conducting a systematic literature review. J. Plan. Educ. Res. **39**(1), 93–112 (2019)

40. Mayer, I.: Qualitative research with a focus on qualitative data analysis. Int. J. Sales Retail. Market. **4**(9), 53–67 (2015)

41. Nowell, L.S., et al.: Thematic analysis: striving to meet the trustworthiness criteria. Int. J. Qual Methods **16**(1), 1609406917733847 (2017)

42. Kumar, D., Pratap, B., Aggarwal, A.: Public trust in state governments in India: who are more confident and what makes them confident about the government? Asian J. Comparat. Polit. **6**(2), 154–174 (2021)

43. Beshi, T.D., Kaur, R.: Public trust in local government: explaining the role of good governance practices. Pub. Organiz. Rev. **20**, 337–350 (2020)

44. Mansoor, M.: Citizens' trust in government as a function of good governance and government agency's provision of quality information on social media during COVID-19. Gov. Inf. Q. **38**(4), 101597 (2021)
45. Mahwai, N., et al.: A scoping review for proposing an eParticipation framework for South African local municipalities. In: 2023 IST-Africa Conference (IST-Africa). IEEE (2023)
46. Terrance, M.T.: E-government and E-participation on improving E-service delivery in bush-buckridge local municipality, South Africa. J. African Films and Diaspora Stud. **6**(2), 99 (2023)
47. Nokele, K.S., Mukonza, R.M.: The Adoption of E-Government in the Department of Home Affairs-Unpacking the Underlying Factors Affecting Adoption of E-Government within the Selected Service Centres in Limpopo Province, South Africa. African J. Govern. Develop. **10**(1), 98–117 (2021)
48. Shibambu, A.: Migration of government records from on-premises to cloud computing storage in South Africa. South African J. Librar. Info. Sci. **88**(1), 1–11 (2022)
49. Kumagai, S., Iorio, F.: Building trust in government through citizen engagement (2020)
50. Kgobe, F.K.L., Mamokhere, J.: Interrogating the effectiveness of public accountability mechanisms in South Africa: can good governance be realized? Int. J. Entrepre. **25**, 1–12 (2021)
51. Sharma, S., Kumar Kar, A., Gupta. M.: Unpacking Digital Accountability: Ensuring efficient and answerable e-governance service delivery. In: Proceedings of the 14th International Conference on Theory and Practice of Electronic Governance (2021)
52. Agostino, D., Saliterer, I., Steccolini, I.: Digitalization, accounting and accountability: A literature review and reflections on future research in public services. Fina. Account. Manage. **38**(2), 152–176 (2022)
53. Gajić, S.S., Pavlović, D.: State capture, hybrid regimes, and security sector reform. J. Region. Secu. **16**(2) (2021)
54. Sutherland, E.: The fourth industrial revolution–the case of South Africa. Politikon **47**(2), 233–252 (2020)
55. Barbosa, J.D.S., Mota, F.P.B.: Adoption of e-government: a study on the role of trust. Revista De Administracao Publica **56**(4), 441–464 (2022)
56. Rao, Y.S., et al.: Digital crime and its impact in present society. Int. J. Eng. Res. Technol. **8**(1), 1–6 (2020)
57. Yang, Y., et al.: Promoting public engagement during the COVID-19 crisis: how effective is the Wuhan local Government's information release? Int. J. Environ. Res. Public Health **18**(1), 118 (2021)
58. Lovari, A., Valentini, C.: Public sector communication and social media: Opportunities and limits of current policies, activities, and practices. The Handbook of Public Sector Communication 315–328 (2020)
59. Maseko, M.M.: Social media, protest and citizen participation in local government: A comparison between the City of Cape Town and Johannesburg metropolitan municipalities: 2010 to 2017 (2022)
60. Nkomo, N., Moyane, S.P.: Implementation of Grassroots E-Government Services in South Africa: A Literature Analysis. African J. Libr. Archi. Info. Sci. **31**(2) (2021)

Utilisation of a Virtual Honeynet to Proactively Secure the South African National Research and Education Network Against Cyberattacks

Heloise Pieterse[1]([✉]) [iD], Graham Barbour[2], André McDonald[2] [iD],
Danielle Badenhorst[2], and Wian Gertenbach[2]

[1] National Integrated Cyberinfrastructure System, CSIR, Pretoria, South Africa
hpieterse@csir.co.za
[2] Defence and Security Cluster, CSIR, Pretoria, South Africa

Abstract. South Africa is witnessing a significant increase in cyberattacks. Although such an increase in cyberattacks can be attributed to various factors, poor investment in cybersecurity technology and lack of awareness are causing South Africa to be a target of interest. While cyberattacks are targeting various sectors, it is the cyberattacks impacting critical infrastructure that are a growing concern. The South African National Research and Education Network (SA NREN) is a high-speed network dedicated to science, research, education and innovation traffic. With the growth of the SA NREN and the continuous increase in cyberattacks affecting South African institutions, proactive steps are required to secure and protect the SA NREN. This responsibility lies with the SA NREN Cybersecurity Incident Response Team (CSIRT), which was established in 2016 to offer protection against cyberattacks. While various proactive measures are currently in place to monitor the SA NREN, the CSIRT continues to explore alternative cost-effective solutions to secure the NREN. This paper investigates the benefits of utilising a novel low-interaction secure shell (SSH) honeynet, referred to as the Virtual Honeynet, to monitor and proactively secure the SA NREN. The Virtual Honeynet uses virtual containers to reduce resource requirements and improve performance. The investigation involved the experimental deployment of the Virtual Honeynet on the SA NREN over a twelve-day period and the evaluation of the captured data. The evaluation conducted focused on extracting behavioural and geographical intelligence from the raw data to guide the deployment of cyber measures to secure the SA NREN. The results presented in this paper confirm the value the Virtual Honeynet offers to the SA NREN as a technology to proactively secure the network.

Keywords: Cyberattacks · Cybersecurity · Honeynet · Network Security · NREN · South Africa

1   Introduction

A continuous increase in cyberattacks has become a growing concern for South Africa. While the country has taken steps to combat cyberattacks with the introduction of the National Cybersecurity Policy Framework (NCPF) in 2015 and the signing of the Cybercrimes Act into law in 2020 [1], South Africa remains a vulnerable target. A reluctance to invest in cybersecurity solutions, minimal cybersecurity awareness campaigns, and the lack of properly trained cybersecurity staff [1, 2] have created endless opportunities for cyberattacks. An evaluation of South Africa's cyberthreat landscape between 2010 and 2020 by Pieterse [3] presented a steady increase in cyberattacks, especially affecting the public sector. However, it is recent attacks against South Africa's critical infrastructure that have become a growing concern.

During 2019, the South African Banking Industry was hit by a wave of ransom-driven distributed denial of service (DDoS) attacks [4]. Shortly thereafter, the City of Johannesburg (CoJ), a metropolitan municipality responsible for local governance, detected a network breach that resulted in a ransomware attack [5]. South Africa's most recent major cyberattack involved Transnet, a state-owned rail, port, and pipeline company, which suffered a ransomware attack in July 2021 [6]. The cyberattack compelled Transnet to declare a force majeure causing significant disruption to transportation services at several ports. Early in 2023, South African Internet Service Provider (ISP), RSAWEB, battled for more than a week to restore all services after a ransomware attack [7]. These cyberattacks confirm a rising tendency to target critical infrastructure and it is only a matter of time before South Africa experiences a highly disruptive cyberattack.

A National Research and Education Network (NREN) provides dedicated network infrastructure, high-speed connectivity, and advanced services to academic and research institutions of a country. It is, therefore, possible to view an NREN as a specialised ISP for the research and education community [8] and forms part of a country's critical infrastructure. The South African NREN (SA NREN) offers high-speed network connectivity to various South African research and education institutions. The South African National Research Network (SANReN) group together with the Tertiary Education and Research Network of South Africa (TENET) constitute SA NREN. The SANReN group designs and builds the network while the TENET team operate the network [8, 9]. As of 2024, the SA NREN connects over 350 sites, namely campuses and offices, across all nine provinces of South Africa at an aggregate bandwidth of more than four terabits per second (4 Tbps) [10]. The growing number of users coupled with high bandwidth and international connectivity presents cyber attackers with an attractive target, particularly targeting SA NREN data and infrastructure [11]. To combat cyberattacks, the SA NREN Cybersecurity Incident Response Team (CSIRT) was established in 2016 to proactively protect and respond to cyber incidents affecting the SA NREN.

The SA NREN CSIRT is an academic-sector CSIRT coordinating proactive services to secure and protect research and education institutions operating on the SA NREN. Due to the large volumes of network activity and the decentralised nature of the SA NREN, the detection of cyberattacks remains a challenging problem [11]. The CSIRT, therefore, requires access to various sensors to enable the continuous monitoring of the SA NREN and the transformation of raw network data into actionable intelligence that can thwart cyberattacks. Past sensors deployed on the SA NREN include network flow collectors, network telescopes, and network honeypots. However, change is constant and the CSIRT must continue to explore alternative sensor solutions to proactively protect the SA NREN.

The focus of this paper is to investigate and explore the benefits offered by the Virtual Honeynet as a technology to proactively protect the SA NREN. The Virtual Honeynet is a novel single-board computer (SBC) implementation of a network of low-interaction Secure Shell (SSH) honeypots. The Virtual Honeynet system uses containers to host the honeypots, thereby reducing system resource requirements and improving the system's capacity to capture and record network activities. An exploratory experiment research methodology was followed and involved the experimental deployment of the Virtual Honeynet on the SA NREN for a twelve-day period. The main objective of the exploratory experiment is to observe the capability offered by the Virtual Honeynet to obtain insights into SA NREN's current cyber threat landscape. The main objective can be achieved by addressing the following research questions:

1. What behavioural trends can be observed by analysing the captured data?
2. What geographical trends can be observed by analysing the captured data?
3. How can observed trends be actioned to proactively improve the SA NREN cybersecurity posture?

The remainder of this paper is structured as follows. Section 2 presents the SA NREN as critical infrastructure while Sect. 3 emphasises the importance of the CSIRT proactively securing the NREN. The novel low-interaction SSH honeynet, which is called the Virtual Honeynet, is introduced and the operational deployment on the SA NREN is discussed in Sect. 4. The data captured by the Virtual Honeynet is analysed in Sect. 5 to address the main objective of this research study. Section 6 considers the results of the research study, and how the results can be applied in practice to secure the SA NREN. The paper is concluded in Sect. 7.

2   SA NREN as Critical Infrastructure

The purpose of a National Research and Education Network (NREN) is to provide backbone network infrastructure, high-speed connectivity and specialised services to the academic and research institutions of a country [12]. The network operates at a national level and is built separately using dedicated fibre optic connections or leases existing high-capacity connections provided by telecommunication providers [12]. The South African NREN was conceptualised in 2003 [13, 14] with the roles and responsibilities of SA NREN distributed between the SANReN group and the TENET [9]. The SANReN group, which is managed and implemented by the Council for Scientific and Industrial Research (CSIR) under contract with the Department of Science and Innovation (DSI), forms a key component of the National Integrated Cyberinfrastructure System (NICIS) and is responsible for the design and building of the SA NREN. The TENET group operates the SA NREN network under the terms of a collaboration agreement with the CSIR [9]. Both groups are also involved in the development and provisioning of value-added services on top of the NREN [8]. Figure 1 presents a high-level overview of the SA NREN backbone infrastructure.

The motivation behind the development of SA NREN is driven by technological, social, and economic factors [12]. From the technological perspective, the SA NREN is to satisfy the high demand for large-scale research and scientific projects such as the Square Kilometre Array Observatory (SKAO), which will become the world's largest radio telescope. The social aspect of the SA NREN ensures collaborative research opportunities across South Africa and international NRENs, as well as the successful participation of South African researchers in the production of global knowledge. Finally, the establishment of the SA NREN assists with economic prosperity and the realisation of associated national development objectives. The SA NREN, therefore, promotes innovation through scientific and technology development.

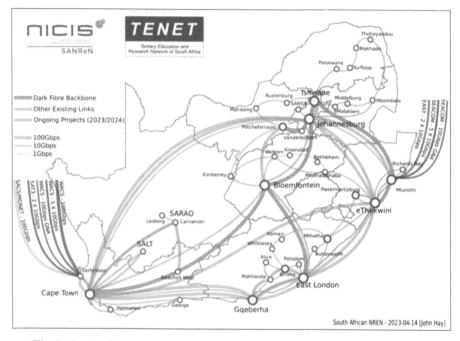

Fig. 1. South African NREN Backbone Map: Terrestrial and Undersea Capacity [15].

The contribution of the NREN to South Africa's critical infrastructure is indisputable. The number of sites connected to the SA NREN continues to grow exponentially. In 2018, the SA NREN supported approximately one million users spread across 151 sites throughout South Africa [14]. As of 2024, the number of connected sites has increased to 350 [10] and offers high-speed connectivity to various users within the academic and research community. The expanding footprint of the SA NREN creates a cyber landscape that presents cyber attackers with the opportunity to exploit for personal, financial, or intellectual gain. To prepare for and respond to the growing threat of cyberattacks against the NREN, the SANReN and TENET groups established an academic sector, coordinating CSIRT [16]. The CSIRT's constituency includes South African public universities, science councils, research organisations and supporting institutions, also commonly referred to as autonomous system (AS) 2018 (TENET) /.ac.za domains.

3   Proactively Securing the SA NREN

The CSIRT for the SA NREN was formally established in 2016 to prevent and respond to cybersecurity incidents. The CSIRT focuses on a proactive and coordinating role to monitor the SA NREN for signs of anomalies, abuse or ongoing cyberattacks [16]. The support offered by the CSIRT to the constituents is through several proactive services intended to prevent the occurrence of cyberattacks [16]. These services include [16]:

- Vulnerability assessments using multiple scanners to evaluate a constituent's network to uncover exploitable weaknesses and vulnerabilities in network devices, servers, and systems.
- Alerts collected via multiple cyber threat intelligence feeds that inform of vulnerable or misconfigured systems detected on the SA NREN, as well as indicators of systems compromised by malware.
- Announcements of weekly articles shared to ensure cybersecurity teams of supported constituents remain up-to-date with cybersecurity trends and developments.

The importance of proactively securing the SA NREN was emphasised by recently published cyberattacks that affected South African universities. In 2021, the University of Mpumalanga fell victim to a cyberattack that nearly resulted in an R100 million loss for the institution [17], while in 2024 a large-scale ransomware attack affected the Tshwane University of Technology [18]. While the number of cyberattacks stated appears minimal, it is important to note that the above-mentioned cyberattacks are the few that have been published publicly. Increasingly more institutions may have been affected or continue to experience cyberattacks unknowingly.

The CSIRT, therefore, requires access to various sensors to enable the continuous monitoring of the SA NREN and the transformation of raw network data into actionable intelligence to prevent cyberattacks. Deployment of cost-effective network sensors (e.g., network telescopes, flow collectors, and honeypots [14]) has previously assisted with the monitoring and detection of malicious activity on the SA NREN.

Network telescopes monitor a portion of routed but unallocated Internet Protocol (IP) address space and all network traffic captured can be considered illegitimate [19]. The exceptions are backscatter traffic and traffic created due to misconfigured systems [20], which can impact the ability to identify suspicious activities on an NREN. The worth of network flow (NetFlow) data to detect and evaluate cyberattacks on the SA NREN has been illustrated by research that focused on distributed reflection denial of service (DRDoS) [14] and Botnet [21] attacks. While NetFlow data is readily available, such data often consists of a mix of legitimate and potentially suspicious traffic and requires extensive analysis to extract actionable intelligence. NetFlow data is, therefore, more suitable for performing a post-cyberattack investigation. Finally, honeypots, such as Cowrie – a medium to high interaction open-source SSH and Telnet honeypot, have been deployed on the SA NREN periodically. A honeypot masquerades as a legitimate service to lure cyber attackers away from the actual targets [20] and offers the ability to capture valuable information about the cyberattack. Such ability is, however, limited if only a single honeypot is revealed, which greatly reduces the likelihood the cyber attacker will target and interact with the honeypot.

The above-mentioned sensors formed part of the Lost Packet Warehousing Service [22], which was a technological solution developed to enable the collection of cyberse-curity data sets and deployed on the SA NREN. Although the purpose of the Lost Packet Warehousing Service was to offer insight into emerging cybersecurity trends from a South African perspective, it also supported the SA NREN. Evaluation of Lost Packet Warehousing Service established that both network telescopes and NetFlow data offer value in protecting the SA NREN but are more suitable for post-cyberattack investi-gations as extensive evaluation of the data collected will be required. Honeypots offer insight into cyber attacker behaviour, which is required to proactively protect the SA NREN, however, deployment of single honeypots might be missed or easily discovered by cyber attackers. Considering the above limitations and with cyber attackers con-tinuously evolving, the CSIRT must explore alternative sensor solutions to proactively protect the SA NREN.

4   Experimental Deployment of the Virtual Honeynet

Honeypots as cybersecurity applications have been the subject of extensive research. These systems have evolved significantly over the past decades, shifting from direct implementations, where an entire device such as a personal computer hosts the honeypot, to more flexible, virtual honeypots, or a hybrid version of both [23–26].

The Honeyd system developed by Provos [27] pioneered the use of virtualisation in the implementation of honeypots and provided a framework for simulating computer systems at a network level. A further improvement was the introduction of the honeynet, or network of honeypots, which increases catchment areas and more accurately simulates a true network environment when compared to a single honeypot. Chang and Tsai [28] detail the implementation of a virtual Honeynet or Honeyfarm, comprising multiple honeypots with distinct IP addresses on one instance of the virtual machine.

Recent research in the field has investigated the use of containers to host honeypots, instead of virtual machines. Primary reasons for the consideration of container-based implementations include enhanced deployment flexibility and efficiency for honeypot configurations [29]. Initial work in this field, undertaken by Memari et al., provided an overview of a lightweight container-based deployment that emulates popular Linux and Windows services to attract cyber attackers [30]. Yu et al. designed a honeynet framework using container-based honeypots [31]. However, a shortcoming of existing honeynet implementations is their inability to expose multiple honeypot IP addresses per physical interface, thereby limiting the attack surface [32].

4.1   Overview of the Virtual Honeynet

The Virtual Honeynet is a novel system that comprises a network of N virtual containers, as illustrated in the system diagram shown in Fig. 2. Each virtual container is a honeypot that hosts the SSH service and allows login attempts from the external network (in the case of the experimental deployment, the SA NREN), thereby providing a means for capturing and recording network activities. The use of virtual containers drastically reduces the resources required to host each honeypot. This feature permits the implementation of the Virtual Honeynet on a cost-effective single-board computer. The Virtual Honeynet used for the experimental deployment was implemented on a Radxa ROCK Pi model E single-board computer [33], with a RK3328 (Cortex-A53) 64-bit quad-core processor operating at 1.3 GHz, and 1 GB of DDR3 memory.

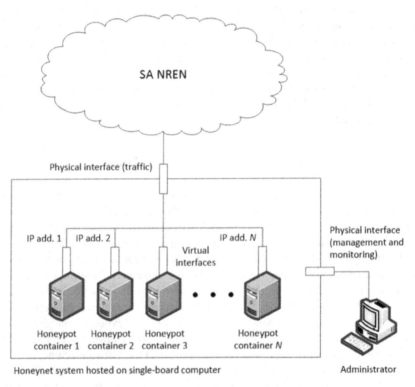

Fig. 2. System diagram of the Virtual Honeynet.

The single-board computer that hosts the Virtual Honeynet was connected to the SA NREN via a single physical Gigabit Ethernet Interface for traffic capture. Each honeypot had a virtual network interface that was assigned a distinct IP address on the SA NREN, thereby exposing multiple concurrent honeypots to the attacker. This novel feature increases the attack surface of the honeynet and improves its information gathering capacity. A network of $N = 11$ honeypots was implemented for the experimental deployment. Whereas the use of virtual containers permits parallel deployment of a larger number of honeypots, the number of honeypots deployed on the SA NREN was restricted by the number of unused IP addresses provided by the operator. The single-board computer presented a second Ethernet Interface to the network administrator for the management of the Virtual Honeynet and the inspection of network traffic collected.

The Virtual Honeynet was implemented as custom software installed on the Ubuntu Linux operating system (Ubuntu Focal server, kernel version 4.4.194–18-rock-chip g3443041f5e70). The custom software uses the Docker platform [34] for the management of virtual containers. The software performs automatic forwarding of traffic between the external network and the network of virtual containers (i.e., the honeynet), as well as the extraction of logs from each container. The software was developed by and is the intellectual property of the CSIR and is not currently available under an open license.

4.2 Observation Period

Evaluation of the Virtual Honeypot involved the experimental deployment of the single-board computer on the SA NREN for a twelve-day period. The motivation behind the experimental deployment of the Virtual Honeynet is two-fold. Firstly, the performance and data capture ability of the Virtual Honeynet are evaluated in a setting representative of the intended operational environment of the technology. The SA NREN is accessible by a large user base and carries high volumes of traffic, which also permitted fatigue testing of the Virtual Honeynet. Secondly, increasing scans and attempted network intrusions are routinely observed on the SA NREN, which allowed for the testing of the proposed single-board computer's capacity to gather information on malicious network activity. The outcome is determining the value the captured and analysed data can offer to proactively secure the SA NREN. The observation period for the experimental deployment, which took place from 26 October 2023 until 6 November 2023, is presented in Fig. 3.

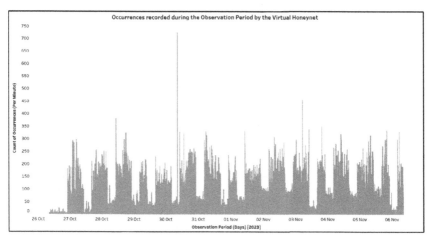

Fig. 3. Count of occurrences recorded during the observation period of the deployed Virtual Honeynet on the SA NREN.

The observation period reveals a relatively consistent pattern of periods resembling high and low activity as recorded by the Virtual Honeynet. Over twelve days, the Virtual Honeynet captured 780 549 occurrences of which 3 097 were from unique IP addresses.

An occurrence is described as an activity or attempted connection recorded by the Virtual Honeynet. While the occurrences collected by the Virtual Honeynet can be deemed abnormal and malicious due to the design and placement of the honeynet, benign traffic due to deployment, and testing were also recorded. Such occurrences were identified and filtered out to exclude any potential bias. The remainder are treated as attempted brute-force attacks. Brute-force attacks are early attempts at perimeter exploitation and are often a precursor to advanced and damaging cyberattacks. DDoS attacks are common threats to NRENs [35], often driven by established botnets, which are networks of compromised computers that attempt to disrupt network availability. Ransomware, which is malicious software demanding a ransom to return access or not expose the exfiltrated data [35], has recently emerged as an increasing threat targeting institutions [18]. By closely observing attempted brute-force attacks, necessary insights can be gathered and turned into actionable intelligence to thwart cyberattacks.

4.3 Observations Across the Honeynet

A key design of the Virtual Honeynet is the deployment of multiple honeypots to increase the attack surface and improve the likelihood that a cyber attacker will interact with one or more honeypots. It is, therefore, possible, to evaluate the effectiveness of the Virtual Honeynet by observing the attempted brute-force attacks across all the honeypots. Figure 4 shows the brute-force attacks collected by the honeypots forming part of the Virtual Honeynet during the observation period.

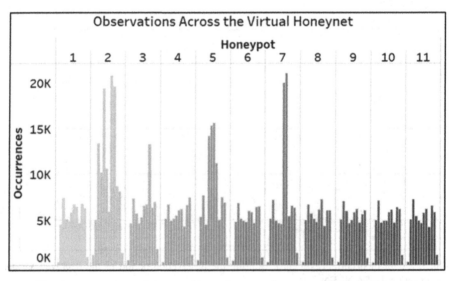

Fig. 4. Observations of attempted brute-force attacks across the Virtual Honeynet.

The occurrences recorded across all the exposed honeypots confirm the success of the Virtual Honeynet in increasing the attack surface. The captured occurrences are further analysed in the subsequent section to enable the extraction of actionable intelligence from the raw data.

5 Data Analysis

The observation period has revealed that the SA NREN is not immune to cyberattacks. The activities detected and recorded by the Virtual Honeynet confirm the SA NREN is continuously exposed to attempted brute-force attacks on SSH. To proactively secure the SA NREN, a better understanding of the captured data is required. The analysis focused on extracting behavioural and geographical intelligence from the raw data to guide the selection of appropriate proactive steps to secure the SA NREN.

5.1 Behavioural Trends

The identification of behavioural trends necessitates the analysis of the captured data to identify meaningful patterns. The Virtual Honeynet captured two data sets that were made available for further analysis:

- **IP Activity**: recorded attempted brute-force attacks per honeypot, inclusive of the time, attacker's IP address and attacked username.
- **User Activity**: recorded attempted brute-force attacks per honeypot, inclusive of used credentials (username and password).

The above-mentioned data sets are further explored in terms of observed attack patterns and SSH credentials attempted during the attacks.

Attack Patterns Evaluation of the IP Activity data set led to the discovery of the patterns presented in Fig. 5. Each pattern is illustrated vertically as a column in Fig. 5 and collectively presents a grouping of blocks representing the occurrences recorded across the Virtual Honeynet. The patterns identified are the following:

- **Recurring**: repeated recording of attempted brute-force attacks targeting the Virtual Honeynet (all honeypots) occurring on one or more days of the observation period. The pattern perceived presents signs of automation.
- **Variability**: deviation of the Recurring pattern with periods of inactivity observed. The lack of consistency can be attributed to several factors, such as intentional modification or unintentional disruptions.
- **Sporadic**: attempted brute-force attacks occurring at irregular intervals witnessed across multiple days of the observation period. The lack of a formal pattern and scatteredness of the attempted brute-force attacks resemble efforts to avoid detection.
- **Consistent**: a larger collection of attempted brute-force attacks targeting a single honeypot occurring successively on one or more days of the observation period.

The four patterns shown in Fig. 5 are representative of the entire IP Activity data set and describe the brute-force attacks attempted against the Virtual Honeynet during the observation period.

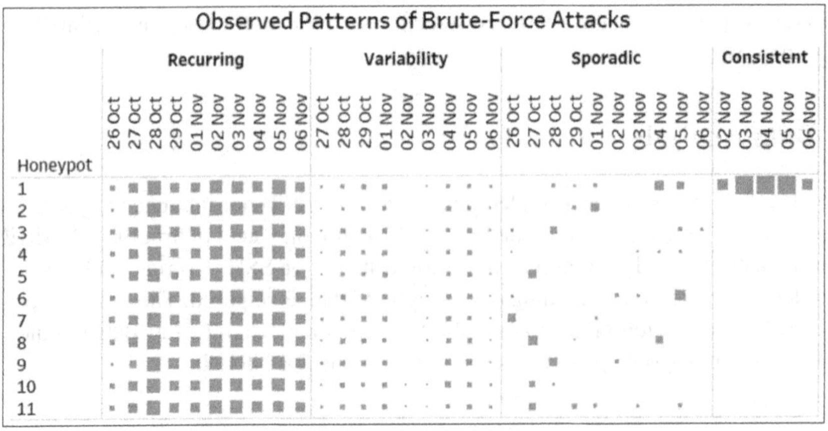

Fig. 5. Observed patterns of brute-force attacks.

To gather further insight, the patterns identified are applied to the top 50 IP addresses of the IP Activity data set. The top 50 IP addresses represent 90% (706 597 occurrences) of all attempted brute-force attacks recorded. Shown in Fig. 6 are the trends observed when applying the identified patterns to the top 50 IP addresses. Each pattern is represented individually as a circle in Fig. 6 and illustrates the occurrences recorded using either a single username (root) or multiple usernames across a single, multiple or all of the available honeypots (entire Virtual Honeynet).

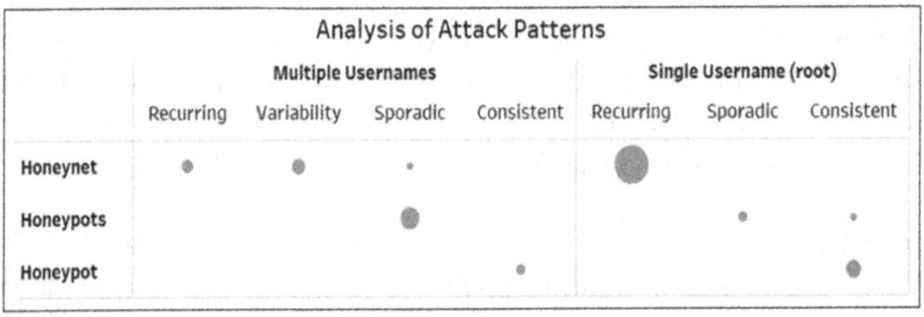

Fig. 6. Analysis of attack patterns to observe key trends.

The trends observed are the following:

- The *root* user is the most targeted which is expected since the *root* user is a common default credential used by vendors for administrative access to Unix-based systems.
- The preferred attack pattern followed is to recurringly target the *root* user on the exposed honeypots across the Virtual Honeynet.
- Attempts to avoid detection by following irregular patterns. Such attacks prefer targeting multiple honeypots, and although attempts against the *root* user are detected, more attempts are detected targeting multiple users.

- Attempted brute-force attacks following the consistent pattern specifically targeting an individual honeypot. Such attacks appear to be more directed, causing higher traffic volumes.

Attempted SSH Credentials Exploration of the User Activity data set focused on the use of SSH credentials (username and password combinations) during the attempted brute-force attacks. Presented in Fig. 7 are the top username and password credential pairs captured by the User Activity data set.

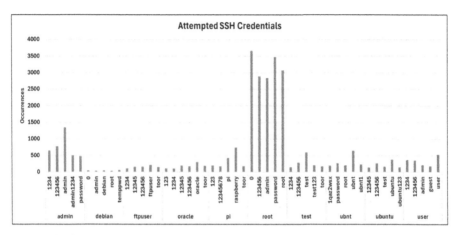

Fig. 7. Top SSH credentials attempted during the recorded brute-force attacks.

In terms of usernames recorded, 1 212 unique usernames were captured with the *root* username accounting for 92% of all observed usernames. The unique passwords attempted were 40 927 and the top password identified was *123456*. The top password observed also topped the most common password list for 2023 [36].

5.2 Geographical Trends

The attempted brute-force attacks collected by the IP Activity data set are further enriched by linking geographical information, namely city, country, autonomous system (AS), and autonomous system number (ASN), to the top 50 captured IP addresses. An AS represents a grouping of networks under the control of a single entity. Using the enriched data set, the geolocation of the top 50 IP addresses is presented in Fig. 8.

The region with the most occurrences collected during the observation period is China. More than 50% of the top 50 IP addresses originated from Nanjing, Tianjin, and Shenzhen, with a total of 583 635 attempted brute-force attacks occurring during the observation period. A significant portion of the IP addresses originating from China (94%) belongs to AS4134, which is the ChinaNET Backbone. AS4134 appears to be an active playground for Advance Persistent Threats (APTs) and is often used to host malware distribution websites [37]. Therefore, all activity associated with AS4134 should be considered high-risk.

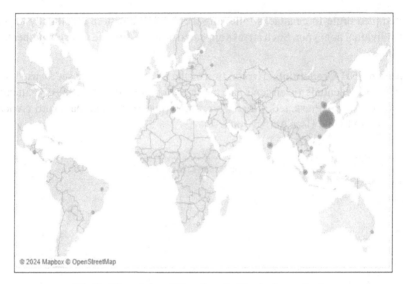
© 2024 Mapbox © OpenStreetMap

Fig. 8. The origins of the attempted brute-force attacks.

Following AS4134 is AS24547, Hebei Mobile Communication Company Limited, of which 33 256 occurrences were recorded during the observation period. Although fewer attempted brute-force attacks were observed coming from AS24547, such attacks are often associated with attempts to spread malware and should also be considered high-risk [38].

The results discussed affirm the importance of considering the geolocation of the attempted brute-force attacks. Having a heightened understanding of the ongoing attacks emanating from a specific region will improve the proactive response should similar attacks be detected in the future affecting the SA NREN.

6 Discussion – Turning Research into Practice

The research was undertaken to explore the benefits offered by the Virtual Honeynet as a proactive measure to secure the SA NREN. The experimental deployment of the Virtual Honeynet enabled the collection of valuable data, which offered insight into the current cyber threat landscape of the SA NREN. The analysis of the captured data presented important findings which must be actioned to ensure continuous proactive protection of the SA NREN against cyberattacks.

6.1 External Monitoring

The patterns observed by analysing the captured data presented attacking trends that require continuous monitoring. Persistent brute-force attacks (resembling recurring or variability patterns) from IP addresses with high confidence of abuse[1] must be filtered

---

[1] https://www.abuseipdb.com/.

or blocked. Elimination of such attacks will reduce unnecessary traffic on the SA NREN and improve the ability to find targeted attacks.

Furthermore, the geographical regions, identifiable by ASNs, from where the brute-force attacks originated must also be continuously evaluated. Such an evaluation should explore the AS for known malicious activities[2] to determine whether traffic from the detected IP addresses should be permitted.

The evaluation should also focus on known threat actors, such as advanced persistent threats (APTs) or known hacker groups, originating from the identified regions. Such threat actors often have well-established techniques, tactics, and procedures (TTPs) that are deployed during cyberattacks and the observations provided by the Virtual Honeynet can support the identification of known behaviour of threat actors.

Both behavioural and geographical trends must also be shared with other CSIRTs and security personnel operating within the SA NREN through appropriate channels to promote awareness and improve the overall security posture of the SA NREN.

6.2 Internal Monitoring

While the intended use of the Virtual Honeynet is to monitor for abnormal or potentially malicious behaviour occurring from systems external to the SA NREN, the internal environment (AS2018) should not be excluded. The Virtual Honeynet presents the opportunity to identify constituents of the SA NREN that are infected with malware or performing malicious activities unknowingly. Such findings can be corroborated using the internally deployed threat intelligence platform and the affected constituent can be informed. The intelligence derived from the data captured by the Virtual Honeynet can also serve as input to internally deployed Security Information and Event Management (SIEM) systems.

6.3 Best Practices

The insights gathered through the analysis of both the IP and User Activity data sets emphasise best practices that should be applied as proactive steps to reduce the cyber threat landscape and secure the SA NREN.

With the SA NREN being exposed to high volumes of continuous brute-force attacks, steps must be taken to limit the exposure of systems operating on the NREN. Only systems supporting services requiring a public-facing IP must be exposed. For services requiring accessibility (e.g., CSIRT services that must be remotely accessible to security personnel), such services should be placed in a separate security zone and made accessible via a virtual private network (VPN) or jump server.

While accessibility to services can be managed, such services can still be vulnerable to attempted attacks should weak credentials be used. The observed brute-force attacks confirmed the use of common credentials and, therefore, it is important that the top-attacked usernames and passwords, especially in combination, are not used by any application. The use of *root* as a username should not be permitted and where possible, password authentication should be disabled. Instead, public key authentication

---

[2] https://urlhaus.abuse.ch/.

(certificates) must be used. Furthermore, the insights gathered regarding the use of username and password combinations during brute-force attacks can be used to enhance cybersecurity policies, as well as support the enforcement of such policies.

The insights provided through the analysis of the data captured by the Virtual Honeynet should be incorporated into cybersecurity awareness campaigns to inform the users of the SA NREN of known threats and the potential impact of cyberattacks.

Applying the best practices identified above, which are supported by the findings observed during data analysis, will reduce the cyber threat landscape of the SA NREN.

7 Conclusion

This study explored the benefits of utilising the Virtual Honeynet to monitor and proactively secure the SA NREN. The experimental deployment of the Virtual Honeynet allowed for the collection of raw data sets, which were analysed to extract intelligence (behavioural and geographical) and guide the selection of proactive steps to improve security. The intelligence obtained has shown that the SA NREN is continuously exposed to attempted brute-force attacks. Such attacks can be averted by transforming the gathered intelligence into actionable steps that can be applied as proactive measures to secure the SA NREN. The findings confirmed the value of the Virtual Honeynet as a technology to proactively secure the NREN. Future development work for the Virtual Honeynet aims to implement honeypot containers that offer additional network services (i.e., other than SSH) to cyber attackers. It is anticipated that these honeypots will improve the volume and diversity of data that may be harvested using the Virtual Honeynet.

Acknowledgements. The authors wish to thank the SANREN CSIRT and NICIS for enabling and facilitating the hosting of the Virtual Honeynet infrastructure on the SA NREN.

References

1. Experts Urge Clearer Direction in South Africa's Cyber Strategy: https://www.infosecurity-magazine.com/news/experts-clearer-south-africa-cyber/. Last accessed 10 March 2024
2. Cyberattacks – South Africa needs an integrated approach to protect critical infrastructure: https://www.dailymaverick.co.za/article/2023-08-03-cyberattacks-in-sa-integrated-plan-needed-to-protect-critical-infrastructure/. Last accessed 10 March 2024
3. Pieterse, H.: The cyber threat landscape in South Africa: A 10-Year review. The African J. Info. Commun. (AJIC) **28**, 1–21 (2021)
4. Bad day for SA's cyber security as banks suffer DDoS attacks, https://www.itweb.co.za/article/bad-day-for-sas-cyber-security-as-banks-suffer-ddos-attacks/LPp6V7r4OVzqDKQz. Last accessed 11 March 2024
5. City of Joburg hit by cyber attack, https://www.itweb.co.za/article/city-of-joburg-hit-by-cyber-attack/dgp45qaG8gZ7X9l8. Last accessed 11 March 2024
6. Transnet identifies, isolates source of disruption to IT systems, https://www.itweb.co.za/article/transnet-identifies-isolates-source-of-disruption-to-it-systems/KPNG8v8Km3Vq4mwD. Last accessed 12 March 2024

7. RSAWeb battles to restore services after cyber attack, https://www.itweb.co.za/article/rsa web-battles-to-restore-services-after-cyber-attack/G98YdMLGdOm7X2PD. Last accessed 12 March 2024

8. Mooi, R., Botha, R.: Prioritizing computer security incident response services for the South African National Research Network (SANReN). In: CONF-IRM 2016 Proceedings, pp. 27–40 (2016)

9. The South African NREN, https://www.sanren.ac.za/south-african-nren/. Last accessed 13 March 2024

10. Trusted networking partner, https://www.tenet.ac.za/network. Last accessed 13 March 2024

11. Mooi, R.: A model for security incident response in the South African National Research and Education Network. Master dissertation. Nelson Mandela Metropolitan University (2014)

12. Murić, G.: Resilience of the Critical Communication Networks Against Spreading Failures - Case of the European National Research and Education Networks. Doctoral dissertation. Technische Universität Dresden (2017)

13. Draai, K., Mooi, R.: Implementing perfSONAR in the South African National Research and Education Network. UbuntuNet Alliance (2015)

14. Burke, I.D., Herbert, A., Mooi, R.: September. Using network flow data to analyse DRDoS attacks, as observed on the SANReN. In: Proceedings of the Annual Conference of the South African Institute of Computer Scientists and Information Technologists (SAICSIT), pp. 164–170. ACM, Port Elizabeth, South Africa (2018)

15. South African NREN Backbone, https://www.sanren.ac.za/backbone/. Last accessed 14 March 2024

16. Responding to cybercrime in SA's higher education and research community, https://www.tenet.ac.za/news/responding-to-cybercrime-in-sa-rne. Last accessed 12 March 2024

17. University of Mpumalanga thwarts R100m hack attempt, https://www.itweb.co.za/article/uni versity-of-mpumalanga-thwarts-r100m-hack-attempt/Kjlyrvw1jmmMk6am. Last accessed 13 March 2024

18. Tshwane University of Technology suffers ransomware attack — thousands of records stolen, https://mybroadband.co.za/news/security/524680-tshwane-university-of-technology-suffers-ransomware-attack-thousands-of-records-stolen.html. Last accessed 14 March 2024

19. Moore, D., Shannon, C., Voelker, G.M., Savage, S.: Network Telescope: Technical Report. Department of Computer Science and Engineering, University of California, San Diego (2004)

20. Hunter, S.O., Irwin, B., Stalmans, E.: Real-time distributed malicious traffic monitoring for honeypots and network telescopes. In: 2013 Information Security for South Africa, pp. 1–9. IEEE, Johannesburg, South Africa (2013)

21. Burke, I.D., Herbert, A.: Tracking botnets on nation research and education network. In: Proceedings of the 19th European Conference on Cyber Warfare and Security, pp. 61–71. Academic Conferences and Publishing International Limited, Reading, UK (2020)

22. Burke, I.D., Motlhabi, M.B., Netshiya, R., Pieterse, H.: Lost packet warehousing service. In: Proceedings of the 16th International Conference on Cyber Warfare and Security, pp. 501–508

23. Watson, D., Riden, J.: The Honeynet Project: Data Collection Tools, Infrastructure, Archives and Analysis. In: 2008 WOMBAT Workshop on Information Security Threats Data Collection and Sharing, pp. 24–30. IEEE Computer Society Press, Amsterdam, Netherlands (2008)

24. Abbasi, F.H., Harris, R.J.: Experiences with a Generation III Virtual Honeynet. In: 2009 Australasian Telecommunication Networks and Applications Conference, ATNAC 2009 – Proceedings, pp. 83–88. IEEE, Canberra, Australia (2009)

25. Wang, J., Zeng, J.: Construction of Large-Scale Honeynet Based on Honeyd. Procedia Engineering 15, 3260–3264 (2011)

26. Sharma, N., Sabo, T., Sran, S.S., Sabo, T.: Detection of Threats in Honeynet Using Honeywall. Int. J. Comp. Sci. Eng. (IJCSE) 3(10), 3332–3336 (2011)

27. Provos, N., Holz, T.: Virtual honeypots: From botnet tracking to intrusion detection, 1ˢᵗ edn. Pearson Education, Boston, USA (2008)

28. Chang, J., Tsai, Y.: Design of virtual honeynet collaboration system in existing security research networks. In: 2010 10th International Symposium on Communications and Information Technologies, pp. 798–803. IEEE, Tokyo, Japan (2010)

29. Felter, W., Ferreira, A., Rajamony, R., Rubio, J.: An updated performance comparison of virtual machines and Linux containers. In: 2015 IEEE International Symposium on Performance Analysis of Systems and Software (ISPASS), pp. 171–172. IEEE Computer Society, Philadelphia, USA (2015)

30. Memari, N., Hashim, S., Samsudin, K.: Container based virtual honeynet for increased network security. In: 2015 5th National Symposium on Information Technology: Towards New Smart World (NSITNSW), pp. 1–6. IEEE, Riyadh, Saudi Arabia (2015)

31. Yu, T., Xin, Y., Zhang, C.: A novel honeynet framework based on container: design and implementation. In: 2023 IEEE 5th International Conference on Civil Aviation Safety and Information Technology (ICCASIT), pp. 892–897. IEEE (2023)

32. DockerTrap: A general-purpose, high-interaction honeypot, https://github.com/mrhavens/DockerTrap. Last accessed 22 March 2024

33. RockpiE – Radxa Wiki, https://wiki.radxa.com/RockpiE/. Last accessed 15 May 2024

34. Docker: Accelerated Container Application Development, https://www.docker.com/. Last accessed 15 May 2024

35. Cybersecurity in an online world, https://www.tenet.ac.za/news/cybersecurity-in-an-online-world. Last accessed 15 May 2024

36. Most overused passwords in the world — make sure yours isn't on the list, https://www.cnbc.com/2023/11/16/most-common-passwords-70percent-can-be-cracked-in-less-than-a-second.html. Last accessed 18 March 2024

37. Malware Digest December 2023, https://www.spamhaus.org/resource-hub/malware/malware-digest-december-2023/. Last accessed 22 March 2024

38. Honeypots: Exploit attempts on vulnerable IoT devices (week 38), https://tehtris.com/en/blog/exploit-attempts-on-vulnerable-iot-devices-week-38/. Last accessed 22 March 2024

Examining Data Governance to Determine How Democratic Data Management Can Be Achieved in Organizations

Jason Stamp and Samwel Dick Mwapwele[(⊠)] [iD]

University of Witwatersrand, Johannesburg Gauteng 2017, South Africa
samwel.mwapwele@wits.ac.za

Abstract. In this age of data-driven decision-making and a data-centric environment, robust data governance is vital for organisational performance and for upholding democratic and fair data practices. Managing data is increasingly challenging with large volumes across systems, evolving regulations, diverse stakeholder interests, and different implementation methods. The research gap is embedded in the realization that data governance is crucial in any organisation, but its implementation faces the demand need to address the horizontal relationships among data providers. The research question is *how can democratic data governance (DDG) be implemented by institutions and organisations to better serve the interests of data providers?*

Employing a systematic literature review, this study is steered by the populations, exposures, and outcomes (PEO) framework to define the review's boundaries. The databases used were Web of Science, ProQuest, and Ebsco-Host. The PRISMA framework was used to ensure a transparent, structured, and exhaustive examination of the selected literature. The inclusion criteria are articles in English, and peer-reviewed literature specifically about democratic data governance. Through thematic analysis, this study explores the obstacles and opportunities of DDG implementation in the 27 articles included.

The key findings are grouped into three themes; data-driven societal challenges, aspects of data governance needed for democratic data governance, and challenges with adapting data governance. Addressing the horizontal relationship between data providers contributes to the policy as it engages with GDPR. The research contributes to the body of knowledge on data governance and the role of privacy.

Keywords: Data governance · Democratic data governance · Data as a democratic medium · Relational · Challenges with data governance

1 Introduction

In this age of data-driven decision-making and a data-centric environment, robust data governance is vital for organizational performance [1–3] and for upholding democratic and fair data practices [4, 5]. Managing data is increasingly challenging with large volumes across systems [3, 6], evolving regulations, diverse stakeholder interests, and different implementation methods [7, 8].

© The Author(s), under exclusive license to Springer Nature Switzerland AG 2024
A. Gerber (Ed.): SAICSIT 2024, CCIS 2159, pp. 421–436, 2024.
https://doi.org/10.1007/978-3-031-64881-6_25

Data governance is a strategic framework essential for effective data use within organizations [1, 2], involving setting data standards, defining ownership, ensuring data quality and security, and meeting legal obligations [1, 8]. Furthermore, it is pivotal for the responsible management and sharing of personal data [3, 7].

Clear delineation of roles and responsibilities within an organization is crucial for effective data governance [1, 9]. While the business is tasked with overseeing data collection and quality, IT plays a supportive role, necessitating robust collaboration between them [6, 9]. Therefore, this study defines data governance as the assignment of data ownership, roles, and responsibilities essential for implementing fair and efficient data-related practices and policies. This encompasses considerations of data quality, collection, storage, and usage within an organization.

The concept of "data as a democratic medium" (DDM) [5] strengthens the capacity of data governance to benefit stakeholders and promote active stakeholder engagement in decision-making and institutional accountability. Unlike the individual-focused "data as an individual medium" (DIM), DDM emphasizes equitable participation and considers both individual and community relationships in data-driven decisions [4, 5]. In DDM, data collectors refer specifically to entities engaged in personal data collection, storage, and use. Data (service) providers refer to entities that provide a platform for data collection and management [10].

[5] contrasts DIM's individual vertical relations between data providers and collectors with DDM's inclusion of horizontal relationships, signifying interconnectedness among data providers. [4] further highlights the importance of horizontal relations in contexts like genetic data use, which can impact related individuals.

DDM, therefore, extends beyond vertical connections to incorporate horizontal relationships among related data providers, advocating for data usage that respects all stakeholders' wishes [4, 8]. Recognizing these, horizontal relationships enhance fair data usage for entire populations [4, 5]. By encouraging stakeholder collaboration in shaping data governance policies, existing power imbalances that may foster discrimination can be dismantled [5, 8]. This research uses the term democratic data governance (DDG) to infer a framework that represents the interests of entire demographics, enabling equitable data collection, management, and use.

Organizations grapple with burgeoning data volumes, necessitating equitable and effective data management and regulatory compliance policies [2, 3]. DDG is crucial in this regard but its implementation faces the demand for the need to address the horizontal relationships among data providers [4, 5, 8]. Therefore, the research gap is found in the demand for addressing the horizontal relationship among data providers. The research question is how can democratic data governance be implemented by institutions and organizations to better serve the interests of data providers?

This research aims to synthesize a unified understanding of democratic data governance [2, 8] by considering the relational interests of data providers [4, 5]. The paper is structured as follows; the next section provides a brief background of the key concepts in the research question followed by the research methodology. That section is followed by the findings and discussion and lastly, a conclusion is provided that considers the research contribution and limitations.

2 Background and Significance

Many organizations grapple with poor data quality, evident in the prevalence of redundant, incomplete, inaccurate, irrelevant, and inconsistent data that impairs value creation [2, 9, 11]. Despite advances in integrated data warehouses for decision-making, data quality challenges linger [11]. Research on 130 Canadian firms revealed an annual revenue loss of 8 to 12% due to poor data quality [12], a finding mirrored in England [13].

The necessity of data quality for enhancing usefulness and efficiency is frequently emphasized [6, 11], underscoring the role of high-quality data in enhancing decision-making and operational efficiency [2, 6]. Thus, prioritizing data quality, especially when mandated by regulation, is crucial for organizations [2, 6].

The dynamic realm of data privacy presents multifaceted challenges for both institutions and individuals [3, 14]. In leading data privacy legislation, the European Union's General Data Protection Regulation (GDPR) stands as a benchmark, establishing principles of informed consent, transparency, and data subject rights [14, 15]. Similarly, the Protection of Personal Information Act (POPIA) in South Africa grants individuals enhanced control over their data, stipulating standards for how businesses should manage such data [16, 17].

POPIA emerges as a pertinent legislative reference for this review, given its South African context, securing its relevance both geographically and legislatively [18, 19]. Both GDPR and POPIA are lauded for their commitment to data protection, sharing several thematic parallels [18, 19]. [19] characterizes POPIA as a stepping stone to GDPR compliance due to their shared attributes and [18] further attributes their resemblance to a shared ambition of transforming data handling and processing in organizations. This alignment is also elucidated through the "Brussels effect", wherein POPIA's foundational principles are seen as an adaptation of GDPR's stringent standards [18], showcasing the latter's legislative influence. However, POPIA lacks certain features, such as Data Protection Impact Assessments (DPIAs) and optional certification processes, marking a distinct divergence [18]. [19] also highlights that GDPR safeguards European citizens' data privacy globally, while POPIA only considers South African citizens' data within its jurisdiction.

While POPIA and GDPR share foundational tenets, GDPR's influence as a blueprint for numerous personal data protection legislations is unmistakable, with a notable inclination towards collaborative governance [18]. Due to its comprehensive and influential framework, GDPR has, therefore, been selected as the primary legislative reference for this review.

[15] delineates the core principles of GDPR, encompassing "purpose limitation, [...] fairness, transparency, [...] individual consent, legal obligations [...], a right to information, of access, of rectification, erasure, and restriction, to data portability, to object and to an explanation in certain cases where one is subjected to decisions based on automated processing". [20] emphasize GDPR's intention to enhance individual control over personal data, explicitly including cookies. However, the intricate and largely arcane nature of information systems, coupled with an induced state of apathy due to data inundation, skews transparency, facilitating manipulation rather than fostering autonomy [15]. This issue is compounded by the allure of convenience and service access, which entices individuals to relinquish their data, compromising self-determination [15].

A study highlighted that even in GDPR-regulated environments, instances were identified where users who refused cookies continued to be surreptitiously tracked, nullifying the intent behind the opt-out choice [20]. Furthermore, websites often resort to obfuscation strategies, utilizing either complex language or subtle placements of opt-out options, thereby complicating the withdrawal process [20]. These practices subvert the foundational tenets of GDPR and cast doubt on the efficacy of regulatory frameworks in safeguarding digital self-determination.

[3] conceptualize data governance as a collective action dilemma, complicated by stakeholders' conflicting interests, free-riding, and trust issues. Reconciling these divergent interests, from individuals to corporations and governments, is crucial [8]. [4] proposes a "relational theory of privacy," acknowledging that regulations reveal both personal data and relational ties. Socio-political implications of data undermine governance models focused on individual rights [5] with privacy extending beyond the individual to the network of relationships and data connections [4].

Data governance is key for achieving data quality, organizational objectives, and regulatory compliance [2, 3]. However, its implementation is fraught with challenges, including unclear guidelines [7, 8] and heightened complexity due to regulatory demands [3]. Organizational attitudes, lack of awareness, and limited knowledge also hinder data governance [3, 6], compounded by insufficient top management support, despite well-defined roles [1, 9]. A "unified standard approach" is necessary [2]. The collective and relational dimensions of data discussed demand a democratic approach to data governance [3, 4]. These insights collectively highlight the need for continuous innovation, flexibility, and collaborative dialogue in managing data privacy and governance complexities in the form of DDG.

3   Research Methodology

Systematic literature reviews (SLRs) are renowned for their rigor and structure, surpassing traditional reviews in transparency and thoroughness [21, 22]. Recognizing the scarcity of systematic research in data governance, [23] underscores the contributions SLRs can make to information systems (IS) research, particularly in data-driven decision-making. An SLR's strength lies in its meticulous methodology, starting with the formulation of a precise research question to guide the review [21]. The reproducibility of SLRs is a significant advantage, enabling other researchers to replicate or build upon the findings, thus advancing knowledge [21].

This research uses SLR and employs the populations, exposures, and outcomes (PEO) framework to refine its scope, as demonstrated in various contexts [24]. Herein, 'Population' refers to data providers, 'Exposure' to democratic data governance strategies, and 'Outcome' to the resultant implications.

A comprehensive literature search is paramount, leveraging electronic databases and manual searches to mitigate publication bias and ensure inclusivity [21]. For this study, three electronic databases i.e., Web of Science, ProQuest, and EbscoHost were used. These databases were selected based on their wide publication of research in data governance, the GDPR, and Information Systems [25, 26].

3.1 Keywords and Search Terms

Using the research question and background section as foundations, the following keywords were created; "data governance", "democratic data governance", "data as a democratic medium", "challenges", and "relational". The keywords were combined to form search terms (queries) employed in the electronic databases as presented in Table 1. The searches were conducted in the databases between August and September of 2023.

Table 1. Databases and Queries

Databases	Queries
Web of Science	• "Data governance" AND Challenges • "Data Governance" AND ("Data as a democratic medium" OR "Democratic data governance") • "Data Governance" AND "Data as a democratic medium" • "Democratic data governance" AND "data governance" • "Data Governance" AND compliance • "Data governance" AND "relational theory"
ProQuest	• "Data governance" AND Challenges • "Data Governance" AND ("Data as a democratic medium" OR "Democratic data governance") • "Data Governance" AND "Data as a democratic medium" • "Democratic data governance" AND "data governance" • "Data Governance" AND compliance • "Data governance" AND "relational theory"
EbscoHost	• "Data governance" AND Challenges • "Data Governance" AND ("Data as a democratic medium" OR "Democratic data governance") • "Data Governance" AND "Data as a democratic medium" • "Democratic data governance" AND "data governance" • "Data Governance" AND compliance • "Data governance" AND "relational theory"

3.2 Inclusion and Exclusion Criteria

Inclusion criteria outline conditions studies must meet to be considered for a systematic literature review (SLR), and exclusion criteria define the parameters for their omission [21, 22]. These criteria are crucial for ensuring the SLR's quality and reliability [21, 22]. Criteria should be precise, relevant, measurable, and aligned with the research question [21]. Factors like the review's aim, study characteristics, resources, and team expertise should also be considered. Although it's ideal to set these criteria early, research is often non-linear [21], necessitating consistent application of criteria throughout the SLR process.

The inclusion criteria for the study were publications made between 2015 and 2023 (GDPR was introduced in 2016 and became enforced in 2018), peer-reviewed journal articles, written in the English language (as both researchers are fluent in English), and relevant to addressing the research question. Articles must fulfill the European context criterion and at least one other democracy-related criterion. Literature lacking geographical context had to explicitly pertain to democratic data governance for inclusion.

To maintain focus and rigor, the review excluded: publications before 2015, non-peer-reviewed materials like grey literature, opinion pieces, commentaries, and news articles to maintain quality within the limited timeframe, non-English articles to streamline the analysis process, and topics irrelevant to the review's scope such as data governance outside European GDPR context. Furthermore, articles on artificial intelligence, healthcare, data governance studies, and literature not specifically addressing democratic data governance challenges were excluded.

3.3 Bias

Caution is advised in interpreting SLR results due to potential biases and selective reporting, emphasizing the need for critical appraisal and transparent reporting [21]. The PRISMA 2020 guidelines stress the importance of bias assessment in systematic reviews, as bias can skew findings and affect decision-making [27]. Transparent, reproducible methods and comprehensive literature searches are crucial to mitigate bias [27, 28]. [28] identify two relevant biases: selection bias and information bias.

Selection bias occurs when a review fails to encapsulate all pertinent studies [28]. For instance, prioritizing recent publications since 2015 enhances relevance but may exclude seminal, and older works. Restricting searches to English or specific databases could also miss important studies [27, 28]. Focusing solely on peer-reviewed primary research articles guarantees quality but could ignore valuable grey literature or secondary research [28]. Selection bias can be mitigated by being transparent i.e. clearly stating and justifying inclusion criteria.

Information bias stems from errors or gaps in study details [28]. Challenges arise during data extraction from primary studies due to discrepancies in definitions or categorizations, complicating the consolidation of findings and increasing classification error risks [28]. Information bias can be mitigated by considering the relevance of an article to the research question.

3.4 Data Extraction

Study selection and quality appraisal are crucial, involving screening against set criteria and quality assessment to ensure relevance and credibility [21, 22]. Data extraction and synthesis follow, with analyses often employing statistical or qualitative methods to discern patterns and knowledge gaps [22].

The initial query [("Data governance") AND (challenges)] on EbscoHost, spanning 2015–2023, returned 855 hits without filters. Refining the search on EbscoHost for peer-reviewed, and full-text, English articles narrowed the results to 290. Subsequent searches across EbscoHost, ProQuest, and Web of Science adhered to the inclusion criteria. Notably, queries on democratic data governance and data as a democratic medium yielded no results on any database, even without filters on ProQuest.

As search queries homed in on democratic data governance, results dwindled substantially. On EbscoHost, queries on challenges of data governance yielded 290 and 510 hits, respectively. When focused on democratic aspects, results were 274 for democratic data governance, but none for "data as a democratic medium". Compliance-related queries returned 168 hits. A sharper decline was evident on ProQuest, with the initial hit for challenges (2843) dropping to zero for "data as a democratic medium", with only 14 for "relational theory". Similarly, Web of Science results plummeted from 173 for challenges, to none for the democratic data governance-focused queries.

From initial searches across EbscoHost, ProQuest, and Web of Science, 1348 articles were identified, which, after removing duplicates, narrowed down to 510. Screening by title relevance led to 271 papers, from which 124 were excluded after assessing their abstracts and conclusions for relevance, leaving 147. These covered data governance in various sectors, such as industry, healthcare, business, and education. Further in-depth review identified 27 articles that directly addressed democratic data governance (DDG), relevant European laws, or the philosophical and ethical foundations of DDG. Figure 1 illustrates this extraction process.

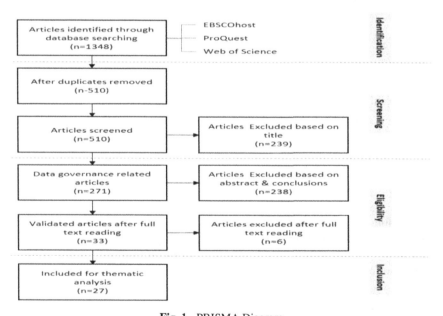

Fig. 1. PRISMA Diagram

[29] analyzed 94 papers from the initial results of 2040 for their SLR on industry 4.0 maturity models. [25] explored determinants of master data quality by examining 15 articles from 2117 that were identified in initial searches. Thus, SLRs may start with a high number of articles in initial searches but only analyze a selected few.

3.5   Quality Assessment and Ranking

Quality assessment in systematic literature reviews is crucial for validating findings, but methods vary among scholars [21, 30]. [30] and [22] both endorse structured evaluations but differ in their implementation. [30] propose a scoring system to quantitatively summarise each criterion, while [22] advocates for a more flexible form that allows for notes and acknowledges that quality criteria can vary across fields.

[21] address the challenges of quality assessment, highlighting the unreliability of scales and advising against their use in Cochrane reviews, contrasting [30]. They argue against a universal tool for quality assessment due to the diversity of existing tools and intricacies involved, suggesting a customized approach instead.

Considering these varied viewpoints, this quality assessment strategy blends structured scoring [30], standardization [22], flexibility, and a comprehensive understanding of quality [21], highlighting the complexity and necessity of a versatile approach tailored to specific research needs. The four criteria identified in Table 2 are meant to capture the demand of the research question, findings in the included article, its number of citations, and coherence in the publication. Each article was ranked based on these criteria as low (poorly addressing the criteria), medium (moderately relevant to the criteria), or high (addressing the criteria) based on the author's agreement.

Table 2. Quality Assessment and Ranking

Criteria	Ranking		
	Low (1)	Medium (2)	High (3)
How does the article effectively tackle the objective of the research question?	0	0	27
How in-depth and in-detail were the findings?	1	9	17
How thoroughly was this research cited?	11	6	12
How coherent is the paper from the introduction to the conclusion?	0	0	27

The Table depicts all articles that addressed the research question and were written coherently. Regarding the level of detail, 17 articles were highly detailed which increases their relevance to the study. About 11 ($\approx$41%) articles are poorly cited. The least cited papers span from 2019 to 2023, with citations ranging from 0 to 16.

3.6   Data Analysis

This study uses thematic analysis (TA). TA is a versatile tool for examining patterns in data governance and its democratic applications, offering insights into stakeholder experiences and interpretations [31]. However, challenges such as unfamiliarity with data, inconsistent coding, and researcher biases can arise [31]. Reflexivity, or the researcher's awareness of their impact on the research, is vital for addressing these challenges.

The thematic analysis process is an extensive work involving six steps [31]. The first step is data familiarity which allowed the researchers to read each article and note initial patterns. The second step is coding and in it, the researchers break down the articles into fragments by giving them labels (codes). The researchers would convene to discuss the different codes used after reading each article with an average agreement of 88%. The third step is theme identification which allows us to cluster related codes and form themes. The fourth step is theme review which allows the researchers to ensure the theme identified in step three adheres to internal homogeneity and external heterogeneity. Some of the themes were grouped as miscellaneous because they did not meet the stated condition. The fifth step is defining themes where the authors would delineate and name each theme, capturing its essence and significance. The last step is reporting, and this manuscript fulfills that purpose.

Table 3. Included articles.

No	Author	Overall ranking
1	[32]	1
2	[33]	1
3	[34]	1
4	[35]	3
5	[3]	2
6	[36]	1
7	[37]	1
8	[38]	2
9	[39]	2
10	[40]	1
11	[41]	1
12	[10]	1
13	[42]	1
14	[43]	3
15	[44]	2
16	[45]	3
17	[46]	2
18	[47]	3
19	[48]	1
20	[49]	1
21	[50]	2
22	[51]	3
23	[52]	1
24	[5]	3
25	[53]	1
26	[54]	3
27	[55]	3

4 Findings and Discussion

Table 3 presents the 27 included articles. Thematic analysis yielded three main themes: (1) data-driven societal challenges, (2) aspects of data governance needed for democratic data governance, and (3) challenges with adapting data governance. The study examines democracy as a vehicle for citizen empowerment, providing them with vital information and the independence to make decisions aligned with their life goals, fostering self-determination [33, 34, 36, 45]. [43] underscore that such empowerment is fundamentally about respecting and safeguarding human rights. [32] and [33] further explore this notion, building on the foundational work by [39] and [40], who identified the centrality of individual rights in data governance.

This research positions democracy at the heart of data governance discussions, advocating for the enhancement of individuals' control over their data and deepening the understanding of data-driven processes [37, 41, 44, 46, 49, 53, 55]. Moreover, the current discourse is shifting from a focus on individual subject rights to a relational perspective that recognizes the interconnectivity of individuals within a society [3, 5, 35, 38].

4.1 Data-Driven Societal Challenges.

Data-driven societal challenges represent the interaction between emerging societal constructs and democratic data governance practices. This theme directly addresses how contemporary digital challenges, such as the dominance of data-centric corporations and the transformative nature of the 4th industrial revolution, potentially impede or shape the realization of democratic governance. Moreover, it underscores the importance of protecting vulnerable populations within this context [40, 41, 53, 55]. These societal challenges are explained in the paragraphs that follow.

Challenges are separated into distinct yet interrelated areas. These include the overpowering influence of data aggregating corporations, the disruptive and pervasive effects of the 4th industrial revolution on societal norms, and the increased susceptibility of vulnerable populations to data mismanagement and exploitation [3, 5, 10, 32–36, 39–43, 45, 47–50, 54, 55].

Societal changes focus on exploration and questions the challenges. Regarding data collection giants, five pivotal issues emerge which are gatekeeping practices that control data access, the exertion of dominance or engagement in abusive tactics, the manipulation of individuals through targeted content, opaque 'black-box' data processing methods, and extensive surveillance practices [5, 10, 33, 35, 40, 41, 43, 45, 48, 50, 53, 55].

For vulnerable populations, eight issues are particularly pronounced: the information overload that obscures privacy and consent, the detailed personal profiling practices leading to 'inference and legibility' issues, a historical mistrust stemming from past misuse of data, and the widespread and often opaque transference of personal data [10, 36, 44, 45, 50, 55]. Further issues include challenges in understanding the nature of one's data, the trade-off between data surrender for convenience, the general unawareness of data privacy concerns, and the complexities surrounding the tracking of data misuse [10, 36, 44, 45, 50, 55].

4.2 Aspects of Data Governance Needed for Democratic Data Governance

The second theme pertains to the essential facets of data governance that need to be incorporated or modified to actualize democratic data governance. Understanding these aspects provides a roadmap toward shaping a data governance structure that inherently respects and realizes democratic values. In the ever-evolving digital landscape, it is not just about controlling and managing data, but about doing so in a manner that embodies the principles of democracy.

These aspects include the core pillars of data governance that are integral to the establishment of democratic data governance. These components of data governance included data stewardship, data quality, respecting stakeholders, data life cycle management, data privacy and security, data architecture and integration, business domains, regulatory compliance, roles and responsibilities, and people-centered governance [3, 32–39, 42–44, 46, 47, 52, 54]. While all pillars are crucial, this study will focus on data stewardship, data quality, respecting stakeholders and people-centered governance.

The core governance pillars can be further explained by splitting them into granular elements. These elements, in tandem, either fortify the ethos of democratic data governance or signify traditional governance practices that might be in tension with democratic ideals. Within data stewardship fiduciaries are duty-bound to prioritize the interests of the data providers, placing their needs above any other interest [5, 10, 33, 53, 55]. General stewardship represents the broader and often traditional responsibilities encompassing the holistic and ethical management of data [34, 39, 52]. Furthermore, individual data sovereignty reinforces the idea that individuals inherently possess rights over their data, transcending mere access and control [3, 5, 33, 35, 36, 39, 42, 48].

In terms of data quality high-quality data is not a luxury but a necessity and characteristics such as accuracy, timeliness, and relevancy are essential traits for ensuring data utility and integrity [3, 5, 36, 38, 42, 45, 49, 55]. Data vocabulary describes unified terminologies that enable seamless data interactions and understanding [37, 47, 48]. Metadata management involves organizing and making sense of data about data, which is to say there is data with the sole purpose of describing and giving context to the data used in business operations [36, 39, 40, 42, 48]. This enables better data control and utilization.

In the democratization of data, stakeholders play pivotal roles, their interests and interactions shaping the data landscape. Identifying stakeholders is important to recognize the key players in the data governance framework [34, 38, 39, 42, 44, 46, 49, 55]. Engagement and collaboration with stakeholders highlight elements of data governance focused on active participation, deliberation, and collaboration of both data providers and data collectors on data matters [3, 33, 34, 39, 42, 44, 45, 49, 52, 55]. Relational Interest delineates the intricate web of stakeholder interests and their inter-relations [3, 5, 10, 32, 35, 36, 38, 40, 41, 44, 45, 49]. Finally, bottom-up stakeholder engagement is a grassroots approach, emphasizing the criticality of individual and community voices in data governance [3, 10, 34, 38, 49].

People-centered data governance philosophies place individuals at the core of data governance decisions. Data ownership recognizes and respects an individual's rights over their data [3, 34, 39–41, 44, 46–48]. Decision-making in a people-centered environment is geared towards empowering individuals in the processes that shape data's destiny [39, 42–44, 52].

4.3 Challenges with Adapting Data Governance

The third theme delves into the aspects encumbering the transition and adjustment of data governance to satisfy the democratic aspirations of the populace. Within this theme, there are challenges, weaving together both age-old impediments consistently faced during the conceptualization and deployment of a data governance framework (complexity, siloed thinking, cost, poor quality, legacy data, poor adoption, lack of expertise and compliance and law), and the novel obstacles emerging in a dynamic digital era (free riding, transparency and accountability, standard understanding of the law, top-down approach) [3, 10, 33, 34, 36, 37, 39, 42, 44, 45, 47–52]. For this study, we will focus on complexity, the law, and costs.

There are distinctions between certain data governance challenges, highlighting specific dimensions and manifestations of these challenges. Complexity is a multifaceted concern, stemming from the intricate nature of today's data ecosystems [3, 36, 38, 39, 47, 52, 55]. Multiple sources due to diverse data origins, lead to integration and harmonization issues [42]. In terms of standardization, the challenge is achieving uniformity across varied data sources and types [3, 38, 39, 47]. The final factor contributing to the complexity of data governance is the high volume of data, which makes effective management a challenging task [3, 36, 40, 42, 44, 49, 52, 55].

In the realm of law (specifically the GDPR), the ambiguous explanations of complex legal verbiage and guidelines hamper the implementation of compliant data governance practices and leave the door open for loopholes to be exploited [33, 44, 50, 54]. Individualistic tick-box consent also proves insufficient in representing people's true interests, relying on formulaic consents rather than genuinely informed choices [5, 33, 41, 48, 50, 51]. Complexity should be considered a standalone challenge representing the difficult task of decoding the multi-layered legal frameworks and their intersections [36, 50–54].

Lastly, there are the cost implications, which represent the financial hurdles to implementing robust data governance. In this regard, legal expenses linked to ensuring regulatory compliance and managing risks must be considered [52, 54]. From a technical standpoint, the cost of investing in the required infrastructure, tools, expertise, and technology must be understood [44, 49, 55].

4.4 Implementation of Democratic Data Governance by Organizations

Institutions and organizations can apply the core pillars of data governance to ensure they serve the interests of data providers and therefore implement democratic data governance. These core pillars are identified in Sect. 4.2. By ensuring these core pillars are addressed, organizations can facilitate the development of democratic data governance not only at an individual level but also relational.

Data providers are however faced with several challenges including those raised by society and those that may affect democratic data governance as explained in Sect. 4.1. Challenges affecting data governance are classified as either old (such as complexity, cost, silo operations, legacy data, and poor quality), or new (such as transparency and accountability, and the presence of the top-down approach) as described in Sect. 4.3. These challenges affect the individuals and communities where data providers operate and may create a negative relationship in some societies.

5 Conclusion

Adoption of data governance frameworks in organizations is hampered by their inaccessibility and inadequate integration stressing the importance of high-level support and resource allocation for successful implementation. The high-level support suffers from the need for horizontal relationships among data providers which is the research gap that the study addresses. The aim of the research was therefore to address how democratic data governance can be implemented by institutions and organizations to better serve the interests of data providers.

Using the systematic literature review approach, the study analyzed 27 articles to address the aim of the research. The three electronic databases used for the study are Web of Science, ProQuest, and EbscoHost. The study considered selection and information bias in the process of creating inclusion criteria, keywords, and search terms, conducting quality appraisal, and thematic analysis.

The findings underscore an urgent call for a shift towards data governance that equitably balances individual and collective needs against data collectors' objectives. Current models, often dominance-driven, starkly oppose democratic principles, posing risks of misuse and surveillance. Democratic data governance is not just a theoretical concept but a vital practicality, requiring the harmonization of progressive laws with advanced technology. In a data-driven era, integrating democratic values into data governance is crucial to protect stakeholder rights and interests. Yet, challenges emerge including complex governance structures, regulatory hurdles, financial limitations, and resistance to change.

Addressing the horizontal relationship between data providers contributes to the policy as it engages with GDPR. The research contributes to the body of knowledge on data governance and the role of privacy which is situated in the intersection of the fields of Information Systems and Ethics.

This research, while comprehensive, is subject to several limitations that delineate the scope and implications of its findings. The study is contextualized primarily within the European Union setting, potentially limiting its applicability to other regions with different regulatory landscapes, politics, legal and cultural dynamics. Moreover, the literature review is confined to English-language sources, which excludes valuable insights from non-English scholarly work. The absence of a proposed framework for democratic data governance is another limitation, as is the reliance on secondary data, foregoing the richness that primary data collection might offer.

Despite these limitations, the current research lays a fertile ground for future scholarly inquiry. The adaptation of traditional governance models to more democratic frameworks presents both challenges and opportunities for further research. Future studies should focus on developing a democratic data governance framework that will consider interdisciplinary research across legal, technological, financial, and social domains. Future work could also conduct comparison studies using different languages and across different regions using other databases such as Scopus, ScienceDirect, IEEE, and Sabinet. Lastly, future work may consider conducting a case study (even multiple case studies).

Declaration of Interest. The authors declare that they have no known competing financial interests or personal relationships that could have appeared to influence the work reported in this paper.

References

1. Vilminko-Heikkinen, R., Pekkola, S.: Changes in roles, responsibilities and ownership in organizing master data management. Int. J. Inf. Manage. **47**, 76–87 (2019)
2. Karkošková, S.: Data governance model to enhance data quality in Financial institutions. Inf. Syst. Manag. **40**, 90–110 (2023)
3. Benfeldt, O., Persson, J.S., Madsen, S.: Data governance as a collective action problem. Inf. Syst. Front. **22**, 299–313 (2020)
4. Costello, R.Á.: Genetic data and the right to privacy: towards a relational theory of privacy? Hum. Rights Law Rev. **22**, 31 (2022)
5. Viljoen, S.: A relational theory of data governance. Yale Law J. **131**, 573–654 (2021)
6. Martins, J., Mamede, H.S., Correia, J.: Risk compliance and master data management in banking – a novel BCBS 239 compliance action-plan proposal. Heliyon **8**, e09627 (2022)
7. Wernick, A., Olk, C., von Grafenstein, M.: Defining data intermediaries: a clearer view through the lens of intellectual property governance. Technol. Regul. 65–77 (2020)
8. Grafenstein, M.V.: Reconciling conflicting interests in data through data governance: an analytical framework (and a brief discussion of the Data Governance Act draft, the AI Regulation draft, as well as the GDPR). HIIG Discuss. Pap. Ser. 2 (2022)
9. Hikmawati, S., Santosa, P.I., Hidayah, I.: Improving data quality and data governance using master data management: a review. Int. J. Inf. Technol. Electr. Eng. **5**, 90–95 (2021)
10. Ho, K.J.M.: Unravelling the Gordian knot for data trusts – The next leap forward for equity? Tulane J. Technol. Intellect. Prop. **25**, 147–212 (2023)
11. Ngueilbaye, A., Wang, H., Mahamat, D.A., Elgendy, I.A., Junaidu, S.B.: Methods for detecting and correcting contextual data quality problems. Intell. Data Anal. **25**, 763–787 (2021)
12. Ghasemaghaei, M., Calic, G.: Can big data improve firm decision quality? The role of data quality and data diagnosticity. Decis. Support. Syst. **120**, 38–49 (2019)
13. Côrte-Real, N., Ruivo, P., Oliveira, T.: Leveraging internet of things and big data analytics initiatives in European and American firms: is data quality a way to extract business value? Inf. Manag. **57**, 103141 (2020)
14. Johnson, G.: Economic research on privacy regulation: lessons from the GDPR and beyond (2022)
15. Schade, F.: Dark sides of data transparency: organized immaturity after GDPR? Bus. Ethics Q. **33**, 473–501 (2023)
16. Da Veiga, A., Vorster, R., Li, F., Clarke, N., Furnell, S.M.: Comparing the protection and use of online personal information in South Africa and the United Kingdom in line with data protection requirements. Inf. Comput. Secur. **28**, 399–422 (2019)
17. de Waal, P.J.: The protection of personal information act (POPIA) and the promotion of access to information act (PAIA): it is time to take note. Curr. Allergy Clin. Immunol. **35**, 232–236 (2022)

18. Bronstein, V.: Prioritising command-and-control over collaborative governance: the role of the information regulator under the protection of personal information act. Potchefstroom Electron. Law J. **25**, 1–41 (2022)

19. Jones, B.: Is POPIA bad business for South Africa? Comparing the GDPR to POPIA and analyzing POPIA's impact on businesses in South Africa. Penn State J. Law Int. Aff. **10**, 218–246 (2021)

20. Sanchez-Rola, I., et al.: Can i opt out yet?: GDPR and the global illusion of cookie control. In: Asia CCS '19: ACM Asia Conference on Computer and Communications Security, pp. 340–351. ACM (2019)

21. Siddaway, A.P., Wood, A.M., Hedges, L.V.: How to do a systematic review: a best practice guide for conducting and reporting narrative reviews, meta-analyses, and meta-syntheses. Annu. Rev. Psychol. **70**, 747–770 (2019)

22. Okoli, C.: A guide to conducting a standalone systematic literature review. Commun. Assoc. Inf. Syst. **37**, 879–910 (2015)

23. Brous, P., Janssen, M., Herder, P.: Next generation data infrastructures: towards an extendable model of the asset management data infrastructure as complex adaptive system. Complexity **2019**, 5415828 (2019)

24. Lindmark, T., Engström, M., Trygged, S.: Psychosocial work environment and well-being of direct-care staff under different nursing home ownership types: a systematic review. J. Appl. Gerontol. **42**, 347–359 (2023)

25. Ibrahim, A., Mohamed, I., Safie, N.: Factors influencing master data quality: a systematic review. Int. J. Adv. Comput. Sci. Appl. **12**, 181–192 (2021)

26. Venkatesh, V., Brown, S.A., Bala, H.: Bridging the qualitative – quantitative divide: guidelines for conducting mixed methods research in information systems. MIS Q. **37**, 21–54 (2013)

27. Page, M.J., McKenzie, J.E., Higgins, J.P.T.: Tools for assessing risk of reporting biases in studies and syntheses of studies: a systematic review. BMJ Open **8**, e019703 (2018). https://doi.org/10.1136/bmjopen-2017-019703

28. Almeida, C.P.B.D., Goulart, B.N.G.D.: How to avoid bias in systematic reviews of observational studies. Rev. CEFAC. **19**, 551–555 (2017)

29. Brossard, P.Y., Minvielle, E., Sicotte, C.: The path from big data analytics capabilities to value in hospitals: a scoping review. BMC Health Serv. Res. **22**, 134 (2022)

30. Kmet, L.M., Lee, R.C., Cook, L.S.: Standard quality assessment criteria for evaluating primary research papers from a variety of fields. Alberta Heritage Foundation for Medical Research, Edmonton, Alta (2004)

31. Braun, V., Clarke, V.: Toward good practice in thematic analysis: avoiding common problems and be(com)ing a knowing researcher. Int. J. Transgender Heal. **24**, 1–6 (2023)

32. Andrusyshyn, B.I., Bilozorov, I.V., Opolska, N.M., Kupina, L.F., Tokarchuk, O.V.: Definition and protection of personal data piculiarities: Ukrainian and European experience. Informatologia **55**, 136–145 (2022)

33. Asgarinia, H., Chomczyk Penedo, A., Esteves, B., Lewis, D.: "Who should I trust with my data?" Ethical and legal challenges for innovation in new decentralized data management technologies. Information **14**, 351–368 (2023)

34. Asswad, J., Gómez, J.M.: Data ownership: a survey. Information **12**, 465 (2021)

35. Belli, L., Doneda, D.C.M.: Municipal data governance: an analysis of Brazilian and European practices. Rev. Direito da Cid. **12**, 40–63 (2020)

36. Cerrillo-Martínez, A., Casadesús-de-Mingo, A.: Data governance for public transparency. El Prof. la Inf. **30**, e300402 (2021)

37. Debruyne, C., Pandit, H.J., Lewis, D., O'Sullivan, D.: "Just-in-time" generation of datasets by considering structured representations of given consent for GDPR compliance. Knowl. Inf. Syst. **62**(9), 3615–3640 (2020). https://doi.org/10.1007/s10115-020-01468-x

38. Coetzee, S., Odijk, M., van Loenen, B., Storm, J., Stoter, J.: Stakeholder analysis of the governance framework of a national SDI dataset – whose needs are met in the buildings and address register of the Netherlands? Int. J. Digit. Earth. **13**, 355–373 (2020)
39. Cuno, S., Bruns, L., Tcholtchev, N., Lämmel, P., Schieferdecker, I.: Data governance and sovereignty in urban data spaces based on standardized ICT reference architectures. Data **4**, 16 (2019)
40. Foster, J., McLeod, J., Nolin, J., Greifeneder, E.: Data work in context: value, risks, and governance. J. Assoc. Inf. Sci. Technol. **69**, 1414–1427 (2018)
41. Hartzog, W.: What is privacy? That's the wrong question. Univ. Chicago Law Rev. **88**, 1677 (2021)
42. Hussain, S.S.I., Vassilios, P., Ioannis, M.: DaLiF: a data lifecycle framework for data-driven governments. J. Big Data. **8**, 89 (2021)
43. Kolesnichenko, O., et al.: Sociological modeling of smart city with the implementation of UN sustainable development goals. Sustain. Sci. **16**, 581–599 (2021)
44. Lupi, L.: City data plan: the conceptualisation of a policy instrument for data governance in smart cities. Urban Sci. **3**, 91 (2019)
45. McMahon, A., Buyx, A., Prainsack, B.: Big data governance needs more collective responsibility: the role of harm mitigation in the governance of data use in medicine and beyond. Med. Law Rev. **28**, 155–182 (2020)
46. Mirko, Z., Ferretti, S., Gabriele, D., Víctor, R.: Data governance through a multi-DLT architecture in view of the GDPR. Cluster Comput. **25**, 4515–4542 (2022)
47. Munoz-Arcentales, A., López-Pernas, S., Pozo, A., Alonso, Á., Salvachúa, J., Huecas, G.: Data usage and access control in industrial data spaces: implementation using FIWARE. Sustainability **12**, 38–85 (2020)
48. Pandit, H.J.: Making sense of solid for data governance and GDPR. Information **14**, 114–154 (2023)
49. Paskaleva, K., Evans, J., Martin, C., Linjordet, T., Yang, D., Karvonen, A.: Data governance in the sustainable smart city. Informatics **4**, 41 (2017)
50. Pike, E.R.: Defending data: toward ethical protections and comprehensive data governance. Emory Law J. **69**, 687–743 (2020)
51. Quelle, C.: Enhancing compliance under the General Data Protection Regulation: the risky upshot of the accountability- and risk-based approach. Eur. J. Risk Regul. **9**, 502–526 (2018)
52. Treacy, S.: Ensuring compliance in the digital era: A knowledge-based dynamic capabilities framework wheel for data-driven organisations. Int. J. Bus. Anal. Intell. **10**, 25–39 (2022)
53. Wu, D., Verhulst, S.G., Pentland, A., Avila, T., Finch, K., Gupta, A.: How data governance technologies can democratize data sharing for community well-being. Data Policy **3**, e14 (2021)
54. Yeung, K., Bygrave, L.A.: Demystifying the modernized European data protection regime: cross-disciplinary insights from legal and regulatory governance scholarship. Regul. Gov. **16**, 137–155 (2022)
55. van Zoonen, L.: Data governance and citizen participation in the digital welfare state. Data Policy **2**, e10 (2020)

An Exploratory Qualitative Study of Disruptive Technology Adoption Among Zimbabwean Small and Medium Enterprises in and Around Harare, Gweru, and Bulawayo

Thomas Mc Donald van der Merwe$^{(\boxtimes)}$ (iD)

University of South Africa, Florida, South Africa
vdmertm@unisa.ac.za

Abstract. In taking advantage of the digital revolution, disruptive technology, which is capacitated by enhancements in computing capacity and Internet bandwidth, not only has the potential to overcome many challenges faced by small-to-medium enterprises but also offers innovative opportunities to create new markets. Identified as a research gap, this paper outlines the state of disruptive technology adoption, estimates its perceived importance, identifies factors that affect its adoption, and gauges government support for providing a conducive environment in randomly selected rural and urban Zimbabwean SMEs. Semi-structured interviews with owners and staff of 12 rural and 12 urban SMEs in and around Harare, Gweru, and Bulawayo were conducted using a qualitative and exploratory approach. Results show its use to be limited, with only two rural and four urban SMEs using disruptive technology. Major factors which limit their use are poor mobile infrastructure, electricity, and the cost of services. Outside four, all urban respondents acknowledged the importance of disruptive technology, with three linking potential usefulness to their business processes. Rural respondents were less convinced, with responses ranging from uncertain, could be, to no need. Other factors identified were poor cash flow, limited knowledge, and no financial support. Despite policies in place, a total absence of government support was reported. The results paint a bleak picture of the current and potential trajectory of disruptive technology adoption in these Zimbabwean SMEs.

Keywords: Disruptive technology adoption · SMEs · Zimbabwe

1 Introduction

In a globally competitive scenario driven by demand, small-to-medium enterprises (SMEs) face many new challenges, including financial, human resources, and organisational limitations [1]. In taking advantage of the digital revolution, disruptive technology (DRT), which is capacitated by enhancements in computing capacity and Internet bandwidth, has the potential to overcome such challenges. DRT was defined in 1995 [2, p. 10] as 'innovations that create an entirely new market through the introduction of a new kind of service or product'. Twelve current or emerging DRT examples are video streaming, digital transport services, virtual reality, online lodging, music streaming, cross-platform instant messaging apps, online encyclopedias, augmented reality, digital currency, collaborative commerce, 3d printing, and online education [3]. One can add chatbots, cybersecurity, artificial intelligence, blockchain, 5G technology, and cloud services to this list. Such technologies have not only enhanced and altered both business and social landscapes and the way people live and work [4] but also impacted the access and cost of products and services [5] and business models and value chains [6]. For example, most emerging online digital retailers do not hold inventory, social media companies own minimal content, and online accommodation providers do not own real estate [4].

A consistent challenge for African SMEs is to effectively embrace DRT while ensuring an inclusive approach that avoids the creation of new digital divides [7]. In Zimbabwe, 60–70% of employment and 65% of the Gross Domestic Product (GDP) are attributed to SMEs with the informal sector being the major employer [8]. Therefore, SMEs are crucial in curbing unemployment and poverty and have shaped the nation's economy [9]. While the adoption of technology by SMEs has been highlighted in various studies around the globe [10–13], no studies have focused on the adoption of DRT by Zimbabwean SMEs.

To address the above shortcoming, this research aims to outline the state of DRT adoption by Zimbabwean SMEs, inclusive of its perceived importance, factors that affect adoption, and government support in place. Although the research distinguishes between rural and urban SMEs, it is not intended as a comparative study.

Specifically, the paper seeks to answer the following research questions:

1. What is the status of DRT adoption by rural and urban SMEs in Zimbabwe?
2. What importance do rural and urban SMEs in Zimbabwe assign to DRT?
3. What factors regulate the adoption of DRT in rural and urban SMEs in Zimbabwe?
4. What key government strategies are in place to improve the adoption of DRT in rural and urban SMEs in Zimbabwe?

The following section reviews the relevant literature to outline the concept of DRT and how it improves competitive advantage for businesses. Section 3 discusses the study's methodology, while Sects. 4 and 5 present the results, analysis, discussion, and further research suggestions.

2   Literature Review

2.1   DRT

The concept of DRT was popularised by Bower and Christensen [2]. According to them, new market players can disrupt established businesses using emerging innovative technologies. DRT often starts as a simple service or product that persistently moves up the market, creating new and radical businesses that displace established competitors. The concept applies to software, hardware, networks, and combined technologies with distinct examples identified by various researchers, including 3D printing, artificial intelligence (AI), solar panels and batteries, distributed manufacturing, augmented reality, drones, robotics, cloud computing, and the Internet of Things [14]. These disruptive technologies can facilitate the delivery of enhanced services. For example, an e-commerce platform which combines the disruptive effect of AI and cloud computing can simultaneously be a multisector retailer, a logistics company, a media company, a health services provider, and a data-infrastructure company [15].

DRT can also alter the competitive basis in any market by introducing product or service dimensions previously unseen within the market [16]. They enable fundamental technological changes, which signify a clear departure from existing practices [17]. Hence, organisations that succeed in adopting DRT ignore existing technology's capabilities and characteristics and seek new ways of applying disruptive innovations [2]. For example, a disruptive online e-commerce retailing system has pushed more consumers to buy products and services at lower prices [18]. This movement has not only brought more benefits to the consumer but has made profitability more difficult for brick-and-mortar stores. On the contrary, the inability to effectively adopt these innovations has led to the downfall of many organisations that have taken a less aggressive approach to adopting DRT and could not enhance products or services [19].

DRT has a transformative effect on economies and societies and has had a significant impact on the cost of, or access to, products or services and how societies and organisations today interact and exchange information [20]. The ability of an SME to exploit DRT effectively and efficiently is vital in guaranteeing survival, customer satisfaction, employment creation, and further growth [21]. Lastly, the broad availability of DRT to ordinary people, businesses, and consumers has been a defining feature in modern times, with new services, products, and markets emerging and spreading rapidly across the globe [20].

2.2 Impact of DRT on SMEs in Developed Countries

The performance of SMEs depends on how the organisation delivers value to its stakeholders and customers [22]. This also relates to how well the SME achieves its goals and objectives. Several factors have been identified as the key to impacting the performance of SMEs, including financial resources, skilled labour, the economic environment, and the attitude of the owner-manager [23]. A key ingredient for the survival and sustenance of SMEs is the ability to adopt DRT effectively [24].

DRT has changed the way business is conducted in SMEs in developed countries and continues to add value to the organisations' existing offerings, which has resulted in enhanced efficient and effective business operations, minimal costs, and increased profits [25]. SMEs can now adopt DRT for the key purpose of enhancing their market share as they utilise these tools to manage labour, capital, and overall business operations and are not capital intensive, which decreases new SMEs' entry barriers [26]. The use of DRT such as cloud computing in SMEs enhances the support of asset-light business models which eventually results in both lower upfront costs and lower operating expenses [14].

The disruptive nature of today's shared resource technologies, including digital supply chains, blockchain systems, and the cloud can also eliminate the need for significant capital expenditures on technology infrastructure for SMEs [24] Technology service rentals have also become popular within the disruptive movement and have enabled a shift in SME behaviour, allowing organisations to have easier access to the latest technology at flexibility and low-cost terms [27]. It is argued that SME business value is amplified and compounded when various disruptive technologies are used in tandem and supported by digital platforms [15].

Many SMEs have begun to disrupt the online retail industry with drone delivery systems, and the digitalisation of the electrical grid using rooftop solar photovoltaic and microgrids has seen SMEs disrupt the power sector [26]. SMEs also see rapid growth, as DRT facilitates scalability, access to larger markets, and opportunities for enhanced innovation through knowledge sharing. Disruptive digital platforms now offer crucial supporting infrastructure through plug-and-play systems and instant access to vast global markets at minimal costs.

Big data has also allowed SMEs to specifically target services and products to consumer preferences, providing customers with enhanced quality of service and product differentiation, forcing other competing firms to innovate [24].

Various studies have identified key technology adoption barriers for SMEs in developing countries. The key basic technology adoption barriers can also be postulated for adopting DRT [28]. In these countries, one of the biggest challenges for SMEs is the lack of knowledge and skill to effectively identify the best technology to adopt within the business [9]. This critical challenge relates to how SMEs can embrace available DRT to add service or product value without incurring exorbitant costs.

The lack of a supportive environment, which includes infrastructure and financial support, is a further barrier to the effective adoption of DRT for SMEs [12]. DRT, which notably includes automation and AI, has struggled to take off in both small and large organisations in developing countries due to job losses coupled with the fact that these emerging markets have cheaper labour costs and a rapidly growing labour force [28]. The digital divide between developed and developing countries also presents a challenge, as this often slows the diffusion of critical DRT in the market [15].

Restrictive regulations have also been identified as a barrier. In most developing countries, outdated policies have introduced restrictions for small and medium enterprises, resulting in the monopolisation of DRT [12]. Finally, owner-manager attitude, political instability, lack of a one-stop facility and access to reliable experts, lack of SME support structures, financial bottlenecks, and restrictive cultures are key barriers to adoption [15].

2.3   Zimbabwean SMEs

There are different debates in the field of ICT4D about technology transfer from developed countries, mainly centered around progressive transformation as an economic and social enabler and disruptive transformation as involving action with unequal effects on different categories of the population [29]. As noted by the author, some scholars are against a 'technology transfer' view that believes all new technologies from first-world countries should be unquestioningly embraced by developing countries. Conversely, several examples exist where developing countries could make strides (for example, with mobile money). In the past decade, Zimbabwean SMEs have contributed just over 60% of the country's GDP annually. They are considered agents of economic empowerment, drive the development of the formal and informal sectors, and have been recognised as critical in the nation's social and economic progress [31]. Despite various government efforts to revive the sector, Zimbabwean SMEs have continued to underperform and remain insignificant economic contributors [32].

Significantly, SMEs in Zimbabwe continue to face various barriers to progress, one of the main identified challenges being poor ICT infrastructure. The use of ICT in most Zimbabwean SMEs is still embryonically characterised by the ineffective utilisation of the Internet and social media for non-commercial purposes [9].

3 Methodology

This study employed an exploratory qualitative approach, which facilitated answering the questions of how, what, and why questions sought by the study objectives. The qualitative approach was appropriate as it provides various interpretative techniques that help decode and translate the meaning of occurring phenomena [33]. It furthermore facilitates the development of new insights into phenomena and issues and develops new concepts [34]. A case study research design [35] was used to contribute knowledge by identifying unknown variables.

Data collection for the study was done through semi-structured interviews to facilitate more insight into business processes. A Zimbabwean national with a PhD and experience in SME research was trained to conduct the interviews.

The participating SMEs were selected using nonprobability purposeful sampling, with 24 randomly selected SMEs from rural, urban, and semi-urban areas in and around Harare, Gweru, and Bulawayo. To cover for limited knowledge, interviews were conducted with two participants at each SME, in all cases, ideally the owner/s.

After a nurturing phase [36], where the general background details on the operations of the SME were discussed and recorded, the purpose of the interview and the term DRT were explained and clarified. Participants were asked to substantiate the extent of DRT use within their businesses, their view on the importance of DRT, what factors they believe regulate adoption, and what government assistance or programmes are in place that could facilitate the use of DRT in their business. Participants were encouraged to elaborate on their responses and freely express their views.

All data collected through the above methods were transcribed and fed into the commercially available Atlas-ti 6.0 software package as a hermeneutic text unit for data analysis. The package is a powerful workbench for qualitatively analysing textual, graphical, audio, and video data bodies. It offers a variety of tools for accomplishing the tasks associated with any systematic approach to "soft" data, that is, material which cannot be sufficiently analysed using formalised, statistical approaches.

Using open coding, the author, experienced in qualitative coding, analysed the interview text by looking for different words or sentences in the statements, thereby classifying part statements with labels to explain the meanings of the different parts [37]. This process involves identifying, naming, categorising, and describing phenomena in the text [38]. Initial codes or labels were assigned to text sections during the first attempt. Rereading the text several times changed some codes with others renamed.

The next step was axial coding, where the meanings behind concepts were compared and categorised to explain the data material and relationships between concepts [37].

The results were then grouped according to the themes guided by the research questions (template analysis), i.e., use, perceived importance, adoption factors and government support.

The following section outlines the results and offers actual data collected during the interviews. It is noted that within a single SME, the two staff members interviewed may have different opinions. Since we are interested in overall experience and knowledge, it is essential to consider all opinions within an SME. For this reason, some staff members from the same SME had different and conflicting views, resulting in seemingly contradictory statements within a single SME and across the presentation of data.

The results are presented separately for the rural and urban areas, with a further distinction between urban and semi-urban areas. Rurality can be defined as territories located at a minimum distance of 8 km or more from a central city [38]. Hence, semi-urban SMEs are near an urban area but not quite rural. In general terms, the population and density of urban areas are higher than rural areas.

4 Results

In this section, results are reported per research questions/theme and as identified using the axial coding techniques stated. Selected answers which effectively support a topic are provided for context.

4.1 Rural SMEs

Table 1 lists the industry, products and services, years in operation, and number of employees for each SME included in the research.

Table 1. Rural SME data

SME	Industry	Product and services	Years in operation	Number of Employees
AR	Retail	Groceries	3	3
B_R	Manufacturing	Brick Making	2	4
C_R	Agriculture	Vegetables	3	4
D_R	Manufacturing	Grinding Mill	2	2
E_R	Retail	Groceries	1	2
F_R	Manufacturing	Furniture	5	3
G_R	Mining	Gold	4	4
H_R	Retail	Clothes	2	2
I_R	Manufacturing	Peanut Butter	1	2
J_R	Transport	Minibus Taxi	1	2
K_R	Agriculture	Vegetables	3	4
L_R	Retail	Bottle store/Butcher	5	4

Of the 12 SMEs, three (C, G, K) were involved in economic activities in the primary sector (two in Agriculture and one in mining), five (B, D, F, I, J) in the secondary sector (four in manufacturing and one in Transport) and four in the tertiary and quaternary sector (retail). Only three SMEs have existed for more than four but less than six years. Likewise, five SMEs have at least four but less than five employees, with the rest three or two. In all cases, the owner was one of the two participants interviewed per SME. The second participant was either a co-owner, supervisor, or general staff. For SMEs B_r, C_r, I_r and K_r, both respondents were co-owners.

Status of DRT Use

The two rural SMEs that make use of DRT are in the retail sector, one making use of mobile payments (H_r, clothing) and the other WhatsApp (L_r, bottle store/butcher). However, the clothing retailer (H_r) highlights that using technology does not necessarily mean intensive, disruptive use. All quotes are 'sic erat scriptum'.

> H_r: *We accept mobile payments through EcoCash for some of our clients who can afford to be on the platform; otherwise, most of our clients can only pay through the local currency or exchange other goods for the service.*

While H and four other SMEs (B_r, F_r, I_r, L_r) use cell phones for business purposes, their use is limited, mainly due to poor network service (and a few others, to be presented later) which limit their use.

> H_r: *We use the cellphone to call customers to come collect their goods, but the network is bad most of the time*
>
> I_r: *We do write our cell phone on the label on the peanut butter tins but we have not received any relevant calls. The network reception is quite bad hence communication is not as fluid as we would want it to be.*

Importance of DRT

Four respondents (C_r, E_r, F_r, I_r) indicated that they are unsure if DRT is important:

> C_r: *Are you aware of any technology that is used by vegetable growers? Maybe it is important for our business, but the question is how.*
>
> F_r: *I don't quite know if technology would be important for a business like ours.*

Another four (D_r, F_r, I_r, K_r) acknowledged that they think it could be:

> D_r; *I think it is important, my son has told me about technology and how it has helped some businesses.*
>
> I_r: *I think it depends on the application of the technology, if applied properly then it would be important.*

Six others (A_r, E_r, G_r, J_r, H_r, L_r) mentioned that they do not need DRT.

B_r: *We track and keep our records in a hard-covered book and as you can observe we use shovels and wooden boxes to make bricks. At this point I would say it is not important since we have not yet seen or experienced a business like ours that uses technology.*

F_r: *We utilise manual tools as you can see here to make the furniture.*

J_r: *In our business of transporting people, we don't quite see the use of technology. Our main tool is the vehicle we use.*

Although not explicitly stated, an impression gained in the responses was that business is largely limited to surrounding rural communities, which may explain why DRT is not seen as essential.

I_r: *Maybe mostly because our clients are from the local community.*

Other responses exposed further factors more important than DRT, covered in the next section.

Factors Regulating the Adoption of DRT
The respondents mentioned several factors, some of which intersect themes.

Cash flow
Four respondents (B_r, D_r, G_r, E_r) highlighted a lack of finance as a reason for not pursuing DRT. The underlying lack includes the cost of diesel, while the impact of COVID-19 is also felt.

B_r: *Our business is very small and we would need to make more money in order for us to start thinking about technology.*

D_r: *The grinding mill relies on diesel which is very expensive and difficult to acquire; hence, we are now only open three to four days a week.*

E_r:*The economic environment makes it very difficult at the moment to think about technology I guess. The lockdown has also not been good for business so I don't know if we will still be open next year.*

Infrastructure
A total of six respondents (A_r, D_r, E_r, F_r, G_r, H_r) mentioned that they do not have access to electricity and that this precludes any use of DRT.

D_r: *Most of these ICT tools require the use of electricity.*

H_r: *I think electricity supply would help with any technology initiatives.*

Poor mobile reception (H_r, L_r) or no mobile infrastructure (F_r, G_r) were mentioned as other main reasons.

Fr: I think you would need proper infrastructure in place as well like mobile networks.

Lr: The network reception is quite bad.

Limited knowledge

Despite an explanation of what DRT is, and across answers, interviewees expressed a lack of knowledge or understanding of DRT. At times, they stated that they would not know where to start, training would be required, or that more information is required. Respondent A_r summarises it succinctly:

> A_r: *I would say knowledge of ICT is key and this lacks in our business. If we knew which tools would be relevant for our business that would help in putting us in the right direction. I_r: think the right skills and training is also key.*

Government Strategies

Sixteen respondents noted that they were unaware of government support, with six indicating that technology support is required.

> G_r: *The government needs to do more for small businesses and listen to our grievances.*
>
> H_r: *It is important for the government to step in and help small businesses to take on more technology.*

For two SMEs, government support has more to do with basic needs such as roads (B_r) and wells (C_r).

Finally, it is noted that no respondents had anything to add to the interview.

4.2   Urban and Semi-urban SMEs

Table 2 provides background data on the semi-urban and urban SMEs included in the study.

Of the 12 SMEs, three (G_u, I_u, K_u) were involved in primary sector economic activities (two in agriculture and one in Mining), four (B_u, F_u, J_u, L_u) in the secondary sector (three in manufacturing and one in Transport) and four (A_u, C_u, D_u, H_u) in the tertiary and quaternary sector (two in retail and one each in Hospitality, Legal and technology). Only three of the SMEs have been in existence for more than six, but less than nine years. Similarly, most SMEs have at least six employees, with one more (seven).

Eight of the SMEs were in an urban area with main employment areas. Except for the bottle store (retail), the other three semi-urban companies participated in primary economic activities i.e., Agriculture (2) and mining (1). As with rural SMEs, the owner was one of the two participants interviewed per SME. The second participant was either a co-owner, supervisor or general staff. For SMEs B_r, $E_{r \text{ and }} I_r$, respondents were co-owners.

Status of DRT Use

Only four of the SMEs used DRT – WhatsApp (E_u, F_u, I_u, respectively, for marketing, to follow market prices before they purchase and to receive orders from clients), a chatbot (E_u), mobile money (H_u), and Skype (E_u). Of these, only E_U, a graphic design company that targets overseas markets, uses multiple DRTs. However, as a non-e-commerce site, they experience problems with international payments.

Table 2: Semi-urban and urban SME data

SME	Industry	Product and services	Years in operation	Number of Employees	Location of SME
A_U	Retail	Groceries	5	4	Urban
B_U	Manufacturing	Metalworks	6	2	Urban
C_U	Hospitality	Lodge	2	6	Urban
D_U	Legal	Legal	6	5	Urban
E_U	Technology	Graphic Design	3	3	Urban
F_U	Manufacturing	Bread	7	7	Semi-Urban
G_U	Agriculture	Tobacco	8	6	Urban
H_U	Retail	Bottle store	8	3	Semi-Urban
I_U	Agriculture	Vegetables	6	5	Semi-Urban
J_U	Manufacturing	Soap	1	6	Urban
K_U	Mining	Gold	2	4	Semi-Urban
L_U	Transport	Minibus Taxi	6	4	Urban

E_u: *However, our challenge has been receiving payments as moving money into this country from outside is a challenge for corporates but for individuals it can be done.*

Importance of DRT

Apart from G_u, all respondents recognised the importance of DRT, although they do not see a current need.

A_u: *I think they would be important.*

C_u: *I think based on your clarification, the technology would be good for any business*

L_u: *Disruptive technologies would be critical for any business especially in these modern times.*

E_u: *I would say any technology is important to any small business these days.*

H_u: *I think based on use in our business it is important as it helps us and our customers and would also help other businesses in this area. It is important because it reduces the cash stress and we can also pay for some orders using mobile money.*

Only three respondents (F_u, H_u, L_u) linked perceived importance to their own business:

H_u: *I on hand (minibus taxis)*

Four respondents (A_u, I_u, B_u, D_u) do not see any need for DRT.

A_u: *As you have observed we use a basic point of sale system comprising a desktop and a receipt printer. That's enough for us for now.*

I_u: *I would say it is important, but for our business now it doesn't pay a critical part.*

B_u: *We are fortunate that we do not need to market as this market is a frequent place for a lot of people.*

D_u: *Our work is mostly referrals, so it might be difficult to see exactly where we can apply disruptive technology.*

Factors Regulating the Adoption of DRT
Cash flow

A lack of cash flow meant that many SMEs (A_u, C_u, F_u, G_u, H_u, I_u, J_u), even if they were interested in DRT, could not afford it for a variety of reasons:

A_u: *It is a bit unstable in the country at the moment to make any changes. A persistent reason for the lack of cash flow is a difficult economic climate.*

C_u: *We would lack the funding to train the staff.*

G_u: *We are facing difficult times especially for tobacco growers so to be able to assign funds for technology at this point would not be feasible.*

J_u: *We are barely making ends meet to get raw materials, so thinking of technology now for our business would be a stretch.*

F_u: *The technology is important because for us we would have to fork out a lot of money to reach out to our clients or even advertise.*

Infrastructure

A lack of suitable infrastructure mostly related to electricity (A_u, E_u, H_u) and Internet reliability and cost (E_u, H_u), even if they made use of advanced technology like solar panels (H_u).

A_u: *I would say electricity because when there is a power outage we have to resort to manual (processes).*

E_u: *We pay an arm and a leg for internet.*

H_u: *The internet and electricity infrastructures are key as I believe this supports these technologies. Now this quality and availability of this infrastructure is very poor in this country and makes it difficult to rely on. The key item I would say is electricity, because without alternative means to charge phones you are completely out. So, electricity is key, now in this area it's constantly down and they sometime take months to fix. So, we have resorted to portable solar panels.*

Owner's role

The role of the owner of an SME in acquiring DRT may play a role (A_u, D_u, K_u):

A_u: *I think they would be important, but that would be up to the owner of course and what he thinks we might do with the technology.*

K_u: *The owner is not keen on changing anything with regards to the operations and frankly I think he doesn't trust technology*

Limited knowledge

Despite an explanation of what DRT is and across questions, interviewees expressed a lack of knowledge or understanding of DRT, at times accompanied by stating that if they were to implement DRT, training would be required or that more information is required since they would not know where to start.

B_u: *The truth is we wouldn't know where to start. I don't know if we will be able to use any of that technology for our business, maybe if we get the information because for years this has been how we have always done our work.*

C_u: *I would not know exactly where to start even if we wanted to. If you have information on where we might be able to get practical training in disruptive technology relevant to our trade, please let us know.*

G_u: *If we had more information on this technology, I would be able to say whether it would be important or not. Think we would need to be trained in technology, but hoping it's not too difficult as most of us here did not go far at school.*

I_u: *Training and knowledge on what vegetable growers can use with regards to disruptive technology, because right now we don't know what else we can use in our business.*

J_u: *The truth is I don't know exactly what we can use or where to find it. We need more information.*

K_u: *Based on your clarification the technology sounds good, but not sure how it would fit for us, or would be important for a business like ours.*

Government Strategies

Only one respondent was aware of government initiatives.

F_u: *It's important for us to get easy loans for us to afford additional tools. The government needs to step in and help us, after all the development of SMEs contributes towards the economy. There are a lot of initiatives that we have heard of which we have not seen being implemented.*

Even if SMEs were to adopt DRT, they (E_u, G_u, I_u, J_u, L_u) would need financial support from the government.

E_u: *The government needs to support small businesses by subsidising internet supply for us.*

I_u: *It would help if there were subsidies in place to cushion the small businessman from the current economic hardships and help toward obtaining more technology.*

J_u: *We need financial support to stay afloat and maybe get the technology.*

As with the rural case, no respondents had anything to add.

5 Discussion

This research aimed to answer several research questions about the use of DRT in rural and urban SMEs in Zimbabwe.

Based on both the number of employees (less than 10, [40]) and constrained by a tendency to be growth-adverse and underdeveloped [41], it is evident that all the randomly selected rural and urban SMEs can be classified as micro businesses. The acronym MSME is therefore more appropriate, but since the selection process was random, we continue to use SME.

The first question covers the status of DRT adoption. From the outset, it is evident that the use of DRT is limited. Only two rural and four urban SMEs make use of any form of DRT. As can be expected, they are either in the secondary or tertiary economic sectors. Although only four rural SMEs make use of mobile phones, other factors combined to limit their use, most notably poor mobile infrastructure. The one urban SME that uses more than one DRT and targets international customers faces a challenge related to international payments with the result that it is not used optimally. The results not only confirm research [19] that highlighted poor general technology adoption levels by SMEs in Zimbabwe, but also align with other research [16] that found that SMEs in developing countries seldom adopt DRT within their business operations. It is noted that interviews were held after the COVID-19 restrictions were lifted. It is reasonable to suggest that the economic impact of the pandemic may also have limited any potential adoption of not only general technology but also DRT.

The second question relates to the importance rural and urban SMEs assigned to DRT. Outside four respondents, all urban respondents acknowledged the importance of DRT, with three linking potential usefulness to their business processes. However, rural respondents were less convinced, with responses ranging from uncertain, could be, to no need. While some of these responses are related to a lack of knowledge and poor infrastructure, it is noteworthy that no rural SME employs more than 4 staff, with the majority in existence for less than 4 years. This is in stark contrast to urban SMEs, where only three SMEs employ less than 4 staff and eight have existed for more than four years. Also, most rural SMEs operate within an immediate rural economic influence sphere, which can be described as limited in the use of technology by customers, a reliance on walk-ins, and subjected to more inhibiting factors. From this perspective, DRT, even if adopted, is less likely to be enabling. For urban SMEs, the results confirm research [27] that most SME owners in an urban area in a developing country are at least aware of the benefits of up-to-date technologies.

The third question considers the factors that regulate DRT adoption in rural and urban SMEs. Poor or no electricity and/or mobile Internet services and/or high cost thereof are consistent factors highlighted by many respondents. The results confirm other research [42] that poor infrastructure is a facilitating condition in rural-based African SMEs. Likewise, poor cash flow, limited knowledge, an absence of government strategies, and financial support were constantly raised across all SMEs. A lack of knowledge has been identified as a critical barrier to DRT adoption in developing countries [16], and the current results support this position. Financial support [12] is also known as a key ingredient for the adoption of DRT. It is noteworthy that no participant had anything to add. Any attempt to explain it further would not have resulted in useful data. At some level, it supports the adage that you cannot throw technology at users and expect them to understand it not for it to work.

In one instance, a staff member indicated that the owner is not open to technology. Although an outlier, the owner's attitude is a known adoption factor [15].

The last question aimed to identify key government strategies to improve DRT adoption in Zimbabwean SMEs. Across SMEs, a total absence of government support, a critical ingredient for driving SME ICT adoption [9], is highlighted. Despite policies in place to improve the country's economy by supporting the SME sector (e.g. the Indigenisation and Empowerment Policy and the Zimbabwe Industrial Development Policy 2012–2016), the current results support earlier research that shows SMEs have little knowledge of such policies. This is not surprising. Even when implemented, they had very little influence [43]. Specifically, the expected growth of the SME sector has not been realised because of a lack of pre-consultation and commitment by the Zimbabwean government [44].

Finally, all respondents had nothing to add to the interview, which confirms overall perceptions that despite pockets of use, respondents are primarily DRT-illiterate, do not view it as crucial, and are merely trying to survive.

6 Conclusion

In conclusion, the overall results paint a bleak picture of DRT adoption in Zimbabwe. Challenges and barriers identified in earlier research in other developing countries are replicated. As such, it raises questions about the potential trajectory of DRT innovation in Zimbabwean SMEs. Stated in simplest terms, DRT is meant to disrupt an already established market or allow lower market segments to be serviced to a higher degree. In the current case, it appears to be far off in the medium, if not long term.

The above results, of course, cannot be generalised. It is suggested that SMEs that use DRT are identified through other sampling methods. Since most research on DRT adoption offers or calls for workable strategies, the intention is to learn from these SMEs and to offer proven and contextual strategies. Whereas exploratory research is useful, there is an urgent need for confirmatory research related to DRT adoption in developing countries. The research by Chishakwe and Smith [27], which uses hypothesis testing, provides an excellent example of this suggested approach.

Acknowledgements. This study was funded by a grant, which allowed the interviewer to conduct the interviews.

Disclosure of Interests. Other than acknowledging contributions from the interviewer for some of the content in this paper, the author has no competing interests to declare. The sole authorship of this paper was approved by the relevant research office.

References

1. Wardati, N.K., Mahendrawathi, E.R.: The impact of social media usage on the sales process in small and medium enterprises (SMEs): a systematic literature review. Proc. Comp. Sci. **161**, 976–983 (2019)

2. Bower, J.L., Christensen, C.M.: Disruptive Technologies: Catching the Wave. HBR (1995) https://www3.yildiz.edu.tr/~naydin/MI2/lectures/Reading/Disruptive%20Technologie% 20Catching%20the%20Wave.pdf. Last accessed 25 Mar 2024
3. Sydle: 12 Examples of Disruptive Technologies You Need to Know https://www.sydle.com/ blog/disruptive-technologies-61aa52868621853d1165bf07. Last accessed 14 June 2023
4. Nagaraj, S.: Marketing analytics for customer engagement: a viewpoint. Int. J. Inf. Syst. Soc. Change **11**(2), 41–55 (2020)
5. Coccia, M.: Sources of technological innovation: radical and incremental innovation problem-driven to support competitive advantage of firms. Tech. Anal. Strat. Manag. **29**(9), 1048–1061 (2017)
6. Cressman, D.: Disruptive Innovation and the Idea Technology. Novation **1**, 18–40 (2019)
7. Arthur, P.: Disruptive technologies, democracy, governance and national elections in Africa: back to the future? In: Arthur, P., Hanson, K., Puplampu, K. (eds) Disruptive Technologies, Innovation and Development in Africa. International Political Economy Series. Palgrave Macmillan, Cham (2020)
8. Kwaramba, N.: The role and importance of key entrepreneurship development. https://www. theindependent.co.zw/2017/05/26/role-importance-key-entrepreneurship-development/. Last accessed 21 Nov 2023 (2017)
9. Makiwa, P., Steyn, R.: An investigation of the government-related factors that inhibit small to medium enterprises' adoption and effective use of information and communication technology in developing countries: the case of Zimbabwe. Commun. Comp. Inf. Sci. **933**, 3–16 (2019)
10. Singh, A., Thakkar, J., Jenamani, M.: An integrated Grey-DEMATEL approach for evaluating ICT adoption barriers in manufacturing SMEs: analysing Indian MSMEs. J. Enterp. Inf. Manag. **35**(6), 1427–1455 (2019)
11. Msuya, C.A., Mjema, E.A., Kundi, B.A: ICT Adoption and use in Tanzania SMEs. Tanzania J. Eng. Technol. **36** (1), 23–34 (2017)
12. Lekhanya, L.M.: The digitalisation of rural entrepreneurship. In: Da Rocha Brito, S.M. (ed.) Entrepreneurship – Trends and Challenges. IntechOpen (2018)
13. Hagsten, E., Kotnik, P.: ICT as facilitator of internationalisation in small-and medium-sized firms. Small Bus. Econ. **48**(2), Special Issue: Entrepreneurship, Innovation and Enterprise Dynamics, 431–446 (2017)
14. Majumdar, D., Banerji, P., Chakrabarti, S.: Disruptive technology and disruptive innovation: ignore at your peril! Technol. Anal. Strat. Manag. **30**(11), 1247–1255 (2018)
15. Niehues, S., Gürpinar, T.: Disruptive technologies: Integration in existing supply chain processes. In: Artificial Intelligence and Digital Transformation in Supply Chain Management: Innovative Approaches for Supply Chains. Proceedings of the Hamburg International Conference of Logistics (HICL), **27**, 265–296. Hamburg University of Technology (TUHH), Institute of Business Logistics and General Management (2019)
16. Kumar, M.D., Chung, J.F., Govindarajo, N.: Technology disruption and business performance in SMEs. Religación Revista de Ciencias Sociales y Humanidades **4**, 130–138 (2019)
17. Renner, B., Fedder, C., Upadhyaya, J.: The adoption of disruptive technologies in the consumer products industry: creating seamless experiences through disruptive technologies. The Deloitte Center for Industry Insights (2019)
18. Obal, M.: Why do incumbents sometimes succeed? Investigating the role of interorganizational trust on the adoption of disruptive technology. Ind. Mark. Manage. **42**(6), 900–908 (2013)
19. Christensen, C.M.: The Innovator's Dilemma. Harper Business Essentials, New York, NJ (2003)
20. Krotov, V.: Predicting the future of disruptive technologies: the method of alternative histories. Bus. Horizons, Elsevier **62**(6), 695–705 (2019)

21. Vorbach, S., Wipfler, H., Schimpf, S.: Business model innovation vs. business model inertia: the role of disruptive technologies. BHM Berg-und Hüttenmännische Monatshefte, **162**(9), 382–385 (2017)
22. Moullin, M.: Performance measurement definitions: linking performance measurement and organisational excellence. Int. J. Health Care Qual. Assur. **20**(3), 181–183 (2007)
23. Slavec, A.: Determinants of SME performance: the impact of entrepreneurial openness and goals economic and social development. In: 7th International Scientific Conference, New York City (2014)
24. Peihani, M.: Financial regulation and disruptive technologies: the case of cloud computing in Singapore. Singapore J. Legal Stud. 77–99 (2017)
25. Schuelke-Leech, B.A.: A model for understanding the orders of magnitude of disruptive technologies. Technol. Forecast. Soc. Change **129**, 261–274 (2018)
26. Singh, D.S.M., Hanafi, N.B.: Disruptive technology and SMEs performance in Malaysia. Int. J. Acad. Res. Bus. Soc. Sci. **9**(12), 140–148 (2019)
27. Chishakwe, D.B., Smith, W.: An analysis of the impact of disruptive technology on the success of small and medium enterprises (SMEs) in a developing nation. A case of King Williams Town, South Africa. African J. Bus. Manag. **6**, 10050–10060 (2012)
28. AlSharji, A., Ahmad, S.Z., Abu Bakar, A.R.: Understanding social media adoption in SMEs: empirical evidence from the United Arab Emirates. J. Entrep. Emerg. Econ. **10**(2), 302–328 (2018)
29. Avgerou, C.: Discourses on ICT and development. Inf. Technol. Int. Dev. **6**(3), 1–18 (2010)
30. Nyoni, T., Bonga, W.G.: Anatomy of the small & medium enterprises (SMEs) critical success factors (CSFs) in Zimbabwe: introducing the 3E model. J. Bus. Manag. (DRJ-JBM) **1**(2), 1–18 (2018)
31. Mugozhi, F., Hlabiso, G.: Determinants of small to medium enterprises' success or failure: an ex-post appraisal of start up business by young entrepreneurs in Zimbabwe. Int. J. Hum. Soc. Stud. **5**(3), 39–46 (2017)
32. Mufudza, T., Jengeta, M., Hove, P.: The usefulness of strategic planning in a turbulent economic environment: a case of Zimbabwe during the period 2007–2009. Bus. Strat. Ser. **14**, 24–29 (2013)
33. Cooper, D.R., Schindler, P.S.: Business Research Methods. McGraw-Hill Irwin, Boston (2008)
34. Leedy, P.D., Ormrod, J.E.: Practical research: Planning and Design, 9th edn. Pearson, UpperSaddle River NJ (2010)
35. Yin, R.K.: Case Study Research Design and Methods, 5th edn. Sage, Thousand Oaks, CA (2014)
36. Fowler, F.J., Mangione, T.W.: Standardized Survey Interviewing. SAGE Publications, Thousand Oaks (1990)
37. Hansen, B.H., Kautz, K.: Grounded theory applied – studying information systems development methodologies in practice. In: 38th Hawaii International Conference on System Sciences. Big Island, HI, USA (2005)
38. Glaser, B.G., A.L.: The Discovery of Grounded Theory: Strategies for Qualitative Research. Aldine Publishing Company, New York (1967)
39. Leibowitz, B.: Rurality and Education. Southern African Rural Students in Higher Education for the Southern African Project. SARiHE Working paper No.1. (2017)
40. POE: Commission Recommendation – the definition of micro, small and medium-sized enterprises. Publications office of the EU. Accessed 23 Oct 2023 (2005). https://publications.eur opa.eu/resource/cellar/1bd0c013-0ba3-4549-b879-0ed797389fa1.0005.02/DOC_2
41. Gherhes, C., Williams, N., Vorley, T., Vasconcelos, A.C.: Distinguishing micro-businesses from SMEs: a systematic review of growth constraints. J. Small Bus. Enterp. Dev. **23**(4), 939–963 (2016)

42. Rahayu, R., Day, J.: E-commerce adoption by SMEs in developing countries: evidence from Indonesia. Eurasian Bus. Rev. **7**. https://doi.org/10.1007/s40821-016-0044-6 (2106)
43. Musabayana, G.T., Mutambara, E., Ngwenya, T.: An empirical assessment of how the government policies influenced the performance of the SMEs in Zimbabwe. J. Innov. Entrepr. **11**(1), 1–20 (2022)
44. Dlamini, B., Schutte, D.P.: An overview of the historical development of Small and Medium Enterprises in Zimbabwe. Small Enterp. Res. **27**(3), 306–322 (2020)

Author Index

A. Gerber (Ed.): SAICSIT 2024, CCIS 2159, pp. 455–456, 2024.
https://doi.org/10.1007/978-3-031-64881-6

Printed in the United States
by Baker & Taylor Publisher Services